The Gigantic Book of Famous Quotations

Over 12,000 Famous Quotations to Inspire, Motivate, Comfort and Amuse You!

By

JOANNE KELLY

JOANNE KELLY

DEDICATION

Dedicated to my supportive husband, Ben, and the many family members and friends who have helped me along the way.

CONTENTS

ACKNOWLEDGMENTS

I would like to acknowledge the wisdom of the many cultural and scientific giants that have made this book possible.

INTRODUCTION

Welcome to my book, The Gigantic Book of Famous Quotations! This book has been a very long time in the making. After all, 12,000 quotes is a huge number of quotations to find, categorise, order, and curate. But from a personal perspective it has been a highly rewarding process.

The process of curating this collection of quotes has enabled me to reflect on quotations from both the past and present that have truly resonated with me. It has given me a better understanding of our collective history as well as the history of my own life. I believe that the wisdom of our cultural and scientific thought leaders through history and the present day, in reflecting on their own lives, offers us a better understanding and acceptance of our own reality. In so doing it enables us to travel though our own lives from a more pragmatic and philosophical perspective.

Within the book quotes are categorised alphabetically so you can easily find the subject that you are interested in. Further, within each category, quotes are ordered alphabetical by the authors name. This will help where you want to find a specific person's thoughts on a particular subject.

I hope you enjoy this book of famous quotations and will refer back to it for years to come as a source of comfort, perspective and amusement. I would be excited to hear what you think of my book and promise to reply to every review. At the same time, as a self-publisher without an editor or company behind me, and with such a vast amount of material to curate, I hope there are few if any errors or omissions. And where they arise, I hope you can, dear reader, be kind about these in review. I have put more time and effort into this work that you can imagine, so I truly hope you enjoy it and feel that it can justify your kind recommendation. I have read that, on average, only one in one hundred people who read a book leave a review. I hope you can be my one in one hundred!

JOANNE KELLY

QUOTATIONS BY CATEGORY

ACCEPTANCE

'If you want a place in the sun, you've got to put up with a few blisters.'
 - Abigail Van Buren

'When you have got an elephant by the hind legs and he is trying to run away, it is best to let him run.'
 - Abraham Lincoln

'The point... is to dwell upon the brightest parts in every prospect, to call off the thoughts when turning upon disagreeable objects, and strive to be pleased with the present circumstances.'
 - Abraham Tucker

'If a ship has been sunk, I can't bring it up. If it is going to be sunk, I can't stop it. I can use my time much better working on tomorrow's problem than by fretting about yesterday's. Besides, if I let those things get me, I wouldn't last long.'
 - Admiral Ernest J. King

'Who except the gods can live without any pain?'
 - Aeschylus

'Against necessity, against its strength, no one can fight and win.'
 - Aeschylus

'An oak and a reed were arguing about their strength. When a strong wind came up, the reed avoided being uprooted by bending and leaning with the gusts of wind. But the oak stood firm and was torn up by the roots.'
 - Aesop

'We may fail of our happiness, strive we ever so bravely; but we are less likely to fail if we measure with judgment our chances and our capabilities.'
 - Agnes Repplier

'Learn to drink the cup of life as it comes.'
 - Agnes Turnbull

'Buddha's doctrine: Man suffers because of his craving to possess and keep forever things which are essentially impermanent... this frustration of the desire to possess is the immediate cause of suffering.'
 - Alan Watts

'Anyone who proposes to do good must not expect people to roll stones out of his way, but must accept his lot calmly, even if they roll a few more upon it.'
 - Albert Schweitzer

'And acceptance is the answer to all my problems today. ... I can find no serenity until I accept that person, place, thing, or situation as being exactly the way it is supposed to be at this moment.'
  - Alcoholics Anonymous

'Don't be sad, don't be angry, if life deceives you! Submit to your grief; your time for joy will come, believe me.'
  - Aleksandr Pushkin

'We must make the best of those ills which cannot be avoided.'
  - Alexander Hamilton

'True freedom lies in the realization and calm acceptance of the fact that there may very well be no perfect answer.'
  - Allen Reid McGinnis

'One completely overcomes only what one assimilates.'
  - Andre Gide

'Results are what you expect; consequences are what you get.'
  - Anonymous

'Cooperation is doing with a smile what you have to do anyhow.'
  - Anonymous

'For so must it be, and help me do my part.'
  - Anonymous

'If you have arthritis, calmly say, I was always complaining about the ruts in the road until I realized that the ruts are the road.'
  - Anonymous

'Resistance causes pain and lethargy. It is when we practice acceptance that new possibilities appear.'
  - Anonymous

'Things turn out best for people who make the best of the way things turn out.'
  - Anonymous

'To expect life to be tailored to our specifications is to invite frustration.'
  - Anonymous

'The beauty of the soul shines out when a man bears with composure one heavy mischance after another, not because he does not feel them, but because he is a man of high and heroic temper.'
  - Aristotle

'The ideal man bears the accidents of life with dignity and grace, making the best of circumstances.'
  - Aristotle

'When we accept tough jobs as a challenge to our ability and wade into them with joy and enthusiasm, miracles can happen.'
- Arland Gilbert

'Trouble will come soon enough, and when he does come receive him as pleasantly as possible ... the more amiably you greet him, the sooner he will go away.'
- Artemus Ward

'I accept life unconditionally. ... Most people ask for happiness on condition. Happiness can only be felt if you don't set any condition.'
- Arthur Rubinstein

'If you are wise, live as you can; if you cannot, live as you would.'
- Baltasar Gracian

'Do not weep; do not wax indignant. Understand.'
- Baruch Spinoza

'The art of living lies less in eliminating our troubles than in growing with them.'
- Bernard M. Baruch

'One cannot get through life without pain. ... What we can do is choose how to use the pain life presents to us.'
- Bernie S. Siegel

'Real life is, to most men ... a perpetual compromise between the ideal and the possible.'
- Bertrand Russell

'Can the Ethiopian change his skin, or the leopard his spots?'
- Bible

'Yet man is born unto trouble, as the sparks fly upward.'
- Bible

'He who attempts to resist the wave is swept away, but he who bends before it abides.'
- Bible

'He who has calmly reconciled his life to fate ... can look fortune in the face.'
- Boethius

'Every man must be content with that glory which he may have at home.'
- Boethius

'I have accepted all and I am free. The inner chains are broken, as well as those outside.'
- C. F. Ramuz

'We cannot change anything unless we accept it. Condemnation does not liberate, it oppresses.'
- Carl Jung

'The greatest and most important problems in life are all in a certain sense insoluble. They can never be solved, but only outgrown.'
- Carl Jung

'Acceptance says, "True, this is my situation at the moment. I'll look unblinkingly at the reality of it. But I'll also open my hands to accept willingly whatever a loving Father sends me."'
- Catharine Marshall

'Acceptance says, True, this is my situation at the moment. I'll look unblinkingly at the reality of it. But I'll also open my hands to accept willingly whatever a loving Father sends me.'
- Catharine Marshall

'He who doesn't accept the conditions of life sells his soul.'
- Charles Baudelaire

'"Okay, I have arthritis, and this is the way arthritis is." Take pain as it comes and you can better master it.'
- Charles Clifford Peale

'There is no quality of human nature so nearly royal as the ability to yield gracefully.'
- Charles Conrad

'The most popular persons are those who take the world as it is, who find the least fault.'
- Charles Dudley Warner

'It is a common observation that those who dwell continually upon their expectations are apt to become oblivious to the requirements of their actual situation.'
- Charles Sanders Peirce

'Being unready and ill-equipped is what you have to expect in life. It is the universal predicament. It is your lot as a human being to lack what it takes. Circumstances are seldom right. You never have the capacities, the strength, the wisdom, the virtue you ought to have. You must always do with less than you need in a situation vastly different from what you would have chosen as appropriate for your special endowments.'
- Charlton Ogburn

'Misfortune comes to all men.'
- Chinese proverb

'The best thing we can do is to make wherever we're lost look as much like home as we can.'
- Christopher Fry

'Flow with whatever may happen and let your mind be free. Stay centered by accepting whatever you are doing. This is the ultimate.'
- Chuang-tzu

'A life of frustration is inevitable for any coach whose man enjoyment is winning.'
- Chuck Noll

'If you aspire to the highest place, it is no disgrace to stop at the second, or even the third, place.'
   - Cicero

'The real world is not easy to live in. It is rough; it is slippery. Without the most clear-eyed adjustments we fall and get crushed.'
   - Clarence Day

'There are things I can't force. I must adjust.'
   - CM. Ward

'The grass must bend when the wind blows across it.'
   - Confucius

'Wood may remain ten years in the water, but it will never become a crocodile.'
   - Congolese proverb

'The secret of success is to be in harmony with existence, to be always calm ... to let each wave of life wash us a little farther up the shore.'
   - Cyril Connolly

'Is life so wretched? Isn't it rather your hands which are too small, your vision which is muddled? You are the one who must grow up.'
   - Dag Hammarskjold

'The survival of the fittest is the ageless law of nature, but the fittest are rarely the strong. The fittest are those endowed with the qualifications for adaptation, the ability to accept the inevitable and conform to the unavoidable, to harmonize with existing or changing conditions.'
   - Dave E. Smalley

'Contentment, and indeed usefulness, comes as the infallible result of great acceptances, great humilities-of not trying to conform to some dramatized version of ourselves.'
   - David Grayson

'He is happy whose circumstances suit his temper; but he is more excellent who can suit his temper to any circumstances.'
   - David Hume

'"Good enough never is" has become the motto of this company.'
   - Debbi Fields

'Happiness ... can exist only in acceptance.'
   - Denis De Rougemont

'A flower falls even though we love it. A weed grows even though we don't love it.'
   - Dogen

'Life leaps like a geyser for those who drill through the rock of inertia.'
   - Dr. Alexis Carrel

'Unhappiness is best defined as the difference between our talents and our expectations.'
- Dr. Edward De Bono

'Nobody has things just as he would like them. The thing to do is to make a success with what material I have. It is a sheer waste of time and soul-power to imagine what I would do if things were different. They are not different.'
- Dr. Frank Crane

'Accept that all of us can be hurt, that all of us can-and surely will at times-fail. Other vulnerabilities, like being embarrassed or risking love, can be terrifying too. I think we should follow a simple rule: if we can take the worst, take the risk.'
- Dr. Joyce Brothers

'Boys, this is only a game. But it's like life in that you will be dealt some bad hands. Take each hand, good or bad, and don't whine and complain, but play it out. If you're men enough to do that, God will help and you will come out well.'
- Dwight D. Eisenhower's mother

'I have learned to live with it all... whatever happens ... all of it.'
- Edelgard

'Genius does what it must, talent does what it can.'
- Edward Bulwer-Lytton

'A private railroad car is not an acquired taste. One takes to it immediately.'
- Eleanor R. Belmont

'I find that it is not the circumstances in which we are placed, but the spirit in which we face them, that constitutes our comfort.'
- Elizabeth T. King

'Whatever is-is best.'
- Ella Wheeler Wilcox

'No life is so hard that you can't make it easier by the way you take it.'
- Ellen Glasgow

'One does not have to stand again the gale. One yields and becomes part of the wind.'
- Emmanuel

'Ask not that events should happen as you will, but let your will be that events should happen as they do, and you shall have peace.'
- Epictetus

'There is only one way to happiness, and that is to cease worrying about things which are beyond the power of our will.'
- Epictetus

'Every new adjustment is a crisis in self-esteem.'
- Eric Hoffer

'I have accepted fear as a part of life -specifically the fear of change ... I have gone ahead despite the pounding in the heart that says: turn back. ...'
- Erica Jong

'Free man is by necessity insecure; thinking man by necessity uncertain.'
- Erich Fromm

'There is no sense in the struggle, but there is no choice but to struggle.'
- Ernie Pyle

'Let a man accept his destiny. No pity and no tears.'
- Euripides

'How base a thing it is when a man will struggle with necessity! We have to die.'
- Euripides

'Much sheer effort goes into avoiding the truth; left to itself, it sweeps in like the tide.'
- Fay Weldon

'The truth does not change according to our ability to stomach it emotionally.'
- Flannery O'Connor

'Nature, to be commanded, must be obeyed.'
- Francis Bacon

'No rose without a thorn.'
- French proverb

'What has always made a hell on earth has been that man has tried to make it his heaven.'
- Friedrich Holderlin

'Man is a pliant animal, a being who gets accustomed to anything.'
- Fyodor Dostoyevsky

'Acceptance is the truest kinship with humanity.'
- G. K. Chesterton

'Make a virtue of necessity.'
- Geoffrey Chaucer

'One's first step in wisdom is to question everything; one's last is to come to terms with everything.'
- Georg Christoph Lichtenberg

'The reasonable man adapts himself to the world; the unreasonable one persists in trying to adapt the world to himself.'
- George Bernard Shaw

'The mind which renounces, once and forever, a futile hope, has its compensations in ever-growing calm.'
- George R. Gissing

'There is no cure for birth or death save to enjoy the interval.'
- George Santayana

'The happy and efficient people in this world are those who accept trouble as a normal detail of human life and resolve to capitalize it when it comes along.'
- H. Bertram Lewis

'Adapt or perish, now as ever, is nature's inexorable imperative.'
- H. G. Wells

'We must learn to accept life and to accept ourselves ... with a shrug and a smile ... because it's all we've got.'
- Harvey Mindess

'It is arrogance to expect that life will always be music.... Harmony, like a following breeze at sea, is the exception. In a world where most things wind up broken or lost, our lot is to tack and tune.'
- Harvey Oxenhorn

'If we can recognize that change and uncertainty are basic principles, we can greet the future and the transformation we are undergoing with the understanding that we do not know enough to be pessimistic.'
- Hazel Henderson

'Everything has its wonders, even darkness and silence, and I learn, whatever state I may be in, therein to be content.'
- Helen Keller

'To repel one's cross is to make it heavier.'
- Henri Frederic Amiel

'When a dog runs at you, whistle for him.'
- Henry David Thoreau

'The mass of men lead lives of quiet desperation.'
- Henry David Thoreau

'The world is not to be put in order, the world is order incarnate. It is for us to put ourselves in unison with this order.'
- Henry Miller

'Acceptance makes any event put on a new face.'
- Henry S. Haskins

'Almost any event will put on a new face when received with cheerful acceptance.'
- Henry S. Haskins

'Into each life some rain must fall, some days must be dark and dreary.'
- Henry Wadsworth Longfellow

'You have come into a hard world. I know of only one easy place in it, and that is the grave.'
- Henry Ward Beecher

'God asks no man whether he will accept life. This is not the choice. You must take it. The only question is how.'
- Henry Ward Beecher

'When I decided to go into politics I weighed the costs. I would get criticism. But I went ahead. So when virulent criticism came I wasn't surprised. I was better able to handle it.'
- Herbert Hoover

'What it is forbidden to be put right becomes lighter by acceptance.'
- Horace

'Better to accept whatever happens.'
- Horace

'To act with common sense, according to the moment, is the best wisdom; and the best philosophy is to do one's duties, to take the world as it comes, submit respectfully to one's lot, and bless the goodness that has given us so much happiness with it, whatever it is.'
- Horace Walpole

'Happiness comes from within a man, from some curious adjustment to life.'
- Hugh Walpole

'Life is 10 percent what you make it, and 90 percent how you take it.'
- Irving Berlin

'Every creator painfully experiences the chasm between his inner vision and its ultimate expression. The chasm is never completely bridged. We all have the conviction, perhaps illusory, that we have much more to say than appears on the paper.'
- Isaac Bashevis Singer

'Happy he who learns to bear what he cannot change!'
- J. C. F. von Schiller

'All I can do is play the game the way the cards fall.'
- James A. Michener

'There is no good in arguing with the inevitable. The only argument available with an east wind is to put on your overcoat.'
- James Russell Lowell

'There is no armor against fate; death lays his icy hands on kings.'
- James Shirley

'It is no use to grumble and complain; It's just as cheap and easy to rejoice; When God sorts out the weather and sends rain-Why, rain's my choice.'
- James Whitcomb Riley

'The chief pang of most trials is not so much the actual suffering itself as our own spirit of resistance to it.'
- Jean Nicholas Grou

'Life is not always what one wants it to be, but to make the best of it, as it is, is the only way of being happy.'
- Jennie Jerome Churchill

'When you make your peace with authority, you become authority.'
- Jim Morrison

'Happy the man who early learns the wide chasm that lies between his wishes and his powers.'
- Johann von Goethe

'The unknown is what it is. And to be frightened of it is what sends everybody scurrying around chasing dreams, illusions, wars, peace, love, hate, all that. Unknown is what it is. Accept that it's unknown, and it's plain sailing.'
- John Lennon

'Man adapts himself to everything, to the best and the worst.'
- Jose Ortega y Gasset

'Maturity is achieved when a person accepts life as full of tension.'
- Joshua L. Liebman

'The most beautiful thing is inevitability of events, and the most ugly thing is trying to resist inevitability.'
- Katharine Butler Hathaway

'Everything in life that we really accept undergoes a change. So suffering must become love. That is the mystery.'
- Katherine Mansfield

'Acceptance is not submission; it is acknowledgement of the facts of a situation. Then deciding what you're going to do about it.'
- Kathleen Casey Theisen

'All that is necessary is to accept the impossible, do without the indispensable, and bear the intolerable.'
- Kathleen Norris

'Happiness is experienced when your life gives you what you are willing to accept.'
- Ken Keyes

'As the soft yield of water cleaves obstinate stone, So to yield with life solves the insolvable: To yield, I have learned, is to come back again.'
  - Lao-Tzu

'For this is wisdom: to live, to take what fate, or the Gods, may give.'
  - Laurence Hope

'There are no conditions to which a man cannot become accustomed.'
  - Leo Tolstoy

'Anxiety is that range of distress which attends willing what cannot be willed.'
  - Leslie H. Farber

'Nothing you write, if you hope to be any good, will ever come out as you first hoped.'
  - Lillian Hellman

'Peace of mind is that mental condition in which you have accepted the worst.'
  - Lin Yutang

'Ours must be the first age whose great goal, on a nonmaterial plane, is not fulfillment but adjustment.'
  - Louis Kronenberger

'You can't fight the desert... you have to ride with it.'
  - Louis L'Amour

'A body shouldn't heed what might be. He's got to do with what is.'
  - Louis L'Amour

'A man shares his days with hunger, thirst, and cold, with the good times and the bad, and the first part of being a man is to understand that.'
  - Louis L'Amour

'She had believed the land was her enemy, and she struggled against it, but you could not make war against a land any more than you could against the sea. One had to learn to live with it, to belong to it, to fit into its seasons and its ways.'
  - Louis L'Amour

'A mountain man tries to live with the country instead of against it.'
  - Louis L'Amour

'To exist is to adapt, and if one could not adapt, one died and made room for those who could.'
  - Louis L'Amour

'One learns to adapt to the land in which one lives.'
  - Louis L'Amour

'What we call reality is an agreement that people have arrived at to make life more livable.'
  - Louise Nevelson

'Every job has drudgery. ... The first secret of happiness is the recognition of this fundamental fact.'
- M. C. Mcintosh

'Each of us does, in effect, strike a series of "deals" or compromises between the wants and longings of the inner self, and an outer environment that offers certain possibilities and sets certain limitations.'
- Maggie Scarf

'Acceptance and Work If you have a job without aggravations, you don't have a job.'
- Malcolm Forbes

'The great soul surrenders itself to fate.'
- Marcus Annaeus Seneca

'Let us train our minds to desire what the situation demands.'
- Marcus Annaeus Seneca

'What must be shall be; and that which is a necessity to him that struggles, is little more than choice to him that is willing.'
- Marcus Annaeus Seneca

'Adapt yourself to the things among which your lot has been cast and love sincerely the fellow creatures with whom destiny has ordained that you shall live.'
- Marcus Aurelius

'Here is a rule to remember when anything tempts you to feel bitter: not, "This is a misfortune," but "To bear this worthily is good fortune."'
- Marcus Aurelius

'Love only what befalls you and is spun for you by fate.'
- Marcus Aurelius

'Vex not thy spirit at the course of things; they heed not thy vexation. How ludicrous and outlandish is astonishment at anything that may happen in life.'
- Marcus Aurelius

'Self-complacency is fatal to progress.'
- Margaret Elizabeth Sangster

'Life's under no obligation to give us what we expect.'
- Margaret Mitchell

'Woman must not accept; she must challenge.'
- Margaret Sanger

'There are some people that you cannot change, you must either swallow them whole or leave them alone.'
- Margot Asquith

'Competition is about passion for perfection, and passion for other people who join in this impossible quest.'
  - Mariah Burton Nelson

'Today I know that I cannot control the ocean tides. I can only go with the flow.... When I struggle and try to organize the Atlantic to my specifications, I sink. If I flail and thrash and growl and grumble, I go under. But if I let go and float, I am borne aloft.'
  - Marie Stilkind

'We must accept finite disappointment, but we must never lose infinite hope.'
  - Martin Luther King, Jr.

'The minute you settle for less than you deserve, you get even less than you settled for.'
  - Maureen Dowd

'A man must live in the world and make the best of it, such as it is.'
  - Michel de Montaigne

'Greatness of soul consists not so much in soaring high and in pressing forward, as in knowing how to adapt and limit oneself.'
  - Michel de Montaigne

'What you can't get out of, get into wholeheartedly.'
  - Mignon McLaughlin

'Science says: "We must live," and seeks the means of prolonging, increasing, facilitating and amplifying life, of making it tolerable and acceptable; wisdom says: "We must die," and seeks how to make us die well.'
  - Miguel de Unamuno

'The individual who is best prepared for any occupation is the one ... able to adapt himself to any situation.'
  - Mortimer Smith

'The idea came to me that I was, am, and will be, but perhaps will not become. This did not scare me. There was for me in being an intensity I did not feel in becoming.'
  - Nina Berberova

'Never deny a diagnosis, but do deny the negative verdict that may go with it.'
  - Norman Cousins

'Part of the happiness of life consists not in fighting battles, but in avoiding them. A masterly retreat is in itself a victory.'
  - Norman Vincent Peale

'The art of life lies in a constant readjustment to our surroundings.'
  - Okakura Kakuzo

'You have to take it as it happens, but you should try to make it happen the way you want to take it.'
  - Old German proverb

'Wisdom never kicks at the iron walls it can't bring down.'
  - Olive Schreiner

'We win half the battle when we make up our minds to take the world as we find it, including the thorns.'
  - Orison Swett Marden

'One of the many lessons that one learns in prison is that things are what they are and will be what they will be.'
  - Oscar Wilde

'There is no such thing as pure pleasure; some anxiety always goes with it.'
  - Ovid

'There are two ways of meeting difficulties: you alter the difficulties, or you alter yourself to meet them.'
  - Phyllis Bottome

'There is a mortal breed most full of futility. In contempt of what is at hand, they strain into the future, hunting impossibilities on the wings of ineffectual hopes.'
  - Pindar

'Those who aim at great deeds must also suffer greatly.'
  - Plutarch

'Since God has been pleased to give us the Papacy, let us enjoy it.'
  - Pope Leo X

'A wise man never refuses anything to necessity.'
  - Publilius Syrus

'No man can have society upon his own terms.'
  - Ralph Waldo Emerson

'Nature magically suits a man to his fortunes, by making them the fruit of his character.'
  - Ralph Waldo Emerson

'Nature is what you may do. There is much you may not do.'
  - Ralph Waldo Emerson

'The resistance to the unpleasant situation is the root of suffering.'
  - Ram Dass

'God, grant me the serenity to accept the things I cannot change, the courage to change the things I can, and the wisdom to know the difference.'
  - Reinhold Niebuhr

'We have fought this fight as long, and as well, as we know how. We have been defeated. There is now but one course to pursue. We must accept the situation.'
- Robert E. Lee

'If you can't fight, and you can't flee, flow.'
- Robert Eliot

'Always fall in with what you're asked to accept.... My aim in life has always been to hold my own with whatever's going. Not against: with.'
- Robert Frost

'I One of the signs of maturity is a healthy respect for reality-a respect that manifests itself in the level of one's aspirations and in the accuracy of one's assessment of the difficulties which separate the facts of today from the bright hopes of tomorrow.'
- Robert H. Davies

'We must like what we have when we don't have what we like.'
- Roger de Rabutin

'A hero is a man who does what he can.'
- Romain Rolland

'No matter how much you feed a wolf, he will always return to the forest.'
- Russian proverb

'When necessity speaks, it demands.'
- Russian proverb

'People are lucky and unlucky ... according to the ratio between what they get and what they have been led to expect.'
- Samuel Butler

'Very few live by choice. Every man is placed in his present condition by causes which acted without his foresight, and with which he did not always willingly cooperate; and therefor you will rarely meet one who does not think the lot of his neighbor better than his own.'
- Samuel Johnson

'I make the most of all that comes and the least of all that goes.'
- Sara Teasdale

'Better bend than break.'
- Scottish proverb

'Anything in life that we don't accept will simply make trouble for us until we make peace with it.'
- Shakti Gawain

'In the face of an obstacle which is impossible to overcome, stubbornness is stupid.'
- Simone de Beauvoir

'It's not a very big step from contentment to complacency.'
- Simone de Beauvoir

'Practice easing your way along. Don't get het up or in a dither. Do your best; take it as it comes. You can handle anything if you think you can. Just keep your cool and your sense of humor.'
- Smiley Blanton

'For those who live neither with religious consolations about death nor with a sense of death (or of anything else) as natural, death is the obscene mystery, the ultimate affront, the thing that cannot be controlled. It can only be denied.'
- Susan Sontag

'It is not necessarily those lands which are the most fertile or most favored in climate that seem to me the happiest, but those in which a long struggle of adaptation between man and his environment has brought out the best qualities of both.'
- T. S. Eliot

'He who cannot do what he wants must make do with what he can.'
- Terence

'There is no man in this world without some manner of tribulation or anguish, though he be king or pope.'
- Thomas a Kempis

'If you bear the cross unwillingly, you make it a burden, and load yourself more heavily; but you must bear it.'
- Thomas a Kempis

'If you cast away one cross, you will certainly find another, and perhaps a heavier.'
- Thomas a Kempis

'Good is not good, where better is expected.'
- Thomas Fuller

'I will not meddle with that which I cannot mend.'
- Thomas Fuller

'When we see ourselves in a situation which must be endured and gone through, it is best to meet it with firmness, and accommodate everything to it in the best way practicable. This lessens the evil, while fretting and fuming only increase your own torments.'
- Thomas Jefferson

'I not only bow to the inevitable, I am fortified by it.'
- Thornton Wilder

'My advice to you is not to inquire why or whither, but just enjoy your ice cream while it's on your plate.'
- Thornton Wilder

'To oppose something is to maintain it.'
- Ursula K. LeGuin

'The greatest evil which fortune can inflict on men is to endow them with small talents and great ambitions.'
- Vauvenargues

'The fishermen know that the sea is dangerous and the storm terrible, but they have never found these dangers sufficient reason for remaining ashore.'
- Vincent van Gogh

'Arrange whatever pieces come your way.'
- Virginia Woolf

'Often the prudent, far from making their destinies, succumb to them.'
- Voltaire

'Better is the enemy of the good.'
- Voltaire

'We do not write as we want, but as we can.'
- W Somerset Maugham

'Life has no smooth road for any of us; and in the bracing atmosphere of a high aim the very roughness stimulates the climber to steadier steps 'til the legend, "over steep ways to the stars," fulfills self.'
- W. C. Doane

'There is no easy path leading out of life, and few are the easy ones that lie within it.'
- Walter Savage Landor

'We cannot conquer fate and necessity, yet we can yield to them in such a manner as to be greater than if we could.'
- Walter Savage Landor

'Happiness is a function of accepting what is.'
- Werner Erhard

'Ride the horse in the direction that it's going.'
- Werner Erhard

'It is almost more important how a person takes his fate than what it is.'
- Wilhelm von Humboldt

'The trouble with most people is that they think with their hopes or fears or wishes rather than with their minds.'
- Will Durant

'The first step toward change is acceptance. Once you accept yourself, you open the door to change. That's all you have to do. Change is not something you do, it's something you allow.'
   - Will Garcia

'I like trees because they seem more resigned to the way they have to live than other things do.'
   - Willa Cather

'It is right it should be so, Man was made for joy and woe; And when this we rightly know, Through the world we safely go.'
   - William Blake

'No traveler e'er reached that blest abode who found not thorns and briers in his road.'
   - William Cowper

'Man is the only animal that laughs and weeps; for he is the only animal that is struck with the difference between what things are and what they might have been.'
   - William Hazlitt

'Acceptance of what has happened is the first step to overcoming the consequence of any misfortune.'
   - William James

'Things past redress are now with me past care.'
   - William Shakespeare

'What cannot be avoided, t'were childish weakness to lament or fear.'
   - William Shakespeare

'The English know how to make the best of things. Their so-called muddling through is simply skill at dealing with the inevitable.'
   - Winston Churchill

'If one has to submit, it is wasteful not to do so with the best grace possible.'
   - Winston Churchill

'If we cannot do what we will, we must will what we can.'
   - Yiddish proverb

ADVERSITY

The habits of a vigorous mind are formed in contending with difficulties.'
- Abigail Adams

'It is not in the still calm of life, or the repose of a pacific station, that great characters are formed. ... Great necessities call out great virtues.'
- Abigail Adams

'The fiery trials through which we pass will light us down in honor or dishonor to the latest generation.'
- Abraham Lincoln

'The human race has had long experience and a fine tradition in surviving adversity. But we now face a task for which we have little experience, the task of surviving prosperity.'
- Alan Gregg

'In the depth of winter, I finally learned that there was in me an invincible summer.'
- Albert Camus

'The struggle to the top is in itself enough to fulfill the human heart. Sisyphus should be regarded as happy.'
- Albert Camus

'I never knew any man in my life who could not bear another's misfortunes perfectly like a Christian.'
- Alexander Pope

'Suffering raises up those souls that are truly great; it is only small souls that are made mean-spirited by it.'
- Alexandra David-Neel

'Suffering! ... We owe to it all that is good in us, all that gives value to life; we owe to it pity, we owe to it courage, we owe to it all the virtues.'
- Anatole France

'Remember that the Devil doesn't sleep, but seeks our ruin in a thousand different ways'
- Angela Merici

'If you do things well, do them better. Be daring, be first, be different, be just.'
- Anita Roddick

'If we had no winter, the spring would not be so pleasant; if we did not sometimes taste of adversity, prosperity would not be so welcome.'
- Anne Bradstreet

'Hope begins in the dark, the stubborn hope that if you just show up and try to do the right thing, the dawn will come. You wait and watch and work: you don't give up.'
- Anne Lamott

'Adversity introduces a man to himself.'
- Anonymous

'Trouble will rain on those who are already wet.'
- Anonymous

'Fire tries gold, misfortune men.'
- Anonymous

'There are times in everyone's life when something constructive is born out of adversity ... when things seem so bad that you've got to grab your fate by the shoulders and shake it.'
- Anonymous

'God will not look you over for medals, degrees or diplomas, but for scars.'
- Anonymous

'Trouble brings experience, and experience brings wisdom.'
- Anonymous

'I didn't know I'd have to be torn down before I could be built up.'
- Anonymous

'Adversity comes with instruction in its hand.'
- Anonymous

'A diamond is a chunk of coal that made good under pressure.'
- Anonymous

'In order to change, we must be sick and tired of being sick and tired.'
- Anonymous

'"The world is a wheel always turning," philosophized Mrs. Pelz. "Those who were high go down low, and those who've been low go up higher."'
- Anzia Yezierska

'Difficulties should act as a tonic. They should spur us to greater exertion.'
- B. C. Forbes

'Do not show your wounded finger, for everything will knock up against it.'
- Baltasar Gracian

'One who was adored by all in prosperity is abhorred by all in adversity.'
- Baltasar Gracian

'For me life is a challenge. And it will be a challenge if I live to be a hundred or if I get to be a trillionaire.'
- Beah Richards

'The English nation is never so great as in adversity.'
- Benjamin Disraeli

'There is no education like adversity.'
- Benjamin Disraeli

'To be thrown upon one's own resources is to be cast into the very lap of fortune, for our faculties then undergo a development and display an energy of which they were previously unsusceptible.'
- Benjamin Franklin

'Those things that hurt, instruct.'
- Benjamin Franklin

'Is there no balm in Gilead? Is there no physician there?'
- Bible

'Weeping may endure for a night, but joy cometh in the morning.'
- Bible

'Thou hast shown thy people hard things: thou hast made us to drink the wine of astonishment.'
- Bible

'In the day of prosperity be joyful, but in the day of adversity consider.'
- Bible

'I am escaped by the skin of my teeth.'
- Bible

'I was lucky I wasn't a better boxer, or that's what I'd be now - a punchy ex-pug.'
- Bob Hope

'Great occasions do not make heroes or cowards; they simply unveil them to the eyes of men. Silently and imperceptibly, as we wake or sleep, we grow strong or weak; and at last some crisis shows what we have become.'
- Brooke Foss Westcott

'Discontent and disorder were signs of energy and hope, not of despair.'
- C. V. Wedgwood

'There is no coming to consciousness without pain.'
- Carl Jung

'I have always grown from my problems and challenges, from the things that don't work out. That's when I've really learned.'
- Carol Burnett

'There is often in people to whom "the worst" has happened an almost transcendent freedom, for they have faced "the worst" and survived it.'
   - Carol Pearson

'Often God has to shut a door in our face, so that He can subsequently open the door through which He wants us to go.'
   - Catharine Marshall

'When it is dark enough, you can see the stars.'
   - Charles A. Beard

'There are three modes of bearing the ills of life: by indifference, by philosophy and by religion.'
   - Charles Caleb Colton

'Problems are the price of progress. Don't bring me anything but trouble.'
   - Charles F. Kettering

'Many men owe the grandeur of their lives to their tremendous difficulties.'
   - Charles Haddon Spurgeon

'I have an inward treasure born within me, which can keep me alive if all the extraneous delights should be withheld; or offered only at a price I cannot afford.'
   - Charlotte Bronte

'You can learn little from victory. You can learn everything from defeat.'
   - Christy Mathewson

'Challenges make you discover things about yourself that you never really knew. They're what make the instrument stretch, what make you go beyond the norm.'
   - Cicely Tyson

'The gem cannot be polished without friction, nor man perfected without trials.'
   - Confucius

'Flowers grow out of dark moments.'
   - Corita Kent

'I long ago came to the conclusion that all life is six to five against.'
   - Damon Runyon

'Who hath not known ill fortune, never knew himself, or his own virtue.'
   - David Mallett

'I have learned in the great University of Hard Knocks a philosophy that no woman who has had an easy life ever acquires. I have learned to live each day as it comes, and not to borrow trouble by dreading tomorrow. It is the dark menace of the future that '
   - Dorothy Dix

'It is only the women whose eyes have been washed clear with tears who get the broad vision that makes them little sisters to all the world.'
  - Dorothy Dix

'They sicken of the calm that know the storm.'
  - Dorothy Parker

'They sicken of calm, who know the storm.'
  - Dorothy Parker

'Man cannot remake himself without suffering, for he is both the marble and the sculptor.'
  - Dr. Alexis Carrel

'A problem is a chance for you to do your best.'
  - Duke Ellington

'And I think that's important, to know how the water's gone over the dam before you start to describe it. It helps to have been over the dam yourself.'
  - E. Annie Proulx

'Never to suffer would have been never to have been blessed.'
  - Edgar Allan Poe

'A good scare is worth more to a man than good advice.'
  - Edgar Watson Howe

'Hot water is my native element. I was in it as a baby, and I have never seemed to get out of it ever since.'
  - Edith Sitwell

'Adversity is a severe instructor. ... He that wrestles with us strengthens our nerves and sharpens our skill. Our antagonist is our helper.'
  - Edmund Burke

'Down you mongrel, Death! Back into your kennel!'
  - Edna Saint Vincent Millay

'Every experience, however bitter, has its lesson, and to focus one's attention on the lesson helps one overcome the bitterness.'
  - Edward Howard Griggs

'They say a reasonable amount o' fleas is good for a dog - it keeps him from broodin' over bein' a dog mebbe.'
  - Edward Noyes Westcott

'Out of suffering have emerged the strongest souls; the most massive characters are seared with scars.'
  - Edwin H. Chapin

'If you suffer, thank God! It is a sure sign that you are alive.'
- Elbert Hubbard

'Every time you meet a situation, though you think at the time it is an impossibility and you go through the torture of the damned, once you have met it and lived through it, you find that forever after you are freer than you were before.'
- Eleanor Roosevelt

'True knowledge comes only through suffering.'
- Elizabeth Barrett Browning

'Woman's discontent increases in exact proportion to her development.'
- Elizabeth Cady Stanton

'At every step the child should be allowed to meet the real experience of life; the thorns should never be plucked from his roses.'
- Ellen Key

'Truth, like the burgeoning of a bulb under the soil, however deeply sown, will make its way to the light.'
- Ellis Peters

'He disposes Doom who hath suffered him.'
- Emily Dickinson

'A wounded deer leaps the highest.'
- Emily Dickinson

'A smooth sea never made a skillful mariner.'
- English proverb

'Difficulties are things that show what men are.'
- Epictetus

'Treasure the memories of past misfortunes; they constitute our bank of fortitude.'
- Eric Hoffer

'Suffering has always been with us, does it really matter in what form it comes? All that matters is how we bear it and how we fit it into our lives.'
- Etty Hillesum

'Were there none who were discontented with what they have, the world would never reach anything better.'
- Florence Nightingale

'Prosperity is not without many fears and distastes, and adversity is not without comforts and hopes.'
- Francis Bacon

'The virtue of prosperity is temperance; the virtue of adversity is fortitude.'
- Francis Bacon

'As there is no worldly gain without some loss, so there is no worldly loss without some gain.... Set the allowance against the loss, and thou shalt find no loss great.'
- Francis Quarles

'Strong people are made by opposition, like kites that go up against the wind.'
- Frank Harris

'When the going gets tough, the tough get going.'
- Frank Leahy

'It is often hard to distinguish between the hard knocks in life and those of opportunity.'
- Frederick Phillips

'Never does a man know the force that is in him till some mighty affection or grief has humanized the soul.'
- Frederick W. Robertson

'Every difficulty slurred over will be a ghost to disturb your repose later on.'
- Fridiric Chopin

'What does not destroy me, makes me strong.'
- Friedrich Nietzsche

'Suffering is the sole origin of consciousness.'
- Fyodor Dostoyevsky

'The secret of a leader lies in the tests he has faced over the whole course of his life and the habit of Taking Action he develops in meeting those tests.'
- Gail Sheehy

'To be tested is good. The challenged life may be the best therapist.'
- Gail Sheehy

'You have learned something. That always feels at first as if you had lost something.'
- George Bernard Shaw

'There is nothing the body suffers which the soul may not profit by.'
- George Meredith

'Wisdom comes by disillusionment.'
- George Santayana

'It is often better to have a great deal of harm happen to one than a little; a great deal may rouse you to remove what a little will only accustom you to endure.'
- Grenville Kleiser

'Trouble is the thing that strong men grow by. Met in the right way, it is a sure-fire means of putting iron into the victim's will and making him a tougher man to down forever after.'
- H. Bertram Lewis

'Even in the deepest sinking there is the hidden purpose of an ultimate rising. Thus it is for all men, from none is the source of light withheld unless he himself withdraws from it. Therefore the most important thing is not to despair.'
- Hasidic saying

'I thank God for my handicaps for, through them, I have found myself, my work, and my God.'
- Helen Keller

'Character cannot be developed in ease and quiet. Only through experience of trial and suffering can the soul be strengthened, vision cleared, ambition inspired, and success achieved.'
- Helen Keller

'Adversity is the trial of principle. Without it a man hardly knows whether he is honest or not.'
- Henry Fielding

'Trouble is only opportunity in work clothes.'
- Henry J. Kaiser

'I'm very grateful that I was too poor to get to art school until I was 21. ... I was old enough when I got there to know how to get something out of it.'
- Henry Moore

'How sublime a thing it is to suffer and be strong.'
- Henry Wadsworth Longfellow

'Forget the times of your distress, but never forget what they taught you.'
- Herbert Gasser

'Necessity is often the spur to genius.'
- Honore de Balzac

'Adversity has the effect of eliciting talents, which, in prosperous circumstances, would have lain dormant.'
- Horace

'Adversity reveals genius, prosperity conceals it.'
- Horace

'When I have listened to my mistakes, I have grown.'
- Hugh Prather

'An earthquake achieves what the law promises but does not in practice maintain - the equality of all men.'
- Ignazio Silone

'I think these difficult times have helped me to understand better than before how infinitely rich and beautiful life is in every way that so many things that one goes around worrying about are of no importance whatsoever.'
- Isak Dinesen

'Opposition inflames the enthusiast, never converts him.'
- J. C. F. von Schiller

'I would never have amounted to anything were it not for adversity. I was forced to come up the hard way.'
- J. C. Penney

'I don't deserve this award, but I have arthritis and I don't deserve that either.'
- Jack Benny

'[A difficult childhood gave me] a kind of cocky confidence. ... I could never have so little that I hadn't had less. It took away my fear.'
- Jacqueline Cochran

'I think my biggest achievement is that after going through a rather difficult time, I consider myself comparatively sane. I'm proud of that.'
- Jacqueline Kennedy Onassis

'Mistakes are often the best teachers.'
- James A. Froude

'Nothing is more desirable than to be released from an affliction, but nothing is more frightening than to be divested of a crutch.'
- James Baldwin

'Everybody's heart is open, you know, when they have recently escaped from severe pain, or are recovering the blessing of health.'
- Jane Austen

'All sorts of spiritual gifts come through privations, if they are accepted.'
- Janet Erskine Stuart

'I think the years I have spent in prison have been the most formative and important in my life because of the discipline, the sensations, but chiefly the opportunity to think clearly, to try to understand things.'
- Jawaharlal Nehru

'Even if misfortune is only good for bringing a fool to his senses, it would still be just to deem it good for something.'
- Jean de la Fontaine

'Life begins on the other side of despair.'
- Jean-Paul Sartre

'I have brightness in my soul, which strains toward Heaven. I am like a bird!'
   - Jenny Lind

'Our trials are tests; our sorrows pave the way for a fuller life when we have earned it.'
   - Jerome P. Fleishman

'Suffering is also one of the ways of knowing you're alive.'
   - Jessamyn West

'It is somehow reassuring to discover that the word "travel" is derived from "travail," denoting the pains of childbirth.'
   - Jessica Mitford

'We only think when we are confronted with a problem.'
   - John Dewey

'If you will call your troubles experiences, and remember that every experience develops some latent force within you, you will grow vigorous and happy, however adverse your circumstances may seem to be.'
   - John Heywood

'A certain amount of opposition is a great help to a man; it is what he wants and must have to be good for anything. Hardship and opposition are the native soil of manhood and self-reliance.'
   - John Neal

'Pain makes man think. Thought makes man wise. Wisdom makes life endurable.'
   - John Patrick

'When the world has once begun to use us ill, it afterwards continues the same treatment with less scruple or ceremony, as men do to a whore.'
   - Jonathan Swift

'The difficulties which I meet with in order to realize my existence are precisely what awaken and mobilize my activities, my capacities.'
   - Jose Ortega y Gasset

'Adversity has the same effect on a man that severe training has on the pugilist - it reduces him to his fighting weight.'
   - Josh Billings

'Of all the advantages which come to any young man ... poverty is the greatest.'
   - Josiah G. Holland

'Much of your pain is the bitter potion by which the physician within you heals your sick self.'
   - Kahlil Gibran

'When I was very young, I tried selling used cars. It didn't last long. I guess that was my good luck too, that I didn't show more promise at it, or I might have been an automobile dealer.'
   - King Vidor

'My luck was my father not striking oil... we'd have been rich. I'd never have set out for Hollywood with my camera, and I'd have had a lot less interesting life.'
- King Vidor

'It is the surmounting of difficulties that makes heroes.'
- Kossuth

'I think hearts are very much like glasses - if they do not break with the first ring, they usually last a considerable time.'
- L. E. Landon

'Supporting myself at an early age was the best training for life I could have possibly received.'
- Lea Thompson

'The most valuable gift I ever received was ... the gift of insecurity ... my father left us. My mother's love might not have prepared me for life the way my father's departure did. He forced us out on the road, where we had to earn our bread.'
- Lillian Gish

'What we want is never simple.'
- Linda Pastan

'Adversity is another way to measure the greatness of individuals. I never had a crisis that didn't make me stronger.'
- Lou Holtz

'Men strive for peace, but it is their enemies that give them strength, and I think if man no longer had enemies, he would have to invent them, for his strength only grows from struggle.'
- Louis L'Amour

'Enemies can be an incentive to survive and become someone in spite of them. Enemies can keep you alert and aware.'
- Louis L'Amour

'Problems are the cutting edge that distinguishes between success and failure. Problems ... create our courage and wisdom.'
- M. Scott Peck

'By becoming more unhappy, we sometimes learn how to be less so.'
- Madame Swetchine

'In my youth, poverty enriched me, but now I can afford wealth.'
- Marc Chagall

'It is grief that develops the powers of the mind.'
- Marcel Proust

'We are healed of a suffering only by experiencing it to the full.'
- Marcel Proust

'The good things that belong to prosperity are to be wished, but the good things that belong to adversity are to be admired.'
- Marcus Annaeus Seneca

'Brave men rejoice in adversity, just as brave soldiers triumph in war.'
- Marcus Annaeus Seneca

'Fire is the test of gold, adversity of strong men.'
- Marcus Annaeus Seneca

'Nothing befalls a man except what is in his nature to endure.'
- Marcus Aurelius

'I have always fought for ideas - until I learned that it isn't ideas but grief, struggle, and flashes of vision which enlighten.'
- Margaret Anderson

'Troubles cured you salty as a country ham, smoky to the taste, thick-skinned and tender inside.'
- Marge Piercy

'If you have been sunned through and through like an apricot on a wall from your earliest days, you are oversensitive to any withdrawal of heat.'
- Margot Asquith

'We say: mad with joy. We should say: wise with grief.'
- Marguerite Yourcenar

'Life can be real tough ... you can either learn from your problems, or keep repeating them over and over.'
- Marie Osmond

'Some knowledge and some song and some beauty must be kept for those days before the world again plunges into darkness.'
- Marion Zimmer Bradley

'A woman has got to love a bad man once or twice in her life to be thankful for a good one.'
- Marjorie Kinnan Rawlings

'Necessity is the mother of "taking chances."'
- Mark Twain

'The ultimate measure of a man is not where he stands in moments of comfort and convenience, but where he stands at times of challenge and controversy.'
- Martin Luther King, Jr.

'I think there is this about the great troubles - they teach us the art of cheerfulness; whereas the small ones cultivate the industry of discontent.'
- Mary Adams

'Sorrow has its reward. It never leaves us where it found us.'
- Mary Baker Eddy

'Experience may be hard but we claim its gifts because they are real, even though our feet bleed on its stones.'
- Mary Parker Follett

'The pain of love is the pain of being alive. It is a perpetual wound.'
- Maureen Duffy

'A clay pot sitting in the sun will always be a clay pot. It has to go through the white heat of the furnace to become porcelain.'
- Mildred W. Struven

'Experience is a good teacher, but she sends in terrific bills.'
- Minna Antrim

'The thought that we are enduring the unendurable is one of the things that keeps us going.'
- Molly Haskell

'A woman is like a tea bag: you never know her strength until you drop her in hot water.'
- Nancy Reagan

'Time engraves our faces with all the tears we have not shed.'
- Natalie Clifford Barney

'Discontent is the first step in the progress of a man or a nation.'
- Oscar Wilde

'It is the north wind that lashes men into Vikings; it is the soft, luscious south wind which lulls them to lotus dreams.'
- Ouida

'A great man does not lose his self-possession when he is afflicted; the ocean is not made muddy by the falling in of its banks.'
- Panchatantra

'Those who have suffered understand suffering and therefore extend their hand.'
- Patti Smith

'They merit more praise who know how to suffer misery than those who temper themselves in contentment.'
- Pietro Aretino

'Prosperity tries the fortunate; adversity the great.'
- Pliny the Younger

'From their errors and mistakes, the wise and good learn wisdom for the future.'
- Plutarch

'Prosperity provideth, but adversity proveth friends.'
- Queen Elizabeth I

'People wish to be settled; only as far as they are unsettled is there any hope for them.'
- Ralph Waldo Emerson

'Bad times have a scientific value. These are occasions a good learner would not miss.'
- Ralph Waldo Emerson

'The effects of opposition are wonderful. There are men who rise refreshed on hearing of a threat, men to whom a crises, which intimidates and paralyzes the majority, comes as graceful and beloved as a bride!'
- Ralph Waldo Emerson

'Every calamity is a spur and valuable hint.'
- Ralph Waldo Emerson

'When a man is pushed, tormented, defeated, he has a chance to learn something; he has been put on his wits ... he has gained facts, learned his ignorance, is cured of the insanity of conceit, has got moderation and real skill.'
- Ralph Waldo Emerson

'Pain, indolence, sterility, endless ennui have also their lesson for you.'
- Ralph Waldo Emerson

'Calamity is the test of integrity.'
- Richardson

'There is not enough darkness in all the world to put out the light of even one small candle.'
- Robert Alden

'Americans are like a rich father who wishes he knew how to give his sons the hardships that made him rich.'
- Robert Frost

'Never complain about your troubles; they are responsible for more than half of your income.'
- Robert R. Updegraff

'To live is to suffer, to survive is to find some meaning in the suffering.'
- Roberta Flack

'Every failure made me more confident. Because I wanted even more to achieve things, as revenge. To show that I could.'
- Roman Polanski

'This struggle of people against their conditions, this is where you find the meaning in life.'
- Rose Chernin

'I've had an unhappy life, thank God.'
- Russell Baker

'Your first big trouble can be a bonanza if you live through it. Get through the first trouble, and you'll probably make it through the next one.'
- Ruth Gordon

'Without the burden of afflictions it is impossible to reach the height of grace. The gift of grace increases as the struggles increase.'
- Saint Rose of Lima

'Necessity makes even the timid brave.'
- Sallust

'In victory even the cowardly like to boast, while in adverse times even the brave are discredited.'
- Sallust

'Adversity has ever been considered as the state in which a man most easily becomes acquainted with himself, being free from flatterers.'
- Samuel Johnson

'Adversity leads us to think properly of our state, and so is most beneficial to us.'
- Samuel Johnson

'(Adversity is) the state in which a man most easily becomes acquainted with himself, being especially free from admirers then.'
- Samuel Johnson

'He knows not his own strength who hath not met adversity.'
- Samuel Johnson

'Night brings our troubles to the light rather than banishes them.'
- Seneca

'No untroubled day has ever dawned for me.'
- Seneca

'Whenever there is chaos, it creates wonderful thinking. I consider chaos a gift.'
- Septima Poinsette Clark

'Pain is the root of knowledge.'
- Simone Weil

'Disappointment is the nurse of wisdom.'
- Sir Boyle Roche

'Adversity is, to me at least, a tonic and a bracer.'
- Sir Walter Scott

'If all our misfortunes were laid in one common heap, whence every one must take an equal portion, most people would be content to take their own and depart.'
- Solon

'The keenest sorrow is to recognize ourselves as the sole cause of all our adversities.'
- Sophocles

'From a fallen tree, all make kindling.'
- Spanish proverb

'You can't have more bugs than a blanketful.'
- Spanish proverb

'He who serves God with what costs him nothing, will do very little service, you may depend on it.'
- Susan Warner

'When things come to the worse, they generally mend.'
- Susanna Moodie

'When one's own problems are unsolvable and all best efforts are frustrated, it is lifesaving to listen to other people's problems.'
- Suzanne Massie

'If you have to be careful because of oppression and censorship, this pressure produces diamonds.'
- Tatyana Tolstaya

'Don't look forward to the day when you stop suffering. Because when it comes, you'll know you're dead.'
- Tennessee Williams

'I have always been pushed by the negative.... The apparent failure of a play sends me back to my typewriter that very night, before the reviews are out. I am more compelled to get back to work than if I had a success.'
- Tennessee Williams

'The saints rejoiced at injuries and persecutions, because in forgiving them they had something to present to God when they prayed to Him.'
- Teresa of Avila

'It constantly happens that the Lord permits a soul to fall so that it may grow humbler.'
- Teresa of Avila

'The burden is equal to the horse's strength.'
- The Talmud

'Restlessness is discontent, and discontent is the first necessity of progress.'
- Thomas A. Edison

'We only really face up to ourselves when we are afraid.'
- Thomas Bernhard

'Adversity is sometimes hard upon a man; but for one man who can stand prosperity, there are a hundred that will stand adversity.'
- Thomas Carlyle

'The block of granite which was an obstacle in the path of the weak becomes a steppingstone in the path of the strong.'
- Thomas Carlyle

'Times of stress and difficulty are seasons of opportunity when the seeds of progress are sown.'
- Thomas F. Woodlock

'Noble discontent is the path to heaven.'
- Thomas W. Higginson

'Emergencies have always been necessary to progress. It was darkness which produced the lamp. It was fog that produced the compass. It was hunger that drove us to exploration. And it took a depression to teach us the real value of a job.'
- Victor Hugo

'Difficulties, opposition, criticism - these things are meant to be overcome, and there is a special joy in facing them and in coming out on top. It is only when there is nothing but praise that life loses its charm and I begin to wonder what I should do about it.'
- Vijaya Lakshmi Pandit

'You'll never find a better sparring partner than adversity.'
- Walt Schmidt

'Constant success shows us but one side of the world; adversity brings out the reverse of the picture.'
- Walter Colton

'Some minds seem almost to create themselves, springing up under every disadvantage and working their solitary but irresistible way through a thousand obstacles.'
- Washington Irving

'Things have got to be wrong in order that they may be deplored.'
- Whitney Griswold

'There are some things you learn best in calm, and some in storm.'
- Willa Cather

'Adversity causes some men to break, others to break records.'
- William A. Ward

'Remorse begets reform.'
- William Cowper

'Difficulties are meant to rouse, not discourage. The human spirit is to grow strong by conflict.'
   - William Ellery Channing

'Too much happens ... Man performs, engenders so much more than he can or should have to bear. That's how he finds that he can bear anything.'
   - William Faulkner

'Unless a man has been kicked around a little, you can't really depend upon him to amount to anything.'
   - William Feather

'Prosperity is a great teacher; adversity is a greater. Possession pampers the mind; privation trains and strengthens it.'
   - William Hazlitt

'The same reason makes a man a religious enthusiast that makes a man an enthusiast in any other way: an uncomfortable mind in an uncomfortable body.'
   - William Hazlitt

'The difficulties and struggles of today are but the price we must pay for the accomplishments and victories of tomorrow.'
   - William J. H. Boetcker

'Be willing to have it so; acceptance of what has happened is the first step to overcoming the consequences of any misfortune.'
   - William James

'Men habitually use only a small part of the powers which they possess and which they might use under appropriate circumstances.'
   - William James

'It is from the level of calamities ... that we learn impressive and useful lessons.'
   - William Makepeace Thackeray

'People don't ever seem to realize that doing what's right is no guarantee against misfortune.'
   - William McFee

'No pain, no palm; no thorns, no throne; no gall, no glory; no cross, no crown.'
   - William Penn

'Sweet are the uses of adversity; Which, like the toad, ugly and venomous, Wears yet a precious jewel in his head.'
   - William Shakespeare

'The man who is swimming against the stream knows the strength of it.'
   - Woodrow Wilson

'I have been in sorrow's kitchen and licked out all the pots. Then I have stood on the peaky mountain wrapped in rainbows, with a harp and sword in my hands.'
  - Zora Neale Hurston

AGING

Wisdom doesn't automatically come with old age. Nothing does - except wrinkles. It's true, some wines improve with age. But only if the grapes were good in the first place.'
- Abigail Van Buren

'No gains without pains.'
- Adlai Stevenson

'It is always in season for old men to learn.'
- Aeschylus

'I never think of the future. It comes soon enough.'
- Albert Einstein

'An old codger, rampant, and still learning.'
- Aldous Huxley

'Growing old is no more than a bad habit which a busy man has no time to form.'
- Andri Maurois

'Age and treachery will triumph over youth and skill.'
- Anonymous

'I was going to take you out to lunch for your birthday . . . but you already are.'
- Anonymous

'I wouldn't say someone is old just because his social security is in Roman numerals or because Mozart played at his senior prom.'
- Anonymous

'If you think a lot of the comments made tonight are not funny, but are immature and tasteless, that's only because the sense of humor is the first thing to go.'
- Anonymous

'Life begins at fifty, but so does bad eyesight, arthritis, and the habit of telling the same story three times to the same listeners.'
- Anonymous

'She's too young for Medicare and too old for me to care.'
- Anonymous

'Once my wife gave me a wonderful birthday present. She let me win an argument.'
- Anonymous

'Pushing fifty is exercise enough.'
- Anonymous

'When we're young we want to change the world. When we're old we want to change the young.'
- Anonymous

'She's not pushing forty, she's dragging it.'
- Anonymous

'Wrinkles - the service stripes of life.'
- Anonymous

'When she told me her age I believed her - why not? she hasn't changed her story for five years.'
- Anonymous

'Remember when we used to laugh at old people when we were young? Do you recall what was so funny?'
- Anonymous

'Middle age is when you have a choice of two temptations and choose the one that will get you home earlier.'
- Anonymous

'When I think of my dad as a little boy, I tend to think of him in black and white.'
- Anonymous

'When Julia Child was asked to what she credited her longevity, she replied, "Red meat and gin."'
- Anonymous

'The age of some women is like the speedometer on a used car - you know it's set back, but you don't know how far.'
- Anonymous

'I hope you live to be as old as your jokes.'
- Anonymous

'Growing old is like being increasingly penalized for a crime you have not committed.'
- Anthony Powell

'A man of sixty has spent twenty years in bed and over three years in eating.'
- Arnold Bennett

'Growing old - it's not nice, but it's interesting.'
- August Strindberg

'Middle age is when your narrow waist and broad mind begin to change places.'
- Ben Klitzner

'All would live long, but none would be old.'
- Benjamin Franklin

'Middle age is when your old classmates are so gray and wrinkled and bald they don't recognize you.'
- Bennett Cerf

'To me, old age is always fifteen years older than I am.'
- Bernard Baruch

'After thirty, a body has a mind of its own.'
- Bette Midler

'Your old men shall dream dreams, your young men shall see visions.'
- Bible

'And he (King David) died in a good old age, full of days, riches and honor.'
- Bible

'Gray hair is God's graffiti.'
- Bill Cosby

'One trouble with growing older is that it gets progressively tougher to find a famous historical figure who didn't amount to much when he was your age.'
- Bill Vaughan

'Women, don't get a tattoo. That butterfly looks great on your breast when you're twenty or thirty, but when you get to be seventy, it stretches into a condor.'
- Billy Elmer

'I don't generally feel anything until noon, then it's time for my nap.'
- Bob Hope

'He's so old his social security number is two digits.'
- Brian Morgan

'Old age, especially an honored old age, has so great authority, that this is of more value than all the pleasures of youth.'
- Cicero

'Old age is by nature rather talkative.'
- Cicero

'Every man who has lived his life to the full should, by the time his senior years are reached, have established a reserve inventory of unfinished thinking.'
- Clarence Randall

'Time goes by: reputation increases, ability declines.'
- Dag Hammarskjold

'Happy the man who gains sagacity in youth, but thrice happy he who retains the fervor of youth in age.'
- Dagobert Runes

'Middle age is having a choice between two temptations and choosing the one that'll get you home earlier.'
  - Dan Bennett

'Middle age is youth without its levity, And age without decay.'
  - Daniel Defoe

'You're only young once, but you can always be immature.'
  - Dave Barry

'There's one advantage to being 102. There's no peer pressure.'
  - Dennis Wolfberg

'She was born in the year of our Lord only knows. The years that a woman subtracts from her age are not lost. They are added to other women's.'
  - Diane de Poitiers

'The really frightening thing about middle age is the knowledge that you'll grow out of it.'
  - Doris Day

'My notion of a wife at forty is that a man should be able to change her, like a banknote, for two twenties.'
  - Douglas Jerrold

'I feel age like an icicle down my back.'
  - Dyson Carter

'The best way to remember your wife's birthday is to forget it once.'
  - E. Joseph Cossman

'I'm very pleased with each advancing year. It stems back to when I was forty. I was a bit upset about reaching that milestone, but an older friend consoled me. 'Don't complain about growing old - many people don't have that privilege.''
  - Earl Warren

'If you want to know how old a woman is . . . ask her sister-in-law.'
  - Edgar Howe

'I was just thinking, when I was a young girl, I never knew what every young girl was supposed to know. And now I am going to be an old lady, I don't know what every old lady is supposed to know.'
  - Edith Bunker

'Life has got to be lived - that's all there is to it. At seventy, I would say the advantage is that you take life more calmly. You know that 'this, too, shall pass!''
  - Eleanor Roosevelt

'He is at an age that whenever a pretty girl smiles at him he immediately looks down to see what is unzipped.'
  - Elmer Pasta

'She claims she just turned thirty, but it must have been a U-turn!'
  - Elmer Pasta

'Many a man that couldn't direct ye to th' drug store on th' corner when he was thirty will get a respectful hearin' when age has further impaired his mind.'
  - Finley Peter Dunne

'Sometimes I feel that I'm not just aging . . . I'm decomposing.'
  - Fletcher Anderson

'The cost of living is going up and the chance of living is going down.'
  - Flip Wilson

'I have learned little from the years that fly; but I have wrung the color from the years.'
  - Frances Pollock

'Middle age occurs when you are too young to take up golf and too old to rush up to the net.'
  - Franklin Pierce Adams

'Old age is like everything else, to make a success of it you got to start young.'
  - Fred Astaire

'If the young only knew; if the old only could.'
  - French saying

'My opportunities were still there, nay, they multiplied tenfold; but the strength and youth to cope with them began to fail, and to need eking out with the shifty cunning of experience.'
  - George Bernard Shaw

'I stay away from natural foods. At my age I need all the preservatives I can get.'
  - George Burns

'You know you're getting old when you stoop to tie your shoes and wonder what else you can do while you're down there.'
  - George Burns

'I must be getting absent-minded. Whenever I complain that things aren't what they used to be, I always forget to include myself.'
  - George Burns

'Before you contradict an old man, my fair friend, you should endeavor to understand him.'
  - George Santayana

'An old man concludeth from his knowing mankind that they know him too, and that maketh him very wary.'
  - George Saville

'Old age takes away from us what we have inherited and gives us what we have earned.'
  - Gerald Brenan

'An old man loved is Winter with flowers.'
   - German proverb

'Old birds are hard to pluck.'
   - German proverb

'So, lively brisk old fellow, don't let age get you down. White hairs or not, you can still be a lover.'
   - Goethe

'Old age is like a plane flying through a storm. Once you are aboard there is nothing you can do.'
   - Golda Meir

'You know you are getting older when "happy hour" is a nap.'
   - Gray Kristofferson

'I have everything I had twenty years ago, only it's all a little bit lower.'
   - Gypsy Rose Lee

'I am just turning 40 and taking my time about it.'
   - Harold Lloyd

'Here's a new day. 0 Pendulum move slowly!'
   - Harold Munro

'For the unlearned, old age is winter; for the learned, it is the season of the harvest.'
   - Hasidic saying

'To know how to grow old is the master-work of wisdom, and one of the most difficult chapters in the great art of living.'
   - Henri Frederic Amiel

'If you live long enough the venerability factor creeps in; you get accused of things you never did and praised for virtues you never had.'
   - I. F. Stone

'Old age is a time of humiliations, the most disagreeable of which, for me, is that I cannot work long at sustained high pressure with no leaks in concentration.'
   - Igor Stravinsky

'One of the delights known to age, and beyond the grasp of youth, is that of 'not going'!'
   - J. B. Priestley

'Let us respect gray hairs, especially our own.'
   - J. P. Senn

'You know you're getting older when you don't care where your wife goes, just so you don't have to go along.'
   - Jacob Braude

'The old repeat themselves and the young have nothing to say. The boredom is mutual.'
   - Jacques Bainville

'If I'd known I was gonna live this long (100 years), I'd have taken better care of myself.'
   - James Hubert Blake

'Actually, being sixty-five isn't so bad. As a matter of fact I rather like being called a sexagenarian. At this time of life it sounds like flattery.'
   - James Humes

'I'm sixty-five, but if there were fifteen months in every year, I'd only be forty-eight.'
   - James Thurber

'When you are forty, half of you belongs to the past. . . And when you are seventy, nearly all of you.'
   - Jean Anouilh

'People who have the most birthdays live the longest.'
   - Jean Bucher

'What makes old age so sad is not that our joys but our hopes cease.'
   - Jean Paul Richter

'Looking fifty is great - if you're sixty.'
   - Joan Rivers

'How beautifully the leaves grow old. How full of light and color are their last days.'
   - John Burroughs

'No Spring, nor Summer beauty hath such grace, As I have seen in one Autumnal face.'
   - John Donne

'As the world is weary of me so am I of it.'
   - John Knox

'No wise man ever wished to be younger.'
   - Jonathan Swift

'Dignity, high station, or great riches are in some sort necessary to old men, in order to keep the younger at a distance, who are otherwise too apt to insult them upon the score of their age.'
   - Jonathan Swift

'Zsa Gabor, when asked which of the Gabor women was the oldest, said "She'll never admit it, but I believe it is Mama." When men grow virtuous in their old age, they only make a sacrifice to God of the devil's leavings.'
   - Jonathan Swift

'Old age is an island surrounded by death.'
   - Juan Montalvo

'I haven't asked you to make me young again. All I want is to go on getting older.'
  - Konrad Adenauer

'Few people know how to be old.'
  - La Rochefoucauld

'I refuse to admit I'm more than fifty-two, even if that does make my sons illegitimate.'
  - Lady Nancy Astor

'Middle age is when anything new in the way you feel is most likely a symptom.'
  - Laurence J. Peter

'First you forget names, then you forget faces, then you forget to pull your zipper up, then you forget to pull your zipper down.'
  - Leo Rosenberg

'The denunciation of the young is a necessary part of the hygiene of older people, and greatly assists the circulation of their blood.'
  - Logan Pearsall Smith

'Old age is the Outpatient's Dept of purgatory.'
  - Lord Cecil

'Of all the things I miss, the thing I miss the most is my mind.'
  - Lotus Weinstock

'The secret of staying young is to live honestly, eat slowly, and lie about your age.'
  - Lucille Ball

'At eighty-eight how do you feel when getting up in the morning? . . . Amazed!'
  - Ludwig von Mises

'They tell you that you'll lose your mind when you grow older. What they don't tell you is that you won't miss it very much.'
  - Malcolm Cowley

'It is the fear of being as dependent as a young child, while not being loved as a child is loved, but merely being kept alive against one's will.'
  - Malcolm Cowley

'When you reach your sixties, you have to decide whether you're going to be a sot or an ascetic. In other words if you want to go on working after you're sixty, some degree of asceticism is inevitable.'
  - Malcolm Muggeridge

'He had come to that time in his life (it varies for every man) when a human being gives himself over to his demon or to his genius, according to a mysterious law which orders him either to destroy or to surpass himself.'
  - Marguerite Yourcenar

'As one cat said to another: Birthdays are like fur balls - the more you have, the more you gag.'
- Maria Morgan

'Wrinkles should merely indicate where smiles have been.'
- Mark Twain

'To an old man any place that's warm is homeland.'
- Maxim Gorky

'We grow neither better nor worse as we get old, but more like ourselves'
- May Lamberton Becker

'Enjoy how sweet, how thoughtful, how kind I'm being on your birthday. Because tomorrow it's back to the same old crap.'
- Melvin Helitzer

'I can't tell you his age, but when he was born the wonder drug was Mercurochrome.'
- Milton Berle

'I refuse to admit that I am more than 52, even if that makes my sons illegitimate.'
- Nancy Lady Astor

'Senescence begins And middle age ends, The day your descendants Outnumber your friends.'
- Ogden Nash

'Middle age: when you're sitting at home on Saturday night and the telephone rings and you hope it isn't for you.'
- Ogden Nash

'Middle age is when you have met so many people that every new person you meet reminds you of someone else and usually is.'
- Ogden Nash

'There is many a good tune played on an old fiddle.'
- Old saying

'Longevity is having a chronic disease and taking care of it.'
- Oliver Wendell Holmes

'A person is always startled when he hears himself seriously called an old man for the first time.'
- Oliver Wendell Holmes

'A man over ninety is a great comfort to all his elderly neighbors: he is a picket-guard at the extreme outpost: and the young folks of sixty and seventy feel that the enemy must get by him before he can come near their camp.'
- Oliver Wendell Holmes

'The young man knows the rules but the old man knows the exceptions.'
- Oliver Wendell Holmes

'To be seventy years young is sometimes far more cheerful and hopeful than to be forty years old.'
- Oliver Wendell Holmes

'An older author is constantly rediscovering himself in the more or less fossilized productions of his earlier years.'
- Oliver Wendell Holmes

'If you think that I am going to bother myself again before I die about social improvement, or read any of those stinking upward and onwarders - you err - I mean to have some good out of being old.'
- Oliver Wendell Holmes

'I really believe that more harm is done by old men who cling to their influence than by young men who anticipate it.'
- Owen D. Young

'Try to accept each other for what you are, and don't point out the fact that the hair he's losing on his head is now growing out of his nose - and his ears.'
- Peg Bundy

'I'm at an age where my back goes out more than I do.'
- Phyllis Diller

'The best contraceptive for old people is nudity.'
- Phyllis Diller

'Age has a good mind and sorry shanks.'
- Pietro Aretino

'The spiritual eyesight improves as the physical eyesight declines.'
- Plato

'The young always have the same problem - how to rebel and conform at the same time. They have now solved this by defying their parents and copying one another.'
- Quentin Crisp

'It is time to be old, To take in sail.'
- Ralph Waldo Emerson

'There are three signs of old age: loss of memory ... I forget the other two.'
- Red Skelton

'There are three ages of man: youth, middle age, and "Gee, you look good."'
- Red Skelton

'Middle age snuffs out more talent than even wars or sudden deaths do.'
- Richard Hughes

'When pain ends, gain ends too.'
- Robert Browning

'Grow old with me! The best is yet to be, The last of life, for which the first was made: Our times are in his hands Who sayeth "a whole I plant, Youth shows but half; Trust God; see all nor be afraid."'
- Robert Browning

'I never dared be radical when young For fear it would make me conservative when old.'
- Robert Frost

'By the time a man gets well into his seventies his continued existence is a mere miracle.'
- Robert Louis Stevenson

'It's an awful thing to grow old by yourself. My wife hasn't had a birthday in seven years.'
- Robert Orben

'My wife never lies about her age. She just tells everyone she's as old as I am. Then she lies about my age.'
- Robert Orben

'I may be forty, but every morning when I get up, I feel like a twenty-year-old. Unfortunately, there's never one around.'
- Robert Orben

'My health is good; it's my age that's bad.'
- Roy Acuff

'The arctic loneliness of age.'
- S. Weir Mitchell

'It's never too late to have a fling For autumn is just as nice as spring And it's never too late to fall in love.'
- Sandy Wilson

'Age is mind over matter. If you don't mind, it doesn't matter.'
- Satchel Paige

'How old would you be if you didn't know how old you are?'
- Satchel Paige

'The age of a woman doesn't mean a thing. The best tunes are played on the oldest fiddles.'
- Sigmund Z. Engel

'The role of a retired person is no longer to possess one.'
- Simone de Beauvoir

'To what do you attribute your advanced age? Well, I suppose I must attribute it to the fact that I have not died.'
- Sir Malcolm Sargent

'The secret to longevity is to keep breathing.'
- Sophie Tucker

'We've reached an age that when construction workers stare at us it's because they figure we might be considering a remodeling job.'
- Susan McClellan

'The difference between being an elder statesman And posing successfully as an elder statesman Is practically negligible.'
- T. S. Eliot

'The years between fifty and seventy are the hardest. You are always asked to do things, and you are not yet decrepit enough to turn them down.'
- T. S. Eliot

'In the last few years everything I'd done up to sixty or so has seemed very childish.'
- T. S. Eliot

'The young feel tired at the end of an Taking Action; The old at the beginning.'
- T. S. Eliot

'For weeks I've been telling him not to buy anything for my birthday, and he still forgot to bring me something.'
- Tanya Noe

'I am long on ideas, but short on time. I expect to live only about a hundred years.'
- Thomas A. Edison

'All the best sands of my life are somehow getting into the wrong end of the hourglass. If I could only reverse it! Were it in my power to do so, would I?'
- Thomas Bailey Aldrich

'To keep the heart unwrinkled, to be hopeful, kindly, cheerful, reverent -that is to triumph over old age.'
- Thomas Bailey Aldrich

'Old foxes want no tutors.'
- Thomas Fuller

'It's a sobering thought: When Mozart was my age, he had been dead for two years.'
- Tom Lehrer

'Age is a high price to pay for maturity.'
- Tom Stoppard

'What can you say when your husband says: 'You can't expect me to remember your birthday when you never look any older.''
- Toni Anderson

'Forty is the old age of youth; fifty is the youth of old age.'
- Victor Hugo

'I advise you to go on living solely to enrage those who are paying your annuities. It is the only pleasure I have left.'
- Voltaire

'Yes, I'm 68, but when I was a boy I was too poor to smoke, so knock off ten years. That makes me 58. And since I never developed the drinking habit, you can knock off ten more years. So I'm 48 - in the prime of my life. Retire? Retire to what?'
- W. A. C. Bennett

'The individual succumbs, but he does not die if he has left something to mankind.'
- Will Durant

'He that has seen both sides of fifty has lived to little purpose if he has no other views of the world than he had when he was much younger.'
- William Cowper

'A man of fifty looks as old as Santa Claus to a girl of twenty.'
- William Feather

'We do not die wholly at our deaths: we have moldered away gradually long before. Faculty after faculty, interest after interest, attachment after attachment disappear: we are torn from ourselves while living.'
- William Hazlitt

'Golden lads and girls all must, As chimney-sweepers, come to dust.'
- William Shakespeare

'Is it not strange that desire should so many years outlive performance?'
- William Shakespeare

'You can live to be a hundred, if you give up all the things that make you want to live to a hundred.'
- Woody Allen

'I'm at the stage of life when if a girl says no to me I'm profoundly grateful to her.'
- Woody Allen

ANGER

Anger makes dull men witty, but it keeps them poor.'
- Anonymous

'An angry man opens his mouth and shuts up his eyes.'
- Anonymous

'He that is slow to anger is better than the mighty; and he that ruleth his spirit than he that taketh a city.'
- Bible

'Anger blows out the lamp of the mind. In the examination of a great and important question, every one should be serene, slow-pulsed, and calm.'
- Charles J. Ingersoll

'Never answer a letter while you are angry.'
- Chinese proverb

'Anger as soon as fed is dead - Tis starving makes it fat.'
- Emily Dickinson

'Many people lose their tempers merely from seeing you keep yours.'
- Frank Moore Colby

'Never forget what a man says to you when he is angry.'
- Henry Ward Beecher

'Anger is momentary madness, so control your passion or it will control you.'
- Horace

'Beware the fury of a patient man.'
- John Dryden

'I never work better than when I am inspired by anger; for when I am angry, I can write, pray, and preach well, for then my whole temperament is quickened, my understanding sharpened, and all mundane vexations and temptations depart.'
- Martin Luther

'There is no passion so much transports the sincerity of judgement as doth anger.'
- Michel de Montaigne

'Never go to bed mad. Stay up and fight.'
- Phyllis Diller

'A good indignation brings out all one's powers.'
- Ralph Waldo Emerson

'Don't get mad, get even.'
- Robert F. Kennedy

'When angry, count four; when very angry, swear.'
- Samuel L. Clemens

'It's my rule never to lose my temper until it would be detrimental to keep it.'
- Sean O'Casey

'Anger is one of the sinners of the soul.'
- Thomas Fuller

'Men often make up in wrath what they want in reason.'
- W. R. Alger

'I was angry with my friend: I told my wrath, my wrath did end. I was angry with my foe: I told it not, my wrath did grow.'
- William Blake

'Heaven has no rage like love to hatred turned, Nor hell a fury like a woman scorned.'
- William Congreve

'Heav'n has no rage, like love to hatred turn'd, Nor Hell a fury, like a woman scorn'd.'
- William Congreve

'Who can refute a sneer?'
- William Paley

ART & CULTURE

'A first rate soup is better than a second rate painting.'
   - Abraham Maslow

Living is a form of not being sure, not knowing what next or how. The moment you know how, you begin to die a little. The artist never entirely knows. We guess. We may be wrong, but we take leap after leap in the dark.'
   - Agnes de Mille

'Every artist preserves deep within him a single source from which, throughout his lifetime, he draws what he is and what he says and when the source dries up the work withers and crumbles.'
   - Albert Camus

'The scholar seeks, the artist finds.'
   - Andre Gide

'A work of art is an exaggeration.'
   - Andre Gide

'All art is a revolt against man's fate.'
   - Andri Malraux

'Art not only imitates nature, but also completes its deficiencies.'
   - Aristotle

'One of the recognizable features of the authentic masterpiece is its capacity to renew itself, to endure the loss of some kinds of immediate relevance while still answering the most important questions men can ask, including new ones they are just learnin'
   - Arnold Stein

'We should comport ourselves with the masterpieces of art as with exalted personages - stand quietly before them and wait till they speak to us.'
   - Arthur Schopenhauer

'I've been 40 years discovering that the Queen of all colors is black.'
   - Auguste Renoir

'One must work, nothing but work, and one must have patience.'
   - Auguste Rodin

'An amateur is an artist who supports himself with outside jobs which enable him to paint. A professional is someone whose wife works to enable him to paint.'
   - Ben Shahn

'I wonder whether Art has a higher function than to make me feel, appreciate, and enjoy natural objects for their art value?'
- Bernard Berenson

'As an artist grows older, he has to fight disillusionment and learn to establish the same relation to nature as an adult as he had when a child.'
- Charles Burchfield

'The song of the brush.'
- Chinese saying

'Art is I, science is we.'
- Claude Bernard

'All profoundly original art looks ugly at first.'
- Clement Greenberg

'Conception, my boy, fundamental brainwork, is what makes the difference in all art.'
- Dante Gabriel Rossetti

'Art isn't something you marry, it's something you rape.'
- Edgar Degas

'Art is based on order. The world is full of 'sloppy Bohemians' and their work betrays them.'
- Eduard Weston

'Man in Canadian art is rarely in command of his environment or ever at home in it.'
- Elizabeth Kilbourn

'If you ask me what I came to do in this world, I, an artist, I will answer you: T am here to live out loud.''
- Emile Zola

'A work of art is a corner of creation seen through a temperament.'
- Entile Zola

'Children, like animals, use all their senses to discover the world. Then artists come along and discover it the same way all over again.'
- Eudora Welty

'Artists are the antennae of the race, but the bullet-headed many will never learn to trust the great artists.'
- Ezra Pound

'Artistic temperament is a disease that afflicts amateurs.'
- G. K. Chesterton

'Caricature is rough truth.'
- George Meredith

'If artists and poets are unhappy, it is after all because happiness does not interest them.'
- George Santayana

'Art is a delayed echo.'
- George Santayana

'An artist may visit a museum but only a pedant can live there.'
- George Santayana

'Pioneers did not produce original works of art, because they were creating original human environments; they did not imagine Utopias because they were shaping them.'
- George Woodcock

'It is not in life but in art that self-fulfillment is to be found.'
- George Woodcock

'Art upsets, science reassures.'
- Georges Braque

'Art is a kind of illness.'
- Giacomo Puccini

'Be regular and orderly in your life like a bourgeois, so that you may be violent and original in your work.'
- Gustave Flaubert

'Nothing can come out of an artist that is not in the man.'
- H. L. Mencken

'Art has no other object than to set aside the symbols of practical utility, the generalities that are conventionally and socially accepted, everything in fact which masks reality from us, in order to set us face to face with reality itself.'
- Henri Bergson

'A work should contain its total meaning within itself and should impress it on the spectator before he even knows the subject.'
- Henri Matisse

'An artist has to take life as he finds it. Life by itself is formless wherever it is. Art must give it form.'
- Hugh MacLennan

'When one admires an artist it is important not to know him personally.'
- Jacinto Benaventey Martinez

'Art distills sensation and embodies it with enhanced meaning in memorable form - or else it is not art.'
- Jacques Barzun

'A work of art cannot be satisfied with being a representation; it should be a presentation.'
   - Jacques Reverdy

'All art is a kind of confession, more or less oblique. All artists, if they are to survive, are forced, at last, to tell the whole story; to vomit the anguish up.'
   - James Baldwin

'The artist, like the God of the creation, remains within or behind or beyond or above his handiwork, invisible, refined, out of existence, indifferent, paring his fingernails.'
   - James Joyce

'The object of art is to give life a shape.'
   - Jean Anouilh

'The painting rises from the brushstrokes as a poem rises from the words. The meaning comes later.'
   - Joan Miro

'Theatre takes place all the time wherever one is and art simply facilitates persuading one this is the case.'
   - John Cage

'When power leads man toward arrogance, poetry reminds him of his limitations. When power narrows the areas of man's concern, poetry reminds him of the richness and diversity of his experience. When power corrupts, poetry cleanses. For art establishes the '
   - John F. Kennedy

'I always suspect an artist who is successful before he is dead.'
   - John Murray Gibbon

'Fine art is that in which the hand, the head, and the heart of man go together.'
   - John Ruskin

'Art gropes, it stalks like a hunter lost in the woods, listening to itself and to everything around it, unsure of itself, waiting to pounce.'
   - John W. Gardner

'History repeats itself, but the special call of an art which has passed away is never reproduced. It is utterly gone out of the world as the song of a destroyed wild bird.'
   - Joseph Conrad

'Drawing is speaking to the eye; talking is painting to the ear.'
   - Joseph Joubert

'In any evolutionary process, even in the arts, the search for novelty becomes corrupting.'
   - Kenneth Boulding

'I am convinced it is a mistake to find an artist human outside his work. If you cannot find him human in and through his work, you are better not to know it when you come to formulate an opinion of his

public value.'
  - Kenneth Winters

'The father of every good work is discontent, and its mother is diligence.'
  - Lajos Kassak

'(Ars longa, vita brevis.) Art is long, life is short. A picture can become for us a highway between a particular thing and a universal feeling.'
  - Lawren Harris

'An artist has been defined as a neurotic who continually cures himself with his art.'
  - Lee Simonson

'Art is a human activity, consisting in this, that one man consciously, by means of external signs, hands on to others feelings he has worked through, and other people are infected by these feelings and also experience them.'
  - Leo Tolstoy

'The fingers must be educated, the thumb is born knowing.'
  - Marc Chagall

'It's not what you see that is art, art is the gap.'
  - Marcel Duchamp

'A picture lives by companionship. It dies by the same token. It is therefore risky to send it out into the world. How often it must be impaired by the eyes of the unfeeling.'
  - Mark Rothko

'Art at its most significant is a Distant Early Warning System that can always be relied on to tell the old culture what is beginning to happen to it.'
  - Marshall McLuhan

'The terror of art lies in the representation of the hidden reality with its shattering effect.'
  - Martin Greenburg

'Illustrations have as much to say as the text. The trick is to say the same thing, but in a different way. It's no good being an illustrator who is saying a lot that is on his or her mind, if it has nothing to do with the text. . . the artist must overrid'
  - Maurice Sendak

'It is well with me only when I have a chisel in my hand.'
  - Michelangelo

'When they asked Michelangelo how he made his statue of David he is reported to have said, "It is easy. You just chip away the stone that doesn't look like David."'
  - Michelangelo

'Designers and free lance artists and editors can set their hourly rates by dividing their annual income needs by 1000.'
- Mike Rider

'Art is not an end in itself, but a means of addressing humanity.'
- Modest Mussorgsky

'Classic means standard as opposed to Romantic: form before meaning as opposed to meaning before form. It grows from inside out, while Romantic grows from outside in.'
- Ned Rorem

'Artists, by definition innocent, don't steal. But they do borrow without giving back.'
- Ned Rorem

'With the pride of the artist, you must blow against the walls of every power that exists, the small trumpet of your defiance.'
- Norman Mailer

'The artist, like the idiot, or clown, sits on the edge of the world, and a push may send him over it.'
- Osbert Sitwell

'Good artists exist simply in what they make, and consequently are perfectly uninteresting in what they are.'
- Oscar Wilde

'Art is man's nature; nature is God's art.'
- P. J. Bailey

'Two boys arrived yesterday with a pebble they said was the head of a dog until I pointed out that it was really a typewriter.'
- Pablo Picasso

'Art washes away from the soul the dust of everyday life.'
- Pablo Picasso

'Every child is an artist. The problem is how to remain an artist once he grows up.'
- Pablo Picasso

'Everything in nature is formed upon the sphere, the cone and the cylinder. One must learn to paint these simple figures and then one can do all that he may wish.'
- Paul Cezanne

'We live in a rainbow of chaos.'
- Paul Cezanne

'Art is either plagiarism or revolution.'
- Paul Gauguin

'Art does not reproduce the visible; rather it makes it visible.'
- Paul Klee

'The more horrifying this world becomes, the more art becomes abstract.'
- Paul Klee

'An artist never really finishes his work, he merely abandons it.'
- Paul Valery

'Works of Art are of an infinite loneliness.'
- Rainer Maria Rilke

'Artists must be sacrificed to their art. Like bees, they must put their lives into the sting they give.'
- Ralph Waldo Emerson

'Perpetual modernness is the measure of merit in every work of art.'
- Ralph Waldo Emerson

'Abstract art is uniquely modern. It is a fundamentally romantic response to modern life - rebellious, individualistic, unconventional, sensitive, irritable.'
- Robert Motherwell

'Painting is silent poetry, and poetry is painting with the gift of speech'
- Simonides

'Interpretation is the revenge of the intellect upon art.'
- Susan Sontag

'Style, like the human body, is specially beautiful when the veins are not prominent and the bones cannot be counted.'
- Tacitus

'Dance is the only art of which we ourselves are the stuff of which it is made.'
- Ted Shawn

'As a painter I shall never signify anything of importance. I feel it absolutely.'
- Vincent van Gogh

'Painting is a faith, and it imposes the duty to disregard public opinion.'
- Vincent van Gogh

'One of the most difficult things to do is to paint darkness which nonetheless has light in it.'
- Vincent van Gogh

'Still, there is a calm, pure harmony, and music inside of me.'
- Vincent van Gogh

'Rembrandt painted about 700 pictures - of these, 3,000 are in existence.'
- Wilhelm Bode

'What's an artist, but the dregs of his work - the human shambles that follows it around?'
- William Gaddis

'The cheap, no matter how charming, how immediate, does not wear so well. It has a way of telling its whole story the first time through.'
- William Littler

'Art is the expression of an enormous preference.'
- Wyndham Lewis

BEAUTY

Beauty is unbearable, drives us to despair, offering us for a minute the glimpse of an eternity that we should like to stretch out over the whole of time.'
- Albert Camus

'The Nature of This Flower is to bloom.'
- Alice Walker

'As a beauty I am not a star, There are others more handsome by far, But my face - I don't mind it For I am behind it. It's the people in front get the jar.'
- Anthony Euwer

'Underneath this stone doth lie As much beauty as could die.'
- Ben Jonson

'Mathematics possesses not only truth, but supreme beauty - a beauty cold and austere, like that of a sculpture.'
- Bertrand Russell

'Beauty is power; a smile is its sword.'
- Charles Reade

'And all the loveliest things there be Come simply, so it seems to me.'
- Edna St. Vincent Millay

'There is no excellent beauty that hath not some strangeness in the proportion.'
- Francis Bacon

'The fountain of beauty is the heart, and every generous thought illustrates the walls of your chamber.'
- Francis Quarles

'Anyone who keeps the ability to see beauty never grows old.'
- Franz Kafka

'Beauty as we feel it is something indescribable; what it is or what it means can never be said.'
- George Santayana

'Beautiful is greater than Good, for it includes the Good.'
- Goethe

'Things are beautiful if you love them.'
- Jean Anouilh

'I'm tired of all the nonsense about beauty being only skin-deep. That's deep enough. What do you want - an adorable pancreas?'
- Jean Kerr

'The excellence of every art is its intensity, capable of making all disagreeable evaporate, from their being in close relationship with beauty and truth.'
- John Keats

'A thing of beauty is a joy forever.'
- John Keats

'Beauty is truth - truth, beauty - that is all Ye know on earth, and all ye need to know.'
- John Keats

'Beauty is truth, truth beauty.'
- John Keats

'There is certainly no absolute standard of beauty. That precisely is what makes its pursuit so interesting.'
- John Kenneth Galbraith

'Remember that the most beautiful things in the world are the most useless, peacocks and lilies for instance.'
- John Ruskin

'The beauty of the animal form is in exact proportion to the amount of moral and intellectual virtue expressed by it.'
- John Ruskin

'Beauty is eternity gazing at itself in a mirror.'
- Kahlil Gibran

'There is no cosmetic for beauty like happiness.'
- Lady Blessington

'It is amazing how complete is the delusion that beauty is goodness.'
- Leo Tolstoy

'Beauty - the adjustment of all parts proportionately so that one cannot add or subtract or change without impairing the harmony of the whole.'
- Leon Battista Alberti

'She walks in beauty like the night Of cloudless climes and starry skies; And all that's best of dark and bright Meet in her aspect and her eyes: Thus mellowed to that tender light Which heaven to gaudy day denies.'
- Lord Byron

'The most natural beauty in the world is honesty and moral truth. For all beauty is truth.'
- Lord Shaftesbury

'Until I saw Chardin's painting, I never realized how much beauty lay around me in my parents' house, in the half-cleared table, in the corner of a tablecloth left awry, in the knife beside the empty oyster shell.'
- Marcel Proust

'Beauty is in the eye of the beholder.'
- Margaret Hungerford

'Beauty is everlasting And dust is for a time.'
- Marianne Moore

'Beauty is the purgation of superfluities.'
- Michelangelo

'That which is striking and beautiful is not always good, but that which is good is always beautiful.'
- Ninon de L'Enclos

'Beauty is potent but money is omnipotent.'
- Old saying

'Do you love me because I'm beautiful, or am I beautiful because you love me?'
- Oscar Hammerstein

'We ascribe beauty to that which is simple; which has no superfluous parts; which exactly answers its ends.'
- Ralph Waldo Emerson

'Beauty without expression tires.'
- Ralph Waldo Emerson

'Though we travel the world over to find the beautiful, we must carry it with us or we find it not.'
- Ralph Waldo Emerson

'Some thoughts always find us young, and keep us so. Such a thought is the love of the universal and eternal beauty.'
- Ralph Waldo Emerson

'Let the beauty you love be what you do. There are a thousand ways to kneel and kiss the earth.'
- Rumi

'Beauty, more than bitterness Makes the heart break.'
- Sara Teasdale

'To do the useful thing, to say the courageous thing, to contemplate the beautiful thing: that is enough for one man's life.'
- T. S. Eliot

'When your inner eyes open, you can find immense beauty hidden within the inconsequential details of daily life. When your inner ears open, you can hear the subtle, lovely music of the universe

everywhere you go.'
    - Timothy Ray Miller

'Ask a toad what is beauty? ... a female with two great round eyes coming out of her little head, a large flat mouth, a yellow belly and a brown back.'
    - Voltaire

'Something wonderful and strange that the artist fashions out of the chaos of the world in the torment of his soul.'
    - W. Somerset Maugham

'Beauty is an ecstasy; it is as simple as hunger. There is really nothing to be said about it.'
    - W. Somerset Maugham

'Exuberance is beauty.'
    - William Blake

'A very beautiful woman hardly ever leaves a clear-cut impression of features and shape in the memory: usually there remains only an aura of living color.'
    - William Bolitho

'Grace is the absence of everything that indicates pain or difficulty, hesitation or incongruity.'
    - William Hazlitt

CHANGE

If one sticks too rigidly to one's principles, one would hardly see anybody.'
   - Agatha Christie

'To remain young one must change.'
   - Alexander Chase

'The art of progress is to preserve order amid change, and to preserve change amid order.'
   - Alfred North Whitehead

'Let a man turn to his own childhood-no further-if he will renew his sense of remoteness, and of the mystery of change.'
   - Alice Meynell

'Never swap horses crossing a stream'
   - American Proverb

'One must never lose time in vainly regretting the past or in complaining against the changes which cause us discomfort, for change is the essence of life.'
   - Anatole France

'Only in growth, reform, and change, paradoxically enough, is true security to be found.'
   - Anne Morrow Lindbergh

'Society can only pursue its normal course by means of a certain progression of changes.'
   - Anonymous

'If you do what you've always done, you'll get what you've always gotten.'
   - Anonymous

'Man would be "otherwise." That's the essence of the specifically human.'
   - Antonio Machado

'Variety is the soul of pleasure.'
   - Aphra Behn

'Very often a change of self is needed more than a change of scene.'
   - Arthur Christopher Benson

'Readjusting is a painful process, but most of us need it at one time or another.'
   - Arthur Christopher Benson

'The absurd man is he who never changes.'
   - Auguste Barthelemy

'We measure success and depth by length and time, but it is possible to have a deep relationship that doesn't always stay the same.'
- Barbara Hershey

'Change is inevitable in a progressive society. Change is constant.'
- Benjamin Disraeli

'Some people are still unaware that reality contains unparalleled beauties. The fantastic and unexpected, the ever-changing and renewing is nowhere so exemplified as in real life itself.'
- Berenice Abbott

'Because things are the way they are, things will not stay the way they are.'
- Bertolt Brecht

'Man needs, for his happiness, not only the enjoyment of this or that, but hope and enterprise and change.'
- Bertrand Russell

'We can say "Peace on Earth." We can sing about it, preach about it or pray about it, but if we have not internalized the mythology to make it happen inside us, then it will not be.'
- Betty Shabazz

'Continuity in everything is unpleasant.'
- Blaise Pascal

'When you're through changing, you're through.'
- Bruce Barton

'All that is not eternal is eternally out of date.'
- C. S. Lewis

'The curious paradox is that when I accept myself just as I am, then I can change.'
- Carl Rogers

'We emphasize that we believe in change because we were born of it, we have lived by it, we prospered and grew great by it. So the status quo has never been our god, and we ask no one else to bow down before it.'
- Carl T. Rowan

'Impermanence is the law of the universe.'
- Carlene Hatcher Polite

'The world hates change, yet it is the only thing that has brought progress.'
- Charles F. Kettering

'The world goes up and the world goes down, And the sunshine follows the rain; And yesterday's sneer and yesterday's frown Can never come over again.'
- Charles Kingsley

'The art of living does not consist in preserving and clinging to a particular mood of happiness, but in allowing happiness to change its form ... happiness, like a child, must be allowed to grow up.'
- Charles L. Morgan

'What is more enthralling to the human mind than this splendid, boundless, colored mutability!-Life in the making?'
- David Grayson

'I have found that sitting in a place where you have never sat before can be inspiring.'
- Dodie Smith

'Earth changes, but thy soul and God stand sure.'
- Elizabeth Barrett Browning

'Change is the watchword of progression. When we tire of well-worn ways, we seek for new. This restless craving in the souls of men spurs them to climb, and to seek the mountain view.'
- Ella Wheeler Wilcox

'All is change; all yields its place and goes.'
- Euripides

'Change is the only evidence of life.'
- Evelyn Waugh

'One of the dreariest spots on life's road is the point of conviction that nothing will ever again happen to you.'
- Faith Baldwin

'He that will not apply new remedies must expect new evils.'
- Francis Bacon

'Things alter for the worse spontaneously, if they be not altered for the better designedly.'
- Francis Bacon

'In all change, well looked into, the germinal good out-vails the apparent ill.'
- Francis Thompson

'Everything passes; everything wears out; everything breaks.'
- French proverb

'Changes are not only possible and predictable, but to deny them is to be an accomplice to one's own unnecessary vegetation.'
- Gail Sheehy

'When people shake their heads because we are living in a restless age, ask them how they would like to life in a stationary one, and do without change.'
- George Bernard Shaw

'Progress is impossible without change, and those who cannot change their minds cannot change anything.'
- George Bernard Shaw

'Life is measured by the rapidity of change, the succession of influences that modify the being.'
- George Eliot

'The old woman I shall become will be quite different from the woman I am now. Another I is beginning.'
- George Sand

'In a moving world re-adaptation is the price of longevity.'
- George Santayana

'Nothing in this world is permanent.'
- German proverb

'We're just getting started. We're just beginning to meet what will be the future-we've got the Model T.'
- Grace Murray Hopper

'Each new season grows from the leftovers from the past. That is the essence of change, and change is the basic law.'
- Hal Borland

'To exist is to change, to change is to mature, to mature is to go on creating oneself endlessly.'
- Henri Bergson

'Things do not change; we change.'
- Henry David Thoreau

'All things must change to something new, to something strange.'
- Henry Wadsworth Longfellow

'Our days are a kaleidoscope. Every instant a change takes place. ... New harmonies, new contrasts, new combinations of every sort. ... The most familiar people stand each moment in some new relation to each other, to their work, to surrounding objects.'
- Henry Ward Beecher

'It is in changing that things find purpose.'
- Heraclitus

'Nothing is permanent but change.'
- Heraclitus

'Everything flows, nothing stays still.'
- Heraclitus

'A living thing is distinguished from a dead thing by the multiplicity of the changes at any moment taking place in it.'
- Herbert Spencer

'The challenges of change are always hard. It is important that we begin to unpack those challenges that confront this nation and realize that we each have a role that requires us to change and become more responsible for shaping our own future.'
- Hillary Rodham Clinton

'Just when I think I have learned the way to live, life changes.'
- Hugh Prather

'Life is always at some turning point.'
- Irwin Edman

'Everything changes but change.'
- Israel Zangwill

'The time is ripe, and rotten-ripe, for change; then let it come.'
- James Russell Lowell

'O visionary world, condition strange, Where naught abiding is but only change.'
- James Russell Lowell

'The basic fact of today is the tremendous.'
- Jawaharlal Nehru

'There is not a single ill-doer who could not be turned to some good.'
- Jean-Jacques Rousseau

'I'm tired of playing worn-out depressing ladies in frayed bathrobes. I'm going to get a new hairdo and look terrific and go back to school and even if nobody notices, I'm going to be the most self-fulfilled lady on the block.'
- Joanne Woodward

'We must always change, renew, rejuvenate ourselves; otherwise we harden.'
- Johann von Goethe

'Life belongs to the living, and he who lives must be prepared for changes.'
- Johann von Goethe

'Arriving at one goal is the starting point to another.'
- John Dewey

'Change is the law of life.'
- John F. Kennedy

'The one unchangeable certainty is that nothing is certain or unchangeable.'
- John F. Kennedy

'Everything changes but change itself.'
- John F. Kennedy

'To live is to change, and to be perfect is to change often.'
- John Henry Cardinal Newman

'If folks can learn to be racist, then they can learn to be antiracist. If being sexist ain't genetic, then, dad gum, people can learn about gender equality.'
- Johnnetta Betsch Cole

'For good and evil, man is a free creative spirit. This produces the very queer world we live in, a world in continuous creation and therefore continuous change and insecurity.'
- Joyce Cary

'All love shifts and changes. I don't know if you can be wholeheartedly in love all the time.'
- Julie Andrews

'Life is change. Growth is optional. Choose wisely.'
- Karen Kaiser Clark

'A person needs at intervals to separate himself from family and companions and go to new places. He must go without his familiars in order to be open to influences, to change.'
- Katharine Butler Hathaway

'None of us knows what the next change is going to be, what unexpected opportunity is just around the corner, waiting to change all the tenor of our lives.'
- Kathleen Norris

'I've learned that you'll never be disappointed if you always keep an eye on uncharted territory, where you'll be challenged and growing and having fun.'
- Kirstie Alley

'The most amazing thing about little children ... was their fantastic adaptability.'
- Kristin Hunter

'People change and forget to tell each other.'
- Lillian Hellman

'The old order changeth, yielding place to new.'
- Lord Alfred Tennyson

'I am not now That which I have been.'
- Lord Byron

'We do not succeed in changing things according to our desire, but gradually our desire changes.'
- Marcel Proust

'For many men, the acquisition of wealth does not end their troubles, it only changes them.'
- Marcus Annaeus Seneca

'Why do we shrink from change? What can come into being save by change?'
- Marcus Aurelius

'There is change in all things. You yourself are subject to continual change and some decay, and this is common to the entire universe.'
- Marcus Aurelius

'The mind of the most logical thinker goes so easily from one point to another that it is not hard to mistake motion for progress.'
- Margaret Collier Graham

'The things we fear most in organizations-fluctuations, disturbances, imbalances-are the primary sources of creativity.'
- Margaret J. Wheatley

'No one can persuade another to change. Each of us guards a gate of change that can only be opened from the inside. We cannot open the gate of another, either by argument or emotional appeal.'
- Marilyn Ferguson

'I've learned only that you never say never.'
- Marina von Neumann Whitman

'Fluidity and discontinuity are central to the reality in which we live.'
- Mary Bateson

'It's quite possible to leave your home for a walk in the early morning air and return a different person- beguiled, enchanted.'
- Mary Chase

'On the human chessboard, all moves are possible.'
- Miriam Schiff

'Impermanence is the very essence of joy-the drop of bitterness that enables one to perceive the sweet.'
- Myrtle Reed

'When you have a baby, you set off an explosion in your marriage, and when the dust settles, your marriage is different from what it was. Not better, necessarily; not worse, necessarily; but different.'
- Nora Ephron

'There are people who not only strive to remain static themselves, but strive to keep everything else so ... their position is almost laughably hopeless.'
- Odell Shepard

'Every saint has a past, and every sinner has a future.'
- Oscar Wilde

'Always! That is the dreadful word ... it is a meaningless word, too.'
- Oscar Wilde

'All things change, nothing is extinguished.'
- Ovid

'Continuity gives us roots; change gives us branches, letting us stretch and grow and reach new heights.'
- Pauline R. Kezer

'You must change in order to survive.'
- Pearl Bailey

'Time, in the turning-over of days, works change for better or worse.'
- Pindar

'I've never met a person, I don't care what his condition, in whom I could not see possibilities. I don't care how much a man may consider himself a failure, I believe in him, for he can change the thing that is wrong in his life anytime he is prepared and'
- Preston Bradley

'Change does not change tradition. It strengthens it. Change is a challenge and an opportunity, not a threat.'
- Prince Phillip of England

'Where the old tracks are lost, new country is revealed with its wonders.'
- Rabindranath Tagore

'Our being is continually undergoing and entering upon changes. ... We must, strictly speaking, at every moment give each other up and let each other go and not hold each other back.'
- Rainer Maria Rilke

'There are no permanent changes because change itself is permanent.'
- Ralph L. Woods

'We change, whether we like it or not.'
- Ralph Waldo Emerson

'Turbulence is a life force. It is opportunity. Let's love turbulence and use it for change.'
- Ramsay Clark

'Wherever we are, it is but a stage on the way to somewhere else, and whatever we do, however well we do it, it is only a preparation to do something else that shall be different.'
- Robert Louis Stevenson

'The healthy being craves an occasional wildness, a jolt from normality, a sharpening of the edge of appetite, his own little festival of the Saturnalia, a brief excursion from his way of life.'
- Robert MacIver

'There is nobody who totally lacks the courage to change.'
- Rollo May

'Someday change will be accepted as life itself.'
- Shirley MacLaine

'I realized that if what we call human nature can be changed, then absolutely anything is possible. And from that moment, my life changed.'
- Shirley MacLaine

'The moral world is as little exempt as the physical world from the law of ceaseless change, of perpetual flux.'
- Sir James Frazer

'All bonafide revolutions are of necessity revolutions of the spirit.'
- Sonia Johnson

'What is actual is actual only for one time, and only for one place.'
- T. S. Eliot

'Would that life were like the shadow cast by a wall or a tree, but it is like the shadow of a bird in flight.'
- Talmud

'Change the fabric of your own soul and your own visions, and you change all.'
- Vachel Lindsay

'A woman's life can really be a succession of lives, each revolving around some emotionally compelling situation or challenge, and each marked off by some intense experience.'
- Wallis Simpson

'There is a certain relief in change, even though it be from bad to worse; as I have found in travelling in a stagecoach, that it is often a comfort to shift one's position and be bruised in a new place.'
- Washington Irving

'Revolutions are not made; they come.'
- Wendell Phillips

'Weep not that the world changes- did it keep a stable, changeless state, it were a cause indeed to weep.'
- William Cullen Bryant

CHILDHOOD

Children are remarkable for their intelligence and ardour, for their curiosity, their intolerance of shams, the clarity and ruthlessness of their vision.'
- Aldous Huxley

'A child thinks twenty shillings and twenty years can scarce ever be spent.'
- Benjamin Franklin

'There are only two things a child will share willingly - communicable diseases and his mother's age.'
- Benjamin Spock

'Out of the mouths of babes and sucklings hast thou ordained strength.'
- Bible

'When I was a child, I spoke as a child, I understood as a child, I thought as a child; but when I became a man I put away childish things.'
- Bible

'Nothing has a stronger influence psychologically on their environment, and especially on their children, than the unlived lives of the parents.'
- Carl Jung

'What children expect from grownups is not to be 'understood', but only to be loved, even though this love may be expressed clumsily or in sternness. Intimacy does not exist between generations - only trust.'
- Carl Zucker

'Beat your child once a day. If you don't know why, he does.'
- Chinese proverb

'We've had bad luck with our kids - they've all grown up.'
- Christopher Morley

'All children wear the sign: 'I want to be important NOW.' Many of our juvenile delinquency problems arise because nobody reads the sign.'
- Dan Pursuit

'Babies are such a nice way to start people.'
- Don Herold

'If a child lives with approval, he learns to live with himself.'
- Dorothy Law Nolte

'Juvenile appraisals of other juveniles make up in clarity what they lack in charity.'
- Edgar Z. Friedenberg

'The events of childhood do not pass but repeat themselves like seasons of the year.'
  - Eleanor Farjeon

'Healthy children will not fear life if their elders have integrity enough not to fear death.'
  - Erik Erikson

'Do not mistake a child for his symptom.'
  - Erik Erikson

'Ask your child what he wants for dinner only if he is buying.'
  - Fran Lebowitz

'The hardest job kids face today is learning good manners without seeing any.'
  - Fred Astaire

'Unlike grownups, children have little need to deceive themselves.'
  - Goethe

'If children grew up according to early indications, we should have nothing but geniuses.'
  - Goethe

'Children need love, especially when they do not deserve it.'
  - Harold S. Hulbert

'There are only two lasting bequests we can hope to give our children. One of these is roots, the other, wings.'
  - Hodding Carter

'Childhood - a period of waiting for the moment when I could send everyone and everything connected with it to hell.'
  - Igor Stravinsky

'Children have never been very good at listening to their elders, but they have never failed to imitate them.'
  - James Baldwin

'Books ... rarely, if ever, talk about what children can make of themselves, about the powers that from the day or moment of birth are present in every child.'
  - John Holt

'Children have more need of models than of critics.'
  - Joseph Joubert

'What's done to children, they will do to society.'
  - Karl Menninger

'A child's a plaything for an hour.'
  - Mary Lamb

'An adolescent is both an impulsive child and a self-starting adult.'
   - Mason Cooley

'William Blake really is important, my cornerstone. Nobody ever told me before he did that childhood was such a damned serious business.'
   - Maurice Sendak

'Of all animals, the boy is the most unmanageable.'
   - Plato

'If a child is to keep alive his inborn sense of wonder without any such gift from the fairies, he needs the companionship of at least one adult who can share it, rediscovering with him the joy, excitement and mystery of the world we live in.'
   - Rachel Carson

'Your children are not dead. They are just waiting until the world deserves them.'
   - Robert Browning

'Give me the children until they are seven and anyone may have them afterwards.'
   - St. Francis Xavier

'The great cathedral space which was childhood.'
   - Virginia Woolf

CHOICE

After a battle is over people talk a lot about how decisions were methodically reached, but actually there's always a hell of a lot of groping around.'
- Admiral Frank Jack Fletcher

'No trumpets sound when the important decisions of our life are made. Destiny is made known silently.'
- Agnes de Mille

'Life is the sum of all your choices.'
- Albert Camus

'Both choices are painful, but only one is therapeutic.'
- Albert M. Wells

'Man is a reasoning, rather than a reasonable, animal.'
- Alexander Hamilton

'The more one does and sees and feels, the more one is able to do, and the more genuine may be one's own appreciation of fundamental things like home, and love, and understanding companionship.'
- Amelia Earhart

'The mania of thinking renders one unfit for every activity.'
- Anatole France

'Full maturity ... is achieved by realizing that you have choices to make.'
- Angela Barron McBride

'Each person has a literature inside them. But when people lose language, when they have to experiment with putting their thoughts together on the spot-that's what I love most. That's where character lives.'
- Anna Deavere Smith

'Authority without wisdom is like a heavy axe without an edge, fitter to bruise than to polish.'
- Anne Bradstreet

'It is better to arm and strengthen your hero, than to disarm and enfeeble your foe.'
- Anne Bronte

'The percentage of mistakes in quick decisions is no greater than in long-drawn-out vacillations, and the effect of decisiveness itself "makes things go" and creates confidence.'
- Anne O'Hare McCormick

'She knew in her heart that to be without optimism, that core of reasonless hope in the spirit, rather than the brain, was a fatal flaw, the seed of death.'
- Anne Perry

'A door must either be shut or open.'
- Anonymous

'You cannot have it both ways.'
- Anonymous

'Where bad's the best, bad must be the choice.'
- Anonymous

'When one bases his life on principle, 99 percent of his decisions are already made.'
- Anonymous

'You cannot sell the cow and sup the milk.'
- Anonymous

'You cannot have your cake and eat it.'
- Anonymous

'Of two evils, choose the less.'
- Anonymous

'One's mind has a way of making itself up in the background, and it suddenly becomes clear what one means to do.'
- Arthur Christopher Benson

'A decision is an Taking Action you must take when you have information so incomplete that the answer does not suggest itself.'
- Arthur Radford

'Life is just an endless chain of judgements. . . . The more imperfect our judgement, the less perfect our success.'
- B. C. Forbes

'If you wait for inspiration you'll be standing on the corner after the parade is a mile down the street.'
- Ben Nicholas

'Nothing is so exhausting as indecision, and nothing is so futile.'
- Bertrand Russell

'You cannot serve God and Mammon.'
- Bible

'We lose the fear of making decisions, great and small, as we realize that should our choice prove wrong we can, if we will, learn from the experience.'
- Bill W.

'In each Taking Action we must look beyond the Taking Action at our past, present and future state, and at others whom it affects, and see the relation of all those things. And then we shall be very cautious.'
- Blaise Pascal

'Say you were standing with one foot in the oven and one foot in an ice bucket. According to the percentage people, you would be perfectly comfortable.'
- Bobby Bragan

'You decide you'll wait for your pitch. Then as the ball starts toward the plate, you think about your stance. And then you think about your swing. And then you realize that the ball that went past you for a strike was your pitch.'
- Bobby Murcer

'Some persons are very decisive when it comes to avoiding decisions.'
- Brendan Francis

'The last, if not the greatest, of the human freedoms: to choose their own attitude in any given circumstance.'
- Bruno Bettelheim

'Decision and determination are the engineer and fireman of our train to opportunity and success.'
- Burt Lawlor

'Of two evils, choose the prettier.'
- Carolyn Wells

'Human foresight often leaves its proudest possessor only a choice of evils.'
- Charles Caleb Colton

'Form the habit of making decisions when your spirit is fresh ... to let dark moods lead is like choosing cowards to command armies.'
- Charles Horton Cooley

'Many of life's circumstances are created by three basic choices: the disciplines you choose to keep, the people you chose to be with, and the laws you choose to obey.'
- Charles Millhuff

'Better to be without logic than without feeling.'
- Charlotte Bronte

'There is a point at which everything becomes simple and there is no longer any question of choice, because all you have staked will be lost if you look back. Life's point of no return.'
- Dag Hammarskjold

'We are not permitted to choose the frame of our destiny. But what we put into it is ours.'
- Dag Hammarskjold

'Optimism is an intellectual choice.'
- Diana Schneider

'It is the characteristic excellence of the strong man that he can bring momentous issues to the fore and make a decision about them. The weak are always forced to decide between alternatives they have not chosen themselves.'
- Dietrich Bonhoeffer

'A problem clearly stated is a problem half solved.'
- Dorothea Brande

'The Pilgrims didn't have any experience when they landed here. Hell, if experience was that important, we'd never have anybody walking on the moon.'
- Doug Rader

'No matter how lovesick a woman is, she shouldn't take the first pill that comes along.'
- Dr. Joyce Brothers

'If you do everything you should do, and do not do anything you should not do, you will, according to the best available statistics, live exactly eighteen hours longer than you would otherwise.'
- Dr. Logain Clendening

'He who has a choice has trouble.'
- Dutch proverb

'When faith is supported by facts or by logic it ceases to be faith.'
- Edith Hamilton

'There are two ways of spreading light: to be the candle or the mirror that reflects it.'
- Edith Wharton

'Choices are the hinges of destiny.'
- Edwin Markham

'Somehow we learn who we really are and then live with that decision.'
- Eleanor Roosevelt

'No question is ever settled until it is settled right.'
- Ella Wheeler Wilcox

'We have resolved to endure the unendurable and suffer what is insufferable.'
- Emperor Hirohito

'You can only predict things after they've happened.'
- Eugene Ionesco

'Imagination took the reins, and Reason, slow-paced, though surefooted, was unequal to a race with so eccentric and flighty a companion.'
- Fanny Burney

'The lame man who keeps the right road outstrips the runner who takes a wrong one ... the more active and swift the latter is, the further he will go astray.'
- Francis Bacon

'Decisions determine destiny.'
- Frederick Speakman

'Between two stools one sits on the ground.'
- French proverb

'Necessity is not an established fact, but an interpretation.'
- Friedrich Nietzsche

'The strongest principle of growth lies in human choice.'
- George Eliot

'Our deeds still travel with us from afar, and what we have been makes us what we are.'
- George Eliot

'Decide on what you think is right, and stick to it.'
- George Eliot

'The beginning of compunction is the beginning of a new life.'
- George Eliot

'The difficulty of life is in the choice.'
- George Moore

'One must either accept some theory or else believe one's own instinct or follow the world's opinion.'
- Gertrude Stein

'Decision is a sharp knife that cuts clean and straight; indecision, a dull one that hacks and tears and leaves ragged edges behind it.'
- Gordon Graham

'Time has told me less than I need to know.'
- Gwen Harwood

'The moment a question comes to your mind, see yourself mentally taking hold of it and disposing of it. In that moment... you learn to become the decider and not the vacillator. Thus you build character.'
- H. Van Anderson

'Not all of your decisions will be correct. None of us is perfect. But if you get into the habit of making decisions, experience will develop your judgment to a point where more and more of your decisions will be right. After all, it is better to be right '
- H. W. Andrews

'Often greater risk is involved in postponement than in making a wrong decision.'
- Harry A. Hopf

'How far would Moses have gone if he had taken a poll in Egypt?'
- Harry S. Truman

'Once a decision was made, I did not worry about it afterward.'
- Harry S. Truman

'Not to decide is to decide.'
- Harvey Cox

'A man must be able to cut a knot, for everything cannot be untied.'
- Henri Frederic Amiel

'Statistics are no substitute for judgement.'
- Henry Clay

'The best we can do is size up the chances, calculate the risks involved, estimate our ability to deal with them, and then make our plans with confidence.'
- Henry Ford

'No country can act wisely simultaneously in every part of the globe at every moment of time.'
- Henry Kissinger

'The absence of alternatives clears the mind marvelously.'
- Henry Kissinger

'There is a time when we must firmly choose the course we will follow, or the relentless drift of events will make the decision for us.'
- Herbert B. Prochnow

'A power greater than any human being helped make this decision.'
- Herbert J. Steifel

'He who postpones the hour of living is like the rustic who waits for the river to run out before he crosses.'
- Horace

'False conclusions which have been reasoned out are infinitely worse than blind impulse.'
- Horace Mann

'In not making the decision, you've made one. Not doing something is the same as doing it.'
- Ivan Bloch

'He who reflects too much will achieve little.'
- J. C. F. von Schiller

'You are the one who must choose your place.'
- James Lane Allen

'Once to every man and nation comes the moment to decide ... And the choice goes by forever t'wixt that darkness and that light.'
- James Russell Lowell

'Where an opinion is general, it is usually correct.'
- Jane Austen

'Do not wait for ideal circumstances, nor the best opportunities; they will never come.'
- Janet Erskine Stuart

'Life is like a game of cards. The hand that is dealt you represents determinism; the way you play it is free will.'
- Jawaharlal Nehru

'If you think too long, you think wrong.'
- Jim Kaat

'You don't get to choose how you're going to die. Or when. You can only decide how you're going to live. Now.'
- Joan Baez

'A man without decision can never be said to belong to himself; he is as a wave of the sea, or a feather in the air which every breeze blows about.'
- John Foster

'Faith ... acts promptly and boldly on the occasion, on slender evidence.'
- John Henry Cardinal Newman

'Pick battles big enough to matter, small enough to win.'
- Jonathan Kozel

'Living is a constant process of deciding what we are going to do.'
- Jose Ortega

'Logic is the art of going wrong with confidence.'
- Joseph Wood Krutch

'In case of doubt, decide in favor of what is correct.'
- Karl Kraus

'I would sort out all the arguments and see which belonged to fear and which to creativeness. Other things being equal, I would make the decision which had the larger number of creative reasons on its side.'
- Katharine Butler Hathaway

'I couldn't claim that I have never felt the urge to explore evil, but when you descend into hell you have to be very careful.'
- Kathleen Raine

'If decisions were a choice between alternatives, decisions would come easy. Decision is the selection and formulation of alternatives.'
    - Kenneth Burke

'The difference between weakness and wickedness is much less than people suppose; and the consequences are nearly always the same.'
    - Lady Marguerite Blessington

'Deliberation often loses a good chance.'
    - Latin proverb

'There is no data on the future.'
    - Laurel Cutler

'Facts are stubborn things, but statistics are more pliable.'
    - Laurence J. Peter

'So what do we do? Anything. Something. So long as we just don't sit there. If we screw it up, start over. Try something else. If we wait until we've satisfied all the uncertainties, it may be too late.'
    - Lee Iacocca

'There comes a time when you've got to say, "Let's get off our asses and go ..." I have always found that if I move with 75 percent or more of the facts I usually never regret it. It's the guys who wait to have everything perfect that drive you crazy.'
    - Lee Iacocca

'We spend our days in deliberating, and we end them without coming to any resolve.'
    - L'Estrange

'Life is the only art that we are required to practice without preparation, and without being allowed the preliminary trials, the failures and botches, that are essential for the training of a mere beginner.'
    - Lewis Mumford

'Decisions, particularly important ones, have always made me sleepy, perhaps because I know that I will have to make them by instinct, and thinking things out is only what other people tell me I should do.'
    - Lillian Hellman

'Logic pervades the world; the limits of the world are also the limits of logic.'
    - Ludwig Wittgenstein

'Rules of society are nothing; one's conscience is the umpire.'
    - Madame Dudevant

'It is always thus, impaled by a state of mind which is destined not to last, that we make our irrevocable decisions.'
    - Marcel Proust

'You wouldn't want to be caught wearing cheap perfume, would you? Then why do you want to wear cheap perfume on your conduct?'
- Margaret Culkin Banning

'I get a little angry about this highhanded scrapping of the look of things. What else have we to go by? How else can the average person form an opinion of a girl's sense of values or even of her chastity except by the looks of her conduct?'
- Margaret Culkin Banning

'The will to be totally rational is the will to be made out of glass and steel: and to use others as if they were glass and steel.'
- Marge Piercy

'Each man must for himself alone decide what is right and what is wrong, which course is patriotic and which isn't. You cannot shirk this and be a man. To decide against your conviction is to be an unqualified and inexcusable traitor, both to yourself and '
- Mark Twain

'Nothing is more difficult, and therefore more precious, than to be able to decide.'
- Napoleon Bonaparte

'Wisdom consists in being able to distinguish among dangers and make a choice of the least harmful.'
- Niccolo Machiavelli

'Decide which is the line of conduct that presents the fewest drawbacks and then follow it out as being the best one, because one never finds anything perfectly pure and unmixed, or exempt from danger.'
- Niccolo Machiavelli

'There is one quality more important than know-how.... This is know-how by which we determine not only how to accomplish our purposes, but what our purposes are to be.'
- Norbert Weiner

'Every year, if not every day, we have to wager our salvation upon some prophecy based upon imperfect knowledge.'
- Oliver Wendell Holmes

'Look for your choices, pick the best one, then go with it.'
- Pat Riley

'What I emphasize is for people to make choices based not on fear, but on what really gives them a sense of fulfillment.'
- Pauline Rose Chance

'Once the "what" is decided, the "how" always follows. We must not make the "how" an excuse for not facing and accepting the "what."'
- Pearl S. Buck

'One faces the future with one's past.'
- Pearl S. Buck

'A true history of human events would show that a far larger proportion of our acts are the result of sudden impulse and accident than of that reason of which we so much boast.'
- Peter Cooper

'Wherever you see a successful business, someone once made a courageous decision.'
- Peter Drucker

'No one knows what he can to do until he tries.'
- Publilius Syrus

'The opportunity is often lost by deliberating.'
- Publilius Syrus

'Choose always the way that seems the best, however rough it may be; custom will soon render it easy and agreeable.'
- Pythagoras

'The most important fact about Spaceship Earth: an instruction book didn't come with it.'
- R. Buckminster Fuller

'As a man thinketh, so is he, and as a man chooseth, so is he.'
- Ralph Waldo Emerson

'God offers to every mind its choice between truth and repose. Take which you please-you can never have both.'
- Ralph Waldo Emerson

'Men and women everywhere must exercise deliberate selection to live wisely.'
- Robert Grant

'It is the mark of a good Taking Action that it appears inevitable, in retrospect.'
- Robert Louis Stevenson

'In the three years I played ball, we won six, lost seventeen and tied two. Some statistician ... calculated that we won 75 percent of the games we didn't lose.'
- Roger M. Blough

'Life is the art of drawing sufficient conclusions from insufficient premises.'
- Samuel Butler

'The tendency of modern science is to reduce proof to absurdity by continually reducing absurdity to proof.'
- Samuel Butler

'Nothing at all will be attempted if all possible objections must first be overcome.'
- Samuel Johnson

'Alternatives, and particularly desirable alternatives, grow only on imaginary trees.'
- Saul Bellow

'No man who has not sat in the assemblies of men can know the light, odd and uncertain ways in which decisions are often arrived at.'
- Sir Arthur Helps

'Our danger is not too few, but too many options ... to be puzzled by innumerable alternatives.'
- Sir Richard Livingstone

'To know just what has do be done, then to do it, comprises the whole philosophy of practical life.'
- Sir William Osier

'How dangerous can false reasoning prove!'
- Sophocles

'History is a stern judge.'
- Svetlana Alliluyeva

'Many persons of high intelligence have notoriously poor judgement.'
- Sydney J. Harris

'There is only one answer to destructiveness and that is creativity.'
- Sylvia Ashton-Warner

'Here's a rule I recommend. Never practice two vices at once.'
- Tallulah Bankhead

'I learn by going where I have to go.'
- Theodore Roethke

'It is the heart always that sees before the head can see.'
- Thomas Carlyle

'Of all paths a man could strike into, there is, at any given moment, a best path which, here and now, it were of all things wisest for him to do. To find this path, and walk in it, is the one thing needful for him.'
- Thomas Carlyle

'We must make the choices that enable us to fulfill the deepest capacities of our real selves.'
- Thomas Merton

'Life is just a series of trying to make up your mind.'
- Timothy Fuller

'You must not change one thing, one pebble, one grain of sand, until you know what good and evil will follow on that act.'
- Ursula K. LeGuin

'We don't have enough time to premeditate all our Taking Actions.'
- Vauvenargues

'Necessity relieves us from the embarrassment of choice.'
- Vauvenargues

'Man does not simply exist, but always decides what his existence will be, what he will become in the next moment.'
- Viktor Frankl

'The last of the human freedoms: to choose one's attitude in any given set of circumstances, to choose one's own way.'
- Viktor Frankl

'Choice of attention ... is to the inner life what choice of Taking Action is to the outer. In both cases, a man is responsible for his choice and must accept the consequences, whatever they may be.'
- W. H. Auden

'When you cannot make up your mind between two evenly balanced courses of Taking Action, choose the bolder.'
- W. J. Slim

'Common sense does not ask an impossible chessboard, but takes the one before it and plays the game.'
- Wendell Phillips

'When possible make the decisions now, even if Taking Action is in the future. A revised decision usually is better than one reached at the last moment.'
- William B. Given

'Conditions are never just right. People who delay Taking Action until all factors are favorable do nothing.'
- William Feather

'A wiser rule would be to make up your mind soberly what you want, peace or war, and then to get ready for what you want; for what we prepare for is what we shall get.'
- William Graham Sumner

'The soul of dispatch is decision.'
- William Hazlitt

'Reason, with most people, means their own opinions.'
- William Hazlitt

'There is no more miserable human being than one in whom nothing is habitual but indecision.'
- William James

'When you have to make a choice and don't make it, that is in itself a choice.'
- William James

'Destiny is not a matter of chance, it is a matter of choice; it is not a thing to be waited for, it is a thing to be achieved.'
  - William Jennings Bryan

COMMITMENT

Your own resolution to success is more important than any other one thing.'
- Abraham Lincoln

'Moderation in war is imbecility.'
- Admiral John Fisher

'Theirs is not to reason why, theirs is but to do or die.'
- Alfred, Lord Tennyson

'We know what happens to people who stay in the middle of the road. They get run over.'
- Aneurin Bevan

'The dedicated life is the life worth living.'
- Annie Dillard

'The man who sees both sides of an issue is very likely on the fence or up a tree.'
- Anonymous

'Our future and our fate lie in our wills more than in our hands, for our hands are but the instruments of our wills.'
- B. C. Forbes

'Nothing can resist a will which will stake even existence upon its fulfillment.'
- Benjamin Disraeli

'The accomplice to the crime of corruption is frequently our own indifference.'
- Bess Myerson

'He did it with all his heart, and prospered.'
- Bible

'The person who makes a success of living is the one who sees his goal steadily and aims for it unswervingly. That is dedication.'
- Cecil B. DeMille

'Sometimes success is due less to ability than zeal. The winner is he who gives himself to his work body and soul.'
- Charles Buxton

'Nothing is so common as unsuccessful men with talent. They lack only determination.'
- Charles Swindoll

'The hottest places in hell are reserved for those who, in a period of moral crisis, maintain their neutrality.'
- Dante Alighieri

'The only place you can win a football game is on the field. The only place you can lose it is in your heart.'
- Darrell Royal

'You can be an ordinary athlete by getting away with less than your best. But if you want to be a great, you have to give it all you've got-your everything.'
- Duke P. Kahanamoku

'Morale is the greatest single factor in successful wars.'
- Dwight D. Eisenhower

'Love me, please, I love you; I can bear to be your friend. So ask of me anything ... I am not a tentative person. Whatever I do, I give up my whole self to it.'
- Edna Saint Vincent Millay

'I could not, at any age, be content to take my place by the fireside and simply look on. Life was meant to be lived. Curiosity must be kept alive. One must never, for whatever reason, turn his back on life.'
- Eleanor Roosevelt

'The only difference between a rut and a grave is their dimensions.'
- Ellen Glasgow

'When I stand before God at the end of my life, I would hope that I would not have a single bit of talent left, and could say, "I used everything you gave me."'
- Erma Bombeck

'It was my tongue that swore; my heart is unsworn.'
- Euripides

'Show me a person who is not an extremist about some things, who is a "middle-of-the-roader" in everything, and I will show you someone who is insecure.'
- G. Aiken Taylor

'It is fatal to enter any war without the will to win it.'
- General Douglas MacArthur

'Wars may be fought with weapons, but they are won by men. It is the spirit of the men who follow, and of the man who leads, that gains the victory.'
- General George S. Patton

'I don't care a damn for your loyal service when you think I am right; when I really want it most is when you think I am wrong.'
- General Sir John Monash

'He who walks in the middle of the road gets hit from both sides.'
- George P. Shultz

'If you deny yourself commitment, what can you do with your life?'
- Harvey Fierstein

'Science may have found a cure for most evils; but it has found no remedy for the worst of them all-the apathy of human beings.'
- Helen Keller

'Now I am steel-set: I follow the call to the clear radiance and glow of the heights.'
- Henrik Ibsen

'There's nothing in the middle of the road but yellow stripes and dead armadillos.'
- Jim Hightower

'If you aren't going all the way, why go at all?'
- Joe Namath

'Strength is a matter of the made-up mind.'
- John Beecher

'The principle of neutrality ... has increasingly become an obsolete conception, and, except under very special circumstances, it is an immoral and shortsighted conception.'
- John Foster Dulles

'Unless you can find some sort of loyalty, you cannot find unity and peace in your active living.'
- Josiah Royce

'There is nothing harder than the softness of indifference.'
- Juan Montalvo

'Let my name stand among those who are willing to bear ridicule and reproach for the truth's sake, and so earn some right to rejoice when the victory is won.'
- Louisa May Alcott

'I never liked the middle ground-the most boring place in the world.'
- Louise Nevelson

'The secret of living is to find a pivot, the pivot of a concept on which you can make your stand.'
- Luigi Pirandello

'We should not permit tolerance to degenerate into indifference.'
- Margaret Chase Smith

'Standing in the middle of the road is very dangerous; you get knocked down by traffic from both sides.'
- Margaret Thatcher

'The will to conquer is the first condition of victory.'
- Marshal Ferdinand Foch

'If a man hasn't discovered something that he will die for, he isn't fit to live.'
- Martin Luther King, Jr.

'It seems safe to say that significant discovery, really creative thinking, does not occur with regard to problems about which the thinker is lukewarm.'
- Mary Henle

'Most people are not for or against anything; the first object of getting people together is to make them respond somehow, to overcome inertia.'
- Mary Parker Follett

'If you don't stand for something, you'll fall for anything.'
- Michael Evans

'A successful marriage requires falling in love many times, always with the same person.'
- Mignon McLaughlin

'If you start to take Vienna, take Vienna.'
- Napoleon Bonaparte

'We're swallowed up only when we are willing for it to happen.'
- Nathalie Sarraute

'Either do not attempt at all, or go through with it.'
- Ovid

'It is by losing himself in the objective, in inquiry, creation, and craft, that a man becomes something.'
- Paul Goodman

'The wonderful thing about saints is that they were human. They lost their tempers, got hungry, scolded God, were egotistical or impatient in their turns, made mistakes and regretted them. Still they went on doggedly blundering toward heaven.'
- Phyllis McGinley

'The middle of the road is where the white line is, and that's the worst place to drive.'
- Robert Frost

'Those who love a cause are those who love the life which has to be led in order to serve it.'
- Simone Weil

'I am seeking, I am striving, I am in it with all my heart.'
- Vincent van Gogh

'Men, like snails, lose their usefulness when they lose direction and begin to bend.'
- Walter Savage Landor

'The height of your accomplishments will equal the depth of your convictions.'
- William F. Scolavino

'Winners are men who have dedicated their whole lives to winning.'
- Woody Hayes

CONVERSATION

A man who listens because he has nothing to say can hardly be a source of inspiration. The only listening that counts is that of the talker who alternately absorbs and expresses ideas.'
- Agnes Repplier

'Not a sentence or a word is independent of the circumstances under which it is uttered.'
- Alfred North Whitehead

'Communication is and should be hell fire and sparks as well as sweetness and light.'
- Aman Vivian Rakoff

'Listen or thy tongue will keep thee deaf.'
- American Indian proverb

'Pollution is nothing but the resources we are not harvesting. We allow them to disperse because we have been ignorant of their value.'
- Buckminster Fuller

'The less men think; the more they talk.'
- Charles Montesquieu

'A ceremony of self-wastage - good talkers are miserable, they know that they have betrayed themselves, that they have taken material which should have a life of its own, to disperse it in noises upon the air.'
- Cyril Connolly

'The real art of conversation is not only to say the right thing in the right place but to leave unsaid the wrong thing at the tempting moment.'
- Dorothy Nevill

'Conversation enriches the understanding, but solitude is the school of genius.'
- Edward Gibbon

'Too much agreement kills a chat.'
- Eldridge Cleaver

'Men always talk about the most important things to perfect strangers.'
- G. K. Chesterton

'She had lost the art of conversation, but not, unfortunately, the power of speech.'
- George Bernard Shaw

'The time to stop talking is when the other person nods his head affirmatively but says nothing.'
- Henry S. Haskins

'He was one of those men whose constitutional inability to make small talk forfeits all one's sympathy, and makes one think that social grace is sometimes a moral duty.'
  - James Morris

'Listening is a magnetic and strange thing, a creative force. The friends who listen to us are the ones we move toward, and we want to sit in their radius. When we are listened to, it creates us, makes us unfold and expand.'
  - Karl Menninger

'Conceit causes more conversation than wit.'
  - La Rochefoucauld

'Never hold any one by the button or the hand in order to be heard out; for if people are unwilling to hear you, you had better hold your tongue than them.'
  - Lord Chesterfield

'Debate is masculine; conversation is feminine.'
  - Louisa May Alcott

'You can never hope to become a skilled conversationalist until you learn how to put your foot tactfully through the television set.'
  - M. Dale Baughman

'Some persons talk simply because they think sound is more manageable than silence.'
  - Margaret Halsey

'Great talkers are trying to fill the gap between themselves and others, but only widen it.'
  - Mason Cooley

'Conversation is the fine art of mutual consideration and communication about matters of common interest that basically have some human importance.'
  - Ordway Tead

'The really important things are said over cocktails and are never done.'
  - Peter F. Drucker

'There is no such thing as conversation. It is an illusion. There are intersecting monologues. That is all.'
  - Rebecca West

'Half the world is composed of people who have something to say and can't and the other half who have nothing to say and keep on saying it.'
  - Robert Frost

'That is the happiest conversation where there is no competition, no vanity, but a calm quiet interchange of sentiments.'
  - Samuel Johnson

'John Wesley's conversation is good, but he is never at leisure. He is always obliged to go at a certain hour. This is very disagreeable to a man who loves to fold his legs and have his talk out as I do.'
    - Samuel Johnson

'When I think over what I have said, I envy dumb people.'
    - Seneca

'You never say a word of yourself, dear Lady Grey. You have that dreadful sin of anti-egotism.'
    - Sydney Smith

'He (Macaulay) has occasional flashes of silence that make his conversation perfectly delightful.'
    - Sydney Smith

'Speech is civilization itself.'
    - Thomas Mann

'The habit of common and continuous speech is a symptom of mental deficiency. It proceeds from not knowing what is going on in other people's minds.'
    - Walter Bagehot

'While the right to talk may be the beginning of freedom, the necessity of listening is what makes the right important.'
    - Walter Lippmann

'Wit is the salt of conversation, not the food.'
    - William Hazlitt

'Silence is one great art of conversation.'
    - William Hazlitt

COPING

Were it not for my little jokes, I could not bear the burdens of this office.'
- Abraham Lincoln

'Let no feeling of discouragement prey upon you, and in the end you are sure to succeed.'
- Abraham Lincoln

'Humor brings insight and tolerance.'
- Agnes Repplier

'Humor is my sword and my shield. It protects me. You can open a door with humor and drive a truck right through.'
- Alan Simpson

'Sometimes only a change of viewpoint is needed to convert a tiresome duty into an interesting opportunity.'
- Alberta Flanders

'Experience is not what happens to you; it is what you do with what happens to you.'
- Aldous Huxley

'Keep your sense of humor. There's enough stress in the rest of your life to let bad shots ruin a game you're supposed to enjoy.'
- Amy Alcott

'When you make a world tolerable for yourself, you make a world tolerable for others.'
- Anais Nin

'A chuckle a day may not keep the doctor away, but it sure does make those times in life's waiting room a little more bearable.'
- Anne Wilson Schaef

'When things go wrong, don't go with them.'
- Anonymous

'Pain is inevitable. Suffering is optional.'
- Anonymous

'The difficulties of life are intended to make us better, not bitter.'
- Anonymous

'Happiness is not the absence of conflict, but the ability to cope with it.'
- Anonymous

'The tragedy is not that things are broken. The tragedy is that they are not mended again.'
- Anonymous

'Turn your stumbling blocks into stepping stones.'
- Anonymous

'The meaning of things lies not in the things themselves, but in our attitude towards them.'
- Antoine de Saint-Exupery

'No matter what has happened, always behave as if nothing had happened.'
- Arnold Bennett

'Little things affect little minds.'
- Benjamin Disraeli

'I'm not happy, I'm cheerful. There's a difference. A happy woman has no cares at all. A cheerful woman has cares but has learned how to deal with them.'
- Beverly Sills

'Losses are comparative, only imagination makes them of any moment.'
- Blaise Pascal

'Losses are comparative, imagination only makes them of any moment.'
- Blaise Pascal

'Nothing is miserable unless you think it so.'
- Boethius

'If you have to be in a soap opera, try not to get the worst role.'
- Boy George

'Comedy is tragedy plus time.'
- Carol Burnett

'A great wind is blowing, and that gives you either imagination or a headache.'
- Catherine the Great

'It seems that we learn lessons when we least expect them but always when we need them the most, and, the true "gift" in these lessons always lies in the learning process itself.'
- Cathy Lee Crosby

'Don't curse the darkness - light a candle.'
- Chinese proverb

'Always take an emergency leisurely.'
- Chinese proverb

'When something bad happens to me, I think I'm able to deal with it in a pretty good way. That makes me lucky. Some people fall apart at the first little thing that happens.'
- Christie Brinkley

'Total absence of humor renders life impossible.'
- Colette

'He who, having lost one ideal, refuses to give his heart and soul to another and nobler, is like a man who declines to build a house on rock because the wind and rain ruined his house on the sand.'
- Constance Naden

'When fate hands you a lemon, make lemonade.'
- Dale Carnegie

'The most unhappy of all men is he who believes himself to be so.'
- David Hume

'Find the grain of truth in criticism - chew it and swallow it.'
- Don Sutton

'Everyday ... life confronts us with new problems to be solved which force us to adjust our old programs accordingly.'
- Dr. Ann Faraday

'Courage, in the final analysis, is nothing but an affirmative answer to the shocks of existence.'
- Dr. Kurt Goldstein

'Let us not be needlessly bitter: certain failures are sometimes fruitful.'
- E. M. Cioran

'Never despair, but if you do, work on in despair.'
- Edmund Burke

'The winds and waves are always on the side of the ablest navigators.'
- Edward Gibbon

'Humor is an antidote to isolation.'
- Elizabeth Janeway

'Warning: Humor may be hazardous to your illness.'
- Ellie Katz

'We are not troubled by things, but by the opinion which we have of things.'
- Epictetus

'On the occasion of every accident that befalls you ... inquire what power you have for turning it to use.'
- Epictetus

'Men are not influenced by things, but by their thoughts about things.'
- Epictetus

'Wrinkles should only indicate where smiles have been.'
- Ethel Barrymore

'This is courage ... to bear unflinchingly what heaven sends.'
- Euripides

'Delicate humor is the crowning virtue of the saints.'
- Evelyn Underhill

'I think we should look forward to death more than we do. Of course everybody hates to go to bed or miss anything but dying is really the only chance we'll get to rest.'
- Florynce Kennedy

'We are never so happy or so unhappy as we think.'
- Francois de La Rochefoucauld

'There are no accidents so unlucky from which clever people are not able to reap some advantage, and none so lucky that the foolish are not able to turn them to their own disadvantage.'
- Francois de La Rochefoucauld

'To jealousy, nothing is more frightful than laughter.'
- Francoise Sagan

'True contentment is the power of getting of any situation all that there is in it.'
- G. K. Chesterton

'Humor is an attitude. It's a way of looking at life and of telling others how you feel about what's happening around you.'
- Gene Perret

'Courage is a perfect sensibility of the measure of danger, and a mental willingness to endure it.'
- General William T. Sherman

'When the rock is hard, we get harder than the rock. When the job is tough, we get tougher than the job.'
- George Cullum

'What counts in making a happy marriage is not so much how compatible you are, but how you deal with incompatibility.'
- George Levinger

'So long as one does not despair, so long as one doesn't look upon life bitterly, things work out fairly well in the end.'
- George Moore

'We must never despair; our situation has been compromising before, and it has changed for the better; so I trust it will again. If difficulties arise, we must put forth new exertion and proportion our efforts to the exigencies of the times.'
- George Washington

'All that is really necessary for survival of the fittest, it seems, is an interest in life, good, bad, or peculiar.'
  - Grace Paley

'The game of life is not so much in holding a good hand as playing a poor hand well.'
  - H. T. Leslie

'Laughter can be more satisfying than honor; more precious than money; more heart-cleansing than prayer.'
  - Harriet Rochlin

'Any man who has had the job I've had and didn't have a sense of humor wouldn't still be here.'
  - Harry S. Truman

'Noble souls, through dust and heat, rise from disaster and defeat the stronger.'
  - Henry Wadsworth Longfellow

'A person without a sense of humor is like a wagon without springs, jolted by every pebble in the road.'
  - Henry Ward Beecher

'We can either change the complexities of life ... or develop ways that enable us to cope more effectively.'
  - Herbert Benson

'We exaggerate misfortune and happiness alike. We are never either so wretched or so happy as we say we are.'
  - Honore de Balzac

'In adversity, remember to keep an even mind.'
  - Horace

'I can complain because rose bushes have thorns, or rejoice because thorn bushes have roses. It's all how you look at it.'
  - J. Kenfield Morley

'Man is only miserable so far as he thinks himself so.'
  - Jacopo Sannazaro

'You gotta play the hand that's dealt you. There may be pain in that hand, but you play it.'
  - James Brady

'Our mistakes won't irreparably damage our lives unless we let them.'
  - James E. Sweeney

'The art of life consists in taking each event which befalls us with a contented mind, confident of good. ... With this method ... rejoice always, though in the midst of sorrows, and possess all things, though destitute of everything.'
  - James Freeman Clarke

'Groan and forget it.'
- Jessamyn West

'To accept whatever comes, regardless of the consequences, is to be unafraid.'
- John Cage

'An error is simply a failure to adjust immediately from a preconception to an actuality.'
- John Cage

'True luck consists not in holding the best cards at the table; luckiest he who knows just when to rise and go home.'
- John Hay

'Your living is determined not so much by what life brings to you as by the attitude you bring to life; not so much by what happens to you as by the way your mind looks at what happens.'
- John Homer Miller

'The mind is its own place, and in itself can make a heaven of hell, a hell of heaven.'
- John Milton

'Nothing is so bad that you have to sit down and go crazy.'
- John Telgen

'Life consists not in holding good cards, but in playing those you do hold well.'
- Josh Billings

'Tears mess up your makeup.'
- Julia Child

'Concern should drive us into Taking Action, not into a depression.'
- Karen Horney

'When we begin to take our failures non-seriously, it means we are ceasing to be afraid of them. It is of immense importance to learn to laugh at ourselves.'
- Katherine Mansfield

'Whatever evil befalls us, we ought to ask ourselves ... how we can turn it into good. So shall we take occasion, from one bitter root, to raise perhaps many flowers.'
- Leigh Hunt

'Happiness does not depend on outward things, but on the way we see them.'
- Leo Tolstoy

'I think laughter may be a form of courage.... As humans we sometimes stand tall and look into the sun and laugh, and I think we are never more brave than when we do that.'
- Linda Ellerbee

'Any man can shoot a gun, and with practice he can draw fast and shoot accurately, but that makes no difference. What counts is how you stand up when somebody is shooting back at you.'
- Louis L'Amour

'Learn to laugh at your troubles and you'll never run out of things to laugh at.'
- Lyn Karol

'If I had no sense of humor, I should long ago have committed suicide.'
- Mahatma Gandhi

'Let us be brave in the face of adversity.'
- Marcus Annaeus Seneca

'Consider how much more you often suffer from your anger and grief than from those very things for which you are angry and grieved.'
- Marcus Aurelius

'If you are distressed by anything external, the pain is not due to the thing itself but to your own estimate of it; and this you have the power to revoke at any moment.'
- Marcus Aurelius

'Laughter is ever young, whereas tragedy, except the very highest of all, quickly becomes haggard.'
- Margaret Sackville

'If you're going to be able to look back on something and laugh about it, you might as well laugh about it now.'
- Marie Osmond

'Humor is the instinct for taking pain playfully.'
- Max Eastman

'Humor is just another defense against the universe.'
- Mel Brooks

'Riches, like glory or health, have no more beauty or pleasure than their possessor is pleased to lend them.'
- Michel de Montaigne

'A sense of humor can help you overlook the unattractive, tolerate the unpleasant, cope with the unexpected, and smile through the unbearable.'
- Moshe Waldoks

'Things are in their essence what we choose to make them. A thing is, according to the mode in which one looks at it.'
- Oscar Wilde

'Whenever you fall, pick something up.'
- Oswald Avery

'Optimism and humor are the grease and glue of life. Without both of them we would never have survived our captivity.'
- Philip Butler

'Courage is to take hard knocks like a man when occasion calls.'
- Plautus

'Anyone can hold the helm when the sea is calm.'
- Publilius Syrus

'A man has no more character than he can command in a time of crisis.'
- Ralph W. Sockman

'What the caterpillar calls a tragedy, the Master calls a butterfly.'
- Richard Bach

'The greatest test of courage on earth is to bear defeat without losing heart.'
- Robert G. Ingersoll

'Humor is the healthy way of feeling "distance" between one's self and the problem, a way of standing off and looking at one's problems with perspective.'
- Rollo May

'Humor is an affirmation of dignity, a declaration of man's superiority to all that befalls him.'
- Romain Gary

'To a brave man, good and bad luck are like his right and left hand. He uses both.'
- Saint Catherine of Siena

'Do not lose your inward peace for anything whatsoever, even if your whole world seems upset.'
- Saint Francis de Sales

'If you are being run out of town, get in front of the crowd and make it look like a parade.'
- Sally Stanford

'One loses many laughs by not laughing at oneself.'
- Sara Jeannette Duncan

'Humor is a means of obtaining pleasure in spite of the distressing effects that interface with it.'
- Sigmund Freud

'Keep strong if possible; in any case, keep cool.'
- Sir Basil Liddell Hart

'To be happy, drop the words "if only" and substitute instead the words "next time."'
- Smiley Blanton

'Almost all our misfortunes in life come from the wrong notions we have about the things that happen to us.'
- Stendhal

'To have courage for whatever comes in life - everything lies in that.'
- Teresa of Avila

'Results? Why, man, I have gotten a lot of results. I know several thousand things that won't work.'
- Thomas A. Edison

'A wise man turns chance into good fortune.'
- Thomas Fuller

'There is no defense against adverse fortune which is so effectual as an habitual sense of humor.'
- Thomas W. Higginson

'A sense of humor judges one's Taking Actions and the Taking Actions of others from a wider reference ... it pardons shortcomings; it consoles failure. It recommends moderation.'
- Thornton Wilder

'Disease can be seen as a call for personal transformation through metamorphosis. It is a transition from the death of your old self into the birth of your new.'
- Tom O'Connor

'Never regret. If it's good, it's wonderful. If it's bad, it's experience.'
- Victoria Holt

'The longer we dwell on our misfortunes, the greater is their power to harm us.'
- Voltaire

'The most important thing in life is not to capitalize on your gains. Any fool can do that. The really important thing is to profit from your losses.'
- William Bolitho

'What can any of us do with his talent but try to develop his vision, so that through frequent failures we may learn better what we have missed in the past.'
- William Carlos Williams

'Good people are good because they've come to wisdom through failure.'
- William Saroyan

'There is nothing either good or bad, but thinking makes it so.'
- William Shakespeare

'There are more serious problems in life than financial ones, and I've had a lot of those. I've been broke before, and will be again. Heart broke? That's serious. Lose a few bucks? That's not.'
- Willie Nelson

'When all that hate energy was focused on me, it was transformed into a fantastic energy. It was supporting me. If you are centered and you can transform all this energy that comes in, it will help you. If you believe it is going to kill you, it will kill '
   - Yoko Ono

COUNCIL

I remember my father telling me the story of the preacher delivering an exhortation to his flock, and as he reached the climax of his exhortation, a man in the front row got up and said, 'O Lord, use me. Use me, O Lord - in an advisory capacity!"
- Adlai Stevenson

'There is little serenity comparable to the serenity of the inexperienced giving advice to the experienced.'
- Anonymous

'Never give advice in a crowd.'
- Arab proverb

'Men of much depth of mind can bear a great deal of counsel; for it does not easily deface their own character, nor render their purposes indistinct.'
- Arthur Helps

'Be frank and explicit. That is the right line to take when you wish to conceal your own mind and to confuse the minds of others.'
- Benjamin Disraeli

'Don't fight forces; use them.'
- Buckminster Fuller

'No man ever listened himself out of a job.'
- Calvin Coolidge

'You must not think, sir, to catch old birds with chaff.'
- Cervantes

'To make pleasure pleasant, shorten.'
- Charles Buxton

'It has seemed to be more necessary to have regard to the weight of words rather than to their number.'
- Cicero

'We only make a dupe of the friend whose advice we ask, for we never tell him all; and it is usually what we have left unsaid that decides our conduct.'
- Diane de Poitiers

'He who can lick can bite.'
- French proverb

'Never give advice unless asked.'
- German proverb

'But one must know where one stands, and where the others wish to go.'
- Goethe

'Good counsel has no price.'
- Guiseppe Mazzini

'The true secret of giving advice is, after you have honestly given it, to be perfectly indifferent whether it is taken or not and never persist in trying to set people right.'
- Hannah Whitall Smith

'Simplicity, simplicity, simplicity. I say, let your affairs be as two or three, and not a hundred or a thousand; instead of a million count half a dozen, and keep your accounts on your thumbnail.'
- Henry David Thoreau

'Whatever advice you give, be short.'
- Horace

'What you don't see with your eyes, don't invent with your tongue.'
- Jewish proverb

'When a man comes to me for advice, I find out the kind of advice he wants, and I give it to him.'
- Josh Billings

'Old men are fond of giving good advice, to console themselves for being no longer in a position to give bad examples.'
- La Rochefoucauld

'We give advice, but we do not inspire conduct.'
- La Rochefoucauld

'Advice is seldom welcome; and those who want it the most always like it the least.'
- Lord Chesterfield

'If you aren't rich, you should always look useful.'
- Louis-Ferdinand Celine

'What is important is to keep learning, to enjoy challenge, and to tolerate ambiguity. In the end there are no certain answers.'
- Marina Horner

'Put all thine eggs in one basket and - watch that basket.'
- Mark Twain

'Fewer things are harder to put up with than the annoyance of a good example.'
- Mark Twain

'It is well enough, when one is talking to a friend, to lodge in an odd word by way of counsel now and then; but there is something mighty irksome in its staring upon one in a letter, where one ought to

see only kind words and friendly remembrances.'
- Mary Lamb

'I give myself, sometimes, admirable advice, but I am incapable of taking it.'
- Mary Wortley Montagu

'The advice of the elders to young men is very apt to be as unreal as a list of the hundred best books.'
- Oliver Wendell Holmes

'The only thing to do with good advice is to pass it on. It is never of any use to oneself.'
- Oscar Wilde

'Thanksgiving comes after Christmas.'
- Peter Kreeft

'A bull does not enjoy fame in two herds.'
- Rhodesian proverb

'Advice is like snow; the softer it falls, the longer it dwells upon, and the deeper it sinks into, the mind.'
- Samuel Taylor Coleridge

'Drink nothing without seeing it; sign nothing without reading it.'
- Spanish proverb

'Never advise anyone to go to war or to marry.'
- Spanish proverb

'Don't offer me advice, give me money.'
- Spanish proverb

'Many receive advice, only the wise profit by it.'
- Syrus

'Admonish your friends privately, but praise them openly.'
- Syrus

'The proverb warns that, "You should not bite the hand that feeds you." But maybe you should, if it prevents you from feeding yourself.'
- Thomas Szasz

''Be yourself!' is about the worst advice you can give to some people.'
- Tom Masson

'If you keep your mind sufficiently open, people will throw a lot of rubbish into it.'
- William A. Orton

'Have more than thou showest, Speak less than thou knowest.'
- William Shakespeare

COURAGE

Courage is sustained by calling up anew the vision of the goal.'
- A. G. Sertillanges

'God grant me the courage not to give up what I think is right, even though I think it is hopeless.'
- Admiral Chester W. Nimitz

'It is easy to be brave from a safe distance.'
- Aesop

'It takes more courage to reveal insecurities than to hide them, more strength to relate to people than to dominate them, more "manhood" to abide by thought-out principles rather than blind reflex. Toughness is in the soul and spirit, not in muscles and an'
- Alex Karras

'The great man is the man who does a thing for the first time.'
- Alexander Smith

'Life is to be entered upon with courage.'
- Alexis de Tocqueville

'True courage is not the brutal force of vulgar heroes, but the firm resolve of virtue and reason.'
- Alfred North Whitehead

'Women have to summon up courage to fulfill dormant dreams.'
- Alice Walker

'Courage to start and willingness to keep everlasting at it are the requisites for success.'
- Alonzo Newton Benn

'Courage is the price that life exacts for granting peace.'
- Amelia Earhart

'Life shrinks or expands in proportion to one's courage.'
- Anais Nin

'One man with courage makes a majority.'
- Andrew Jackson

'If one cannot invent a really convincing lie, it is often better to stick to the truth.'
- Angela Thirkell

'No blame should attach to telling the truth.'
- Anita Brookner

'The naked truth is always better than the best-dressed lie.'
- Ann Landers

'It isn't for the moment you are stuck that you need courage, but for the long uphill climb back to sanity and faith and security.'
- Anne Morrow Lindbergh

'It takes as much courage to have tried and failed as it does to have tried and succeeded.'
- Anne Morrow Lindbergh

'Truth, that fair goddess who comes always with healing in her wings.'
- Anne Shannon Monroe

'The brave venture anything.'
- Anonymous

'You're only as sick as your secrets.'
- Anonymous

'A brave arm makes a short sword long.'
- Anonymous

'We run away all the time to avoid coming face to face with ourselves.'
- Anonymous

'Nothing ventured, nothing gained.'
- Anonymous

'A bold heart is half the battle.'
- Anonymous

'None are so blind as those who will not see.'
- Anonymous

'Whatever you are trying to avoid won't go away until you confront it.'
- Anonymous

'The weapon of the brave is in his heart.'
- Anonymous

'A man of courage never wants weapons.'
- Anonymous

'Bad weather always looks worse through a window.'
- Anonymous

'The best way out of a problem is through it.'
- Anonymous

'Valor is nobleness of the mind.'
    - Anonymous

'To fight a bull when you are not scared is nothing. And to not fight a bull when you are scared is nothing. But to fight a bull when you are scared is something.'
    - Anonymous

'Courage is the right disposition toward fear.'
    - Anonymous

'The will of God will not take you where the grace of God cannot keep you.'
    - Anonymous

'Despair gives courage to a coward.'
    - Anonymous

'Courage is what it takes to stand up and speak; courage is also what it takes to sit down and listen.'
    - Anonymous

'It is often wonderful how putting down on paper a clear statement of a case helps one to see, not perhaps the way out, but the way in.'
    - Arthur Christopher Benson

'Admitting errors clears the score and proves you wiser than before.'
    - Arthur Guiterman

'Courage is never letting your Taking Actions be influenced by your fears.'
    - Arthur Koestler

'The fly ought to be used as the symbol of impertinence and audacity, for whilst all other animals shun man more than anything else, and run away even before he comes near them, the fly lights upon his very nose.'
    - Arthur Schopenhauer

'I became more courageous by doing the very things I needed to be courageous for-first, a little, and badly. Then, bit by bit, more and better. Being avidly-sometimes annoyingly-curious and persistent about discovering how others were doing what I wanted '
    - Audre Lorde

'When it comes to betting on yourself ... you're a chicken-livered coward if you hesitate.'
    - B. C. Forbes

'Knowledge without courage is sterile.'
    - Baltasar Gracian

'He who finds Fortune on his side should go briskly ahead, for she is wont to favor the bold.'
    - Baltasar Gracian

'In politics, guts is all.'
- Barbara Castle

'You don't develop courage by being happy in your relationships everyday. You develop it by surviving difficult times and challenging adversity.'
- Barbara De Angelis

'Life is the acceptance of responsibilities, or their evasion; it is a business of meeting obligations, or avoiding them.'
- Ben Ames Williams

'Courage is fire, and bullying is smoke.'
- Benjamin Disraeli

'You can't expect to win unless you know why you lose.'
- Benjamin Lipson

'Yesterday I dared to struggle. Today I dare to win.'
- Bernadette Devlin

'In true courage there is always an element of choice, of an ethical choice, and of anguish, and also of Taking Action and deed. There is always a flame of spirit in it, a vision of some necessity higher than oneself.'
- Brenda Ueland

'Courage is not simply one of the virtues, but the form of every virtue at the testing point.'
- C. S. Lewis

'No great thing conies to any man unless he has courage.'
- Cardinal James Gibbons

'Valor is a gift. Those having it never know for sure if they have it till the test comes. And those having it in one test never know for sure if they will have it when the next test comes.'
- Carl Sandburg

'Catch courage.'
- Carolyn Heilbrun

'That cowardice is incorrigible which the love of power cannot overcome.'
- Charles Caleb Colton

'Courage is generosity of the highest order, for the brave are prodigal of the most precious things.'
- Charles Caleb Colton

'Courage is a peculiar kind of fear.'
- Charles Kennedy

'The most mortifying infirmity in human nature ... is, perhaps, cowardice.'
- Charles Lamb

'The difference between getting somewhere and nowhere is the courage to make an early start.'
   - Charles M. Schwab

'Courage is the virtue which champions the cause of right.'
   - Cicero

'A man of courage is also full of faith.'
   - Cicero

'Courage is the ladder on which all other virtues mount.'
   - Clare Boothe Luce

'To see what is right, and not do it, is want of courage.'
   - Confucius

'The superior man makes the difficulty to be overcome his first interest; success comes only later.'
   - Confucius

'To know what is right and not do it is the worst cowardice.'
   - Confucius

'Often the test of courage is not to die, but to live.'
   - Conte Vittorio Alfieri

'Optimism and self-pity are the positive and negative poles of modern cowardice.'
   - Cyril Connolly

'The great virtue in life is real courage that knows how to face facts and live beyond them.'
   - D. H. Lawrence

'Life only demands from you the strength you possess.'
   - Dag Hammarskjold

'Only one feat is possible: not to have run away.'
   - Dag Hammarskjold

'Courage is ... the knowledge of how to fear what ought to be feared and how not to fear what ought not to be feared.'
   - David Ben-Gurion

'We learn courageous Taking Action by going forward whenever fear urges us back.'
   - David Seabury

'Courage is as often the outcome of despair as of hope; in the one case we have nothing to lose, in the other everything to gain.'
   - Diane de Poitiers

'Act boldly and unseen forces will come to your aid.'
   - Dorothea Brande

'Courage is fear that has said its prayers.'
- Dorothy Bernard

'Courage ... is nothing less than the power to overcome danger, misfortune, fear, injustice, while continuing to affirm inwardly that life, with all its sorrows, is good; that everything is meaningful, even if in a sense beyond our understanding; and that '
- Dorothy Thompson

'Courage is to feel the daily daggers of relentless steel and keep on living.'
- Douglas Malloch

'Courage is doing what you're afraid to do. There can be no courage unless you're scared.'
- Eddie Rickenbacker

'If you knew how cowardly your enemy is, you would slap him.'
- Edgar Watson Howe

'Bravery is the knowledge of the cowardice in the enemy.'
- Edgar Watson Howe

'Experience shows that exceptions are as true as rules.'
- Edith Ronald Mirrielees

'If I ever said in grief or pride, I tired of honest things, I lied.'
- Edna Saint Vincent Millay

'At the bottom of a good deal of bravery ... lurks a miserable cowardice. Men will face powder and steel because they cannot face public opinion.'
- Edwin H. Chapin

'What one has to do usually can be done.'
- Eleanor Roosevelt

'The best protection any woman can have ... is courage.'
- Elizabeth Cady Stanton

'All we are asked to bear we can bear. That is a law of the spiritual life. The only hindrance to the working of this law, as of all benign laws, is fear.'
- Elizabeth Goudge

'There is in the end no remedy but truth. It is the one course that cannot be evil.'
- Ellis Peters

'Courage is a quietness, not martial music made Born of facing up to life, even when afraid.'
- Emily Sargent Councilman

'A change of heart is the essence of all other change, and it has brought about me a reeducation of the mind.'
- Emmeline Pethick-Lawrence

'So when the crisis is upon you, remember that God, like a trainer of wrestlers, has matched you with a tough and stalwart antagonist... that you may prove a victor at the Great Games.'
- Epictetus

'Fortune favors the audacious.'
- Erasmus

'It takes courage to lead a life. Any life.'
- Erica Jong

'Everyone has a talent. What is rare is the courage to follow that talent to the dark place where it leads.'
- Erica Jong

'It takes a lot of courage to show your dreams to someone else.'
- Erma Bombeck

'Cowardice, as distinguished from panic, is almost always simply a lack of ability to suspend the functioning of the imagination.'
- Ernest Hemingway

'Courage is grace under pressure.'
- Ernest Hemingway

'Courage is the integrating strength that causes one to overcome tragedy.'
- Eugene E. Brussell

'To persevere, trusting in what hopes he has, is courage. The coward despairs.'
- Euripides

'A coward turns away, but a brave man's choice is danger.'
- Euripides

'Courage which goes against military expediency is stupidity, or, if it is insisted upon by a commander, irresponsibility.'
- Field Marshal Erwin Rommel

'The peril of the hour moved the British to tremendous exertions, just as always in a moment of extreme danger things can be done which had previously been thought impossible. Mortal danger is an effective antidote for fixed ideas.'
- Field Marshal Erwin Rommel

'If one is willing to do a thing he is afraid to do, he does not have to ... face a situation fearlessly, and [if] there is no situation to face; it falls away of its own weight.'
- Florence Scovel Shinn

'Soldiers, strike the foe in the face!'
- Florus

'Courage does not always march to airs blown by a bugle, it is not always wrought out of the fabric ostentation wears.'
- Frances Rodman

'Courage is a virtue only so far as it is directed by prudence.'
- Francois de Fenelon

'Perfect courage means doing unwitnessed what we would be capable of with the world looking on.'
- Francois de La Rochefoucauld

'If the word frankly or sincerely is not uttered in the first ten minutes-or let us speak openly-then you are not in the presence of a genuine businessman, and he will certainly go bankrupt.'
- Francoise Mallet-Joris

'With them I gladly shared my all and learned the great truth that where God guides, He provides.'
- Frank N. D. Buchman

'Why not go out on a limb? Isn't that where the fruit is?'
- Frank Scully

'Bravery is being the only one who knows you're afraid.'
- Franklin P. Jones

'Courage is the best slayer-courage which attacketh, for in every attack there is the sound of triumph.'
- Friedrich Nietzsche

'We ought to face our destiny with courage.'
- Friedrich Nietzsche

'The paradox of courage is that a man must be a little careless of his life in order to keep it.'
- G. K. Chesterton

'Courage is almost a contradiction in terms. It means a strong desire to live taking the form of readiness to die.'
- G. K. Chesterton

'Only those are fit to live who are not afraid to die.'
- General Douglas MacArthur

'Courage is fear holding on a minute longer.'
- General George S. Patton

'All men are afraid in battle. The coward is the one who lets his fear overcome his sense of duty. Duty is the essence of manhood.'
- General George S. Patton

'War is fear cloaked in courage.'
- General William Westmoreland

'The fly that doesn't want to be swatted is most secure when it lights on the fly-swatter.'
- Georg Christoph Lichtenberg

'You don't learn to hold your own in the world by standing on guard, but by attacking, and getting well-hammered yourself.'
- George Bernard Shaw

'Any coward can fight a battle when he's sure of winning.'
- George Eliot

'Because a fellow has failed once or twice or a dozen times, you don't want to set him down as a failure till he's dead or loses his courage-and that's the same thing.'
- George Horace Lorimer

'When it comes to the pinch, human beings are heroic.'
- George Orwell

'Have the courage of your desire.'
- George R. Gissing

'The human spirit is stronger than anything that can happen to it.'
- George. C. Scott

'Awakening begins when a man realizes that he is going nowhere, and does not know where to go.'
- Georges Gurdjieff

'Audacity, more audacity, always audacity.'
- Georges Jacques Danton

'To create one's own world in any of the arts takes courage.'
- Georgia O'Keeffe

'Great things are done more through courage than through wisdom.'
- German proverb

'He who has the courage to laugh is almost as much the master of the world as he who is ready to die.'
- Giacomo Leopardi

'I have met brave women who are exploring the outer edge of human possibility, with no history to guide them, and with a courage to make themselves vulnerable that I find moving beyond words.'
- Gloria Steinem

'Truth is the vital breath of Beauty; Beauty the outward form of Truth.'
- Grace Aguilar

'It is brave to be involved.'
- Gwendolyn Brooks

'Courage ought to have eyes as well as arms.'
  - H. G. Bohn

'The trouble with lying and deceiving is that their efficiency depends entirely upon a clear notion of the truth that the liar and deceiver wishes to hide.'
  - Hannah Arendt

'In the darkest hour the soul is replenished and given strength to continue and endure.'
  - Heart Warrior Chosa

'There is plenty of courage among us for the abstract, but not for the concrete.'
  - Helen Keller

'How, then, find the courage for Taking Action? By slipping a little into unconsciousness, spontaneity, instinct which holds one to the earth and dictates the relatively good and useful. ... By accepting the human condition more simply, and candidly, by dreading '
  - Henri Frederic Amiel

'The frontiers are not east or west, north or south, but wherever a man fronts a fact.'
  - Henry David Thoreau

'However mean your life is, meet it and live it; do not shun it and call it hard names. It is not so bad as you are.'
  - Henry David Thoreau

'Where there is a brave man, in the thickest of the fight, there is the post of honor.'
  - Henry David Thoreau

'There is something healthy and invigorating about direct Taking Action.'
  - Henry Miller

'No one has yet computed how many imaginary triumphs are silently celebrated by people each year to keep up their courage.'
  - Henry S. Haskins

'The bravest are the tenderest. The loving are the daring.'
  - Henry Wadsworth Longfellow

'Go forth to meet the shadowy Future without fear and with a manly heart.'
  - Henry Wadsworth Longfellow

'Failure is only postponed success as long as courage "coaches" ambition. The habit of persistence is the habit of victory.'
  - Herbert Kaufman

'It is better by noble boldness to run the risk of being subject to half of the evils we anticipate than to remain in cowardly listlessness for fear of what might happen.'
  - Herodotus

'It is the bold man who every time does best, at home or abroad.'
- Homer

'A decent boldness ever meets with friends.'
- Homer

'All happiness depends on courage and work.'
- Honore de Balzac

'In times of stress, be bold and valiant.'
- Horace

'It is courage, courage, courage, that raises the blood of life to crimson splendor. Live bravely and present a brave front to adversity!'
- Horace

'Fools, through false shame, conceal their open wounds.'
- Horace

'Courage is the fear of being thought a coward.'
- Horace Smith

'We all carry it within us: supreme strength, the fullness of wisdom, unquenchable joy. It is never thwarted, and cannot be destroyed.'
- Huston Smith

'Spiritual cowardice is not only weakness but wickedness.'
- J. B. Gambrell

'Everyone will be taxed according to his means.'
- J. C. F. von Schiller

'He that is overcautious will accomplish little.'
- J. C. F. von Schiller

'Who dares nothing, need hope for nothing.'
- J. C. F. von Schiller

'God helps the brave.'
- J. C. F. von Schiller

'The truth will set you free, but first it will make you miserable.'
- James A. Garfield

'It takes courage to know when you ought to be afraid.'
- James A. Michener

'One of the biggest factors in success is the courage to undertake something.'
- James A. Worsham

'Greatness, in the last analysis, is largely bravery-courage in escaping from old ideas and old standards.'
- James Harvey Robinson

'You will never do anything in this world without courage.'
- James Lane Allen

'Fate loves the fearless.'
- James Russell Lowell

'Let us not look back in anger, nor forward in fear, but around us in awareness.'
- James Thurber

'You don't change the course of history by turning the faces of portraits to the wall.'
- Jawaharlal Nehru

'To say yes, you have to sweat and roll up your sleeves and plunge both hands into life up to the elbows. It is easy to say no, even if saying no means death.'
- Jean Anouilh

'Until the day of his death, no man can be sure of his courage.'
- Jean Anouilh

'True miracles are created by men when they use the courage and intelligence that God gave them.'
- Jean Anouilh

'Women and men of retiring timidity are cowardly only in dangers which affect themselves, but the first to rescue when others are endangered.'
- Jean Paul Richter

'How many feasible projects have miscarried through despondency, and been strangled in their birth by a cowardly imagination?'
- Jeremy Collier

'It takes courage to live-courage and strength and hope and humor. And courage and strength and hope and humor have to be bought and paid for with pain and work and prayers and tears.'
- Jerome P. Fleishman

'When you're my size in the pros, fear is a sign that you're not stupid.'
- Jerry Levias

'Talent is helpful in writing, but guts are absolutely necessary.'
- Jessamyn West

'When you have no choice, mobilize the spirit of courage.'
- Jewish proverb

'Act, and God will act.'
- Joan of Arc

'It's weak and despicable to go on wanting things and not trying to get them.'
- Joanna Field

'You look at a guy who's being brave. He's afraid, or he wouldn't be brave. If he isn't afraid, he's stupid.'
- Joe Torre

'Cowards cannot see that their greatest safety lies in dauntless courage.'
- Johann Kaspar Lavater

'The man with insight enough to admit his limitations comes nearest to perfection.'
- Johann von Goethe

'Nature reacts not only to physical disease, but also to moral weakness; when the danger increases, she gives us greater courage.'
- Johann von Goethe

'What you can do, or dream you can do, begin it; boldness has genius, power and magic in it.'
- Johann von Goethe

'Confidence ... is directness and courage in meeting the facts of life.'
- John Dewey

'Between cowardice and despair, valor is gendered.'
- John Donne

'Fortune befriends the bold.'
- John Dryden

'None but the brave deserve the fair.'
- John Dryden

'There is, in addition to a courage with which men die, a courage by which men must live.'
- John F. Kennedy

'If you are scared to go to the brink, you are lost.'
- John Foster Dulles

'The only cowards are sinners; fighting the fight is all.'
- John G. Neihardt

'Courage does not consist in calculation, but in fighting against chances.'
- John Henry Cardinal Newman

'The highest courage is to dare to appear to be what one is.'
- John Lancaster Spalding

'Get in front of the ball, you won't get hurt. That's what you've got a chest for, young man.'
- John McGraw

'The real gift of love is self disclosure.'
- John Powell

'Courage and perseverance have a magical talisman, before which difficulties disappear, and obstacles vanish into air.'
- John Quincy Adams

'God gives us always strength enough, and sense enough, for everything He wants us to do.'
- John Ruskin

'There is no such thing as bravery, only degrees of fear.'
- John Wainwright

'Courage is being scared to death ... and saddling up anyway.'
- John Wayne

'All men would be cowards if they durst.'
- John Wilmot, Earl of Rochester

'An excuse is a lie guarded.'
- Jonathan Swift

'Courage that grows from constitution often forsakes a man ... courage which arises from a sense of duty acts in a uniform manner.'
- Joseph Addison

'The last thing a woman will consent to discover in a man whom she loves, or on whom she simply depends, is want of courage.'
- Joseph Conrad

'Facing it-always facing it-that's the way to get through. Face it!'
- Joseph Conrad

'The man who most vividly realizes a difficulty is the man most likely to overcome it.'
- Joseph Farrell

'The highest courage is not to be found in the instinctive acts of men who risk their lives to save a friend or slay a foe; the physical fearlessness of a moment or an hour is not to be compared with immolation of months or years for the sake of wisdom or '
- Joseph H. Odell

'A great man is one who seizes the vital issue in a complex question, what we might call the jugular vein of the whole organism, and spends his energies upon that.'
- Joseph Rickaby

'I discovered I always have choices and sometimes it's only a choice of attitude.'
- Judith M. Knowlton

'Courage is more than standing for a firm conviction. It includes the risk of questioning that conviction.'
- Julian Weber Gordon

'Leap, and the net will appear.'
- Julie Cameron

'As a rule, what is out of sight disturbs men's minds more seriously than what they see.'
- Julius Caesar

'Genius is an infinite capacity for taking life by the scruff of the neck.'
- Katharine Hepburn

'Everyone thought I was bold and fearless and even arrogant, but inside I was always quaking.'
- Katharine Hepburn

'Risk! Risk anything! ... Do the hardest thing on earth for you. Act for yourself. Face the truth.'
- Katherine Mansfield

'When moral courage feels that it is in the right, there is no personal daring of which it is incapable.'
- Leigh Hunt

'I have often though morality may perhaps consist solely in the courage of making a choice.'
- Leon Blum

'In difficult situations, when hope seems feeble, the boldest plans are safest.'
- Livy

'Instead of looking at life as a narrowing funnel, we can see it ever widening to choose the things we want to do, to take the wisdom we've learned and create something.'
- Liz Carpenter

'What is more mortifying than to feel that you have missed the plum for want of courage to shake the tree?'
- Logan Pearsall Smith

'Fear is the single strongest motivating force in our lives. ... The more frightened you become, the better your chances of achieving success.'
- Lois Korey

'I'm not funny. What I am is brave.'
- Lucille Ball

'I'd rather give my life than be afraid to give it.'
- Lyndon B. Johnson

'We cannot solve life's problems except by solving them.'
- M. Scott Peck

'Trouble, like the hill ahead, straightens out when you advance upon it.'
- Marcelene Cox

'Fortune reveres the brave, and overwhelms the cowardly.'
- Marcus Annaeus Seneca

'Knowledge of sin is the beginning of salvation.'
- Marcus Annaeus Seneca

'Sometimes even to live is an act of courage.'
- Marcus Annaeus Seneca

'Courage is a scorner of things which inspire fear.'
- Marcus Annaeus Seneca

'There is nothing in the world so much admired as a man who knows how to bear unhappiness with courage.'
- Marcus Annaeus Seneca

'Courage leads starward, fear toward death.'
- Marcus Annaeus Seneca

'The first rule is to keep an untroubled spirit. The second is to look things in the face and know them for what they are.'
- Marcus Aurelius

'There are some women who seem to be born without fear, just as there are people who are born without the ability to feel pain. ... Providence appears to protect such women, maybe out of astonishment.'
- Margaret Atwood

'There is no power on earth more formidable than the truth.'
- Margaret Lee Runbeck

'Courage is rarely reckless or foolish ... courage usually involves a highly realistic estimate of the odds that must be faced.'
- Margaret Truman

'The spirit of man is an inward flame; a lamp the world blows upon but never puts out.'
- Margot Asquith

'The incurable ills are the imaginary ills'
- Marie von Ebner-Eschenbach

'It takes great courage to break with one's past history and stand alone.'
- Marion Woodman

'Courage is resistance to fear, mastery of fear-not absence of fear.'
- Mark Twain

'We must constantly build dykes of courage to hold back the flood of fear.'
- Martin Luther King, Jr.

'Courage to be is the key to revelatory power of the feminist revolution.'
- Mary Daly

'If we have the courage and tenacity of our forebears, who stood firmly like a rock against the lash of slavery, we shall find a way to do for our day what they did for theirs.'
- Mary McLeod Bethune

'Be content to stand in the light, and let the shadow fall where it will.'
- Mary W. Stewart

'There is a courage of happiness as well as a courage of sorrow.'
- Maurice Maeterlinck

'We must have courage to bet on our ideas, on the calculated risk, and to act. Everyday living requires courage if life is to be effective and bring happiness.'
- Maxwell Maltz

'Courage is the most important of all virtues, because without it we can't practice any other virtue with consistency.'
- Maya Angelou

'The elegance of honesty needs no adornment.'
- Merry Browne

'The Bible tells us that a sparrow does not fall without God's notice. I know he will help us meet our responsibilities through his guidance.'
- Michael Cardone

'Cowardice is the mother of cruelty.'
- Michel de Montaigne

'Valor is stability, not of legs and arms, but of courage and the soul.'
- Michel de Montaigne

'Courage can't see around corners, but goes around them anyway.'
- Mignon McLaughlin

'If you are brave too often, people will come to expect it of you.'
- Mignon McLaughlin

'The only courage that matters is the kind that gets you from one moment to the next.'
- Mignon McLaughlin

'valor lies just halfway between rashness and cowardice.'
- Miguel de Cervantes

'He who loses wealth loses much; he who loses a friend loses more; but he who loses his courage loses all.'
- Miguel de Cervantes

'The guts carry the feet, not the feet the guts.'
- Miguel de Cervantes

'Faint heart never won fair lady.'
- Miguel de Cervantes

'If you suppress grief too much, it can well redouble.'
- Moliere

'However confused the scene of our life appears, however torn we may be who now do face that scene, it can be faced, and we can go on to be whole.'
- Muriel Rukeyser

'Courage is like love, it must have hope for nourishment.'
- Napoleon Bonaparte

'With audacity one can undertake anything.'
- Napoleon Bonaparte

'Fatalism is a lazy man's way of accepting the inevitable.'
- Natalie Clifford Barney

'Optimism is the foundation of courage.'
- Nicholas Murray Butler

'Necessity does the work of courage.'
- Nicholas Murray Butler

'Courage is clearly a readiness to risk self-humiliation.'
- Nigel Dennis

'Many become brave when brought to bag.'
- Norwegian proverb

'Wealth lost-something lost; Honor lost-much lost; Courage lost-all lost.'
- Old German proverb

'rouble creates a capacity to handle it.'
- Oliver Wendell Holmes

'Happy the man who ventures boldly to defend what he holds dear.'
- Ovid

'Fortune and Love befriend the bold.'
- Ovid

'Fortune and love favor the brave.'
- Ovid

'It takes vision and courage to create- it takes faith and courage to prove.'
- Owen D. Young

'Introversion, at least if extreme, is a sign of mental and spiritual immaturity.'
- Pearl S. Buck

'In this unbelievable universe in which we live, there are no absolutes. Even parallel lines, reaching into infinity, meet somewhere yonder.'
- Pearl S. Buck

'Truth is always exciting. Speak it, then; life is dull without it.'
- Pearl S. Buck

'When we know what we want to prove, we go out and find our facts. They are always there.'
- Pearl S. Buck

'Being "brave" means doing or facing something frightening. ... Being "fearless" means being without fear.'
- Penelope Leach

'Men perish by the sword, cowards by disease.'
- Phillippus

'Among wellborn spirits courage does not depend on age.'
- Pierre Corneille

'Courage is a kind of salvation.'
- Plato

'Courage is knowing what not to fear.'
- Plato

'Courage is its own reward.'
- Plautus

'Courage in danger is half the battle.'
- Plautus

'Courage is what preserves our liberty, safety, life, and our homes and parents, our country and children. Courage comprises all things.'
- Plautus

'Courage easily finds its own eloquence.'
- Plautus

'He shall fare well who confronts circumstances aright.'
   - Plutarch

'Bravery and faith bring both material and spiritual rewards.'
   - Preston Bradley

'Audacity has made kings.'
   - Prosper Jolyot de Crebillion

'Audacity augments courage; hesitation, fear.'
   - Publilius Syrus

'Cowards falter, but danger is often overcome by those who nobly dare.'
   - Queen Elizabeth I

'I would often be a coward, but for the shame of it.'
   - Ralph Connor

'You can surmount the obstacles in your path if you are determined, courageous and hardworking. ...
Do not fear to pioneer, to venture down new paths of endeavor.'
   - Ralph J. Bunche

'The test of courage comes when we are in the minority.'
   - Ralph W. Sockman

'Do not be too timid and squeamish. ... All life is an experiment. The more experiments you make, the
better.'
   - Ralph Waldo Emerson

'Whatever you do, you need courage. ... To map out a course of Taking Action and follow it to an end
requires some of the same courage which a soldier needs.'
   - Ralph Waldo Emerson

'Every man has his own courage, and is betrayed because he seeks in himself the courage of other
persons.'
   - Ralph Waldo Emerson

'Nature arms each man with some faculty which enables him to do easily some feat impossible to any
other.'
   - Ralph Waldo Emerson

'Courage consists of the power of self-recovery.'
   - Ralph Waldo Emerson

'We can easily become as much slaves to precaution as we can to fear.'
   - Randolph Bourne

'Courage is the power to let go of the familiar.'
   - Raymond Lindquist

'I'm not afraid of too many things, and I got that invincible kind of attitude from my father.'
   - Reinhold Niebuhr

'We need the courage to start and continue what we should do, and courage to stop what we shouldn't do.'
   - Richard L. Evans

'Have the courage to live. Anyone can die.'
   - Robert Cody

'The world is not perishing for the want of clever or talented or well-meaning men. It is perishing for the want of men of courage and resolution.'
   - Robert J. McCracken

'Courage is the footstool of the Virtues, upon which they stand.'
   - Robert Louis Stevenson

'Keep your fears to yourself, but share your courage with others.'
   - Robert Louis Stevenson

'Courage is required not only in a person's occasional crucial decision for his own freedom, but in the little hour-to-hour decisions which place the bricks in the structure of his building of himself into a person who acts with freedom and responsibility.'
   - Rollo May

'Courage is the basic virtue for everyone so long as he continues to grow, to move ahead.'
   - Rollo May

'The hallmark of courage in our age of conformity is the capacity to stand on one's convictions-not obstinately or defiantly (these are gestures of defensiveness, not courage) nor as a gesture of retaliation, but simply because these are what one believes.'
   - Rollo May

'To say a person is a coward has no more meaning than to say he is lazy: It simply tells us that some vital potentiality is unrealized or blocked.'
   - Rollo May

'I'm a real pussycat-with an iron tail.'
   - Rona Barrett

'There are at least two kinds of cowards. One kind always lives with himself, afraid to face the world. The other kind lives with the world, afraid to face himself.'
   - Roscoe Snowden

'That's what being young is all about. You have the courage and the daring to think that you can make a difference.'
   - Ruby Dee

'Courage is very important. Like a muscle, it is strengthened by use.'
  - Ruth Gordon

'The confession of evil works is the first beginning of good works.'
  - Saint Augustine

'Courage is the greatest of all the virtues. Because if you haven't courage, you may not have an opportunity to use any of the others.'
  - Samuel Johnson

'Courage is a quality so necessary for maintaining virtue that it is always respected even when it is associated with vice.'
  - Samuel Johnson

'If you have enough fantasies, you're ready, in the event that something happens.'
  - Sheila Ballantyne

'Defending the truth is not something one does out of a sense of duty or to allay guilt complexes, but is a reward in itself.'
  - Simone de Beauvoir

'Courage is the thing. All goes if courage goes.'
  - Sir James M. Barrie

'Courage is the lovely virtue-the rib of Himself that God sent down to His children.'
  - Sir James M. Barrie

'Where life is more terrible than death, it is the truest valor to dare to live.'
  - Sir Thomas Browne

'To the timid and hesitating everything is impossible because it seems so.'
  - Sir Walter Scott

'Truth is not introduced into the individual from without, but was within him all the time.'
  - Soren Kierkegaard

'Have the courage to face a difficulty lest it kick you harder than you bargain for.'
  - Stanislaus

'What God expects us to attempt, He also enables us to achieve.'
  - Stephen Olford

'Courage permits the caliber of performance to continue at its peak, until the finish line is crossed.'
  - Stuart Walker

'Courage is the ability to solve problems realistically in the presence of fear.'
  - Stuart Walker

'Hail, Caesar, those who are about to die salute thee.'
- Suetonius

'You cannot weave truth on a loom of lies.'
- Suzette Haden Elgin

'Should I, after tea and cakes and ices, have the strength to force the moment to its crisis?'
- T. S. Eliot

'Nothing is as valuable to a man as courage.'
- Terence

'To have courage for whatever comes in life-everything lies in that.'
- Teresa of Avila

'I am not afraid of a fight; I have to do my duty, come what may.'
- Therese of Lisieux

'Be courageous! ... I have seen many depressions in business. Always America has come out stronger and more prosperous. Be as brave as your fathers before you. Have faith! Go forward.'
- Thomas A. Edison

'The courage we desire and prize is not the courage to die decently, but to live manfully.'
- Thomas Carlyle

'He who is afraid of every nettle should not piss in the grass.'
- Thomas Fuller

'Tender-handed stroke a nettle, and it stings you for your pains; Grasp it like a man of mettle, and it soft as silk remains.'
- Thomas Fuller

'A coward's fear can make a coward valiant.'
- Thomas Fuller

'We would be cowards, if we had courage enough.'
- Thomas Fuller

'He that handles a nettle tenderly is soonest stung.'
- Thomas Fuller

'Within us all there are wells of thought and dynamos of energy which are not suspected until emergencies arise. Then oftentimes we find that it is comparatively simple to double or triple our former capacities and to amaze ourselves by the results achieve'
- Thomas J. Watson

'Honesty is the first chapter of the book of wisdom.'
- Thomas Jefferson

'We have what we seek. It is there all the time, and if we give it time, it will make itself known to us.'
   - Thomas Merton

'There is at least one thing more brutal than the truth, and that is the consequence of saying less than the truth.'
   - Ti-Grace Atkinson

'He who knows how to suffer everything can dare everything.'
   - Vauvenargues

'Nothing but courage can guide life.'
   - Vauvenargues

'Sorrow is a fruit. God does not allow it to grow on a branch that is too weak to bear it.'
   - Victor Hugo

'This is the art of courage: to see things as they are and still believe that the victory lies not with those who avoid the bad, but those who taste, in living awareness, every drop of the good.'
   - Victoria Lincoln

'Freedom is not for the timid.'
   - Vijaya Lakshmi Pandit

'What would life be if we had no courage to attempt anything?'
   - Vincent van Gogh

'Prudence which degenerates into timidity is very seldom the path to safety.'
   - Viscount Cecil

'Often the test of courage is not to die but to live.'
   - Vittorio Conte Alfieri

'Imposing limitations on yourself is cowardly because it protects you from having to try, and perhaps failing.'
   - Vladimir Zworykin

'Exigencies create the necessary ability to meet and conquer them.'
   - Wendell Phillips

'Courage is always the surest wisdom.'
   - Wilfred Grenfell

'There is a time when to avoid trouble is to store up trouble, and when to seek for a lazy and a cowardly peace is to court a still greater danger.'
   - William Barclay

'On many of the great issues of our time, men have lacked wisdom because they have lacked courage.'
   - William Benton

'All problems become smaller if you don't dodge them, but confront them.'
- William F. Halsey

'Our energy is in proportion to the resistance it meets. We attempt nothing great but from a sense of the difficulties we have to encounter; we persevere in nothing great but from a pride in overcoming them.'
- William Hazlitt

'No man will succeed unless he is ready to face and overcome difficulties, and is prepared to assume responsibilities.'
- William J. H. Boetcker

'Life is a battle in which we fall from wounds we receive in running away.'
- William L. Sullivan

'Attacking is the only secret. Dare and the world always yields; or if it beats you sometimes, dare it again, and it will succumb.'
- William Makepeace Thackeray

'Cowards die many times before their deaths; the valiant never taste of death but once.'
- William Shakespeare

'But screw your courage to the sticking place and we'll not fail.'
- William Shakespeare

'Courage mounteth with occasion.'
- William Shakespeare

'Many women miss their greatest chance of happiness through a want of courage in a decisive moment.'
- Winifred Gordon

'Courage is the first of the human qualities because it is the quality which guarantees all the others.'
- Winston Churchill

'Success is never found. Failure is never fatal. Courage is the only thing.'
- Winston Churchill

'We shall draw from the heart of suffering itself the means of inspiration and survival.'
- Winston Churchill

'Without courage, all other virtues lose their meaning.'
- Winston Churchill

'God gave burdens, also shoulders.'
- Yiddish proverb

CRITICISM

He has a right to criticize, who has a heart to help.'
    - Abraham Lincoln

'The factor in human life provocative of a noble discontent is the gradual emergence of a sense of criticism, founded upon appreciation of beauty, and of intellectual distinction, and of duty.'
    - Alfred North Whitehead

'Don't judge any man until you have walked two moons in his moccasins.'
    - American Indian saying

'The good critic is he who narrates the adventures of his soul among masterpieces.'
    - Anatole France

'Any fool can criticize, and many of them do.'
    - Archbishop C. Garbett

'Reprove not a scorner, lest he hate thee; rebuke a wise man and he will love thee.'
    - Bible

'Critics are like eunuchs in a harem: they know how it's done, they've seen it done every day, but they're unable to do it themselves.'
    - Brendan Behan

'A critic is a legless man who teaches running.'
    - Channing Pollock

'In judging others, folks will work overtime for no pay.'
    - Charles Edwin Carruthers

'Asking a working writer what he thinks about critics is like asking a lamppost how it feels about dogs.'
    - Christopher Hampton

'His words leap across rivers and mountains, but his thoughts are still only six inches long.'
    - E. B. White

'To escape criticism - do nothing, say nothing, be nothing.'
    - Elbert Hubbard

'It is not expected of critics that they should help us to make sense of our lives; they are bound only to attempt the lesser feat of making sense of the ways we try to make sense of our lives.'
    - Frank Kermode

'The critic is an overgoer with pen-envy.'
    - Geoffrey Hartman

'It is easy - terribly easy - to shake a man's faith in himself. To take advantage of that, to break a man's spirit is devil's work.'
- George Bernard Shaw

'Analysis kills spontaneity. The grain once ground into flour springs and germinates no more.'
- Henri Frederic Amiel

'Two and two continue to make four, in spite of the whine of the amateur for three, or the cry of the critic for five.'
- James McNeill Whistler

'Nature fits all her children with something to do He who would write and can't write, can surely review.'
- James Russell Lowell

'I don't want to see the uncut version of anything.'
- Jean Kerr

'To many people dramatic criticism must seem like an attempt to tattoo soap bubbles.'
- John Mason Brown

'Book reviewers are little old ladies of both sexes.'
- John O'Hara

'A critic is a man who knows the way but can't drive the car.'
- Kenneth Tynan

'Constant, indiscriminate approval devalues because it is so predictable.'
- Kit Reed

'Of all the cants which are canted in this canting world, tho' the cant of hypocrites may be the worst, the cant of criticism is the most tormenting.'
- Laurence Sterne

'If you are willing to take the punishment, you're halfway through the battle. That the issues may be trivial, the battle ugly, is another point.'
- Lillian Hellman

'A critic at best is a waiter at the great table of literature.'
- Louis Dudek

'Tomorrow night I appear for the first time before a Boston audience - 4000 critics.'
- Mark Twain

'I am sitting in the smallest room in my house. I have your review in front of me. Soon it will be behind me.'
- Max Reger

'Henry James chews more than he bites off.'
- Mrs. Henry Adams

'Nature, when she invented, manufactured and patented her authors, contrived to make critics out of the chips that were left.'
- Oliver Wendell Holmes

'When critics disagree, the artist is in accord with himself.'
- Oscar Wilde

'Vilify! Vilify! Some of it will always stick.'
- Pierre Beaumarchais

'Always bring money along with your complaints.'
- Plautus

'A guest sees more in an hour than the host in a year.'
- Polish proverb

'More and more people think of the critic as an indispensable middle man between writer and reader, and would no more read a book alone, if they could help it, than have a baby alone.'
- Randall Jarrell

'The critic is the duenna in the passionate affair between playwrights, actors and audiences - a figure dreaded, and occasionally comic, but never welcome, never loved.'
- Robertson Davies

'The test of a good critic is whether he knows when and how to believe on insufficient evidence.'
- Samuel Butler

'Critics are biased, and so are readers. (Indeed, a critic is a bundle of biases held loosely together by a sense of taste.) But intelligent readers soon discover how to allow for the windage of their own and a critic's prejudices.'
- Whitney Balliett

DEATH

Call no man happy till he is dead.'
  - Aeschylus

'Though this may be play to you, Tis death to us.'
  - Aesop

'I have a rendezvous with Death At some disputed barricade.'
  - Alan Seecer

'Till tired, he sleeps, and life's poor play is o'er.'
  - Alexander Pope

'The Lord gave, and the Lord hath taken away; blessed be the name of the Lord.'
  - Anonymous

'In the midst of life we are in death.'
  - Anonymous

'Earth to earth, ashes to ashes, dust to dust, in sure and certain hope of the resurrection.'
  - Anonymous

'Yet a little sleep, a little slumber, a little folding of the hands to sleep.'
  - Anonymous

'Man that is born of a woman hath but a short time to live, and is full of misery. He cometh up, and is cut down, like a flower; he fleeth as it were a shadow, and never continueth in one stay.'
  - Anonymous

'Why fear death? It is the most beautiful adventure in life.'
  - Charles Frohman

'I lived in Miami for a while, in a section with a lot of really old people. The average age in my apartment house was dead.'
  - Gabe Kaplan

'There is no death! the stars go down To rise upon some other shore, And bright in Heaven's jeweled crown, They shine for ever more.'
  - John L. McCreery

'Sunset and evening star, And one clear call for me! And may there be no moaning of the bar When I put out to sea.'
  - Lord Alfred Tennyson

'God's finger touched him, and he slept.'
  - Lord Alfred Tennyson

'Death, so called, is a thing which makes men weep, And yet a third of life is pass'd in sleep.'
- Lord Byron

'We begin to die as soon as we are born, and the end is linked to the beginning.'
- Marcus Manilius

'Strange - is it not? - that of the myriads who Before us passed the door of Darkness through, Not one returns to tell us of the road Which to discover we must travel too.'
- Omar Khayyam

'For he who lives more lives than one More deaths than one must die.'
- Oscar Wilde

'First our pleasures die - and then Our hopes, and then our fears - and when These are dead, the debt is due, Dust claims dust - and we die too.'
- Percy Bysshe Shelley

'Now I am about to take my last voyage, a great leap in the dark.'
- Thomas Hobbes

'Nothing can happen more beautiful than death.'
- Walt Whitman

'Is death the last sleep? No, it is the last final awakening.'
- Walter Scott

'To die: - to sleep: No more; and, by a sleep to say we end The heart-ache and the thousand natural shocks That flesh is heir to, 'tis a consummation Devoutly to be wished.'
- William Shakespeare

'I am dying, Egypt, dying.'
- William Shakespeare

'Nothing in his life Became him like the leaving it.'
- William Shakespeare

'Death lies on her, like an untimely frost Upon the sweetest flower of all the field.'
- William Shakespeare

ECONOMICS

By pursuing his own interest (the individual) frequently promotes that of the society more effectually than when he really intends to promote it. I have never known much good done by those who affected to trade for the public good.'
   - Adam Smith

'People of the same trade seldom meet together, even for merriment and diversion, but the conversation ends in a conspiracy against the public, or in some contrivance to raise prices.'
   - Adam Smith

'It is an economic axiom as old as the hills that goods and services can be paid for only with goods and services.'
   - Albert J. Nock

'Power over a man's subsistence amounts to a power over his will.'
   - Alexander Hamilton

'Business? It's quite simple. It's other people's money.'
   - Alexandre Dumas

'Business is a combination of war and sport.'
   - Andri Maurois

'Nothing in fine print is ever good news.'
   - Andy Rooney

'After an eight-hour day, workers require three overtime hours to produce two regular hours of results.'
   - Anonymous

'Christmas is over and Business is Business.'
   - Anonymous

'No one leads the orchestra without turning his back on the crowd.'
   - Anonymous

'To make a long story short, . . . there's nothing like having the boss walk in.'
   - Anonymous

'The motto in the workaholic Silicon Valley is "Stop for lunch and you are lunch."'
   - Anonymous

'Live together like brothers and do business like strangers.'
   - Anonymous

'The whole world knows we have it made in America . . . made in China, made in Mexico, made in Japan.'
- Anonymous

'To be a leader you need a lot of people dumb enough to follow.'
- Anonymous

'If a cluttered desk is an indication of a cluttered mind, what is indicated by an empty desk?'
- Anonymous

'The secret of business is to know something that nobody else knows.'
- Aristotle Onassis

'Anti-intellectualism has long been the anti-Semitism of the business man.'
- Arthur Schopenhauer

'The nature of business is swindling.'
- August Bebel

'Whose merchants are princes.'
- Bible

'Wist ye not that I must be about my Father's business ?'
- Bible

'Expenditure rises to meet income.'
- C. Northcote Parkinson

'The business of America is business.'
- Calvin Coolidge

'Pounds are the sons, not of pounds, but of pence.'
- Charles Buxton

'All business proceeds on beliefs, on judgements of probabilities, and not on certainties.'
- Charles W. Eliot

'Those who can, do; those who can't, teach; and those who can do neither, administer.'
- Collet Calverley

'There can be no return to prosperity while the government (of Ontario) believes that taking money from the people who have earned it and giving it away to the people who haven't, in exchange for their votes and regardless of merit, is the essence of fairn'
- Conrad Black

'Big business is basic to the very life of this country; and yet many -perhaps most - Americans have a deep-seated fear and an emotional repugnance to it. Here is monumental contradiction.'
- David Lilienthal

'The consumer is not a moron; she is your wife.'
  - David Ogilvy

'One of the best ways to persuade others is with your ears - by listening to them.'
  - Dean Rusk

'To convert an hourly wage to an approximate yearly salary, double the wage and change the decimal to a comma.'
  - Don Tichnor

'Call on a business man at business times only, and on business, transact your business and go about your business, in order to give him time to finish his business.'
  - Duke of Wellington

'Mere parsimony is not economy . . . expense, and great expense, may be an essential part of true economy.'
  - Edmund Burke

'Corporations cannot commit treason, nor be outlawed, nor excommunicated, for they have no souls.'
  - Edward Coke

'The solid wealth of insurance companies and the success of those who organize gambling are some indication of the profits to be derived from the efficient use of chance.'
  - Edward de Bono

'Remember that when an employee enters your office, he is in a strange land.'
  - Erwin H. Schell

'When you've got them by their wallets, their hearts and minds will follow.'
  - Fern Naito

'Christmas is over, and Business is Business.'
  - Franklin Pierce Adams

'Managers don't have to cook the books to manipulate earnings; they often have all the power they need in the leeway built into accounting rules.'
  - Fred S. Worthy

'The Bell System is like a damn big dragon. You kick it in the tail, and two years later, it feels it in its head.'
  - Frederick Kappel

'The price spoils the pleasure.'
  - French proverb

'Competition means decentralized planning by many separate persons.'
  - Friedrich Hayek

'Barbaric accuracy - whimpering humility.'
  - G. C. Lichtenberg

'Twenty generations ago - around the year 1390 - you had 1,048,576 ancestors. In the 21st generation of your family that number will double again.'
  - Genealogical Research Library

'Inflation is defined as the quality that makes balloons larger and candy bars smaller.'
  - General Features Corporation

'I often feel like the director of a cemetery. I have a lot of people under me, but nobody listens!'
  - General John Gavin

'No-wher so bisy a man as he ter nas, And yet he semed bisier that he was.'
  - Geoffrey Chaucer

'All professions are a conspiracy against the country.'
  - George Bernard Shaw

'I am a Millionaire. That is my religion.'
  - George Bernard Shaw

'Labor is not a commodity, or a standard, or a means to an ulterior end, but an end in itself.'
  - George Brockway

'In show business the key word is honesty. Once you've learned to fake that, the rest is easy.'
  - George Burns

'In matters of commerce the fault of the Dutch Is offering too little and asking too much. The French are with equal advantage content, So we clap on Dutch bottoms just 20%.'
  - George Canning

'Whose bread I eat, his song I sing.'
  - German proverb

'Don't be humble. You're not that great.'
  - Golda Meir

'It takes no more actual sagacity to carry on the everyday hawking and haggling of the world, or to ladle out its normal doses of bad medicine and worse law, than it takes to operate a taxi cab or fry a pan of fish.'
  - H. L. Mencken

'I don't believe in just ordering people to do things. You have to sort of grab an oar and row with them.'
  - Harold Geneen

'One man's wage rise is another man's price increase.'
  - Harold Wilson

'What recommends commerce to me is its enterprise and bravery. It does not clasp its hands and pray to Jupiter.'
- Henry David Thoreau

'I think that there is nothing, not even crime, more opposed to poetry, to philosophy, ay, to life itself than this incessant business.'
- Henry David Thoreau

'It is not the employer who pays wages - he only handles the money. It is the product that pays wages.'
- Henry Ford

'Net - the biggest word in the language of business.'
- Herbert Casson

'Few have heard of Fra Luca Parioli, the inventor of double-entry bookkeeping, but he has probably had more influence on human life than has Dante or Michelangelo.'
- Herbert J. Muller

'A criminal is a person with predatory instincts who has not sufficient capital to form a corporation.'
- Howard Scott

'After being on the road so much I want to spend more time with my family, who I hear are wonderful people.'
- Howie Mandel

'A man isn't a man until he has to meet a payroll.'
- Ivan Shaffer

'That which is everybody's business, is nobody's business.'
- Izaak Walton

'Executive ability is deciding quickly and getting somebody else to do the work.'
- J. C. Pollard

'Business is like oil. It won't mix with anything but business.'
- J. Graham

'In all modern depressions, recessions, or growth-correction, as variously they are called, we never miss the goods that are not produced. We miss only the opportunities for the labor - for the jobs - that are not provided.'
- J. K. Galbraith

'In economics, the majority is always wrong.'
- J. K. Galbraith

'People of privilege will always risk their complete destruction rather than surrender any material part of their advantage.'
- J. K. Galbraith

'Capital is past savings accumulated for future production.'
- Jackson Martindell

'The Middle East is a region where oil is thicker than blood.'
- James Holland

'A company is judged by the president it keeps.'
- James Hulbert

'Entrepreneurship is the last refuge of the trouble-making individual.'
- James K. Glassman

'You are never giving, nor can you ever give, enough service.'
- James R. Cook

'The forces in a capitalist society, if left unchecked, tend to make the rich richer and the poor poorer.'
- Jawaharlal Nehru

'Good management consists of showing average people how to do the work of superior people.'
- John D. Rockefeller

'The ability to deal with people is as purchasable a commodity as sugar or coffee. And I pay more for that ability than for any other under the sun.'
- John D. Rockefeller

'The corporation is an artificial being, invisible, intangible, and existing only in contemplation of law.'
- John Marshall

'The best way to destroy the capitalist system is to debauch the currency. By a continuing process of inflation, governments can confiscate, secretly and unobserved, an important part of the wealth of their citizens.'
- John Maynard Keynes

'The big-business mergers and the big-labor mergers have the appearance of dinosaurs mating.'
- John Naisbitt

'One of the best-kept secrets in America is that people are aching to make a commitment, if they only had the freedom and environment in which to do so.'
- John Naisbitt

'The happiest time in any man's life is when he is in red-hot pursuit of a dollar with a reasonable prospect of overtaking it.'
- Josh Billings

'Had there been a computer a hundred years ago, it would probably have predicted that by now there would be so many horse-drawn vehicles it would be impossible to clear up all the manure.'
- K. William Kapp

'We have yet to find a significant case where the company did not move in the direction of the chief executive's home.'
  - Ken Patton

'In a hierarchy every employee tends to rise to his level of incompetence.'
  - Laurence J. Peter

'Management is now where the medical profession was when it decided that working in a drug store was not sufficient training to become a doctor.'
  - Lawrence Appley

'Business is more exciting than any game.'
  - Lord Beaverbrook

'Without some dissimulation no business can be carried on at all.'
  - Lord Chesterfield

'Patience is a most necessary quality for business; many a man would rather you heard his story than grant his request.'
  - Lord Chesterfield

'Business is religion, and religion is business. The man who does not make a business of his religion has a religious life of no force, and the man who does not make a religion of his business has a business life of no character.'
  - Maltbie Babcock

'Commerce is greedy. Ideology is blood-thirsty.'
  - Mason Cooley

'Committee: A group of men who keep minutes and waste hours.'
  - Milton Berle

'What kind of society isn't structured on greed? The problem of social organization is how to set up an arrangement under which greed will do the least harm; capitalism is that kind of a system.'
  - Milton Friedman

'There is only one social responsibility of business - to use its resources and engage in activities designed to increase its profits without deception or fraud.'
  - Milton Friedman

'The big print giveth and the fine print taketh away.'
  - Monsignor J. Fulton Sheen

'Benefits should be granted little by little, so that they may be better enjoyed.'
  - Niccolo Machiavelli

'An expert is one who knows more and more about less and less.'
  - Nicholas M. Butler

'Capitalism in the United States has undergone profound modification, not just under the New Deal but through a consensus that continued to grow after the New Deal. Government in the U.S. today is a senior partner in every business in the country.'
- Norman Cousins

'Expansion means complexity and complexity decay.'
- Northcote Parkinson

'It might be termed the Law of Triviality. Briefly stated, it means that the time spent on any item of the agenda will be in adverse proportion to the sum involved.'
- Northcote Parkinson

'Today's sales should be better than yesterday's - and worse than tomorrow's.'
- Old saying

'If you fail to plan, you plan to fail.'
- Old saying

'It is not the crook in modern business that we fear, but the honest man who does not know what he is doing.'
- Owen D. Young

'Anybody can cut prices, but it takes brains to produce a better article.'
- P. D. Armour

'Going to work for a large company is like getting on a train. Are you going sixty miles an hour or is the train going sixty miles an hour and you're just sitting still?'
- Paul Getty

'Few great men could pass Personnel.'
- Paul Goodman

'You build on cost and you borrow on value.'
- Paul Reichmann

'A businessman is a hybrid of a dancer and a calculator.'
- Paul Valery

'Adults are always asking little kids what they want to be when they grow up 'cause they're looking for ideas.'
- Paula Poundstone

'Luck is infatuated with the efficient.'
- Persian proverb

'Profitability is the sovereign criterion of the enterprise.'
- Peter Drucker

'Along this tree From root to crown Ideas flow up And vetoes down.'
- Peter Drucker

'There are an enormous number of managers who have retired on the job.'
- Peter F. Drucker

'The manager with the in-basket problem does not yet understand that he must discipline himself to take care of activities that fail to excite him.'
- Priscilla Elfrey

'Things have to be made to happen in a way you want them to happen. Without management, without the intervention of organized willpower the desired result simply cannot be obtained.'
- Robert Heller

'Crime is a logical extension of the sort of behavior that is often considered perfectly respectable in legitimate business.'
- Robert Rice

'The big unions served a noble purpose once, and bless them for it. Now they're part of the problem and must give way if America is to move and to participate in management and achieve reasonable productivity.'
- Robert Townsend

'As one retiring chief executive said to his successor "Yesterday was the last day you heard the truth from your subordinates."'
- Robert W. McMurry

'Man exploits man. Under communism, it's just the opposite.'
- Russian saying

'Chaplin is no businessman - all he knows is that he can't take anything less.'
- Sam Goldwyn

'There are two times in a man's life when he should not speculate: when he can't afford it, and when he can.'
- Samuel L. Clemens

'Never burn bridges. Today's junior jerk, tomorrow's senior partner.'
- Sigourney Weaver

'They (corporations) cannot commit treason, nor be outlawed, nor excommunicated, for they have no souls.'
- Sir Edward Coke

'The white man knows how to make everything, but he does not know how to distribute it.'
- Sitting Bull

'Gross National Product is our Holy Grail.'
- Stuart Udall

'We demand that big business give people a square deal; in return we must insist that when anyone engaged in big business honesty endeavors to do right, he shall himself be given a square deal.'
- Theodore Roosevelt

'I succeed him; no one could replace him.'
- Thomas Jefferson

'All business sagacity reduces itself in the last analysis to a judicious use of sabotage.'
- Thorstein Veblen

'Business is really more agreeable than pleasure; it interests the whole mind . . . more deeply. But it does not look as if it did.'
- Walter Bagehot

'A decorator can make lots of money - assuming she wins the lottery.'
- Wendy Morgan

'A holding company is the people you give your money to while you're being searched.'
- Will Rogers

'Don't gamble; take all your savings and buy some good stock and hold it till it goes up, then sell it. If it don't go up, don't buy it.'
- Will Rogers

'When two men in business always agree, one of them is unnecessary.'
- William Wrigley

'The way to stop financial "joy-riding" is to arrest the chauffeur, not the automobile.'
- Woodrow Wilson

EXUBERANCE

'With renunciation life begins.'
- Amelia Barr

'Our passions are ourselves.'
- Anatole France

'I prefer the errors of enthusiasm to the indifference of wisdom.'
- Anatole France

'The clue is not to ask in a miserly way-the key is to ask in a grand manner.'
- Ann Wigmore

'No one keeps up his enthusiasm automatically. Enthusiasm must be nourished with new Taking Actions, new aspirations, new efforts, new vision. Compete with yourself; set your teeth and dive into the job of breaking your own record. It is one's own fault if his en'
- Anonymous

'Let a man in a garret burn with enough intensity, and he will set fire to the world.'
- Antoine de Saint-Exupery

'Enthusiasm can only be aroused by two things: first, an ideal which takes the imagination by storm, and second, a definite, intelligible plan for carrying that ideal into practice.'
- Arnold J. Toynbee

'Enthusiasm moves the world.'
- Arthur James Balfour

'As I grow older, part of my emotional survival plan must be to actively seek inspiration instead of passively waiting for it to find me.'
- Bebe Moore Campbell

'Every production of genius must be the production of enthusiasm.'
- Benjamin Disraeli

'Energy and persistence conquer all things.'
- Benjamin Franklin

'What hunger is in relation to food, zest is in relation to life.'
- Bertrand Russell

'I really do believe I can accomplish a great deal with a big grin. I know some people find that disconcerting, but that doesn't matter.'
- Beverly Sills

'And whatsoever ye do, do it heartily.'
  - Bible

'Practice being excited.'
  - Bill Foster

'There is a passion for perfection which you rarely see fully developed, but... in successful lives it is never wholly lacking.'
  - Bliss Carman

'Through zeal, knowledge is gotten; through lack of zeal, knowledge is lost.'
  - Buddha

'We would accomplish many more things if we did not think of them as impossible.'
  - C. Malesherbez

'Winning isn't everything. Wanting to win is.'
  - Catfish Hunter

'Most great men and women are not perfectly rounded in their personalities, but are instead people whose one driving enthusiasm is so great it makes their faults seem insignificant.'
  - Charles A. Cerami

'Success is due less to ability than to zeal.'
  - Charles Buxton

'All we need to make us really happy is something to be enthusiastic about.'
  - Charles Kingsley

'It is the greatest shot of adrenaline to be doing what you've wanted to do so badly. You almost feel like you could fly without the plane.'
  - Charles Lindbergh

'A man can succeed at almost anything for which he has unlimited enthusiasm.'
  - Charles M. Schwab

'If you're a champion, you have to have it in your heart.'
  - Chris Evert

'The method of the enterprising is to plan with audacity and execute with vigor.'
  - Christian Bovee

'Zest is the secret of all beauty. There is no beauty that is attractive without zest.'
  - Christian Dior

'Enthusiasm is the most beautiful word on earth.'
  - Christian Morgenstern

'Charm is a cunning self-forgetfulness.'
- Christina Stead

'What one has, one ought to use; and whatever he does, he should do with all his might.'
- Cicero

'Every man without passions has within him no principle of Taking Action, nor motive to act.'
- Claude Helvetius

'When enthusiasm is inspired by reason; controlled by caution; sound in theory; practical in application; reflects confidence; spreads good cheer; raises morale; inspires associates; arouses loyalty; and laughs at adversity, it is beyond price.'
- Coleman Cox

'You will do foolish things, but do them with enthusiasm.'
- Colette

'Boredom is the fear of self.'
- Comtesse Diane

'Be still when you have nothing to say; when genuine passion moves you, say what you've got to say, and say it hot.'
- D. H. Lawrence

'Flaming enthusiasm, backed up by horse sense and persistence, is the quality that most frequently makes for success.'
- Dale Carnegie

'Whatever course you have chosen for yourself, it will not be a chore but an adventure if you bring to it a sense of the glory of striving, if your sights are set far above the merely secure and mediocre.'
- David Sarnoff

'Whatever you attempt, go at it with spirit. Put some in!'
- David Starr Jordan

'If you have the will to win, you have achieved half your success; if you don't, you have achieved half your failure.'
- David V. A. Ambrose

'Only passions, great passions, can elevate the soul to great things.'
- Denis Diderot

'If you're not happy every morning when you get up, leave for work, or start to work at home-if you're not enthusiastic about doing that, you're not going to be successful.'
- Donald M. Kendall

'A continued atmosphere of hectic passion is very trying if you haven't got any of your own.'
- Dorothy L. Sayers

'What counts is not necessarily the size of the dog in the fight, but the size of the fight in the dog.'
- Dwight D. Eisenhower

'My enthusiasms ... constitute my reserves, my unexploited resources, perhaps my future.'
- E. M. Cioran

'Every man is enthusiastic at times. One man has enthusiasm for thirty minutes, another man has it for thirty days. But it is the man who has it for thirty years who makes a success in life.'
- Edward B. Butler

'Nothing is so contagious as enthusiasm; it moves stones, it charms brutes. Enthusiasm is the genius of sincerity, and truth accomplishes no victories without it.'
- Edward Bulwer-Lytton

'Optimism, unaccompanied by personal effort, is merely a state of mind and not fruitful.'
- Edward L. Curtis

'The measure of an enthusiasm must be taken between interesting events. It is between bites that the lukewarm angler loses heart.'
- Edwin Way Teale

'The great composer does not set to work because he is inspired, but becomes inspired because he is working. Beethoven, Wagner, Bach and Mozart settled down day after day to the job in hand with as much regularity as an accountant settles down each day to '
- Ernest Newman

'This, indeed, is one of the eternal paradoxes of both life and literature-that without passion little gets done; yet, without control of that passion, its effects are largely ill or null.'
- F. L. Lucas

'You see me in my most virile moment when you see me doing what I do. When I am directing, a special energy comes upon me. ... It is only when I am doing my work that I feel truly alive. It is like having sex.'
- Federico Fellini

'Reason alone is insufficient to make us enthusiastic in any matter.'
- Francois de La Rochefoucauld

'If we resist our passions, it is more from their weakness than from our strength.'
- Francois de La Rochefoucauld

'The passions are the only orators which always persuade.'
- Francois de La Rochefoucauld

'Nothing great in the world has been accomplished without passion.'
- George Hegel

'We can accomplish almost anything within our ability if we but think that we can!'
- George Matthew Adams

'A faint endeavor ends in a sure defeat.'
- Hannah Moore

'Without passion man is a mere latent force and possibility, like the flint which awaits the shock of the iron before it can give forth its spark.'
- Henri Frederic Amiel

'Enthusiasm is nothing more or less than faith in Taking Action.'
- Henry Chester

'None are so old as those who have outlived enthusiasm.'
- Henry David Thoreau

'There is nothing greater than enthusiasm.'
- Henry Moore

'In things pertaining to enthusiasm, no man is sane who does not know how to be insane on proper occasions.'
- Henry Ward Beecher

'Energy, even like the Biblical grain of mustard-seed, will move mountains.'
- Hosea Ballou

'Knowledge is power, but enthusiasm pulls the switch.'
- Ivern Ball

'Someone's always saying, "It's not whether you win or lose," but if you feel that way, you're as good as dead.'
- James Caan

'To sing is to love and affirm, to fly and soar, to coast into the hearts of the people who listen, to tell them that life is to live, that love is there, that nothing is a promise, but that beauty exists, and must be hunted for and found.'
- Joan Baez

'A willing heart adds feather to the heel.'
- Joanna Baillie

'O lovely Sisters! is it true That they are all inspired by you, And write by inward magic charm'd, And high enthusiasm warm'd?'
- Joanna Baillie

'Energy will do anything that can be done in this world.'
- Johann von Goethe

'What a man knows only through feeling can be explained only through enthusiasm.'
- Joseph Joubert

'Pm convinced that it's energy and humor. The two of them combined equal charm.'
  - Judith Krantz

'Drama is very important in life: You have to come on with a bang. You never want to go out with a whimper.'
  - Julia Child

'Vitality! That's the pursuit of life, isn't it?'
  - Katharine Hepburn

'Enthusiasm is the divine particle in our composition: with it we are great, generous, and true; without it, we are little, false, and mean.'
  - L. E. Landon

'Do it big or stay in bed.'
  - Larry Kelly

'He fights with spirit as well as with the sword.'
  - Latin proverb

'The only thing that keeps a man going is energy. And what is energy but liking life?'
  - Louis Auchincloss

'The aim of military training is not just to prepare men for battle, but to make them long for it.'
  - Louis Simpson

'Enthusiasm signifies God in us.'
  - Madame de Stael

'A man can be short and dumpy and getting bald but if he has fire, women will like him.'
  - Mae West

'People who never get carried away should be.'
  - Malcolm Forbes

'I have always had a dread of becoming a passenger in life.'
  - Margareth II, Queen of Denmark

'When the habitually even-tempered suddenly fly into a passion, that explosion is apt to be more impressive than the outburst of the most violent amongst us.'
  - Margery Allingham

'No one grows old by living, only by losing interest in living.'
  - Marie Beynon Ray

'It is not opposition but indifference which separates men.'
  - Mary Parker Follett

'The great man is he who does not lose his childlike heart.'
- Mencius

'All passions exaggerate; it is because they do that they are passions.'
- Nicolas de Chamfort

'Human nature, if it healthy, demands excitement; and if it does not obtain its thrilling excitement in the right way, it will seek it in the wrong. God never makes bloodless stoics; He makes no passionless saints.'
- Oswald Chambers

'No one has it who isn't capable of genuinely liking others, at least at the actual moment of meeting and speaking. Charm is always genuine; it may be superficial but it isn't fake.'
- P. D. James

'Enthusiasm is life.'
- Paul Scofield

'When his enthusiasm goes, he's through as a player.'
- Pete Rose

'The world belongs to the energetic.'
- Ralph Waldo Emerson

'Nothing great was ever achieved without enthusiasm.'
- Ralph Waldo Emerson

'Passion, though a bad regulator, is a powerful spring.'
- Ralph Waldo Emerson

'Vigor is contagious, and whatever makes us either think or feel strongly adds to our power and enlarges our field of Taking Action.'
- Ralph Waldo Emerson

'What is man but his passion?'
- Robert Penn Warren

'It is energy, the central element of which is will, that produces the miracles of enthusiasm in all ages. It is the mainspring of what is called force of character and the sustaining power of all great Taking Action.'
- Samuel Smiles

'We always attract into our lives whatever we think about most, believe in most strongly, expect on the deepest level, and imagine most vividly.'
- Shakti Gawain

'You can have anything you want if you want it desperately enough. You must want it with an inner exuberance that erupts through the skin and joins the energy that created the world.'
- Sheila Graham

'Energy is equal to desire and purpose.'
  - Sheryl Adams

'I rate enthusiasm even above professional skill.'
  - Sir Edward Appleton

'Life is enthusiasm, zest.'
  - Sir Laurence Olivier

'You've got to sing like you don't need the money. You've got to love like you'll never get hurt. You've got to dance like there's nobody watching. You've got to come from the heart, if you want it to work.'
  - Susanna Clark

'Enthusiasm is the most important thing in life.'
  - Tennessee Williams

'To bring one's self to a frame of mind and to the proper energy to accomplish things that require plain hard work continuously is the one big battle that everyone has. When this battle is won for all time, then everything is easy.'
  - Thomas A. Buckner

'The difference between one man and another is not mere ability ... it is energy.'
  - Thomas Arnold

'Give me a man who sings at his work.'
  - Thomas Carlyle

'Enthusiasm for one's goal to lessens the disagreeableness of working toward it.'
  - Thomas Eakins

'The real difference between men is energy.'
  - Thomas Fuller

'Faith that the thing can be done is essential to any great achievement.'
  - Thomas N. Carruther

'Man never rises to great truths without enthusiasm.'
  - Vauvenargues

'If you aren't fired with enthusiasm, you will be fired with enthusiasm.'
  - Vince Lombardi

'Let us go singing as far as we go; the road will be less tedious.'
  - Virgil

'The real secret of success is enthusiasm. Yes, more than enthusiasm, I would say excitement. I like to see men get excited. When they get excited they make a success of their lives.'
  - Walter Chrysler

'To burn always with this hard gemlike flame. To maintain this ecstasy, is success in life.'
  - Walter Pater

'Years wrinkle the face, but to give up enthusiasm wrinkles the soul.'
  - Watterson Lowe

'There is only one big thing-desire. And before it, when it is big, all is little.'
  - Willa Cather

'A strong passion for any object will ensure success, for the desire of the end will point out the means.'
  - William Hazlitt

'Zeal will do more than knowledge.'
  - William Hazlitt

'The world belongs to the Enthusiast who keeps cool.'
  - William McFee

'Success is going from failure to failure without loss of enthusiasm.'
  - Winston Churchill

FAITH

'Above all am I convinced of the need, irrevocable and inescapable, of every human heart, for God. No matter how we try to escape, to lose ourselves in restless seeking, we cannot separate ourselves from our divine source. There is no substitute for God.'
   - A. J. Cronin

'An act of God was defined as "something which no reasonable man could have expected."'
   - A. P. Herbert

'A church is a hospital for sinners, not a museum for saints.'
   - Abigail Van Buren

'Then comes the insight that All is God. One still realizes that the world is as it was, but it does not matter, it does not affect one's faith.'
   - Abraham Heschel

Let us have faith that right makes might; and in that faith, let us, to the end, dare to do our duty as we understand it.'
   - Abraham Lincoln

'Without the assistance of the Divine Being ... I cannot succeed. With that assistance, I cannot fail.'
   - Abraham Lincoln

'We trust, sir, that God is on our side. It is more important to know that we are on God's side.'
   - Abraham Lincoln

'Zen is a way of liberation, concerned not with discovering what is good or bad or advantageous, but what is.'
   - Alan Watts

'Faith is, above all, openness; an act of trust in the unknown.'
   - Alan Watts

'Don't wait for the Last Judgment. It takes place every day.'
   - Albert Camus

'God is clever, but not dishonest.'
   - Albert Einstein

'The deep emotional conviction of the presence of a superior reasoning power, which is revealed in the incomprehensible universe, forms my idea of God.'
   - Albert Einstein

'I can't believe that God plays dice with the universe.'
   - Albert Einstein

'Our human resources, as marshalled by the will, were not sufficient; they failed utterly.... Every day is a day when we must carry the vision of God's will into all our activities.'
- Alcoholics Anonymous

'To all things clergic I am allergic.'
- Alexander Woollcott

'Faith is believing before receiving.'
- Alfred A. Montapert

'The total absence of humor in the Bible is one of the most singular things in all literature.'
- Alfred North Whitehead

'The experience of God, or in any case the possibility of experiencing God, is innate.'
- Alice Walker

'Infidel, n: in New York, one who does not believe in the Christian religion; in Constantinople, one who does.'
- Ambrose Bierce

'Heathen, n. A beknighted creature who has the folly to worship something that he can see and feel.'
- Ambrose Bierce

'Man is a dog's ideal of what God should be.'
- Andri Malraux

'An outward and visible sign of an inward and spiritual grace.'
- Anonymous

'Everybody should believe in something; I believe I'll have another drink.'
- Anonymous

'What we are is God's gift to us. What we become is our gift to God.'
- Anonymous

'When we lose God, it is not God who is lost.'
- Anonymous

'Some people talk about finding God, as if He could get lost.'
- Anonymous

'God is no enemy to you. He asks no more than that He hear you call Him "Friend."'
- Anonymous

'If Jesus was Jewish, how come he has a Mexican name?'
- Anonymous

'B.I.B.L.E. = Basic Instructions Before Leaving Earth.'
- Anonymous

'Conscience gets a lot of credit that belongs to cold feet.'
- Anonymous

'As the little boy said to the Sunday School teacher after being told the reason we are on Earth is to help others: "Then what are the others here for?"'
- Anonymous

'The world's shortest sermon: "When in doubt... don't!"'
- Anonymous

'Let's all give God a great big hand. I've seen the last page of the bible and it's going to turn out all right.'
- Anonymous

'The Church of England is the Tory party at prayer.'
- Anonymous

'His clear conscience is a result of a poor memory.'
- Anonymous

'The test for a prophet is in the Bible. It is this. "When a prophet speaketh in the name of the Lord, if the thing follow not, nor come to pass, that is the thing which the Lord hath not spoken."'
- Anonymous

'God created man and then woman, but the atheist created himself.'
- Anonymous

'Faith is like electricity. You can't see it, but you can see the light.'
- Anonymous

'We have no choice but to be guilty God is unthinkable if we are innocent.'
- Archibald MacLeish

'God has many names, though He is only one Being.'
- Aristotle

'God seems to have the receiver off the hook.'
- Arthur Koestler

'Christ - an anarchist who succeeded.'
- Axel Munthe

'Believe in something larger than yourself.'
- Barbara Bush

'If triangles had a God, he would have three sides.'
- Baron de Montesquieu

'Pardon, not wrath, is God's best attribute.'
- Bayard Taylor

'Forgetfulness of self is remembrance of God.'
- Bayazid Al-Bistami

'Yes, I am a Jew, and when the ancestors of the right honorable gentlemen were brutal savages in an unknown land, mine were priests in the Temple of Solomon.'
- Benjamin Disraeli

'If men are so wicked with religion, what would they be without it?'
- Benjamin Franklin

'Fear is the denomination of the Old Testament; belief is the denomination of the New.'
- Benjamin Whichcote

'The Blessed Virgin used me like a broom, and then put me back in my place.'
- Bernadette Soubirous

'I have fought a good fight, I have finished my course, I have kept the faith.'
- Bible

'The kingdom of God is within you.'
- Bible

'Trust in the Lord with all thine heart, and lean not unto thine own understanding. In all thy ways acknowledge Him, and He shall direct thy paths.'
- Bible

'The things which are impossible with men are possible with God.'
- Bible

'God is love.'
- Bible

'Do you not know that you are God's temple and that God's spirit dwells within you?'
- Bible

'All things are possible to him who believes.'
- Bible

'Oh my Father, if it be possible, let this cup pass from me: nevertheless, not as I will, but as thou wilt.'
- Bible

'For what is your life? It is even a vapor, that appeareth for a little time, and then vanisheth away.'
- Bible

'His countenance was like lightning, and his raiment white as snow.'
- Bible

'It is better to dwell in a corner of the housetop, than with a brawling woman in a wide house.'
- Bible

'The next day John seethe Jesus coming unto him and saith. Behold the Lamb of God, which taketh away the sins of the world.'
- Bible

'He that is not with me is against me.'
- Bible

'I am fearfully and wonderfully made.'
- Bible

'Be not curious in unnecessary matters: for more things are shewed unto thee than men understand.'
- Bible

'Neither do men light a candle and put it under a bushel, but on a candlestick; and it giveth light unto all that are in the house.'
- Bible

'Ye have not chosen me, but I have chosen you.'
- Bible

'How beautiful upon the mountains are the feet of him that bringeth good tidings, that publisheth peace.'
- Bible

'Bone of my bones, and flesh of my flesh: she shall be called woman.'
- Bible

'I know thy works, that thou art neither cold nor hot: I would thou wert cold or hot.'
- Bible

'The letter killeth, but the spirit giveth life.'
- Bible

'They are as stubble before the wind, and as chaff that the storm carrieth away.'
- Bible

'A prophet is not without honor, save in his own country.'
- Bible

'Unto everyone that hath shall be given, and he shall have abundance: but from him that hath not shall be taken away even that which he hath.'
- Bible

'For if the trumpet give an uncertain sound, who shall prepare himself to the battle?'
- Bible

'Be not deceived; God is not mocked: for whatsoever a man soweth, that shall he also reap.'
- Bible

'I know thy pride, and the naughtiness of thine heart.'
- Bible

'Borne the burden and heat of the day.'
- Bible

'Watchman, what of the night?'
- Bible

'The whole head is sick, and the whole heart faint.'
- Bible

'Seek not out the things that are too hard for thee, neither search the things that are above thy strength.'
- Bible

'My days are swifter than a weaver's shuttle.'
- Bible

'The wilderness and the solitary place shall be glad for them and the desert shall rejoice, and blossom as the rose.'
- Bible

'We have piped unto you, and ye have not danced; we have mourned to you, and ye have not wept.'
- Bible

'The fathers have eaten a sour grape, and the children's teeth are set on edge.'
- Bible

'Man goeth to his long home, and the mourners go about the streets.'
- Bible

'Millions of angels are at God's command.'
- Billy Graham

'The nearer the church, the further from God.'
- Bishop Lancelot Andrewes

'It is the heart which experiences God, not the reason.'
- Blaise Pascal

'The good news is that Jesus is coming back. The bad news is that he's really pissed off.'
- Bob Hope

'I do benefits for all religions. ... I'd hate to blow the hereafter on a technicality.'
- Bob Hope

'The Holy Spirit . . . wants to flow through us and realize all these wonderful possibilities in the world - if we only open ourselves and allow it to happen.'
- Br. David Steindl-Rast

'Man appoints, and God disappoints.'
- Cervantes

'The three great apostles of practical atheism, that make converts without persecuting and retain them without preaching are Wealth, Health and Power.'
- Charles Caleb Colton

'Men will wrangle for religion, write for it, fight for it, die for it, anything but live for it.'
- Charles Caleb Colton

'As for a future life, every man must judge for himself between conflicting vague possibilities.'
- Charles Darwin

'The mystery of the beginning of all things is insoluble by us; and I for one must be content to remain agnostic.'
- Charles Darwin

'My creed is this: Happiness is the only good. The place to be happy is here. The time to be happy is now. The way to be happy is to help make others so.'
- Charles J. Ingersoll

'My theology, briefly, Is that the universe Was dictated But not signed.'
- Christopher Morley

'Father expected a good deal of God. He didn't actually accuse God of inefficiency, but when he prayed his tone was loud and angry, like that of a dissatisfied guest in a carelessly managed hotel.'
- Clarence Day

'It is not my ability, but my response to God's ability, that counts.'
- Corrie ten Boom

'To think you are separate from God is to remain separate from your own being.'
- D. M. Street

'Let God love you through others and let God love others through you.'
- D. M. Street

'God does not die on the day when we cease to believe in a personal deity, but we die on the day when our lives cease to be illuminated by the steady radiance, renewed daily, of a wonder, the source of which is beyond all reason.'
- Dag Hammarskjold

'Faith is our direct link to universal wisdom, reminding us that we know more than we have heard or read or studied that we have only to look, listen, and trust the love and wisdom of the Universal Spirit

working through us all.'
 - Dan Millman

'The worst moment for the atheist is when he is really thankful, and has nobody to thank.'
 - Dante Gabriel Rossetti

'No statement about God is simply, literally true. God is far more than can be measured, described, defined in ordinary language, or pinned down to any particular happening.'
 - David Jenkins

'If you can't be kind, at least be vague.'
 - David Powers

'When I use the word spirituality, I don't necessarily mean religion; I mean whatever it is that helps you feel connected to something that is larger than yourself.'
 - Dean Ornish

'Religion is a way of walking, not a way of talking.'
 - Dean William R. Inge

'To tolerate everything is to teach nothing.'
 - Dr. F. J. Kinsman

'God does not pay weekly, but he pays at the end.'
 - Dutch proverb

'The writers against religion, whilst they oppose every system, are wisely careful never to set up any of their own.'
 - Edmund Burke

'The soul can split the sky in two, and let the face of God shine through.'
 - Edna Saint Vincent Millay

'The various modes of worship which prevailed in the Roman world were all considered by the people as equally true; by the philosopher as equally false; and by the magistrate as equally useful.'
 - Edward Gibbon

'By night an atheist half-believes in God.'
 - Edward Young

'Whoever falls from God's right hand is caught into His left.'
 - Edwin Markham

'The Vatican is against surrogate mothers. Good thing they didn't have that rule when Jesus was born.'
 - Elayne Boosler

'My ancestors wandered lost in the wilderness for forty years because even in biblical times men would not stop to ask directions.'
 - Elayne Boosler

'Mystic: a person who is puzzled before the obvious, but who understands the non-existent.'
   - Elbert Hubbard

'Souls are made of dawn-stuff and starshine.'
   - Elbert Hubbard

'He is more within us than we are ourselves.'
   - Elizabeth Ann Seton

'The accidents of life separate us from our dearest friends, but let us not despair. God is like a looking glass in which souls see each other. The more we are united to Him by love, the nearer we are to those who belong to Him.'
   - Elizabeth Ann Seton

'The Father most tender, Father of all, my immense God-I His atom.'
   - Elizabeth Ann Seton

'The Ten Commandments don't tell you what you ought to do: They only put ideas into your head.'
   - Elizabeth Bibesco

'Your mind cannot possibly understand God. Your heart already knows. Minds were designed for carrying out the orders of the heart.'
   - Emmanuel

'When I was a kid, I used to pray every night for a new bicycle. Then I realized that the Lord, in his wisdom, didn't work that way. So I just stole one and asked him to forgive me.'
   - Emo Philips

'God gives the milk but not the pail.'
   - English proverb

'The soul is awakened through service.'
   - Erica Jong

'I think if you ask people what their concept of heaven is, they would say, if they are honest, that it is a big department store, with new things every week - all the money to buy them, and maybe a little more than the neighbours.'
   - Erich Fromm

'A consciousness of God releases the greatest power of all.'
   - Ernest Holmes

'There is but one ultimate Power. This Power is to each one what he is to it.'
   - Ernest Holmes

'Sometimes I try my hand at turning out small profundities and uncertain short stories, but I always end up with just one single word: God.'
   - Etty Hillesum

'Try thyself first, and after call in God. For to the worker God himself lends aid.'
  - Euripides

'If we're not growing, we must feel guilty, because we are not fulfilling Christ's demand.'
  - Eva Burrows

'A firm belief atthracts facts. They come out iv holes in the ground an' cracks in th' wall to support belief, but they run away fr'm doubt.'
  - Finley Peter Dunne

'It is left only to God and to the angels to be lookers on.'
  - Francis Bacon

'Atheism is rather in the lip than in the heart of Man.'
  - Francis Bacon

'He that hath no cross deserves no crown.'
  - Francis Quarles

'If you begin to live life looking for the God that is all around you, every moment becomes a prayer.'
  - Frank Bianco

'The first Sunday I sang in the church choir, two hundred people changed their religion.'
  - Fred Allen

'Faith is not being sure where you're going but going anyway.'
  - Fredrick Buechner

'What is there in man so worthy of honor and reverence as this, that he is capable of contemplating something higher than his own reason, more sublime than the whole universe- that Spirit which alone is self-subsis-tent, from which all truth proceeds, with'
  - Friedrich Jacobi

'The abdomen is the reason why man does not easily take himself for a god.'
  - Friedrich Nietzsche

'Though the mills of God grind slowly, yet they grind exceeding small; Though with patience He stands waiting, with exactness grinds he all.'
  - Friedrich von Logau

'No man hates God without first hating himself.'
  - Fulton J. Sheen

'An atheist is a man who has no invisible means of support.'
  - Fulton Sheen

'When people cease to believe in God, they don't believe in nothing; they believe in anything.'
  - G. K. Chesterton

'The Bible tells us to love our neighbors, and also to love our enemies; probably because they are generally the same people.'
- G. K. Chesterton

'If I saw the gates of hell open and I stood on the brink of the abyss, I would not despair, I would not lose hope of mercy, because I would trust in You, my God.'
- Gemma Galgani

'Oh, if everyone knew how beautiful Jesus is, how amiable He is! Fhey would all die from love.'
- Gemma Galgani

'We have grasped the mystery of the atom and rejected the Sermon on the Mount.'
- General Omar N. Bradley

'Beware of the man whose God is in the skies.'
- George Bernard Shaw

'Religion is a great force - the only real motive force in the world; but you must get at a man through his own religion, not through yours.'
- George Bernard Shaw

'Christianity might be a good thing if anyone ever tried it.'
- George Bernard Shaw

'If you can't have faith in what is held up to you for faith, you must find things to believe in yourself, for life without faith in something is too narrow a space to live.'
- George Edward Woodberry

'The first condition of human goodness is something to love; the second, something to revere.'
- George Eliot

'I could prove God statistically.'
- George Gallup

'Not only then has each man his individual relation to God, but each man has his peculiar relation to God.'
- George Macdonald

'Each religion, by the help of more or less myth which it takes more or less seriously, proposes some method of fortifying the human soul and enabling it to make its peace with its destiny.'
- George Santayana

'My atheism, like that of Spinoza, is true piety towards the universe and denies only gods fashioned by men in their own image, to be servants of their human interests.'
- George Santayana

'There is literally nothing that I ever asked to do, that I asked the blessed Creator to help me to do, that I have not been able to accomplish.'
- George Washington Carver

'All my life I have risen regularly at four o'clock and have gone into the woods and talked to God. There He gives me my orders for the day.'
- George Washington Carver

'A comprehended God is no God at all.'
- Gerhard Tersteegen

'We Jews have a secret weapon in our struggle with the Arabs - we have no place to go.'
- Golda Meir

'God is not dead but alive and well and working on a much less ambitious project.'
- Graffiti

'Moral indignation is jealousy with a halo.'
- H. G. Wells

'God is a comedian whose audience is afraid to laugh.'
- H. L. Mencken

'A Puritan is a person who lives in the fear that someone, somewhere, may be having a good time.'
- H. L. Mencken

'Conscience is the inner voice that warns us somebody may be looking.'
- H. L. Mencken

'Puritanism - the haunting fear that someone, somewhere may be happy.'
- H. L. Mencken

'My wife converted me to religion. I never believed in hell until I married her.'
- Hal Roach

'Many a humble soul will be amazed to find that the seed it sowed in weakness, in the dust of daily life, has blossomed into immortal flowers under the eye of the Lord.'
- Harriet Beecher Stowe

'God is not a cosmic bellboy for whom we can press a button to get things done.'
- Harry Emerson Fosdick

'Nothing in human life, least of all in religion, is ever right until it is beautiful.'
- Harry Emerson Fosdick

'Faith is the substance of things hoped for, the evidence of things not seen.'
- Hebrews

'It is extremely difficult for a Jew to be converted, for how can he bring himself to believe in the divinity of - another Jew?'
- Heinrich Heine

'It must require an inordinate share of vanity and presumption after enjoying so much that is good and beautiful on earth, to ask the Lord for immortality in addition to it all.'
- Heinrich Heine

'God Himself is not secure, having given man dominion over His work.'
- Helen Keller

'The million little things that drop into your hands The small opportunities each day brings He leaves us free to use or abuse And goes unchanging along His silent way.'
- Helen Keller

'Faith is the strength by which a shattered world shall emerge into the light.'
- Helen Keller

'I wanted to become an atheist but I gave it up. They have no holidays.'
- Henny Youngman

'I don't fly on account of my religion. I'm a devout coward.'
- Henny Youngman

'I know what I'm giving up for Lent: my New Year's resolutions.'
- Henny Youngman

'The spiritual life does not remove us from the world but leads us deeper into it.'
- Henri J. M. Nouwen

'One religion is as true as another.'
- Henry Burton

'It's only by forgetting yourself that you draw near to God.'
- Henry David Thoreau

'Live your beliefs and you can turn the world around.'
- Henry David Thoreau

'I believe God is managing affairs and that He doesn't need any advice from me. With God in charge, I believe everything will work out for the best in the end.'
- Henry Ford

'God is to me that creative Force, behind and in the universe, who manifests Himself as energy, as life, as order, as beauty, as thought, as conscience, as love.'
- Henry Sloane Coffin

'The soul ... is audible, not visible.'
- Henry Wadsworth Longfellow

'The strength of a man consists in finding out the way in which God is going, and going in that way too.'
- Henry Ward Beecher

'I believe in the incomprehensibility of God.'
- Honore de Balzac

'Every morning I spend fifteen minutes filling my mind full of God, and so there's no room left for worry thoughts.'
- Howard Chandler Christy

'Get down on your knees and thank God you are on your feet.'
- Irish saying

'If you can't believe in God the chances are your God is too small.'
- J. B. Phillips

'I have never yet met a healthy person who worries very much about his health or a really good person who worries much about his own soul.'
- J. B. S. Haldane

'God speaks to all individuals through what happens to them moment by moment.'
- J. P. DeCaussade

'Courage is not afraid to weep, and she is not afraid to pray, even when she is not sure who she is praying to.'
- J. Ruth Gendler

'I never went to bed in my life and I never ate a meal in my life without saying a prayer. I know my prayers have been answered thousands of times, and I know that I never said a prayer in my life without something good coming of it.'
- Jack Dempsey

'God comes at last when we think he is farthest off.'
- James Howell

'Do not have your concert first and tune your instruments afterwards. Begin the day with God.'
- James Hudson Taylor

'One's religion is whatever he is most interested in.'
- James M. Barrie

'God'll send the bill to you.'
- James Russell Lowell

'Whom the heart of man shuts out, Sometimes the heart of God takes in.'
- James Russell Lowell

'Darkness is strong, and so is Sin, But surely God endures forever!'
- James Russell Lowell

'I don't go to church. Kneeling bags my nylons.'
- Jan Sterling

'I love God, and when you get to know Him, you find He's a Livin' Doll.'
   - Jane Russell

'I thank the goodness and the grace Which on my birth have smiled, And made me, in these Christian days, A happy Christian child.'
   - Jane Taylor

'Every man thinks God is on his side. The rich and powerful know he is.'
   - Jean Anouilh

'God is an unutterable sigh, planted in the depths of the soul.'
   - Jean Paul Richter

'God, that dumping ground of our dreams.'
   - Jean Rostand

'When you recover or discover something that nourishes your soul and brings joy, care enough about yourself to make room for it in your life.'
   - Jean Shinoda Bolen

'In a world filled with causes for worry and anxiety . . . we need the peace of God standing guard over our hearts and minds.'
   - Jerry W. McCant

'When caught reading the Bible, W.C. Fields said I'm looking for loopholes.' The Bible is nothing but a succession of civil rights struggles by the Jewish people against their oppressors.'
   - Jesse Jackson

'My debt to you, Beloved, Is one I cannot pay In any coin of any realm On any reckoning day.'
   - Jessie Rittenhouse

'He maketh his sun to rise on the evil and on the good, and sendeth rain on the just and on the unjust.'
   - Jesus Christ

'If you bring forth what is within you, what you bring forth will save you. If you do not bring forth what is within you, what you do not bring forth will destroy you.'
   - Jesus Christ

'The best minister is the human heart; the best teacher is time; the best book is the world; the best friend is God.'
   - Jewish saying

'God dwells wherever man lets Him in.'
   - Jewish saying

'God answers all our prayers. Sometimes the answer is yes. Sometimes the answer is no. Sometimes the answer is, you've got to be kidding!'
   - Jimmy Carter

'The Pope is barely Catholic enough for some converts.'
  - John Ayscough

'Yet, in the maddening maze of things, And tossed by storm and flood, To one fixed trust my spirit clings; I know that God is good!'
  - John Greenleaf Whittier

'Before me, even as behind, God is, and all is well.'
  - John Greenleaf Whittier

'Who fathoms the Eternal Thought? Who talks of scheme and plan? The Lord is God! He needeth not The poor device of man.'
  - John Greenleaf Whittier

'The English of the Bible has a pithiness and raciness, a homely tang, a terse sententiousness, an idiomatic flavor which comes home to men's business and bosoms ... a nobility of diction and ... a rhythmic quality . . . unrivaled in its beauty.'
  - John Livingston Lowes

'God, when he makes the prophet, does not unmake the man.'
  - John Locke

'God doth not need Either man's work or his own gifts; who best Bear His mild yoke, they serve Him best; His state Is kingly; thousands at His bidding speed And post o'er land and ocean without rest - They also serve who only stand and wait.'
  - John Milton

'You have not converted a man because you have silenced him.'
  - John Morley

'Here on earth, God's work must surely be our own.'
  - John. F. Kennedy

'A true love of God must begin with a delight in his holiness.'
  - Jonathan Edwards

'I'm not really a Jew; just Jewish, not the whole hog.'
  - Jonathan Miller

'The person who has a firm trust in the Supreme Being is powerful in his power, wise by his wisdom, happy by his happiness.'
  - Joseph Addison

'I always say my God will take care of me. If it's my time I'll go, and if it's not I won't. I feel that He really has a lot of important things for me to do. And He's going to make sure that I'm here to do them.'
  - Joycelyn Elders

'I am afraid I shall not find Him, but I shall still look for Him. If He exists, He may be appreciative of my efforts.'
- Jules Renard

'The more of himself man attributes to God, the less he has left in himself.'
- Karl Marx

'Religion is the opium of the people.'
- Karl Marx

'Religion is the opiate of the people.'
- Karl Marx

'He was of the faith chiefly in the sense that the Church he currently did not attend was Catholic.'
- Kingsley Amis

'Religion converts despair, which destroys, into resignation, which submits.'
- Lady Blessington

'God will be present, whether asked or not.'
- Latin proverb

'Conscience: That which makes a boy tell his mother before his sister does.'
- Laurence J. Peter

'God loves us the way we are but He loves us too much to leave us that way.'
- Leighton Ford

'The fact that I can plant a seed and it becomes a flower, share a bit of knowledge and it becomes another's, smile at someone and receive a smile in return, are to me continual spiritual exercises.'
- Leo Buscaglia

'Faith is the force of life.'
- Leo Tolstoy

'Why is it when we talk to God we are said to be praying, and when God talks to us we're said to be schizophrenic?'
- Lily Tomlin

'There lives more faith in honest doubt, Believe me, than in half the creeds.'
- Lord Alfred Tennyson

'While I cannot be regarded as a pillar, I must be regarded as a buttress of the church, because I support it from outside.'
- Lord Melbourne

'To love one that is great, is almost to be great one's self.'
- Madame Necker

'I generally avoid temptation, unless I can't resist it.'
- Mae West

'I consider myself a Hindu, Christian, Moslem, Jew, Buddhist, and Confucian.'
- Mahatma Gandhi

'To them that ask, where have you seen the Gods, or how do you know for certain there are Gods, that you are so devout in their worship? I answer: Neither have I ever seen my own soul, and yet I respect and honor it.'
- Marcus Aurelius

'He loves, He hopes, He waits. Our Lord prefers to wait Himself for the sinner for years rather than keep us waiting an instant.'
- Maria Goretti

'Hunting God is a great adventure.'
- Marie DeFloris

'They understand but little who understand only what can be explained.'
- Marie von Ebner-Eschenbach

'Religion is the way we honor our ancestors' errors.'
- Mark M. Otoysao

'Heaven goes by favor; if it went by merit, you would stay out and your dog would go in.'
- Mark Twain

'It ain't those parts of the Bible that I can't understand that bother me, it's the parts that I do understand.'
- Mark Twain

'That kind of so-called housekeeping where they have six Bibles and no cork-screw.'
- Mark Twain

'I didn't want to pray to God 'cause I didn't want him to know where I was.'
- Marsha Dobb

'When something good happens, it's a miracle, and you should wonder what God is saving up for you later.'
- Marshall Brickman

'Here I stand. I can do no otherwise. God help me. Amen.'
- Martin Luther

'All who call on God in true faith, earnestly from the heart, will certainly be heard, and will receive what they have asked and desired.'
- Martin Luther

'God uses lust to impel men to marry, ambition to office, avarice to earning, and fear to faith. God led me like an old blind goat.'
- Martin Luther

'Every law of matter or the body, supposed to govern man, is rendered null and void by the law of Life, God.'
- Mary Baker Eddy

'God is incorporeal, divine, supreme, infinite. Mind, Spirit, Soul, Principle, Life, Truth, Love.'
- Mary Baker Eddy

'Divine love always has met and always will meet every human need.'
- Mary Baker Eddy

'Fo those leaning on the sustaining infinite, today is big with blessings.'
- Mary Baker Eddy

'I would rather walk with God in the dark than go alone in the light.'
- Mary Gardiner Brainard

'God does not ask your ability, or your inability. He asks only your availability.'
- Mary Kay Ash

'Man is a venerating animal. He venerates as easily as he purges himself. When they take away from him the gods of his fathers, he looks for others abroad.'
- Max Jacob

'God is what man finds that is divine in himself. God is the best way man can behave in the ordinary occasions of life, and the farthest point to which man can stretch himself.'
- Max Lerner

'The finding of God is the coming to one's own self.'
- Meher Baba

'Some people want to see God with their eyes as they see a cow, and to love Him as they love their cow-for the milk and cheese and profit it brings them. This is how it is with people who love God for the sake of outward wealth or inward comfort.'
- Meister Eckhart

'A New England conscience doesn't keep you from doing anything; it just keeps you from enjoying it.'
- Morris Mandel

'I believe there is no god but Allah alone and Muhammed is his prophet.'
- Muslim Creed

'For the rest of my life I'm going to trust that God is always at work in all things, and give Him thanks long before my simplest prayers are answered.'
- Nancy Parker Brummett

'We were born to make manifest the glory of God that is within us. It's not just in some of us, it's in everyone.'
   - Nelson Mandela

'God loves you. God doesn't want anyone to be hungry and oppressed. He just puts his big arms around everybody and hugs them up against himself.'
   - Norman Vincent Peale

'The bible should be taught so early and so thoroughly that it sinks straight to the bottom of the mind where everything that comes along can settle on it.'
   - Northrop Frye

'One unquestioned text we read, All doubt beyond, all fear above; Nor crackling pile nor cursing creed Can burn or blot it: God is Love.'
   - Oliver Wendell Holmes

'A minister is coming down every generation nearer and nearer to the common level of the useful citizen - no oracle at all, but a man of more than average moral instincts, who if he knows anything, knows how little he knows.'
   - Oliver Wendell Holmes

'Men are idolaters, and want something to look at and kiss and hug, or throw themselves down before; they always did, they always will, and if you don't make it of wood, you must make it of words.'
   - Oliver Wendell Holmes

'We have grasped the mystery of the atom, and rejected the Sermon on the Mount.'
   - Omar Bradley

'God can dream a bigger dream for you than you can dream for yourself, and your role on Earth is to attach yourself to that divine force and let yourself be released to it.'
   - Oprah Winfrey

'I can believe anything, provided it is incredible.'
   - Oscar Wilde

'Jesus was born on a bank holiday and died on a bank holiday. We can therefore assume that when he returns again it will also be on a bank holiday.'
   - P. G. Johnson

'God is really another artist. He invented the giraffe, the elephant and the cat. He has no real style. He just goes on trying other things.'
   - Pablo Picasso

'It's clear why they only served bread and wine at the Last Supper. It was a potluck . . . organized by men.'
   - Patti Page

'"What do you think of God," the teacher asked. After a pause, the young pupil replied, "He's not a think, he's a feel."'
- Paul Frost

'"You are accepted!" ... accepted by that which is greater than you and the name of which you do not know. Do not ask the name now, perhaps you will know it later. Do not try to do anything, perhaps later you will do much. Do not seek for anything, do not '
- Paul Tillich

'Walk boldly and wisely. ... There is a hand above that will help you on.'
- Philip James Bailey

'Life has a practice of living you if you don't live it.'
- Philip Larlcin

'Talking about God is not at all the same thing as experiencing God, or acting out God through our lives.'
- Phillip Hewett

'God pays, but not weekly wages.'
- Polish proverb

'The light of God surrounds me, The love of God enfolds me, The power of God protects me, The Presence of God watches over me, Wherever I am, God is.'
- Prayer Card

'The idea that He would take his attention away from the universe in order to give me a bicycle with three speeds is just so unlikely I can't go along with it.'
- Quentin Crisp

'God is a verb, not a noun.'
- R. Buckminster Fuller

'Faith is not knowledge of what the mystery of the universe is, but the conviction that there is a mystery, and that it is greater than us.'
- Rabbi David Wolpe

'God is like a mirror. The mirror never changes, but everybody who looks at it sees something different.'
- Rabbi Harold Kushner

'Faith is the bird that feels the light and sings when the dawn is still dark.'
- Rabindranath Tagore

'In every out-thrust headland, in every curving beach, in every grain of sand, there is the story of the earth.'
- Rachel Carson

'Some things have to be believed to be seen.'
- Ralph Hodgson

'AH I have seen teaches me to trust the Creator for all I have not seen.'
- Ralph Waldo Emerson

'God enters by a private door into every individual.'
- Ralph Waldo Emerson

'To Be is to live with God.'
- Ralph Waldo Emerson

'There is a crack in everything God has made.'
- Ralph Waldo Emerson

'The merit claimed for the Anglican Church is that, if you let it alone, it will let you alone.'
- Ralph Waldo Emerson

'Excite the soul, and the weather and the town and your condition in the world all disappear; the world itself loses its solidity, nothing remains but the soul and the Divine Presence in which it lives.'
- Ralph Waldo Emerson

'We are a rather big-headed little species in a vast cosmos which can do without us very well.'
- Rev. George Carey

'I'm not ok - you're not ok, and that's ok.'
- Rev. William Sloane Coffin

'Remember that everything has God's fingerprints on it.'
- Richard Carlson

'I wouldn't put it past God to arrange a virgin birth if he wanted to, but I very much doubt if he would because it seems to be contrary to the way in which he deals with persons and brings his wonders out of natural personal relationships.'
- Right Rev. David Jenkins

'Don't be agnostic - be something.'
- Robert Frost

'With soap baptism is a good thing.'
- Robert G. Ingersoll

'I have a hard time believing that billions of years ago two protozoa bumped into each other under a volcanic cesspool and evolved into Cindy Crawford.'
- Robert G. Lee

'If a blade of grass can grow in a concrete walk and a fig tree in the side of a mountain cliff, a human being empowered with an invincible faith can survive all odds the world can throw against his

tortured soul.'
- Robert H. Schuller

'What if the meek inherited the Earth and we had to defend ourselves from Martians?'
- Robert Orben

'I don't see why religion and science can't get along. What's wrong with counting our blessings with a computer?'
- Robert Orben

'God is usually on the side of big squadrons and against little ones.'
- Roger de Bussy-Rabutin

'Gawd knows, and 'E won't split on a pal.'
- Rudyard Kipling

'God, to be God, must transcend what is. He must be the maker of what ought to be.'
- Rufus M. Jones

'If the thunder is not loud, the peasant forgets to cross himself.'
- Russian proverb

'Christ has made my soul beautiful with the jewels of grace and virtue.'
- Saint Agnes

'So great was my joy in God that I took no heed of looking at the angels and the saints, because all their goodness and all their beauty was from Him and in Him.'
- Saint Angela of Foligno

'Our condition is most noble, being so beloved of the Most High God that He was willing to die for our sake- which He would not have done if man had not been a most noble creature and of great worth.'
- Saint Angela of Foligno

'Our perfection certainly consists in knowing God and ourselves.'
- Saint Angela of Foligno

'Faith is to believe what we do not see; the reward of this faith is to see what we believe.'
- Saint Augustine

'It is impossible to fulfill the law concerning love for Me, God eternal, apart from the law concerning love for your neighbors.'
- Saint Catherine of Siena

'As in heaven Your will is punctually performed, so may it be done on earth by all creatures, particularly in me and by me.'
- Saint Elizabeth of Hungary

'I need nothing but God, and to lose myself in the heart of God.'
- Saint Margaret Mary Alacoque

'Oysters are more beautiful than any religion . . . there's nothing in Christianity or Buddhism that quite matches the sympathetic unselfishness of an oyster.'
- Saki

'You can do very little with faith, but you can do nothing without it.'
- Samuel Butler

'To be of no Church is dangerous.'
- Samuel Johnson

'There's no reason to bring religion into it. I think we ought to have as great a regard for religion as we can, so as to keep it out of as many things as possible.'
- Sean O'Casey

'Eventually I lost interest in trying to control my life, to make things happen in a way that I thought I wanted them to be. I began to practice surrendering to the universe and finding out what "it" wanted me to do.'
- Shakti Gawain

'By learning to contact, listen to, and act on our intuition, we can directly connect to the higher power of the universe and allow it to become our guiding force.'
- Shakti Gawain

'I could be whatever I wanted to be if I trusted that music, that song, that vibration of God that was inside of me.'
- Shirley MacLaine

'When a man is freed of religion, he has a better chance to live a normal and wholesome life.'
- Sigmund Freud

'There was never law, or sect, or opinion did so much magnify goodness, as the Christian religion doth.'
- Sir Francis Bacon

'Coincidence is God's way of performing miracles anonymously.'
- Sophy Burnham

'Most people believe that the Christian commandments are intentionally a little too severe - like setting a clock half an hour ahead to make sure of not being late in the morning.'
- Soren Kierkegaard

'God delays, but doesn't forget.'
- Spanish proverb

'Faith is to believe what we do not see; and the reward of this faith is to see what we believe.'
- St. Augustine

'Lord, who art always the same, give that I know myself, give that I know Thee.'
- St. Augustine

'The glory of God is in man fully alive.'
  - St. Irenaeus

'I am one of those who would rather sink with faith than swim without it.'
  - Stanley Bladwin

'When you have succeeded in enshrining God within your heart, you will see Him everywhere.'
  - Swami Sivananda

'The best thing must be to flee from all to the All.'
  - Teresa of Avila

'Holy church-that mother who is also a queen because she is a king's bride.'
  - Teresa of Avila

'How is it, Lord, that we are cowards in everything save in opposing Thee?'
  - Teresa of Avila

'After all, what's a cult? It just means not enough people to make a minority.'
  - The Globe and Mail

'Give God time.'
  - The Koran

'Three things are good in little measure and evil in large: yeast, salt and hesitation.'
  - The Talmud

'Jesus makes the bitterest mouthful taste sweet.'
  - Therese of Lisieux

'For the multitude of worldly friends profiteth not, nor may strong helpers anything avail, nor wise counselors give profitable counsel, nor the cunning of doctors give consolation, nor riches deliver in time of need, nor a secret place to defend, if Thou,'
  - Thomas a Kempis

'Man proposes; God disposes.'
  - Thomas a Kempis

'A humble knowledge of oneself is a surer road to God than a deep searching of the sciences.'
  - Thomas a Kempis

'His religion at best is an anxious wish, - like that of Rebelais, a great Perhaps.'
  - Thomas Carlyle

'A good life is the only religion.'
  - Thomas Fuller

'There is a good deal too strange to be believed, nothing is too strange to have happened.'
  - Thomas Hardy

'I will not fear, for you are ever with me, and you will never leave me to face my perils alone.'
- Thomas Merton

'There is not a flower that opens, not a seed that falls into the ground, and not an ear of wheat that nods on the end of its stalk in the wind that does not preach and proclaim the greatness and the mercy of God to the whole world.'
- Thomas Merton

'Soul appears when we make room for it.'
- Thomas Moore

'My own mind is my own church.'
- Thomas Paine

'The world is my country, all mankind are my brethren, and to do good is my religion.'
- Thomas Paine

'Every conjecture we can form with regard to the works of God has as little probability as the conjectures of a child with regard to the works of a man.'
- Thomas Reid

'If you talk to God, you are praying; if God talks to you, you have schizophrenia.'
- Thomas Szasz

'The most beautiful of all emblems is that of God, whom Timaeus of Locris describes under the image of "A circle whose center is everywhere and whose circumference is nowhere."'
- Voltaire

'If God made us in his image, we have certainly returned the compliment.'
- Voltaire

'If God did not exist, it would be necessary to invent him.'
- Voltaire

'God is a circle whose center is everywhere and circumference nowhere.'
- Voltaire

'Faith consists in believing when it is beyond the power of reason to believe. It is not enough that a thing be possible for it to be believed.'
- Voltaire

'A Unitarian very earnestly disbelieves what everyone else believes.'
- W. Somerset Maugham

'Men prefer to believe that they are degenerated angels, rather than elevated apes.'
- W. Winwood Roade

'In the faces of men and women I see God.'
- Walt Whitman

'Men will wrangle for religion; write for it; fight for it; die for it; anything but - live it.'
- Walter Colton

'Faith means intense, usually confident, belief that is not based on evidence sufficient to command assent from every reasonable person.'
- Walter Kaufmann

'Many families think of church as if it was a convention - they send one delegate.'
- Wayne Day

'One on God's side is a majority.'
- Wendell Phillips

'If there's a God, why are there such things as famine and The Jerry Springer Show.'
- Wendy Morgan

'The service we render others is really the rent we pay for our room on Earth.'
- Wilfred Grenfell

'Faith is the continuation of reason.'
- William Adams

'Faith is knowing there is an ocean because you have seen a brook.'
- William Arthur Ward

'The Old and New Testaments are the Great Code of Art.'
- William Blake

'Religion, if in heavenly truths attired, Needs only to be seen to be admired.'
- William Cowper

'The God of many men is little more than their court of appeal against the damnatory judgement passed on their failures by the opinion of the world.'
- William James

'Nothing hath separated us from God but our own will, or rather our own will is our separation from God.'
- William Law

'Religion is nothing else but love to God and man.'
- William Penn

'I have never understood why it should be considered derogatory to the Creator to suppose that He has a sense of humor.'
- William Ralph Inge

'The church exists for the sake of those outside it.'
- William Temple

'Audible at five miles, painful at three, and lethal at one.'
- Winchester Cathedral

'How to make God laugh. Tell him your future plans.'
- Woody Allen

'The worst that you can say about him (God) is that basically he's an underachiever.'
- Woody Allen

'You want to make God laugh? Tell him your future plans.'
- Woody Allen

'If I could only see one miracle, just one miracle. Like a burning bush, or the seas part, or my uncle Sasha pick up a check.'
- Woody Allen

'If only God would give me a clear sign, like making a large deposit in my name at a Swiss bank.'
- Woody Allen

'I don't believe in God. Just try getting a plumber on the weekend.'
- Woody Allen

'I was thrown out of college for cheating on the metaphysics exam; I looked into the soul of the boy next to me.'
- Woody Allen

'Because you cannot see him, God is everywhere.'
- Yasunari Kawabata

'The world is more exacting than God himself.'
- Yiddish proverb

'God will provide - if only God would provide until he provides.'
- Yiddish proverb

'The purpose of life on earth is that the soul should grow - So Growl By doing what is right.'
- Zelda Fitzgerald

FAMILY

It is my pleasure that my children are free and happy, and unrestrained by parental tyranny. Love is the chain whereby to bind a child to its parents.'
- Abraham Lincoln

'A mother's love for her child is like nothing else in the world. It knows no aw, no pity, it dares all things and crushes down remorselessly all that stands in its path.'
- Agatha Christie

'Youth I Stay close to the young, and a little rubs off.'
- Alan Jay Lerner

'Sometimes our light goes out but is blown into flame by another human being. Each of us owes deepest thanks to those who have rekindled this light.'
- Albert Schweitzer

'Whenever I'm with my [teenager], I feel as though I have to spend the whole time avoiding land mines.'
- Amy Tan

'It takes about five years for a walnut tree to produce nuts, but this is not true of a family tree.'
- Anonymous

'A scout is a boy who dresses like a schmuck. A scoutmaster is a schmuck who dresses like a boy.'
- Anonymous

'When I reprimanded my son for hair like Michael Jackson, he said: "I don't see the problem you wear yours like Michael Jordan."'
- Anonymous

'Sis, I've been wondering . . . On my birthday mom always gives me five thousand dollars. How much does she give you?'
- Anonymous

'A child prodigy is one with highly imaginative parents.'
- Anonymous

'To encourage my little kid to eat I'd sometimes say: "Just pretend it's sand."'
- Anonymous

'Children have become so expensive that only the poor can afford them.'
- Anonymous

'Few mistakes can be made by a mother-in-law who is willing to baby-sit.'
- Anonymous

'Keep in mind ... to a dog you are family, to a cat you are staff.'
- Anonymous

'It appears there's a little too much chlorine in their gene pool.'
- Anonymous

'My kid asked if he could borrow ten dollars. When I only gave him five dollars he said, "Okay, since you owe me the other five dollars, we'll call it even."'
- Anonymous

'Friendship is a single soul dwelling in two bodies.'
- Aristotle

'The parents exist to teach the child, but also they must learn what the child has to teach them; and the child has a very great deal to teach them.'
- Arnold Bennett

'To us, family means putting your arms around each other and being there.'
- Barbara Bush

'Children are the true connoisseurs. What's precious to them has no price - only value.'
- Bel Kaufman

'Honor your father and your mother.'
- Bible

'Human beings are the only creatures on Earth that allow children to come back home.'
- Bill Cosby

'Grown men can learn from very little children for the hearts of little children are pure. Therefore, the Great Spirit may show to them many things which older people miss.'
- Black Elk

'Teaching kids to count is fine, but teaching them what counts is best.'
- Bob Talbert

'They are doing away with drive-ins. Now where are the teenagers going to go to not watch a movie?'
- Bob Thomas

'Big sisters are the crabgrass in the lawn of life.'
- Charles Schulz

'The family with an old person in it possesses a jewel.'
- Chinese saying

'Children have a remarkable talent for not taking the adult world with the kind of respect we are so confident it ought to be given. To the irritation of authority figures of all sorts, children expend considerable energy in "clowning around." They refuse '
- Conrad Hyers

'You can make more friends in two months by becoming more interested in other people than you can in two years by trying to get people interested in you.'
- Dale Carnegie

'True friendship comes when silence between two people is comfortable.'
- Dave Tyson Gentry

'The best way to keep children home is to make the home atmosphere pleasant - and let the air out of the tires.'
- Dorothy Parker

'Few things are more delightful than grandchildren fighting over your lap.'
- Doug Larson

'Those who love the young best stay young longer.'
- Edgar Friedenberg

'When a friend is in trouble, don't annoy him by asking if there is anything you can do. Think up something appropriate and do it.'
- Edgar Watson Howe

'It is great to have friends when one is young, but indeed it is still more so when you are getting old. When we are young, friends are, like everything else, a matter of course. In the old days we know what it means to have them.'
- Edvard Grieg

'A friend is someone who knows all about you and loves you just the same.'
- Elbert Hubbard

'Of all the things which wisdom provides to make us entirely happy, much the greatest is the possession of friendship.'
- Epicurus

'Family life got better and we got our car back - as soon as we put "I love Mom" on the license plate.'
- Erma Bombeck

'Never lend your car to someone you've given birth to.'
- Erma Bombeck

'I read one psychologist's theory that said, "Never strike a child in your anger." When could I strike him? When he is kissing me on my birthday? When he's recuperating from measles? Do I slap the Bible out of his hand on Sunday?'
- Erma Bombeck

'In family life, love is the oil that eases friction, the cement that binds closer together, and the music that brings harmony.'
- Eva Burrows

'Ask your child what he wants for dinner only if he's buying.'
- Fran Lebowitz

'Since there is nothing so well worth having as friends, never lose a chance to make them.'
- Francesco Guicciardini

'It is infinitely more useful for a child to hear a story told by a person than by computer. Because the greatest part of the learning experience lies not in the particular words of the story but in the involvement with the individual reading it.'
- Frank Smith

'My father never raised his hand to any one of his children - except in self-defense.'
- Fred Allen

'Family love is messy, clinging, and of an annoying and repetitive pattern, like bad wallpaper.'
- Friedrich Nietzsche

'[A mother] discovers with great delight that one does not love one's children just because they are one's children but because of the friendship formed while raising them.'
- Gabriel Garcia Marquez

'Insanity runs in my family. It practically gallops.'
- Gary Grant

'So, like a forgotten fire, a childhood can always flare up again within us.'
- Gaston Bachelard

'Happiness is having a large, loving, caring, close-knit family ... in another city.'
- George Burns

'We are given children to test us and make us more spiritual.'
- George Will

'The Family is the Country of the heart. There is an angel in the Family who, by the mysterious influence of grace, of sweetness, and of love, renders the fulfillment of duties less wearisome, sorrows less bitter. The only pure joys unmixed with sadness.'
- Giuseppe Mazzini

'Why, a four-year-old child could understand this report. Run out and find me a four-year-old child.'
- Groucho Marx

'Blessed be childhood, which brings down something of heaven into the midst of our rough earthliness.'
- Henri Amiel

'Every man should have a fair-sized cemetery in which to bury the faults of his friends.'
- Henry Brooks Adams

'Friends will not only live in harmony, but in melody.'
  - Henry David Thoreau

'The most I can do for my friend is simply to be his friend.'
  - Henry David Thoreau

'The only artists for whom I would make way are - children. For me the paintings of children belong side by side with the works of the masters.'
  - Henry Miller

'The most important thing a father can do for his children is to love their mother.'
  - Henry Ward Beecher

'All of us collect fortunes when we are children. A fortune of colors, of lights, and darkness, of movement, of tensions. Some of us have the fantastic chance to go back to his fortune when grown up.'
  - Ingmar Bergman

'Let's face it, there's lots of spoiled kids out there . . . because you can't spank Grandma.'
  - Janet Anderson

'I love being a great-grandparent, but what I hate is being the mother of a grandparent.'
  - Janet Anderson

'Treat your friends as you do your pictures, and place them in their best light.'
  - Jennie Jerome Churchill

'There's no way that moving in with your parents is a sign that your life is on track.'
  - Jerry Seinfeld

'God could not be everywhere, therefore he made mothers.'
  - Jewish saying

'There's no way to be a perfect mother and a million ways to be a good one.'
  - Jill Churchill

'Watching your daughter being collected by her date feels like handing over a million-dollar Stradivarius to a gorilla.'
  - Jim Bishop

'I hate housework! You make the beds, you do the dishes - and six months later you have to start all over again.'
  - Joan Rivers

'Children are the world's most valuable resource and its best hope for the future.'
  - John F. Kennedy

'Old friends are best. King James used to call for his old shoes; they were the easiest for his feet.'
  - John Selden

'Friendship improves happiness, and abates misery, by doubling our joy, and dividing our grief.'
- Joseph Addison

'The greatest sweetener of human life is Friendship.'
- Joseph Addison

'Adults are just children who earn money.'
- Kenneth Branagh

'Each of us has a spark of life inside us, and our highest endeavor ought to be to set off that spark in one another.'
- Kenny Ausubel

'Never brag about your ancestors coming over on the Mayflower; the immigration laws weren't as strict in those days.'
- Lew Lehr

'The last step in parental love involves the release of the beloved; the willing cutting of the cord that would otherwise keep the child in a state of emotional dependence.'
- Lewis Mumford

'So if you have a grandma, Thank the Good Lord up above, And give Grandmama hugs and kisses, For grandmothers are to love.'
- Lois Wyse

'If I had known how wonderful it would be to have grandchildren, I'd have had them first.'
- Lois Wyse

'Bringing a child into the world is the greatest act of hope there is.'
- Louise Hart

'Parents are often so busy with the physical rearing of children that they miss the glory of parenthood, just as the grandeur of the trees is lost when raking leaves.'
- Marcelene Cox

'When I was a boy of fourteen, my father was so ignorant I could hardly stand to have the old man around. But when I got to be twenty-one, I was astonished at how much the old man had learned in seven years.'
- Mark Twain

'Family is just accident. . . . They don't mean to get on your nerves. They don't even mean to be your family, they just are.'
- Marsha Norman

'I've just been to a debutant ball where all the girls were wearing low-cut gowns. It's clear why they're called coming out parties.'
- Martin Fenton

'It is not what you give your friend, but what you are willing to give him, that determines the quality of your friendship.'
- Mary Dixon Thayer

'I think a dysfunctional family is any family with more than one person in it.'
- Mary Karr

'My son has taken up meditation - at least it's better than sitting doing nothing.'
- Max Kaufman

'The great man is he that does not lose his child-heart.'
- Mencius

'There is little less trouble in governing a private family than a whole kingdom.'
- Michel Montaigne

'None but a mule denies his family.'
- Moroccan proverb

'Smile at each other, smile at your wife, smile at your husband, smile at your children, smile at each other - it doesn't matter who it is and that will help you to grow up in greater love for each other.'
- Mother Teresa

'The best inheritance a parent can give his children is a few minutes of his time each day.'
- O. A. Battista

'Children begin by loving their parents. After a time they judge them. Rarely, if ever, do they forgive them.'
- Oscar Wilde

'You know your children are growing up when they stop asking where they came from and refuse to tell you where they're going.'
- P. O'Brien

'What do we teach our children? . . . We should say to each of them: Do you know what you are? You are a marvel. You are unique . . . You may become a Shakespeare, a Michelangelo, a Beethoven. You have the capacity for anything.'
- Pablo Casals

'Children are the bridge to heaven.'
- Persian proverb

'The Jewish man with parents still alive is a fifteen-year-old boy and will remain a fifteen-year-old boy until they die.'
- Philip Roth

'What God is to the world, parents are to their children.'
- Philo

'Cleaning your house while your children are still growing is like shoveling the walk before it stops snowing.'
- Phyllis Diller

'In most states you can get a driver's license when you're sixteen years old, which made a lot of sense to me when I was sixteen years old but now seems insane.'
- Phyllis Diller

'The whole world is my family.'
- Pope John XXIII

'Each time a new baby is born there is a possibility of reprieve. Each child is a new being, a potential prophet, a new spiritual prince, a new spark of light precipitated into the outer darkness.'
- R. D. Laing

'The glory of friendship is not the outstretched hand, nor the kindly smile, nor the joy of companionship; it is the spiritual inspiration that comes to one when he discovers that someone else believes in him and is willing to trust him.'
- Ralph Waldo Emerson

'A friend might well be reckoned the masterpiece of nature.'
- Ralph Waldo Emerson

'The only way to have a friend is to be one.'
- Ralph Waldo Emerson

'One of the most obvious facts about grownups to a child is that they have forgotten what it is like to be a child.'
- Randall Jarrell

'Friendships are fragile things, and require as much care in handling as any other fragile and precious thing.'
- Randolph Bourne

'Never raise your hands to your kids. It leaves your groin unprotected.'
- Red Buttons

'Adolescence is when children start trying to bring up their parents.'
- Richard Armour

'Have children while your parents are still young enough to take care of them.'
- Rita Rudner

'In America there are two classes of travel - first class and with children.'
- Robert Benchley

'Home is the place, when you have to go there, they have to take you in.'
- Robert Frost

'One laugh of a child will make the holiest day more sacred still.'
  - Robert G. Ingersoll

'I take my children everywhere, but they always find their way back home.'
  - Robert Orben

'I don't want to say anything about my kids . . . but I go to PTA meetings under an assumed name!'
  - Robert Orben

'We're supposed to take our problems to a family adviser. Personally, I've never met a family adviser. They're all off somewhere listening to dirty stories.'
  - Robert Orben

'The reason grandparents and grandchildren get along so well is that they have a common enemy.'
  - Sam Levenson

'Insanity is hereditary; you get it from your children.'
  - Sam Levenson

'What a great blessing is a friend with a heart so trusty you may safely bury all your secrets in it.'
  - Seneca

'It is not the talking that counts between friends, it is the never needing to say what counts.'
  - Shawn Green

'Unconditional love is loving your kids for who they are, not for what they do ... it isn't something you will achieve every minute of every day. But it is the thought we must hold in our hearts every day.'
  - Stephanie Marston

'The real question isn't whether or not you love your kids, but how well you are able to demonstrate your love and caring so that your children really feel loved.'
  - Stephanie Marston

'Remember, no matter how many candles you blow out this year, there's one gal who will always think of you as young, strong and handsome - your mother.'
  - Susan D. Anderson

'I want you to know how I feel about my Italian heritage, so I'd like to say a few words in Italian: Verdi, Pavarotti, DiMaggio, Valentino, De Niro, Giuliani. . .'
  - Susan Lucci

'The happiest moments of my life have been the few which I have passed at home in the bosom of my family.'
  - Thomas Jefferson

'My father told me marijuana would cause me brain damage - because if he caught me doing it he was going to break my head.'
  - Tom Dreesen

'We were so poor we had no hot water. But it didn't matter because we had no bathtub to put it in anyway.'
- Tom Dreesen

'There are no seven wonders of the world in the eyes of a child. There are seven million.'
- Walt Streightiff

'A real friend is one who walks in when the rest of the world walks out.'
- Walter Winchell

'As long as I continue to hear "normal" people telling me I am too childish, I know I'm doing just fine.'
- Wayne Dyer

'By giving children lots of affection, you can help fill them with love and acceptance of themselves. Then that's what they will have to give away.'
- Wayne Dyer

'Perfect love sometimes does not come until the first grandchild.'
- Welsh proverb

'To be a good friend remember that we are human magnets: that like attracts like and that as we give we get.'
- Wilfred Peterson

'No man has ever lived that had enough of children's gratitude or woman's love.'
- William Butler Yeats

'Of course if you like your kids, if you love them from the moment they begin, you yourself begin all over again, in them and with them.'
- William Saroyan

'Where does the family start? It starts with a young man falling in love with a girl - no superior alternative has yet been found.'
- Winston Churchill

'Friendship is the only cement that will ever hold the world together.'
- Woodrow Wilson

'The best thing to do is to behave in a manner befitting one's age. If you are sixteen and under, try not to go bald.'
- Woody Allen

'Honor your father and mother, even as you honor God, for all three were partners in your creation.'
- Zohar

FEAR

I, a stranger and afraid In a world I never made.'
 - A. E. Housman

'Excessive fear is always powerless.'
 - Aeschylus

'When men are ruled by fear, they strive to prevent the very changes that will abate it.'
 - Alan Paton

'This is the century of fear.'
 - Albert Camus

'Nothing is more despicable than respect based on fear.'
 - Albert Camus

'A fanatic is a man who consciously over-compensates a secret doubt.'
 - Aldous Huxley

'The only way to get rid of my fears is to make films about them.'
 - Alfred Hitchcock

'I have come to realize that all my trouble with living has come from fear and smallness within me.'
 - Angela L. Wozniak

'I am never afraid of what I know.'
 - Anna Sewell

'We're frightened of what makes us different.'
 - Anne Rice

'Fear is the prison of the heart.'
 - Anonymous

'Only your mind can produce fear.'
 - Anonymous

'All fear is bondage.'
 - Anonymous

'Once men are caught up in an event they cease to be afraid. Only the unknown frightens men.'
 - Antoine de St. Exupery

'The worst sorrows in life are not in its losses and misfortunes, but its fears.'
 - Arthur Christopher Benson

'The only thing I am afraid of is fear.'
   - Arthur Wellesley

'Fear is the main source of superstition, and one of the main sources of cruelty.'
   - Bertrand Russell

'All forms of fear produce fatigue.'
   - Bertrand Russell

'Neither a man nor a crowd nor a nation can be trusted to act humanely or to think sanely under the influence of a great fear.'
   - Bertrand Russell

'The fear of the Lord is the beginning of knowledge.'
   - Bible

'Only the self-deceived will claim perfect freedom from fear.'
   - Bill W.

'We are always afraid to start something that we want to make very good, true, and serious.'
   - Brenda Ueland

'Of all the passions, fear weakens judgment most.'
   - Cardinal de Retz

'The only thing we have to fear on this planet is man.'
   - Carl Jung

'No power is strong enough to be lasting if it labors under the weight of fear.'
   - Cicero

'Fear can be headier than whisky, once man has acquired a taste for it.'
   - Donald Dowries

'The most destructive element in the human mind is fear. Fear creates aggressiveness; aggressiveness engenders hostility; hostility engenders fear-a disastrous circle.'
   - Dorothy Thompson

'Only when we are no longer afraid do we begin to live.'
   - Dorothy Thompson

'We fear the thing we want the most.'
   - Dr. Robert Anthony

'No passion so effectually robs the mind of all its powers of acting and reasoning as fear.'
   - Edmund Burke

'There is no devil but fear.'
   - Elbert Hubbard

'Fear is created not by the world around us, but in the mind, by what we think is going to happen.'
- Elizabeth Gawain

'Fear comes from uncertainty. When we are absolutely certain, whether of our worth or worthlessness, we are almost impervious to fear. Thus a feeling of utter unworthiness can be a source of courage.'
- Eric Hoffer

'The only thing we have to fear is fear itself.'
- F. D. Roosevelt

'Fear is the fire that melts Icarian wings.'
- Florence Earle Coates

'How very little can be done under the spirit of fear.'
- Florence Nightingale

'I can stand what I know. It's what I don't know that frightens me.'
- Frances Newton

'Nothing is terrible except fear itself.'
- Francis Bacon

'We promise according to our hopes, and perform according to our fears.'
- Francois de La Rochefoucauld

'So let me assert my firm belief that the only thing we have to fear is fear itself - nameless, unreasoning, unjustified terror which paralyzes needed efforts to convert retreat into advance.'
- Franklin D. Roosevelt

'The only thing we have to fear is fear itself-nameless, unreasoning, unjustified terror which paralyzes needed efforts to convert retreat into advance.'
- Franklin Delano Roosevelt

'Fear, true fear, is a savage frenzy. Of all the insanities of which we are capable, it is surely the most cruel.'
- Georges Bernanos

'Fear makes the wolf bigger than he is.'
- German proverb

'In grief we know the worst of what we feel, But who can tell the end of what we fear?'
- Hannah More

'To hate and to fear is to be psychologically ill... it is, in fact, the consuming illness of our time.'
- Harry A. Overstreet

'Nothing is so much to be feared as fear.'
- Henry David Thoreau

'Fear is an acid which is pumped into one's atmosphere. It causes mental, moral and spiritual asphyxiation, and sometimes death; death to energy and all growth.'
   - Horace Fletcher

'We are largely the playthings of our fears. To one, fear of the dark; to another, of physical pain; to a third, of public ridicule; to a fourth, of poverty; to a fifth, of loneliness ... for all of us, our particular creature waits in ambush.'
   - Horace Walpole

'The horse does abominate the camel; the mighty elephant is afraid of a mouse; and they say that the lion, which scorneth to turn his back upon the stoutest animal, will tremble at the crowing of a cock.'
   - Increase Mather

'Fear is the parent of cruelty.'
   - James A. Froude

'Horror is a feeling that cannot last long; human nature is incapable of supporting it.'
   - James de Mille

'Fear is an insidious virus. Given a breeding place in our minds ... it will eat away our spirit and block the forward path of our endeavors.'
   - James F. Bell

'A man who is afraid will do anything.'
   - Jawaharlal Nehru

'There is perhaps nothing so bad and so dangerous in life as fear.'
   - Jawaharlal Nehru

'God! Is there anything uglier than a frightened man!'
   - Jean Anouilh

'There seemed to be endless obstacles ... it seemed that the root cause of them all was fear.'
   - Joanna Field

'We must travel in the direction of our fear.'
   - John Berryman

'Fear is like fire. If controlled it will help you; if uncontrolled, it will rise up and destroy you. Men's Taking Actions depend to a great extent upon fear. We do things either because we enjoy doing them or because we are afraid not to do them.'
   - John F. Milburn

'The craven's fear is but selfishness, like his merriment.'
   - John Greenleaf Whittier

'Fear, if allowed free rein, would reduce all of us to trembling shadows of men, for whom only death could bring release.'
   - John M. Wilson

'Where no hope is left, is left no fear.'
- John Milton

'Power does not corrupt. Fear corrupts, perhaps the fear of a loss of power.'
- John Steinbeck

'How does one kill fear, I wonder? How do you shoot a specter through the heart, slash off its spectral head, take it by the spectral throat?'
- Joseph Conrad

'When did reason ever direct our desires or our fears?'
- Juvenal

'If you let fear of consequence prevent you from following your deepest instinct, then your life will be safe, expedient and thin.'
- Katharine Butler Hathaway

'We all choke, and the man who says he doesn't choke is lying like hell.'
- Lee Trevino

'We all fear what we don't know-it's natural.'
- Leo Buscaglia

'Just as courage imperils life, fear protects it.'
- Leonardo da Vinci

'If a man harbors any sort of fear, it percolates through all his thinking, damages his personality, makes him landlord to a ghost.'
- Lloyd C. Douglas

'A man who says he has never been scared is either lying or else he's never been any place or done anything.'
- Louis L'Amour

'People wish to learn to swim and at the same time to keep one foot on the ground.'
- Marcel Proust

'If we let things terrify us, life will not be worth living.'
- Marcus Annaeus Seneca

'We are more often frightened than hurt; and we suffer more from imagination than from reality.'
- Marcus Annaeus Seneca

'Where fear is, happiness is not.'
- Marcus Annaeus Seneca

'Fear has a smell, as Love does.'
- Margaret Atwood

'Nothing in life is to be feared. It is only to be understood.'
    - Marie Curie

'The human race is a race of cowards; and I am not only marching in that procession but carrying a banner.'
    - Mark Twain

'There is nothing in the universe that I fear, but that I shall not know all my duty or fail to do it.'
    - Mary Lyon

'Many fears are born of fatigue and loneliness.'
    - Max Ehrmann

'The thing I fear most is fear.'
    - Michel de Montaigne

'One of the effects of fear is to disturb the senses and cause things to appear other than what they are.'
    - Miguel de Cervantes

'He who fears something gives it power over him.'
    - Moorish proverb

'Let us not fear the hidden. Or each other.'
    - Muriel Rukeyser

'Fear is not an unknown emotion to us.'
    - Neil Armstrong

'Fear is secured by a dread of punishment.'
    - Niccolo Machiavelli

'Men hesitate less to injure a man who makes himself loved than to injure one who makes himself feared, for their love is held by a chain of obligation which, because of men's wickedness, is broken on every occasion for the sake of selfish profit; but thei'
    - Niccolo Machiavelli

'As many people die from an excess of timidity as from bravery.'
    - Norman Mailer

'Fear of losing is what makes competitors so great. Show me a gracious loser and I'll show you a perennial loser.'
    - O. J. Simpson

'The suspense is terrible. I hope it will last.'
    - Oscar Wilde

'Fear is the most devastating of all human emotions. Man has no trouble like the paralyzing effects of fear.'
- Paul Parker

'Fear always springs from ignorance.'
- Ralph Waldo Emerson

'There's nothing I'm afraid of like scared people.'
- Robert Frost

'Men who look young, act young, and everlastingly harp on the fact that they are young-but who nevertheless think and act with a degree of caution what would be excessive in their grandfathers-are the curses of the world.'
- Robertson Davies

'Every day I wake up a little afraid. Only a fool is never afraid.'
- Ron Meyer

'When fear is excessive it can make many a man despair.'
- Saint Thomas Aquinas

'O, how vain and vile a passion is this fear! What base, uncomely things it makes men do.'
- Samuel Johnson

'What begins in fear usually ends in folly.'
- Samuel Taylor Coleridge

'The more I traveled the more I realized that fear makes strangers of people who should be friends.'
- Shirley MacLaine

'In doubt, fear is the worst of prophets.'
- Statius

'I will show you fear in a handful of dust.'
- T. S. Eliot

'If your desires be endless, your cares and fears will be so, too.'
- Thomas Fuller

'Great self-destruction follows upon unfounded fear.'
- Ursula K. LeGuin

'There is nothing that fear or hope does not make men believe.'
- Vauvenargues

'Fear is the proof of a degenerate mind.'
- Virgil

'The flocks fear the wolf, the crops the storm, and the trees the wind.'
  - Virgil

'Fear follows crime, and is its punishment.'
  - Voltaire

'Fear is the most damnable, damaging thing to human personality in the whole world.'
  - William Faulkner

'Fear, born of that stern matron, Responsibility.'
  - William McFee

'A man's doubts and fears are his worst enemies.'
  - William Wrigley

FOCUS

'A straight path never leads anywhere except to the objective.'
- Andre Gide

'The effectiveness of work increases according to geometrical progression if there are no interruptions.'
- Andre Maurois

'Concentrate your energies, your thoughts and your capital. ... The wise man puts all his eggs in one basket and watches the basket.'
- Andrew Carnegie

'The field of consciousness is tiny. It accepts only one problem at a time.'
- Antoine de Saint-Exupery

'The secret of concentration is the secret of self-discovery. You reach inside yourself to discover your personal resources, and what it takes to match them to the challenge.'
- Arnold Palmer

'One cannot both feast and become rich.'
- Ashanti proverb

'To be able to concentrate for a considerable time is essential to difficult achievement.'
- Bertrand Russell

'For him who has no concentration, there is no tranquility.'
- Bhagaved Gita

'This one thing I do ... I press toward the mark.'
- Bible

'A full mind is an empty baseball bat.'
- Branch Rickey

'Other people's interruptions of your work are relatively insignificant compared with the countless times you interrupt yourself.'
- Brendan Francis

'I can't concentrate on golf or bowling. Those bowling pins aren't going to hurt me. I can concentrate in the ring because someone is trying to kill me.'
- Carmen Basilio

'I go at what I am about as if there was nothing else in the world for the time being.'
- Charles Lingsley

'A bird can roost but on one branch. A mouse can drink no more than its fill from a river.'
- Chinese proverb

'Successful minds work like a gimlet, to a single point.'
- Christian Bovee

'Concentrate on finding your goal, then concentrate on reaching it.'
- Colonel Michael Friedman

'Give me a man who says this one thing I do, and not these fifty things I dabble in.'
- Dwight L. Moody

'The difference in men does not lie in the size of their hands, nor in the perfection of their bodies, but in this one sublime ability of concentration: to throw the weight with the blow, to live an eternity in an hour.'
- Elbert Hubbard

'One man; two loves. No good ever comes of that.'
- Euripides

'While the work or play is on ... don't constantly feel you ought to be doing the other.'
- Franklin P. Adams

'The perplexity of life arises from there being too many interesting things in it for us to be interested properly in any of them.'
- G. K. Chesterton

'The immature mind hops from one thing to another; the mature mind seeks to follow through.'
- Harry A. Overstreet

'No horse gets anywhere until he is harnessed. No steam or gas ever drives anything until it is confined. No Niagara is ever turned into light and power until it is tunneled. No life ever grows great until it is focused, dedicated, disciplined.'
- Harry Emerson Fosdick

'Nothing interferes with my concentration. You could put on an orgy in my office and I wouldn't look up. Well, maybe once.'
- Isaac Asimov

'If I have ever made any valuable discoveries, it has been owing more to patient attention than to any other talent.'
- Isaac Newton

'A single idea, if it is right, saves us the labor of an infinity of experiences.'
- Jacques Maritain

'One thought driven home is better than three left on base.'
- James Liter

'Beware of dissipating your powers; strive constantly to concentrate them.'
  - Johann von Goethe

'The secret to success in any human endeavor is total concentration.'
  - Kurt Vonnegut

'Become so wrapped up in something that you forget to be afraid.'
  - Lady Bird Johnson

'The ability to concentrate and to use your time well is everything.'
  - Lee Iacocca

'Those who set out to serve both God and Mammon soon discover that there is no God.'
  - Logan Pearsall Smith

'There is time enough for everything in the course of the day if you do but one thing at once; but there is not time enough in the year if you will do two things at a time.'
  - Lord Chesterfield

'When one is learning, one should not think of play; and when one is at play, one should not think of learning.'
  - Lord Chesterfield

'Concentration is everything. On the day I'm performing, I don't hear anything anyone says to me.'
  - Luciano Pavarotti

'No man will swim ashore and take his baggage with him.'
  - Marcus Annaeus Seneca

'A man should remove not only unnecessary acts, but also unnecessary thoughts, for then superfluous activity will not follow.'
  - Marcus Aurelius

'Each man is capable of doing one thing well. If he attempts several, he will fail to achieve distinction in any.'
  - Plato

'To do two things at once is to do neither.'
  - Publilius Syrus

'If you direct your whole thought to work itself, none of the things which invade eyes or ears will reach the mind.'
  - Quintilian

'Do whatever you do intensely.'
  - Robert Henri

'When a man knows he is to be hanged in a fortnight, it concentrates his mind wonderfully.'
  - Samuel Johnson

'A man may be so much of everything that he is nothing of everything.'
    - Samuel Johnson

'It is only when I dally with what I am about, look back and aside, instead of keeping my eyes straight forward, that I feel these cold sinkings of the heart.'
    - Sir Walter Scott

'Purity of heart is to will one thing.'
    - Soren Kierkegaard

'You can't ring the bells and, at the same time, walk in the procession.'
    - Spanish proverb

'I like to laugh, but on the court, it is my work. I try to smile, but it is so difficult. I concentrate on the ball, not on my face.'
    - Steffi Graf

'All good is gained by those whose thought and life are kept pointed close to one main thing, not scattered abroad upon a thousand.'
    - Stephen McKenna

'I've learned ruthless concentration. I can write under any circumstances ... street noises, loud talk, music, you name it.'
    - Sylvia Porter

'If you don't concentrate, you'll end up on your rear.'
    - Tai Babilonia

'If there is anything that can be called genius, it consists chiefly in the ability to give that attention to a subject which keeps it steadily in the mind, till we have surveyed it accurately on all sides.'
    - Thomas Reid

'When I come into a game in the bottom of the ninth, bases loaded, no one out and a one-run lead ... it takes people off my mind.'
    - Tug McGraw

'One arrow does not bring down two birds.'
    - Turkish proverb

'Attention to a subject depends upon our interest in it.'
    - Tyron Edwards

'Choice of attention, to pay attention to this and ignore that, is to the inner life what choice of Taking Action is to the outer.'
    - W. H. Auden

'The real essence of work is concentrated energy.'
    - Walter Bagehot

'The first law of success ... is concentration: to bend all the energies to one point, and to go directly to that point, looking neither to the right nor the left.'
   - William Matthews

FOOD

'A hungry man is not a free man.'
- Adlai Stevenson

'There is no such thing as a little garlic.'
- Anonymous

'A good meal makes a man feel more charitable toward the whole world than any sermon.'
- Arthur Pendenys

'To get the best results, you must talk to your vegetables.'
- Charles, Prince of Wales

'No man is lonely while eating spaghetti - it requires so much attention.'
- Christopher Morley

'Cheese - milk's leap toward immortality.'
- Clifton Fadiman

'The one way to get thin is to re-establish a purpose in life.'
- Cyril Connolly

'Food is an important part of a balanced diet.'
- Fran Lebowitz

'A good meal ought to begin with hunger.'
- French proverb

'There is no such thing as a pretty good omelette.'
- French proverb

'There is no love sincerer than the love of food.'
- George Bernard Shaw

'Kissing don't last: cookery do.'
- George Meredith

'If you wish to grow thinner, diminish your dinner.'
- H. S. Leigh

'Hunger is not debatable.'
- Harry Hopkins

'If you ask the hungry man how much is two and two, he replies four loaves.'
- Hindu proverb

'More die in the United States of too much food than of too little.'
- J. K. Galbraith

'All happiness depends on a leisurely breakfast.'
- John Gunther

'A smiling face is half the meal.'
- Latvian proverb

'I feel a recipe is only a theme, which an intelligent cook can play each time with a variation.'
- Madame Benoit

'To a man with an empty stomach, food is god.'
- Mahatma Gandhi

'At the end of every diet, the path curves back toward the trough.'
- Mason Cooley

'Never eat more than you can lift.'
- Miss Piggy

'A gourmet is just a glutton with brains.'
- Philip W. Haberman

'It is a hard matter, my fellow citizens, to argue with the belly, since it has no ears.'
- Plutarch

'Fish, to taste right, must swim three times - in water, in butter and in wine.'
- Polish proverb

'Even were a cook to cook a fly, he would keep the breast for himself.'
- Polish proverb

'Hunger is the best sauce.'
- Proverbs

'A man is in general better pleased when he has a good dinner upon his table, than when his wife talks Greek.'
- Samuel Johnson

'A great step toward independence is a good-humored stomach.'
- Seneca

'Vegetarianism is harmless enough, though it is apt to fill a man with wind and self-righteousness.'
- Sir Robert Hutchinson

'Dinner, a time when . . . one should eat wisely but not too well, and talk well but not too wisely.'
- W. Somerset Maugham

'To eat well in England you should have breakfast three times a day.'
- W. Somerset Maugham

'It's a very odd thing As odd as can be That whatever Miss T. eats Turns into Miss T.'
- Walter de la Mare

'Toots Shore's restaurant is so crowded nobody goes there anymore.'
- Yogi Berra

FORGIVENESS

It is almost impossible to throw dirt on someone without getting a little on yourself.'
  - Abigail Van Buren

'This only grant me, that my means may lie too low for envy, for contempt too high.'
  - Abraham Cowley

'Just to be is a blessing. Just to live is holy.'
  - Abraham Heschel

'Ask the gods nothing excessive.'
  - Aeschylus

'Be content with your lot; one cannot be first in everything.'
  - Aesop

'I like living. I have sometimes been wildly, despairingly, acutely miserable, racked with sorrow, but through it all I still know quite certainly that just to be alive is a grand thing.'
  - Agatha Christie

'If there is a sin against life, it consists perhaps not so much in despairing of life as in hoping for another, and in eluding the implacable grandeur of this life.'
  - Albert Camus

'Anger dwells only in the bosom of fools.'
  - Albert Einstein

'Resentment is the "number one" offender. It destroys more alcoholics than anything else. From it stem all forms of spiritual disease, for we have been not only mentally and physically ill, we have been spiritually sick.'
  - Alcoholics Anonymous

'Most human beings have an almost infinite capacity for taking things for granted.'
  - Aldous Huxley

'To understand is to forgive, even oneself.'
  - Alexander Chase

'To err is human; to forgive, divine.'
  - Alexander Pope

'To err is human, to forgive, divine.'
  - Alexander Pope

'How shall I love the sin, yet keep the sense, And love the offender, yet detest the offence?'
  - Alexander Pope

'One never hugs one's good luck so affectionately as when listening to the relation of some horrible misfortunes which has overtaken others.'
- Alexander Smith

'Tis better to have loved and lost than never to have loved at all.'
- Alfred, Lord Tennyson

'Happiness is composed of misfortunes avoided.'
- Alphonse Karr

'It is not customary to love what one has.'
- Anatole France

'I wept because I had no shoes, until I saw a man who had no feet.'
- Ancient Persian saying

'Welcome everything that comes to you, but do not long for anything else.'
- Andre Gide

'Long only for what you have.'
- Andre Gide

'When life's problems seem overwhelming, look around and see what other people are coping with. You may consider yourself fortunate.'
- Ann Landers

'Think of all the beauty still left around you and be happy.'
- Anne Frank

'My gratitude for good writing is unbounded; I'm grateful for it the way I'm grateful for the ocean.'
- Anne Lamott

'One cannot collect all the beautiful shells on the beach.'
- Anne Morrow Lindbergh

'One can never pay in gratitude; one can only pay "in kind" somewhere else in life.'
- Anne Morrow Lindbergh

'The heart has always the pardoning power.'
- Anne-Sophie Swetchine

'Seeds of discouragement will not grow in the thankful heart.'
- Anonymous

'It is easier to forgive an enemy than a friend.'
- Anonymous

'Thank God for dirty dishes; they have a tale to tell. While other folks go hungry, we're eating pretty well. With home, and health, and happiness, we shouldn't want to fuss; For by this stack of evidence,

God's very good to us.'
- Anonymous

'Resentments are burdens we don't need to carry.'
- Anonymous

'Even though we can't have all we want, we ought to be thankful we don't get all we deserve.'
- Anonymous

'If you can't be thankful for what you receive, be thankful for what you escape.'
- Anonymous

'To be content with little is difficult; to be content with much, impossible.'
- Anonymous

'The greatest wealth is contentment with a little.'
- Anonymous

'They may not deserve forgiveness, but I do.'
- Anonymous

'Life is hard. Next to what?'
- Anonymous

'A Christian could even give thanks for Hell, because Hell was a threat and a warning to keep him in the right way.'
- Anonymous

'He is not rich that possesses much, but he that is content with what he has.'
- Anonymous

'More than enough is too much.'
- Anonymous

'He who is content in his poverty is wonderfully rich.'
- Anonymous

'A wise man cares not for what he cannot have.'
- Anonymous

'Those who can't forget are worse off than those who can't remember.'
- Anonymous

'He has enough who is contented with little.'
- Anonymous

'No one is satisfied with his fortune, or dissatisfied with his intellect.'
- Antoinette Deshouliere

'Any man can seek revenge; it takes a king or prince to grant a pardon.'
- Arthur J. Rehrat

'To be alive, to be able to see, to walk ... it's all a miracle. I have adapted the technique of living life from miracle to miracle.'
- Arthur Rubinstein

'The happiness of any given life is to be measured not by its joys and pleasures, but by the extent to which it has been free from suffering, from positive evil.'
- Arthur Schopenhauer

'Hatred is a death wish for the hated, not a life wish for anything else.'
- Audre Lorde

'It's a grand thing to be able to take your money in your hand and to think no more of it when it slips away from you than you would a trout that would slip back into the stream.'
- Augusta Gregory

'A prudent man will think more important what fate has conceded to him, than what it has denied.'
- Baltasar Gracian

'Resentment is weak and lowers your self-esteem.'
- Barbara Sher

'If you desire many things, many things will seem but a few.'
- Benjamin Franklin

'Ambition has its disappointments to sour us, but never the good fortune to satisfy us.'
- Benjamin Franklin

'A wise man will desire no more than what he may get justly, use soberly, distribute cheerfully, and leave contently.'
- Benjamin Franklin

'What a miserable thing life is: you're living in clover, only the clover isn't good enough.'
- Bertolt Brecht

'It isn't important to come out on top. What matters is to come out alive.'
- Bertolt Brecht

'Give us this day our daily bread. And forgive us our debts, as we forgive our debtors.'
- Bible

'And be content with such things as ye have.'
- Bible

'Judge not, that ye be not judged.'
- Bible

'Let all bitterness, and wrath, and anger, and clamor, and evil speaking, be put away from you, with all malice; and be ye kind to one another, tenderhearted, forgiving one another, even as God, for Christ's sake, hath forgiven you.'
- Bible

'Forgive us our trespasses, as we forgive them that trespass against us.'
- Bible

'Sometimes the best deals are the ones you don't make.'
- Bill Veeck

'So long as we can lose any happiness, we possess some.'
- Booth Tarkington

'Those who are free of resentful thoughts surely find peace.'
- Buddha

'Holding on to anger is like grasping a hot coal with the intent of throwing it at someone else; you are the one who gets burned.'
- Buddha

'Only with a new ruler do you realize the value of the old.'
- Burmese proverb

'Man never has what he wants, because what he wants is everything.'
- C. F. Ramuz

'Revenge may not be a particularly high consciousness-oriented activity.'
- Carrie Fisher

'I learned that true forgiveness includes total self-acceptance. And out of acceptance wounds are healed and happiness is possible again.'
- Catharine Marshall

'The forgiving state of mind is a magnetic power for attracting good.'
- Catherine Ponder

'Forgiveness is all-powerful. Forgiveness heals all ills.'
- Catherine Ponder

'I forgive myself for having believed for so long that... I was never good enough to have, get, be what I wanted.'
- Ceanne DeRohan

'Happiness is a way station between too much and too little.'
- Channing Pollock

'True contentment depends not upon what we have; a tub was large enough for Diogenes, but a world was too little for Alexander.'
- Charles Caleb Colton

'Reflect upon your present blessings, of which every man has many; not on your past misfortunes, of which all men have some.'
- Charles Dickens

'Thank God every morning when you get up that you have something to do which must be done, whether you like it or not.'
- Charles Kingsley

'Many promising reconciliations have broken down because while both parties came prepared to forgive, neither party came prepared to be forgiven.'
- Charles William

'Something of vengeance I had tasted for the first time; as aromatic wine it seemed, on swallowing, warm and racy; its after-flavor, metallic and corroding, gave me a sensation as if I had been poisoned.'
- Charlotte Bronte

'Life appears to me too short to be spent in nursing animosity or registering wrong.'
- Charlotte Bronte

'The use we make of our fortune determines as to its sufficiency. A little is enough if used wisely, and too much is not enough if expended foolishly.'
- Christian Bovee

'Forgiveness is the act of admitting we are like other people.'
- Christina Baldwin

'How we remember, what we remember, and why we remember form the most personal map of our individuality.'
- Christina Baldwin

'A thankful heart is not only the greatest virtue, but the parent of all other virtues.'
- Cicero

'If only every man would make proper use of his strength and do his utmost, he need never regret his limited ability.'
- Cicero

'The covetous man is always poor.'
- Claudian

'There are people who have money and people who are rich.'
- Coco Chanel

'What a wonderful life I've had! I only wish I'd realized it sooner.'
- Colette

'Gratitude weighs heavy on us only when we no longer feel it.'
- Comtesse Diane

'To be wronged is nothing unless you continue to remember it.'
- Confucius

'No one has yet had the courage to memorialize his wealth on his tombstone. A dollar mark would not look well there.'
- Corra May Harris

'Forgiveness is an act of the will, and the will can function regardless of the temperature of the heart.'
- Corrie ten Boom

'When something does not insist on being noticed, when we aren't grabbed by the collar or struck on the skull by a presence or an event, we take for granted the very things that most deserve our gratitude.'
- Cynthia Ozick

'How Forgiveness Helps Us Forgiveness is the answer to the child's dream of a miracle by which what is broken is made whole again, what is soiled is again made clean.'
- Dag Hammarskjold

'While you fear missing a meal, you aren't fully aware of the meals you do eat.'
- Dan Millman

'Of all the people in the world, those who want the most are those who have the most.'
- David Grayson

'If you haven't forgiven yourself something, how can you forgive others?'
- Dolores Huerta

'This is another day! Are its eyes blurred With maudlin grief for any wasted past? A thousand thousand failures shall not daunt! Let dust clasp dust, death, death; I am alive!'
- Don Marquis

'We don't need to increase our goods nearly as much as we need to scale down our wants. Not wanting something is as good as possessing it.'
- Donald Horban

'Until you make peace with who you are, you'll never be content with what you have.'
- Doris Mortman

'Hate smolders and eventually destroys, not the hated but the hater.'
- Dorothy Thompson

'The world is full of people looking for spectacular happiness while they snub contentment.'
- Doug Larson

'Hate is a prolonged form of suicide.'
  - Douglas V. Steere

'To what extent is any given man morally responsible for any given act? We do not know.'
  - Dr. Alexis Carrel

'You will never be the person you can be if pressure, tension and discipline are taken out of your life.'
  - Dr. James G. Bilkey

'Anger repressed can poison a relationship as surely as the crudest words.'
  - Dr. Joyce Brothers

'The best proof of love is trust.'
  - Dr. Joyce Brothers

'The angry people are those people who are most afraid.'
  - Dr. Robert Anthony

'I thank You God for this most amazing day; for the leaping greenly spirits of trees and a blue true dream of sky; and for everything which is natural which is infinite which is yes.'
  - e. e. cummings

'The real tragedy of life is not being limited to one talent, but in failing to use that one talent.'
  - Edgar Watson Howe

'I know now that patriotism is not enough; I must have no hatred and bitterness toward anyone.'
  - Edith Cavell

'For one mother, joy is the quiet pleasure found in gently rubbing shampoo into her young child's hair. For another woman it's taking a long walk alone, while for yet another it's reveling in a much-anticipated vacation.'
  - Eileen Stukane

'We never ask God to forgive anybody except when we haven't.'
  - Elbert Hubbard

'To have a full stomach and fixed income are no small things .'
  - Elbert Hubbard

'I have the greatest of all riches: that of not desiring them.'
  - Eleonora Duse

'Blessed are those who can give without remembering and take without forgetting.'
  - Elizabeth Asquith Bibesco

'Good, to forgive; Best, to forget.'
  - Elizabeth Barrett Browning

'All your youth you want to have your greatness taken for granted; when you find it taken for granted, you are unnerved.'
- Elizabeth Bowen

'Remember that not to be happy is not to be grateful.'
- Elizabeth Carter

'My mother used to say, "He who angers you conquers you."'
- Elizabeth Kenny

'We are told that people stay in love because of chemistry, or because they remain intrigued with each other, because of many kindnesses, because of luck. ... But part of it has got to be forgiveness and gratefulness.'
- Ellen Goodman

'The mere sense of living is joy enough.'
- Emily Dickinson

'My friends are my estate.'
- Emily Dickinson

'Anger as soon as fed is dead, 'tis starving makes it fat.'
- Emily Dickinson

'We never know the worth of water till the well is dry.'
- English proverb

'Freedom is not procured by a full enjoyment of what is desired, but by controlling the desire.'
- Epictetus

'He is a man of sense who does not grieve for what he has not, but rejoices in what he has.'
- Epictetus

'Bear and forbear.'
- Epictetus

'Do not spoil what you have by desiring what you have not; remember that what you now have was once among the things only hoped for.'
- Epicurus

'Whoever does not regard what he has as most ample wealth is unhappy, though he is master of the world.'
- Epicurus

'Nothing is enough to the man for whom enough is too little.'
- Epicurus

'The summit of pleasure is the elimination of all that gives pain.'
- Epicurus

'Who does not thank for little will not thank for much.'
    - Estonian proverb

'The externals are simply so many props; everything we need is within us.'
    - Etty Hillesum

'The moment an individual can accept and forgive himself, even a little, is the moment in which he becomes to some degree lovable.'
    - Eugene Kennedy

'Slight not what is near though aiming at what is far.'
    - Euripides

'Sufficiency's enough for men of sense.'
    - Euripides

'He is not rich that possesses much, but he that covets no more; and he is not poor that enjoys little, but he that wants too much.'
    - Francis Beaumont

'The beginning of men's rebellion against God was, and is, the lack of a thankful heart.'
    - Francis Schaeffer

'Mankind, by the perverse depravity of their nature, esteem that which they have most desired as of no value the moment it is possessed, and torment themselves with fruitless wishes for that which is beyond their reach.'
    - Francois de Fenelon

'One forgives to the degree that one loves.'
    - Francois de La Rochefoucauld

'One is never fortunate or as unfortunate as one imagines.'
    - Francois de La Rochefoucauld

'No man can be satisfied with his attainment, although he may be satisfied with his circumstances.'
    - Frank Swinnerton

'When we cannot get what we love, we must love what is within our reach.'
    - French proverb

'The tulip is, among flowers, what the peacock is among birds. A tulip lacks scent, a peacock has an unpleasant voice. The one takes pride in its garb, the other in its tail.'
    - French proverb

'He who curbs his desires will always be rich enough.'
    - French proverb

'That which does not kill me makes me stronger.'
    - Friedrich Nietzsche

'The way to love anything is to realize that it may be lost.'
- G. K. Chesterton

'True contentment... is the power of getting out of any situation all that there is in it. It is arduous, and it is rare.'
- G. K. Chesterton

'It matters very little whether a man is discontented in the name of pessimism or progress, if his discontent does in fact paralysis his power of appreciating what he has got.'
- G. K. Chesterton

'Forgiving means to pardon the unpardonable, faith means believing the unbelievable, and hoping means to hope when things are hopeless.'
- G. K. Chesterton

'Forgiving those who hurt us is the key to personal peace.'
- G. Weatherly

'What strange perversity is it that induces a man to set his heart on doing those things which he has not succeeded in, and makes him slight those in which his achievement has been respectable.'
- Gamaliel Bradford

'True affluence is not needing anything.'
- Gary Snyder

'Too much is unwholesome.'
- Georg Christoph Lichtenberg

'The secret of forgiving everything is to understand nothing.'
- George Bernard Shaw

'Hatred is like fire-it makes even light rubbish deadly.'
- George Eliot

'Forgiveness is the giving, and so the receiving, of life.'
- George Macdonald

'The superiority of the distant over the present is only due to the mass and variety of the pleasures that can be suggested, compared with the poverty of those that can at any time be felt.'
- George Santayana

'Happiness lies, first of all, in health.'
- George William Curtis

'It is strange what a contempt men have for the joys that are offered them freely.'
- Georges Duhamel

'I can have peace of mind only when I forgive rather than judge.'
- Gerald Jampolsky

'Forgiveness means letting go of the past.'
- Gerald Jampolsky

'Forgiveness is the way to true health and happiness.'
- Gerald Jampolsky

'Contentment is worth more than riches.'
- German proverb

'You can be happy indeed if you have breathing space from pain.'
- Giacomo Leopardi

'The end of pain we take as happiness.'
- Giacomo Leopardi

'Silent gratitude isn't much use to anyone.'
- Gladys Browyn Stern

'Not being beautiful was the true blessing. ... Not being beautiful forced me to develop my inner resources. The pretty girl has a handicap to overcome.'
- Golda Meir

'Nothing will content him who is not content with a little.'
- Greek proverb

'Nothing's easier than believing we understand experiences we've never had.'
- Gwen Bristow

'I remember those happy days and often wish I could speak into the ears of the dead the gratitude which was due to them in life and so ill-returned.'
- Gwyn Thomas

'Forgiveness is the noblest vengeance.'
- H. G. Bohn

'The Pilgrims made seven times more graves than huts. No Americans have been more impoverished than these who, nevertheless, set aside a day of thanksgiving.'
- H. U. Westermayer

'Be content with what thou hast received, and smooth thy frowning forehead.'
- Hafez

'Forgiveness is the key to Taking Action and freedom.'
- Hannah Arendt

'A man who accustoms himself to buy superfluities is often in want of necessities.'
- Hannah Farnham Lee

'Forgive all who have offended you, not for them, but for yourself.'
- Harriet Uts Nelson

'Bitterness imprisons life; love releases it.'
- Harry Emerson Fosdick

'Every man treats himself as society treats the criminal.'
- Harvey Fergusson

'God will forgive me the foolish remarks I have made about Him just as I will forgive my opponents the foolish things they have written about me, even though they are spiritually as inferior to me as I to thee, O God!'
- Heinrich Heine

'God will forgive me, that is His business.'
- Heinrich Heine

'I used to store my anger and it affected my play. Now I get it out. I'm never rude to my playing partner. I'm very focused on the ball. Then it's over.'
- Helen Alfredsson

'People are more than the worst thing they have ever done in their lives.'
- Helen Prejean

'That man is richest whose pleasures are the cheapest.'
- Henry David Thoreau

'A man is rich in proportion to the things he can afford to let alone.'
- Henry David Thoreau

'Be glad of life because it gives you the chance to love, and to work, and to play and to look up at the stars.'
- Henry Van Dyke

'"I can forgive, but I cannot forget" is only another way of saying, "I will not forgive." Forgiveness ought to be like a canceled note-torn in two and burned up so that it never can be shown against one.'
- Henry Ward Beecher

'God pardons like a mother, who kisses the offense into everlasting forgetfulness.'
- Henry Ward Beecher

'The unthankful heart... discovers no mercies; but let the thankful heart sweep through the day and, as the magnet finds the iron, so it will find, in every hour, some heavenly blessings!'
- Henry Ward Beecher

'The unthankful heart... discovers no mercies; but the thankful heart... will find, in every hour, some heavenly blessings.'
- Henry Ward Beecher

'My country ... gave me schooling, independence of Taking Action and opportunity for service. ... I am indebted to my country beyond any human power to repay.'
- Herbert Hoover

'If you hate a person, you hate something in him that is part of yourself.'
- Hermann Hesse

'There is satiety in all things, in sleep, and love-making, in the loveliness of singing and the innocent dance.'
- Homer

'Some troubles, like a protested note of a solvent debtor, bear interest.'
- Honore de Balzac

'Anger is a short madness.'
- Horace

'Let him who has enough wish for nothing more.'
- Horace

'Only a stomach that rarely feels hungry scorns common things.'
- Horace

'Forgiveness is man's deepest need and highest achievement.'
- Horace Bushnell

'Moderation is the key to lasting enjoyment.'
- Hosea Ballou

'Oh, my friend, it's not what they take away from you that counts-it's what you do with what you have left.'
- Hubert H. Humphrey

'You cannot shake hands with a clenched fist.'
- Indira Gandhi

'Forgiveness is the sweetest revenge.'
- Isaac Friedmann

'To be angry about trifles is mean and childish; to rage and be furious is brutish; and to maintain perpetual wrath is akin to the practice and temper of devils; but to prevent and suppress rising resentment is wise and glorious, is manly and divine.'
- Isaac Watts

'As long as you don't forgive, who and whatever it is will occupy a rent-free space in your mind.'
- Isabelle Holland

'Health is ... a blessing that money cannot buy.'
- Izaak Walton

'Not what we have, but what we enjoy, constitutes our abundance.'
- J. Petit-Senn

'One of life's gifts is that each of us, no matter how tired and downtrodden, finds reasons for thankfulness.'
- J. Robert Maskin

'Generally the man with a good wife, or the woman with a good husband, or the children with good parents discover too late the goodness they overlooked while it was in full bloom.'
- James Douglas

'Good heavens, of what uncostly material is our earthly happiness composed ... if we only knew it. What incomes have we not had from a flower, and how unfailing are the dividends of the seasons.'
- James Russell Lowell

'Health is the vital principle of bliss.'
- James Thomson

'My private measure of success is daily. If this were to be the last day of my life would I be content with it? To live in a harmonious balance of commitments and pleasures is what I strive for.'
- Jane Rule

'He is poor who does not feel content.'
- Japanese proverb

'Gratitude is the memory of the heart.'
- Jean Baptiste Massieu

'Better to suffer than to die.'
- Jean de la Fontaine

'We are never content with our lot.'
- Jean de la Fontaine

'To be able to dispense with good things is tantamount to possessing them.'
- Jean Francois Regnard

'Humanity is never so beautiful as when praying for forgiveness, or else forgiving another.'
- Jean Paul Richter

'I may not amount to much, but at least I am unique.'
- Jean-Jacques Rousseau

'The happiest is he who suffers the least pain; the most miserable, he who enjoys the least pleasure.'
- Jean-Jacques Rousseau

'For me it's not possible to forget, and I don't understand people who, when the love is ended, can bury the other person in hatred or oblivion. For me, a man I have loved becomes a kind of brother.'
- Jeanne Moreau

'The private and personal blessings we enjoy-the blessings of immunity, safeguard, liberty and integrity- deserve the thanksgiving of a whole life.'
  - Jeremy Taylor

'It is very easy to forgive others their mistakes; it takes more grit and gumption to forgive them for having witnessed your own.'
  - Jessamyn West

'I have looked on a lot of women with lust. I've committed adultery in my heart many times. God recognizes I will do this and forgives me.'
  - Jimmy Carter

'No longer forward nor behind I look in hope or fear; But, grateful, take the good I find, The best of now and here.'
  - John Greenleaf Whittier

'Enough is as good as a feast.'
  - John Heywood

'A sound mind in a sound body is a short but full description of a happy state in this world.'
  - John Locke

'Men ... always think that something they are going to get is better than what they have got.'
  - John Oliver Hobbes

'Considering the fortune you might have lost, you'll have to admit you're rich already.'
  - John Rothchild

'There is no wealth but life.'
  - John Ruskin

'Sunshine is delicious, rain is refreshing, wind braces us up, snow is exhilarating; there is really no such thing as bad weather, only different kinds of good weather.'
  - John Ruskin

'Forgiveness is the most tender part of love.'
  - John Sheffield

'We spend our time searching for security and hate it when we get it.'
  - John Steinbeck

'I have learned to seek my happiness by limiting my desires, rather than in attempting to satisfy them.'
  - John Stuart Mill

'What you really value is what you miss, not what you have.'
  - Jorge Luis Borges

'A man should always consider ... how much more unhappy he might be than he is.'
  - Joseph Addison

'Looking for Silver Linings Our real blessings often appear to us in the shape of pains, losses and disappointments.'
- Joseph Addison

'Who would care to question the ground of forgiveness or compassion?'
- Joseph Conrad

'Not what we have, but what we use, not what we see, but what we choose-these are the things that mar or bless human happiness.'
- Joseph Fort Newton

'Forgiveness is the highest and most difficult of all moral lessons.'
- Joseph Jacobs

'Think of the ills from which you are exempt.'
- Joseph Joubert

'Happy is the man who can do only one thing: in doing it, he fulfills his destiny.'
- Joseph Joubert

'Luckily, I never feel at one time more than half my pains.'
- Joseph Joubert

'The happiness which is lacking makes one think even the happiness one has unbearable.'
- Joseph Roux

'Happiness is itself a kind of gratitude.'
- Joseph Wood Krutch

'It ain't so much trouble to get rich as it is to tell when we have got rich.'
- Josh Billings

'There is no revenge so complete as forgiveness.'
- Josh Billings

'A BMW can't take you as far as a diploma.'
- Joyce A. Myers

'Experience is how life catches up with us and teaches us to love and forgive each other.'
- Judy Collins

'People call me an optimist, but I'm really an appreciator ... years ago, I was cured of a badly infected finger with antibiotics when once my doctor could have recommended only a hot water soak or, eventually, surgery.... When I was six years old and had '
- Julian Simon

'How few are our real wants, and how easy is it to satisfy them! Our imaginary ones are boundless and insatiable.'
- Julius Charles Hare

'Yes, there is a Nirvanah: it is in leading your sheep to a green pasture, and in putting your child to sleep, and in writing the last line of your poem.'
  - Kahlil Gibran

'Joy is the simplest form of gratitude.'
  - Karl Barth

'One may have been a fool, but there's no foolishness like being bitter.'
  - Kathleen Norris

'Hate is all a lie, there is no truth in hate.'
  - Kathleen Norris

'We always have enough to be happy if we are enjoying what we do have- and not worrying about what we don't have.'
  - Ken Keyes

'To be upset over what you don't have is to waste what you do have.'
  - Ken Keyes

'The hardest thing is to take less when you can get more.'
  - Kin Hubbard

'Nobody ever forgets where he buried a hatchet.'
  - Kin Hubbard

'Friends are the thermometer by which we may judge the temperature of our fortunes.'
  - Lady Marguerite Blessington

'He who is contented is rich.'
  - Lao-Tzu

'We are content to forgo joy when pain is also lost.'
  - Latin proverb

'I figure if I have my health, can pay the rent and I have my friends, I call it "content."'
  - Lauren Bacall

'Only the brave know how to forgive. ... A coward never forgave; it is not in his nature.'
  - Laurence Sterne

'It is possible to own too much. A man with one watch knows what time it is; a man with two watches is never quite sure.'
  - Lee Segall

'Why do some people always see beautiful skies and grass and lovely flowers and incredible human beings, while others are hard-pressed to find anything or any place that is beautiful?'
  - Leo Buscaglia

'Was it always my nature to take a bad time and block out the good times, until any success became an accident and failure seemed the only truth?'
- Lillian Hellman

'How can they say my life is not a success? Have I not for more than sixty years gotten enough to eat and escaped being eaten?'
- Logan Pearsall Smith

'Hate would destroy him who hated.'
- Louis L'Amour

'Man needs so little ... yet he begins wanting so much.'
- Louis L'Amour

'Revenge could steal a man's life until there was nothing left but emptiness.'
- Louis L'Amour

'A man can lose sight of everything else when he's bent on revenge, and it ain't worth it.'
- Louis L'Amour

'Anger is a killing thing: it kills the man who angers, for each rage leaves him less than he had been before-it takes something from him.'
- Louis L'Amour

'Were a man to order his life by the rules of true reason, a frugal substance joined to a contented mind is for him great riches.'
- Lucretius

'It is right to be contented with what we have, never with what we are.'
- Mackintosh

'Who understands much, forgives much.'
- Madame de Stael

'Anger and worry are the enemies of clear thought.'
- Madeleine Brent

'It is better to be looked over than overlooked.'
- Mae West

'Too much of a good thing can be wonderful.'
- Mae West

'Keeping score of old scores and scars, getting even and one-upping, always make you less than you are.'
- Malcolm Forbes

'Too many people overvalue what they are not and undervalue what they are.'
- Malcolm Forbes

'Be on the lookout for mercies. The more we look for them, the more of them we will see.... Better to loose count while naming your blessings than to lose your blessings to counting your troubles.'
- Maltbie D. Babcock

'No evil is without its compensation ... it is not the loss itself, but the estimate of the loss, that troubles us.'
- Marcus Annaeus Seneca

'We can be thankful to a friend for a few acres or a little money; and yet for the freedom and command of the whole earth, and for the great benefits of our being, our life, health, and reason, we look upon ourselves as under no obligation.'
- Marcus Annaeus Seneca

'There is nothing so bitter that a patient mind cannot find some solace for it.'
- Marcus Annaeus Seneca

'The heart is great which shows moderation in the midst of prosperity.'
- Marcus Annaeus Seneca

'Malice drinks one-half of its own poison.'
- Marcus Annaeus Seneca

'Failure changes for the better, success for the worse.'
- Marcus Annaeus Seneca

'Not he who has little, but he who wishes more, is poor.'
- Marcus Annaeus Seneca

'A man can refrain from wanting what he has not, and cheerfully make the best of a bird in the hand.'
- Marcus Annaeus Seneca

'What is the proper limit for wealth? It is, first, to have what is necessary; and, second, to have what is enough.'
- Marcus Annaeus Seneca

'Whom they have injured, they also hate.'
- Marcus Annaeus Seneca

'He who receives a benefit with gratitude repays the first installment on his debt.'
- Marcus Annaeus Seneca

'Try to live the life of the good man who is more than content with what is allocated to him.'
- Marcus Aurelius

'Take full account of the excellencies which you possess, and in gratitude remember how you would hanker after them, if you had them not.'
- Marcus Aurelius

'I can pardon everybody's mistakes except my own.'
  - Marcus Porcius Cato

'The days are too short even for love; how can there be enough time for quarreling?'
  - Margaret Gatty

'Pain is no longer pain when it is past.'
  - Margaret Junkin Preston

'Life is the first gift, love is the second, and understanding the third.'
  - Marge Piercy

'We must give ourselves more earnestly and intelligently and generously than we have to the happy duty of appreciation.'
  - Mariana Griswold Van Rensselaer

'The enslaver is enslaved, the hater, harmed.'
  - Marianne Moore

'Joy is what happens to us when we allow ourselves to recognize how good things really are.'
  - Marianne Williamson

'Stretch out your hand! Let no human soul wait for a benediction.'
  - Marie Corelli

'Even a stopped clock is right twice a day.'
  - Marie von Ebner-Eschenbach

'Rage and bitterness do not foster femininity. They harden the heart and make the body sick.'
  - Marion Woodman

'Speak not against anyone whose burden you have not weighed yourself.'
  - Marion Zimmer Bradley

'The fragrance of the violet sheds on the heel that has crushed it.'
  - Mark Twain

'To be satisfied with what one has; that is wealth. As long as one sorely needs a certain additional amount, that man isn't rich.'
  - Mark Twain

'Once a woman has forgiven a man, she must not reheat his sins for breakfast.'
  - Marlene Dietrich

'There is a gigantic difference between earning a great deal of money and being rich.'
  - Marlene Dietrich

'Forgiveness is God's command.'
  - Martin Luther

'Reject hatred without hating.'
- Mary Baker Eddy

'Courage and clemency are equal virtues.'
- Mary Delariviere Manley

'In hatred as in love, we grow like the thing we brood upon. What we loathe, we graft into our very soul.'
- Mary Renault

'I am convinced, the longer I live, that life and its blessings are not so entirely unjustly distributed as when we are suffering greatly we are inclined to suppose.'
- Mary Todd Lincoln

'It made me gladsome to be getting some education, it being like a big window opening.'
- Mary Webb

'One is as one is, and the love that can't encompass both is a poor sort of love.'
- Marya Mannes

'Is there no end to this escalation of desire?'
- Marya Mannes

'Appreciation is yeast, lifting ordinary to extraordinary.'
- Mary-Ann Petro

'Is it so small a thing to have enjoyed the sun, to have lived light in the spring, to have loved, to have thought, to have done?'
- Matthew Arnold

'I thank Thee first because I was never robbed before; second, because although they took my purse they did not take my life; third, because although they took my all, it was not much; and fourth because it was I who was robbed, and not I who robbed.'
- Matthew Henry

'The one who deals the mortal blow receives the mortal wound.'
- Maude Parker

'Thanksgiving is a sure index of spiritual health.'
- Maurice Dametz

'There must be more to life than having everything.'
- Maurice Sendak

'Too many people miss the silver lining because they're expecting gold.'
- Maurice Setter

'Happiness always looks small while you hold it in your hands, but let it go, and you learn at once how big and precious it is.'
- Maxim Gorky

'If the only prayer you say in your whole life is "Thank you," that would suffice.'
- Meister Eckhart

'Her breasts and arms ached with the beauty of her own forgiveness.'
- Meridel Le Sueur

'If you want an accounting of your worth, count your friends.'
- Merry Browne

'In the country of the blind, the one-eyed man is king.'
- Michael Apostolius

'We are all of us richer than we think we are.'
- Michel de Montaigne

'What you have become is the price you paid to get what you used to want.'
- Mignon McLaughlin

'Let us forget and forgive injuries.'
- Miguel de Cervantes

'There are many excuses for the person who made the mistake of confounding money and wealth. Like many others they mistook the sign for the thing signified.'
- Millicent Garrett Fawcett

'By putting his hand around my neck, he slowly strangled himself.'
- Minako Ohba

'The weak can never forgive. Forgiveness is the attribute of the strong.'
- Mohandas Gandhi

'The human heart in its perversity finds it hard to escape hatred and revenge.'
- Moses Luzzatto

'After my mother's death, I began to see her as she had really been.... It was less like losing someone than discovering someone.'
- Nancy Hale

'Who is content with nothing possesses all things.'
- Nicolas Boileau

'Life is an adventure in forgiveness.'
- Norman Cousins

'When you pray for anyone you tend to modify your personal attitude toward him.'
- Norman Vincent Peale

'You can't appreciate home until you've left it, money till it's spent, your wife till she's joined a woman's club, nor Old Glory till you see it hanging on a broomstick on the shanty of a consul in a foreign town.'
- O. Henry

'Hatred is a passion requiring one hundred times the energy of love. Keep it for a cause, not an individual. Keep it for intolerance, injustice, stupidity. For hatred is the strength of the sensitive. Its power and its greatness depend on the selflessness '
- Olive Moore

'Philosophy ... should not pretend to increase our present stock, but make us economists of what we are possessed of.'
- Oliver Goldsmith

'Grateful for the blessing lent of simple tastes and mind content!'
- Oliver Wendell Holmes

'The man who thinks his wife, his baby, his house, his horse, his dog, and himself severely unequalled, is almost sure to be a good-humored person.'
- Oliver Wendell Holmes

'Keep a grateful journal. Every night, list five things that you are grateful for. What it will begin to do is change your perspective of your day and your life.'
- Oprah Winfrey

'You cannot hate other people without hating yourself.'
- Oprah Winfrey

'Always forgive your enemies; nothing annoys them so much.'
- Oscar Wilde

'The basis of optimism is sheer terror.'
- Oscar Wilde

'Happy the man who can count his sufferings.'
- Ovid

'Few love what they may have.'
- Ovid

'Today I forgive all those who have ever offended me. I give my love to all thirsty hearts, both to those who love me and to those who do not love me.'
- Paramahansa Yogananda

'Enjoy the successes that you have, and don't be too hard on yourself when you don't do well. Too many times we beat up on ourselves. Just relax and enjoy it.'
- Patty Sheehan

'A man with ambition and love for his blessings here on earth is ever so alive. Having been alive, it won't be so hard in the end to lie down and rest.'
- Pearl Bailey

'Love is an act of endless forgiveness, a tender look which becomes a habit.'
- Peter Ustinov

'It is manlike to punish but godlike to forgive.'
- Peter von Winter

'I seek the utmost pleasure and the least pain.'
- Plautus

'How unhappy is he who cannot forgive himself.'
- Publilius Syrus

'Avarice is as destitute of what it has as poverty is of what it has not.'
- Publilius Syrus

'The whole human race loses by every act of personal vengeance.'
- Rae Foley

'His heart was as great as the world, but there was no room in it to hold the memory of a wrong.'
- Ralph Waldo Emerson

'Want is a growing giant whom the coat of Have was never large enough to cover.'
- Ralph Waldo Emerson

'When I first open my eyes upon the morning meadows and look out upon the beautiful world, I thank God I am alive.'
- Ralph Waldo Emerson

'For everything you have missed, you have gained something else.'
- Ralph Waldo Emerson

'Forgiveness is the final form of love.'
- Reinhold Niebuhr

'May we never let the things we can't have, or don't have, spoil our enjoyment of the things we do have and can have.'
- Richard L. Evans

'Without forgiveness life is governed ... by an endless cycle of resentment and retaliation.'
- Robert Assaglioli

'Abandon your animosities and make your sons Americans!'
- Robert E. Lee

'Who covets more is evermore a slave.'
- Robert Herrick

'To forgive is the highest, most beautiful form of love. In return, you will receive untold peace and happiness.'
- Robert Muller

'If you count all your assets, you always show a profit.'
- Robert Quillen

'If the will remains in protest, it stays dependent on that which it is protesting against.'
- Rollo May

'Double-no, triple-our troubles and we'd still be better off than any other people on earth.'
- Ronald Reagan

'I've had an exciting life; I married for love and got a little money along with it.'
- Rose Fitzgerald Kennedy

'Birds sing after a storm; why shouldn't people feel as free to delight in whatever remains to them?'
- Rose Fitzgerald Kennedy

'The best things in life are appreciated most after they have been lost.'
- Roy L. Smith

'Each day comes bearing its own gifts. Untie the ribbons.'
- Ruth Ann Schabacker

'If thou covetest riches, ask not but for contentment, which is an immense treasure.'
- Sa'di

'Forgiveness is the remission of sins. For it is by this that what has been lost, and was found, is saved from being lost again.'
- Saint Augustine

'Many a man curses the rain that falls upon his head, and knows not that it brings abundance to drive away hunger.'
- Saint Basil

'It is in pardoning that we are pardoned.'
- Saint Francis of Assisi

'Money and time are the heaviest burdens of life, and the unhappiest of all mortals are those who have more of either than they know how to use.'
- Samuel Johnson

'The knowledge that something remains yet unenjoyed impairs our enjoyment of the good before us.'
- Samuel Johnson

'Life is a progress from want to want, not from enjoyment to enjoyment.'
- Samuel Johnson

'I have no riches but my thoughts. Yet these are wealth enough for me.'
- Sara Teasdale

'Nor need we power or splendor, wide hall or lordly dome; the good, the true, the tender-these form the wealth of home.'
- Sarah Josepha Hale

'Dwelling on the negative simply contributes to its power.'
- Shirley MacLaine

'Not the power to remember, but its very opposite, the power to forget, is a necessary condition for our existence.'
- Sholem Asch

'If we go down into ourselves, we find that we possess exactly what we desire.'
- Simone Weil

'Grace fills empty spaces, but it can only enter where there is a void to receive it, and it is grace itself which makes this void.'
- Simone Weil

'Fire destroys that which feeds it.'
- Simone Weil

'Content may dwell in all stations. To be low, but above contempt, may be high enough to be happy.'
- Sir Thomas Browne

'Life may be hard, but it's also wonderful.'
- Small Change

'If all misfortunes were laid in one common heap whence everyone must take an equal portion, most people would be contented to take their own and depart.'
- Socrates

'How many things there are which I do not want.'
- Socrates

'Nothing in excess.'
- Solon

'If there's no bread, cakes are very good.'
- Spanish proverb

'He who limps still walks.'
- Stanislaw Lee

'Over a period of time it's been driven home to me that I'm not going to be the most popular writer in the world, so I'm always happy when anything in any way is accepted.'
- Stephen Sondheim

'Jesus, please teach me to appreciate what I have before time forces me to appreciate what I had.'
- Susan L. Lenzkes

'There's no point in burying a hatchet if you're going to put up a marker on the site.'
- Sydney J. Harris

'I have gout, asthma, and seven other maladies, but am otherwise very well.'
- Sydney Smith

'Forgive others often, yourself never.'
- Syrus

'All fortune belongs to him who has a contented mind.'
- The Panchatantra

'Know all and you will pardon all.'
- Thomas a Kempis

'We should learn, by reflection on the misfortunes of others, that there is nothing singular in those which befall ourselves.'
- Thomas Fitzosborne

'He that cannot forgive others breaks the bridge over which he must pass himself; for every man has need to be forgiven.'
- Thomas Fuller

'There is no banquet but some dislike something in it.'
- Thomas Fuller

'He is not poor that hath not much, but he that craves much.'
- Thomas Fuller

'Better a little fire to warm us than a great one to burn us.'
- Thomas Fuller

'He is rich that is satisfied.'
- Thomas Fuller

'Happiness is not being pained in body, or troubled in mind.'
- Thomas Jefferson

'Greediness of getting more, deprives ... the enjoyment of what it had got.'
- Thomas Sprat

'The stupid neither forgive nor forget; the naive forgive and forget; the wise forgive, but do not forget.'
- Thomas Szasz

'An easy thing, O Power Divine, To thank thee for these gifts of Thine, For summer's sunshine, winter's snow, For hearts that kindle, thoughts that glow; But when shall I attain to this- To thank Thee for the things I miss?'
- Thomas W. Higginson

'Moderate desires constitute a character fitted to acquire all the good which the world can yield. He who has this character is prepared, in whatever situation he is, therewith to be content and has learned the science of being happy.'
- Timothy Dwight

'There are men who are happy without knowing it.'
- Vauvenargues

'If we get everything that we want, we will soon want nothing that we get.'
- Vernon Luchies

'If you would but exchange places with the other fellow, how much more you could appreciate your own position.'
- Victor E. Gardner

'Hate is not a good counselor.'
- Victoria Wolff

'Reconciliation is more beautiful than victory.'
- Violeta Barrios de Chamorro

'Too happy would you be, did ye but know your own advantages!'
- Virgil

'To every disadvantage there is a corresponding advantage.'
- W. Clement Stone

'Much unhappiness results from our inability to remember the nice things that happen to us.'
- W. N. Rieger

'Not what we say about our blessings, but how we use them, is the true measure of our thanksgiving.'
- W. T. Purkiser

'Whoever is not in his coffin and the dark grave, let him know he has enough.'
- Walt Whitman

'We are no longer happy so soon as we wish to be happier.'
- Walter Savage Landor

'I tell you, there is no such thing as creative hate!'
- Willa Cather

'God gave you a gift of 86,400 seconds today. Have you used one to say "thank you"?'
- William A. Ward

'You never know what is enough unless you know what is more than enough.'
- William Blake

'The cut worm forgives the plow.'
- William Blake

'To carry a grudge is like being stung to death by one bee.'
- William H. Walton

'Anyone is to be pitied who has just sense enough to perceive his deficiencies.'
- William Hazlitt

'The greatest saint in the world is not he who prays most or fasts most; it is not he who gives alms, or is most eminent for temperance, chastity or justice. It is he who is most thankful to God.'
- William Law

'That daily life is really good one appreciates when one wakes from a horrible dream, or when one takes the first outing after a sickness. Why not realize it now?'
- William Lyon Phelps

'The difficulties, hardships and trials of life, the obstacles ... are positive blessings. They knit the muscles more firmly, and teach self-reliance.'
- William Matthews

'One well-cultivated talent, deepened and enlarged, is worth one hundred shallow faculties.'
- William Matthews

'The average man is rich enough when he has a little more than he has got.'
- William Ralph Inge

'Be grateful for yourself... be thankful.'
- William Saroyan

'Poor and content is rich, and rich enough.'
- William Shakespeare

'He is well paid that is well satisfied.'
- William Shakespeare

'Happy thou art not; for what thou hast not, still thou striv'est to get; and what thou hast, forget'est.'
- William Shakespeare

'Let me embrace thee, sour adversity, for wise men say it is the wisest course.'
- William Shakespeare

'My crown is called content, a crown that seldom kings enjoy.'
- William Shakespeare

'Independence may be found in comparative as well as in absolute abundance; I mean where a person contracts his desires within the limits of his fortune.'
- William Shenstone

'Every dog has its day, but it's not every dog that knows when he's having it.'
- Winifred Gordon

'The talent for being happy is appreciating and liking what you have, instead of what you don't have.'
- Woody Allen

'Forgetting is the cost of living cheerfully.'
- Zoe Akins

FRIENDSHIP

'Nothing is more limiting than a closed circle of acquaintanceship where every avenue of conversation has been explored and social exchanges are fixed in a known routine.'
- A. J. Cronin

'A word of advice, don't give it.'
- A. J. Volicos

'Acquaintance I would have, but when it depends not on the number, but the choice of friends.'
- Abraham Cowley

'I desire so to conduct the affairs of this administration that if at the end ... I have lost every other friend on earth, I shall at least have one friend left, and that friend shall be down inside of me.'
- Abraham Lincoln

'Don't believe your friends when they ask you to be honest with them. All they really want is to be maintained in the good opinion they have of themselves.'
- Albert Camus

'To associate with other like-minded people in small purposeful groups is for the great majority of men and women a source of profound psychological satisfaction.'
- Aldous Huxley

'There is nothing meritorious but virtue and friendship.'
- Alexander Pope

'Every organism requires an environment of friends, partly to shield it from violent changes, and partly to supply it with its wants.'
- Alfred North Whitehead

'If it's very painful for you to criticize your friends-you're safe in doing it. But if you take the slightest pleasure in it, that's the time to hold your tongue.'
- Alice Duer Miller

'No person is your friend who demands your silence, or denies your right to grow.'
- Alice Walker

'Is solace anywhere more comforting than in the arms of sisters?'
- Alice Walker

'If I made it, it's half because I was game enough to take a lot of punishment along the way and half because there were a lot of people who cared enough to help me.'
- Althea Gibson

'The great difference between voyages rests not in ships but in the people you meet on them.'
- Amelia Barr

'Friends Make Life Bearable But I have certainty enough, For I am sure of you.'
   - Amelia Barr

'What I cannot love, I overlook.'
   - Anais Nin

'Each friend represents a world in us, a world possibly not born until they arrive, and it is only by this meeting that a new world is born.'
   - Anais Nin

'[Families] are made to make you forget yourself occasionally, so that the beautiful balance of life is not destroyed.'
   - Anais Nin

'I cannot concentrate all my friendship on any single one of my friends because no one is complete enough in himself.'
   - Anais Nin

'One out of four people in this country is mentally imbalanced. Think of your three closest friends and if they seem okay, then you're the one.'
   - Ann Landers

'Fond as we are of our loved ones, there comes at times during their absence an unexplained peace.'
   - Ann Shaw

'If ever two were one, then surely we. If ever man were loved by wife, then thee.'
   - Anne Bradstreet

'The loneliness you get by the sea is personal and alive. It doesn't subdue you and make you feel abject. It's stimulating loneliness.'
   - Anne Morrow Lindbergh

'There's no friend like someone who has known you since you were five.'
   - Anne Stevenson

'We challenge one another to be funnier and smarter. ... It's the way friends make love to one another.'
   - Annie Gottlieb

A true friend is the best possession.'
   - Anonymous

'The rich know not who is his friend.'
   - Anonymous

'Love your friend with his fault.'
   - Anonymous

'The best rule of friendship is to keep your heart a little softer than your head.'
- Anonymous

'Books and friends should be few but good.'
- Anonymous

'Keep good men company, and you shall be of their number.'
- Anonymous

'Good company upon the road is the shortest cut.'
- Anonymous

'As the psychiatrist said to the cannibal at the end of a session: "Your problem is easy you're just fed up with people."'
- Anonymous

'The company makes the feast.'
- Anonymous

'One enemy is too many; a hundred friends too few.'
- Anonymous

'Friendship is a plant which must be often watered.'
- Anonymous

'Friends come and go, enemies linger.'
- Anonymous

'A man is known by the company he keeps.'
- Anonymous

'With friends like you - who needs enemas.'
- Anonymous

'A hedge between keeps friendships green.'
- Anonymous

'There are two kinds of people in the world: those who come into a room and say, "Here I am!" and those who come in and say, "Oh, there you are."'
- Anonymous

'Sudden friendship, sure repentance.'
- Anonymous

'To have a good friend is one of the highest delights of life; to be a good friend is one of the noblest and most difficult undertakings.'
- Anonymous

'When good cheer is lacking, our friends will be packing.'
- Anonymous

'If we were all given by magic the power to read each other's thoughts, I suppose the first effect would be to dissolve all friendships.'
- Anonymous

'He that lies down with dogs shall rise up with fleas.'
- Anonymous

'Friendship increases in visiting friends, but not in visiting them too often.'
- Anonymous

'The best mirror is an old friend.'
- Anonymous

'There is no physician like a true friend.'
- Anonymous

'Friends are folks who excuse you when you have made a fool of yourself.'
- Anonymous

'A real friend helps us think our best thoughts, do our noblest deeds, be our finest selves.'
- Anonymous

'Have but few friends, though many acquaintances.'
- Anonymous

'There are only two people who can tell you the truth about yourself-an enemy who has lost his temper and a friend who loves you dearly.'
- Antisthenes

'Man is a knot, a web, a mesh into which relationships are tied. Only those relationships matter.'
- Antoine de Saint-Exupery

'There is no hope or joy except in human relations.'
- Antoine de Saint-Exupery

'A new friend is like new wine; when it has aged you will drink it with pleasure.'
- Apocrypha

'A faithful friend is the medicine of life.'
- Apocrypha

'A wise man associating with the vicious becomes an idiot; a dog traveling with good men becomes a rational being.'
- Arab proverb

'Without friends no one would choose to live, though he had all other goods.'
- Aristotle

'Wishing to be friends is quick work, but friendship is a slow-ripening fruit.'
- Aristotle

'In poverty and other misfortunes of life, true friends are a sure refuge.'
- Aristotle

'Between friends there is no need of justice.'
- Aristotle

'We should behave to our friends as we would wish our friends to behave to us.'
- Aristotle

'Friends are an aid to the young, to guard them from error; to the elderly, to attend to their wants and to supplement their failing power of Taking Action; to those in the prime of life, to assist them to noble deeds.'
- Aristotle

'My best friend is the man who in wishing me well wishes it for my sake.'
- Aristotle

'Trouble is a sieve through which we sift our acquaintances. Those too big to pass through are our friends.'
- Arlene Francis

'It is well, when judging a friend, to remember that he is judging you with the same godlike and superior impartiality.'
- Arnold Bennett

'A loyal friend laughs at your jokes when they're not so good, and sympathizes with your problems when they're not so bad.'
- Arnold Glasow

'A good friend can tell you what is the matter with you in a minute. He may not seem such a good friend after telling.'
- Arthur Brisbane

'I never enter a new company without the hope that I may discover a friend, perhaps the friend, sitting there with an expectant smile. That hope survives a thousand disappointments.'
- Arthur Christopher Benson

'No greater burden can be born by an individual than to know none who cares or understands.'
- Arthur H. Stainback

'I observed once to Goethe ... that when a friend is with us we do not think the same of him as when he is away. He replied, "Yes! because the absent friend is yourself, and he exists only in your head;

whereas the friend who is present has an individualit'
  - Arthur Schopenhauer

'Friendship is a word the very sight of which in print makes the heart warm.'
  - Augustine Birrell

'A home-made friend wears longer than one you buy in the market.'
  - Austin O'Malley

'The way to make a true friend is to be one. Friendship implies loyalty, esteem, cordiality, sympathy, affection, readiness to aid, to help, to stick, to fight for, if need be. ... Radiate friendship and it will return sevenfold.'
  - B. C. Forbes

'The real friend is he or she who can share all our sorrow and double our joys.'
  - B. C. Forbes

'Friends are a second existence.'
  - Baltasar Gracian

'There is no wilderness like a life without friends; friendship multiplies blessings and minimizes misfortunes; it is a unique remedy against adversity, and it soothes the soul.'
  - Baltasar Gracian

'Friendship multiplies the good of life and divides the evil. Tis the sole remedy against misfortune, the very ventilation of the soul.'
  - Baltasar Gracian

'I think togetherness is a very important ingredient to family life. It's a cliché and we use it too much but I think for a husband and wife, the way to stay close is to do things together and share.'
  - Barbara Bush

'A new acquaintance is like a new book. I prefer it, even if bad, to a classic.'
  - Benjamin Disraeli

'There is a magic in the memory of a schoolboy friendship. It softens the heart, and even affects the nervous system of those who have no heart.'
  - Benjamin Disraeli

'Be slow in choosing a friend, slower in changing.'
  - Benjamin Franklin

'A sense of duty is useful in work, but offensive in personal relations. People wish to be liked, not endured with patient resignation.'
  - Bertrand Russell

'Keep the other person's well-being in mind when you feel an attack of soul-purging truth coming on.'
  - Betty White

'Faithful are the wounds of a friend, but the kisses of an enemy are deceitful.'
- Bible

'Iron sharpeneth man; so a man sharpeneth the countenance of his friend.'
- Bible

'Saul and Jonathan were lovely and pleasant in their lives, and in their death they were not divided.'
- Bible

'Thine own friend, and thy father's friend, forsake not.'
- Bible

'Greater love hath no man than this, that a man lay down his life for his friends.'
- Bible

'Forsake not an old friend, for the new is not comparable to him; a new friend is as new wine.'
- Bible

'We are both great men, but I have succeeded better in keeping it a profound secret than he has.'
- Bill Nye

'If I don't have friends, then I ain't nothing.'
- Billie Holiday

'If we all told what we know of one another, there would not be four friends in the world'
- Blaise Pascal

'The two most important things in life are good friends and a strong bull pen.'
- Bob Lemon

'My friend thought he was not gonna make it. Then he started thinking positive. Now he's positive he's not gonna make it.'
- Brother Sammy Shore

'True friends ... face in the same direction, toward common projects, interests, goals.'
- C. S. Lewis

'The man who trusts other men will make fewer mistakes than he who distrusts them.'
- Camillo Di Cavour

'Brotherhood is the very price and condition of man's survival.'
- Carlos P. Romulo

'And we find at the end of a perfect day, The soul of a friend we've made.'
- Carrie Jacobs Bond

'Writers seldom choose as friends those self-contained characters who are never in trouble, never unhappy or ill, never make mistakes, and always count their change when it is handed to them.'
- Catherine Drinker Bowen

'Most of our misfortunes are comments of our friends upon them.'
- Charles Caleb Colton

'True friendship is like sound health; the value of it is seldom known until it be lost.'
- Charles Caleb Colton

'The wise man's ... friendship is capable of going to extremes with many people, evoked as it is by many qualities.'
- Charles Dudley Warner

'Five years from now you will be pretty much the same as you are today except for two things: the books you read and the people you get close to.'
- Charles Jones

''Tis the privilege of friendship to talk nonsense, and have her nonsense respected.'
- Charles Lamb

'Lead the life that will make you kindly and friendly to everyone about you, and you will be surprised what a happy life you will live.'
- Charles M. Schwab

'If we would build on a sure foundation in friendship, we must love friends for their sake rather than for our own.'
- Charlotte Bronte

'I can trust my friends. ... These people force me to examine myself, encourage me to grow.'
- Cher

'Do not remove a fly from your friend's forehead with a hatchet.'
- Chinese proverb

'It is easier to visit friends than to live with them.'
- Chinese proverb

'Man's best support is a very dear friend.'
- Cicero

'Friendship was given by nature to be an assistant to virtue, not a companion in vice.'
- Cicero

'A friend is, as it were, a second self.'
- Cicero

'Friendship is nothing else than an accord in all things, human and divine, conjoined with mutual goodwill and affection.'
- Cicero

'Friendship makes prosperity more brilliant, and lightens adversity by dividing and sharing it.'
- Cicero

'Loyalty is what we seek in friendship.'
   - Cicero

'As in the case of wines that improve with age, the oldest friendships ought to be the most delightful.'
   - Cicero

'The shifts of fortune test the reliability of friends.'
   - Cicero

'Women rely on friends. ... That's where we draw sustenance and find safety. We can count on our women friends when we need a good laugh or a good cry.'
   - Cokie Roberts

'Parents are friends that life gives us; friends are parents that the heart chooses.'
   - Comtesse Diane

'Have no friends not equal to yourself.'
   - Confucius

'Though Love be deeper, Friendship is more wide.'
   - Corinne Roosevelt Robinson

'The friendships which last are those wherein each friend respects the other's dignity to the point of not really wanting anything from him.'
   - Cyril Connolly

'Do not protect yourself by a fence, but rather by your friends.'
   - Czech proverb

'Can you understand how cruelly I feel the lack of friends who will believe in me a bit?'
   - D. H. Lawrence

'Friendship needs no words-it is solitude delivered from the anguish of loneliness.'
   - Dag Hammarskjold

'Those who cannot give friendship will rarely receive it, and never hold it.'
   - Dagobert D. Runes

'Half the secret of getting along with people is consideration of their values; the other half is tolerance in one's own views.'
   - Daniel Frohman

'Friendship is neither a formality nor a mode: it is rather a life.'
   - David Grayson

'No real friendship is ever made without an initial clashing which discloses the metal of each to each.'
   - David Grayson

'The essence of true friendship is to make allowance for another's little lapses.'
- David Storey

'In prosperity friends do not leave you unless desired, whereas in adversity they stay away of their own accord.'
- Demetrius

'Trouble shared is trouble halved.'
- Dorothy L. Sayers

'Constant use had not worn ragged the fabric of their friendship.'
- Dorothy Parker

'Scratch a lover, and find a foe.'
- Dorothy Parker

'In reality, we are still children. We want to find a playmate for our thoughts and feelings.'
- Dr. Wilhelm Stekhel

'Our happiness in this world depends on the affections we are able to inspire.'
- Duchess Prazlin

'When one friend washes another, both become clean.'
- Dutch proverb

'Probably no man ever had a friend he did not dislike a little; we are all so constituted by nature that no one can possibly entirely approve of us.'
- Edgar Watson Howe

'Friends are like a pleasant park where you wish to go; while you may enjoy the flowers, you may not eat them.'
- Edgar Watson Howe

'Instead of loving your enemies, treat your friends a little better.'
- Edgar Watson Howe

'I suppose there is one friend in the life of each of us who seems not a separate person, however dear and beloved, but an expansion, an interpretation, of one's self.'
- Edith Wharton

'Friends are the family we choose for ourselves.'
- Edna Buchanan

'My heart is warm with the friends I make, And better friends I'll not be knowing; Yet there isn't a train I wouldn't take, No matter where it's going.'
- Edna St. Vincent Millay

'Friendship, like credit, is highest where it is not used.'
- Elbert Hubbard

'Beware of the danger signals that flag problems: silence, secretiveness, or sudden outburst.'
- Eleanor H. Porter

'Friendship with oneself is all-important, because without it one cannot be friends with anyone else.'
- Eleanor Roosevelt

'A cheer, then, for the noblest breast That fears not danger's post; And like the lifeboat, proves a friend, When friends are wanted most.'
- Eliza Cook

'My friend and I have built a wall Between us thick and wide: The stones of it are laid in scorn And plastered high with pride.'
- Elizabeth Cutter Morrow

'The desire to be and have a sister is a primitive and profound one that may have everything or nothing to do with the family a woman is born to. It is a desire to know and be known by someone who shares blood and body, history and dreams.'
- Elizabeth Fishel

'Sisters define their rivalry in terms of competition for the gold cup of parental love. It is never perceived as a cup which runneth over, rather a finite vessel from which the more one sister drinks, the less is left over for the others.'
- Elizabeth Fishel

'Both within the family and without, our sisters hold up our mirrors: our images of who we are and of who we can dare to become.'
- Elizabeth Fishel

'The most beautiful discovery true friends make is that they can grow separately without growing apart.'
- Elizabeth Foley

'The richer your friends, the more they will cost you.'
- Elizabeth Marbury

'The particular human chain we're a part of is central to our individual identity.'
- Elizabeth Stone

'We flatter those we scarcely know, We please the fleeting guest, And deal full many a thoughtless blow To those who love us best.'
- Ella Wheeler Wilcox

'Laugh, and the world laughs with you; weep and you weep alone.'
- Ella Wheeler Wilcox

'All love that has not friendship for its base, Is like a mansion built upon the sand.'
- Ella Wheeler Wilcox

'There is only one thing better than making a new friend, and that is keeping an old one.'
- Elmer G. Letterman

'Here's a toast to someone who's truly a best friend - a person who goes around telling good things behind your back.'
- Elmer Pasta

'Many a person has held close, throughout their entire lives, two friends that always remained strange to one another, because one of them attracted by virtue of similarity, the other by difference.'
- Emil Ludwig

'Love is like the wild-rose briar; Friendship is like the holly-tree. The holly is dark when the rose briar blooms, But which will bloom most constantly?'
- Emily Bronte

'My only sketch, profile, of heaven is a large blue sky, and larger than the biggest I have seen in June- and in it are my friends-every one of them.'
- Emily Dickinson

'It is not so much our friends' help that helps us, as the confidence of their help.'
- Epicurus

'He does good to himself who does good to his friend.'
- Erasmus

'Nothing is ever lost by courtesy. It is the cheapest of pleasures, costs nothing, and conveys much. It pleases him who gives and receives and thus, like mercy, is twice blessed.'
- Erastus Wiman

'Advice is what we ask for when we already know the answer but wish we didn't.'
- Erica Jong

'You hear a lot of dialogue on the death of the American family. Families aren't dying. They're merging into big conglomerates.'
- Erma Bombeck

'The best time to make friends is before you need them.'
- Ethel Barrymore

'I would prefer as a friend a good man who is ignorant than one more clever who is evil, too.'
- Euripides

'Every man is like the company he is wont to keep.'
- Euripides

'Real friendship is shown in times of trouble; prosperity is full of friends.'
- Euripides

'1 loathe a friend ... who takes his friend's prosperity but will not voyage with him in his grief.'
- Euripides

'Friendship is a strong and habitual inclination in two persons to promote the good and happiness of one another.'
- Eustace Budgell

'Friends are relatives you make for yourself.'
- Eustache Deschamps

'We cherish our friends not for their ability to amuse us, but for ours to amuse them.'
- Evelyn Waugh

'We cherish our friends not for their ability to amuse us but for ours to amuse them.'
- Evelyn Waugh

'Character builds slowly, but it can be torn down with incredible swiftness.'
- Faith Baldwin

'Affinities are rare. They come but a few times in a life. It is awful to risk losing one when it arrives.'
- Florence H. Winterburn

'I have learned that to have a good friend is the purest of all God's gifts, for it is a love that has no exchange of payment.'
- Frances Farmer

'A friend can tell you things you don't want to tell yourself.'
- Frances Ward Weller

'Only friends will tell you the truths you need to hear to make ... your life bearable.'
- Francine Du Plessix Gray

'The worst solitude is to be destitute of sincere friendship.'
- Francis Bacon

'There is no man that imparteth his joys to his friends, but he joyeth the more; and no man that imparteth his griefs to his friends, but he grieveth the less.'
- Francis Bacon

'The best preservative to keep the mind in health is the faithful admonition of a friend.'
- Francis Bacon

'Those that lack friends to open themselves unto are cannibals of their own hearts.'
- Francis Bacon

'We need two kinds of acquaintances, one to complain to, while we boast to the others. -Logan Pearsall Smith No one person can possibly combine all the elements supposed to make up what everyone means by friendship.'
- Francis Marion Crawford

'That friendship will not continue to the end which is begun for an end.'
- Francis Quarles

'A true friend is the greatest of all blessings, and that which we take the least care of all to acquire.'
- Francois de La Rochefoucauld

'Friendship is only a reciprocal conciliation of interests.'
- Francois de La Rochefoucauld

'It is more shameful to distrust our friends than to be deceived by them.'
- Francois de La Rochefoucauld

'I want no men around me who have not the knack of making friends.'
- Frank A. Vanderlip

'Many a friendship-long, loyal, and self-sacrificing-rested at first upon no thicker a foundation than a kind word.'
- Frederick W. Faber

'Tell me whom you frequent, and I will tell you who you are.'
- French proverb

'A friend should be a master at guessing and keeping still.'
- Friedrich Nietzsche

'Women can form a friendship with a man very well; but to preserve it, a slight physical antipathy most probably helps.'
- Friedrich Nietzsche

'Sometimes we owe a friend to the lucky circumstance that we give him no cause for envy.'
- Friedrich Nietzsche

'Shared joys make a friend, not shared sufferings.'
- Friedrich Nietzsche

'My philosophy is: anyone or anything that gives you knowledge inspires you.'
- Gabrielle Reece

'One is taught by experience to put a premium on those few people who can appreciate you for what you are.'
- Gail Godwin

'She is one of my best friends. Why, I've known her ever since we were the same age.'
- Galen Cooper

'Old friends, we say, are best, when some sudden disillusionment shakes our faith in a new comrade.'
- Gelett Burgess

'The only service a friend can really render is to keep up your courage by holding up to you a mirror in which you can see a noble image of yourself.'
  - George Bernard Shaw

'Give me the avowed, the erect and manly foe, Bold I can meet, perhaps may turn the blow; But of all plagues, good Heaven, thy wrath can send, Save, oh save me from the candid friend!'
  - George Canning

'Flatterers look like friends, as wolves like dogs.'
  - George Chapman

'I am quite sure that no friendship yields its true pleasure and nobility of nature without frequent communication, sympathy and service.'
  - George E. Woodberry

'Best friend, my well-spring in the wilderness!'
  - George Eliot

'Animals are such agreeable friends- they ask no questions, they pass no criticisms.'
  - George Eliot

'Wear a smile and have friends; wear a scowl and have wrinkles.'
  - George Eliot

'Perhaps the most delightful friendships are those in which there is much agreement, much disputation, and yet more personal liking.'
  - George Eliot

'Love demands infinitely less than friendship.'
  - George Jean Nathan

'Fortify yourself with a flock of friends! You can select them at random, write to one, dine with one, visit one, or take your problems to one. There is always at least one who will understand, inspire, and give you the lift you may need at the time.'
  - George Matthew Adams

'One's friends are that part of the human race with which one can be human.'
  - George Santayana

'Friendship is almost always the union of a part of one mind with a part of another; people are friends in spots.'
  - George Santayana

'It is characteristic of spontaneous friendship to take on, without enquiry and almost at first sight, the unseen doings and unspoken sentiments of our friends; the part known gives us evidence enough that the unknown part cannot be much amiss.'
  - George Santayana

'To cement a new friendship, especially between foreigners or persons of a different social world, a spark with which both were secretly charged must fly from person to person, and cut across the accidents of place and time.'
- George Santayana

'Be courteous to all, but intimate with few; and let those few be well-tried before you give them your confidence.'
- George Washington

'True friendship is a plant of slow growth and must undergo and withstand the shocks of adversity before it is entitled to the appellation.'
- George Washington

'Taking Actions, not words, are the true criterion of the attachment of friends.'
- George Washington

'Associate yourself with men of good quality if you esteem your own reputation, for 'tis better to be alone than in bad company.'
- George Washington

'I have always differentiated between two types of friends; those who want proofs of friendship, and those who do not. One kind loves me for myself, and the others for themselves.'
- Gerard de Nerval

'Time's passage through the memory is like molten glass that can be opaque or crystallize at any given moment at will: a thousand days are melted into one conversation, one glance, one hurt, and one hurt can be shattered and sprinkled over a thousand.'
- Gloria Naylor

'Old as she was, she still missed her daddy sometimes.'
- Gloria Naylor

'That is the best-to laugh with someone because you think the same things are funny.'
- Gloria Vanderbilt

'The lion is ashamed, it's true, when he hunts with the fox.'
- Gotthold Ephraim Lessing

'To those who know thee not, no words can paint! And those who know thee, know all words are faint!'
- Hannah Moore

'Confidence is the foundation of friendship. If we give it, we will receive it.'
- Harry E. Humphreys

'Today a man discovered gold and fame, Another flew the stormy seas; Another set an unarmed world aflame, One found the germ of a disease. But what high fates my path attend for I-today-I found a friend.'
- Helen Barker Parker

'Now and then one sees a face which has kept its smile pure and undefiled. Such a smile transfigures; such a smile, if the artful but know it, is the greatest weapon a face can have.'
  - Helen Hunt Jackson

'My friends have made the story of my life. In a thousand ways they have turned my limitations into beautiful privileges, and enabled me to walk serene and happy in the shadow cast by my deprivation.'
  - Helen Keller

'A friend in power is a friend lost.'
  - Henry Adams

'Friendship needs a certain parallelism of life, a community of thought, a rivalry of aim.'
  - Henry Adams

'Accident counts for much in companionship, as in marriage.'
  - Henry Adams

'There is not so good an understanding between any two, but the exposure by the one of a serious fault in the other will produce a misunderstanding in proportion to its heinousness.'
  - Henry David Thoreau

'The language of friendship is not words, but meanings.'
  - Henry David Thoreau

'How often we find ourselves turning our backs on our actual friends, that we may go and meet their ideal cousins.'
  - Henry David Thoreau

'A man cannot be said to succeed in this life who does not satisfy one friend.'
  - Henry David Thoreau

'Ah, how good it feels! The hand of an old friend.'
  - Henry Wadsworth Longfellow

'There's nothing worth the wear of winning but laughter, and the love of friends.'
  - Hilaire Belloc

'A man becomes like those whose society he loves.'
  - Hindu proverb

'Since we are mortal, friendships are best kept to a moderate level, rather than sharing the very depths of our souls.'
  - Hippolytus

'A sympathetic friend can be quite dear as a brother.'
  - Homer

'Two friends-two bodies with one soul inspired.'
  - Homer

'Old friends are the great blessing of one's later years. ... They have a memory of the same events and have the same mode of thinking.'
- Horace Walpole

'In a friend you find a second self.'
- Isabelle Norto

'Good company and good discourse are the very sinews of virtue.'
- Izaak Walton

'When our friends are alive, we see the good qualities they lack; dead, we remember only those they possessed.'
- J. Petit-Senn

'Chance makes our parents, but choice makes our friends.'
- Jacques Delille

'We cannot tell the precise moment when friendship is formed. As in filling a vessel drop by drop, there is at last a drop which makes it run over. So in a series of kindnesses there is, at last, one which makes the heart run over.'
- James Boswell

'Should auld acquaintances be forgot, And never brought to mind? Should auld acquaintance be forgot, And days o'auld lang syne?'
- James Drummond Burns

'Friendship without self-interest is one of the rare and beautiful things of life.'
- James F. Byrnes

'I have come to esteem history as a component of friendships. In my case at least friendships are not igneous but sedimentary.'
- Jane Howard

'Call it a clan, call it a network, call it a tribe, call it a family: Whatever you call it, whoever you are, you need one.'
- Jane Howard

'Who ran to help me when I fell And would some pretty story tell Or kiss the place to make it well? My mother.'
- Jane Taylor

'Nothing wounds a friend like a want of confidence.'
- Jean Baptiste LaCordaire

'Two persons cannot long be friends if they cannot forgive each other's little failings.'
- Jean de la Bruyere

'What a wonderful thing it is to have a good friend. He identifies your innermost desires, and spares you the embarrassment of disclosing them to him yourself.'
   - Jean de la Fontaine

'Seek those who find your road agreeable, your personality and mind stimulating, your philosophy acceptable, and your experiences helpful. Let those who do not, seek their own kind.'
   - Jean-Henri Fabre

'Treat your fiends as you do your picture, and place them in their best light.'
   - Jennie Jerome Churchill

'He [Winston Churchill] has a future and I have a past, so we should be all right.'
   - Jennie Jerome Churchill

'Treat your friends as you do your picture, and place them in their best light.'
   - Jennie Jerome Churchill

'The family is the building block for whatever solidarity there is in society.'
   - Jill Ruckelshaus

'The easiest kind of relationship for me is with ten thousand people. The hardest is with one.'
   - Joan Baez

'It is better to be deceived by one's friends than to deceive them.'
   - Johann von Goethe

'Go to the place where the thing you wish to know is native; your best teacher is there. ... You acquire a language most readily in the country where it is spoken, you study mineralogy best among miners, and so with everything else.'
   - Johann von Goethe

'My life seems to have become suddenly hollow, and I do not know what is hanging over me. I cannot even put the shadow that has fallen on me into words. At least into written words. I would give a great deal for a friend's voice.'
   - John Addington Symonds

'In prosperity our friends know us; in adversity we know our friends.'
   - John Churton Collins

'To accept a favor from a friend is to confer one.'
   - John Churton Collins

'Friendships, like marriages, are dependent on avoiding the unforgivable.'
   - John D. MacDonald

'Who friendship with a knave hath made, is judged a partner in the trade.'
   - John Gay

'Make all good men your well-wishers, and then, in the years' steady sifting, some of them will turn into friends.'
- John Hay

'Friends are the sunshine of life.'
- John Hay

'It takes a long time to grow an old friend.'
- John Leonard

'A cheerful friend is like a sunny day, which sheds its brightness on all around.'
- John Lubbock

'I am learning to live close to the lives of my friends without ever seeing them. No miles of any measurement can separate your soul from mine.'
- John Muir

'Any man will usually get from other men what he is expecting from them. If he is looking for friendship, he will likely receive it. If his attitude is that of indifference, it will beget indifference. And if a man is looking for a fight, he will in all li'
- John Richelsen

'Every time I paint a portrait I lose a friend.'
- John Singer Sargent

'111 company is like a dog, who dirts those most whom he loves best.'
- Jonathan Swift

'True happiness ... arises, in the first place, from the enjoyment of one's self, and in the next from the friendship and conversation of a few select companions.'
- Joseph Addison

'When my friends lack an eye, I look at them in profile.'
- Joseph Joubert

'Friendship admits of difference of character, as love does that of sex.'
- Joseph Roux

'We call that person who has lost his father, an orphan; and a widower, that man who has lost his wife. But that man who has known that immense unhappiness of losing a friend, by what name do we call him? Here every language holds its peace in impotence.'
- Joseph Roux

'Remember that you are all people and that all people are you.'
- Joy Harjo

'We have no more right to put our discordant states of mind into the lives of those around us and rob them of their sunshine and brightness than we have to enter their houses and steal their silverware.'
- Julia Seton

'The only way not to break a friendship is not to drop it.'
- Julie Holz

'Nobody who is afraid of laughing, and heartily too, at his friend can be said to have a true and thorough love for him.'
- Julius Charles Hare

'Friendship is always a sweet responsibility, never an opportunity.'
- Kahlil Gibran

'The support of one's personality is friends. A part of one's self and a real foundation and existence.'
- Katharine Butler Hathaway

'I always felt that the great high privilege, relief and comfort of friendship was that one had to explain nothing.'
- Katherine Mansfield

'I am treating you as my friend, asking you to share my present minuses in the hope I can ask you to share my future pluses.'
- Katherine Mansfield

'Friendship is an art, and very few persons are born with a natural gift for it.'
- Kathleen Norris

'You never know how many friends you have until you rent a cottage at the beach.'
- Kraig Kristofferson

'It is not enough to succeed, a friend must fail.'
- La Rochefoucauld

'It is not the services we render them, but the services they render us, that attaches people to us.'
- Labiche et Martin

'It was such a joy to see thee. I wish I could tell how much thee is to my life. I always turn to thee as a sort of rest.'
- Lady Henry Somerset

'If you always live with those who are lame, you will yourself learn to limp.'
- Latin proverb

'You can always tell a real friend; when you've made a fool of yourself he doesn't feel you've done a permanent job.'
- Laurence J. Peter

'We need old friends to help us grow old and new friends to help us stay young.'
- Letty Cottin Pogrebin

'Friendships aren't perfect and yet they are very precious. For me, not expecting perfection all in one place was a great release.'
- Letty Cottin Pogrebin

'[My father] was generous with his affection, given to great, awkward, engulfing hugs, and I can remember so clearly the smell of his hugs, all starched shirt, tobacco, Old Spice, and Cutty Sark. Sometimes I think I've never been properly hugged since.'
- Linda Ellerbee

'We all need somebody to talk to. It would be good if we talked ... not just pitter-patter, but real talk. We shouldn't be so afraid, because most people really like this contact; that you show you are vulnerable makes them free to be vulnerable.'
- Liv Ullmann

'We need new friends. Some of us are cannibals who have eaten their old friends up; others must have ever-renewed audiences before whom to re-enact an ideal version of their lives.'
- Logan Pearsall Smith

'Don't tell your friends their social faults; they will cure the fault and never forgive you.'
- Logan Pearsall Smith

'Plant a seed of friendship; reap a bouquet of happiness.'
- Lois L. Kaufman

'Friendship is love without his wings!'
- Lord Byron

'Distrust all those who love you extremely upon a very slight acquaintance and without any viable reason.'
- Lord Chesterfield

'Friendship cannot live with ceremony, nor without civility.'
- Lord Halifax

'Nature has been for me, for as long as I remember, a source of solace, inspiration, adventure, and delight; a home, a teacher, a companion.'
- Lorraine Anderson

'"Stay" is a charming word in a friend's vocabulary.'
- Louisa May Alcott

'Female friendships that work are relationships in which women help each other belong to themselves.'
- Louise Bernikow

'You will find yourself refreshed by the presence of cheerful people. Why not make earnest effort to confer that pleasure on others?...Half the battle is gained if you never allow yourself to say anything gloomy.'
- Lydia M. Child

'It is easier to forgive an enemy than it is a friend.'
- Madame Dorothee Deluzy

'One who's our friend is fond of us; one who's fond of us isn't necessarily our friend.'
- Marcus Annaeus Seneca

'He who looks for advantage out of friendship strips it all of its nobility.'
- Marcus Annaeus Seneca

'It isn't easy to be the person who sometimes has to try to preserve your happiness at the expense of your fun.'
- Margaret Culkin Banning

'If you want to be listened to, you should put in time listening.'
- Marge Piercy

'In real friendship the judgment, the genius, the prudence of each party become the common property of both.'
- Maria Edgeworth

'Being considerate of others will take you and your children further in life than any college or professional degree.'
- Marian Wright Edelman

'Great friendship is never without anxiety.'
- Marie de Rabutin-Chantal

'Oh Dear! How unfortunate I am not to have anyone to weep with!'
- Marie de Rabutin-Chantal

'In meeting again after a separation, acquaintances ask after our outward life, friends after our inner life.'
- Marie von Ebner-Eschenbach

'Families will not be broken. Curse and expel them, send their children wandering, drown them in floods and fires, and old women will make songs of all these sorrows and sit in the porches and sing them on mild evenings.'
- Marilynne Robinson

'It should be part of our private ritual to devote a quarter of an hour every day to the enumeration of the good qualities of our friends. When we are not active we fall back idly upon defects, even of those whom we most love.'
- Mark Rutherford

'There ain't no surer way to find out whether you like people or hate them than to travel with them.'
- Mark Twain

'Good friends, good books and a sleepy conscience: this is the ideal life.'
- Mark Twain

'The proper office of a friend is to side with you when you are in the wrong. Nearly everybody will side with you when you are in the right.'
- Mark Twain

'It is the weak and confused who worship the pseudo-simplicities of brutal directness.'
- Marshall McLuhan

'Friendship is the bread of the heart.'
- Mary Russell Mitford

'It's the folks that depend on us for this and for the other that we most do miss.'
- Mary Webb

'Even where the affections are not strongly moved by any superior excellence, the companions of our childhood always possess a certain power over our minds which hardly any later friend can obtain.'
- Mary Wollstonecraft Shelley

'Solitude is one thing and loneliness is another.'
- May Sarton

'The most called-upon prerequisite of a friend is an accessible ear.'
- Maya Angelou

'Friendship is one mind in two bodies.'
- Mencius

'If you press me to say why I loved him, I can say no more than because he was he, and I was I.'
- Michel de Montaigne

'It's important to our friends to believe that we are unreservedly frank with them, and important to our friendship that we are not.'
- Mignon McLaughlin

'Tell me thy company, and I'll tell thee what thou art.'
- Miguel de Cervantes

'A man must eat a peck of salt with his friend before he knows him.'
- Miguel de Cervantes

'The more we love our friends, the less we flatter them; it is by excusing nothing that pure love shows itself.'
- Moliere

'Friendship is honey, but don't eat it all.'
- Moroccan proverb

'Kind words can be short and easy to speak, but their echoes are truly endless.'
- Mother Teresa

'The hardest of all is learning to be a well of affection, and not a fountain, to show them that we love them, not when we feel like it, but when they do.'
    - Nan Fairbrother

'Sooner or later you've heard all your best friends have to say. Then comes the tolerance of real love.'
    - Ned Rorem

'Hold a true friend with both your hands.'
    - Nigerian proverb

'To find a friend one must close one eye. To keep him ... two.'
    - Norman Douglas

'My helpless friend, your helplessness is the most powerful plea which rises up to the tender father-heart of God. You think that everything is closed to you because you cannot pray. My friend, your helplessness is the very essence of prayer.'
    - O. Hallesby

'Never befriend the oppressed unless you are prepared to take on the oppressor.'
    - Ogden Nash

'Don't flatter yourself that friendship authorizes you to say disagreeable things to your intimates. The nearer you come into relation with a person, the more necessary do tact and courtesy become.'
    - Oliver Wendell Holmes

'Except in cases of necessity, which are rare, leave your friend to learn unpleasant things from his enemies; they are ready enough to tell him.'
    - Oliver Wendell Holmes

'Without wearing any mask we are conscious of, we have a special face for each friend.'
    - Oliver Wendell Holmes

'Friendship is the pleasing game of interchanging praise.'
    - Oliver Wendell Holmes

'Lots of people want to ride with you in the limo, but what you want is someone who will take the bus with you when the limo breaks down.'
    - Oprah Winfrey

'If our friends' idealizations of us need the corrective of our own experience, it may be true also that our own sordid view of our lives needs the corrective of our friends' idealizations.'
    - Oscar W. Firkins

'A cruel story runs on wheels, and every hand oils the wheels as they run.'
    - Ouida

'Truth is a rough, honest, helter-skelter terrier, that none like to see brought into their drawing rooms.'
    - Ouida

'When you are young and without success, you have only a few friends. Then, later on, when you are rich and famous, you still have a few ... if you are lucky.'
- Pablo Picasso

'There is a magnet in your heart that will attract true friends. That magnet is unselfishness, thinking of others first... when you learn to live for others, they will live for you.'
- Paramahansa Yogananda

'A friend is like a poem.'
- Persian proverb

'O summer friendship, whose flat-tering leaves shadowed us in our prosperity, With the least gust, drop off in the autumn of adversity.'
- Philip Massinger

'I keep my friends as misers do their treasure because, of all the things granted us by wisdom, none is greater or better than friendship.'
- Pietro Aretino

'Your wealth is where your friends are.'
- Plautus

'What is thine is mine, and all mine is thine.'
- Plautus

'Forget your woes when you see your friend.'
- Priscian

'We die as often as we lose a friend.'
- Publilius Syrus

'Friendship neither finds nor makes equals.'
- Publilius Syrus

'Unless you bear with the faults of a friend you betray your own.'
- Publilius Syrus

'The thicker one gets with some people, the thinner they become.'
- Puzant Thomain

'Don't ask of your friends what you yourself can do.'
- Quintus Ennius

'Love your friends as if they would some day hate you.'
- R. D. Hicks

'A friend is one before whom I may think aloud.'
- Ralph Waldo Emerson

'We take care of our health, we lay up money, we make our roof tight and our clothing sufficient, but who provides wisely that he shall not be wanting in the best property of all-friends.'
   - Ralph Waldo Emerson

'The condition which high friendship demands is the ability to do without it.'
   - Ralph Waldo Emerson

'A friend is a person with whom I may be sincere. Before him, I may think aloud.'
   - Ralph Waldo Emerson

'Go oft to the house of thy friend, for weeds choke the unused path.'
   - Ralph Waldo Emerson

'How casually and unobservedly we make all our most valued acquaintances.'
   - Ralph Waldo Emerson

'The secret of success in society is a certain heartiness and sympathy.'
   - Ralph Waldo Emerson

'Friendship requires more time than poor busy men can usually command.'
   - Ralph Waldo Emerson

'Every man passes his life in the search after friendship.'
   - Ralph Waldo Emerson

'A man's growth is seen in the successive choirs of his friends.'
   - Ralph Waldo Emerson

'It is one of the blessings of old friends that you can afford to be stupid with them.'
   - Ralph Waldo Emerson

'A man with few friends is only half-developed; there are whole sides of his nature which are locked up and have never been expressed. He cannot unlock them himself, he cannot even discover them; friends alone can stimulate him and open him.'
   - Randolph Bourne

'There is a definite process by which one made people into friends, and it involved talking to them and listening to them for hours at a time.'
   - Rebecca West

'Nobody likes having salt rubbed into their wounds, even if it is the salt of the earth.'
   - Rebecca West

'So often the truth is told with hate, and lies are told with love.'
   - Rita Mae Brown

'Years and years of happiness only make us realize how lucky we are to have friends that have shared and made that happiness a reality.'
   - Robert E. Frederick

'To be social is to be forgiving.'
- Robert Frost

'The art of friendship has been little cultivated in our society.'
- Robert J. Havighurst

'A friend is a present you give to yourself.'
- Robert Louis Stevenson

'The truth that is suppressed by friends is the readiest weapon of the enemy.'
- Robert Louis Stevenson

'Friendship will not stand the strain of very much good advice for very long.'
- Robert Lynd

'Friendship is mutual blackmail elevated to the level of love.'
- Robin Morgan

'Jimmy and I were always partners.'
- Rosalynn Carter

'I know what things are good: friendship and work and conversation.'
- Rupert Brooke

'In a world that holds books and babies and canyon trails, why should one condemn oneself to live day in, day out with people one does not like, and sell oneself to chaperone and correct them?'
- Ruth Benedict

'He alone has lost the art to live who cannot win new friends.'
- S. Weir Mitchell

'No medicine is more valuable, none more efficacious, none better suited to the cure of all our temporal ills than a friend to whom we may turn for consolation in time of trouble, and with whom we may share our happiness in time of joy.'
- Saint Alfred of Rievaulx

'The reward of friendship is itself. The man who hopes for anything else does not understand what true friendship is.'
- Saint Alfred of Rievaulx

'If two friends ask you to judge a dispute, don't accept, because you will lose one friend; on the other hand, if two strangers come with the same request, accept, because you will gain one friend.'
- Saint Augustine

'Friendship requires great communication.'
- Saint Francis de Sales

'A quarrel between friends, when made up, adds a new tie to friendship, as ... the callosity formed 'round a broken bone makes it stronger than before.'
- Saint Francis de Sales

'Friendship is the source of the greatest pleasures, and without friends even the most agreeable pursuits become tedious.'
- Saint Thomas Aquinas

'There is nothing on this earth more to be prized than true friendship.'
- Saint Thomas Aquinas

'To like and dislike the same things, this is what makes a solid friendship.'
- Sallust

'A friend who cannot at a pinch remember a thing or two that never happened is as bad as one who does not know how to forget.'
- Samuel Butler

'An old friend never can be found, and nature has provided that he cannot easily be lost.'
- Samuel Johnson

'Friendship is a union of spirits, a marriage of hearts, and the bond there of virtue.'
- Samuel Johnson

'Friendship, peculiar boon of Heaven, The noble mind's delight and pride, To men and angels only given, To all the lower world denied.'
- Samuel Johnson

'Men only become friends by community of pleasures.'
- Samuel Johnson

'If a man does not make new acquaintances as he advances through life, he will soon find himself left alone.'
- Samuel Johnson

'Friendship is seldom lasting but between equals, or where the superiority on one side is reduced by some equivalent advantage on the other.'
- Samuel Johnson

'Always set high value on spontaneous kindness. He whose inclination prompts him to cultivate your friendship of his own accord will love you more than one whom you have been at pains to attach to you.'
- Samuel Johnson

'It is foolish to make experiments upon the constancy of a friend, as upon the chastity of a wife.'
- Samuel Johnson

'The feeling of friendship is like that of being comfortably filled with roast beef.'
- Samuel Johnson

'No man is much pleased with a companion who does not increase, in some respect, his fondness of himself.'
- Samuel Johnson

'That friendship may be at once fond and lasting, there must not only be equal virtue on each part, but virtue of the same kind; not only the same end must be proposed, but the same means must be approved by both.'
- Samuel Johnson

'The family unit plays a critical role in our society and in the training of the generation to come.'
- Sandra Day O'Connor

'To act the part of a true friend requires more conscientious feeling than to fill with credit and complacency any other station or capacity in social life.'
- Sarah Ellis

'The growth of true friendship may be a lifelong affair.'
- Sarah Orne Jewett

'Yes'm, old friends is always best, 'less you can catch a new one that's fit to make an old one out of.'
- Sarah Orne Jewett

'Friends are lost by calling often and calling seldom.'
- Scottish proverb

'Give and take makes good friends.'
- Scottish proverb

'Where there is lasting love, there is a family.'
- Shere Hite

'Let him have the key of thy heart, who hath the lock of his own.'
- Sir Thomas Browne

'I like a highland friend who will stand by me not only when I am in the right, but when I am a little in the wrong.'
- Sir Walter Scott

'The chain of friendship, however bright, does not stand the attrition of constant close contact.'
- Sir Walter Scott

'Be slow to fall into friendship; but when thou art in, continue firm and constant.'
- Socrates

'Be slow to fall into friendship, but when thou art in continue firm and constant.'
- Socrates

'He that walketh with wise men shall be wise.'
- Solomon

'A friend is one who withholds judgment no matter how long you have his unanswered letter.'
 - Sophie Irene Loeb

'To throw away an honest friend is, as it were, to throw your life away.'
 - Sophocles

'One who knows how to show and to accept kindness will be a friend better than any possession.'
 - Sophocles

'You win the victory when you yield to friends.'
 - Sophocles

'Rather throw away that which is dearest to you, your own life, than turn away a good friend.'
 - Sophocles

'It is better to weep with wise men than to laugh with fools.'
 - Spanish proverb

'Life without a friend is death without a witness.'
 - Spanish proverb

'Friends and wine should be old.'
 - Spanish proverb

'Flattery makes friends, truth enemies.'
 - Spanish proverb

'Money can't buy friends, but you can get a better class of enemy.'
 - Spike Milligan

'A friend in need is a friend indeed.'
 - Susan Ferrier

'One can find traces of every life in each life.'
 - Susan Griffin

'Before a secret is told, one can often feel the weight of it in the atmosphere.'
 - Susan Griffin

'Friendship's a noble name, 'tis love refined.'
 - Susannah Centlivre

'Madam, I have been looking for a person who disliked gravy all my life; let us swear eternal friendship.'
 - Sydney Smith

'Life is partly what we make it, and partly what it is made by the friends we choose.'
 - Tehyi Hsieh

'Of my friends, I am the only one I have left.'
- Terence

'I should like to tell you again of my bitter troubles so that mutually, by recounting our grief, we can lighten each other's sorrow.'
- The Kanteletar

'A friend is someone you can do nothing with, and enjoy it.'
- The Optimist

'By associating with good and evil persons a man acquires the virtues and vices which they possess, even as the wind blowing over different places takes along good and bad odors.'
- The Panchatantra

'I have friends in overalls whose friendship I would not swap for the favor of the kings of the world.'
- Thomas A. Edison

'Hope is a pleasant acquaintance, but an unsafe friend.'
- Thomas Chandler Haliburton

'A good friend is my nearest relation.'
- Thomas Fuller

'A wise man may look ridiculous in the company of fools.'
- Thomas Fuller

'Friendship that flames goes out in a flash.'
- Thomas Fuller

'No man can be happy without a friend, nor be sure of his friend till he is unhappy.'
- Thomas Fuller

'We shall never have friends if we expect to find them without fault.'
- Thomas Fuller

'Be a friend to thyself, and others will be so too.'
- Thomas Fuller

'Better fare hard with good men than feast with bad.'
- Thomas Fuller

'Blessed are they who have the gift of making friends, for it is one of God's best gifts. It involves many things, but above all, the power of getting out of one's self, and appreciating whatever is noble and loving in another.'
- Thomas Hughes

'We secure our friends not by accepting favors but by doing them.'
- Thucydides

'There are worse words than cuss words; there are words that hurt.'
- Tillie Olsen

'Here's a dime. Call all your friends.'
- Tom Meany

'Friendship is a furrow in the sand.'
- Tongan proverb

'Who seeks a faultless friend remains friendless.'
- Turkish proverb

'Satan's friendship reaches to the prison door.'
- Turkish proverb

'None is so rich as to throw away a friend.'
- Turkish proverb

'The friend of my adversity I shall always cherish most. I can better trust those who helped to relieve the gloom of my dark hours than those who are so ready to enjoy with me the sunshine of my prosperity.'
- Ulysses S. Grant

'However deep our devotion may be to parents or to children, it is our contemporaries alone with whom understanding is instinctive and entire.'
- Vera Brittain

'I feel the need of relations and friendship, of affection, of friendly intercourse. ... I cannot miss these things without feeling, as does any other intelligent man, a void and a deep need.'
- Vincent van Gogh

'I have lost friends, some by death ... others by sheer inability to cross the street.'
- Virginia Woolf

'Some people go to priests; others to poetry; I to my friends.'
- Virginia Woolf

'As there are some flowers which you should smell but slightly to extract all that is pleasant in them ... so there are some men with whom a slight acquaintance is quite sufficient to draw out all that is agreeable; a more intimate one would be unsafe and '
- Walter Savage Landor

'Friendship may sometimes step a few paces in advance of truth.'
- Walter Savage Landor

'Only solitary men know the full joys of friendship. Others have their family; but to a solitary and an exile his friends are everything.'
- Willa Cather

'The bird, a nest; the spider, a web; man, friendship.'
- William Blake

'One thing everybody in the world wants and needs is friendliness.'
- William E. Holler

'Politeness is an inexpensive way of making friends.'
- William Feather

'True friendship is self-love at second hand.'
- William Hazlitt

'We often choose a friend as we do a mistress, for no particular excellence in themselves, but merely from some circumstance that flatters our self-love.'
- William Hazlitt

'We are fonder of visiting our friends in health than in sickness. We judge less favorably of their characters when any misfortune happens to them; and a lucky hit, either in business or reputation, improves even their personal appearance in our eyes.'
- William Hazlitt

'It is well there is no one without fault; for he would not have a friend in the world. He would seem to belong to a different species.'
- William Hazlitt

'To be capable of steady friendship or lasting love are the two greatest proofs, not only of goodness of heart, but of strength of mind.'
- William Hazlitt

'Most men's friendships are too inarticulate.'
- William James

'The first thing to learn in intercourse with others is non-interference with their own peculiar ways of being happy, provided those ways do not assume to interfere with ours.'
- William James

'A true friend unbosoms freely, advises justly, assists readily, adventures boldly, takes all patiently, defends courageously, and continues a friend unchangeably.'
- William Penn

'There can be no friendship when there is no freedom. Friendship loves the free air, and will not be fenced up in straight and narrow enclosures.'
- William Penn

'A friend should bear his friend's infirmities.'
- William Shakespeare

'Those friends thou hast, and their adoption tried, grapple them to thy soul with hoops of steel.'
- William Shakespeare

'The best way to keep your friends is not to give them away.'
- Wilson Mizner

'You cannot be friends upon any other terms than upon the terms of equality.'
- Woodrow Wilson

'It seems to me that trying to live without friends is like milking a bear to get cream for your morning coffee. It is a whole lot of trouble, and then not worth much after you get it.'
- Zora Neale Hurston

FUTURE

'There was a wise man in the East whose constant prayer was that he might see today with the eyes of tomorrow.'
- Alfred Mercier

'I believe the future is only the past again, entered through another gate.'
- Arthur Wing Pinero

'The present is great with the future'
- Baron von Leibnitz

'Till the sun grows cold, And the stars are old, And the leaves of the Judgment Book unfold.'
- Bayard Taylor

'When all else is lost, the future still remains.'
- Christian Nestell Bovee

'Take therefore no thought for the morrow; for the morrow shall take thought for the things of itself. Sufficient unto the day is the evil thereof.'
- Matthew

'There was the Door to which I found no key; There was the Veil through which I might not see.'
- Omar Khayyam

'I know of no way of judging the future but by the past.'
- Patrick Henry

'Tis the sunset of life gives me mystical lore, And coming events cast their shadows before.'
- Thomas Campbell

GENIUS

'The difference between genius and stupidity is that genius has its limits.'
  - Anonymous

'Genius is only great patience.'
  - Anonymous

'The parting genius is with sighing sent.'
  - Anonymous

'There is no great genius without a mixture of madness.'
  - Aristotle

'It takes immense genius to represent, simply and sincerely, what we see in front of us.'
  - Edmond Duranty

'The poet's scrolls will outlive the monuments of stone. The Genius survives; all else is claimed by death.'
  - Edmund Spenser

'Genius does what it must, and talent does what it can.'
  - Edward G. Bulwer-Lytton

'Gift, like genius, I often think only means an infinite capacity for taking pains.'
  - Ellice Hopkins

'Genius as such can neither be explained nor treated away; only, at times, its delay and inhibition and its perversion to destructive or self-destructive ends.'
  - Erik Erikson

'Too often we forget that genius ... depends upon the data within its reach, that Archimedes could not have devised Edison's inventions.'
  - Ernest Dimnet

'The lamp of genius burns quicker than the lamp of life.'
  - Friedrich von Schiller

'Everyone is a genius at least once a year; a real genius has his original ideas closer together.'
  - G. C. Lichtenberg

'Sometimes men come by the name of genius in the same way that certain insects come by the name of centipede - not because they have a hundred feet, but because most people can't count above fourteen.'
  - G. C. Lichtenberg

'Genius develops in quiet places, character out in the full current of human life.'
- Goethe

'Doing easily what others find is difficult is talent; doing what is impossible for talent is genius.'
- Henri Frederic Amiel

'Before I was a genius I was a drudge.'
- Ignace Jan Paderewski

'Three-fifths of him genius and two-fifths sheer fudge.'
- James Russell Lowell

'Talent is that which is in a man's power; genius is that in whose power a man is.'
- James Russell Lowell

'When a true genius appears in the world you may know him by this sign, that the dunces are all in confederacy against him.'
- Jonathan Swift

'Men of genius are the worst possible models for men of talent.'
- Murray D. Edwards

'There is a thin line between genius and insanity. I have erased this line.'
- Oscar Levant

'The public is wonderfully tolerant. It forgives everything except genius.'
- Oscar Wilde

'The genius of Einstein leads to Hiroshima.'
- Pablo Picasso

'To believe your own thought, to believe that what is true for you in your private heart is true for all men - that is genius.'
- Ralph Waldo Emerson

'In every work of genius we recognize our own rejected thoughts; they come back to us with a certain alienated majesty.'
- Ralph Waldo Emerson

'In the republic of mediocrity, genius is dangerous.'
- Robert G. Ingersoll

'Every man of genius is considerably helped by being dead.'
- Robert S. Lund

'The true genius is a mind of large general powers, accidentally determined to some particular direction.'
- Samuel Johnson

'Genius is one per cent inspiration and ninety-nine per cent perspiration.'
   - Thomas Alva Edison

'The mark of genius is an incessant activity of mind. Genius is a spiritual greed.'
   - V. S. Pritchett

'Genius is a promontory jutting out of the infinite.'
   - Victor Hugo

'Genius is an African who dreams up snow.'
   - Vladimir Nabokov

'Geniuses are the luckiest of mortals because what they must do is the same as what they most want to do.'
   - W. H. Auden

'Improvement makes straight roads; but the crooked roads without improvement are roads of genius.'
   - William Blake

'Genius, in truth, means little more than the faculty of perceiving in an unhabitual way.'
   - William James

GOALS

'Every man is said to have his peculiar ambition.'
   - Abraham Lincoln

'Life has ... taught me not to expect success to be the inevitable result of my endeavors. She taught me to seek sustenance from the endeavor itself, but to leave the result to God.'
   - Alan Paton

'The only ones among you who will be really happy are those who will have sought and found how to serve.'
   - Albert Schweitzer

'One should want only one thing and want it constantly. Then one is sure of getting it. But I desire everything, and consequently get nothing.'
   - Andre Gide

'He who wants to do everything will never do anything.'
   - Andre Maurois

'Your goal should be out of reach but not out of sight.'
   - Anita DeFrantz

'The streams which would otherwise diverge to fertilize a thousand meadows, must be directed into one deep narrow channel before they can turn a mill.'
   - Anna Jameson

'What exactly is success? For me it is to be found not in applause, but in the satisfaction of feeling that one is realizing one's ideal.'
   - Anna Pavlova

'We all live with the objective of being happy; our lives are all different, and yet the same.'
   - Anne Frank

'A schedule defends from chaos and whim. It is a net for catching days. It is a scaffolding on which a worker can stand and labor with both hands at sections of time.'
   - Annie Dillard

'Having a dream isn't stupid. ... It's not having a dream that's stupid.'
   - Anonymous

'Set short term goals and you'll win games. Set long term goals and you'll win championships!'
   - Anonymous

'Aim at nothing and you'll succeed.'
   - Anonymous

'Life has a meaning only if one barters it day by day for something other than itself.'
- Antoine de Saint-Exupery

'There were angry men confronting me and I caught the flashing of defiant eyes, but above me and within me, there was a spirit stronger than them all.'
- Antoinette Brown Blackwell

'A woman finds the natural lay of the land almost unconsciously; and not feeling it incumbent on her to be guide and philosopher to any successor, she takes little pains to mark the route by which she is making her ascent.'
- Antoinette Brown Blackwell

'If you cry "Forward," you must make plain in what direction to go.'
- Anton Chekhov

'All men seek one goal: success or happiness.'
- Aristotle

'I probably hold the distinction of being one movie star who, by all laws of logic, should never have made it. At each stage of my career, I lacked the experience.'
- Audrey Hepburn

'It is when things go hardest, when life becomes most trying, that there is greatest need for having a fixed goal. When few comforts come from without, it is all the more necessary to have a fount to draw on from within.'
- B. C. Forbes

'It's not enough to just swing at the ball. You've got to loosen your girdle and really let it fly.'
- Babe Didrikson Zaharias

'Someday, someone will follow in my footsteps and preside over the White House as the President's spouse. And I wish him well.'
- Barbara Bush

'I never intended to become a run-of-the-mill person.'
- Barbara Jordaon

'I truly believe that before I retire from public office, I'll be voting for a woman for president.'
- Barbara Mikulski

'To be what we are, and to become what we are capable of becoming, is the only end of life.'
- Baruch Spinoza

'If you don't know where you are going, how can you expect to get there?'
- Basil S. Walsh

'The secret of success is constancy to purpose.'
- Benjamin Franklin

'The tragedy of life doesn't lie in not reaching your goal. The tragedy lies in having no goal to reach.'
  - Benjamin Mays

'Tell them that as soon as I can walk I'm going to fly!'
  - Bessie Coleman

'My passions were all gathered together like fingers that made a fist. Drive is considered aggression today; I knew it then as purpose.'
  - Bette Davis

'Those who attain any excellence commonly spend life in one pursuit; for excellence is not often granted upon easier terms. -Samuel Johnson No man can serve two masters: for either he will hate the one, and love the other; or else he will hold to the one, '
  - Bible

'I'm always making a comeback but nobody ever tells me where I've been.'
  - Billie Holiday

'You have to have a dream so you can get up in the morning.'
  - Billy Wilder

'No matter what the competition is, I try to find a goal that day and better that goal.'
  - Bonnie Blair

'It doesn't matter what anybody thinks of what I do. The clock doesn't lie.'
  - Bonnie Blair

'Men cannot for long live hopefully unless they are embarked upon some great unifying enterprise, one for which they may pledge their lives, their fortunes and their honor.'
  - C. A. Dykstra

'Purpose is what gives life a meaning.'
  - C. H. Parkhurst

'Laboring toward distant aims sets the mind in a higher key, and puts us at our best.'
  - C. H. Parkhurst

'Aim at heaven and you get earth thrown in; aim at earth and you get neither.'
  - C. S. Lewis

'There are people who want to be everywhere at once, and they get nowhere.'
  - Carl Sandburg

'Get out of the blocks, run your race, stay relaxed. If you run your race, you'll win. Channel your energy. Focus.'
  - Carol Lewis

'Lack of something to feel important about is almost the greatest tragedy a man may have.'
  - Charles C. Noble

'You must have long-range goals to keep you from being frustrated by short-range failures.'
- Charles C. Noble

'A windmill is eternally at work to accomplish one end, although it shifts with every variation of the weathercock, and assumes ten different positions in a day.'
- Charles Caleb Colton

'The state of the world today demands that women become less modest and dream/plan/act/risk on a larger scale.'
- Charlotte Bunch

'Life is about enjoying yourself and having a good time.'
- Cher

'Never try to catch two frogs with one hand.'
- Chinese proverb

'One cannot manage too many affairs: like pumpkins in the water, one pops up while you try to hold down the other.'
- Chinese proverb

'Happy the man who knows his duties!'
- Christian Furchtegott Gellert

'It is necessary to try to surpass one's self always; this occupation ought to last as long as life.'
- Christina Augusta

'There's a very fine line between a groove and a rut; a fine line between eccentrics and people who are just plain nuts.'
- Christine Lavin

'There are three ingredients in the good life: learning, earning and yearning.'
- Christopher Morley

'So long as I believe I have to do certain things, I will just go right ahead. That's how I run my life.'
- Corazan Aquino

'The measure of a life, after all, is not its duration, but its donation.'
- Corrie ten Boom

'Only he who keeps his eye fixed on the far horizon will find his right road.'
- Dag Hammarskjold

'I am searching for that which every man seeks-peace and rest.'
- Dante Alighieri

'A life that hasn't a definite plan is likely to become driftwood.'
- David Sarnoff

'The world stands aside to let anyone pass who knows where he is going.'
  - David Starr Jordan

'Be a life long or short, its completeness depends on what it was lived for.'
  - David Starr Jordan

'Goals are dreams with deadlines.'
  - Diana Scharf Hunt

'Unhappiness is in not knowing what we want and killing ourselves to get it.'
  - Don Herold

'The goal of all civilization, all religious thought, and all that sort of thing is simply to have a good time. But man gets so solemn over the process that he forgets the end.'
  - Don Marquis

'There is only one real sin and that is to persuade oneself that the second best is anything but second best.'
  - Doris Lessing

'You cannot do good work if you take your mind off the work to see how the community is taking it.'
  - Dorothy L. Sayers

'Having a goal is a state of happiness.'
  - E. J. Bartek

'The man who succeeds above his fellows is the one who early in life discerns his object and toward that object habitually directs his powers. Even genius itself is but fine observation strengthened by fixity of purpose.'
  - Edward Bulwer-Lytton

'Too low they build, who build beneath the stars.'
  - Edward Young

'If we want a free and peaceful world, if we want to make the deserts bloom and man grow to greater dignity as a human being-we can do it.'
  - Eleanor Roosevelt

'What an immense power over the life is the power of possessing distinct aims. The voice, the dress, the look, the very motions of a person, define and alter when he or she begins to live for a reason.'
  - Elizabeth Stuart Phelps

'He who demands little gets it.'
  - Ellen Glasgow

'When one paints an ideal, one does not need to limit one's imagination.'
  - Ellen Key

'The brain is wider than the sky.'
- Emily Dickinson

'First say to yourself what you would be, and then do what you have to do.'
- Epictetus

'There is only one meaning of life: the act of living itself.'
- Erich Fromm

'The only people who attain power are those who crave for it.'
- Erich Kastner

'Know what you want to do-then do it. Make straight for your goal and go undefeated in spirit to the end.'
- Ernestine Schumann-Heink

'You must learn day by day, year by year, to broaden your horizon. The more things you love, the more you are interested in, the more you enjoy, the more you are indignant about, the more you have left when anything happens.'
- Ethel Barrymore

'The American people can have anything they want; the trouble is, they don't know what they want.'
- Eugene V. Debs

'What does so-called success or failure matter if only you have succeeded in doing the thing you set out to do. The doing is all that really counts.'
- Eva Le Gallienne

'Remember if people talk behind your back, it only means you're two steps ahead!'
- Fannie Flagg

'One of the most important factors, not only in military matters but in life as a whole, is ... the ability to direct one's whole energies towards the fulfillment of a particular task.'
- Field Marshal Erwin Rommel

'People don't pay much attention to you when you are second best. I wanted to see what it felt like to be number one.'
- Florence Griffith Joyner

'Man can only receive what he sees himself receiving.'
- Florence Scovel Shinn

'Promises that you make to yourself are often like the Japanese plum tree-they bear no fruit.'
- Frances Marion

'Only he who can see the invisible can do the impossible.'
- Frank Gaines

'The man who fails because he aims astray, or because he does not aim at all, is to be found everywhere.'
- Frank Swinnerton

'Happiness lies in the joy of achievement and the thrill of creative effort.'
- Franklin Delano Roosevelt

'I am not sending messages with my feet. All I ever wanted was not to come up empty. I did it for the dough, and the old applause.'
- Fred Astaire

'Many are stubborn in pursuit of the path they have chosen, few in pursuit of the goal.'
- Friedrich Nietzsche

'He who has a why to live for can bear almost any how.'
- Friedrich Nietzsche

'Life exists for the love of music or beautiful things.'
- G. K. Chesterton

'There is one thing which gives radiance to everything. It is the idea of something around the corner.'
- G. K. Chesterton

'The true object of human life is play.'
- G. K. Chesterton

'The object of war is not to die for your country, but to make the other bastard die for his.'
- General George S. Patton

'Never undertake anything for which you wouldn't have the courage to ask the blessings of heaven.'
- Georg Christoph Lichtenberg

'This is true joy of life-being used for a purpose that is recognized by yourself as a mighty one ... instead of being a feverish, selfish little clod of ailments and grievances, complaining that the world will not devote itself to making you happy.'
- George Bernard Shaw

'Use your health, even to the point of wearing it out. That is what it is for. Spend all you have before you die; do not outlive yourself.'
- George Bernard Shaw

'Give a man health and a course to steer, and he'll never stop to trouble about whether he's happy or not.'
- George Bernard Shaw

'In the multitude of middle-aged men who go about their vocations in a daily course determined for them much in the same way as they tie their cravats, there is always a good number who once meant to shape their own deeds and alter the world a little.'
- George Eliot

'Life has a value only when it has something valuable as its object.'
  - George Hegel

'In this life we get only those things for which we hunt, for which we strive, and for which we are willing to sacrifice.'
  - George Matthew Adams

'Human happiness and moral duty are inseparably connected.'
  - George Washington

'Your world is as big as you make it.'
  - Georgia Douglas Johnson

'Who begins too much accomplishes little.'
  - German proverb

'Catching something is purely a byproduct of our fishing. It is the act of fishing that wipes away all grief, lightens all worry, dissolves all fear and anxiety.'
  - Gladys Taber

'I can honestly say that I was never affected by the question of the success of an undertaking. If I felt it was the right thing to do, I was for it regardless of the possible outcome.'
  - Golda Meir

'Obstacles are those frightful things you see when you take your eyes off the goal.'
  - Hannah More

'My father used to play with my brother and me in the yard. Mother would come out and say, "You're tearing up the grass." "We're not raising grass," Dad would reply. "We're raising boys."'
  - Harmon Killebrew

'The poor man is not he who is without a cent, but he who is without a dream.'
  - Harry Kemp

'Nearly every glamorous, wealthy, successful career woman you might envy now started out as some kind of schlepp.'
  - Helen Gurley Brown

'You can have your titular recognition. I'll take money and power.'
  - Helen Gurley Brown

'True happiness ... is not attained through self-gratification, but through fidelity to a worthy purpose.'
  - Helen Keller

'One of the sources of pride in being a human being is the ability to bear present frustrations in the interests of longer purposes.'
  - Helen Merrell Lynd

'To seek one's goals and to drive toward it, steeling one's heart, is most uplifting!'
- Henrik Ibsen

'In the long run men hit only what they aim at. Therefore, though they should fall immediately, they had better aim at something high.'
- Henry David Thoreau

'If one advances confidently in the direction of his dreams, and endeavors to live the life which he has imagined, he will meet with a success unexpected in common hours.'
- Henry David Thoreau

'Not only must we be good, but we must also be good for something.'
- Henry David Thoreau

'There is no happiness except in the realization that we have accomplished something.'
- Henry Ford

'What our deepest self craves is not mere enjoyment, but some supreme purpose that will enlist all our powers and give unity and direction to our life.'
- Henry J. Golding

'True happiness, we are told, consists in getting out of one's self, but the point is not only to get out; you must stay out, and to stay out, you must have some absorbing errand.'
- Henry James

'Happiness is not the end of life; character is.'
- Henry Ward Beecher

'He who never sacrificed a present to a future good, or a personal to a general one, can speak of happiness only as the blind speak of color.'
- Horace Mann

'The very first condition of lasting happiness is that a life should be full of purpose, aiming at something outside self.'
- Hugh Black

'We have believed-and we do believe now-that freedom is indivisible, that peace is indivisible, that economic prosperity is indivisible.'
- Indira Gandhi

'My motto: sans limites.'
- Isadora Duncan

'He who begins many things finishes but few.'
- Italian proverb

'There is more to life than just existing and having a pleasant time.'
- J. C. F. von Schiller

'Why should I deem myself to be a chisel, when I could be the artist?'
- J. C. F. von Schiller

'Aim at the sun, and you may not reach it; but your arrow will fly far higher than if aimed at an object on a level with yourself.'
- J. Hawes

'The proper function of man is to live-not to exist.'
- Jack London

'For me it's the challenge-the challenge to try to beat myself or do better than I did in the past. I try to keep in mind not what I have accomplished but what I have to try to accomplish in the future.'
- Jackie Joyner-Kersee

'I might have been born in a hovel but I am determined to travel with the wind and the stars.'
- Jacqueline Cochran

'An aim in life is the only fortune worth finding.'
- Jacqueline Kennedy Onassis

'To grow and know what one is growing towards-that is the source of all strength and confidence in life.'
- James Baillie

'I take it that what all men are really after is some form of, perhaps only some formula of, peace.'
- James Conrad

'Nations, like individuals, have to limit their objectives or take the consequences.'
- James Reston

'Not failure, but low aim, is crime.'
- James Russell Lowell

'He who hunts two hares leaves one and loses the other.'
- Japanese proverb

'In everything one must consider the end.'
- Jean de la Fontaine

'We're half the people, we should be half the Congress.'
- Jeannette Rankin

'What else are we gonna live by if not dreams? We need to believe in something. What would really drive us crazy is to believe this reality we run into every day is all there is. If I don't believe that there's a happy ending out there-that will-you-marry-'
- Jill Robinson

'Normal is not something to aspire to, it's something to get away from.'
- Jodie Foster

'It is in self-limitation that a master first shows himself.'
- Johann von Goethe

'A useless life is an early death.'
- Johann von Goethe

'Let us live, while we are alive!'
- Johann von Goethe

'Life's objective is life itself.'
- Johann von Goethe

'Once you say you're going to settle for second, that's what happens to you.'
- John F. Kennedy

'The object of war is to survive it.'
- John Irving

'The great business of life is to be, to do, to do without, and to depart.'
- John Morley

'A person can grow only as much as his horizon allows.'
- John Powell

'Life is a petty thing unless it is moved by the indomitable urge to extend its boundaries.'
- Jose Ortega y Gasset

'To live means to have ... a mission to fulfill-and in the measure in which we avoid setting our life to something, we make it empty.'
- Jose Ortega y Gasset

'Follow your bliss. Find where it is and don't be afraid to follow it.'
- Joseph Campbell

'Without duty, life is soft and boneless.'
- Joseph Joubert

'Each time I leaped I seemed to touch the sky and when I regained earth it seemed to be mine alone.'
- Josephine Baker

'Only when men are connected to large, universal goals are they really happy-and one result of their happiness is a rush of creative activity.'
- Joyce Carol Oates

'To have a reason to get up in the morning, it is necessary to possess a guiding principle. A belief of some kind. A bumper sticker, if you will.'
- Judith Guest

'He who wishes to fulfill his mission in the world must be a man of one idea, one great overmastering purpose, overshadowing all his aims, and guiding and controlling his entire life.'
- Julius Bate

'The most comprehensive formulation of therapeutic goals is the striving for wholeheartedness: to be without pretense, to be emotionally sincere, to be able to put the whole of oneself into one's feelings, one's work, one's beliefs.'
- Karen Horney

'The purpose of life is life.'
- Karl Lagerfeld

'Our being is subject to all the chances of life. There are so many things we are capable of, that we could be or do. The potentialities are so great that we never, any of us, are more than one-fourth fulfilled.'
- Katherine Anne Porter

'We can do whatever we wish to do provided our wish is strong enough. ... What do you want most to do? That's what I have to keep asking myself, in the face of difficulties.'
- Katherine Mansfield

'Before you begin a thing, remind yourself that difficulties and delays quite impossible to foresee are ahead. ... You can only see one thing clearly and that is your goal. Form a mental vision of that and cling to it through thick and thin.'
- Kathleen Norris

'If ambition doesn't hurt you, you haven't got it.'
- Kathleen Norris

'I always ask the question, "Is this what I want in my life?"'
- Kathy Ireland

'Strong lives are motivated by dynamic purposes.'
- Kenneth Hildebrand

'Happiness is the overcoming of not unknown obstacles toward a known goal.'
- L. Ron Hubbard

'When you reach for the stars, you may not quite get one, but you won't come up with a handful of mud, either.'
- Leo Burnett

'I think the purpose of life is to be useful, to be responsible, to be honorable, to be compassionate. It is, after all, to matter: to count, to stand for something, to have made some difference that you lived at all.'
- Leo C. Rosten

'A novelist must know what his last chapter is going to say and one way or another work toward that last chapter. ... To me it is utterly basic, yet it seems like it's a great secret.'
- Leon Uris

'He turns not back who is bound to a star.'
- Leonardo da Vinci

'Shoot for the moon. Even if you miss it, you will land among the stars.'
- Les Brown

'If I had one wish for my children, it would be that each of them would reach for goals that have meaning for them as individuals.'
- Lillian Carter

'You have to erect a fence and say, "Okay, scale this."'
- Linda Ronstadt

'There are two things to aim at in life: first, to get what you want, and after that to enjoy it. Only the wisest of mankind achieve the second.'
- Logan Pearsall Smith

'Aim at perfection in everything, though in most things it is unattainable. However they who aim at it, and persevere, will come much nearer to it than those whose laziness and despondency make them give it up as unattainable.'
- Lord Chesterfield

'Firmness of purpose is one of the most necessary sinews of character and one of the best instruments of success. Without it, genius wastes its efforts in a maze of inconsistencies.'
- Lord Chesterfield

'He might never really do what he said, but at least he had it in mind. He had somewhere to go.'
- Louis L'Amour

'I want to be great, or nothing. I won't be a commonplace dauber, so I don't intend to try any more.'
- Louisa May Alcott

'Far away in the sunshine are my highest inspirations. I many not reach them, but I can look up and see the beauty, believe in them and try to follow where they lead.'
- Louisa May Alcott

'Every true man, sir, who is a little above the level of the beasts and plants, lives so as to give a meaning and a value to his own life.'
- Luigi Pirandello

'The self-confidence one builds from achieving difficult things and accomplishing goals is the most beautiful thing of all.'
- Madonna

'I have the same goal I've had ever since I was a little girl. I want to rule the world.'
- Madonna

'Everything's in the mind. That's where it all starts. Knowing what you want is the first step toward getting it.'
- Mae West

'People can have many different kinds of pleasure. The real one is that for which they will forsake the others.'
- Marcel Proust

'You can change your beliefs so they empower your dreams and desires. Create a strong belief in yourself and what you want.'
- Marcia Wieder

'There's some end at last for the man who follows a path; mere rambling is interminable.'
- Marcus Annaeus Seneca

'Our plans miscarry because they have no aim. When a man does not know what harbor he is making for, no wind is the right wind.'
- Marcus Annaeus Seneca

'A man's happiness: to do the things proper to man.'
- Marcus Aurelius

'Without a purpose, nothing should be done.'
- Marcus Aurelius

'The one thing worth living for is to keep one's soul pure.'
- Marcus Aurelius

'A man's worth is no greater than the worth of his ambitions.'
- Marcus Aurelius

'The true worth of a man is to be measured by the objects he pursues.'
- Marcus Aurelius

'People think that at the top there isn't much room. They tend to think of it as an Everest. My message is that there is tons of room at the top.'
- Margaret Thatcher

'If you just set out to be liked, you would be prepared to compromise on anything at any time, and you would achieve nothing.'
- Margaret Thatcher

'[My father] said, Don't grow up to be a woman, and what he meant by that was, a housewife ... without any interests.'
- Maria Goeppert Mayer

'I was born to be a remarkable woman; it matters little in what way or how. ... I shall be famous or I will die.'
- Marie Bashkirtseff

'From his cradle to the grave, a man never does a single thing which has any first and foremost object save one-to secure peace of mind, spiritual comfort, for himself.'
- Mark Twain

'Duties are what make life most worth living. Lacking them, you are not necessary to anyone.'
- Marlene Dietrich

'I think the key is for women not to set any limits.'
- Martina Navratilova

'I've always had such high expectations for myself. I'm aware of them, but I can't relax them.'
- Mary Decker Slaney

'A good goal is like a strenuous exercise-it makes you stretch.'
- Mary Kay Ash

'There is a place in God's sun for the youth "farthest down" who has the vision, the determination, and the courage to reach it.'
- Mary McLeod Bethune

'Leader and followers are both following the invisible leader-the common purpose.'
- Mary Parker Follett

'Nothing contributes so much to tranquilize the mind as a steady purpose-a point on which the soul may fix its intellectual eye.'
- Mary Wollstonecraft Shelley

'If I smashed the traditions it was because I knew no traditions.'
- Maude Adams

'You seldom get what you go after unless you know in advance what you want.'
- Maurice Switzer

'Growth is not concerned with itself.'
- Meridel Le Sueur

'The great and glorious masterpiece of man is to know how to live to purpose.'
- Michel de Montaigne

'The soul that has no established aim loses itself.'
- Michel de Montaigne

'The great and glorious masterpiece of man is how to live with a purpose.'
- Michel de Montaigne

'No wind serves him who addresses his voyage to no certain port.'
- Michel de Montaigne

'It's a sign of your own worth sometimes if you are hated by the right people.'
- Miles Franklin

'No pleasure philosophy, no sensuality, no place nor power, no material success can for a moment give such inner satisfaction Action as the sense of living for good purpose.'
- Minot Simons

'You decide what it is you want to accomplish and then you lay out your plans to get there, and then you just do it. It's pretty straightforward.'
- Nancy Ditz

'Fortunate is the person who has developed the self-control to steer a straight course toward his objective in life, without being swayed from his purpose by either commendation or condemnation.'
- Napoleon Hill

'One principle reason why men are so often useless is that they ... divide and shift their attention among a multitude of objects and pursuits.'
- Nathaniel Emmons

'The business of life is to enjoy oneself; everything else is a mockery.'
- Norman Douglas

'Life is an end in itself, and the only question as to whether it is worth living is whether you have had enough of it.'
- Oliver Wendell Holmes

'We are all in the gutter, but some of us are looking at the stars.'
- Oscar Wilde

'Pleasure is the only thing to live for. Nothing ages like happiness.'
- Oscar Wilde

'The man who seeks one thing in life, and but one May hope to achieve it before life be done. But he who seeks all things wherever he goes Only reaps from the hopes which around him he sows A harvest of barren regrets.'
- Owen Meredith

'Reach high, for stars lie hidden in your soul. Dream deep, for every dream precedes the goal.'
- Pamela Vaull Starr

'Enjoyment is not a goal, it is a feeling that accompanies important ongoing activity.'
- Paul Goodman

'We need to restore the full meaning of that old word, duty. It is the other side of rights.'
- Pearl S. Buck

'I am comforted by life's stability, by earth's unchangeableness. What has seemed new and frightening assumes its place in the unfolding of knowledge.'
- Pearl S. Buck

'Happiness is the natural flower of duty.'
- Phillips Brooks

'As you emphasize your life, you must localize and define it... you cannot do everything.'
- Phillips Brooks

'He who serves two masters has to lie to one.'
- Portuguese proverb

'Great is the road I climb, but... the garland offered by an easier effort is not worth the gathering.'
- Propertius

'He is conscious of touching the highest pinnacle of fulfillment... when he is consumed in the service of an idea, in the conquest of the goal pursued.'
- R. Briffault

'I am always more interested in what I am about to do than in what I have already done.'
- Rachel Carson

'We aim above the mark to hit the mark. Every act hath some falsehood or exaggeration in it.'
- Ralph Waldo Emerson

'I take it as a prime cause of the present confusion of society that it is too sickly and too doubtful to use pleasure as a test of value.'
- Rebecca West

'I never took a position we were going to be a good ball club. I took the position we were going to be a winning ball club.'
- Red Auerbach

'I finally figured out the only reason to be alive is to enjoy it.'
- Rita Mae Brown

'Man's reach should exceed his grasp, or what's a heaven for?'
- Robert Browning

'The purpose of life is a life of purpose.'
- Robert Byrne

'An aspiration is a joy forever, a possession as solid as a landed estate, a fortune which we can never exhaust and which gives us year by year a revenue of pleasurable activity.'
- Robert Louis Stevenson

'I looked on child rearing not only as a work of love and duty but as a profession that was fully as interesting and challenging as any honorable profession in the world and one that demanded the best

I could bring to it.'
- Rose Fitzgerald Kennedy

'I'm not going to let my life revolve around losing weight. I have other things to do.'
- Rosie O'Donnell

'The happiest excitement in life is to be convinced that one is fighting for all one is worth on behalf of some clearly seen and deeply felt good.'
- Ruth Benedict

'The main obligation is to amuse yourself.'
- S. J. Perelman

'All animals except man know that the ultimate of life is to enjoy it.'
- Samuel Butler

'Choosing a goal and sticking to it changes everything.'
- Scott Reed

'It's expectation that differentiates you from the dead.'
- Sheila Ballantyne

'You can't assume the responsibility for everything you do-or don't do.'
- Simone de Beauvoir

'What most counts is not to live, but to live aright.'
- Socrates

'The greyhound that starts many hares kills none.'
- Spanish proverb

'If you would be Pope, you must think of nothing else.'
- Spanish proverb

'Unless in one thing or another we are straining toward perfection, we have forfeited our manhood.'
- Stephen McKenna

'To have no set purpose in one's life is the harlotry of the will.'
- Stephen McKenna

'There is no such thing as expecting too much.'
- Susan Cheever

'I care not what your education is, elaborate or nothing, what your mental calibre is, great or small, that man who concentrates all his energies of body, mind and soul in one direction is a tremendous man.'
- T. DeWitt Talmage

'Nothing is more terrible than activity without insight.'
- Thomas Carlyle

'If you run after two hares, you will catch neither.'
- Thomas Fuller

'One may miss the mark by aiming too high, as too low.'
- Thomas Fuller

'Seek happiness for its own sake, and you will not find it; seek for duty, and happiness will follow, as the shadow comes with the sunshine.'
- Tyron Edwards

'The most absurd and reckless aspirations have sometimes led to extraordinary success.'
- Vauvenargues

'Where no plan is laid, where the disposal of time is surrendered merely to the chance of incident, chaos will soon reign.'
- Victor Hugo

'When the shriveled skin of the ordinary is stuffed out with meaning, it satisfies the senses amazingly.'
- Virginia Woolf

'Pleasure is the object, duty and the goal of all rational creatures.'
- Voltaire

'Great minds have purposes, others have wishes.'
- Washington Irving

'When we ... devote ourselves to the strict and unsparing performance of duty, ihen happiness comes of itself.'
- Wilhelm von Humboldt

'Never mind your happiness; do your duty.'
- Will Durant

'The fact that I was a girl never damaged my ambitions to be a pope or an emperor.'
- Willa Cather

'That is happiness: to be dissolved into something completely great.'
- Willa Cather

'Happiness is essentially a state of going somewhere, wholeheartedly, one-directionally, without regret or reservation.'
- William H. Sheldon

'I can tell you how to get what you want: You've just got to keep a thing in view and go for it and never let your eyes wander to right or left or up or down. And looking back is fatal.'
- William J. Lock

'The greatest use of life is to spend it for something that will outlast it.'
   - William James

'A determinate purpose of life, and steady adhesion to it through all disadvantages, are indispensable conditions of success.'
   - William M. Punshion

'Unless you give yourself to some great cause, you haven't even begun to live.'
   - William P. Merrill

'A lot of young girls have looked to their career paths and have said they'd like to be chief. There's been a change in the limits people see.'
   - Wilma Pearl Mankiller

GREATNESS

'A great secret of success is to go through life as a man who never gets used up.'
- Albert Schweitzer

'Great men are not always wise.'
- Bible

'Greatness is a road leading towards the unknown.'
- Charles de Gaulle

'None think the great unhappy, but the great.'
- Edward Young

'Only great men may have great faults.'
- French proverb

'The world knows nothing of its greatest men.'
- Henry Taylor

'Everything great in the world comes from neurotics. They alone have founded our religions, and composed our masterpieces. Never will the world know all it owes to them, nor all they have suffered to enrich us.'
- Marcel Proust

'In great moments life seems neither right nor wrong, but something greater: it seems inevitable.'
- Margaret Sherwood

'Behind every great man there is a surprised woman.'
- Maryon Pearson

'The great are great only because we are on our knees. Let us rise!'
- Max Stirner

'Every calling is great when greatly pursued.'
- Oliver Wendell Holmes

'All the great blessings of my life are present in my thoughts today.'
- Phoebe Cary

'Clever men are impressed in their differences from their fellows. Wise men are conscious of their resemblance to them.'
- R. H. Tawney

'All great men come out of the middle classes.'
- Ralph Waldo Emerson

'A great part of courage is the courage of having done the thing before.'
- Ralph Waldo Emerson

'A great man stands on God. A small man stands on a great man.'
- Ralph Waldo Emerson

'I'm a great believer in luck. I find the harder I work, the more I have of it.'
- Stephen Leacock

'Great and good are seldom the same man.'
- Thomas Fuller

'Life is a great surprise. I do not see why death should not be an even greater one.'
- Vladimir Nabokov

HAPPINESS

'I have known some quite good people who were unhappy, but never an interested person who was unhappy.'
- A. C. Benson

'If this world affords true happiness, it is to be found in a home where love and confidence increase with the years, where the necessities of life come without severe strain, where luxuries enter only after their cost has been carefully considered.'
- A. Edward Newton

'The formula for complete happiness is to be very busy with the unimportant.'
- A. Edward Newton

'The formula for complete happiness is to be very busy.'
- A. Edward Newton

'If you have not often felt the joy of doing a kind act, you have neglected much, and most of all yourself.'
- A. Neilen

'Most folk are about as happy as they make up their minds to be.'
- Abraham Lincoln

'I went back to being an amateur, in the sense of somebody who loves what she is doing. If a professional loses the love of work, routine sets in, and that's the death of work and life.'
- Ada Bethune

'To seek after beauty as an end, is a wild goose chase, a will-o'-the-wisp, because it is to misunderstand the very nature of beauty, which is the normal condition of a thing being as it should be.'
- Ada Bethune

'What can be added to the happiness of man who is in health, out of debt, and has a clear conscience?'
- Adam Smith

'It is not easy to find happiness in ourselves, and it is not possible to find it elsewhere.'
- Agnes Repplier

'We cannot really love anybody with whom we never laugh.'
- Agnes Repplier

'The tourist may complain of other tourists, but he would be lost without them.'
- Agnes Repplier

'It is in his pleasure that a man really lives.'
- Agnes Repplier

'I am happy and content because I think I am.'
- Alain-Rene Lesage

'To be happy, we must not be too concerned with others.'
- Albert Camus

'But what is happiness except the simple harmony between a man and the life he leads?'
- Albert Camus

'Happiness? That's nothing more than health and a poor memory.'
- Albert Schweitzer

'Life becomes harder for us when we live for others, but it also becomes richer and happier.'
- Albert Schweitzer

'Happiness is something you get as a by-product in the process of making something else.'
- Aldous Huxley

'It is not the level of prosperity that makes for happiness but the kinship of heart to heart and the way we look at the world. Both attitudes are within our power, so that a man is happy so long as he chooses to be happy, and no one can stop him.'
- Aleksandr Solzhenitsyn

'False happiness is like false money; it passes for a long time as well as the true, and serves some ordinary occasions; but when it is brought to the touch, we find the lightness and alloy, and feel the loss.'
- Alexander Pope

'Amusement is the happiness of those who cannot think.'
- Alexander Pope

'The happiness of a man in this life does not consist in the absence, but in the mastery, of his passions.'
- Alfred, Lord Tennyson

'Happiness is not a matter of events; it depends upon the tides of the mind.'
- Alice Meynell

'Celebrate the happiness that friends are always giving, make every day a holiday and celebrate just living!'
- Amanda Bradley

'It is always the simple that produces the marvelous.'
- Amelia Barr

'A good message will always find a messenger.'
- Amelia Barr

'We hear voices in solitude, we never hear in the hurry and turmoil of life; we receive counsels and comforts we get under no other condition.'
- Amelia Barr

'Happiness, to some, is elation; to others it is mere stagnation.'
- Amy Lowell

'Scatter seeds of kindness everywhere you go; Scatter bits of courtesy-watch them grow and grow. Gather buds of friendship, keep them till full-blown; You will find more happiness than you have ever known.'
- Amy R. Raabe

'I will not be just a tourist in the world of images, just watching images passing by which I cannot live in, make love to, possess as permanent sources of joy and ecstasy.'
- Anais Nin

'What we call happiness is what we do not know.'
- Anatole France

'In order to be utterly happy the only thing necessary is to refrain from comparing this moment with other moments in the past, which I often did not fully enjoy because I was comparing them with other moments of the future.'
- Andre Gide

'To win one's joy through struggle is better than to yield to melancholy.'
- Andre Gide

'Few are they who have never had the chance to achieve happiness ... and fewer those who have taken that chance.'
- Andre Maurois

'The first recipe for happiness is: Avoid too lengthy meditations on the past.'
- Andre Maurois

'You leave home to seek your fortune and, when you get it, you go home and share it with your family.'
- Anita Baker

'The best things in life aren't things.'
- Ann Landers

'We can sometimes love what we do not understand, but it is impossible completely to understand what we do not love.'
- Anna Jameson

'The right to happiness is fundamental.'
- Anna Pavlova

'The truth is, laughter always sounds more perfect than weeping. Laughter flows in a violent riff and is effortlessly melodic. Weeping is often fought, choked, half strangled, or surrendered to with humiliation.'
- Anne Rice

'And when our baby stirs and struggles to be born it compels humility: what we began is now its own.'
- Anne Ridler

'To love deeply in one direction makes us more loving in all others.'
- Anne-Sophie Swetchine

'All happiness is in the mind.'
- Anonymous

'The really happy man is one who can enjoy the scenery on a detour.'
- Anonymous

'Who will present pleasure refrain, shall in time to come the more pleasure obtain.'
- Anonymous

'No pleasure without pain.'
- Anonymous

'Happiness consists of living each day as if it were the first day of your honeymoon and the last day of your vacation.'
- Anonymous

'Pleasure is not pleasant unless it cost dear.'
- Anonymous

'Happy is he that chastens himself.'
- Anonymous

'When you dig another out of their troubles, you find a place to bury your own.'
- Anonymous

'The best way for a person to have happy thoughts is to count his blessings and not his cash.'
- Anonymous

'Laughter is the best medicine.'
- Anonymous

'Sadness and gladness succeed each other.'
- Anonymous

'Happiness is often the result of being too busy to be miserable.'
- Anonymous

'Why not learn to enjoy the little things-there are so many of them.'
- Anonymous

'He who leaves his house in search of happiness pursues a shadow.'
- Anonymous

'Enjoy yourself. These are the "good old days" you're going to miss in the years ahead.'
- Anonymous

'Some pursue happiness, others create it.'
- Anonymous

'It is comparison that makes men happy or miserable.'
- Anonymous

'Do all the good you can, By all the means you can, In all the ways you can, In all the places you can, At all the times you can.'
- Anonymous

'It isn't our position, but our disposition, that makes us happy.'
- Anonymous

'Let him that would be happy for a day, go to the barber; for a week, marry a wife; for a month, buy him a new horse; for a year, build him a new house; for all his lifetime, be an honest man.'
- Anonymous

'Being asked one day what was the surest way of remaining happy in this world, the Emperor Sigismund of Germany replied: "Only do in health what you have promised to do when you were sick."'
- Anonymous

'If ignorance is bliss, why aren't there more happy teenagers?'
- Anonymous

'You cannot always have happiness, but you can always give happiness.'
- Anonymous

'Better be happy than wise.'
- Anonymous

'Men are made for happiness, and anyone who is completely happy has a right to say to himself: "I am doing God's will on earth."'
- Anton Chekhov

'Different men seek ... happiness in different ways and by different means.'
- Aristotle

'Happiness is the meaning and the purpose of life, the whole aim and end of human existence'
- Aristotle

'Happiness seems to require a modicum of external prosperity.'
- Aristotle

'Happiness depends upon ourselves.'
- Aristotle

'Happiness is an expression of the soul in considered Taking Actions.'
- Aristotle

'Congenial labor is the secret of happiness.'
- Arthur Christopher Benson

'Happiness belongs to those who are sufficient unto themselves. For all external sources of happiness and pleasure are, by their very nature, highly uncertain, precarious, ephemeral and subject to chance.'
- Arthur Schopenhauer

'Money is human happiness in the abstract; he, then, who is no longer capable of enjoying human happiness in the concrete devotes himself utterly to money.'
- Arthur Schopenhauer

'I find my joy of living in the fierce and ruthless battles of life.'
- August Strindberg

'Happiness is that state of consciousness which proceeds from the achievement of one's values.'
- Ayn Rand

'My happiness is not the means to any end. It is the end. It is its own goal. It is its own purpose.'
- Ayn Rand

'Money, or even power, can never yield happiness unless it be accompanied by the goodwill of others.'
- B. C. Forbes

'Everything holds its breath except spring. She bursts through as strong as ever.'
- B. M. Bower

'Surfeits of happiness are fatal.'
- Baltasar Gracian

'Whether you are talking about education, career, or service, you are talking about life. And life must really have joy. It's supposed to be fun.'
- Barbara Bush

'If you aren't good at loving yourself, you will have a difficult time loving anyone, since you'll resent the time and energy you give another person that you aren't even giving to yourself.'
- Barbara De Angelis

'Love is a force more formidable than any other. It is invisible-it cannot be seen or measured, yet it is powerful enough to transform you in a moment, and offer you more joy than any material possession could.'
- Barbara De Angelis

'It's what you do that makes your soul, not the other way around.'
- Barbara Kingsolver

'Sometimes the strength of motherhood is greater than natural laws.'
- Barbara Kingsolver

'The real winners in life are the people who look at every situation with an expectation that they can make it work or make it better.'
- Barbara Pletcher

'A good laugh makes any interview, or any conversation, so much better.'
- Barbara Walters

'We cannot hold a torch to light another's path without brightening our own.'
- Ben Sweetland

'The U.S. Constitution doesn't guarantee happiness, only the pursuit of it. Your have to catch up with it yourself.'
- Benjamin Franklin

'Happiness consists more in small conveniences or pleasures that occur every day, than in great pieces of good fortune that happen but seldom.'
- Benjamin Franklin

'Spiritual life is like a moving sidewalk. Whether you go with it or spend your whole life running against it, you're still going to be taken along.'
- Bernadette Roberts

'A great obstacle to happiness is to expect too much happiness.'
- Bernard de Fontenelle

'The simple truth is that happy people generally don't get sick.'
- Bernie S. Siegel

'Getting what you go after is success; but liking it while you are getting it is happiness.'
- Bertha Damon

'Everyone chases after happiness, not noticing that happiness is at their heels.'
- Bertolt Brecht

'What's joy to one is a nightmare to the other.'
- Bertolt Brecht

'If all our happiness is bound up entirely in our personal circumstances, it is difficult not to demand of life more than it has to give.'
- Bertrand Russell

'Continuity of purpose is one of the most essential ingredients of happiness in the long run, and for most men this comes chiefly through their work.'
- Bertrand Russell

'A happy life must be to a great extent a quiet life, for it is only in an atmosphere of quiet that true joy can live.'
- Bertrand Russell

'To be without some of the things you want is an indispensable part of happiness.'
- Bertrand Russell

'A sure way to lose happiness, I found, is to want it at the expense of everything else.'
- Bette Davis

'To fulfill a dream, to be allowed to sweat over lonely labor, to be given the chance to create, is the meat and potatoes of life. The money is the gravy.'
- Bette Davis

'He that despiseth his neighbor sinneth; but he that hath mercy on the poor, happy is he.'
- Bible

'He that is of a merry heart hath a continual feast.'
- Bible

'Behold, we count them happy which endure. Ye have heard of the patience of Job.'
- Bible

'. . . the little hills rejoice on every side. The pastures are clothed with flocks; the valleys also are covered over with corn; they shout for joy, they also sing.'
- Bible

'The joyfulness of a man prolongeth his days.'
- Bible

'All men have happiness as their object: there are no exceptions. However different the means they employ, they aim at the same end.'
- Blaise Pascal

'Instinct teaches us to look for happiness outside ourselves.'
- Blaise Pascal

'Everyone, without exception, is searching for happiness.'
- Blaise Pascal

'All I can say about life is, Oh God, enjoy it!'
  - Bob Newhart

'It is only by expressing all that is inside that purer and purer streams come.'
  - Brenda Ueland

'If you pursue happiness you'll never find it.'
  - C. P. Snow

'So they speak soothingly about progress and the greatest possible happiness, forgetting that happiness is itself poisoned if the measure of suffering has not been fulfilled.'
  - Carl Jung

'A happy life is made up of little things ... a gift sent, a letter written, a call made, a recommendation given, transportation provided, a cake made, a book lent, a check sent.'
  - Carol Holmes

'It's no good saying one thing and doing another.'
  - Catherine Cookson

'First health, then wealth, then pleasure, and do not owe anything to anybody.'
  - Catherine the Great

'If you want to die happily, learn to live; if you would live happily, learn to die.'
  - Celio Calcagnini

'The greatest happiness of the greatest number.'
  - Cesare Beccaria

'Happiness is a way station between too little and too much.'
  - Channing Pollock

'A multitude of small delights constitute happiness.'
  - Charles Baudelaire

'Happiness ... leads none of us by the same route.'
  - Charles Caleb Colton

'To be obliged to beg our daily happiness from others bespeaks a more lamentable poverty than that of him who begs his daily bread.'
  - Charles Caleb Colton

'The man of pleasure, by a vain attempt to be more happy than any man can be, is often more miserable than most men.'
  - Charles Caleb Colton

'False happiness renders men stern and proud, and that happiness is never communicated. True happiness renders kind and sensible, and that happiness is always shared.'
  - Charles de Montesquieu

'No one can sincerely try to help another without helping himself.'
   - Charles Dudley Warner

'New Year's Day is every man's birthday.'
   - Charles Lamb

'My life has no purpose, no direction, no aim, no meaning, and yet I'm happy. I can't figure it out. What am I doing right?'
   - Charles M. Schulz

'It has never been given to a man to attain at once his happiness and his salvation.'
   - Charles Peguy

'Make one person happy each day and in forty years you will have made 14,600 human beings happy for a little time, at least.'
   - Charley Willey

'Happiness quite unshared can scarcely be called happiness; it has no taste.'
   - Charlotte Bronte

'To attain happiness in another world we need only to believe something; to secure it in this world, we must do something.'
   - Charlotte P. Gilman

'Happiness to a dog is what lies on the other side of a door.'
   - Charlton Ogburn

'Happiness to a dog is what lies on the other side of the door.'
   - Charlton Ogburn

'Anyone who's a great kisser I'm always interested in.'
   - Cher

'Make happy those who are near, and those who are far will come.'
   - Chinese proverb

'Happiness is not a horse, you cannot harness it.'
   - Chinese proverb

'A bit of fragrance always clings to the hand that gives you roses.'
   - Chinese proverb

'With happiness comes intelligence to the heart.'
   - Chinese proverb

'Contentment is not happiness. An oyster may be contented. Happiness is compounded of richer elements.'
   - Christian Bovee

'My heart is like a singing bird.'
- Christina Georgina Tossetti

'Perfect happiness is the absence of striving for happiness.'
- Chuang-tzu

'A life of frustration is inevitable for any coach whose main enjoyment is winning.'
- Chuck Noll

'I never admired another's fortune so much that I became dissatisfied with my own.'
- Cicero

'A happy life consists in tranquility of mind.'
- Cicero

'There is no other solution to man's progress but the day's honest work, the day's honest decisions, the day's generous utterances, and the day's good deed.'
- Clare Boothe Luce

'No social system will bring us happiness, health and prosperity unless it is inspired by something greater than materialism.'
- Clement R. Attlee

'Hope costs nothing.'
- Colette

'Be happy. It's one way of being wise.'
- Colette

'At rare moments in history, by a series of accidents never to be repeated, arise flower societies in which the cult of happiness is paramount, hedonistic, mindless, intent upon the glorious physical instant.'
- Colm MacInnes

'The way of a superior man is threefold: Virtuous, he is free from anxieties; wise, he is free from perplexities; bold, he is free from fear.'
- Confucius

'Is life worth living? Aye, with the best of us, Heights of us, depths of us- Life is the test of us!'
- Corinne Roosevelt Robinson

'Happiness lies in the fulfillment of the spirit through the body.'
- Cyril Connolly

'Happiness is not a possession to be prized, it is a quality of thought, a state of mind.'
- Daphne du Maurier

'Happiness ... loves to see men work. She loves sweat, weariness, self-sacrifice. She will not be found in the palaces, but lurking in cornfields and factories, and hovering over littered desks.'
  - David Grayson

'Back of tranquility lies always captured unhappiness.'
  - David Grazin

'Happiness is Taking Action.'
  - David Thomas

'Happy people plan Taking Actions, they don't plan results.'
  - Dennis Wholey

'Happiness is a by-product of helping others.'
  - Denny Miller

'A mother's arms are more comforting than anyone else's.'
  - Diana, Princess of Wales

'I don't want to get to the end of my life and find that I lived just the length of it. I want to have lived the width of it as well.'
  - Diane Ackerman

'One of the things I keep learning is that the secret of being happy is doing things for other people.'
  - Dick Gregory

'Happiness comes fleetingly now and then, To those who have learned to do without it And to them only.'
  - Don Marquis

'It is better to be happy for a moment and be burned up with beauty than to live a long time and be bored all the while.'
  - Don Marquis

'Happiness is the interval between periods of unhappiness.'
  - Don Marquis

'Happiness comes fleetingly now and then to those who have learned to do without it, and to them only.'
  - Don Marquis

'In the Orient people believed that the basis of all disease was unhappiness. Thus to make a patient happy again was to restore him to health.'
  - Donald Law

'What matters most is that we learn from living.'
  - Doris Lessing

'Laughter is by definition healthy.'
  - Doris Lessing

'Happiness grows at our own firesides, and is not to be picked in strangers' gardens.'
  - Douglas Jerrold

'Happiness is mostly a by-product of doing what makes us feel fulfilled.'
  - Dr. Benjamin Spock

'Like swimming, riding, writing or playing golf, happiness can be learned.'
  - Dr. Boris Sokoloff

'Those who are the most happy appear to know it the least; happiness is something that for the most part seems to mainly consist in not knowing it.'
  - Dr. Joyce Brothers

'Those who have easy, cheerful attitudes tend to be happier than those with less pleasant temperaments regardless of money, "making it" or success.'
  - Dr. Joyce Brothers

'When you come right down to it, the secret of having it all is loving it all.'
  - Dr. Joyce Brothers

'Joy is the feeling of grinning on the inside.'
  - Dr. Melba Colgrove

'Man is happy only as he finds a work worth doing-and does it well.'
  - E. Merrill Root

'Happiness has many roots, but none more important than security.'
  - E. R. Stettinius

'Suspicion of happiness is in our blood.'
  - E. V. Lucas

'Man's real life is happy, chiefly because he is ever expecting that it soon will be so.'
  - Edgar Allan Poe

'They seemed to come suddenly upon happiness as if they had surprised a butterfly in the winter woods.'
  - Edith Wharton

'If only we'd stop trying to be happy we'd have a pretty good time.'
  - Edith Wharton

'The secret of happiness is to admire without desiring.'
  - EH. Bradley

'Get happiness out of your work or you may never know what happiness is.'
- Elbert Hubbard

'Life without absorbing occupation is hell.'
- Elbert Hubbard

'Life has got to be lived-that's all that there is to it.'
- Eleanor Roosevelt

'Happiness is not a goal, it is a byproduct.'
- Eleanor Roosevelt

'Though language forms the preacher, 'Tis "good works" make the man.'
- Eliza Cook

'Treat a horse like a woman and a woman like a horse. And they'll both win for you.'
- Elizabeth Arden

'Change is an easy panacea. It takes character to stay in one place and be happy there.'
- Elizabeth Clarke Dunn

'When you're in your nineties and looking back, it's not going to be how much money you made or how many awards you've won. It's really what did you stand for. Did you make a positive difference for people?'
- Elizabeth Dole

'A caress is better than a career.'
- Elizabeth Marbury

'The major job was getting people to understand that they had something within their power that they could use.'
- Ella Baker

'Love lights more fires than hate extinguishes, And men grow better as the world grows old.'
- Ella Wheeler Wilcox

'Talk happiness. The world is sad enough without your woe. No path is wholly rough.'
- Ella Wheeler Wilcox

'The genius of happiness is still so rare, is indeed on the whole the rarest genius. To possess it means to approach life with the humility of a beggar, but to treat it with the proud generosity of a prince; to bring to its totality the deep understanding '
- Ellen Key

'Eating is not merely a material pleasure. Eating well gives a spectacular joy to life and contributes immensely to goodwill and happy companionship. It is of great importance to the morale.'
- Elsa Schiapirelli

'The only way to happiness is never to give happiness a thought.'
- Elton Trueblood

'To live is so startling it leaves little time for anything else.'
- Emily Dickinson

'Eden is that old-fashioned house we dwell in every day without suspecting our abode until we drive away.'
- Emily Dickinson

'Where thou art, that is home.'
- Emily Dickinson

'For each ecstatic instant We must an anguish pay In keen and quivering ratio To the ecstasy.'
- Emily Dickinson

'The attributes of a great lady may still be found in the rule of the four S's: Sincerity, Simplicity, Sympathy, and Serenity.'
- Emily Post

'A joy that's shared is a joy made double.'
- English proverb

'The essence of philosophy is that a man should so live that his happiness shall depend as little as possible on external things.'
- Epictetus

'It is the chiefest point of happiness that a man is willing to be what he is.'
- Erasmus

'The happiness of most people is not ruined by great catastrophes or fatal errors, but by the repetition of slowly destructive little things.'
- Ernest Dimnet

'May you have warmth in your igloo, oil in your lamp, and peace in your heart.'
- Eskimo proverb

'We learn the inner secret of happiness when we learn to direct our inner drives, our interest, and our attention to something besides ourselves.'
- Ethel Percy Andrus

'Happiness hates the timid!'
- Eugene O'Neill

'Happiness is brief It will not stay. God batters at its sails.'
- Euripides

'That man is happiest who lives from day to day and asks no more, garnering the simple goodness of a life.'
- Euripides

'It is those who have a deep and real inner life who are best able to deal with the irritating details of outer life.'
- Evelyn Underhill

'When love is out of your life, you're through in a way. Because while it is there it's like a motor that's going, you have such vitality to do things, big things, because love is goosing you all the time.'
- Fanny Brice

'For me it is sufficient to have a corner by my hearth, a book and a friend, and a nap undisturbed by creditors or grief.'
- Fernandez de Andrada

'I love, and the world is mine!'
- Florence Earle Coates

'The attainment of justice is the highest human endeavor.'
- Florence Ellinwood Allen

'Seldom can the heart be lonely, If it seeks a lonelier still; Self-forgetting, seeking only Emptier cups of love to fill.'
- Frances Ridley Havergal

'They are happy men whose natures sort with their vocations.'
- Francis Bacon

'If we have not peace within ourselves, it is in vain to seek it from outward sources.'
- Francois de La Rochefoucauld

'A man's happiness or unhappiness depends as much on his temperament as on his destiny.'
- Francois de La Rochefoucauld

'No sooner is it a little calmer with me than it is almost too calm, as though I have the true feeling of myself only when I am unbearably unhappy.'
- Franz Kafka

'To make a man happy, fill his hands with work.'
- Frederick E. Crane

'To make a man happy, fill his hands with work, his heart with affection, his mind with purpose, his memory with useful knowledge, his future with hope, and his stomach with food.'
- Frederick E. Crane

'If I were to suggest a general rule for happiness, I would say "Work a little harder; Work a little longer; Work!"'
- Frederick H. Ecker

'Man is preceded by forest followed by desert.'
- French graffiti

'Perhaps the best function of parenthood is to teach the young creature to love with safety, so that it may be able to venture unafraid when later emotion comes; the thwarting of the instinct to love is the root of all sorrow and not sex only but divinity '
- Freya Stark

'There can be no happiness if the things we believe in are different from the things we do.'
- Freya Stark

'The will of man is his happiness.'
- Friedrich von Schiller

'We are all happy, if we only knew it.'
- Fyodor Dostoyevsky

'Man is fond of counting his troubles, but he does not count his joys. If he counted them up as he ought to, he would see that every lot has enough happiness provided for it.'
- Fyodor Dostoyevsky

'The true object of all human life is play.'
- G. K. Chesterton

'No man can be merry unless he is serious.'
- G. K. Chesterton

'Happiness is a mystery like religion, and it should never be rationalized.'
- G. K. Chesterton

'Happy is he who still loves something he loved in the nursery: He has not been broken in two by time; he is not two men, but one, and he has saved not only his soul, but his life.'
- G. K. Chesterton

'The more the heart is sated with joy, the more it becomes insatiable.'
- Gabrielle Roy

'She knew what all smart women knew: Laughter made you live better and longer.'
- Gail Parent

'No one gives joy or sorrow. ... We gather the consequences of our own deeds.'
- Garuda Purana

'Everyone only goes around the track once in life, and if you don't enjoy that trip, it's pretty pathetic.'
- Gary Rogers

'There is work that is work and there is play that is play; there is play that is work and work that is play. And in only one of these lie happiness.'
- Gelett Burgess

'We have no more right to consume happiness without producing it than to consume wealth without producing it.'
   - George Bernard Shaw

'The only way to avoid being miserable is not to have enough leisure to wonder whether you are happy or not.'
   - George Bernard Shaw

'The secret of being miserable is to have leisure to bother about whether you are happy or not.'
   - George Bernard Shaw

'Happiness and beauty are by-products. Folly is the direct pursuit of happiness and beauty.'
   - George Bernard Shaw

'I look better, feel better, make love better, and I'll tell you something else ... I never lied better.'
   - George Burns

''Tis what I love determines how I love.'
   - George Eliot

'Have a variety of interests. ... These interests relax the mind and lessen tension on the nervous system. People with many interests live, not only longest, but happiest.'
   - George Matthew Allen

'There is only one happiness in life, to love and be loved.'
   - George Sand

'One is happy as a result of one's own efforts-once one knows the necessary ingredients of happiness-simple tastes, a certain degree of courage, self-denial to a point, love of work, and, above all, a clear conscience.'
   - George Sand

'Happiness lies in the consciousness we have of it.'
   - George Sand

'Knowledge of what is possible is the beginning of happiness.'
   - George Santayana

'Happiness is the only sanction in life; where happiness fails, existence remains a mad and lamentable experiment.'
   - George Santayana

'I believe in the possibility of happiness, if one cultivates intuition and outlives the grosser passions, including optimism.'
   - George Santayana

'All the goodness, beauty, and perfection of a human being belong to the one who knows how to recognize these qualities.'
   - Georgette Leblanc

'Anarchy is against the law.'
- Graffiti

'When I was young I used to think that wealth and power would bring me happiness. I was right.'
- Graham Wilson

'Painting's not important. The important thing is keeping busy.'
- Grandma Moses

'He who would be happy should stay at home.'
- Greek proverb

'The habit of being uniformly considerate toward others will bring increased happiness to you.'
- Grenville Kleiser

'Human life is basically a comedy. Even its tragedies often seem comic to the spectator, and not infrequently they actually have comic touches to the victim. Happiness probably consists largely in the capacity to detect and relish them.'
- H. L. Mencken

'Love from one being to another can only be that two solitudes come nearer, recognize and protect and comfort each other.'
- Han Suyin

'Love, by its very nature, is unworldly, and it is for this reason rather than its rarity that it is not only apolitical but anti-political, perhaps the most powerful of all anti-political human forces.'
- Hannah Arendt

'Happiness consists in the full employment of our faculties in some pursuit.'
- Harriet Martineau

'Being happy is something you have to learn. I often surprise myself by saying, "Wow, this is it. I guess I'm happy. I've got a home that I love. A career that I love. I'm even feeling more and more at peace with myself." If there's something else to happi'
- Harrison Ford

'The principles we live by, in business and in social life, are the most important part of happiness.'
- Harry Harrison

'I have smelt all the aromas there are in the fragrant kitchen they call Earth; and what we can enjoy in this life, I surely have enjoyed just like a lord!'
- Heinrich Heine

'When one door of happiness closes, another opens; but often we look so long at the closed door that we do not see the one which has been opened for us.'
- Helen Keller

'Joy is the holy fire that keeps our purpose warm and our intelligence aglow.'
- Helen Keller

'Love is like a beautiful flower which I may not touch, but whose fragrance makes the garden a place of delight just the same.'
- Helen Keller

'To live we must conquer incessantly, we must have the courage to be happy.'
- Henri Frederic Amiel

'This is life! It can harden and it can exalt!'
- Henrik Ibsen

'Man is the artificer of his own happiness.'
- Henry David Thoreau

'There is no happiness in having or in getting, but only in giving.'
- Henry Drummond

'Happiness ... consists in giving, and in serving others.'
- Henry Drummond

'Live all you can; it's a mistake not to. It doesn't so much matter what you do in particular, so long as you have your life. If you haven't had that, what have you had?'
- Henry James

'No man is more cheated than the selfish man.'
- Henry Ward Beecher

'I believe that a worthwhile life is defined by a kind of spiritual journey and a sense of obligation.'
- Hillary Rodham Clinton

'True happiness consists in making others happy.'
- Hindu proverb

'Those who seek happiness miss it, and those who discuss it, lack it.'
- Holbrook Jackson

'Your readiest desire is your path to joy ... even if it destroys you.'
- Holbrook Jackson

'And may I live the remainder of my life ... for myself; may there be plenty of books and many years' store of the fruits of the earth!'
- Horace

'You will live wisely if you are happy in your lot.'
- Horace

'Real happiness is cheap enough, yet how dearly we pay for its counterfeit.'
- Hosea Ballou

'The happiest people I have known in this world have been the Saints-and, after these, the men and women who get immediate and conscious enjoyment from little things.'
- Hugh Walpole

'If we cannot live so as to be happy, let us at least live so as to deserve it.'
- Immanuel Hermann von Fichte

'Happiness is good health and a bad memory.'
- Ingrid Bergman

'Even if we can't be happy, we must always be cheerful.'
- Irving Kristol

'One must never look for happiness: one meets it by the way.'
- Isabelle Eberhardt

'I don't think that... one gets a flash of happiness once, and never again; it is there within you, and it will come as certainly as death.'
- Isak Dinesen

'We women ought to put first things first. Why should we mind if men have their faces on the money, as long as we get our hands on it?'
- Ivy Baker Priest

'There are four things a child needs: plenty of love, nourishing food, regular sleep, and lots of soap and water.'
- Ivy Baker Priest

'We can build upon foundations anywhere, if they are well and truly laid.'
- Ivy Compton-Burnett

'Happiness comes more from loving than being loved; and often when our affection seems wounded it is only our vanity bleeding. To love, and to be hurt often, and to love again-this is the brave and happy life.'
- J. E. Buckrose

'I believe the recipe for happiness to be just enough money to pay the monthly bills you acquire, a little surplus to give you confidence, a little too much work each day, enthusiasm for your work, a substantial share of good health, a couple of real frien'
- J. Kenfield Morley

'The medals don't mean anything and the glory doesn't last. It's all about your happiness. The rewards are going to come, but my happiness is just loving the sport and having fun performing.'
- Jackie Joyner-Kersee

'I don't think being an athlete is unfeminine. I think of it as a kind of grace.'
- Jackie Joyner-Kersee

'Seek to do good, and you will find that happiness will run after you.'
- James Freeman Clarke

'The secret of happiness is not in doing what one likes, but in liking what one has to do.'
- James M. Barrie

'That sanguine expectation of happiness which is happiness itself.'
- Jane Austen

'Why not seize the pleasure at once? How often is happiness destroyed by preparation, foolish preparation?'
- Jane Austen

'There is nothing like staying at home for real comfort.'
- Jane Austen

'Parents, however old they and we may grow to be, serve among other things to shield us from a sense of our doom. As long as they are around, we can avoid the fact of our mortality; we can still be innocent children.'
- Jane Howard

'Happiness is not perfected until it is shared.'
- Jane Porter

'People genuinely happy in their choices seem less often tempted to force them on other people than those who feel martyred and broken by their lives.'
- Jane Rule

'Beauty is a radiance that originates from within and comes from inner security and strong character.'
- Jane Seymour

'The most exquisite pleasure is giving pleasure to others.'
- Jean de la Bruyere

'What families have in common the world around is that they are the place where people learn who they are and how to be that way.'
- Jean Illsley Clarke

'Happiness: a good bank account, a good cook and a good digestion.'
- Jean-Jacques Rousseau

'Age does not protect you from love but love to some extent protects you from age.'
- Jeanne Moreau

'The greatest happiness of the greatest number is the foundation of morals and legislation.'
- Jeremy Bentham

'Let your boat of life be light, packed only with what you need-a homely home and simple pleasures, one or two friends worth the name, someone to love and to love you, a cat, a dog, enough to eat and

enough to wear, and a little more than enough to drink, '
- Jerome K. Jerome

'Accept the pain, cherish the joys, resolve the regrets; then can come the best of benedictions-"If I had my life to live over, I'd do it all the same."'
- Joan Mcintosh

'This will be triumph! This will be happiness! Yea, that very thing, happiness, which I have been pursuing all my life, and have never yet overtaken.'
- Joanna Baillie

'Let how you live your life stand for something, no matter how small and incidental it may seem.'
- Jodie Foster

'Love and respect are the most important aspects of parenting, and of all relationships.'
- Jodie Foster

'Who is the happiest of men? He who values the merits of others, And in their pleasure takes joy, even as though t'were his own.'
- Johann von Goethe

'A reasonable man needs only to practice moderation to find happiness.'
- Johann von Goethe

'He is happiest, be he king or peasant, who finds peace in his home.'
- Johann von Goethe

'Even the lowliest, provided he is whole, can be happy, and in his own . way, perfect.'
- Johann von Goethe

'Happiness is not in our circumstances, but in ourselves. It is not something we see, like a rainbow, or feel, like the heat of a fire. Happiness is something we are.'
- John B. Sheerin

'Happiness sneaks in through a door you didn't know you left open.'
- John Barrymore

'The bird of paradise alights only on the hand that does not grasp.'
- John Berry

'Happiness comes most to persons who seek it least, and think least about it. It is not an object to be sought, it is a state to be induced. It must follow and not lead. It must overtake you, and not you overtake it.'
- John Burroughs

'Few persons realize how much of their happiness, such as it is, is dependent upon their work.'
- John Burroughs

'The road to happiness lies in two simple principles: find what it is that interests you and that you can do well, and when you find it put your whole soul into it-every bit of energy and ambition and natural ability you have.'
   - John D. Rockefeller III

'To find out what one is fitted to do, and to secure an opportunity to do it, is the key to happiness.'
   - John Dewey

'Only man clogs his happiness with care, destroying what is, with thoughts of what may be.'
   - John Dryden

'If all were gentle and contented as sheep, all would be as feeble and helpless.'
   - John Lancaster Spalding

'Best trust the happy moments. ... The days that make us happy make us wise.'
   - John Masefield

'I know well that happiness is in little things.'
   - John Ruskin

'When men are rightly occupied, their amusement grows out of their work, as the color-petals out of a fruitful flower.'
   - John Ruskin

'When I have been unhappy, I have heard an opera ... and it seemed the shrieking of winds; when I am happy, a sparrow's chirp is delicious to me. But it is not the chirp that makes me happy, but I that make it sweet.'
   - John Ruskin

'Unquestionably, it is possible to do without happiness; it is done involuntarily by nineteen-twentieths of mankind.'
   - John Stuart Mill

'Ask yourself whether you are happy, and you will cease to be so.'
   - John Stuart Mill

'Not only is there a right to be happy, there is a duty to be happy. So much sadness exists in the world that we are all under obligation to contribute as much joy as lies within our powers.'
   - John Sutherland Bonnell

'True happiness is of a retired nature and an enemy to pomp and noise; it arises, in the first place, from the enjoyment of one's self; and, in the next, from the friendship and conversations of a few select companions.'
   - Joseph Addison

'The grand essentials to happiness in this life are something to do, something to love and something to hope for.'
   - Joseph Addison

'A man should always consider how much he has more than he wants, and how much more unhappy he might be than he really is.'
- Joseph Addison

'Happiness, happiness ... the flavor is with you-with you alone, and you can make it as intoxicating as you please.'
- Joseph Conrad

'Enjoy your happiness while you have it, and while you have it do not too closely scrutinize its foundation.'
- Joseph Farrell

'Without duty, life is soft and bone less.'
- Joseph Joubert

'It is an aspect of all happiness to suppose that we deserve it.'
- Joseph Joubert

'Misery is almost always the result of thinking.'
- Joseph Joubert

'When unhappy, one doubts everything; when happy, one doubts nothing.'
- Joseph Roux

'I look at what I have not and think myself unhappy; others look at what I have and think me happy.'
- Joseph Roux

'Man is that he might have joy.'
- Joseph Smith

'If we could learn how to balance rest against effort, calmness against strain, quiet against turmoil, we would assure ourselves of joy in living and psychological health for life.'
- Josephine Rathbone

'Don't mistake pleasures for happiness. They are a different breed of dog.'
- Josh Billings

'If you ever find happiness by hunting for it, you will find it, as the old woman did her lost spectacles, safe on her nose all the time.'
- Josh Billings

'Love is the same as like except you feel sexier.'
- Judith Viorst

'Suffering is not a prerequisite for happiness.'
- Judy Tatelbaum

'Little deeds of kindness, little words of love, Help to make earth happy like the heaven up above.'
- Julia A. Fletcher Carney

'Moderation. Small helpings. Sample a little bit of everything. These are the secrets of happiness and good health.'
- Julia Child

'The secret of a happy marriage is finding the right person. You know they're right if you love to be with them all of the time.'
- Julia Child

'I don't think about whether people will remember me or not. I've been an okay person. I've learned a lot. I've taught people a thing or two. That's what's important.'
- Julia Child

'I think the inner person is the most important. ... I would like to see an invention that keeps the mind alert. That's what is important.'
- Julia Child

'We deem those happy who from the experience of life have learned to bear its ills, without being overcome by them.'
- Juvenal

'To love is to receive a glimpse of heaven.'
- Karen Sunde

'In about the same degree as you are helpful, you will be happy.'
- Karl Reiland

'If you always do what interests you, at least one person is pleased.'
- Katharine Hepburn

'If you obey all the rules you miss all the fun.'
- Katharine Hepburn

'There is only one history of any importance, and it is the history of what you once believed in, and the history of what you came to believe in.'
- Kay Boyle

'People who postpone happiness are like children who try chasing rainbows in an effort to find the pot of gold at the rainbow's end. ... Your life will never be fulfilled until you are happy here and now.'
- Ken Keyes

'It's pretty hard to tell what does bring happiness. Poverty and wealth have both failed.'
- Kin Hubbard

'Happiness walks on busy feet.'
- Kitte Turmell

'We are never so happy, nor so unhappy, as we suppose ourselves to be.'
- La Rochefoucauld

'We are never so happy nor so unhappy as we imagine.'
- La Rochefoucauld

'Virtue, like a dowerless beauty, has more admirers than followers.'
- Lady Marguerite Blessington

'Happiness consists not in having much, but in being content with little.'
- Lady Marguerite Blessington

'Happiness is a rare plant that seldom takes root on earth-few ever enjoyed it, except for a brief period; the search after it is rarely rewarded by the discovery, but there is an admirable substitute for it... a contented spirit.'
- Lady Marguerite Blessington

'Live virtuously, and you cannot die too soon, or live too long.'
- Lady R. Russell

'Seek not happiness too greedily, and be not fearful of unhappiness.'
- Lao-Tzu

'Manifest plainness, Embrace simplicity, Reduce selfishness, Have few desires.'
- Lao-Tzu

'I am beginning to learn that it is the sweet, simple things of life which are the real ones after all.'
- Laura Ingalls Wilder

'I don't sit around thinking that I'd like to have another husband; only another man would make me think that way.'
- Lauren Bacall

'Paradise is exactly like where you are right now ... only much, much better.'
- Laurie Anderson

'Happiness comes only when we push our brains and hearts to the farthest reaches of which we are capable.'
- Leo C. Rosten

'Man is meant for happiness and this happiness is in him, in the satisfaction of the daily needs of his existence.'
- Leo Tolstoy

'I cannot and will not cut my conscience to fit this year's fashions.'
- Lillian Hellman

'The older you get, the more you realize that kindness is synonymous with happiness.'
- Lionel Barrymore

'Inspiration never arrived when you were searching for it.'
- Lisa Alther

'What you become is what counts.'
   - Liz Smith

'To live as fully, as completely as possible, to be happy ... is the true aim and end to life.'
   - Llewelyn Powers

'The test of enjoyment is the remembrance which it leaves behind.'
   - Logan Pearsall Smith

'All who would win joy, must share it; happiness was born a twin.'
   - Lord Byron

'Pleasure is a reciprocal; no one feels it who does not at the same time give it. To be pleased, one must please.'
   - Lord Chesterfield

'There is always something left to love. And if you ain't learned that, you ain't learned nothing.'
   - Lorraine Hansbury

'Love is the only thing we can carry with us when we go, and it makes the end so easy.'
   - Louisa May Alcott

'Love is a great beautifier.'
   - Louisa May Alcott

'I was in love with the whole world and all that lived in its rainy arms.'
   - Louise Erdrich

'Our Thoughts Determine Our Happiness High above hate I dwell, 0 storms! Farewell.'
   - Louise Imogen Guiney

'Love is the great miracle cure. Loving ourselves works miracles in our lives.'
   - Louise L. Hay

'The world of those who are happy is different from the world of those who are not.'
   - Ludwig Wittgenstein

'No music is so pleasant to my ears as that word-father.'
   - Lydia M. Child

'The cure for all ills and wrongs, the cares, the sorrows and the crimes of humanity, all lie in the one word 'love.' It is the divine vitality that everywhere produces and restores life.'
   - Lydia M. Child

'Happiness is the perpetual possession of being well deceived.'
   - Lytton Strachey

'I am convinced that we must train not only the head, but the heart and hand as well.'
   - Madame Chiang Kai-Shek

'The true way to soften one's troubles is to solace those of others.'
   - Madame De Maintenon

'Happiness is when what you think, what you say, and what you do are in harmony.'
   - Mahatma Gandhi

'Happiness is not something you get, but something you do.'
   - Marcelene Cox

'Unhappy is the man, though he rule the world, who doesn't consider himself supremely blessed.'
   - Marcus Annaeus Seneca

'A man's as miserable as he thinks he is.'
   - Marcus Annaeus Seneca

'A happy life is one which is in accordance with its own nature.'
   - Marcus Annaeus Seneca

'No man can live happily who regards himself alone, who turns everything to his own advantage. Thou must live for another if thou wishest to live for thyself.'
   - Marcus Annaeus Seneca

'The happiness of your life depends upon the quality of your thoughts.'
   - Marcus Aurelius

'To live happily is an inward power of the soul.'
   - Marcus Aurelius

'If thou workest at that which is before thee ... expecting nothing, fearing nothing, but satisfied with thy present activity according to Nature, and with heroic truth in every word and sound which thou utterest, thou wilt live happy. And there is no man '
   - Marcus Aurelius

'The Eskimos had fifty-two names for snow because it was important to them; there ought to be as many for love.'
   - Margaret Atwood

'Time is compressed like the fist I close on my knee ... I hold inside it the clues and solutions and the power for what I must do now.'
   - Margaret Atwood

'The nice thing about teamwork is that you always have others on your side.'
   - Margaret Carty

'Conscience, as I understand it, is the impulse to do the right thing because it is right, regardless of personal ends, and has nothing whatever to do with the ability to distinguish between right and wrong.'
   - Margaret Collier Graham

'A house is not a home unless it contains food and fire for the mind as well as the body.'
- Margaret Fuller

'Happiness is not a station to arrive at, but a manner of traveling.'
- Margaret Lee Runbeck

'What happiness is there which is not purchased with more or less of pain?'
- Margaret Oliphant

'What a richly colored strong warm coat is woven when love is the warp and work is the woof.'
- Marge Piercy

'My father got me strong and straight and slim And I give thanks to him. My mother bore me glad and sound and sweet, I kiss her feet.'
- Marguerite Wilkinson

'The human heart, at whatever age, opens only to the heart that opens in return.'
- Maria Edgeworth

'We can be wise from goodness and good from wisdom.'
- Marie von Ebner-Eschenbach

'I don't want to make money. I just want to be wonderful.'
- Marilyn Monroe

'To get the full value of a joy you must have somebody to divide it with.'
- Mark Twain

'Happiness is a Swedish sunset; it is there for all, but most of us look the other way and lose it.'
- Mark Twain

'To be busy is man's only happiness.'
- Mark Twain

'The greater part of our happiness or misery depends on our dispositions, and not our circumstances.'
- Martha Washington

'Hire the best. Pay them fairly. Communicate frequently. Provide challenges and rewards. Believe in them. Get out of their way and they'll knock your socks off.'
- Mary Ann Allison

'Small kindnesses, small courtesies, small considerations, habitually practiced in our social intercourse, give a greater charm to the character than the display of great talents and accomplishments.'
- Mary Ann Kelty

'To live and let live, without clamor for distinction or recognition; to wait on divine Love; to write truth first on the tablet of one's own heart-this is the sanity and perfection of living, and my human ideal.'
- Mary Baker Eddy

'To serve thy generation, this thy fate: "Written in water," swiftly fades thy name; But he who loves his kind does, first or late, A work too great for fame.'
- Mary Clemmer

'Build a little fence of trust Around today; Fill the space with loving work, And therein stay.'
- Mary Frances Butts

'Seek not outside yourself, heaven is within.'
- Mary Lou Cook

'I have had more than half a century of such happiness. A great deal of worry and sorrow, too, but never a worry or a sorrow that was not offset by a purple iris, a lark, a bluebird, or a dewy morning glory.'
- Mary McLeod Bethune

'Invest in the human soul. Who knows, it might be a diamond in the rough.'
- Mary McLeod Bethune

'Knowledge is the prime need of the hour.'
- Mary McLeod Bethune

'To be kind to all, to like many and love a few, to be needed and wanted by those we love, is certainly the nearest we can come to happiness.'
- Mary Roberts Rinehart

'Resolve to be thyself; and know that who finds himself, loses his misery.'
- Matthew Arnold

'Love is the only effective counter to death.'
- Maureen Duffy

'Happiness will never be any greater than the idea we have of it.'
- Maurice Maeterlinck

'Why is it that people who cannot show feeling presume that that is a strength and not a weakness?'
- May Sarton

'Each moment in time we have it all, even when we think we don't.'
- Melody Beattie

'I'm happier. ... I guess I made up my mind to be that way.'
- Merle Haggard

'For the happiest life, days should be rigorously planned, nights left open to chance.'
- Mignon McLaughlin

'Everyone speaks of it, few know it.'
- Mme. Jeanne P. Roland

'Not all of us have to possess earth-shaking talent. Just common sense and love will do.'
    - Myrtle Auvil

'For the rational, psychologically healthy man, the desire for pleasure is the desire to celebrate his control over reality. For the neurotic, the desire for pleasure is the desire to escape from reality.'
    - Nathaniel Branden

'If solid happiness we prize, within our breast this jewel lies, And they are fools who roam; the world has nothing to bestow, From our own selves our bliss must flow, And that dear hut-our home.'
    - Nathaniel Cotton

'Happiness is a butterfly which, when pursued, is always beyond our grasp, but, if you will sit down quietly, may alight upon you.'
    - Nathaniel Hawthorne

'Happiness is a resultant of the relative strengths of positive and negative feelings rather than an absolute amount of one or the other.'
    - Norman Bradburn

'Happiness is not so much in having as sharing. We make a living by what we get, but we make a life by what we give.'
    - Norman MacEwan

'Our society allows people to be absolutely neurotic and totally out of touch with their feelings and everyone else's feelings, and yet be very respectable.'
    - Ntozake Shange

'There are only two things that are absolute realities, love and knowledge, and you can't escape them.'
    - Olive Schreiner

'There is nothing ridiculous in love.'
    - Olive Schreiner

'Life is a romantic business, but you have to make the romance.'
    - Oliver Wendell Holmes

'But here's what I've learned in this war, in this country, in this city: to love the miracle of having been born.'
    - Oriana Fallaci

'In this world there are only two tragedies. One is not getting what one wants, and the other is getting it.'
    - Oscar Wilde

'What is it that love does to a woman? Without it, she only sleeps; with it alone, she lives.'
    - Ouida

'An easygoing husband is the one indispensable comfort of life.'
- Ouida

'Happiness is never stopping to think if you are.'
- Palmer Sondreal

'From the moment we walk out the door until we come back home our sensibilities are so assaulted by the world that we have to soak up as much love as we can get, simply to arm ourselves.'
- Patty Duke

'Unhappiness indicates wrong thinking, just as ill health indicates a bad regimen.'
- Paul Bourget

'We must not seek happiness in peace, but in conflict.'
- Paul Claudel

'Happiness is the cheapest thing in the world ... when we buy it for someone else.'
- Paul Flemming

'I am one of those people who just can't help getting a kick out of life - even when it's a kick in the teeth.'
- Paula Adler

'You have much more power when you are working for the right thing than when you are working for the wrong thing.'
- Peace Pilgrim

'People see God every day, they just don't recognize Him.'
- Pearl Bailey

'The sweetest joy, the wildest woe is love.'
- Pearl Bailey

'Growth itself contains the germ of happiness.'
- Pearl S. Buck

'Our Taking Actions are the springs of our happiness or misery.'
- Philip Skelton

'The general rule is that people who enjoy life also enjoy marriage.'
- Phyllis Battelle

'Where there is laughter there is always more health than sickness.'
- Phyllis Bottome

'We never enjoy perfect happiness; our most fortunate successes are mingled with sadness; some anxieties always perplex the reality of our satisfaction.'
- Pierre Corneille

'Without pleasure man would live like a fool and soon die.'
- Pierre de Beaumarchais

'The most satisfying thing in life is to have been able to give a large part of oneself to others.'
- Pierre Teilhard de Chardin

'The man who makes everything that leads to happiness depend upon himself, and not upon other men, has adopted the very best plan for living happily.'
- Plato

'Success can also cause misery. The trick is not to be surprised when you discover it doesn't bring you all the happiness and answers you thought it would.'
- Prince

'No man is happy unless he believes he is.'
- Publilius Syrus

'If a man has important work, and enough leisure and income to enable him to do it properly, he is in possession of as much happiness as is good for any of the children of Adam.'
- R. H. Tawney

'Caring about others, running the risk of feeling, and leaving an impact on people, brings happiness.'
- Rabbi Harold Kushner

'As the sergeant said to the recruit: "You might as well be happy, mate - no one cares if you ain't."'
- Ralph Ricketts

'The happiest man is he who learns from nature the lesson of worship.'
- Ralph Waldo Emerson

'The high prize of life, the crowning fortune of man, is to be born with a bias to some pursuit which finds him in employment and happiness.'
- Ralph Waldo Emerson

'Discontent is want of self-reliance; it is infirmity of will.'
- Ralph Waldo Emerson

'Five great enemies to peace inhabit us: avarice, ambition, envy, anger and pride. If those enemies were to be banished, we should infallibly enjoy perpetual peace.'
- Ralph Waldo Emerson

'A man is relieved and gay when he has put his heart into his work and done his best.'
- Ralph Waldo Emerson

'Nothing can bring you peace but yourself.'
- Ralph Waldo Emerson

'To fill the hour, and leave no crevice ... that is happiness.'
- Ralph Waldo Emerson

'Simplicity, clarity, singleness: these are the attributes that give our lives power and vividness and joy.'
- Richard Halloway

'What is the worth of anything, But for the happiness 'twill bring?'
- Richard Owen Cambridge

'Enjoy the little things, for one day you may look back and realize they were the big things.'
- Robert Brault

'Make us happy and you make us good.'
- Robert Browning

'Employment... is so essential to human happiness that indolence is justly considered the mother of misery.'
- Robert Burton

'Happiness makes up in height for what it lacks in length.'
- Robert Frost

'Few rich men own their own property. Their property owns them.'
- Robert G. Ingersoll

'My creed is that: Happiness is the only good. The place to be happy is here. The time to be happy is now. The way to be happy is to make others so.'
- Robert G. Ingersoll

'It takes great wit and interest and energy to be happy. The pursuit of happiness is a great activity. One must be open and alive. It is the greatest feat man has to accomplish.'
- Robert Henri

'Family life is the source of the greatest human happiness.'
- Robert J. Havighurst

'Deliberately to pursue happiness is not the surest way of achieving it. Seek it for its own sake and I doubt whether you will find it.'
- Robert J. McCracken

'There is no duty so much underrated as the duty of being happy.'
- Robert Louis Stevenson

'We live in an ascending scale when we live happily, one thing leading to another in an endless series.'
- Robert Louis Stevenson

'To forget oneself is to be happy.'
- Robert Louis Stevenson

'The world is so full of a number of things, I'm sure we should all be as happy as kings.'
- Robert Louis Stevenson

'Happiness is to be found along the way, not at the end of the road, for then the journey is over and it is too late.'
- Robert R. Updegraff

'All times are beautiful for those who maintain joy within them; but there is no happy or favorable time for those with disconsolate or orphaned souls.'
- Rosalia Castro

'Taking joy in life is a woman's best cosmetic.'
- Rosalind Russell

'There's a thread that binds all of us together, pull one end of the thread, the strain is felt all down the line.'
- Rosamond Marshall

'Happiness is something that comes into our lives through doors we don't even remember leaving open.'
- Rose Wilder Lane

'Remember that happiness is a way of travel - not a destination.'
- Roy M. Goodman

'A garden isn't meant to be useful. It's for joy.'
- Rumer Godden

'Happiness is a small and unworthy goal for something as big and fancy as a whole lifetime, and should be taken in small doses.'
- Russell Baker

'The needle of our conscience is as good a compass as any.'
- Ruth Wolff

'Order your soul; reduce your wants; live in charity; associate in Christian community; obey the laws; trust in Providence.'
- Saint Augustine

'All the wealth of the world cannot be compared with the happiness of living together happily united.'
- Saint Mary Margaret d'Youville

'Parenting, at its best, comes as naturally as laughter. It is automatic, involuntary, unconditional love.'
- Sally James

'All animals except man know that the principle business of life is to enjoy it.'
- Samuel Butler

'When someone does something good, applaud! You will make two people happy.'
- Samuel Goldwyn

'That kind of life is most happy which affords us most opportunities of gaining our own esteem.'
- Samuel Johnson

'Such is the state of life that none are happy but by the anticipation of change. The change itself is nothing; when we have made it the next wish is to change again.'
- Samuel Johnson

'Pleasure is very seldom found where it is sought. Our brightest blazes are commonly kindled by unexpected sparks.'
- Samuel Johnson

'There is certainly no greater happiness than to be able to look back on a life usefully and virtuously employed, to trace our own progress in existence by such tokens as excite neither shame nor sorrow.'
- Samuel Johnson

'Nothing is more hopeless than a scheme of merriment.'
- Samuel Johnson

'It is by studying little things that we attain the great knowledge of having as little misery and as much happiness as possible.'
- Samuel Johnson

'Learn how to feel joy.'
- Seneca

'If an Arab in the desert were suddenly to discover a spring in his tent, and so would always be able to have water in abundance, how fortunate he would consider himself; so too, when a man who ... is always turned toward the outside, thinking that his hap'
- Seren Kierkegaard

'Every family is a "normal" family- no matter whether it has one parent, two, or no children at all.'
- Shere Hite

'Within our family there was no such thing as a person who did not matter. Second cousins thrice removed mattered.'
- Shirley Abbott

'Just as a cautious businessman avoids investing all his capital in one concern, so wisdom would probably admonish us also not to anticipate all our happiness from one quarter alone.'
- Sigmund Freud

'The little things are infinitely the most important.'
- Sir Arthur Conan Doyle

'Work is the true elixir of life. The busiest man is the happiest man.'
- Sir Theodore Martin

'Living well and beautifully and justly are all one thing.'
- Socrates

'From birth to age eighteen, a girl needs good parents. From eighteen to thirty-five, she needs good looks. From thirty-five to fifty-five, she needs a good personality. From fifty-five on, she needs good cash.'
  - Sophie Tucker

'Best to live lightly, unthinkingly.'
  - Sophocles

'Our happiness depends on wisdom all the way.'
  - Sophocles

'When a man has lost all happiness, he's not alive. Call him a breathing corpse.'
  - Sophocles

'Most men pursue pleasure with such breathless haste that they hurry past it.'
  - Soren Kierkegaard

'Unshared joy is an unlighted candle.'
  - Spanish proverb

'Family jokes, though rightly cursed by strangers, are the bond that keeps most families alive.'
  - Stella Benson

'To describe happiness is to diminish it.'
  - Stendhal

'Happiness comes of the capacity to feel deeply, to enjoy simply, to think freely, to risk life, to be needed.'
  - Storm Jameson

'Happiness ... is achieved only by making others happy.'
  - Stuart Cloete

'One of the quickest ways to become exhausted is by suppressing your feelings.'
  - Sue Patton Thoele

'Sooner or later we all discover that the important moments in life are not the advertised ones, not the birthdays, the graduations, the weddings, not the great goals achieved. The real milestones are less prepossessing. They come to the door of memory.'
  - Susan B. Anthony

'In violent and chaotic times such as these, our only chance for survival lies in creating our own little islands of sanity and order, in making little havens of our homes.'
  - Susan Kaufman

'Fear less, hope more; eat less, chew more; whine less, breathe more; talk less, say more; love more, and all good things will be yours.'
  - Swedish proverb

'If you want others to be happy, practice compassion. If you want to be happy, practice compassion.'
- The Dalai Lama

'Work and love-these are the basics. Without them there is neurosis.'
- Theodor Reik

'This is wisdom: to love wine, beauty, and the heavenly spring. That's sufficient-the rest is worthless.'
- Theodore De Banville

'Blessed is he who has found his work; let him ask no other blessedness. He has a work, a life-purpose. ... Get your happiness out of your work or you will never know what real happiness is. ... Even in the meanest sorts of labor, the whole soul of a man i'
- Thomas Carlyle

'To complain that life has no joys while there is a single creature whom we can relieve by our bounty, assist by our counsels or enliven by our presence, is... just as rational as to die of thirst with the cup in our hands.'
- Thomas Fitzosborne

'He is happy that knoweth not himself to be otherwise.'
- Thomas Fuller

'It is neither wealth nor splendor, but tranquility and occupation, which give happiness.'
- Thomas Jefferson

'Our greatest happiness does not depend on the condition of life in which chance has placed us, but is always the result of a good conscience, good health, occupation and freedom in all just pursuits.'
- Thomas Jefferson

'Happiness is not being pained in body nor troubled in mind.'
- Thomas Jefferson

'It is necessary to the happiness of man that he be mentally faithful to himself.'
- Thomas Paine

'Every minute your mouth is turned down you lose sixty seconds of happiness.'
- Tom Walsh

'Servitude debases men to the point where they end up liking it.'
- Vauvenargues

'The entire sum of existence is the magic of being needed by just one person.'
- Vi Putnam

'The supreme happiness of life is the conviction that we are loved.'
- Victor Hugo

'It is the very pursuit of happiness that thwarts happiness.'
- Viktor Frankl

'Happy [is] the man who has learned the cause of things and has put under his feet all fear, inexorable fate, and the noisy strife of the hell of greed.'
- Virgil

'If you observe a really happy man, you will find ... that he is happy in the course of living life twenty-four crowded hours of each day.'
- W. Beran Wolfe

'To be happy means to be free, not from pain or fear, but from care or anxiety.'
- W. H. Auden

'It is nonsense to speak of 'higher' and 'lower' pleasures. To a hungry man it is, rightly, more important that he eat than that he philosophize.'
- W. H. Auden

'Most true happiness comes from one's inner life, from the disposition of the mind and soul. Admittedly, a good inner life is difficult to achieve, especially in these trying times. It takes reflection and contemplation and self-discipline.'
- W. L. Shirer

'Where there is great love, there are always wishes.'
- Willa Cather

'I am enjoying to a full that period of reflection which is the happiest conclusion to a life of Taking Action.'
- Willa Cather

'Joy has nothing to do with material things, or with a man's outward circumstance ... a man living in the lap of luxury can be wretched, and a man in the depths of poverty can overflow with joy.'
- William Barclay

'Happiness is like a cat. If you try to coax it or call it, it will avoid you. It will never come. But if you pay no attention to it and go about your business, you'll find it rubbing against your legs and jumping into your lap.'
- William Bennett

'Life delights in life.'
- William Blake

'Mirth is better than fun, and happiness is better than mirth.'
- William Blake

'Joy is the will which labors, which overcomes obstacles, which knows triumph.'
- William Butler Yeats

'Happiness depends, as Nature shows, Less on exterior things than most suppose.'
- William Cowper

'Existence is a strange bargain. Life owes us little; we owe it everything. The only true happiness comes from squandering ourselves for a purpose.'
- William Cowper

'The happiest people are those who are too busy to notice whether they are or not.'
- William Feather

'Some of us might find happiness if we quit struggling so desperately for it.'
- William Feather

'We must be doing something to be happy.'
- William Hazlitt

'Why is it that so many people are afraid to admit that they are happy?'
- William Lyon Phelps

'If happiness truly consisted in physical ease and freedom from care, then the happiest individual... would be, I think, an American cow.'
- William Lyon Phelps

'Happiness is the light on the water. The water is cold and dark and deep.'
- William Maxwell

'If thou wouldst be happy ... have an indifference for more than what is sufficient.'
- William Penn

'The happy people are those who are producing something.'
- William Ralph Inge

'The happiest people seem to be those who have no particular cause for being happy except that they are so.'
- William Ralph Inge

'The greatest happiness you can have is knowing that you do not necessarily require happiness.'
- William Saroyan

'I don't want to live-I want to love first, and live incidentally.'
- Zelda Fitzgerald

'It is in virtue that happiness consists, for virtue is the state of mind which tends to make the whole of life harmonious.'
- Zeno

'Loving, like prayer, is a power as well as a process. It's curative. It is creative.'
- Zona Gale

'Love, I find, is like singing. Everybody can do enough to satisfy themselves, though it may not impress the neighbors as being very much.'
- Zora Neale Hurston

'I want a busy life, a just mind, and a timely death.'
- Zora Neale Hurston

'I love myself when I am laughing.'
- Zora Neale Hurston

HEALTH

'Thank heaven, I have given up smoking again! . . . God! I feel fit. A different man. Irritable, moody, depressed, rude, perhaps . . . but the lungs are fine.'
- A. P. Herbert

'To improve your memory, lend people money.'
- Anonymous

'My husband wasn't listening when the doctor asked for "a urine, stool, and semen sample" . . . so I just told him they wanted his shorts.'
- Anonymous

'I get my exercise being a pallbearer for those of my friends who believed in regular running and calisthenics.'
- Anonymous

'doctor to stout patient: You've been swallowing your food again.'
- Anonymous

'He who has health has hope, and he who has hope has everything.'
- Arabian proverb

'Stressed spelled backwards is desserts.'
- Barbara Enberg

'God heals and the doctor takes the fee.'
- Ben Franklin

'There must be something to acupuncture - after all, you never see any sick porcupines.'
- Bob Goddard

'Health food makes me sick.'
- Calvin Trillin

'His idea of exercise is walking to his vitamins.'
- Casey Fenton

'Ladies and gentlemen, after what I've been through, I am happy just to be wearing clothes that open in the front.'
- David Letterman

'I won't say I'm out of condition now - but I even puff going downstairs.'
- Dick Gregory

'She is such a health food nut, she thinks a grape is wine in pill form.'
- Elmer Pasta

'I've been on a constant diet for the last two decades. I've lost a total of 789 pounds. By all accounts, I should be hanging from a charm bracelet.'
- Erma Bombeck

'The trouble with jogging is that, by the time you realize you're not in shape for it, it's too far to walk back.'
- Franklin P. Jones

'I've been on every diet in the world. The best one is the BBC diet: Buy Bigger Clothes.'
- Gary Owens

'You can't lose weight without exercise. But I've got a philosophy about exercise. I don't think you should punish your legs for something your mouth did. Drag your lips around the block once or twice.'
- Gary Owens

'The good Lord never gives you more than you can handle. Unless you die of something.'
- Guindon Cartoon

'If I am ever stuck on a respirator or a life support system, I definitely want to be unplugged but not until I get down to size eight.'
- Henriette Montel

'Diets are for people who are thick and tired of it.'
- Jacob Braude

'I'm Jewish. I don't work out. If God had wanted us to bend over, he would have put diamonds on the floor.'
- Joan Rivers

'I know lots more old drunks than old doctors.'
- Joe E. Lewis

'Lord, if you can't make me thin - can you make all my friends fat?'
- Judy Hampton

'For fast-acting relief, try slowing down.'
- Lily Tomlin

'Health is not a condition of matter, but of Mind.'
- Mary Baker Eddy

'The first wealth is health.'
- Ralph Waldo Emerson

'I burned sixty calories. That should take care of a peanut I had in 1962.'
- Rita Rudner

'Whenever I feel like exercise, I lie down until the feeling passes.'
- Robert M. Hutchins

'Have you noticed when you go on a diet, the first thing you lose is your temper.'
- Robert Orben

'Your medical tests are in. You're short, fat, and bald.'
- Tom Wilson

'I'm not that much into working out. My philosophy - no pain, no pain.'
- Toni Anderson

'You don't get ulcers from what you eat. You get them from what's eating you.'
- Vicki Baum

'The art of medicine consists of amusing the patient while nature cures the disease.'
- Voltaire

'The fate of a nation has often depended on the good or bad digestion of a prime minister.'
- Voltaire

'I never drink water because of the disgusting things that fish do in it.'
- W. C. Fields

'My doctor gave me six months to live, but when I couldn't pay the bill, he gave me six months more.'
- Walter Mattbau

'Health lies in labor, and there is no royal road to it but through toil.'
- Wendell Phillips

'They say the Japanese don't experience menopause or hot flashes. If that's the case, why are they the number-one fan-producing country in the world?'
- Wendy Morgan

'I don't give my weight. I weigh a hundred and plenty.'
- Wendy Morgan

'My husband lost a lot of weight on a new diet, and I resent it. It's simple, he just doesn't eat when I'm talking.'
- Wendy Morgan

HISTORY

'History is something that never happened, written by a man who wasn't there.'
- Anonymous

'Assassination has never changed the history of the world.'
- Benjamin Disraeli

'The economic interpretation of history does not necessarily mean that all events are determined solely by economic forces. It simply means that economic facts are the ever recurring decisive forces, the chief points in the process of history.'
- Edward Bernstein

'History is indeed little more than the register of the crimes, follies, and misfortunes of mankind.'
- Edward Gibbon

'The historian is a prophet looking backwards.'
- Friedrich von Schlegel

'Human history is in essence a history of ideas.'
- H. G. Wells

'What is history but a fable agreed upon?'
- Napoleon

'There is properly no history, only biography.'
- Ralph Waldo Emerson

'All history is a lie!'
- Sir Robert Walpole

'History, a distillation of rumor'
- Thomas Carlyle

HOPE

'Hell is the place where one has ceased to hope.'
- A. J. Cronin

'An act of God was defined as something which no reasonable man could have expected.'
- A. P. Herbert

'Hope! of all ills that men endure The only cheap and universal cure.'
- Abraham Cowley

'Dreams grow holy put in Taking Action; work grows fair through starry dreaming. But where each flows on unmingling, both are fruitless and in vain.'
- Adelaide Proctor

'Hope springs eternal in the human breast; Man never is, but always to be blest.'
- Alexander Pope

'Hope springs eternal in the human breast.'
- Alexander Pope

'All human wisdom is summed up in two words-wait and hope.'
- Alexandre Dumas

'Hope is desire and expectation rolled into one.'
- Ambrose Bierce

'A genius is one who shoots at something no one else can see-and hits it.'
- Anonymous

'Everybody lives for something better to come.'
- Anonymous

'Hope is the anchor of the soul, the stimulus to Taking Action, and the incentive to achievement.'
- Anonymous

'Hope sees the invisible, feels the intangible and achieves the impossible.'
- Anonymous

'Faith, hope, and charity-if we had more of the first two, we'd need less of the last.'
- Anonymous

'Hope is the last thing to abandon the unhappy.'
- Anonymous

'When you get to the end of your rope, tie a knot and hang on.'
- Anonymous

'To hope is not to demand.'
- Anonymous

'Hope is putting faith to work when doubting would be easier.'
- Anonymous

'Hope and Happiness Hope is grief's best music.'
- Anonymous

'A rock pile ceases to be a rock pile the moment a single man contemplates it, bearing within him the image of a cathedral.'
- Antoine de Saint-Exupery

'Hope is a waking dream.'
- Aristotle

'All acts performed in the world begin in the imagination.'
- Barbara Grizzuti Harrison

'There is no hope unmingled with fear, and no fear unmingled with hope.'
- Baruch Spinoza

'Refusal to hope is nothing more than a decision to die.'
- Bernie S. Siegel

'Extreme hopes are born of extreme misery.'
- Bertrand Russell

'And thou shalt be secure because there is hope.'
- Bible

'Now the God of hope fills you with all joy and peace in believing, that ye may abound in hope.'
- Bible

'To all the living there is hope, for a living dog is better than a dead lion.'
- Bible

'Prisoners of hope.'
- Bible

'Guido the plumber and Michelangelo obtained their marble from the same quarry, but what each saw in the marble made the difference between a nobleman's sink and a brilliant sculpture.'
- Bob Kail

'Hope is the parent of faith.'
- C. A. Bartol

'Hope is an echo, hope ties itself yonder, yonder.'
- Carl Sandburg

'Faith walks simply, childlike, between the darkness of human life and the hope of what is to come.'
- Catherine de Hueck Doherty

'When you say a situation or a person is hopeless, you are slamming the door in the face of God.'
- Charles L. Allen

'Without hope men are only half alive. With hope they dream and think and work.'
- Charles Sawyer

'I believe that you cannot go any further than you can think. I certainly believe if you don't desire a thing, you will never get it.'
- Charleszetta Waddles

'To the sick, while there is life there is hope.'
- Cicero

'There are no hopeless situations; there are only men who have grown hopeless about them.'
- Clare Boothe Luce

'Nobody really cares if you're miserable, so you might as well be happy.'
- Cynthia Nelms

'The engineering is secondary to the vision.'
- Cynthia Ozick

'Man can only become what he is able to consciously imagine, or to "image forth."'
- Dane Rudhyar

'The gift we can offer others is so simple a thing as hope.'
- Daniel Berrigan

'Abandon hope, all ye who enter here.'
- Dante Alighieri

'We live on the leash of our senses.'
- Diane Ackerman

'Man's mind is not a container to be filled but rather a fire to be kindled.'
- Dorothea Brande

'By going over your day in imagination before you begin it, you can begin acting successfully at any moment.'
- Dorothea Brande

'Hope is a satisfaction unto itself, and need not be fulfilled to be appreciated.'
- Dr. Fred O. Henker

'Hope is the major weapon against the suicide impulse.'
- Dr. Karl Menninger

'Hope is an adventure, a going forward, a confident search for a rewarding life.'
- Dr. Karl Menninger

'Hope is the positive mode of awaiting the future.'
- Emil Brunner

'Hope is the thing with feathers that perches in the soul and sings the tune without words and never stops at all.'
- Emily Dickinson

'Hope is the thing with feathers That perches in the soul, And sings the tune without the words, And never stops at all.'
- Emily Dickinson

'Hope for the best, but prepare for the worst.'
- English proverb

'We do not really feel grateful toward those who make our dreams come true; they ruin our dreams.'
- Eric Hoffer

'It is the around-the-corner brand of hope that prompts people to Taking Action, while the distant hope acts as an opiate.'
- Eric Hoffer

'Ten thousand men possess ten thousand hopes.'
- Euripides

'One should ... be able to see things as hopeless and yet be determined to make them otherwise.'
- F. Scott Fitzgerald

'Hope is a good breakfast, but it is a bad supper.'
- Francis Bacon

'Hope is the last thing that dies in man.'
- Francois de La Rochefoucauld

'Everyone who has ever built anywhere a "new heaven" first found the power thereto in his own hell.'
- Friedrich Nietzsche

'Strong hope is a much greater stimulant of life than any single realized joy could be.'
- Friedrich Nietzsche

'Hope is the power of being cheerful in circumstances which we know to be desperate.'
- G. K. Chesterton

'Hope is the poor man's bread.'
- Gary Herbert

'A woman's hopes are woven of sunbeams; a shadow annihilates them.'
- George Eliot

'Hope never abandons you, you abandon it.'
- George Weinberg

'Hope is a risk that must be run.'
- Georges Bernanos

'Other men see only a hopeless end, but the Christian rejoices in an endless hope.'
- Gilbert M. Beeken

'Hope is a very unruly emotion.'
- Gloria Steinem

'In time of trouble avert not thy face from hope, for the soft marrow abideth in the hard bone.'
- Hafez

'Man can live about forty days without food, about three days without water, about eight minutes without air ... but only for one second without hope.'
- Hal Lindsey

'It is characteristic of genius to be hopeful and aspiring.'
- Harriet Martineau

'The important thing is not that we can live on hope alone, but that life is not worth living without it.'
- Harvey Milk

'Optimism is the faith that leads to achievement. Nothing can be done without hope or confidence.'
- Helen Keller

'Honor begets honor, trust begets trust, faith begets faith, and hope is the mainspring of life.'
- Henry L. Stimson

'Hope has as many lives as a cat or a king.'
- Henry Wadsworth Longfellow

'Hope is a light diet, but very stimulating.'
- Honore de Balzac

'Never despair.'
- Horace

'Hope is the last thing ever lost.'
- Italian proverb

'Have hope. Though clouds environs now, And gladness hides her face in scorn, Put thou the shadow from thy brow - No night but hath its morn.'
- J. C. F. von Schiller

'If we were logical, the future would be bleak indeed. But we are more than logical. We are human beings, and we have faith, and we have hope, and we can work.'
- Jacques Cousteau

'To hope is to enjoy.'
- Jacques Delille

'Hope is a vigorous principle ... it sets the head and heart to work, and animates a man to do his utmost.'
- Jeremy Collier

'Hold your head high, stick your chest out. You can make it. It gets dark sometimes but morning comes. ... Keep hope alive.'
- Jesse Jackson

'Hope is the second soul of the unhappy.'
- Johann von Goethe

'Our greatest good, and what we least can spare, is hope.'
- John Armstrong

'Hope is the first thing to take some sort of Taking Action.'
- John Armstrong

'We should not let our fears hold us back from pursuing our hopes.'
- John F. Kennedy

'Vision is the art of seeing things invisible.'
- Jonathan Swift

'He who does not hope to win has already lost.'
- Jose Joaquin Olmedo

'At first we hope too much; later on, not enough.'
- Joseph Roux

'A daydreamer is prepared for most things.'
- Joyce Carol Oates

'Grass grows at last above all graves.'
- Julia Dorr

'Stars will blossom in the darkness, Violets bloom beneath the snow.'
- Julia Dorr

'All shall be well, and all shall be well, and all manner of things shall be well.'
- Julian of Norwich

'Hope ... is not a feeling; it is something you do.'
- Katherine Paterson

'My faith is important. I have nothing without it.'
- Kathy Ireland

'We all live under the same sky, but we don't all have the same horizon.'
- Konrad Adenauer

'Hope is not a dream, but a way of making dreams become reality.'
- L. J. Cardinal Suenens

'Hope, deceitful as it is, serves at least to lead us to the end of life along an agreeable road.'
- La Rochefoucauld

'Hope is one of those things in life you cannot do without.'
- LeRoy Douglas

'The slow compromise, or even surrender, of our fondest hopes is a regular feature of normal human life.'
- Leston L. Havens

'Hope is like a road in the country; there was never a road, but when many people walk on it, the road comes into existence.'
- Lin Yutang

'The wind was cold off the mountains and I was a naked man with enemies behind me, and nothing before me but hope.'
- Louis L'Amour

'Little girls are cute and small only to adults. To one another they are not cute. They are life-sized.'
- Margaret Atwood

'It has never been, and never will be, easy work! But the road that is built in hope is more pleasant to the traveler than the road built in despair, even though they both lead to the same destination.'
- Marion Zimmer Bradley

'You can't depend on your eyes when your imagination is out of focus.'
- Mark Twain

'Lord save us all from ... a hope tree that has lost the faculty of putting out blossoms.'
- Mark Twain

'Every thing that is done in the world is done by hope.'
- Martin Luther

'Even the cry from the depths is an affirmation: why cry if there is no hint of hope of hearing?'
- Martin Marty

'The happy ending is our national belief.'
- Mary McCarthy

'Clouds and darkness surround us, yet heaven is just, and the day of triumph will surely come, when justice and truth will be vindicated. Our wrongs will be made right, and we will once more taste the blessings of freedom.'
- Mary Todd Lincoln

'Hope is but the dream of those that wake.'
- Matthew Prior

'Oh, what a valiant faculty is hope.'
- Michel de Montaigne

'Hope says to us constantly, "Go on, go on," and leads us thus to the grave.'
- Mme. de Maintenon

'We want to create hope for the person ... we must give hope, always hope.'
- Mother Teresa

'It's never too late-in fiction or in life-to revise.'
- Nancy Thayer

'A leader is a dealer in hope.'
- Napoleon Bonaparte

'The human body experiences a powerful gravitational pull in the direction of hope. That is why the patient's hopes are the physician's secret weapon. They are the hidden ingredients in any prescription.'
- Norman Cousins

'In the face of uncertainty, there is nothing wrong with hope.'
- O. Carl Simonton

'When you're depressed, the whole body is depressed, and it translates to the cellular level. The first objective is to get your energy up, and you can do it through play. It's one of the most powerful ways of breaking up hopelessness and bringing energy i'
- O. Carl Simonton

'It is a long lane that has no turning.'
- Old saying

'Hope, like the gleaming taper's light, adorns and cheers our way; And still, as darker grows the night, emits a lighter ray.'
- Oliver Goldsmith

'Youth fades; love droops, the leaves of friendship fall; A mother's secret hope outlives them all.'
- Oliver Wendell Holmes

'The hopeful man sees success where others see failure, sunshine where others see shadows and storm.'
- Orison Swett Marden

'There is no medicine like hope, no incentive so great, and no tonic so powerful as expectation of something tomorrow.'
- Orison Swett Marden

'Take hope from the heart of man and you make him a beast of prey.'
- Ouida

'Hope, that star of life's tremulous ocean.'
- Paul Moon James

'Hope is a song in a weary throat.'
- Pauli Murray

'When hope is taken away from the people, moral degeneration follows swiftly after.'
- Pearl S. Buck

'To eat bread without hope is still slowly to starve to death.'
- Pearl S. Buck

'We must have hope or starve to death.'
- Pearl S. Buck

'If winter comes, can spring be far behind?'
- Percy Bysshe Shelley

'No hope, no Taking Action.'
- Peter Levi

'Just as dumb creatures are snared by food, human beings would not be caught unless they had a nibble of hope.'
- Petronius

'Hope is the pillar that holds up the world. Hope is the dream of a waking man.'
- Pliny the Elder

'Hope deferred maketh the heart sick.'
- Proverbs

'A feeble man can see the farms that are fenced and tilled, the houses that are built. The strong man sees the possible houses and farms. His eye makes estates as fast as the sun breeds clouds.'
- Ralph Waldo Emerson

'Hope and patience are two sovereign remedies for all, the surest reposals, the softest cushions to lean on in adversity.'
- Robert Burton

'I always entertain great hopes.'
- Robert Frost

'Hope is the only bee that makes honey without flowers.'
- Robert G. Ingersoll

'I suppose it can be truthfully said that hope is the only universal liar who never loses his reputation for veracity.'
- Robert G. Ingersoll

'In the night of death, hope sees a star, and listening love can hear the rustle of a wing.'
- Robert G. Ingersoll

'"Wait'll next year!" is the favorite cry of baseball fans, football fans, hockey fans, and gardeners.'
- Robert Orben

'Some one once said to me, 'Reverend Schuller, I hope you live to see all your dreams fulfilled.' I replied, T hope not, because if I live and all my dreams are fulfilled, I'm dead.' It's unfulfilled dreams that keep you alive.'
- Robert Schuller

'Who against hope believed in hope.'
- Romans

'Wonder ... music heard in the heart, is voiceless.'
- Rosemary Dobson

'True vision is always twofold. It involves emotional comprehensions as well as physical perception.'
- Ross Parmenter

'Hope is necessary in every condition. The miseries of poverty, sickness and captivity would, without this comfort, be insupportable.'
- Samuel Johnson

'Hope is itself a species of happiness, and, perhaps, the chief happiness which this world affords.'
- Samuel Johnson

'In all pleasure hope is a considerable part.'
- Samuel Johnson

'Man's many desires are like the small metal coins he carries about in his pocket. The more he has the more they weight him down.'
- Satya Sai Baba

'You can always trust information given you by people who are crazy; they have an access to truth not available through regular channels.'
- Sheila Ballantyne

'Hope is brightest when it dawns from fears.'
- Sir Walter Scott

'Who is the wise man? He who sees what's going to be born.'
- Solomon

'Just because a man lacks the use of his eyes doesn't mean he lacks vision.'
- Stevie Wonder

'Hope is the belief, more or less strong, that joy will come; desire is the wish it may come.'
- Sydney Smith

'While there's life, there's hope.'
- Terence

'Hope is patience with the lamp lit.'
- Tertullian

'Hope is one of the principal springs that keep mankind in motion.'
- Thomas Fuller

'If it were not for hopes, the heart would break.'
- Thomas Fuller

'Great hopes make great men.'
- Thomas Fuller

'Appetite, with an opinion of attaining, is called hope; the same, without such opinion, despair.'
- Thomas Hobbes

'I steer my bark with hope in my heart, leaving fear astern.'
- Thomas Jefferson

'For what human ill does not dawn seem to be an alleviation?'
- Thornton Wilder

'My imagination makes me human and makes me a fool; it gives me all the world and exiles me from it.'
- Ursula K. LeGuin

'Hope is not the conviction that something will turn out well but the certainty that something makes sense, regardless of how it turns out.'
- Vaclav Havel

'Patience is the art of hoping.'
- Vauvenargues

'Hope is the word which God has written on the brow of every man.'
- Victor Hugo

'Hope is some extraordinary spiritual grace that God gives us to control our fears, not to oust them.'
- Vincent NcNabb

'The sickening pang of hope deferr'd.'
- Walter Scott

'A fool sees not the same tree that a wise man sees.'
- William Blake

'None are completely wretched but those who are without hope, and few are reduced so low as that.'
- William Hazlitt

'True hope is swift and flies with swallow's wings; Kings it makes Gods, and meaner creatures kings.'
- William Shakespeare

'The miserable have no medicine but hope.'
- William Shakespeare

'Hope arouses, as nothing else can arouse, a passion for the possible.'
- William Sloane Coffin

'One need not hope in order to undertake; nor succeed in order to persevere.'
- William the Silent

HUMOR

'Nonsense is an assertion of man's spiritual freedom in spite of all the oppressions of circumstance.'
- Aldous Huxley

'Wit is far more often a shield than a lance.'
- Anonymous

'He who laughs, lasts.'
- Anonymous

'Hum our is the only test of gravity, and gravity of humor, for a subject which will not bear raillery is suspicious, and a jest which will not bear serious examination is false wit.'
- Aristotle

'Comedy is tragedy - plus time.'
- Carol Burnett

'The teller of a mirthful tale has latitude allowed him. We are content with less than absolute truth.'
- Charles Lamb

'Anything awful makes me laugh. I misbehaved once at a funeral.'
- Charles Lamb

'humor is the contemplation of the finite from the point of view of the infinite.'
- Christian Morgenstern

'A humorist is a man who feels bad but who feels good about it.'
- Don Herold

'The great humorist forgets himself in his delighted contemplation of other people.'
- Douglas Bush

'humor plays close to the big, hot fire, which is the truth, and the reader feels the heat.'
- E. B. White

'humor can be dissected, as a frog can, but the thing dies in the process.'
- E. B. White

'A joke is an epigram on the death of a feeling.'
- Friedrich Nietzsche

'If it's sanity you're after There's no recipe like Laughter. Laugh it off.'
- Henry Rutherford Elliot

'Mirthfulness is in the mind and you cannot get it out. It is just as good in its place as conscience or veneration.'
- Henry Ward Beecher

'He that jokes confesses.'
- Italian proverb

'There are things of deadly earnest that can only be safely mentioned under cover of a joke.'
- J. J. Procter

'humor is richly rewarding to the person who employs it. It has some value in gaining and holding attention. But it has no persuasive value at all.'
- J. K. Galbraith

'A comedian is a fellow who finds other comedians too humorous to mention.'
- Jack Herbert

'Humor is emotional chaos remembered in tranquility.'
- James Thurber

'No one is more profoundly sad than he who laughs too much.'
- Jean Paul Richter

'The difficulty with humorists is that they will mix what they believe with what they don't; whichever seems likelier to win an effect.'
- John Updike

'Caricature: putting the face of a joke upon the body of a truth.'
- Joseph Conrad

'Laughter is the sensation of feeling good all over and showing it principally in one spot.'
- Josh Billings

'Laughter is the closest thing to the grace of God.'
- Karl Barth

'The role of a comedian is to make the audience laugh, at a minimum of once every fifteen seconds.'
- Lenny Bruce

'Wit is the only wall Between us and the dark.'
- Mark Van Doren

'Look at Jewish history. Unrelieved lamenting would be intolerable. So, for every ten Jews beating their breasts, God designated one to be crazy and amuse the breast-beaters. By the time I was five I knew I was that one.'
- Mel Brooks

'humor is just another defense against the universe.'
- Mel Brooks

'If there's anything I hate it's the word humorist - I feel like countering with the word seriousist.'
  - Peter de Vries

'A satirist is a man who discovers unpleasant things about himself and then says them about other people.'
  - Peter McArthur

'Comedy is simply a funny way of being serious.'
  - Peter Ustinov

'humor is the most engaging cowardice. With it myself I have been able to hold some of my enemy in play far out of gunshot.'
  - Robert Frost

'The love of truth lies at the root of much humor.'
  - Robertson Davies

'You can pretend to be serious, but you can't pretend to be witty.'
  - Sacha Guitry

'The ability to laugh at life is right at the top, with love and communication, in the hierarchy of our needs. humor has much to do with pain; it exaggerates the anxieties and absurdities we feel, so that we gain distance and through laughter, relief.'
  - Sara Davidson

'The best definition of humor I know is: humor may be defined as the kindly contemplation of the incongruities of life, and the artistic expression thereof. I think this is the best I know because I wrote it myself.'
  - Stephen Leacock

'You encourage a comic man too much, and he gets silly.'
  - Stephen Leacock

'Any man will admit if need be that his sight is not good, or that he cannot swim or shoots badly with a rifle, but to touch upon his sense of humor is to give him mortal affront.'
  - Stephen Leacock

'He deserves paradise who makes his companions laugh.'
  - The Koran

'Novelist Peter de Vries, like Adlai Stevenson and Mark Twain, has suffered from the American assumption that anyone with a sense of humor is not to be taken seriously.'
  - Timothy Foote

'Laughter is the shortest distance between two people.'
  - Victor Borge

'humor is the first of the gifts to perish in a foreign tongue.'
  - Virginia Woolf

'We are all here for a spell, get all the good laughs you can.'
    - Will Rogers

'Everything is funny as long as it is happening to somebody else.'
    - Will Rogers

'A jest's prosperity lies in the ear of him that hears it, never in the tongue Of him that makes it.'
    - William Shakespeare

IGNORANCE

'Not ignorance, but ignorance of ignorance is the death of knowledge.'
- Alfred North Whitehead

'Ignoramus: a person unacquainted with certain kinds of knowledge familiar to yourself and having certain other kinds that you know nothing about.'
- Ambrose Bierce

'Truth can be outraged by silence quite as cruelly as by speech.'
- Amelia Barr

'To be ignorant of one's ignorance is the malady of the ignorant.'
- Amos Bronson Alcott

'Lack of understanding is a great power. Sometimes it enables men to conquer the world.'
- Anatole France

'My doctrine is this, that if we see cruelty or wrong that we have the power to stop, and do nothing, we make ourselves sharers in the guilt.'
- Anna Sewell

'When Columbus started out he didn't know where he was going, when he got there he didn't know where he was, and when he got back he didn't know where he had been.'
- Anonymous

'Little wit in the head makes much work for the feet.'
- Anonymous

'Sometimes it proves the highest understanding not to understand.'
- Baltasar Gracian

'The greatest wisdom often consists in ignorance.'
- Baltasar Gracian

'Ignorance never settles a question.'
- Benjamin Disraeli

'What makes a good pinch hitter? I wish the hell I knew.'
- Bobby Murcer

'Nothing sways the stupid more than arguments they can't understand.'
- Cardinal de Retz

'Ordinary people believe only in the possible. Extraordinary people visualize not what is possible or probable, but rather what is impossible. And by visualizing the impossible, they begin to see it as

possible.'
  - Cherie Carter-Scott

'I am not ashamed to confess that I am ignorant of what I do not know.'
  - Cicero

'I am not ashamed to confess that I am ignorant of what. I do not know.'
  - Cicero

'Success is often achieved by those who don't know that failure is inevitable.'
  - Coco Chanel

'Education is learning what you didn't even know you didn't know.'
  - Daniel Boorstin

'The Wright brothers flew through the smoke screen of impossibility.'
  - Dorothea Brande

'God may have been waiting for centuries for somebody ignorant enough of the impossible to do that thing.'
  - Dr. J. A. Holmes

'all ignorance toboggans into know and trudges up to ignorance again.'
  - e. e. cummings

'Painting is easy when you don't know how, but very difficult when you do.'
  - Edgar Degas

'Unprovided with original learning, unformed in the habits of thinking, unskilled in the arts of composition, I resolved to write a book.'
  - Edward Gibbon

'To some people, the impossible is impossible.'
  - Elizabeth Asquith Bisco

'Most of the basic truths of life sound absurd at first hearing.'
  - Elizabeth Goudge

'The work will teach you how to do it.'
  - Estonian proverb

'At first people refuse to believe that a strange new thing can be done, then they begin to hope it can be done, then they see it can be done-then it is done and all the world wonders why it was not done centuries ago.'
  - Frances Hodgson Burnett

'There is more stupidity around than hydrogen and it has longer shelf life.'
  - Frank Zappa

'All I know about humor is that I don't know anything about it.'
  - Fred Allen

'Curiosity is the one thing invincible in Nature.'
  - Freya Stark

'Against stupidity the very gods Themselves contend in vain.'
  - Friedrich von Schiller

'The good thing about being young is that you are not experienced enough to know you cannot possibly do the things you are doing.'
  - Gene Brown

'I don't know what I'm doing. I don't know what actors do.'
  - Geraldine Page

'When an idea is wanting, a word can always be found to take its place.'
  - Goethe

'There is nothing more frightening than ignorance in Taking Action.'
  - Goethe

'And here, poor fool, with all my lore I stand no wiser than before.'
  - Goethe

'When we are not sure, we are alive.'
  - Graham Greene

'An impossibility does not disturb us until its accomplishment shows what fools we were.'
  - Henry S. Haskins

'Ignorance is no excuse, it's the real thing.'
  - Irene Peter

'Today, if you are not confused, you are not thinking clearly.'
  - Irene Peter

'Every true genius is bound to be naive.'
  - J. C. F. von Schiller

'Her own mother lived the latter years of her life in the horrible suspicion that electricity was dripping invisibly all over the house.'
  - James Thurber

'You can do one of two things; just shut up, which is something I don't find easy, or learn an awful lot very fast, which is what I tried to do.'
  - Jane Fonda

'To write a good love letter you ought to begin without knowing what you mean to say, and to finish without knowing what you have written.'
- Jean-Jacques Rousseau

'To measure up to all that is demanded of him, a man must overestimate his capacities.'
- Johann von Goethe

'The true test of character is ... how we behave when we don't know what to do.'
- John Holt

'People think the Beatles know what's going on. We don't. We're just doing it.'
- John Lennon

'The empty vessel giveth a greater sound than the full barrel.'
- John Lyly

'It is a blind goose that cometh to the fox's sermon.'
- John Lyly

'It is a sign of strength, not of weakness, to admit that you don't know all the answers.'
- John P. Loughrane

'The trouble ain't that people are ignorant: it's that they know so much that ain't so.'
- Josh Billings

'The good Lord set definite limits on man's wisdom, but set no limits on his stupidity - and that's just not fair.'
- Konrad Adenauer

'Whatever people in general do not understand, they are always prepared to dislike; the incomprehensible is always the obnoxious.'
- L. E. Landon

'I have always wanted to be somebody, but I see now I should have been more specific.'
- Lily Tomlin

'Life is my college. May I graduate well, and earn some honors!'
- Louisa May Alcott

'Whenever two good people argue over principles, they are both right.'
- Marie von Ebner-Eschenbach

'Once you start asking questions, innocence is gone.'
- Mary Astor

'Aerodynamically, the bumblebee shouldn't be able to fly, but the bumble bee doesn't know it so it goes on flying anyway.'
- Mary Kay Ash

'Men are always averse to enterprises in which they foresee difficulties.'
- Niccolo Machiavelli

'A weak mind does not accumulate force enough to hurt itself; stupidity often saves a man from going mad.'
- Oliver Wendell Holmes

'Great things are accomplished by those who do not feel the impotence of man. This ... is a precious gift.'
- Paul Valery

'The young do not know enough to be prudent, and therefore they attempt the impossible-and achieve it, generation after generation.'
- Pearl S. Buck

'It is our duty as men and women to proceed as though limits to our abilities do not exist.'
- Pierre Teilhard de Chardin

'No one knows what he can do until he tries.'
- Publilius Syrus

'Nothing in this world can one imagine beforehand, not the least thing. Everything is made up of so many unique particulars that cannot be foreseen.'
- Rainer Maria Rilke

'If I cannot brag of knowing something, then I brag of not knowing it, at any rate, brag.'
- Ralph Waldo Emerson

'All decisions are made on insufficient evidence.'
- Rita Mae Brown

'Progress results only from the fact that there are some men and women who refuse to believe that what they know to be right cannot be done.'
- Russell W. Davenport

'The little I know, I owe to my ignorance.'
- Sacha Guitry

'Some of my best friends are illusions. Been sustaining me for years.'
- Sheila Ballantyne

'I know it was wonderful, but I don't know how I did it.'
- Sir Laurence Olivier

'So long as we think dugout canoes are the only possibility-all that is real or can be real-we will never see the ship, we will never feel the free wind blow.'
- Sonia Johnson

'One learns by doing the thing; for though you think you know it, you have no certainty until you try.'
- Sophocles

'Intelligence is really a kind of taste: taste in ideas.'
- Susan Sontag

'If ignorance is indeed bliss, it is a very low grade of the article.'
- Tehyi Hsieh

'Where ignorance is bliss, Tis folly to be wise.'
- Thomas Gray

'Where there is an unknowable, there is a promise.'
- Thornton Wilder

'Basic research is what I'm doing when I don't know what I'm doing.'
- Wernher von Braun

'Everybody is ignorant, only on different subjects.'
- Will Rogers

'I don't know what humor is.'
- Will Rogers

'In baseball, you don't know nothing.'
- Yogi Berra

IMAGINATION

'Imagination is more important than knowledge.'
   - Albert Einstein

'Fools act on imagination without knowledge, pedants act on knowledge without imagination.'
   - Alfred North Whitehead

'From ghoulies and ghosties and long-leggedy beasties And things that go bump in the night, good
Lord, deliver us!'
   - Anonymous

'It is good to know the truth, but it is better to speak of palm trees.'
   - Arabic proverb

'It was a year when Frankie thought about the world. And she did not see it as a round school globe,
with the countries neat and different-colored. She thought of the world as huge and cracked and
loose and turning a thousand miles an hour.'
   - Carson McCullers

'To make a prairie it takes clover and one bee one clover, and a bee, and revelry. The revelry alone will
do, if bees are few.'
   - Emily Dickinson

'I admit that twice two makes four is an excellent thing, but if we are to give everything its due, twice
two makes five is sometimes a very charming thing too.'
   - Fyodor Dostoyevsky

'Imagination frames events unknown, In wild, fantastic shapes of hideous ruin, And what it fears,
creates.'
   - Hannah More

'Imagination is a poor substitute for experience.'
   - Havelock Ellis

'The value of a sentiment is the amount of sacrifice you are prepared to make for it.'
   - John Galsworthy

'Ever let the Fancy roam, Pleasure never is at home.'
   - John Keats

'The imagination of a boy is healthy, and the mature imagination of a man is healthy, but there is a
space of life between, in which the soul is in ferment, the character undecided, the way of life
uncertain.'
   - John Keats

'Imagination is the eye of the soul.'
- Joseph Joubert

'He who has imagination without learning has wings but no feet.'
- Joseph Joubert

'Let us leave pretty women to men without imagination.'
- Marcel Proust

'Saddle your dreams afore you ride 'am.'
- Mary Webb

'The human race is governed by its imagination.'
- Napoleon

'Inspiration could be called inhaling the memory of an act never experienced.'
- Ned Rorem

'Imagination disposes of everything; it creates beauty, justice, and happiness, which is everything in this world.'
- Pascal

'Reason respects the differences, and imagination the similitudes of things.'
- Percy Bysshe Shelley

'The eyes are not responsible when the mind does the seeing.'
- Publilius Syrus

'The sky is the daily bread of the eyes.'
- Ralph Waldo Emerson

'Were it not for imagination, a man would be as happy in the arms of a chambermaid as of a duchess.'
- Samuel Johnson

'His imagination resembled the wings of an ostrich. It enabled him to run, though not to soar.'
- Thomas Babington Macaulay

'Imagination grows by exercise, and contrary to common belief, is more powerful in the mature than in the young.'
- W. Somerset Maugham

INSPIRATIONAL

'Beware of trying to accomplish anything by force.'
- Angela Merici

'Discontent is the first step in progress. No one knows what is in him till he tries, and many would never try if they were not forced to.'
- Basil W. Maturin

'For every man there exists a bait which he cannot resist swallowing.'
- Friedrich Nietzsche

'It is the spur of ignorance, the consciousness of not understanding, and the curiosity about that which lies beyond that are essential to our progress.'
- John Pierce

'The moment somebody says to me, "This is very risky," is the moment it becomes attractive to me.'
- Kate Capshaw

'The pitcher cries for water to carry and a person for work that is real.'
- Marge Piercy

'If you're good to your staff when things are going well, they'll rally when times go bad.'
- Mary Kay Ash

'Never let go of that fiery sadness called desire.'
- Patti Smith

'Praise out of season, or tactlessly bestowed, can freeze the heart as much as blame.'
- Pearl S. Buck

'What you are must always displease you, if you would attain to that which you are not.'
- Saint Augustine

'All progress is based upon a universal, innate desire on the part of every living organism to live beyond its income.'
- Samuel Butler

KNOWLEDGE

'As we acquire more knowledge, things do not become more comprehensible, but more mysterious.'
   - Albert Schweitzer

'The learned is happy, nature to explore, the fool is happy, that he knows no more.'
   - Alexander Pope

'Strange how much you've got to know Before you know how little you know.'
   - Anonymous

'All men by nature desire to know.'
   - Aristotle

'Grace is given of God, but knowledge is bought in the market.'
   - Arthur Hugh Clough

'To be conscious that you are ignorant is a great step to knowledge.'
   - Benjamin Disraeli

'In all affairs, love, religion, politics or business, it's a healthy idea, now and then, to hang a question mark on things you have long taken for granted.'
   - Bertrand Russell

'There is much pleasure to be gained from useless knowledge.'
   - Bertrand Russell

'He that increaseth knowledge increascth sorrow.'
   - Bible

'We should live and learn; but by the time we've learned, it's too late to live.'
   - Carolyn Wells

'We owe almost all our knowledge not to those who have agreed, but to those who have differed.'
   - Charles Caleb Colton

'I do not pretend to know what many ignorant men are sure of.'
   - Clarence Darrow

'There was never an age in which useless knowledge was more important than in our own.'
   - Cyril Joad

'The only good is knowledge, and the only evil ignorance.'
   - Diogenes

'Little minds are interested in the extraordinary; great minds in the commonplace.'
   - Elbert Hubbard

'Knowledge is power.'
- Francis Bacon

'Then I began to think, that it is very true which is commonly said, that the one-half of the world knoweth not how the other half liveth.'
- Francois Rabelais

'Better know nothing than half-know many things.'
- Friedrich Nietzsche

'Everybody gets so much common information all day long that they lose their common sense.'
- Gertrude Stein

'The first problem for all of us, men and women, is not to learn, but to unlearn.'
- Gloria Steinem

'A man only understands what is akin to something already existing in himself.'
- Henri Frederic Amiel

'They know enough who know how to learn.'
- Henry Adams

'To know that we know what we know, and that we do not know what we do not know, that is true knowledge.'
- Henry David Thoreau

'Anyone who stops learning is old, whether at twenty or eighty. Anyone who keeps learning stays young. The greatest thing in life is to keep your mind young.'
- Henry Ford

'One cannot know everything.'
- Horace

'Our knowledge can only be finite, while our ignorance must necessarily be infinite.'
- Karl Popper

'He who knows others is learned; He who knows himself is wise.'
- Lao-Tsze

'Pocket all your knowledge with your watch and never pull it out in company unless desired.'
- Lord Chesterfield

'The specialist is a man who fears the other subjects.'
- Martin H. Fisher

'There are times I think I am not sure of something which I absolutely know.'
- Mongkut, King of Siam

'It ain't the things you don't know what gets you into trouble; it's the things you know for sure what ain't so.'
- Negro Saying

'The simplest questions are the hardest to answer.'
- Northrop Frye

'Ten lands are sooner known than one man.'
- Old saying

'President Reagan didn't always know what he knew.'
- Oliver North

'I am not young enough to know everything.'
- Oscar Wilde

'He that hath knowledge spareth his words.'
- Proverbs

'Our knowledge is the amassed thought and experience of innumerable minds.'
- Ralph Waldo Emerson

'There are two kinds of statistics, the kind you look up and the kind you make up.'
- Rex Stout

'I have tried to know absolutely nothing about a great many things, and I have succeeded fairly well.'
- Robert Benchley

'One of the greatest joys known to man is to take a flight into ignorance in search of knowledge.'
- Robert Lynd

'We're drowning in information and starving for knowledge.'
- Rutherford D. Rogers

'The public do not know enough to be experts, yet know enough to decide between them.'
- Samuel Butler

'Man is not weak - knowledge is more than equivalent to force. The master of mechanics laughs at strength.'
- Samuel Johnson

'Knowledge is of two kinds; we know a subject ourselves, or we know where we can find information upon it.'
- Samuel Johnson

'A man must carry knowledge with him, if he would bring home knowledge.'
- Samuel Johnson

'I take all knowledge to be my province.'
- Sir Francis Bacon

'For knowledge, too, is itself a power.'
- Sir Francis Bacon

'Know thyself.'
- Socrates

'As for me, all I know is that I know nothing.'
- Socrates

'Zeal without knowledge is fire without light.'
- Thomas Fuller

'Sit down before fact as a little child, be prepared to give up every preconceived notion, follow humbly wherever and to whatever abyss nature leads, or you shall learn nothing.'
- Thomas Huxley

'Every great advance in natural knowledge has involved the absolute rejection of authority.'
- Thomas Huxley

'If a little knowledge is dangerous - where is the man who has so much as to be out of danger?'
- Thomas Huxley

'Our knowledge is a receding mirage in an expanding desert of ignorance.'
- Will Durant

'It isn't what we don't know that gives us trouble, it's what we know that ain't so.'
- Will Rogers

'All that men really understand is confined to a very small compass; to their daily affairs and experience; to what they have an opportunity to know; and motives to study or practice. The rest is affectation and imposture.'
- William Hazlitt

'We know what we are, but know not what we may be.'
- William Shakespeare

'And seeing ignorance is the curse of God, Knowledge the wing wherewith we fly to heaven.'
- William Shakespeare

LAW

'Appeal in law: to put the dice into the box for another throw.'
- Ambrose Bierce

'Litigant: a person about to give up his skin for the hope of retaining his bone.'
- Ambrose Bierce

'The law, in its majestic equality, forbids the rich as well as the poor to sleep under bridges, to beg in the streets, and to steal bread.'
- Anatole France

'Any fool can make a rule, and every fool will mind it.'
- Anonymous

'The law locks up both man and woman Who steals the goose from off the common, But lets the great felon loose Who steals the common from the goose.'
- Anonymous

'When the 30-year-old lawyer died he said to St. Peter, "How can you do this to me? - a heart attack at my age? I'm only 30." Replied St. Peter: "When we looked at your total hours billed we figured you were 95."'
- Anonymous

'A man may as well open an oyster without a knife, as a lawyer's mouth without a fee.'
- Barten Holyday

'Divorce is a game played by lawyers.'
- Cary Grant

'If there were no bad people, there would be no good lawyers.'
- Charles Dickens

'When you have no basis for an argument, abuse the plaintiff.'
- Cicero

'Lawyers and painters can soon change white to black.'
- Danish proverb

'Show me the man and I'll show you the law.'
- David Ferguson

'You are remembered for the rules you break.'
- Douglas MacArthur

'Law and order is one of the steps taken to maintain injustice.'
- Edward Bond

'In America, an acquittal doesn't mean you're innocent, it means you beat the rap. My clients lose even when they win.'
- F. Lee Bailey

'Fragile as reason is and limited as law is as the institutionalized medium of reason, that's all we have standing between us and the tyranny of mere will and the cruelty of unbridled, undisciplined feeling.'
- Felix Frankfurter

'To some lawyers, all facts are created equal.'
- Felix Frankfurter

'An appeal is when ye ask wan court to show its contempt for another court.'
- Finley Peter Dunne

'No matter whether the Constitution follows the flag or not, the Supreme Court follows the election returns.'
- Finley Peter Dunne

'Revenge is a kind of wild justice, which the more man's nature runs to, the more ought law to weed it out.'
- Francis Bacon

'I understand you undertake to overthrow my undertaking.'
- Gertrude Stein

'A judge is a law student who marks his own examination papers.'
- H. L. Mencken

'Law school taught me one thing: how to take two situations that are exactly the same and show how they are different.'
- Hart Pomerantz

'It usually takes 100 years to make a law, and then, after it's done its work, it usually takes 100 years to be rid of it.'
- Henry Ward Beecher

'Those who are too lazy and comfortable to think for themselves and be their own judges obey the laws. Others sense their own laws within them.'
- Hermann Hesse

'Well, I don't know as I want a lawyer to tell me what I cannot do. I hire him to tell me how to do what I want to do.'
- J. P. Morgan

'Lawyers are the only persons in whom ignorance of the law is not punished.'
- Jeremy Bentham

'Law ... begins when someone takes to doing something someone else does not like.'
- Karl Llewellyn

'An excess of law inescapably weakens the rule of law.'
  - Laurence H. Tribe

'The aim of law is the maximum gratification of the nervous system of man.'
  - Learned Hand

'Every skilled person is to be believed with reference to his own art.'
  - Legal maxim

'The law of England is a very strange one; it cannot compel anyone to tell the truth. . . . But what the law can do is to give you seven years for not telling the truth.'
  - Lord Darling

'That is the beauty of the Common Law, it is a maze and not a motorway.'
  - Lord Diplock

'In cross-examination, as in fishing, nothing is more ungainly than a fisherman pulled into the water by his catch.'
  - Louis Nizer

'Lawyers are men who hire out their words and anger.'
  - Martial

'Every new time will give its law.'
  - Maxim Gorky

'Whatever is enforced by command is more imputed to him who exacts than to him who performs.'
  - Michel de Montaigne

'Lawyers spend a great deal of time shoveling smoke.'
  - Oliver Wendell Holmes

'Law is the witness and external deposit of our moral life. Its history is the history of the moral development of the race.'
  - Oliver Wendell Holmes

'The life of the law has not been logic: it has been experience.'
  - Oliver Wendell Holmes

'The adversary system is a kind of warfare in mufti.'
  - R. I. Fitzhenry

'A successful lawsuit is the one worn by a policeman.'
  - Robert Frost

'A jury consists of twelve persons chosen to decide who has the better lawyer.'
  - Robert Frost

'The law must be stable and yet it must not stand still.'
- Roscoe Pound

'A lawyer's dream of heaven - every man reclaimed his property at the resurrection, and each tried to recover it from all his forefathers.'
- Samuel Butler

'In England, justice is open to all - like the Ritz Hotel.'
- Sir James Mathew

'Laws are the spider's webs which, if anything small falls into them they ensnare it, but large things break through and escape.'
- Solon

'Laws, like the spider's web, catch the fly and let the hawk go free.'
- Spanish proverb

'No man is above the law and no man is below it: nor do we ask any man's permission when we ask him to obey it.'
- Theodore Roosevelt

'A vague uneasiness; the police. It's like when you suddenly understand you have to undress in front of the doctor.'
- Ugo Betti

'I know of no method to secure the repeal of bad or obnoxious laws so effective as their stringent execution.'
- Ulysses S. Grant

'And whether you're an honest man, or whether you're a thief, depends on whose solicitor has given me my brief.'
- W. S. Gilbert

'Law is nothing unless close behind it stands a warm, living public opinion.'
- Wendell Phillips

'Far more has been accomplished for the welfare and progress of mankind by preventing bad Taking Actions than by doing good ones.'
- William Lyon Mackenzie King

'It is as if the ordinary language we use every day has a hidden set of signals, a kind of secret code.'
- William Stafford

LEADERSHIP

'The slave begins by demanding justice and ends by wanting to wear a crown. He must dominate in his turn.'
- Albert Camus

'I've got to follow them - I am their leader.'
- Alexandre Ledru-Rollin

'A chief is a man who assumes responsibility. He says, 'I was beaten'; he does not say 'My men were beaten.''
- Antoine de Saint-Exupery

'Winston has written four volumes about himself and called it 'World Crisis'.'
- Arthur Balfour

'If I advance, follow me! If I retreat, cut me down! If I die, avenge me!'
- Benito Mussolini

''Ah, John A., John A., how I love you! How I wish I could trust you!'
- Canadian Liberal politician

'A true leader always keeps an element of surprise up his sleeve, which others cannot grasp but which keeps his public excited and breathless.'
- Charles de Gaulle

'Every man of Taking Action has a strong dose of egotism, pride, hardness and cunning. But all those things will be forgiven him, indeed, they will be regarded as high qualities, if he can make them the means to achieve great ends.'
- Charles de Gaulle

'A leader may symbolize and express what is best in his people, like Pericles, or what is worst, like Hitler, but he cannot successfully express what is only in his heart and not in theirs.'
- Charles Yost

'Winston Churchill - fifty per cent genius, fifty per cent bloody fool.'
- Clement Attlee

'It is better to have a lion at the head of an army of sheep, than a sheep at the head of an army of lions.'
- Daniel Defoe

'It is said that Mr. Gladstone could persuade most people of most things, and himself of anything.'
- Dean William R. Inge

'I know I have the body of a weak and feeble woman, but I have the heart and stomach of a King, and of a King of England too.'
- Elizabeth I

'He who would rule must hear and be deaf, see and be blind.'
- German proverb

'Dictators ride to and fro upon tigers from which they dare not dismount.'
- Hindu proverb

'Achilles absent, was Achilles still.'
- Homer

'I suppose leadership at one time meant muscles; but today it means getting along with people.'
- Indira Gandhi

'In Pierre Elliott Trudeau, Canada has at last produced a political leader worthy of assassination.'
- Irving Layton

'Dictators are rulers who always look good until the last ten minutes.'
- Jan Masaryk

'With a good conscience our only sure reward, with history the final judge of our deeds, let us go forth to lead the land we love asking His blessing and His help, but knowing that here on earth God's work must truly be our own.'
- John F. Kennedy

'Every woman's man, and every man's woman.'
- Julius Caesar

'Where there are no tigers, a wildcat is very self-important.'
- Korean proverb

'If I advance, follow me! If I retreat, kill me! If I die, avenge me!'
- La Rochefoucauld

'As for the best leaders, the people do not notice their existence. The next best, the people honor and praise. The next, the people fear, and the next the people hate. When the best leader's work is done, the people say, 'we did it ourselves!''
- Lao-Tzu

'To lead the people, walk behind them.'
- Lao-Tzu

'A frightened captain makes a frightened crew.'
- Lister Sinclair

'To lead means to direct and to exact, and no man dares do either - he might be unpopular. What authority we are given now is a trinity: the grin, the generality, and God (the Word).'
  - Marya Mannes

'I have no family. My only responsibility is the welfare of Quebec. I belong to the province.'
  - Maurice Duplessis

'There are two levers for moving men - interest and fear.'
  - Napoleon Bonaparte

'Follow me, if I advance; kill me if I retreat; revenge me if I die!'
  - Ngo Dinh Diem

'The reward of a general is not a bigger tent - but command.'
  - Oliver Wendell Holmes

'If you shoot at a king you must kill him.'
  - Ralph Waldo Emerson

'It is a characteristic of all movements and crusades that the psychopathic element rises to the top.'
  - Robert Lindner

'It is much safer to obey than to rule.'
  - Thomas a Kempis

'The final test of a leader is that he leaves behind in other men the conviction and the will to carry on.'
  - Walter Lippmann

'To get others to come into our ways of thinking, we must go over to theirs; and it is necessary to follow, in order to lead.'
  - William Hazlitt

'I really believe my greatest service is in the many unwise steps I prevent.'
  - William Lyon Mackenzie King

'I have never accepted what many people have kindly said, namely that I have inspired the nation. It was the nation and the race dwelling all around the globe that had the lion heart. I had the luck to be called upon to give the roar.'
  - Winston Churchill

'I have nothing to offer but blood, toil, tears and sweat.'
  - Winston Churchill

'When you come into the presence of a leader of men, you know that you have come into the presence of fire - that it is best not uncautiously to touch that man - that there is something that makes it dangerous to cross him.'
  - Woodrow Wilson

LEARNING

'The true teacher defends his pupils against his own personal influence.'
- A. B. Alcott

'Intelligence appears to be the thing that enables a man to get along without Learning. Learning appears to be the thing that enables a man to get along without the use of his intelligence.'
- A. E. Wiggan

'The freshmen bring a little knowledge in and the seniors take none out, so it accumulates through the years.'
- A. Lawrence Lowell

'A good Learning should leave much to be desired.'
- Alan Gregg

'The Jews have always been students, and their greatest study is themselves.'
- Albert Goldman

''Tis Learning forms the common mind; Just as the twig is bent the tree's inclined.'
- Alexander Pope

'The antithesis between a technical and a liberal Learning is fallacious. There can be no adequate technical Learning which is not liberal, and no liberal Learning which is not technical.'
- Alfred North Whitehead

'Learning with inert ideas is not only useless; it is above all things harmful.'
- Alfred North Whitehead

'Learning, n: that which discloses to the wise and disguises from the foolish their lack of understanding.'
- Ambrose Bierce

'Creative minds have always been known to survive any kind of bad training.'
- Anna Freud

'Bumper sticker: My kid beat the heck out of the student of the month.'
- Anonymous

'When asked to spell Mississippi the boy asked, "The river or the state?"'
- Anonymous

'Bumper sticker: Driver carries no cash - he has a son in college.'
- Anonymous

'Boy handing over his report card: Of course I seem stupid to my teachers . . . they're all college graduates.'
- Anonymous

'She's an honor student. She's always saying, "Yes, Your Honor. No, Your Honor."'
- Anonymous

'There are a hundred thousand useless words in the English language, but they come in handy in college football yells.'
- Anonymous

'Everyone is in awe of the lion tamer in a cage with half a dozen lions - everyone but a school bus driver.'
- Anonymous

'One little six-year-old took home a note saying he need not come to school since he was "too stupid to learn." That boy was Thomas Edison.'
- Anonymous

'A kindergarten teacher is a woman who knows how to make little things count.'
- Anonymous

'Soon learnt, soon forgotten.'
- Anonymous

'Some drink from the fountain of knowledge - others just gargle.'
- Anonymous

'Last words when sending our boy to college: "If there's anything you want, call us and we'll show you how to live without it."'
- Anonymous

'Letter home from, college boy: "There are 370 boys here - I wish there were 369."'
- Anonymous

'Those who go to college and never get out are called professors.'
- Anonymous

'The investigation of the meaning of words is the beginning of Learning.'
- Antisthenes

'Learning is what survives when what has been learnt has been forgotten.'
- B. F. Skinner

'If a man empties his purse into his head, no one can take it from him.'
- Benjamin Franklin

'A gentleman need not know Latin, but he should at least have forgotten it.'
- Brander Matthews

'We didn't feel so good when we took our son to college and saw a sign on the liquor store - Back to School Sale.'
- Brian Morgan

'One looks back with appreciation to the brilliant teachers, but with gratitude to those who touched our human feelings. The curriculum is so much necessary raw material, but warmth is a vital element for the growing plant and for the soul of the child.'
- Carl Jung

'It is of interest to note that while some dolphins are reported to have learned English - up to fifty words used in correct context - no human being has been reported to have learned dolphinese.'
- Carl Sagan

'Do you know the difference between a kayak and a college student? A kayak tips.'
- Chad Morgan

'Pedantry crams our heads with learned lumber and takes out brains to make room for it.'
- Charles Caleb Colton

'One could get a first-class Learning from a shelf of books five feet long.'
- Charles William Eliot

'What greater or better gift can we offer the republic than to teach and instruct our youth?'
- Cicero

'Creatures whose main spring is curiosity will enjoy the accumulating of fact, far more than the pausing at times to reflect on those facts.'
- Clarence Day

'I find the three major administrative problems on a campus are sex for the students, athletics for the alumni and parking for the faculty.'
- Clark Kerr

'He couldn't get into Harvard even if he had the dean's wife at gunpoint.'
- Dave Barry

'Passing the SAT: My personal theory is that it has to do with how much money you send them in the mail. I think the amounts they tell you to send are actually just suggested minimum donations - if you get my drift.'
- Dave Barry

'Universities are the cathedrals of the modern age. They shouldn't have to justify their existence by utilitarian criteria.'
- David Lodge

'Today's public Learning system is a failed monopoly: bureaucratic, rigid and in unsteady control of dissatisfied captive markets.'
- David T. Kearns

'College is the best time of your life. When else are your parents going to spend several thousand dollars a year just for you to go to a strange town and get drunk every night?'
   - David Wood

'If you think Learning is expensive - try ignorance.'
   - Derek Bok

'You can lead a man up to the university, but you can't make him think.'
   - Finley Peter Dunne

'And if the student finds that this is not to his taste, well, that is regrettable. Most regrettable. His taste should not be consulted; it is being formed.'
   - Flannery O'Connor

'He who would learn to fly one day must first learn to stand and walk and run and climb and dance; one cannot fly into flying.'
   - Friedrich Nietzsche

'Most men of Learning are more superstitious than they admit - nay, than they think.'
   - G. C. Lichtenberg

'Good teaching is l/4th preparation and 3/4ths theatre.'
   - Gail Godwin

'Whenever I'm asked what college I attended, I'm tempted to reply, Thornton Wilder'.'
   - Garson Kanin

''Whom are you?' he asked, for he had been to night school.'
   - George Ade

'One father is more than 100 schoolmasters.'
   - George Herbert

'A child educated only at school is an uneducated child.'
   - George Santayana

'Whatever is good to know is difficult to learn.'
   - Greek proverb

'The Romans would never have had time to conquer the world if they had been obliged to learn Latin first of all.'
   - Heinrich Heine

'Nothing in Learning is so astonishing as the amount of ignorance it accumulates in the form of inert facts.'
   - Henry Adams

'Arrogance, pedantry, and dogmatism are the occupational diseases of those who spend their lives directing the intellects of the young.'
- Henry S. Canby

'It's strange how few of the world's great problems are solved by people who remember their algebra.'
- Herbert Prochnow

'Schoolhouses are the republican line of fortifications.'
- Horace Mann

'Learning commences at the mother's knee, and every word spoken within the hearsay of little children tends towards the formation of character.'
- Hosea Ballou

'The average PhD thesis is nothing but a transference of bones from one graveyard to another.'
- J. Frank Dobie

'The test and the use of man's Learning is that he finds pleasure in the exercise of his mind.'
- Jacques Barzun

'Learning is indoctrination, if you're white - subjugation if you're black.'
- James Baldwin

'Learning today, more than ever before, must see clearly the dual objectives: Learning for living and educating for making a living.'
- James Mason Wood

'You could do anything in your room at college. You could smoke pot, live in a coed dorm, have a girl. But you couldn't have a . . . hot plate!'
- Jay Leno

'I used to keep my college roommate from reading my personal mail by hiding it in her textbooks.'
- Joan Welsh

'A university is what a college becomes when the faculty loses interest in students.'
- John Ciardi

'To make your children capable of honesty is the beginning of Learning.'
- John Ruskin

'John Milton called his school, Christ College, 'a stony-hearted stepmother'. The ultimate goal of the Learningal system is to shift to the individual the burden of pursuing his Learning.'
- John W. Gardner

'Schoolmasters and parents exist to be grown out of.'
- John Wolfenden

'Learning should be gentle and stern, not cold and lax.'
- Joseph Joubert

'My husband managed to cram four years of college into five.'
- Judy Hampton

'Fathers send their sons to college either because they went to college, or because they didn't.'
- L. L. Hendren

'"Do you think your boy will forget all he learned in college?" "I hope so. He can't make a living drinking."'
- Larry Wilde

'By learning you will teach; by teaching you will learn.'
- Latin proverb

'I won't say ours was a tough school, but we had our own coroner. We used to write essays like "What I'm Going to Be if I Grow Up."'
- Lenny Bruce

'The university is the last remaining platform for national dissent.'
- Leon Eisenberg

'When there are two PhD's in a developing country, one is Head of State and the other is in exile.'
- Lord Samuel

'On many American campuses the only qualification for admission was the ability actually to find the campus and then discover a parking space.'
- Malcolm Bradbury

'Learning is the process of driving a set of prejudices down your throat.'
- Martin H. Fischer

'You don't understand anything until you learn it more than one way.'
- Marvin Minsky

'Graduation Speech: You'll have to excuse me if I cry. I've been a little teary-eyed all week; the sadness, the joy, . . . the fact that I'm off my parents' payroll.'
- Melissa Amernick

'Tell me and I'll forget. Show me, and I may not remember. Involve me, and I'll understand.'
- Native American saying

'We must reject that most dismal and fatuous notion that Learning is a preparation for life.'
- Northrop Frye

'Learning is an admirable thing, but it is well to remember from time to time that nothing that is worth knowing can be taught.'
- Oscar Wilde

'I forget what I was taught. I only remember what I have learnt.'
- Patrick White

'Let the schools teach the nobility of labor and the beauty of human service: but the superstitions of ages past? Never!'
- Peter Cooper

'All learning has an emotional base.'
- Plato

'There is a time in every man's Learning when he arrives at the conviction that envy is ignorance; that imitation is suicide; that he must take himself for better, for worse as his portion.'
- Ralph Waldo Emerson

'I pay the School Master, but 'tis the school boys that educate my son.'
- Ralph Waldo Emerson

'The things taught in schools are not an Learning but the means of Learning.'
- Ralph Waldo Emerson

'Learning to learn is to know how to navigate in a forest of facts, ideas and theories, a proliferation of constantly changing items of knowledge. Learning to learn is to know what to ignore but at the same time not rejecting innovation and research.'
- Raymond Queneau

'A one-book man is either a slow learner or an ill-equipped teacher.'
- Robert Burke

'Learning is the ability to listen to almost anything without losing your temper or your self-confidence.'
- Robert Frost

'I went to a high school that was so dangerous, the school newspaper had an obituary column.'
- Rocky Ray

'If you educate a man you educate a person, but if you educate a woman, you educate a family.'
- Rudy Manikan

'If you hit a pony over the nose at the outset of your acquaintance, he may not love you but he will take a deep interest in your movements ever afterwards.'
- Rudyard Kipling

'There is less flogging in our great schools than formerly, but then less is learned there; so that what the boys get at one end they lose at the other.'
- Samuel Johnson

'Training is everything. The peach was once a bitter almond; cauliflower is nothing but cabbage with a college Learning.'
- Samuel L. Clemens

'It is in fact a part of the function of Learning to help us to escape, not from our own time - for we are bound by that - but from the intellectual and emotional limitations of our time.'
- T. S. Eliot

'No one can become really educated without having pursued some study in which he took no interest. For it is part of Learning to interest ourselves in subjects for which we have no aptitude.'
- T. S. Eliot

'Learning makes a man fit company for himself.'
- Thomas Fuller

'It was going all wrong at my college interview until I nonchalantly asked, "Do you need any large donations for new buildings?"'
- Todd Anderson

'There is that indescribable freshness and unconsciousness about an illiterate person that humbles and mocks the power of the noblest expressive genius.'
- Walt Whitman

'The schools ain't what they used to be and never was.'
- Will Rogers

'There is nothing so stupid as an educated man, if you get off the thing that he was educated in.'
- Will Rogers

'Learning is not the-filling of a pail, but the lighting of a fire.'
- William Butler Yeats

'It is a greater work to educate a child, in the true and larger sense of the word, than to rule a state.'
- William Ellery Channing

'Some men are graduated from college cum laude, some are graduated summa cum laude, and some are graduated mirabile dictu.'
- William Howard Taft

LIFE

'The loveliest of trees, the cherry now is hung with bloom along the bough, and stands about the woodland ride wearing white for Eastertide.'
   - A. E. Housman

'Clay lies still but blood's a rover; Breath's a ware that will not keep Up, lad; when the journey's over There'll be time enough to sleep.'
   - A. E. Housman

'It is not the years in your life but the life in your years that counts.'
   - Adlai Stevenson

'Our insignificance is often the cause of our safety.'
   - Aesop

'He who despairs of the human condition is a coward, but he who has hope for it is a fool.'
   - Albert Camus

'Love . . . includes fellowship in suffering, in joy and in effort.'
   - Albert Schweitzer

'At any given moment life is completely senseless. But viewed over a period, it seems to reveal itself as an organism existing in time, having a purpose, tending in a certain direction.'
   - Aldous Huxley

'The natural rhythm of human life is routine punctuated by orgies.'
   - Aldous Huxley

'The vanity of human life is like a river, constantly passing away, and yet constantly coming on.'
   - Alexander Pope

'Every man's road in life is marked by the graves of his personal likings.'
   - Alexander Smith

'All the things I really like to do are either immoral, illegal or fattening.'
   - Alexander Woollcott

'There are two ways to slide easily through life; to believe everything or doubt everything. Both ways save us from thinking.'
   - Alfred Korzybski

'Life is an offensive, directed against the repetitious mechanism of the universe.'
   - Alfred North Whitehead

'The Grand essentials of happiness are: something to do, something to love, and something to hope for.'
- Allan K. Chalmers

'Enjoy life. Think of all the women who passed up dessert on the Titanic.'
- Anonymous

'Life is a handful of short stories, pretending to be a novel.'
- Anonymous

'I expect to pass through this world but once. Any good therefore that I can do, or any kindness that I can show to any fellow creature, let me do it now. Let me not defer or neglect it, for I shall not pass this way again.'
- Anonymous

'Life is a jig saw puzzle with most of the pieces missing.'
- Anonymous

'There is no better exercise for strengthening the heart than reaching down and lifting up another.'
- Anonymous

'A single event can awaken within us a stranger totally unknown to us. To live is to be slowly born.'
- Antoine de Saint-Exupery

'The closing years of life are like the end of a masquerade party, when the masks are dropped.'
- Arthur Schopenhauer

'I try to take one day at a time, but sometimes several days attack me at once.'
- Ashleigh Brilliant

'We come and we cry, and that is life; we yawn and we depart, and that is death!'
- Ausone de Chancel

'Our whole life is like a play.'
- Ben Jonson

'For life in general, there is but one decree: youth is a blunder, manhood a struggle, old age a regret.'
- Benjamin Disraeli

'Were the offer made true, I would engage to run again, from beginning to end, the same career of life. All I would ask should be the privilege of an author, to correct, in a second edition, certain errors of the first.'
- Benjamin Franklin

'Dost thou love life? Then do not squander time, for that is the stuff life is made of.'
- Benjamin Franklin

'Don't do things to not die, do things to enjoy living. The by-product may be not dying.'
- Bernie S. Siegel

'The good life, as I conceive it, is a happy life. I do not mean that if you are good you will be happy - I mean that if you are happy you will be good.'
- Bertrand Russell

'To fear love is to fear life, and those who fear life are already three parts dead.'
- Bertrand Russell

'All that a man hath will he give for his life.'
- Bible

'Give me neither poverty nor riches; feed me with food convenient for me.'
- Bible

'Life is seldom as unendurable as, to judge by the facts, it logically ought to be.'
- Brooks Atkinson

'Love your neighbor as yourself, but don't take down the fence.'
- Carl Sandburg

'Life is pain and the enjoyment of love is an anesthetic.'
- Cesare Pavese

'The expression often used by Mr. Herbert Spencer of the Survival of the Fittest is more accurate and is sometimes equally convenient.'
- Charles Darwin

'People in the West are always getting ready to live.'
- Chinese proverb

'If we all discovered that we only had five minutes left to say all that we wanted to say, every telephone booth would be occupied by people calling other people to tell them that they loved them.'
- Christopher Morley

'The first half of our lives is ruined by our parents and the second half by our children.'
- Clarence Darrow

'There is time for work. And time for love. That leaves no other time.'
- Coco Chanel

'The power of habit and the charm of novelty are the two adverse forces which explain the follies of mankind.'
- Comtesse Diane

'Life is ours to be spent, not to be saved.'
- D. H. Lawrence

'Life only demands from the strength you possess. Only one feat is possible - not to have run away.'
- Dag Hammarskjold

'Sometimes I wish life had a fast-forward button.'
- Dan Chopin

'Sloppy, raggedy-assed old life. I love it. I never want to die.'
- Dennis Trudell

'Love's like the measles - all the worse when it comes late in life.'
- Douglas Jerrold

'Everything I did in my life that was worthwhile I caught Hell for.'
- Earl Warren

'I love humanity but I hate people.'
- Edna St. Vincent Millay

'It is not true that life is one damn thing after another- it's one damn thing over and over.'
- Edna St. Vincent Millay

'My candle burns at both ends; It will not last the night; But, ah, my foes, and, oh, my friends - It gives a lovely light.'
- Edna St. Vincent Millay

'Life is the game that must be played: This truth at least, good friends, we know; So live and laugh, nor be dismayed As one by one the phantoms go.'
- Edwin Arlington Robinson

'You've got to keep fighting - you've got to risk your life every six months to stay alive.'
- Elia Kazan

'To love means not to impose your own powers on your fellow man but offer him your help. And if he refuses it, to be proud that he can do it on his own strength.'
- Elisabeth Kubler-Ross

'Love doesn't make the world go round, Love is what makes the ride worthwhile.'
- Elizabeth Barrett Browning

'Love is anterior to life Posterior to death Initial of creation, and The exponent of breath.'
- Emily Dickinson

'No one is to be despaired of as long as he breathes. (While there is life there is hope.)'
- Erasmus

'Love is the only sane and satisfactory answer to the problem of human existence.'
- Erich Fromm

'Who will tell whether one happy moment of love or the joy of breathing or walking on a bright morning and smelling the fresh air, is not worth all the suffering and effort which life implies.'
- Erich Fromm

'The real reason for not committing suicide is because you always know how swell life gets again after the hell is over.'
- Ernest Hemingway

'Life is a game of whist. From unseen sources The cards are shuffled, and the hands are dealt. I do not like the way the cards are shuffled, But yet I like the game and want to play.'
- Eugene F. Ware

'Life is for each man a solitary cell whose walls are mirrors.'
- Eugene O'Neill

'I haven't heard of anybody who wants to stop living on account of the cost.'
- F. McKinney Hubbard

'Magnificently unprepared for the long littleness of life.'
- Frances Cornford

'It matters not how long we live, but how.'
- Francis Bailey

'He who has a why to live can bear with almost any how.'
- Friedrich Nietzsche

'His saying was: live and let live.'
- Friedrich von Schiller

'A tragedy means always a man's struggle with that which is stronger than man.'
- G. K. Chesterton

'This is the true joy in life, the being used for a purpose recognized by yourself as a mighty one; the being thoroughly worn out before you are thrown on the scrap heap.'
- George Bernard Shaw

'Hurried and worried until we're buried, and there's no curtain call, Life's a very funny proposition, after all.'
- George M. Cohan

'Most people get a fair amount of fun out of their lives, but on balance life is suffering and only the very sound or the very foolish imagine otherwise.'
- George Orwell

'Life in common among people who love each other is the ideal of happiness.'
- George Sand

'There is only one happiness in life: to love and be loved.'
- George Sand

'There is no cure for birth and death, save to enjoy the interval.'
- George Santayana

'Love is letting go of fear.'
- Gerald Jampolsky

'He alone deserves liberty and life who daily must win them anew.'
- Goethe

'Every man's life is a fairy-tale written by God's fingers.'
- Hans Christian Andersen

'The man who has no inner life is the slave of his surroundings.'
- Henri Frederic Amiel

'The Indian Summer of life should be a little sunny and a little sad, like the season, and infinite in wealth and depth of tone - but never hustled.'
- Henry Adams

'Cats and monkeys - monkeys and cats - all human life is there.'
- Henry James

'Life, as it is called, is for most of us one long postponement.'
- Henry Miller

'The one thing we can never get enough of is love. And the one thing we never give enough of is love.'
- Henry Miller

'Tell me not, in mournful numbers, Life is but an empty dream!'
- Henry Wadsworth Longfellow

'After the game, the king and pawn go into the same box.'
- Italian proverb

'Real life seems to have no plots.'
- Ivy Compton-Burnett

'The world is made up of people who never quite get into the first team and who just miss the prizes at the flower show.'
- Jacob Bronowski

'Life is but a day at most.'
- James Drummond Burns

'Every life is many days, day after day. We walk through ourselves, meeting robbers, ghosts, giants, old men, young men, wives, widows, brothers-in-love. But always meeting ourselves.'
- James Joyce

'All men should strive to learn before they die what they are running from, and to, and why.'
- James Thurber

'Life is a tragedy for those who feel, and a comedy for those who think.'
  - Jean de la Bruyere

'One returns to the place one came from.'
  - Jean de la Fontaine

'The flower is the poetry of reproduction. It is the example of the eternal seductiveness of life.'
  - Jean Giraudoux

'Age does not protect you from love. But love, to some extent, protects you from age.'
  - Jeanne Moreau

'When the power of love overcomes the love of power, the world will know peace.'
  - Jimi Hendrix

'You only live once - but if you work it right, once is enough.'
  - Joe E. Lewis

'Love does not dominate; it cultivates.'
  - Johann Wolfgang von Goethe

'A proverb is no proverb to you till life has illustrated it.'
  - John Keats

'Oh for a life of sensations rather than of thoughts.'
  - John Keats

'The great business of life is to be, to do, to do without and to depart.'
  - John Morley

'We are most alive when we're in love.'
  - John Updike

'May you live all the days of your life.'
  - Jonathan Swift

'Without duty, life is soft and boneless; it cannot hold itself together.'
  - Joseph Joubert

'My advice to those who are about to begin, in earnest, the journey of life, is to take their heart in one hand and a club in the other.'
  - Josh Billings

'Love looks through a telescope; envy through a microscope.'
  - Josh Billings

'Oh, how daily life is. (Ah, que la vie est quotidienne.)'
  - Jules Laforgue

'Life without love is like a tree without blossom and fruit.'
- Kahlil Gibran

'All of life is more or less what the French would call s'imposer - to be able to create one's own terms for what one does.'
- Kenneth Tynan

'If you're on the merry-go-round, you have to go round.'
- Kent Thompson

'And remember, my sentimental friend, that a heart is not judged by how much you love, but by how much you are loved by others.'
- L. Frank Baum

'The world is a beautiful place to be born into if you don't mind some people dying all the time or maybe only starving some of the time which isn't half so bad if it isn't you.'
- Laurence Ferlinghetti

'If love is the answer, could you please rephrase the question?'
- Lily Tomlin

'We're all in this together - by ourselves.'
- Lily Tomlin

'The trouble with the rat race is that even if you win, you're still a rat.'
- Lily Tomlin

'It is now life and not art that requires the willing suspension of disbelief.'
- Lionel Trilling

'Love is like pi - natural, irrational, and very important.'
- Lisa Hoffman

'The white flower of a blameless life.'
- Lord Alfred Tennyson

'Life is ever since man was born, licking honey from a thorn.'
- Louis Ginsberg

'One must choose in life between boredom and suffering.'
- Madame de Stael

'Where there is love there is life.'
- Mahatma Gandhi

'St. Teresa of Avila described our life in this world as like a night at a second-class hotel.'
- Malcolm Muggeridge

'In our life there is a single color, as on an artist's palette, which provides the meaning of life and art. It is the color of love.'
- Marc Chagall

'There can be no peace of mind in love, since the advantage one has secured is never anything by a fresh starting-point for further desires.'
- Marcel Proust

'The art of living is more like that of wrestling than of dancing. The main thing is to stand firm and be ready for an unforeseen attack.'
- Marcus Aurelius

'Life is a stranger's sojourn, a night at an inn.'
- Marcus Aurelius

'Death and taxes and childbirth. There's never any convenient time for any of them.'
- Margaret Mitchell

'Life would be infinitely happier if we could only be born at the age of eighty and gradually approach eighteen.'
- Mark Twain

'Christian life consists in faith and charity.'
- Martin Luther

'Strait is the gate and narrow is the way which leadeth unto life.'
- Matthew

'In the arithmetic of love, one plus one equals everything, and two minus one equals nothing.'
- Mignon McLaughlin

'The true meaning of life is to plant trees, under whose shade you do not expect to sit.'
- Nelson Henderson

'Life is made up of sobs, sniffles and smiles, with sniffles predominating.'
- O. Henry

'Life is not having been told that the man has just waxed the floor.'
- Ogden Nash

'Man wants but little here below nor wants that little long.'
- Oliver Goldsmith

'Life is Taking Action and passion; therefore, it is required of a man that he should share the passion and Taking Action of the time, at peril of being judged not to have lived.'
- Oliver Wendell Holmes

'I am on the side of the unregenerate who affirm the worth of life as an end in itself, as against the saints who deny it.'
- Oliver Wendell Holmes

'Love is the master key which opens the gates of happiness.'
- Oliver Wendell Holmes

'Life is painting a picture, not doing a sum.'
- Oliver Wendell Holmes

'Ah Love! could you and I with him conspire To grasp this sorry Scheme of Things entire Would we not shatter it to bits - and then Re-mould it nearer to the Heart's Desire?'
- Omar Khayyam

'Men know life too early, women know life too late.'
- Oscar Wilde

'Keep love in your heart. A life without it is like a sunless garden when the flowers are dead.'
- Oscar Wilde

'The character of human life, like the character of the human condition, like the character of all life, is "ambiguity": the inseparable mixture of good and evil, the true and false, the creative and destructive forces - both individual and social.'
- Paul Tillich

'What the world really needs is more love and less paperwork.'
- Pearl Bailey

'If you won't be better tomorrow than you were today, then what do you need tomorrow for?'
- Rabbi Nahman of Bratslav

'Let your life lightly dance on the edges of Time like dew on the tip of a leaf.'
- Rabindranath Tagore

'For one human being to love another: that is perhaps the most difficult of our tasks; the ultimate, the last test and proof, the work for which all other work is but preparation.'
- Rainer Maria Rilke

'Out of sleeping a waking, Out of waking a sleep.'
- Ralph Waldo Emerson

'In the morning a man walks with his whole body; in the evening, only with his legs.'
- Ralph Waldo Emerson

'The whole of what we know is a system of compensations. Each suffering is rewarded; each sacrifice is made up; every debt is paid.'
- Ralph Waldo Emerson

'Life consists in what a man is thinking of all day.'
- Ralph Waldo Emerson

'If there is another world, he lives in bliss If there is none, he made the best of this.'
- Robert Burns

'O Life! thou art a galling load, Along a rough, a weary road, to wretches such as I.'
- Robert Burns

'In three words I can sum up everything I've learned about life. It goes on.'
- Robert Frost

'The essence of love is kindness.'
- Robert Louis Stevenson

'There are days when it takes all you've got just to keep up with the losers.'
- Robert Orben

'This is the Law of the Yukon, that only the strong shall thrive; That surely the weak shall perish, and only the fit survive.'
- Robert W. Service

'I like life. It's something to do. Somewhere on this globe every 10 seconds, there is a woman giving birth to a child. She must be found and stopped.'
- Sam Levenson

'Life is one long process of getting tired.'
- Samuel Butler

'To live is like to love - all reason is against it, and all healthy instinct for it.'
- Samuel Butler

'The joy of life is variety; the tenderest love requires to be renewed by intervals of absence.'
- Samuel Johnson

'The love of life is necessary to the vigorous prosecution of any undertaking.'
- Samuel Johnson

'Man arrives as a novice at each age of his life.'
- Sebastien Chamfort

'As is a tale, so is life: not how long it is, but how good it is, is what matters.'
- Seneca

'Basically, I'm interested in friendship, sex and death.'
- Sharon Riis

'Life as we find it is too hard for us; it entails too much pain, too many disappointments, impossible tasks. We cannot do without palliative remedies.'
- Sigmund Freud

'Life is a long lesson in humility.'
- Sir James M. Barrie

'Life can only be understood backwards; but it must be lived forwards.'
- Soren Kierkegaard

'It is a misery to be born, a pain to live, a trouble to die.'
- St. Bernard of Clairvaux

'Life, we learn too late, is in the living, in the tissue of every day and hour.'
- Stephen Leacock

'And whatever it is that keeps widening your heart, that's Mary, too, not only the power inside you but the love. And when you get down to it, Lily, that's the only purpose grand enough for a human life. Not just to love - but to persist in love.'
- Sue Monk Kidd

'Birth, copulation and death. That's all the facts when you come to brass tacks.'
- T. S. Eliot

'I have measured out my life with coffee spoons.'
- T. S. Eliot

'Where love is, no room is too small.'
- Talmud

'Life is all memory, except for the one present moment that goes by you so quickly you hardly catch it going.'
- Tennessee Williams

'I wish to preach not the doctrine of ignoble ease, but the doctrine of the strenuous life.'
- Theodore Roosevelt

'The tragedy of life is not so much what men suffer, but rather what they miss.'
- Thomas Carlyle

'One life - a little gleam of Time between two Eternities.'
- Thomas Carlyle

'Love is ever the beginning of Knowledge as fire is of light.'
- Thomas Carlyle

'Measurement of life should be proportioned rather to the intensity of the experience than to its actual length.'
- Thomas Hardy

'If way to the Better there be, it exacts a full look at the Worst.'
- Thomas Hardy

'Life is what happens to us while we are making other plans.'
- Thomas la Mance

'It is love, not reason, that is stronger than death.'
- Thomas Mann

'The truth that many people never understand, until it is too late, is that the more you try to avoid suffering the more you suffer because smaller and more insignificant things begin to torture you in proportion to your fear of being hurt.'
- Thomas Merton

'Population, when unchecked, increases in a geometrical ratio. Subsistence only increases in an arithmetical ratio.'
- Thomas Robert Malthus

'Life is better than death, I believe, if only because it is less boring and because it has fresh peaches in it.'
- Thomas Walker

'Is not this the true romantic feeling - not to desire to escape life, but to prevent life from escaping you.'
- Thomas Wolfe

'We live in what is, but we find 1,000 ways not to face it. Great theatre strengthens our faculty to face it.'
- Thornton Wilder

'They say a person needs just three things to be truly happy in this world: someone to love, something to do, and something to hope for.'
- Tom Bodett

'Love is like the truth, sometimes it prevails, sometimes it hurts.'
- Victor M. Garcia

'Life is a luminous halo, a semi-transparent envelope surrounding us from the beginning.'
- Virginia Woolf

'Ofttimes the test of courage becomes rather to live than to die.'
- Vittorio Conte Alfieri

'We never live, but we are always in the expectation of living.'
- Voltaire

'Love is a canvas furnished by nature and embroidered by imagination.'
- Voltaire

'Among those whom I like or admire, I can find no common denominator, but among those whom I love, I can: all of them make me laugh.'
- W. H. Auden

'Life isn't long enough for love and art.'
- W. Somerset Maugham

'The great pleasure in life is doing what people say you cannot do.'
- Walter Bagehot

'One hour of life, crowded to the full with glorious Taking Action, and filled with noble risks, is worth whole years of those mean observances of paltry decorum.'
- Walter Scott

'Loving people live in a loving world. Hostile people live in a hostile world. Same world.'
- Wayne W. Dyer

'Life is a long preparation for something that never happens.'
- William Butler Yeats

'Be intent upon the perfection of the present day.'
- William Law

'Such as we are made of, such we be.'
- William Shakespeare

'One man in his time plays many parts.'
- William Shakespeare

'Out, out, brief candle! Life's but a walking shadow.'
- William Shakespeare

'If music be the food of love, play on; Give me excess of it, that, surfeiting, The appetite may sicken, and so die. That strain again! it had a dying fall: O, it came o'er my ear like the sweet sound.'
- William Shakespeare

'Without a measureless and perpetual uncertainty, the drama of human life would be destroyed.'
- Winston Churchill

'Neither a lofty degree of intelligence nor imagination nor both together go to the making of genius. Love, love, love, that is the soul of genius.'
- Wolfgang Amadeus Mozart

LITERATURE

'A novel is never anything but a philosophy put into images.'
- Albert Camus

'The essay is a literary device for saying almost everything about almost anything.'
- Aldous Huxley

'A perfect judge will read each word of wit with the same spirit that its author writ.'
- Alexander Pope

'In literature as in love we are astounded by what is chosen by others.'
- Andre Maurois

'In literary history, generation follows generation in a rage.'
- Annie Dillard

'Good children's literature appeals not only to the child in the adult, but to the adult in the child.'
- Anonymous

'Literature is a power to be possessed, not a body of objects to be studied.'
- Anonymous

'One hears about life all the time from different people with very different narrative gifts.'
- Anthony Powell

'Medicine is my lawful wife. Literature is my mistress.'
- Anton Chekhov

'Literature is the art of writing something that will be read twice; journalism what will be grasped at once.'
- Cyril Connolly

'When I read Shakespeare I am struck with wonder that such trivial people should muse and thunder in such lovely language.'
- D. H. Lawrence

'Literature is mostly about sex and not much about having children; and life is the other way around.'
- David Lodge

'Literature flourishes best when it is half a trade and half an art.'
- Dean William R. Inge

'Those expressions are omitted which cannot with propriety be read aloud in the family.'
- Dr. Thomas Bowdler

'Science is uneasy with beginnings. Mythology is concerned above all with what happened "in the beginning". Its signature is "Once upon a time".'
- Dudley Young

'When a man can observe himself suffering and is able, later, to describe what he's gone through, it means he was born for literature.'
- Edouard Bourdet

'The walls are the publishers of the poor.'
- Eduardo Galeano

'The short story is the art form that deals with the individual when there is no longer a society to absorb him, and when he is compelled to exist, as it were, by his own inner light.'
- Frank O'Connor

'The man who writes about himself and his own time is the only man who writes about all people and about all time.'
- George Bernard Shaw

'Published memoirs indicate the end of a man's activity, and that he acknowledges the end.'
- George Meredith

'A literary movement consists of five or six people who live in the same town and hate each other cordially.'
- George Moore

'To be a good diarist, one must have a little snouty, sneaky mind.'
- Harold Nicolson

'Literature is my Utopia. Here I am not disfranchised. No barrier of the senses shuts me out from the sweet, gracious discourse of my book-friends. They talk to me without embarrassment or awkwardness.'
- Helen Keller

'What is a diary as a rule? A document useful to the person who keeps it, dull to the contemporary who reads it and invaluable to the student, centuries afterwards, who treasures it!'
- Helen Terry

'Oh! Let us never, never doubt What nobody is sure about.'
- Hilaire Belloc

'The llama is a woolly sort of fleecy hairy goat, with an indolent expression and an undulating throat like an unsuccessful literary man.'
- Hilaire Belloc

'The great standard of literature as to purity and exactness of style is the Bible.'
- Hugh Blair

'Fiction reveals truth that reality obscures.'
- Jessamyn West

'Biography is one of the new terrors of death.'
- John Arbuthnot

'Chaucer, I confess, is a rough diamond; and must be polished e'er he shines.'
- John Dryden

'Literature was formerly an art and finance a trade: today it is the reverse.'
- Joseph Roux

'A novel is a static thing that one moves through; a play is a dynamic thing that moves past one.'
- Kenneth Tynan

'I am never long, even in the society of her I love, without yearning for the company of my lamp and my library.'
- Lord Byron

'The answers you get from literature depend upon the questions you pose.'
- Margaret Atwood

'Biographies are but the clothes and buttons of the man - the biography of the man himself cannot be written.'
- Mark Twain

'The universe is made up of stories, not of atoms.'
- Muriel Rukeyser

'The difference between literature and journalism is that journalism is unreadable, and literature is not read.'
- Oscar Wilde

'It has come to be practically a sort of rule in literature that a man, having once shown himself capable of original writing, is entitled thenceforth to steal from the writings of others at discretion.'
- Ralph Waldo Emerson

'I can find my biography in every fable that I read.'
- Ralph Waldo Emerson

'The novel is a prose narrative of some length that has something wrong with it.'
- Randall Jarrell

'All that non-fiction can do is answer questions. It's fiction's business to ask them.'
- Richard Hughes

'What is an epigram? A dwarfish whole, its body brevity, and wit its soul.'
- Samuel Taylor Coleridge

'The first thing to be done by a biographer in estimating character is to examine the stubs of the victim's cheque books.'
- Silas W. Mitchell

'A novel is a mirror carried along a main road.'
- Stendhal

'The classics are only primitive literature. They belong to the same class as primitive machinery and primitive music and primitive medicine.'
- Stephen Leacock

'Literature is the orchestration of platitudes.'
- Thornton Wilder

'A biography is considered complete if it merely accounts for six or seven selves, whereas a person may well have as many as a thousand.'
- Virginia Woolf

'Contemporary literature can be classified under three headings: the neurotic, the erotic and the tommy-rotic.'
- W. Giese

'Literature is the effort of man to indemnify himself for the wrongs of his condition.'
- Walter Savage Landor

LOVE

'It has been wisely said that we cannot really love anybody at whom we never laugh.'
   - Agnes Repplier

'Love cannot accept what it is. Everywhere on earth it cries out against kindness, compassion, intelligence, everything that leads to compromise. Love demands the impossible, the absolute, the sky on fire, inexhaustible springtime, life after death, and de'
   - Albert Camus

'We always deceive ourselves twice about the people we love - first to their advantage, then to their disadvantage.'
   - Albert Camus

'No, this trick won't work. . . . How on earth are you ever going to explain in terms of chemistry and physics so important a biological phenomenon as first love?'
   - Albert Einstein

'Gravitation cannot be held responsible for people falling in love.'
   - Albert Einstein

'The art of love ... is largely the art of persistence.'
   - Albert Ellis

'What dire offence from am'rous causes springs. What mighty contests rise from trivial things.'
   - Alexander Pope

'I have learned not to worry about love; but to honor its coming with all my heart.'
   - Alice Walker

'Man loves little and often, woman much and rarely.'
   - Anonymous

'There is no fear in love; but perfect love casteth out fear.'
   - Anonymous

'In the act of loving someone you arm them against you.'
   - Anonymous

'The mystery of love is greater than the mystery of death.'
   - Anonymous

'Love is like war, easy to begin but hard to end.'
   - Anonymous

'Love is what makes two people sit in the middle of a bench when there is plenty of room at both ends.'
- Anonymous

'Some love lasts a lifetime. True love lasts forever.'
- Anonymous

'True love cannot be found where it truly does not exist, nor can it be hidden where it truly does.'
- Anonymous

'The first sigh of love is the last of wisdom.'
- Antoine Bret

'Love does not consist in gazing at each other, but in looking together in the same direction.'
- Antoine de Saint-Exupery

'True love begins when nothing is looked for in return.'
- Antoine de Saint-Exupery

'Love is composed of a single soul inhabiting two bodies.'
- Aristotle

'The porcupine, whom one must handle gloved, may be respected, but is never loved.'
- Arthur Guiterman

'The loving are the daring.'
- Bayard Taylor

'Love is the magician that pulls man out of his own hat.'
- Ben Hecht

'We are all born for love, ... It is the principle of existence and its only end.'
- Benjamin Disraeli

'The magic of first love is our ignorance that it can ever end.'
- Benjamin Disraeli

'Without love, what are we worth? Eighty-nine cents! Eighty-nine cents worth of chemicals walking around lonely.'
- Benjamin Franklin

'If you would be loved, love and be lovable.'
- Benjamin Franklin

'I thought I was in love once, and then later I thought maybe it was just an inner-ear imbalance.'
- Benton Fraser

'Many people when they fall in love look for a little haven of refuge from the world, where they can be sure of being admired when they are not admirable, and praised when they are not praiseworthy.'
- Bertrand Russell

'Love is strong as death; jealousy is cruel as the grave.'
- Bible

'Many waters cannot quench love, neither can the floods drown it.'
- Bible

'Whither thou goest, I will go; and where thou lodgest, I will lodge; thy people shall be my people, and thy God my God.'
- Bible

'He that loveth his brother abideth in the light, and there is none occasion of stumbling in him.'
- Bible

'Above all things have devoted love among yourselves, for love covers a multitude of sins.'
- Bible

'Beloved, let us love one another: for love is of God; and every one that loveth is born of God, and knoweth God.'
- Bible

'People who throw kisses are hopelessly lazy.'
- Bob Hope

'What we can do for another is the test of powers; what we can suffer is the test of love.'
- Brooke Foss Westcott

'Love is like a friendship caught on fire. In the beginning a flame, very pretty, often hot and fierce, but still only light and flickering. As love grows older, our hearts mature and our love becomes as coals, deep-burning and unquenchable.'
- Bruce Lee

'Do not waste time bothering whether you "love" your neighbor; act as if you did. As soon as we do this we find one of the great secrets. When you are behaving as if you loved someone, you will presently come to love him. If you injure someone you dislike,'
- C. S. Lewis

'Though our feelings come and go, God's love for us does not.'
- C. S. Lewis

'The higher animals are in a sense drawn into Man when he loves them and makes them (as he does) much more nearly human than they would otherwise be.'
- C. S. Lewis

'Where love rules, there is no will to power and where power predominates, love is lacking. The one is the shadow of the other.'
- Carl G. Jung

'Being in therapy is great. I spend an hour just talking about myself. It's kinda like being the guy on a date.'
- Caroline Rhea

'What is irritating about love is that it is a crime that requires an accomplice.'
- Charles Baudelaire

'If you cannot inspire a woman with love of you, fill her above the brim with love of herself; all that runs over will be yours.'
- Charles Caleb Colton

'We have lived and loved together Through many changing years; We have shared each other's gladness, And wept each other's tears.'
- Charles Jefferys

'Tell me who admires and loves you, and I will tell you who you are.'
- Charles-Augustin Sainte-Beuve

'Our first and last love is - self-love.'
- Christian Nestell Bovee

'Come live with me, and be my love, And we will all the pleasures prove, That valleys, groves, or hills, or fields, Or woods and steepy mountains, yield.'
- Christopher Marlowe

'It is an extra dividend when you like the girl you've fallen in love with.'
- Clark Gable

'Love is. the flower of life, and blossoms unexpectedly and without law, and must be plucked where it is found, and enjoyed for the brief hour of its duration.'
- D. H. Lawrence

'I recently read that love is entirely a matter of chemistry. That must be why my wife treats me like toxic waste.'
- David Bissonette

'To love and be loved is to feel the sun from both sides.'
- David Viscott

'Love me without fear Trust me without questioning Need me without demanding Want me without restrictions Accept me without change Desire me without inhibitions For a love so free . . . Will never fly away.'
- Dick Sutphen

'Love is like quicksilver in the hand. Leave the fingers open and it stays. Clutch it, and it darts away.'
- Dorothy Parker

'unlove's the heavenless hell and homeless home . . . lovers alone wear sunlight.'
- e. e. cummings

'No woman ever falls in love with a man unless she has a better opinion of him than he deserves.'
- Edgar Watson Howe

'After all, my erstwhile dear, my no longer cherished, need we say it was no love, just because it perished?'
- Edna St. Vincent Millay

'And if I loved you Wednesday, well, what is that to you? I do not love you Thursday - so much is true.'
- Edna St. Vincent Millay

''Tis not love's going hurts my days, but that it went in little ways.'
- Edna St. Vincent Millay

'Love must have wings to fly away from love, And to fly back again.'
- Edwin Arlington Robinson

'I love thee to the depth and breadth and height my soul can reach.'
- Elizabeth Barrett Browning

'When you love someone, all your saved-up wishes start coming out.'
- Elizabeth Bowen

'Love is moral even without legal marriage, but marriage is immoral without love.'
- Ellen Key

'Love is a deep well from which you may drink often, but into which you may fall but once.'
- Ellye Howell Glover

'Love in its essence is spiritual fire.'
- Emmanuel Swedenborg

'Two's a company, three's a crowd.'
- English proverb

'Love means to commit oneself without guarantee, to give oneself completely in the hope that our love will produce love in the loved person. Love is an act of faith, and whoever is of little faith is also of little love.'
- Erich Fromm

'Immature love says "I love you because I need you." Mature love says "I need you because I love you."'
- Erich Fromm

'But one always returns to one's first loves.'
- Etienne

'Of all the paths [that] lead to a woman's love Pity's the straightest.'
- Francis Beaumont

'True love is like ghosts, which everybody talks about and few have seen.'
- Francois de La Rochefoucauld

'No love, no friendship can cross the path of our destiny without leaving some mark on it forever.'
- Francois Mauriac

'Respect is love in plain clothes.'
- Frankie Byrne

'Human love is often but the encounter of two weaknesses.'
- Franqois Mauriac

'Love makes the time pass. Time makes love pass.'
- French proverb

'There is one who kisses, and the other who offers a cheek.'
- French proverb

'It's love, it's love that makes the world go round.'
- French Song

'Every theory of love, from Plato down, teaches that each individual loves in the other sex what he lacks in himself.'
- G. Stanley Hall

'A romp in the hay lingers like the first line of a song, but your true love is the one you make a life with and write more than a line about, you write a whole book.'
- Garrison Keillor

'The fickleness of the woman I love is equaled by the infernal constancy of the women who love me.'
- George Bernard Shaw

'Love is a gross exaggeration of the difference between one person and everybody else.'
- George Bernard Shaw

'Love is nature's second son.'
- George Chapman

'But there's nothing half so sweet in life as love's young dream.'
- George Moore

'Someone asked me why women don't gamble as much as men do, and I gave the commonsensical reply that we don't have as much money. That was a true and incomplete answer. In fact, women's

total instinct for gambling is satisfied by marriage.'
- Gloria Steinem

'Never forget the three powerful resources you always have available to you: love, prayer and forgiveness.'
- H. Jackson Brown

'Love is the delusion that one woman differs from another.'
- H. L. Mencken

'The irony of love is that it guarantees some degree of anger, fear and criticism.'
- Harold H. Bloomfield

'I love a lassie, a bonnie, bonnie lassie, She's as pure as the lily in the dell. She's as sweet as the heather, The bonnie, bloomin' heather, Mary, ma Scotch Blue-bell.'
- Harry Lauder

'All thoughts, all passions, all delights, Whatever stirs this mortal frame, All are but ministers of Love, And feed his sacred flame.'
- Hartley Coleridge

'Whom the Lord loveth he chasteneth.'
- Hebrews

'I believe that life is given us so that we may grow in love, and I believe that God is in me as the sun is in the color and fragrance of a flower.'
- Helen Keller

'Falling in love consists merely in uncorking the imagination and bottling the common-sense.'
- Helen Rowland

'You can't buy love, but you can pay heavily for it.'
- Henny Youngman

'Of all the girls that are so smart There's none like pretty Sally; She is the darling of my heart, And lives in our alley.'
- Henry Carey

'When the satisfTaking Action or the security of another person becomes as significant to one as one's own satisfTaking Action or security, then the state of love exists.'
- Henry Stack Sullivan

'Time is too slow for those who wait, too swift for those who fear, too long for those who grieve, too short for those who rejoice, but for those who love, time is eternity.'
- Henry Van Dyke

'First love is a kind of vaccination which saves a man from catching the complaint the second time.'
- Honore de Balzac

'True love is eternal, infinite, and always like itself. It is equal and pure, without violent demonstrations: it is seen with white hairs and is always young in the heart.'
  - Honore de Balzac

'The most wonderful of all things in life is the discovery of another human being with whom one's relationship has a growing depth, beauty and joy as the years increase. This inner progressiveness of love between two human beings is a most marvelous thing;'
  - Hugh Walpole

'A man loves his sweetheart the most, his wife the best, but his mother the longest.'
  - Irish proverb

'In how many lives does Love really play a dominant part? The average taxpayer is no more capable of a 'grand passion' than of a grand opera.'
  - Israel Zangwill

'Love rules without rules. (Amore regge senza legge.)'
  - Italian proverb

'Oh my luoe's like a red, red rose, That's newly sprung in June; Oh my love's like the melody That's sweetly played in tune.'
  - James Drummond Burns

'A lady of forty-seven who has been married twenty-seven years and has six children knows what love really is and once described it for me like this: 'Love is what you've been through with somebody.''
  - James Thurber

'As one who cons at evening o'er an album all alone, And muses on the faces of the friends that he has known, So I turn the leaves of Fancy, till in shadowy design I find the smiling features of an old sweetheart of mine.'
  - James Whitcomb Riley

'Little privations are easily endured when the heart is better treated than the body.'
  - Jean-Jacques Rousseau

'True love brings up everything you're allowing a mirror to be held up to you daily.'
  - Jennifer Aniston

'True love is night jasmine, a diamond in darkness, the heartbeat no cardiologist has ever heard. It is the most common of miracles, fashioned of fleecy clouds a handful of stars tossed into the night sky.'
  - Jim Bishop

'In the race for love, I was scratched.'
  - Joan Davis

'Love, all love of other sights controls. And makes one little room an everywhere.'
  - John Donne

'If yet I have not all thy love, love Dear, I shall never have it all.'
  - John Donne

'I am two fools, I know, for loving, and saying so.'
  - John Donne

'All kings, and all their favorites, All glory of honours, beauties, wits, The sun itself, which makes time, as they pass, Is elder by a year now than it was When thou and I first one another saw. All other things to their destruction draw, Only our love '
  - John Donne

'"I'm sorry that I spell'd the word; I hate to go above you, Because" - the brown eyes lower fell, - "Because, you see, I love you!"'
  - John Greenleaf Whittier

'A thing of beauty is a joy forever; Its loveliness increases; it will never Pass into nothingness.'
  - John Keats

'I have been astonished that men could die martyrs for their religion I have shudder'd at it. I shudder no more. I could be martyr'd for my religion Love is my religion And I could die for that. I could die for you.'
  - John Keats

'Love in a hut, with water and a crust, Is - Love, forgive us! - cinders, ashes, dust.'
  - John Keats

'So dear I love him, that with him all deaths I could endure, without him live no life.'
  - John Milton

'No one can do me any good by loving me; I have more love than I need or could do any good with; but people do me good by making me love them - which isn't easy.'
  - John Ruskin

'When love and skill work together expect a masterpiece.'
  - John Ruskin

'Tis the most tender part of love, each other to forgive.'
  - John Sheffield

'We are so fond of each other because our ailments are the same.'
  - Jonathan Swift

'How wise are they that are but fools in love!'
  - Joshua Cooke

'Love doesn't grow on the trees like apples in Eden - it's something you have to make and you must use your imagination to make it too, just like anything else. It's all work, work.'
  - Joyce Carey

'Love is like an hourglass, with the heart filling up as the brain empties.'
- Jule Renard

'Love is not blind - it sees more, not less. But because it sees more, it is willing to see less.'
- Julius Gordon

'The chemist who can extract from his heart's elements compassion, respect, longing, patience, regret, surprise, and forgiveness and compound them into one can create that atom which is called love.'
- Kahlil Gibran

'There is only one path to Heaven. On Earth, we call it Love.'
- Karen Goldman

'"The whole world loves a lover" is an interesting theory, but a very bad legal defense.'
- Keith Sullivan

'The reason why lovers and their mistresses never tire of being together is that they are always talking of themselves.'
- La Rochefoucauld

'If we are to judge of love by its consequences, it more nearly resembles hatred than friendship.'
- La Rochefoucauld

'Being deeply loved by someone gives you strength, while loving someone deeply gives you courage.'
- Lao-Tzu

'Love is a kind of military service.'
- Latin proverb

'Pale hands I loved beside the Shalimar, Where are you now? Who lies beneath your spell? Whom do you lead on Rapture's roadway, far, Before you agonize them in farewell?'
- Laurence Hope

'Love is always bestowed as a gift - freely, willingly and without expectation. We don't love to be loved; we love to love.'
- Leo Buscaglia

'To love one's neighbors, to love one's enemies, to love everything - to love God in all His manifestations - human love serves to love those dear to us but to love one's enemies we need divine love.'
- Leo Tolstoy

''Tis better to have loved and lost, Than never to have loved at all.'
- Lord Alfred Tennyson

'Man's love is of man's life a thing apart, 'Tis woman's whole existence.'
- Lord Byron

'Love is an ocean of emotions, entirely surrounded by expenses.'
- Lord Dewar

'I no longer cared about survival - I merely loved.'
- Loren Eiseley

'Love is the irresistible desire to be desired irresistibly.'
- Louis Ginsberg

'I have learned that only two things are necessary to keep one's wife happy. First, let her think she's having her own way. And second, let her have it.'
- Lyndon B. Johnson

'They say love is blind . . . and marriage is an institution. Well, I'm nor ready for an instirurion for rhe blind just yet.'
- Mae West

'Love is a conflict between reflexes and reflections.'
- Magnus Hirschfeld

'Whenever you are confronted with an opponent, conquer him with love.'
- Mahatma Gandhi

'Love in France is a comedy; in England a tragedy; in Italy an opera seria; and in Germany a melodrama.'
- Marguerite Blessington

'Love is what we were borne with. Fear is what we learned here.'
- Marianne Williamson

'We don't believe in rheumatism and true love until after the first attack.'
- Marie von Ebner-Eschenbach

'To get the full value of joy you must have someone to divide it with.'
- Mark Twain

'Love seems the swiftest but it is the slowest of all growths. No man or woman really knows what perfect love is until they have been married a quarter of a century.'
- Mark Twain

'Love is a madness; if thwarted it develops fast.'
- Mark Twain

'To keep the fire burning brightly there's one easy rule: Keep the two logs together, near enough to keep each other warm and far enough apart - about a finger's breadth - for breathing room. Good fire, good marriage, same rule.'
- Marnie Reed Crowell

'Hatred paralyzes life; love releases it. Hatred confuses life; love harmonizes it. Hatred darkens life; love illumines it.'
- Martin Luther King, Jr.

'A youth with his first cigar makes himself sick; a youth with his first girl makes everybody sick.'
- Mary Wilson Little

'When one loves somebody, everything is clear - where to go, what to do - it all takes care of itself and one doesn't have to ask anybody about anything.'
- Maxim Gorky

'You can't put a price tag on love, but you can on all its accessories.'
- Melanie Clark

'Love one another and you will be happy. It's as simple and as difficult as that.'
- Michael Leunig

'No one has ever loved anyone the way everyone wants to be loved.'
- Mignon McLaughlin

'There's no love lost between us.'
- Miguel de Cervantes

'Tell me thy company and I will tell thee what thou art.'
- Miguel de Cervantes

'When you are in love with someone you want to be near him all the time, except when you are out buying things and charging them to him.'
- Miss Piggy

'Love with men is not a sentiment, but an idea.'
- Mme. de Girardin

'Love is often a fruit of marriage.'
- Moliere

'Love makes of the wisest man a fool, and of the most foolish woman, a sage.'
- Moritz G. Saphir

'The bravest thing that men do is love women.'
- Mort Sahl

'Americans, who make more of marrying for love than any other people, also break up more of their marriages, but the figure reflects not so much the failure of love as the determination of people not to live without it.'
- Morton Hunt

'Love blinds us to faults, hatred to virtues.'
- Moses Ibn Ezra

'If you judge people, you have no time to love them.'
  - Mother Teresa

'Love is a fruit in season at all times, and within reach of every hand.'
  - Mother Teresa

'[Being in love] is something like poetry. Certainly, you can analyze it and expound its various senses and intentions, but there is always something left over, mysteriously hovering between music and meaning.'
  - Muriel Spark

'One of the things my life has taught me is how important it is to try to say, "I love you" in ways that can be preserved, looked at, and read when you are alone or when there is adversity or when circumstances bring separation. In any case, . . . saying "'
  - Nancy Reagan

'The only victory over love is flight.'
  - Napoleon

'Selfishness is one of the qualities apt to inspire love.'
  - Nathaniel Hawthorne

'Speak to me of love, said St Francis to the almond tree, and the tree blossomed.'
  - Nicholas Kazantzakis

'The highest prize in a world of men is the most beautiful woman available on your arm and living there in her heart loyal to you.'
  - Normal Mailer

'Treasure the love you receive above all. It will survive long after your gold and good health have vanished.'
  - Og Mandino

'We're born alone, we live alone, we die alone. Only through our love and friendship can we create the illusion for the moment that we're not alone.'
  - Orson Welles

'If you want to be loved, be lovable.'
  - Ovid

'Young men wish: love, money and health. One day, they'll say: health, money and love.'
  - Paul Geraldy

'What we call love is the desire to awaken and to keep awake in another's body, heart and mind, the responsibility of flattering, in our place, the self of which we are not very certain.'
  - Paul Geraldy

'Love is a spendthrift, leaves its arithmetic at home, is always 'in the red'.'
  - Paul Scherer

'The first duty of love is to listen.'
- Paul Tillich

'Love: Two minds without a single thought.'
- Philip Barry

'Love - a grave mental disease.'
- Plato

'At the touch of love, everyone becomes a poet.'
- Plato

'The greater love is a mother's; then comes a dog's; then a sweetheart's.'
- Polish proverb

'Everybody in love is blind.'
- Propertius

'Better is a dinner of herbs where love is, than a stalled ox and hatred therewith.'
- Proverbs

'Love consists in this, that two solitudes protect and touch and greet each other.'
- Rainer Maria Rilke

'Love, you know, seeks to make happy rather than to be happy.'
- Ralph Connor

'All mankind love a lover.'
- Ralph Waldo Emerson

'Give all to love; obey thy heart.'
- Ralph Waldo Emerson

'Man begins by loving love and ends by loving a woman. Woman begins by loving a man and ends by loving love.'
- Remy de Gourmont

'I believe in love, but I don't sit around waiting for it.'
- Renee Zellweger

'I could not love thee, dear, so much Loved I not honor more.'
- Richard Lovelace

'He who for love hath undergone The worst that can befall, Is happier thousandfold than one Who never loved at all.'
- Richard Monckton Milnes

'To love her was a liberal education.'
- Richard Steele

'Because God is love, the most important lesson He wants you to learn on earth is how to love.'
- Rick Warren

'They gave each other a smile with a future in it.'
- Ring Lardner

'To see her is to love her, And love but her forever; For Nature made her what she is, And never made another.'
- Robert Burns

'No cord nor cable can so forcibly draw, or hold so fast, as love can do with a twined thread.'
- Robert Burton

'The hours I spent with thee, dear heart, Are as a string of pearls to me; I could them over, every one apart, My rosary, my rosary.'
- Robert Cameron Rogers

'You've got to love what's lovable, and hate what's hateable. It takes brains to see the difference.'
- Robert Frost

'You say to me-ward's your affection's strong; Pray love me little, so you love me long.'
- Robert Herrick

'What the heart gives away is never gone.... It is kept in the hearts of others.'
- Robin St. John

'Love is the fulfilling of the law.'
- Romans

'Some pray to marry the man they love, My prayer will somewhat vary: I humbly pray to Heaven above That I love the man I marry.'
- Rose Pastor Stokes

'Sing, for faith and hope are high - None so true as you and I - Sing the Lovers' Litany: "Love like ours can never die!"'
- Rudyard Kipling

'From success you get a lot of things, but not that great inside thing that love brings you.'
- Sam Goldwyn

'Love at first sight is easy to understand; it's when two people have been looking at each other for a lifetime that it becomes a miracle.'
- Sam Levenson

'A man is only as good as what he loves.'
- Saul Bellow

'Love and work are the cornerstones of our humanness.'
- Sigmund Freud

'True love's the gift which God has given To man alone beneath the heaven: It is not fantasy's hot fire, Whose wishes soon as granted fly; It liveth not in fierce desire.'
- Sir Walter Scott

'Blue eyes say, "Love me or I die"; black eyes say, "Love me or I kill thee."'
- Spanish proverb

'Where there is love, there is pain.'
- Spanish proverb

'Since love grows within you, so beauty grows. For love is the beauty of the soul.'
- St. Augustine

'Many a man in love with a dimple makes the mistake of marrying the whole girl.'
- Stephen Leacock

'When love is strong, a man and a woman can make their bed on a sword's blade. When love grows weak, a bed of 60 cubits is not large enough.'
- Talmud

'How delicious is the winning of a kiss at love's beginning.'
- Thomas Campbell

'Love, the itch, and a cough cannot be hid.'
- Thomas Fuller

'Love lives on propinquity, but dies on contact.'
- Thomas Hardy

'He who loves the more is the inferior and must suffer.'
- Thomas Mann

'We are obliged to love one another. We are not strictly bound to "like" one another.'
- Thomas Merton

'The heart that has truly loved never forgets but as truly loves on to the close.'
- Thomas More

'Alas!, how light a cause may move dissention between hearts that love!'
- Thomas More

'You can always get someone to love you - even if you have to do it yourself.'
- Tom Masson

'We waste time looking for the perfect lover, instead of creating the perfect love.'
- Tom Robbins

'Love doesn't just sit there, like a stone; it has to be made, like bread, remade all the time, made new.'
- Ursula K. Le Guin

'Men love because they are afraid of themselves, afraid of the loneliness that lives in them, and need someone in whom they can lose themselves as smoke loses itself in the sky.'
- V. F. Calverton

'The greatest happiness in life is the conviction that we are loved - loved for ourselves, or rather, loved in spite of ourselves.'
- Victor Hugo

'Love conquers all.'
- Virgil

'A woman can forgive a man for the harm he does her . . . but she can never forgive him for the sacrifices he makes on her account.'
- W. Somerset Maugham

'Love is what happens to men and women who don't know each other.'
- W. Somerset Maugham

'And love is loveliest when embalm'd in tears.'
- Walter Scott

'Wine comes in at the mouth and love comes in at the eye; that's all we shall know for truth before we grow old and die.'
- William Butler Yeats

'Heaven has no rage like love to hatred turned.'
- William Congreve

'Love sought is good, but given unsought is better.'
- William Shakespeare

'Love is not love which alters when it alteration finds.'
- William Shakespeare

'Men have died from time to time, and worms have eaten them - but not for love.'
- William Shakespeare

'Love is a smoke raised with the fume of sighs; Being purged, a fire sparkling in lovers' eyes; Being vex'd a sea nourish'd with lovers' tears: What is it else? a madness most discreet, A choking gall and a preserving sweet.'
- William Shakespeare

'Ay me! for aught that I ever could read, Could ever hear by tale or history, The course of true love never did run smooth.'
- William Shakespeare

'Give me my Romeo; and, when he shall die. Take him, and cut him out in little stars, And he will make the face of heaven so fine, That all the world will be in love with night, And pay no worship to the

garish sun.'
  - William Shakespeare

'I love thee, I love but thee With a love that shall not die Till the sun grows cold And the stars grow old.'
  - William Shakespeare

'Love looks not with the eyes, but with the mind; And therefore is winged Cupid painted blind.'
  - William Shakespeare

'Werther had a love for Charlotte, Such as words could never utter; Would you know how first he met her? She was cutting bread and butter.'
  - William Thackeray

'That best portion of a good man's life, His little, nameless, unremembered acts Of kindness and of love.'
  - William Wordsworth

'Romance without finance is no good.'
  - Willie The Lion' Smith

'I sold my memoirs of my love life to Parker Brothers and they are going to make a game out of it.'
  - Woody Allen

'I was nauseous and tingly all over. I was either in love or I had smallpox.'
  - Woody Allen

'Nobody has ever measured, not even poets, how much the heart can hold.'
  - Zelda Fitzgerald

MARRIAGE

'Marriage is neither heaven nor hell; it is simply purgatory.'
- Abraham Lincoln

'There is so little difference between husbands you might as well keep the first.'
- Adela Rogers St. John

'An archaeologist is the best husband a woman can have; the older she gets, the more interested he is in her.'
- Agatha Christie

'If you want to read about love and marriage you've got to buy two separate books.'
- Alan King

'So heavy is the chain of wedlock that it needs two to carry it, and sometimes three.'
- Alexandre Dumas

'Marriage, n: the state or condition of a community consisting of a master, a mistress, and two slaves, making, in all, two.'
- Ambrose Bierce

'Marriage is not a ritual or an end. It is a long, intricate, intimate dance together and nothing matters more than your own sense of balance and your choice of partner.'
- Amy Bloom

'A happy marriage is a long conversation which always seems too short.'
- Andre Maurois

'Heaven will be no heaven to me if I do not meet my wife there.'
- Andrew Jackson

'A simple enough pleasure, surely, to have breakfast alone with one's husband, but how seldom married people in the midst of life achieve it.'
- Anne Morrow Lindbergh

'My wife is the most wonderful woman in the world, and that's not just my opinion - it's hers.'
- Anonymous

'There are no perfect people - except, of course, my wife's first husband.'
- Anonymous

'"So you want to become my son-in-law." "Not exactly. I just want to marry your daughter."'
- Anonymous

'Leisure time is when your wife can't find you'
- Anonymous

'When my wife was asked, "Do you take this man for richer or poorer . . ." she answered, "For richer."'
- Anonymous

'I remember when I got married. I remember where I got married. But for the life of me, I can't remember why I got married.'
- Anonymous

'Marriage is a romance in which the hero dies in the first chapter.'
- Anonymous

'A husband always prefers his wife's mother-in-law to his own.'
- Anonymous

'No man is truly married until he understands every word his wife is NOT saying.'
- Anonymous

'You don't marry someone you can live with - you marry the person who you cannot live without.'
- Anonymous

'A man and a woman marry because both of them don't know what to do with themselves.'
- Anton Chekhov

'It is better for a woman to marry a man who loves her than a man she loves.'
- Arab proverb

'The only thing that holds a marriage together is the husband being big enough to step back and see where the wife was wrong.'
- Archie Bunker

'I married the first man I ever kissed. When I tell this to my children, they just about throw up.'
- Barbara Bush

'It destroys one's nerves to be amiable every day to the same human being.'
- Benjamin Disraeli

'No man is regular in his attendance at the House of Commons until he is married.'
- Benjamin Disraeli

'Every woman should marry - and no man.'
- Benjamin Disraeli

'Where there's marriage without love, there will be love without marriage.'
- Benjamin Franklin

'You can bear your own faults, and why not a fault in your wife?'
- Benjamin Franklin

'Keep your eyes wide open before marriage, half shut afterwards.'
- Benjamin Franklin

'It is not good that the man should be alone.'
  - Bible

'Bone of my bones, and flesh of my flesh.'
  - Bible

'Marriage is a lottery in which men stake their liberty, and women their happiness.'
  - Bible

'With this ring I thee wed, with my body I thee worship, and with all my worldly goods I thee endow.'
  - Bible

'A prudent wife is from the Lord.'
  - Bible

'Whoso findeth a wife findeth a good thing.'
  - Bible

'Marriage is a great institution, and no family should be without it.'
  - Channing Pollock

'There isn't a wife in the world who has not taken the exact measure of her husband, weighed him and settled him in her own mind, and knows him as well as if she had ordered him after designs and specifications of her own.'
  - Charles Warner

'Married couples who love each other tell each other a thousand things without talking.'
  - Chinese proverb

'A deaf husband and a blind wife are always a happy couple.'
  - Danish proverb

'There is a French saying: "Love is the dawn of marriage, and marriage is the sunset of love."'
  - De Finod

'Any married man should forget his mistakes - no use two people remembering the same thing.'
  - Duane Dewel

'To marry once is a duty, twice a folly, thrice is madness.'
  - Dutch proverb

'I wanted to marry her when I saw the moonlight shining on the barrel of her father's shotgun.'
  - Eddie Albert

'A man should be taller, older, heavier, uglier and hoarser than his wife.'
  - Edgar Watson Howe

'Polygamy: an endeavour to get more out of life than there is in it.'
  - Elbert Hubbard

'There is a radicalism in all getting, and a conservatism in all keeping. Lovemaking is radical, while marriage is conservative.'
- Eric Hoffer

'Bigamy is having one husband too many. Monogamy is the same.'
- Erica Jong

'Marriage has no guarantees. If that's what you're looking for, go live with a car battery.'
- Erma Bombeck

'Look for a sweet person. Forget rich.'
- Estee Lauder

'If thee marries for money, thee surely will earn it.'
- Ezra Bowen

'What is instinct? It is the natural tendency in one when filled with dismay to turn to his wife.'
- Finley Peter Dunne

'Father giving advice to son: Never do anything once around the house that you don't want to do for the rest of your life.'
- Frank Briggs

'A good husband should always bore his wife.'
- Fred Jacob

'The whole world is strewn with snares, traps, gins and pitfalls for the capture of men by women.'
- George Bernard Shaw

'Weeping bride, laughing wife; laughing bride, weeping wife.'
- German proverb

'I've given my memoirs far more thought than any of my marriages. You can't divorce a book.'
- Gloria Swanson

'My husband will never chase another woman. He's too fine, too decent, too old.'
- Grade Allen

'I was married by a judge. I should have asked for a jury.'
- Groucho Marx

'Politics doesn't make strange bedfellows - marriage does.'
- Groucho Marx

'One of the best hearing aids a man can have is an attentive wife.'
- Groucho Marx

'Men have a much better time of it than women. For one thing, they marry later. For another thing, they die earlier.'
  - H. L. Mencken

'No matter how happily a woman may be married, it always pleases her to discover that there is a nice man who wishes she were not.'
  - H. L. Mencken

'The double standard of morality will survive in this world so long as the woman whose husband has been lured away is favoured with the sympathetic tears of other women, and a man whose wife has made off is laughed at by other men.'
  - H. L. Mencken

'Often the difference between a successful marriage and a mediocre one consists of leaving about three or four things a day unsaid.'
  - Harlan Miller

'Behind every successful man you'll find a woman who has nothing to wear.'
  - Harold Coffin

'When you realize you want to spend the rest of your life with somebody, you want the rest of your life to start as soon as possible.'
  - Harry Burns

'Matrimony, - the high sea for which no compass has yet been invented.'
  - Heinrich Heine

'In olden times sacrifices were made at the altar, a custom which is still continued.'
  - Helen Rowland

'A husband is what is left of a lover, after the nerve has been extracted.'
  - Helen Rowland

'The secret of a happy marriage remains a secret.'
  - Henny Youngman

'Marriage is something you have to give your whole mind to.'
  - Henrik Ibsen

'His designs were strictly honorable, as the phrase is: that is, to rob a lady of her fortune by way of marriage.'
  - Henry Fielding

'The majority of husbands remind me of an orangutan trying to play the violin.'
  - Honore de Balzac

'A woman must be a genius to create a good husband.'
  - Honore de Balzac

'The calmest husbands make the stormiest wives.'
  - Isaac Disraeli

'There is more difference within the sexes than between them.'
  - Ivy Compton-Burnett

'There is probably nothing like living together for blinding people to each other.'
  - Ivy Compton-Burnett

'The young man who wants to marry happily should pick out a good mother and marry one of her daughters - any one will do.'
  - J. Ogden Armour

'she: Before we got married, you told me you were well-off. he: I was, and I didn't know it.'
  - Jacob Braude

'Marriage is like a violin. After the beautiful music is over, the strings are still attached.'
  - Jacob Braude

'I was the best man at the wedding. So why is she marrying him?'
  - Jerry Seinfeld

'Sexiness wears thin after a while and beauty fades, but to be married to a man who makes you laugh every day, ah, now that's a real treat.'
  - Joanne Woodward

'Every marriage tends to consist of an aristocrat and a peasant, of a teacher and a learner.'
  - John Updike

'Marriage is our last, best chance to grow up.'
  - Joseph Barth

'Marrying for love may be a bit risky, but it is so honest that God can't help but smile on it.'
  - Josh Billings

'Let there be spaces in your togetherness.'
  - Kahlil Gibran

'Marriage: a job. Happiness or unhappiness has nothing to do with it.'
  - Kathleen Norris

'Modern American marriage is like a wire fence. The woman's the wire -the posts are the husband's.'
  - Langdon Mitchell

'Marriage is three parts love and seven parts forgiveness of sins.'
  - Langdon Mitchell

'No laborer in the world is expected to work for room, board, and love -except the housewife.'
  - Letty Cottin Pogrebin

'Married women are kept women, and they are beginning to find it out.'
- Logan Pearsall Smith

'Marriages are made in Heaven.'
- Lord Alfred Tennyson

'Only two things are necessary to keep one's wife happy. One is to let her think she is having her own way, and the other, to let her have it.'
- Lyndon B. Johnson

'One of the best things about marriage is that it gets young people to bed at a decent hour.'
- M. M. Musselman

'I never married because I have three pets at home that answer the same purpose as a husband. I have a dog that growls every morning, a parrot that swears all afternoon, and a cat that comes home late at night.'
- Marie Corelli

'Behind every successful man is a surprised woman!'
- Maryon Pearson

'What therefore God hath joined together let not man put asunder.'
- Matthew

'A good marriage would be between a blind wife and a deaf husband.'
- Michel de Montaigne

'Marriage is the deep, deep peace of the double bed after the hurly-burly of the chaise longue.'
- Mrs. Patrick Campbell

'A virtuous wife is a man's best treasure.'
- Muhammad

'I'm an extinct volcano.'
- Nancy Lady Astor

'I married beneath me - all women do.'
- Nancy Lady Astor

'Something old, something new, Something borrowed, something blue.'
- Old English Rhyme

'Husband and wife come to look alike at last.'
- Oliver Wendell Holmes

'All women become like their mothers. That is their tragedy. No man does. That's his.'
- Oscar Wilde

'Marriage is the one subject on which all women agree and all men disagree.'
- Oscar Wilde

'Men marry because they are tired, women because they are curious: both are disappointed.'
- Oscar Wilde

'If thou wouldst marry wisely, marry thine equal.'
- Ovid

'Never get married in the morning, because you never know who you'll meet that night.'
- Paul Hornung

'The woman cries before the wedding; the man afterward.'
- Polish proverb

'A rich widow weeps with one eye and signals with the other.'
- Portuguese proverb

'When a man opens the car door for his wife, it's either a new car or a new wife.'
- Prince Philip

'Is not marriage an open question, when it is alleged, from the beginning of the world, that such as are in the institution wish to get out, and such as are out wish to get in.'
- Ralph Waldo Emerson

'A wise woman will always let her husband have her way.'
- Richard Brinsley Sheridan

'Love is a fever which marriage puts to bed and cures.'
- Richard J. Needham

'When I eventually met Mr. Right I had no idea that his first name was Always.'
- Rita Rudner

'Marriage is one long conversation checkered by disputes.'
- Robert Louis Stevenson

'As a general thing, people marry most happily with their own kind. The trouble lies in the fact that people usually marry at an age when they do not really know what their own kind is.'
- Robertson Davies

'A wife encourages her husband's egoism in order to exercise her own.'
- Russell Green

'An ideal wife is one who remains faithful to you but tries to be just as if she weren't.'
- Sacha Guitry

'Marriage has many pains, but celibacy has no pleasures.'
- Samuel Johnson

'Marriages would in general be as happy, and often more so, if they were all made by the Lord Chancellor.'
- Samuel Johnson

'Nothing flatters a man as much as the happiness of his wife; he is always proud of himself as the source of it.'
- Samuel Johnson

'Whenever you want to marry someone, go have lunch with his ex-wife.'
- Shelley Winters

'Pains do not hold a marriage together. It is threads, hundreds of tiny threads which sew people together through the years. That's what makes a marriage last - more than passion or even sex.'
- Simone Signoret

'A man finds himself seven years older the day after his marriage.'
- Sir Francis Bacon

'He that hath a wife and children hath given hostages to fortune; for they are impediments to great enterprises, either of virtue or mischief.'
- Sir Francis Bacon

'Woe to the house where the hen crows and the rooster keeps still.'
- Spanish proverb

'A wife is the joy of a man's heart.'
- Talmud

'Keep thy eyes wide open before marriage; and half shut afterward.'
- Thomas Fuller

'Any marriage, happy or unhappy, is infinitely more interesting and significant than any romance, however passionate.'
- W. H. Auden

'Henry VIII had so many wives because his dynastic sense was very strong whenever he saw a maid of honor.'
- Will Cuppy

'Thus grief still treads upon the heels of pleasure, Marry'd in hast, we may repent at leisure.'
- William Congreve

'In my conscience I believe the baggage loves me, for she never speaks well of me herself, nor suffers anybody else to rail at me.'
- William Congreve

'What is there in the vale of life Half so delightful as a wife When Friendship, love and peace combine To stamp the marriage bond divine?'
- William Cowper

'Men are April when they woo, December when they wed; maids are May when they are maids, but the sky changes when they are wives.'
- William Shakespeare

'Remember, it is as easy to marry a rich woman as a poor woman.'
- William Thackeray

'My most brilliant achievement was my ability to be able to persuade my wife to marry me.'
- Winston Churchill

'Conrad Hilton was very generous to me in the divorce settlement. He gave me 5,000 Gideon Bibles.'
- Zsa Gabor

MEN

'That all men are equal is a proposition to which, at ordinary times, no sane individual has ever given his assent.'
- Aldous Huxley

'A man is never so weak as when a woman is telling him how strong he is.'
- Anonymous

'When I was very young, I kissed my first woman, and smoked my first cigarette on the same day. Believe me, never since have I wasted any more time on tobacco.'
- Arturo Toscanini

'I love men, not because they are men, but because they are not women.'
- Christina, Queen of Sweden

'I wish Adam had died with all his ribs in his body.'
- Dion Boucicault

'A good cigar is as great a comfort to a man as a good cry is to a woman.'
- Edward Bulwer-Lytton

'What's with you men? Would hair stop growing on your chest if you asked directions somewhere?'
- Erma Bombeck

'If a man hears much that a woman says, she is not beautiful.'
- Henry S. Haskins

'The only time a woman really succeeds in changing a male is when he's a baby.'
- Jacob Braude

'Men don't get cellulite. God might just be a man.'
- Rita Rudner

MONEY

'Philanthropist: a rich (and usually bald) old gentleman who has trained himself to grin while his conscience is picking his pocket.'
- Ambrose Bierce

'Gentlemen prefer bonds.'
- Andrew Mellon

'Why is there so much month left at the end of the money?'
- Anonymous

'We were awfully poor. But we had a lot of things that money can't buy . . . like unpaid bills.'
- Anonymous

'When you want really big money, you usually find yourself talking to people who didn't go to Eton.'
- Anonymous

'Definition of the upper crust: A bunch of crumbs held together by dough.'
- Anonymous

'The man who invented slow-motion movies got his idea while watching a Scotsman reach for a check in a restaurant.'
- Anonymous

'By the time a man is rich enough to sleep late, he's too old to enjoy it.'
- Anonymous

'Money is human happiness in the abstract.'
- Arthur Schopenhauer

'It isn't enough for you to love money - it's also necessary that money should love you.'
- Baron Rothschild

'If you would know the value of money, go and try to borrow some.'
- Benjamin Franklin

'The love of money is the root of all evil.'
- Bible

'Wine maketh merry: but money answereth all things.'
- Bible

'Jesus went into the temple... overthrew the tables of the money changers, and the seats of them that sold doves.'
- Bible

'Not greedy of filthy lucre.'
    - Bible

'He that maketh haste to be rich shall not be innocent.'
    - Bible

'Money won't buy happiness, but it will pay the salaries of a large research staff to study the problem.'
    - Bill Vaughan

'Never invest your money in anything that eats or needs repairing.'
    - Billy Rose

'"Mommy, we're not going to be poor again, are we?" "Not as long as you have that rare blood type."'
    - Brett Butler

'They make money the old-fashioned way. They inherit it.'
    - Brian Morgan

'I never been in no situation where havin' money made it any worse.'
    - Clinton Jones

'What some people mistake for the high cost of living is really the cost of living high.'
    - Doug Larson

'If a man has money, it is usually a sign too, that he knows how to take care of it; don't imagine his money is easy to get simply because he has plenty of it.'
    - Edgar Watson Howe

'There is only one thing for a man to do who is married to a woman who enjoys spending money, and that is to enjoy earning it.'
    - Edgar Watson Howe

'Money isn't everything - but it's a long way ahead of what comes next.'
    - Edmund Stockdale

'Money is the wise man's religion.'
    - Euripides

'Money is like muck - not good unless it be spread.'
    - Francis Bacon

'Riches are for spending.'
    - Francis Bacon

'There are plenty of good five-cent cigars in the country. The trouble is they cost a quarter. What the country really needs is a good five-cent nickle.'
    - Franklin P. Adams

'To be clever enough to get all that money, one must be stupid enough to want it.'
   - G. K. Chesterton

'A fool and his money are soon parted.'
   - George Buchanan

'Money is always there but the pockets change; it is not in the same pockets after a change, and that is all there is to say about money.'
   - Gertrude Stein

'Money is good for bribing yourself through the inconveniences of life.'
   - Gottfried Reinhardt

'Penny wise, pound foolish.'
   - Henry Burton

'Money is not required to buy one necessity of the soul.'
   - Henry David Thoreau

'Money is the fruit of evil as often as the root of it.'
   - Henry Fielding

'Interest works night and day in fair weather and in foul. It gnaws at a man's substance with invisible teeth.'
   - Henry Ward Beecher

'There's nothing an economist should fear so much as applause.'
   - Herbert Marshall

'Money doesn't always bring happiness. People with $10 million are no happier than people with $9 million.'
   - Hobart Brown

'The darkest hour of any man's life is when he sits down to plan how to get money without earning it.'
   - Horace Greeley

'I'm so happy to be rich, I'm willing to take all the consequences.'
   - Howard Ahmanson

'The farmer's way of saving money: to be owed by someone he trusted.'
   - Hugh MacLennan

'Money swore an oath that nobody who did not love it should ever have it.'
   - Irish proverb

'Right now I have enough money to last me the rest of my life - unless I buy something.'
   - Jackie Mason

'There's another advantage in being poor. The doctor will cure you faster.'
- Jacob Braude

'Money, it turned out, was exactly like sex; you thought of nothing else if you didn't have it and thought of other things if you did.'
- James Baldwin

'With money in your pocket, you are wise, and you are handsome, and you sing well too.'
- Jewish proverb

'You can't force anyone to love you or to lend you money.'
- Jewish proverb

'If the rich could hire other people to die for them, the poor would make a wonderful living.'
- Jewish proverb

'How to double your money: Fold it over once and put it back in your pocket.'
- Jim Dodds

'It doesn't matter if you're rich or poor, as long as you've got money.'
- Joe E. Lewis

'I don't like money actually, but it quiets my nerves.'
- Joe Louis

'Bankruptcy is a legal proceeding in which you put your money in your pants pocket and give your coat to your creditors.'
- Joey Adams

'Making money is fun, but it's pointless if you don't use the power it brings.'
- John Bentley

'Money, like a queen, gives rank and beauty .'
- Latin proverb

'The wretchedness of being rich is that you live with rich people.'
- Logan Pearsall Smith

'Make money and the whole world will conspire to call you a gentleman.'
- Mark Twain

'Money is the poor people's credit card.'
- Marshall McLuhan

'Money is not an aphrodisiac: the desire it may kindle in a female eye is more for the cash than the carrier.'
- Marya Marines

'If you would know what the Lord God thinks of money, you have only to look at those to whom he gives it.'
- Maurice Baring

'Money is something you got to make in case you don't die.'
- Max Asnas

'We forget that money gives its value - that someone exchanged work for it.'
- Neal O'Hara

'When people ask me if I have any spare change, I tell them I have it at home in my spare wallet.'
- Nick Arnette

'But then one is always excited by descriptions of money changing hands. It's much more fundamental than sex.'
- Nigel Dennis

'Some people's money is merited and other people's is inherited.'
- Ogden Nash

'Ah, take the Cash, and let the Credit go, Nor heed the rumble of a distant Drum!'
- Omar Khayyam

'When I was young, I thought money was the most important thing in life. Now that I'm old - I know it is.'
- Oscar Wilde

'I'd like to live like a poor man - only with lots of money.'
- Pablo Picasso

'The rich aren't like us, they pay less taxes.'
- Peter de Vries

'When I had money everyone called me brother.'
- Polish proverb

'Laws go where dollars please.'
- Portuguese proverb

'My doctor said I look like a million dollars - green and wrinkled.'
- Red Skelton

'If you like easygoing, monogamous men, stay away from billionaires.'
- Rita Rudner

'Never ask of money spent Where the spender thinks it went. Nobody was ever meant To remember or invent What he did with every cent.'
- Robert Frost

'Men are more often bribed by their loyalties and ambitions than by money.'
- Robert H. Jackson

'Inflation is determined by money supply growth.'
- Roger Bootle

'Money is the most egalitarian force in society. It confers power on whoever holds it.'
- Roger Starr

'Money can't buy happiness, but it will certainly get you a better class of memories.'
- Ronald Reagan

'When money speaks the truth is silent.'
- Russian proverb

'When you have told anyone you have left him a legacy, the only decent thing to do is to die at once.'
- Samuel Butler

'A good mind possesses a kingdom: a great fortune is a great slavery.'
- Seneca

'Money can't buy you happiness, but it does bring you a more pleasant form of misery.'
- Spike Milligan

'How do you make a million? You start with $900,000.'
- Stephen Lewis

'Be the business never so painful, you may have it done for money.'
- Thomas Fuller

'God makes, and apparel shapes: but it's money that finishes the man.'
- Thomas Fuller

'Money dignifies what is frivolous if unpaid for.'
- Virginia Woolf

'When it is a question of money, everybody is of the same religion.'
- Voltaire

'When asked to borrow money: "I'll see what my lawyer says. . . . And if he says yes, I'll get another lawyer."'
- W. C. Fields

'A rich man is nothing but a poor man with money.'
- W. C. Fields

'Money is like a sixth sense, and you can't make use of the other five without it.'
- W. Somerset Maugham

'The almighty dollar, that great object of universal devotion throughout our land, seems to have no genuine devotees in these peculiar villages.'
- Washington Irving

'He says he's not broke, but he is trying to sell his kidney and corneas.'
- Wendy Morgan

'To make money, buy some good stock, hold it until it goes up, and then sell it. If it doesn't go up, don't buy it.'
- Will Rogers

'The petty economies of the rich are just as amazing as the silly extravagances of the poor.'
- William Feather

'Take care of the pence, and the pounds will take care of themselves.'
- William Lowndes

'In the bad old days, there were three easy ways of losing money - racing being the quickest, women the pleasantest and farming the most certain.'
- William Pitt Amherst

'Neither a borrower nor a lender be for loan oft loses both itself and friend, and borrowing dulls the edge of husbandry.'
- William Shakespeare

'Another good thing about being poor is that when you are seventy your children will not have you declared legally insane in order to gain control of your estate.'
- Woody Allen

'When asked what he would do if he found a million dollars: "I would try to find the person that lost it, and if he was poor - I'd give it back."'
- Yogi Berra

MOTIVATION

'People who fight fire with fire usually end up with ashes.'
   - Abigail Van Buren

'Most people would rather be seen through than not seen at all.'
   - Ada Levenson

'One must not lose desires. They are mighty stimulants to creativeness, to love and to long life.'
   - Alexander A. Bogomoletz

'Love makes the wildest spirit tame, and the tamest spirit wild.'
   - Alexis Delp

'I want to do it because I want to do it.'
   - Amelia Earhart

'You will accomplish more by kind words and a courteous manner than by anger or sharp rebuke, which should never be used except in necessity.'
   - Angela Merici

'Anxiety and conscience are a powerful pair of dynamos. Between them, they have ensured that I shall work hard, but they cannot ensure that one shall work at anything worthwhile.'
   - Arnold J. Toynbee

'One man with a dream, at pleasure, Shall go forth and conquer a crown, And three with a new song's measure, Can trample an empire down.'
   - Arthur O'Shaughnessy

'What allows us, as human beings, to psychologically survive life on earth, with all of its pain, drama, and challenges, is a sense of purpose and meaning.'
   - Barbara De Angelis

'To feel valued, to know, even if only once in a while, that you can do a job well is an absolutely marvelous feeling.'
   - Barbara Walters

'I tried to treat them like me, and some of them weren't.'
   - Bill Russell

'We do not content ourselves with the life we have in ourselves; we desire to live an imaginary life in the minds of others, and for this purpose we endeavor to shine.'
   - Blaise Pascal

'Lust and force are the source of all our Taking Actions; lust causes voluntary Taking Actions, force involuntary ones.'
   - Blaise Pascal

'Hardships, poverty and want are the best incentives, and the best foundation, for the success of man.'
- Bradford Merrill

'Some people change their ways when they see the light, others when they feel the heat.'
- Caroline Schoeder

'If you can learn from hard knocks, you can also learn from soft touches.'
- Carolyn Kenmore

'I praise loudly; I blame softly.'
- Catherine II

'What you praise you increase.'
- Catherine Ponder

'Applause is the spur of noble minds, the end and aim of weak ones.'
- Charles Caleb Colton

'We must each find our separate meaning in the persuasion of our days until we meet in the meaning of the world.'
- Christopher Fry

'We are all motivated by a keen desire for praise, and the better a man is, the more he is inspired by glory.'
- Cicero

'Diplomacy is the art of letting someone have your way.'
- Daniele Vare

'Taking Action springs not from thought, but from a readiness for responsibility.'
- Dietrich Bonhoeffer

'I don't make deals for the money. I've got enough, much more than I'll never need. I do it to do it. Other people paint beautifully on canvas or write wonderful poetry. I like making deals, preferably big deals. That's how I get my kicks.'
- Donald Trump

'If each of us were to confess his most secret desire, the one that inspires all his plans, all his Taking Actions, he would say: "I want to be praised."'
- E. M. Cioran

'A loafer never works except when there is a fire; then he will carry out more furniture than anybody.'
- Edgar Watson Howe

'What men and women need is encouragement. ... Instead of always harping on a man's faults, tell him of his virtues. Try to pull him out of his rut of bad habits.'
- Eleanor H. Porter

'No leader can be too far ahead of his followers.'
- Eleanor Roosevelt

'Some people are molded by their admirations, others by their hostilities.'
- Elizabeth Bowen

'Those who are lifting the world upward and onward are those who encourage more than criticize.'
- Elizabeth Harrison

'Good humor, like the jaundice, makes every one of its own complexion.'
- Elizabeth Inchbald

'Just don't give up trying to do what you really want to do. Where there is love and inspiration, I don't think you can go wrong.'
- Ella Fitzgerald

'The passion to get ahead is sometimes born of the fear lest we be left behind.'
- Eric Hoffer

'To have a grievance is to have a purpose in life.'
- Eric Hoffer

'The virtues and the vices are all put in motion by interest.'
- Francois de La Rochefoucauld

'Happiness is in the taste, and not in the things themselves; we are happy from possessing what we like, not from possessing what others like.'
- Francois de La Rochefoucauld

'Interest speaks all sorts of tongues, and plays all sorts of parts, even that of disinterestedness.'
- Francois de La Rochefoucauld

'Love teaches even asses to dance.'
- French proverb

'Because it's there.'
- G. H. L. Mallory

'To hear how special and wonderful we are is endlessly enthralling.'
- Gail Sheehy

'Men are not against you; they are merely for themselves.'
- Gene Fowler

'As long as I have a want, I have a reason for living. Satisfaction is death.'
- George Bernard Shaw

'What makes life dreary is want of motive.'
- George Eliot

'It seems to me we can never give up longing and wishing while we are alive. There are certain things we feel to be beautiful and good, and we must hunger for them.'
- George Eliot

'Acting was a way out at first. A way out of not knowing what to do, a way of focusing ambitions. And the ambition wasn't for fame. The ambition was to do an interesting job.'
- Harrison Ford

'Words are less needful to sorrow than to joy.'
- Helen Hunt Jackson

'It is not merely cruelty that leads men to love war, it is excitement.'
- Henry Ward Beecher

'To sink a six-foot putt with thirty million people looking over your shoulder, convince yourself that, if you miss it, you will be embarrassed and poor.'
- Jack Nicklaus

'In my experience, there is only one motivation, and that is desire. No reasons or principle contain it or stand against it.'
- Jane Smiley

'There are only two stimulants to one's best efforts: the fear of punishment, and the hope of reward.'
- John M. Wilson

'The greatest efforts of the race have always been traceable to the love of praise, as the greatest catastrophes to the love of pleasure.'
- John Ruskin

'When you get hungry enough, you find yourself speaking Spanish pretty well.'
- Josh Gibson

'I wish it, I command it. Let my will take the place of a reason.'
- Juvenal

'Praise is the only gift for which people are really grateful.'
- Lady Marguerite Blessington

'We accept the verdict of the past until the need for change cries out loudly enough to force upon us a choice between the comforts of further inertia and the irksomeness of Taking Action.'
- Louis L'Amour

'It is for the superfluous things of life that men sweat.'
- Marcus Annaeus Seneca

'It is easier to influence strong than weak characters in life.'
- Margot Asquith

'You have to know exactly what you want out of your career. If you want to be a star, you don't bother with other things.'
- Marilyn Home

'Necessity is the mother of taking chances.'
- Mark Twain

'Accurate information is a key part of motivation.'
- Mary Ann Allison

'There are two things that people want more than sex and money- recognition and praise.'
- Mary Kay Ash

'Everyone has an invisible sign hanging from their neck saying, "Make me feel important." Never forget this message when working with people.'
- Mary Kay Ash

'The speed of the leader is the speed of the gang.'
- Mary Kay Ash

'We treat our people like royalty. If you honor and serve the people who work for you, they will honor and serve you.'
- Mary Kay Ash

'Sandwich every bit of criticism between two heavy layers of praise.'
- Mary Kay Ash

'They never die, who have the future in them.'
- Meridel Le Sueur

'Football linemen are motivated by a more complicated, self-determining series of factors than the simple fear of humiliation in the public gaze, which is the emotion that galvanizes the backs and receivers.'
- Merlin Olsen

'Fear, desire, hope still push us on toward the future.'
- Michel de Montaigne

'Take away the cause, and the effect ceases.'
- Miguel de Cervantes

'Urgent necessity prompts many to do things.'
- Miguel de Cervantes

'A man will fight harder for his interests than for his rights.'
- Napoleon Bonaparte

'There are only two forces that unite men-fear and interest.'
- Napoleon Bonaparte

'Where the willingness is great, the difficulties cannot be great.'
- Niccolo Machiavelli

'The breakfast of champions is not cereal, it's the opposition.'
- Nick Seitz

'My advice about acting? Speak clearly, don't bump into people, and if you must have motivation, think of your pay packet on Friday.'
- Noel Coward

'Don't let other people tell you what you want.'
- Pat Riley

'You can't underestimate the power of fear.'
- Patricia Nixon

'There's only one good reason to be a writer-we can't help it! We'd all like to be successful, rich and famous, but if those are our goals, we're off on the wrong foot. ... I just wanted to earn enough money so I could work at home on my writing.'
- Phyllis Whitney

'Wealth ... and poverty: the one is the parent of luxury and indolence, and the other of meanness and vicious-ness, and both of discontent.'
- Plato

'Necessity, who is the mother of our invention.'
- Plato

'Human behavior flows from three main sources: desire, emotion, and knowledge.'
- Plato

'Poverty, Frost, Famine, Rain, Disease, are the beadles and guardsmen that hold us to Common Sense.'
- Ralph Waldo Emerson

'Money and women. They're the two strongest things in the world. There are things you do for a woman you wouldn't do for anything else. Same with money.'
- Satchel Paige

'There isn't much that tastes better than praise from those who are wise and capable.'
- Selma Lagerlof

'The secret of discipline is motivation. When a man is sufficiently motivated, discipline will take care of itself.'
- Sir Alexander Paterson

'I happened on the idea of fitting an engine to a bicycle simply because I did not want to ride crowded trains and buses.'
- Soichire Honda

'It's so hard when I have to, and so easy when I want to.'
- Sondra Anice Barnes

'I believe in using words, not fists.'
- Susan Sarandon

'Money never remains just coins and pieces of paper. Money can be translated into the beauty of living, a support in misfortune, an education, or future security.'
- Sylvia Porter

'All I want out of life is that when I walk down the street, folks will say, "There goes the greatest hitter who ever lived."'
- Ted Williams

'A team that has character doesn't need stimulation.'
- Tom Landry

'Your distress about life might mean you have been living for the wrong reason, not that you have no reason for living.'
- Tom O'Connor

'When the flag is unfurled, all reason is in the trumpet.'
- Ukrainian proverb

'Great men undertake great things because they are great; fools, because they think them easy.'
- Vauvenargues

'I always felt that I hadn't achieved what I wanted to achieve. I always felt I could get better. That's the whole incentive.'
- Virginia Wade

'We talk on principle, but we act on interest.'
- Walter Savage Landor

'Everyone expects to go further than his father went; everyone expects to be better than he was born and every generation has one big impulse in its heart-to exceed all the other generations of the past in all the things that make life worth living.'
- William Allen White

MUSIC

'If a literary man puts together two words about music, one of them will be wrong.'
- Aaron Copland

'After silence, that which comes nearest to expressing the inexpressible is music.'
- Aldous Huxley

'Light quirks of music, broken and uneven, make the soul dance upon a jig of heaven.'
- Alexander Pope

'Canned music is like audible wallpaper.'
- Alistair Cooke

'Music is another planet.'
- Alphonse Daudet

'The basic difference between classical music and jazz is that in the former the music is always graver than its performance - whereas the way jazz is performed is always more important than what is being played.'
- Andre Previn

'Oboe - an ill woodwind that nobody blows good.'
- Anonymous

'Harpists spend half their life tuning and the other half playing out of tune.'
- Anonymous

'In the Negro melodies of America I find all that is needed for a great and noble school of music.'
- Antonin Dvorak

'Mozart is sunshine.'
- Antonin Dvorak

'Rests always sound well.'
- Arnold Schoenberg

'Handel was a man of the world; but Bach was a world of a man.'
- Arnold Stevenson

'Music is only sound expressing certain patterns, so to what extent is that sound architecture and to what extent theatre?'
- Arthur Brown

'The public doesn't want new music; the main thing that it demands of a composer is that he be dead.'
- Arthur Honegger

'I am tired before the concert, not afterward.'
- Artur Rubinstein

'The notes I handle no better than many pianists. But the pauses between the notes - ah, that is where the art resides!'
- Artur Schnabel

'The sonatas of Mozart are unique; they are too easy for children, and too difficult for artists.'
- Artur Schnabel

'God tells me how he wants the music played - and you get in his way.'
- Arturo Toscanini

'Music should strike fire from the heart of man, and bring tears from the eyes of woman.'
- Beethoven

'I am an arrogant and impatient listener, but in the case of a few composers, a very few, when I hear a work I do not like, I am convinced that it is my own fault. Verdi is one of those composers.'
- Benjamin Britten

'A jazz musician is a juggler who uses harmonies instead of oranges.'
- Benny Green

'Wagner's music is better than it sounds.'
- Bill Nye

'I think popular music in this country is one of the few things in the twentieth century that have made giant strides in reverse.'
- Bing Crosby

'Chamber music - a conversation between friends.'
- Catherine Drinker Bowen

'Discord occasions a momentary distress to the ear, which remains unsatisfied, and even uneasy, until it hears something better.'
- Charles Burney

'I have sat through an Italian opera, til, for sheer pain, and inexplicable anguish, I have rushed out into the noisiest places of the crowded street, to solace myself with sounds which I was not obliged to follow and get rid of the distracting torment of '
- Charles Lamb

'Sentimentally I am disposed to harmony; but organically I am incapable of a tune.'
- Charles Lamb

'Music is your own experience, your thoughts, your wisdom. If you don't live it, it won't come out of your horn.'
- Charlie Parker

'A symphony is a stage play with the parts written for instruments instead of for actors.'
- Colin Wilson

'Music produces a kind of pleasure which human nature cannot do without.'
- Confucius

'Jazz is about the only form of art existing today in which there is freedom of the individual without the loss of group contact.'
- Dave Brubeck

'The Sonata is an essentially dramatic art form, combining the emotional range in vivid presentation of a full-size stage drama with the terseness of a short story.'
- Donald Francis Tovey

'Opera is when a guy gets stabbed in the back and instead of bleeding he sings.'
- Ed Gardner

'When people hear good music, it makes them homesick for something they never had, and never will have.'
- Edgar Watson Howe

'I am sure my music has a taste of codfish in it.'
- Edvard Grieg

'I do not mind what language an opera is sung in so long as it is the language I don't understand.'
- Edward Appleton

'You know what you do when you shit, singing is the same thing, only up!'
- Enrico Caruso

'The good composer is slowly discovered, the bad composer is slowly found out.'
- Ernest Newman

'For most singers the first half of the career involves extending one's repertoire, the second half trimming it.'
- Ethan Mordden

'Generally music feedeth that disposition of the spirits which it findeth.'
- Francis Bacon

'Classic music is th' kind that we keep thinkin'll turn into a tune.'
- Frank McKinney

'Music with dinner is an insult, both to the cook and the violinist.'
- G. K. Chesterton

'Hell is full of musical amateurs.'
- George Bernard Shaw

'From Mozart I learnt to say important things in a conversational way.'
- George Bernard Shaw

'Music sweeps by me as a messenger carrying a message that is not for me.'
- George Eliot

'The harp that once through Tara's halls The soul of music shed, Now hangs as mute on Tara's walls, As if that soul were fled.'
- George Moore

'Conductors must give unmistakable and suggestive signals to the orchestra, not choreography to the audience.'
- George Szell

'Wagner has lovely moments but awful quarters of an hour.'
- Gioacchino Rossini

'One cannot judge 'Lohengrin' from a first hearing, and I certainly do not intend to hear it a second time.'
- Gioacchino Rossini

'How wonderful opera would be if there were no singers.'
- Gioacchino Rossini

'Mozart is the human incarnation of the divine force of creation.'
- Goethe

'Never compose anything unless the not composing of it becomes a positive nuisance to you.'
- Gustav Hoist

'Opera in English is, in the main, just about as sensible as baseball in Italian.'
- H. L. Mencken

'Going to the opera, like getting drunk, is a sin that carries its own punishment with it and that a very severe one.'
- Hannah More

'He was dying all his life.'
- Hector Berlioz

'Music is a strange thing. I would almost say it is a miracle. For it stands halfway between thought and phenomenon, between spirit and matter.'
- Heinrich Heine

'Music is the universal language of mankind.'
- Henry Wadsworth Longfellow

'It is the best of all trades to make songs, and the second best to sing them.'
- Hilaire Belloc

'The musician who always plays on the same string, is laughed at.'
- Horace

'I know that the twelve notes in each octave and the varieties of rhythm offer me opportunities that all of human genius will never exhaust.'
- Igor Stravinsky

'Too many pieces of music finish too long after the end.'
- Igor Stravinsky

'Music is given to us specifically to make order of things, to move from an anarchic, individualistic state to a regulated, perfectly concious one, which alone insures vitality and durability.'
- Igor Stravinsky

'Such sweet compulsion doth in music lie.'
- John Milton

'Jazz will endure just as long as people hear it through their feet instead of their brains.'
- John Philip Sousa

'Mozart's music gives us permission to live.'
- John Updike

'Music, the greatest good that mortals know, and all of heaven we have below.'
- Joseph Addison

'Music is the art of thinking with sounds.'
- Jules Combarieu

'Music touches places beyond our touching.'
- Keith Bosley

'Music is the shorthand of emotion.'
- Leo Tolstoy

'Soprano, basso, even the contralto Wished him five fathom under the Rialto.'
- Lord Byron

'What we play is life.'
- Louis Armstrong

'Beethoven can write music, thank God - but he can do nothing else on earth.'
- Ludwig van Beethoven

'Richard Wagner, a musician who wrote music which is better than it sounds.'
- Mark Twain

'The devil does not stay where music is.'
- Martin Luther

'A nation creates music - the composer only arranges it.'
- Mikhail Glinka

'Don't play what's there, play what's not there.'
- Miles Davis

'A legend is an old man with a cane known for what he used to do.'
- Miles Davis

'She was an aging singer who had to take every note above 'A' with her eyebrows.'
- Montague Glass

'Nothing is better than music.... It has done more for us than we have the right to hope for.'
- Nadia Boulanger

'Jazz is the only music in which the same note can be played night after night but differently each time.'
- Ornette Coleman

'Throughout my career, nervousness and stage-fright have never left me before playing. And each of the thousands of concerts I have played at, I feel as bad as I did the very first time.'
- Pablo Casals

'Let us not forget that the greatest composers were also the greatest thieves. They stole from everyone and everywhere.'
- Pablo Casals

'Jazz came to America 300 years ago in chains.'
- Paul Whiteman

'The function of pop music is to be consumed.'
- Pierre Boulez

'Who hears music, feels his solitude peopled at once.'
- Robert Browning

'Why should the devil have all the good tunes?'
- Rowland Hill

'Had I learned to fiddle, I should have done nothing else.'
- Samuel Johnson

'Swans sing before they die - 'twere no bad thing, did certain persons die before they sing.'
- Samuel Taylor Coleridge

'An ear for music is very different from a taste for music. I have no ear whatever; I could not sing an air to save my life; but I have the intensest delight in music, and can detect good from bad.'
- Samuel Taylor Coleridge

'Twelve Highlanders and a bagpipe make a rebellion.'
- Scottish proverb

'He could fiddle all the bugs off a sweet-potato vine.'
- Stephen Vincent Benet

'Music first and last should sound well, should allure and enchant the ear. Never mind the inner significance.'
- Thomas Beecham

'Who is there that, in logical words, can express the effect music has on us? A kind of inarticulate, unfathomable speech, which leads us to the edge of the Infinite and lets us for moments gaze into that!'
- Thomas Carlyle

'Music is well said to be the speech of angels.'
- Thomas Carlyle

'No one can any longer write in the fat style of Strauss. That was killed by Stravinsky. He stripped the body of much of its clothes. Music is the craft of building structures with sound and that is what Stravinsky represents.'
- Vladimir Nabokov

'Music hath charms to soothe a savage breast, to soften rocks, or bend a knotted oak.'
- William Congreve

'Music hath charms to soothe the savage breast.'
- William Congreve

'The man that hath no music in himself, Nor is no moved with concord of sweet sounds, Is fit for treasons, stratagems and spoils.'
- William Shakespeare

'I write as a sow piddles.'
- Wolfgang Amadeus Mozart

NATURE

'When elephants fight it is the grass that suffers.'
- African saying

'Look deep, deep into nature, and then you will understand everything better.'
- Albert Einstein

'All gardening is landscape painting.'
- Alexander Pope

'As long as the Earth can make a spring every year, I can. As long as the Earth can flower and produce nurturing fruit, I can, because I'm the Earth. I won't give up until the Earth gives up.'
- Alice Walker

'Today a new sun rises for me; everything lives, everything is animated, everything seems to speak to me of my passion, everything invites me to cherish it.'
- Anne De Lenclos

'In all things of nature there is something of the marvelous.'
- Aristotle

'To demand 'sense' is the hallmark of nonsense. Nature does not make sense. Nothing makes sense.'
- Ayn Rand

'If you watch how nature deals with adversity, continually renewing itself, you can't help but learn.'
- Bernie Siegel

'Speak to the earth, and it shall teach thee.'
- Bible

'This is the day the Lord had made. We will rejoice and be glad in it.'
- Bible

'There is one glory of the sun and another glory of the moon and another glory of the stars: for one star differeth from another star in glory.'
- Bible

'Consider the lilies of the field, how they grow; they neither toil nor spin; yet I tell you, even Solomon in all his glory was not arrayed like one of these.'
- Bible

'The greatest joy in nature is the absence of man.'
- Bliss Carman

'Grass is the forgiveness of nature - her constant benediction. Forests decay, harvests perish, flowers vanish, but grass is immortal.'
- Brian Ingalls

'Who are we? We find that we live on an insignificant planet of a humdrum star lost in a galaxy tucked away in some forgotten corner of a universe in which there are far more galaxies than people.'
- Carl Sagan

'Light may be shed on man and his origins.'
- Charles Darwin

'I have called this principle, by which each slight variation, if useful, is preserved, by the term natural selection.'
- Charles Darwin

'Pleasure for an hour, a bottle of wine; pleasure for a year, marriage; pleasure for a lifetime, a garden.'
- Chinese saying

'The beauty of the world and the orderly arrangement of everything celestial makes us confess that there is an excellent and eternal nature, which ought to be worshiped and admired by all mankind.'
- Cicero

'I never knew how soothing trees are - many trees and patches of open sunlight, and tree presences; it is almost like having another being.'
- D. H. Lawrence

'The whole of nature is a conjugation of the verb to eat, in the active and passive.'
- Dean William R. Inge

'The kiss of sun for pardon, The song of the birds for mirth One is nearer God's Heart in a garden Than anywhere else on earth.'
- Dorothy Gurney

'Earth's crammed with Heaven, And every common bush afire with God.'
- E. B. Browning

'What mighty battles have I seen and heard waged between the trees and the west wind - an Iliad fought in the fields of air.'
- Edith M. Thomas

'The course of nature is the art of God.'
- Edward Young

'If you wish to know the divine, feel the wind on your face and the warm sun on your hand.'
- Eido Tai Shimano Roshi

'The dinosaur's eloquent lesson is that if some bigness is good, an overabundance of bigness is not necessarily better.'
- Eric Johnston

'God Almighty first planted a garden. And indeed it is the purest of human pleasures.'
- Francis Bacon

'We cannot command Nature except by obeying her.'
- Francis Bacon

'Nature abhors a vacuum.'
- Francois Rabelais

'Is dishwater dull? Naturalists with microscopes have told me that it teems with quiet fun.'
- G. K. Chesterton

'By nature's kindly disposition, most questions which it is beyond man's power to answer do not occur to him at all.'
- George Santayana

'Nobody sees a flower - really - it is so small it takes time - we haven't time - and to see takes time, like to have a friend takes time.'
- Georgia O'Keeffe

'Every flower is a soul blossoming in Nature.'
- Gerard de Nerval

'Man is a complex being: he makes deserts bloom and lakes die.'
- Gil Stern

'Nothing is worth more than this day.'
- Goethe

'The unnatural - that too is natural.'
- Goethe

'When I would recreate myself, I seek the darkest wood, the thickest and most interminable, and to the citizen, most dismal swamp. I enter a swamp as a sacred place - a sanctum sanctorum. There is the strength, the marrow of Nature.'
- Henry David Thoreau

'The finest workers in stone are not copper or steel tools, but the gentle touches of air and water working at their leisure with a liberal allowance of time.'
- Henry David Thoreau

'The bluebird carries the sky on his back.'
- Henry David Thoreau

'I frequently tramped eight or ten miles through the deepest snow to keep an appointment with a beech tree, or a yellow birch, or an old acquaintance among the pines.'
- Henry David Thoreau

'For many years I was self-appointed inspector of snowstorms and rainstorms, and did my duty faithfully, though I never received one cent for it.'
- Henry David Thoreau

'Flowers have an expression of countenance as much as men or animals. Some seem to smile, some have a sad expression, some are pensive and diffident, others again are plain, honest and upright.'
- Henry Ward Beecher

'Everything in nature acts in conformity with law.'
- Immanuel Kant

'I have always been delighted at the prospect of a new day, a fresh try, one more start, with perhaps a bit of magic waiting somewhere behind the morning.'
- J. B. Priestly

'It was one of those perfect summer days - the sun was shining, a breeze was blowing, the birds were singing, and the lawnmower was broken.'
- James Dent

'After rain comes fair weather.'
- James Howell

'Nature is usually wrong.'
- James McNeill Whistler

'For Art may err, but Nature cannot miss.'
- John Dryden

'The universe is not hostile, nor yet is it friendly. It is simply indifferent.'
- John Hughes Holmes

'Accuse not Nature, she hath done her part; Do thou but thine!'
- John Milton

'The radiance in some places is so great as to be fairly dazzling . . . every crystal, every flower a window opening into heaven, a mirror reflecting the Creator.'
- John Muir

'The clearest way into the Universe is through a forest wilderness.'
- John Muir

'Climb the mountains and get their good tidings: Nature's peace will flow into you as sunshine into flowers, the winds will blow their freshness into you, and the storms, their energy and cares will drop off like autumn leaves.'
- John Muir

'There is something haunting in the light of the moon; it has all the dispassionateness of a disembodied soul, and something of its inconceivable mystery.'
- Joseph Conrad

'All gardeners live in beautiful places because they make them so.'
- Joseph Joubert

'When a man wantonly destroys a work of man we call him a vandal; when a man destroys one of the works of God, we call him a sportsman.'
- Joseph Wood Krutch

'Forget not that the earth delights to feel your bare feet and the winds long to play with your hair.'
- Kahlil Gibran

'Don't knock the weather; nine-tenths of the people couldn't start a conversation if it didn't change once in a while.'
- Kin Hubbard

'Nature is not human-hearted.'
- Lao-Tzu

'I chatter, chatter, as I flow To join the brimming river, For men may come and men may go, But I go on forever.'
- Lord Alfred Tennyson

'I love not man the less, but nature more.'
- Lord Byron

'Flowers always make people better, happier, and more helpful; they are sunshine, food, and medicine to the soul.'
- Luther Burbank

'Yesterday is not ours to recover, but tomorrow is ours to win or lose.'
- Lyndon B. Johnson

'Like a gardener, I believe that what goes down must come up.'
- Lynwood L. Giacomini

'Monotony is the law of nature. Look at the monotonous manner in which the sun rises. The monotony of necessary occupations is exhilarating and life-giving.'
- Mahatma Gandhi

'Weather means more when you have a garden. There's nothing like listening to a shower and thinking how it is soaking in around your green beans.'
- Marcelene Cox

'The nicest thing about the promise of spring is that sooner or later she'll have to keep it.'
- Mark Beltaire

'I love the challenge of starting at zero every day and seeing how much I can accomplish.'
- Martha Stewart

'Our Lord has written the promise of resurrection, not in books alone but in every leaf of springtime.'
- Martin Luther

'Normal day, let me be aware of the treasure you are. Let me learn from you, love you, bless you before you depart. Let me not pass you by in quest of some rare and perfect tomorrow.'
- Mary Jean Iron

'Today is a new day. You will get out of it just what you put into it. . . If you have made mistakes, even serious mistakes, there is always another chance for you. . . . for this thing that we call "failure" is not the falling down, but the staying down.'
- Mary Pickford

'Nature, with equal mind, sees all her sons at play, sees man control the wind, the wind sweep man away.'
- Matthew Arnold

'Next time a sunrise steals your breath or a meadow of flowers leave you speechless, remain that way. Say nothing, and listen as heaven whispers, "Do you like it? I did it just for you."'
- Max Lucado

'Nature is a catchment of sorrows.'
- Maxine Kumin

'Rivers and rocks and trees have always been talking to us, but we've forgotten how to listen.'
- Michael Roads

'The AmenT of Nature is always a flower.'
- Oliver Wendell Holmes

'When I look at the future, it's so bright, it burns my eyes.'
- Oprah Winfrey

'Nature tops the list of potent tranquilizers and stress reducers. The mere sound of moving water has been shown to lower blood pressure.'
- Patch Adams

'Nature thrives on patience; man on impatience.'
- Paul Boese

'The world is full of poetry. The air is living with its spirit; and the waves dance to the music of its melodies, and sparkle in its brightness.'
- Percival

'The universe is like a safe to which there is a combination, but the combination is locked up in the safe.'
- Peter de Vries

'The soil, in return for her service, keeps the tree tied to her; the sky asks nothing and leaves it free.'
- Rabindranath Tagore

'Nature is too thin a screen; the glory of the omnipresent God bursts through everywhere.'
- Ralph Waldo Emerson

'Adopt the pace of nature: her secret is patience.'
- Ralph Waldo Emerson

'The creation of a thousand forests is in one acorn.'
- Ralph Waldo Emerson

'Earth laughs in flowers.'
- Ralph Waldo Emerson

'Nature is reckless of the individual. When she has points to carry, she carries them'
- Ralph Waldo Emerson

'What is a weed? A plant whose virtues have not yet been discovered.'
- Ralph Waldo Emerson

'Nature is saturated with deity.'
- Ralph Waldo Emerson

'Write it on your heart that every day is the best day in the year.'
- Ralph Waldo Emerson

'To the dull mind all nature is leaden. To the illumined mind the whole world burns and sparkles with light.'
- Ralph Waldo Emerson

'The mastery of nature is vainly believed to be an adequate substitute for self-mastery.'
- Reinhold Niebuhr

'Nature uses only the longest threads to weave her patterns, so each small piece of her fabric reveals the organization of the entire tapestry.'
- Richard Feynman

'Gie me a spark o' nature's fire, that's a' the learning I desire.'
- Robert Burns

'In nature there are neither rewards nor punishments - there are consequences.'
- Robert G. Ingersoll

'There is nothing in which the birds differ more from man than the way in which they can build and yet leave a landscape as it was before.'
- Robert Lynd

'Spring is nature's way of saying, "Let's party!"'
- Robin Williams

'God's miracles are to be found in nature itself; the wind and waves, the wood that becomes a tree - all of these are explained biologically, but behind them is the hand of God.'
- Ronald Reagan

'Every new day begins with possibilities. It's up to us to fill it with the things that move us toward progress and peace.'
- Ronald Reagan

'The woods were made for the hunter of dreams, The brooks for the fishes of song.'
- Sam Walter Foss

'The sun gives us light, but the moon provides inspiration. If you look at the sun without shielding your eyes, you'll go blind. If you look at the moon without covering your eyes, you'll become a poet.'
- Serge Bouchard

'From the intrinsic evidence of His creation, the Great Architect of the Universe now begins to appear as a pure mathematician .'
- Sir James Jeans

'A vacuum is a hell of a lot better than some of the stuff that nature replaces it with.'
- Tennessee Williams

'Deep in their roots, all flowers keep the light.'
- Theodore Roethke

'After a debauch of thundershower, the weather takes the pledge and signs it with a rainbow.'
- Thomas Bailey Aldrich

'We lose our souls if we lose the experience of the forest, the butterflies, the song of the birds, if we can't see the stars at night.'
- Thomas Berry

'When the oak is felled the whole forest echoes with its fall, but a hundred acorns are sown in silence by an unnoticed breeze.'
- Thomas Carlyle

'The sun - my almighty physician.'
- Thomas Jefferson

'Nature, like a kind and smiling mother, lends herself to our dreams and cherishes our fancies.'
- Victor Hugo

'Men argue, nature acts.'
- Voltaire

'Nature has always had more force than education.'
- Voltaire

'I believe a leaf of grass is no less than the journey-work of the stars.'
- Walt Whitman

'To him who in the love of Nature holds Communion with her visible forms, she speaks A various language.'
- William Cullen Bryant

'One touch of nature makes the whole world kin.'
- William Shakespeare

'To hold, as 't were, the mirror up to nature.'
- William Shakespeare

'Come forth into the light of things. Let nature be your teacher.'
- William Wordsworth

'My heart leaps up when I behold a rainbow in the sky.'
- William Wordsworth

'Nature never did betray the heart that loved her.'
- William Wordsworth

'Nature is a volume of which God is the author.'
- William Wordsworth

'I wanted to say something about the universe. There's God, angels, plants... and horseshit.'
- Zero Mostel

OPTIMISM & PESSIMISM

'In the midst of winter, I finally learned that there was in me an invincible summer.'
- Albert Camus

'An optimist is a guy that has never had much experience.'
- Don Marquis

'A pessimist is one who has been compelled to live with an optimist.'
- Elbert Hubbard

'Pessimism is only the name that men of weak nerves give to wisdom.'
- Elbert Hubbard

'Still round the corner there may wait, a new road, or a secret gate.'
- J. R. R. Tolkien

'The optimist claims we live in the best of all possible worlds, and the pessimist fears this is true.'
- James Branch Cabell

'My pessimism goes to the point of suspecting the sincerity of the pessimists.'
- Jean Rostand

'When Fortune empties her chamber pot on your head, smile and say 'We are going to have a summer shower.''
- John A. Macdonald

'There is a budding morrow in midnight.'
- John Keats

'An optimist is a fellow who believes what's going to be will be postponed.'
- Kin Hubbard

'The world gets better every day - then worse again in the evening.'
- Kin Hubbard

'Pessimist - one who, when he has the choice of two evils, chooses both.'
- Oscar Wilde

'When I look in the glass I see that every line in my face means pessimism, but in spite of my face - that is my experience - I remain an optimist.'
- Richard Jeffries

'When things come to the worst, they generally mend.'
- Susanna Moodie

'One cloud is enough to eclipse all the sun.'
    - Thomas Fuller

'The progress of rivers to the ocean is not so rapid as that of man to error.'
    - Voltaire

'A man he seems of cheerful yesterdays And confident tomorrows.'
    - William Wordsworth

PARENTHOOD

'Parenthood remains the greatest single preserve of the amateur.'
   - Alvin Toffler

'Anything which parents have not learned from experience they can now learn from their children.'
   - Anonymous

'A mother is a person who if she is not there when you get home from school you wouldn't know how to get your dinner, and you wouldn't feel like eating it anyway.'
   - Anonymous

'The best way to bring up some children is short.'
   - Anthony J. Pettito

'Parents are sometimes a bit of a disappointment to their children. They don't fulfill the promise of their early years.'
   - Anthony Powell

'I demand for the unmarried mother, as a sacred channel of life, the same reverence and respect as for the married mother; for Maternity is a cosmic thing and once it has come to pass, our conventions must not be permitted to blaspheme it.'
   - Ben Lindsey

'The fundamental defect of fathers is that they want their children to be a credit to them.'
   - Bertrand Russell

'Train a child in the way he should go, and when he is old he will not depart from it.'
   - Bible

'Our sons, who so easily recognize our errors, and rightly denounce them, will have to confess their own, later on, and they may be as bad as ours, perhaps worse.'
   - Bruce Hutchison

'Parents accept their obsolescence with the best grace they can muster. . . they do all they can to make it easy for the younger generation to surpass the older, while secretly dreading the rejection that follows.'
   - Christopher Lasch

'It is the malady of our age that the young are so busy teaching us that they have no time left to learn.'
   - Eric Hoffer

'The mother-child relationship is paradoxical and, in a sense, tragic. It requires the most intense love on the mother's side, yet this very love must help the child grow away from the mother and to become fully independent.'
   - Erich Fromm

'Perhaps host and guest is really the happiest relation for father and son.'
- Evelyn Waugh

'No matter how old a mother is, she watches her middle-aged children for signs of improvement.'
- Florida Scott-Maxwell

'A father is a banker provided by nature.'
- French proverb

'When one has not had a good father, one must create one.'
- Friedrich Nietzsche

'Who doesn't desire his father's death?'
- Fyodor Dostoyevsky

'The best brought-up children are those who have seen their parents as they are. Hypocrisy is not the parents' first duty.'
- George Bernard Shaw

'Parentage is a very important profession, but no test of fitness, for it is ever imposed in the interests of the Children.'
- George Bernard Shaw

'Who takes the child by the hand takes the mother by the heart.'
- German proverb

'What the mother sings to the cradle goes all the way down to the coffin.'
- Henry Ward Beecher

'A mother who is really a mother is never free.'
- Honore de Balzac

'The thing about having a baby is that thereafter you have it.'
- Jean Kerr

'Your children need your presence more than your presents.'
- Jesse Jackson

'God could not be everywhere and therefore he made mothers.'
- Jewish proverb

'I must study politics and war, that my sons may have the liberty to study mathematics and philosophy, geography, natural history, and naval architecture, navigation, commerce, and agriculture, in order to give their children a right to study painting, poe'
- John Adams

'Every parent is at some time the father of the unreturned prodigal, with nothing to do but keep his house open to hope.'
- John Ciardi

'Everyone likes to think that he has done reasonably well in life, so that it comes as a shock to find our children believing differently. The temptation is to tune them out; it takes much more courage to listen.'
- John D. Rockefeller III

'People should be free to find or make for themselves the kinds of educational experiences they want their children to have.'
- John Holt

'To bring up a child in the way he should go, travel that way yourself once in a while.'
- Josh Billings

'Whatever you would have your children become, strive to exhibit in your own lives and conversation.'
- Lydia H. Sigourney

'Every beetle is a gazelle in the eyes of its mother.'
- Moorish proverb

'Parents are the bones on which children cut their teeth.'
- Peter Ustinov

'A Jewish man with parents alive is a 15-year-old boy, and will remain a 15-year-old boy until they die.'
- Philip Roth

'Don't limit a child to your own learning, for he was born in another time.'
- Rabbinical saying

'Diogenes struck the father when the son swore.'
- Robert Burton

'You don't have to deserve your mother's love. You have to deserve your father's. He's more particular.'
- Robert Frost

'Insanity is hereditary - you can get it from your children.'
- Sam Levenson

'A rich child often sits in a poor mother's lap.'
- Spanish proverb

'An ounce of mother is worth a pound of clergy.'
- Spanish proverb

'To become a father is not hard, to be a father is, however.'
- Wilhelm Busch

'Tired mothers find that spanking takes less time than reasoning and penetrates sooner to the seat of the memory.'
- Will Durant

'Mother is the name for God in the lips and hearts of children.'
  - William Makepeace Thackeray

PASSION

'The ruling passion, be it what it will, The ruling passion conquers reason still.'
- Alexander Pope

'Law and love are the same - romantic in concept but the actual practice can give you a yeast infection.'
- Ally McBeal

'If love is blind, why is lingerie so popular?'
- Anonymous

'Love - a wildly misunderstood although highly desirable malfunction of the heart which weakens the brain, causes eyes to sparkle, cheeks to glow, blood pressure to rise and the lips to pucker.'
- Anonymous

'Knowledge of mankind is a knowledge of their passions.'
- Benjamin Disraeli

'The human race has been set up. Someone, somewhere, is playing a practical joke on us. Apparently, women need to feel loved to have sex. Men need to have sex to feel loved. How do we ever get started?'
- Billy Connolly

'Women need a reason to have sex. Men just need a place.'
- Billy Crystal

'The big difference between sex for money and sex for free is that sex for money usually costs a lot less.'
- Brendan Behan

'You call it madness, but I call it love.'
- Don Byas

'I prefer love over sex.'
- Enrique Iglesias

'I have loved to the point of madness; that which is called madness, that which to me, is the only sensible way to love.'
- Francoise Sagan

'Acting is not very hard. The most important things are to be able to laugh and cry. If I have to cry, I think of my sex life. And if I have to laugh, well, I think of my sex life.'
- Glenda Jackson

'To be in love is merely to be in a state of perpetual anesthesia: To mistake an ordinary young man for a Greek god or an ordinary young woman for a goddess.'
- H. L. Mencken

'Love ain't nothing but sex misspelled.'
- Harlan Ellison

'Passion is universal humanity. Without it religion, history, romance and art would be useless.'
- Honore de Balzac

'Sex without love is as hollow and ridiculous as love without sex.'
- Hunter S. Thompson

'Passion makes the world go round. Love just makes it a safer place.'
- Ice T

'A kiss is a lovely trick designed by nature to stop speech when words become superfluous.'
- Ingrid Bergman

'I need sex for a clear complexion, but I'd rather do it for love.'
- Joan Crawford

'Take heed lest passion sway Thy judgment to do aught, which else free will Would not admit.'
- John Milton

'Love is of all passions the strongest, for it attacks simultaneously the head, the heart and the senses.'
- Lao-Tzu

'She walks in beauty, Like the night of cloudless climes and starry skies; And all that's best of dark and bright Meet in her aspect and her eyes.'
- Lord Byron

'Love is an exploding cigar we willingly smoke.'
- Lynda Barry

'I have found men who didn't know how to kiss. I've always found time to teach them.'
- Mae West

'In my sex fantasy, nobody ever loves me for my mind.'
- Nora Ephron

'It does not matter what you do in the bedroom as long as you do not do it in the street and frighten the horses.'
- Patrick Campbell

'Soul meets soul on lover's lips.'
- Percy Bysshe Shelly

'Sex is a conversation carried out by other means. If you get on well out of bed, half the problems of bed are solved.'
- Peter Ustinov

'Love is an irresistible desire to be irresistibly desired.'
- Robert Frost

'If we seek the pleasures of love, passion should be occasional, and common sense continual.'
- Robertson Davies

'Anyone can be passionate, but it takes real lovers to be silly.'
- Rose Franken

'Love is not altogether a delirium, yet it has many points in common therewith.'
- Thomas Carlyle

'A lover without indiscretion is no lover at all.'
- Thomas Hardy

'Passions unguided are for the most part mere madness.'
- Thomas Hobbes

'Love is only a dirty trick played on us to achieve continuation of the species.'
- W. Somerset Maugham

'Give me that man That is not passion's slave.'
- William Shakespeare

'Sex alleviates tension. Love causes it.'
- Woody Allen

'I know nothing about sex, because I was always married.'
- Zsa Gabor

PATIENCE

'The slow rhythm of waiting.'
  - Adrian Cowell

'Hasten slowly.'
  - Augustus Caesar

'He that can have patience can have what he will.'
  - Benjamin Franklin

'With time and patience the mulberry leaf becomes a silk gown.'
  - Chinese proverb

'Never think that God's delays are God's denials. Hold on; hold fast; hold out. Patience is genius.'
  - Comte de Buffon

'A handful of patience is worth more than a bushel of brains.'
  - Dutch proverb

'Patience makes a woman beautiful in middle age.'
  - Elliot Paul

'People in a hurry cannot think, cannot grow, nor can they decay. They are preserved in a state of perpetual puerility.'
  - Eric Hoffer

'Patience has its limits. Take it too far, and it's cowardice.'
  - George Jackson

'Life on the farm is a school of patience; you can't hurry the crops or make an ox in two days.'
  - Henri Fournier Alain

'All things come round to him who will but wait.'
  - Henry Wadsworth Longfellow

'Patience and passage of time do more than strength and fury.'
  - Jean de la Fontaine

'By time and toil we sever What strength and rage could never.'
  - Jean de la Fontaine

'The more haste, the less speed.'
  - John Heywood

'Never cut what you can untie.'
  - Joseph Joubert

'Patience is a bitter plant but it has sweet fruit.'
  - Old proverb

'What can't be cured, must be endured.'
  - Old saying

'There is nothing so bitter, that a patient mind cannot find some solace for it.'
  - Seneca

'Have patience with all things, but chiefly have patience with yourself. Do not lose courage in considering your own imperfections, but instantly set about remedying them - every day begin the task anew.'
  - St. Francis de Sales

'Patience, that blending of moral courage with physical timidity.'
  - Thomas Hardy

'There are no short cuts to Heaven, only the ordinary way of ordinary things.'
  - Vincent McNabb

'I am as poor as Job, my lord, but not so patient.'
  - William Shakespeare

'How poor are they that have not patience! What wound did ever heal but by degrees?'
  - William Shakespeare

'And makes us rather bear those ills we have Than fly to others that we know not of?'
  - William Shakespeare

PEACE

'Get into the habit of looking for the silver lining of the cloud, and, when you have found it, continue to look at it, rather than at the leaden gray in the middle. It will help you over many hard places.'
  - A. A. Willitts

'If the pursuit of peace is both old and new, it is also both complicated and simple. It is complicated, for it has to do with people, and nothing in this universe baffles man as much as man himself.'
  - Adlai Stevenson

'Be brave enough to live creatively. The creative is the place where no one else has ever been. You have to leave the city of your comfort and go into the wilderness of your intuition. You cannot get there by bus, only by hard work, risking and by not quit'
  - Alan Alda

'There are two means of refuge from the miseries of life: music and cats.'
  - Albert Schweitzer

'Until he extends his circle of compassion to all living things, man will not find peace.'
  - Albert Schweitzer

'Peace at any price.'
  - Alphonse de Lamartine

'Peace: in international affairs, a period of cheating between two periods of fighting.'
  - Ambrose Bierce

'Know thyself. Don't accept your dog's admiration as conclusive evidence that you are wonderful.'
  - Ann Landers

'Everyone has inside of him a piece of good news. The good news is that you don't know how great you can bel How much you can love! What you can accomplish! And what your potential is I'
  - Anne Frank

'Picture yourself placing your problem inside a pale, yellow balloon, letting it go, watching it drift until it is a tiny pastel dot in the sky.'
  - Barbara Markoff

'Peace is not an absence of war, it is a virtue, a state of mind, a disposition for benevolence, confidence, justice.'
  - Benedict Spinoza

'Even peace may be purchased at too high a price.'
  - Benjamin Franklin

'Trust yourself. You know more than you think you do.'
  - Benjamin Spock

'There is no psychiatrist in the world like a puppy licking your face.'
- Bern Williams

'Diseases can be our spiritual flat tires - disruptions in our lives that seem to be disasters at the time but end by redirecting our lives in a meaningful way.'
- Bernie Siegel

'Look at everything as though you were seeing it either for the first or last time. Then your time on earth will be filled with glory.'
- Betty Smith

'Peace be with you.'
- Bible

'Glory to God, in the highest, and on earth peace, good will toward men.'
- Bible

'Peace be to this house.'
- Bible

'Mercy and truth are met together: righteousness and peace have kissed each other.'
- Bible

'Peace be within thy walls, and prosperity within they palaces.'
- Bible

'The wolf also shall dwell with the lamb, and the leopard shall lie down with the kid.'
- Bible

'Ask, and it shall be given you; seek, and ye shall find; knock, and it shall be opened unto you. For every one that asketh, receiveth; and he that seeketh, findeth; and to him that knocketh it shall be opened.'
- Bible

'They shall beat their swords into ploughshares, and their spears into pruninghooks; nation shall not lift up sword against nation neither shall they learn war any more.'
- Bible

'Her ways are ways of pleasantness, and all her paths are peace.'
- Bible

'Each of us makes his own weather, determines the color of the skies in the emotional universe which he inhabits.'
- Bishop Fulton J. Sheen

'Nothing splendid has ever been achieved except by those who dared to believe that something inside of them was superior to circumstance.'
- Bruce Barton

'Everyone has got it in him, if he will only make up his mind and stick at it. None of us is born with a stop-valve on his powers or with a set limit to his capacities. There is no limit possible to the expansion of each one of us.'
- Charles Schwab

'I prefer the most unfair peace to the most righteous war.'
- Cicero

'Time spent with cats is never wasted.'
- Colette

'It is impossible to keep a straight face in the presence of one or more kittens.'
- Cynthia E. Varnado

'There are no makers of peace because the making of peace is at least as costly as the making of war - at least as exigent.'
- Daniel Berrigan

'Today, let's give thanks for life. For life itself. For simply being born!'
- Daphne Rose Kingma

'They sicken of the calm who know the storm.'
- Dorothy Parker

'Pessimism never won any battle.'
- Dwight D. Eisenhower

'I think that people want peace so much that one of these days governments had better get out of their way and let them have it.'
- Dwight D. Eisenhower

'We merely want to live in peace with all the world, to trade with them, to commune with them, to learn from their culture as they may learn from ours, so that the products of our toil may be used for our schools and our roads and our churches and not for '
- Dwight D. Eisenhower

'I keep the telephone of my mind open to peace, harmony, health, love, and abundance. Then whenever doubt, anxiety, or fear try to call me, they keep getting a busy signal and soon they'll forget my number.'
- Edith Armstrong

'It is the mind that maketh good of ill, that maketh wretch or happy, rich or poor.'
- Edmund Spenser

'It isn't enough to talk about peace; one must believe in it. And it isn't enough to believe in it; one must work at it.'
- Eleanor Roosevelt

'Life is a mirror and will reflect back to the thinker what he thinks into it.'
- Ernest Holmes

'There is no such thing as inner peace, there is only nervousness and death.'
- Fran Lebowitz

'Peace, like charity, begins at home.'
- Franklin D. Roosevelt

'Whoever said you can't buy happiness forgot about little puppies.'
- Gene Hill

'One sword keeps another in the sheath.'
- George Herbert

'Before the war, and especially before the Boer War, it was summer all the year round.'
- George Orwell

'To be prepared for war is one of the most effectual means of preserving peace.'
- George Washington

'Choose to experience peace rather than conflict.'
- Gerald Jampolsky

'You don't have to have fought in a war to love peace.'
- Geraldine Ferraro

'Stop the mindless wishing that things would be different. Rather than wasting time and emotional and spiritual energy in explaining why we don't have what we want, we can start to pursue other ways to get it.'
- Greg Anderson

'It is understanding that gives us an ability to have peace. When we understand the other fellow's viewpoint, and he understands ours, then we can sit down and work out our differences.'
- Harry S. Truman

'Keep your face to the sunshine and you cannot see the shadow.'
- Helen Keller

'Enthusiasm is the greatest asset in the world. It beats money and power and influence.'
- Henry Chester

'The dog is the god of frolic.'
- Henry Ward Beecher

'God gave us our memories so that we might have roses in December.'
- J. M. Barrie

'No matter what level of your ability, you have more potential than you can ever develop in a lifetime.'
- James McCay

'It is the ultimate wisdom of the mountains that we are never so much human as when we are striving for what is beyond our grasp, and that there is no battle worth the winning save that against our own ignorance and fear.'
- James Ramsey Ullman

'I have always thought of a dog lover as a dog that was in love with another dog.'
- James Thurber

'You can't look at a sleeping cat and be tense.'
- Jane Pauley

'Out of difficulties grow miracles.'
- Jean de la Bruyere

'Man is so made that whenever anything fires his soul, impossibilities vanish.'
- Jean de la Fontaine

'Once you hear the details of victory, it is hard to distinguish it from a defeat.'
- Jean-Paul Sartre

'Cats are smarter than dogs. You can't get eight cats to pull a sled through snow.'
- Jeff Valdez

'We're all only fragile threads, but what a tapestry we make.'
- Jerry Ellis

'Peace is a daily, a weekly, a monthly process, gradually changing opinions, slowly eroding old barriers, quietly building new structures. And however undramatic the pursuit of peace, the pursuit must go on.'
- John F. Kennedy

'It takes two to make peace.'
- John F. Kennedy

'Peace hath her victories, No less renowned than war.'
- John Milton

'We cannot tell what may happen to us in the strange medley of life. But we can decide what happens in us - how we take it, what we do with it - and that is what really counts in the end.'
- Joseph Newton

'Cats seem to go on the principle that it never does any harm to ask for what you want.'
- Joseph Wood Krutch

'Money will buy a pretty good dog but it won't buy the wag of his tail.'
- Josh Billings

'A dog Is the only thing on earth that loves you more than he loves himself.'
- Josh Billings

'Every beauty and greatness in this world is created by a single thought or emotion inside a man. Every thing we see today, made by past generations, was, before its appearance, a thought in the mind of a man or an impulse in the heart of a woman.'
- Kahlil Gibran

'Could we change our attitude, we should not only see life differently, but life itself would come to be different. Life would undergo a change of appearance because we ourselves had undergone a change in attitude.'
- Katherine Mansfield

'There are two big forces at work, external and internal. We have very little control over external forces such as tornadoes, earthquakes, floods, disasters, illness, and pain. What really matters is the internal force. How do I respond to those disasters?'
- Leo Buscaglia

'Peace is the first thing the angels sang. Peace is the mark of the sons of God. Peace is the nurse of love. Peace is the mother of unity. Peace is the rest of blessed souls. Peace is the dwelling place of eternity.'
- Leo the Great

'The war-drum throbb'd no longer, and the battle flags were furl'd In the parliament of man, the federation of the world.'
- Lord Alfred Tennyson

'If peace cannot be maintained with honor, it is no longer peace.'
- Lord Russell

'I am a man of peace, God knows how I love peace; but I hope I shall never be such a coward as to mistake oppression for peace.'
- Louis Kossuth

'No matter how little money and how few possessions you own, having a dog makes you rich.'
- Louis Sabin

'I'm not afraid of storms for I'm learning how to sail my ship.'
- Louisa May Alcott

'It doesn't hurt to be optimistic. You can always cry later.'
- Lucimar Santos de Lima

'The quickest way to change your attitude toward pain is to accept the fact that everything that happens to us has been designed for our spiritual growth.'
- M. Scott Peck

'A dog wags its tail with its heart.'
- Martin Buxbaum

'Dogs come when they're called; cats take a message and get back to you.'
- Mary Bly

'We are each gifted in a unique and important way. It is our privilege and our adventure to discover our own special light.'
- Mary Dunbar

'Dogs laugh, but they laugh with their tails.'
- Max Eastman

'Within you right now is the power to do things you never dreamed possible. This power becomes available to you just as soon as you can change your beliefs.'
- Maxwell Maltz

'Help us to be the always hopeful gardeners of the spirit who know that without darkness nothing comes to birth as without light nothing flowers.'
- May Sarton

'Living with a dog is one way to retain something of a child's spirit.'
- Michael Rosen

'If we have no peace, it is because we have forgotten that we belong to each other.'
- Mother Teresa

'If they want peace, nations should avoid the pin-pricks that precede cannon-shots.'
- Napoleon

'War is an invention of the human mind. The human mind can invent peace.'
- Norman Cousins

'People become really quite remarkable when they start thinking that they can do things. When they believe in themselves they have the first secret of success.'
- Norman Vincent Peale

'Deep within man dwell those slumbering powers; powers that would astonish him, that he never dreamed of possessing; forces that would revolutionize his life if aroused and put into Taking Action.'
- Orison S. Marden

'Our thoughts and imaginations are the only real limits to our possibilities,'
- Orison S. Marden

'One for whom the pebble has value must be surrounded by treasures wherever he goes.'
- Par Lagerkvist

'Peace is a virtual, mute, sustained victory of potential powers against probable greeds.'
- Paul Valery

'Whenever something good happens, write it down. Buy a special notebook . . . and use it to list all the good in your life.'
- Peter McWilliams

'Positive thoughts (joy, happiness, fulfillment, achievement, worthiness) have positive results (enthusiasm, calm, well-being, ease, energy, love). - Negative thoughts (judgment, unworthiness, mistrust, resentment, fear) produce negative results (tension, '
- Peter McWilliams

'The power which resides in man is new in nature, and none but he knows what that is which he can do, nor does he until he has tried.'
- Ralph Waldo Emerson

'The peace of the man who has foresworn the use of the bullet seems to me not quite peace, but a canting impotence.'
- Ralph Waldo Emerson

'What lies behind us and what lies before us are small matter compared to what lies within us.'
- Ralph Waldo Emerson

'Exhilaration of life can be found only with an upward look. This is an exciting world. It is cram-packed with opportunity. Great moments wait around every corner.'
- Richard Devos

'I wonder if other dogs think poodles are members of a weird religious cult.'
- Rita Rudner

'The average pencil is seven inches long, with just a half-inch eraser - in case you thought optimism was dead.'
- Robert Brault

'You can do anything you wish to do, have anything you wish to have, be anything you wish to be.'
- Robert Collier

'The place to improve the world is first in one's own heart and head and hands.'
- Robert Persig

'Dogs are not our whole life, but they make our lives whole.'
- Roger Caras

'The greatest pleasure of a dog is that you may make a fool of yourself with him, and not only will he not scold you, but he will make a fool of himself, too.'
- Samuel Butler

'Cats are angels with fur.'
- Sark

'Most of us can, as we choose, make of this world either a palace or a prison.'
- Sir John Lubbock

'When fire and water are at war it is the fire that loses.'
- Spanish proverb

'Where they make a desert, they call it peace.'
- Tacitus

'The only way to bring peace to the earth is to learn to make our own life peaceful.'
- The Buddha

'I am not discouraged, because every wrong attempt discarded is another step forward.'
- Thomas Alva Edison

'If we did all the things we are capable of doing, we would literally astound ourselves.'
- Thomas Alva Edison

'Before a painter puts a brush to his canvas he sees his picture mentally. ... If you think of yourself in terms of a painting, what do you see? ... Is the picture one you think worth painting? . . . You create yourself in the image you hold in your mind.'
- Thomas Dreier

'I have never advocated war, except as a means of peace.'
- Ulysses S. Grant

'The more we sweat in peace the less we bleed in war.'
- Vijaya Lakshmi Pandit

'There is very little difference in people, but that little difference makes a big difference. The little difference is attitude. The big difference is whether it is positive or negative.'
- W. Clement Stone

'What is defeat? Nothing but education, nothing but the first step toward something better.'
- Wendell Phillips

'Peace rules the day, where reason rules the mind.'
- William Collins

'That they may have a little peace, even the best dogs are compelled to snarl occasionally.'
- William Feather

'Great emergencies and crises show us how much greater our vital resources are than we had supposed.'
- William James

'Be not afraid of life. Believe that life is worth living, and your belief will help create the fact.'
- William James

'Peace won by compromise is usually a short-lived achievement.'
- Winfield Scott

PEOPLE

'God must have loved the plain people: He made so many of them.'
    - Abraham Lincoln

'You can fool some of the people all of the time, and all of the people some of the time, but you cannot fool all of the people all the time.'
    - Abraham Lincoln

'We here highly resolve that these dead shall not have died in vain; that this nation, under God, shall have a new birth of freedom, and that government of the people, by the people, and for the people, shall not perish from the earth.'
    - Abraham Lincoln

'The voice of the people is the voice of God.'
    - Alcuin

'The two kinds of people on earth that I mean Are the people who lift and the people who lean.'
    - Ella Wheeler Wilcox

'The second, sober thought of the people is seldom wrong, and always efficient.'
    - Martin Van Buren

'The people are the only sure reliance for the preservation of our liberty.'
    - Thomas Jefferson

PHILOSOPHY

'A man of business may talk of philosophy; a man who has none may practise it.'
- Alexander Pope

'It takes a very unusual mind to undertake the analysis of the obvious.'
- Alfred North Whitehead

'I have a simple philosophy. Fill what's empty. Empty what's full. And scratch where it itches.'
- Alice Roosevelt Longworth

'Philosophy: A route of many roads leading from nowhere to nothing.'
- Ambrose Bierce

'In philosophy an individual is becoming himself.'
- Bernard Lonergan

'Three passions, simple but overwhelmingly strong, have governed my life: the longing for love, the search for knowledge and unbearable pity for the suffering of mankind.'
- Bertrand Russell

'Science is what you know, philosophy is what you don't know.'
- Bertrand Russell

'To teach how to live with uncertainty, and yet without being paralyzed by hesitation, is perhaps the chief thing that philosophy in our age can still do for those who study it.'
- Bertrand Russell

'It is easy to build a philosophy. It doesn't have to run.'
- Charles F. Kettering

'I've developed a new philosophy - I only dread one day at a time.'
- Charles M. Schulz

'Romanticism is the expression of man's urge to rise above reason and common sense, just as rationalism is the expression of his urge to rise above theology and emotion.'
- Charles Yost

'When you have only two pennies left in the world, buy a loaf of bread with one. and a lily with the other.'
- Chinese proverb

'Be a philosopher but, amid all your philosophy be still a man.'
- David Hume

'One's task is not to turn the world upside down, but to do what is necessary at the given place and with a due consideration of reality.'
- Dietrich Bonhoeffer

'Queen of arts, and daughter of heaven.'
- Edmund Burke

'Here is the beginning of philosophy: a recognition of the conflicts between men, a search for their cause, a condemnation of mere opinion .. . and the discovery of a standard of judgement.'
- Epictetus

'All philosophy lies in two words, sustain and abstain.'
- Epictetus

'The philosopher is Nature's pilot. And there you have our difference: to be in hell is to drift: to be in heaven is to steer.'
- George Bernard Shaw

'Every day look at a beautiful picture, read a beautiful poem, listen to some beautiful music, and if possible, say some reasonable thing.'
- Goethe

'In other words, apart from the known and the unknown, what else is there?'
- Harold Pinter

'In philosophy, it is not the attainment of the goal that matters, it is the things that are met with by the way.'
- Havelock Ellis

'The philosophy of one century is the common sense of the next.'
- Henry Ward Beecher

'Philosophy goes no further than probabilities, and in every assertion keeps a doubt in reserve.'
- James Froude

'Philosophy will clip an Angel's wings Conquer all mysteries by rule and line, Empty the haunted air, the gnomed mine -Unweave a rainbow.'
- John Keats

'Whence? wither? why? how? - these questions cover all philosophy.'
- Joseph Joubert

'Anything that comes easy, comes wrong.'
- Josephine Tessier

'Philosophy has a fine saying for everything - for Death it has an entire set.'
- Laurence Sterne

'A blind man in a dark room - looking for a black hat which isn't there.'
   - Lord Bowen

'Philosophy is doubt.'
   - Michel de Montaigne

'The opposite of a correct statement is a false statement. But the opposite of a profound truth may well be another profound truth.'
   - Niels Bohr

'Philosophy is a good horse in the stable, but an errant jade on a journey.'
   - Oliver Goldsmith

'All philosophies, if you ride them home, are nonsense; but some are greater nonsense than others.'
   - Samuel Butler

'A little philosophy inclineth man's mind to atheism; but depth in philosophy bringeth men's minds about to religion.'
   - Sir Francis Bacon

'Philosophy - the purple bullfinch in the lilac tree.'
   - T. S. Eliot

'The discovery of what is true and the practice of that which is good are the two most important objects of philosophy.'
   - Voltaire

'The unrest which keeps the never-stopping clock metaphysics going is the thought that the non-existence of this world is just as possible as its existence.'
   - William James

'Adversity's sweet milk, philosophy.'
   - William Shakespeare

'There are more things in heaven and earth, Horatio, Than are dreamt of in your philosophy.'
   - William Shakespeare

'For there was never yet philosopher That could endure the toothache patiently.'
   - William Shakespeare

POETRY

'One of Wordsworth's Lake District neighbours remarked, upon hearing of the poet's death "I suppose his son will carry on the business."'
- Anonymous

'It is Homer who has chiefly taught other poets the art of telling lies skillfully.'
- Aristotle

'Poetry is the opening and closing of a door, leaving those who look through to guess what is seen during a moment.'
- Carl Sandburg

'Poetry is the journal of a sea animal living on land, wanting to fly in the air.'
- Carl Sandburg

'The courage of the poet is to keep ajar the door that leads into madness.'
- Christopher Morley

'Most people do not believe in anything very much and our greatest poetry is given to us by those that do.'
- Cyril Connolly

'A good poem is a contribution to reality. The world is never the same once a good poem has been added to it. A good poem helps to change the shape and significance of the universe, helps to extend everyone's knowledge of himself and the world around him.'
- Dylan Thomas

'The essentials of poetry are rhythm, dance and the human voice.'
- Earle Birney

'The mind that finds its way to wild places is the poet's; but the mind that never finds its way back is the lunatic's.'
- G. K. Chesterton

'Popular poets are the parish priests of the Muse, retailing her ancient divinations to a long since converted public.'
- George Santayana

'Poets and painters are outside the class system, or rather they constitute a special class of their own, like the circus people and the gypsies.'
- Gerald Brenan

'Color, which is the poet's wealth, is so expensive that most take to mere outline sketches and become men of science.'
- Henry David Thoreau

'Before verse can be human again it must learn to be brutal.'
- J. M. Synge

'A drainless shower of light is poesy; 'tis the supreme of power; 'tis might half slumb'ring on its own right arm.'
- John Keats

'An art in which the artist by means of rhythm and great sincerity can convey to others the sentiment which he feels about life.'
- John Masefield

'Science is for those who learn; poetry for those who know.'
- Joseph Roux

'Poetry is all nouns and verbs.'
- Marianne Moore

'Poetry is the impish attempt to paint the color of the wind.'
- Maxwell Bodenheim

'Poetry is not a profession, it's a destiny.'
- Mikhail Dudan

'Poets aren't very useful, because they aren't consumeful or very produceful.'
- Ogden Nash

'When I feel inclined to read poetry I take down my dictionary. The poetry of words is quite as beautiful as that of sentences. The author may arrange the gems effectively but their shape and lustre have been given by the attrition of ages.'
- Oliver Wendell Holmes

'When you write in prose you say what you mean. When you write in rhyme you say what you must.'
- Oliver Wendell Holmes

'Not reading poetry amounts to a national pastime here.'
- Phyllis McGinley

'Poetry must be as new as foam, and as old as the rock.'
- Ralph Waldo Emerson

'A good poet is someone who manages, in a lifetime of standing out in thunderstorms, to be struck by lightning five or six times.'
- Randall Jarrell

'Writing free verse is like playing tennis with the net down.'
- Robert Frost

'Poetry is a way of taking life by the throat.'
- Robert Frost

'A poem begins with a lump in the throat; a homesickness or alovesickness. It is a reaching-out toward expression; an effort to find fulfillment. A complete poem is one where an emotion has found its thought and the thought has found words.'
- Robert Frost

'Poetry should be common in experience but uncommon in books.'
- Robert Frost

'There's no money in poetry, but then there's no poetry in money either.'
- Robert Graves

'I don't really feel my poems are mine at all. I didn't create them out of nothing. I owe them to my relations with other people.'
- Robert Graves

'For what is a poem but a hazardous attempt at self-understanding: it is the deepest part of autobiography.'
- Robert Penn Warren

'There are nine and sixty ways of constructing tribal lays, and every single one of them is right.'
- Rudyard Kipling

'I wish our clever young poets would remember my homely definitions of prose and poetry; that is, prose - words in their best order; poetry - the best words in their best order.'
- Samuel Taylor Coleridge

'Poetry is the language of a state of crisis.'
- Stephane Mallarme

'For me, poetry is an evasion of the real job of writing prose.'
- Sylvia Plath

'When a great poet has lived, certain things have been done once for all, and cannot be achieved again.'
- T. S. Eliot

'The poet's mind is ... a receptacle for seizing and storing up numberless feelings, phrases, images, which remain there until all the particles which can unite to form a new compound are present together.'
- T. S. Eliot

'No honest poet can ever feel quite sure of the permanent value of what he has written: he may have wasted his time and messed up his life for nothing.'
- T. S. Eliot

'Poetry is a mug's game.'
- T. S. Eliot

'When a poet's mind is perfectly equipped for its work, it is constantly amalgamating disparate experiences.'
- T. S. Eliot

'If Galileo had said in verse that the world moved, the Inquisition might have let him alone.'
- Thomas Hardy

'In poetry, you must love the words, the ideas and the images and rhythms with all your capacity to love anything at all.'
- Wallace Stevens

'The poet is the priest of the invisible.'
- Wallace Stevens

'To have great poets there must be great audiences too.'
- Walt Whitman

'Of our conflicts with others we make rhetoric; of our conflicts with ourselves we make poetry.'
- William Butler Yeats

'Most joyful let the Poet be, it is through him that all men see.'
- William Ellery Channing

POLITICS

'Democracy is the government of the people, by the people, for the people.'
  - Abraham Lincoln

'As I would not be a slave, so I would not be a master. This expresses my idea of democracy.'
  - Abraham Lincoln

'Honest statesmanship is the wise employment of individual meannesses for the public good.'
  - Abraham Lincoln

'They pick a president, and then for four years they pick on him.'
  - Adlai Stevenson

'An independent is a guy who wants to take the politics out of politics.'
  - Adlai Stevenson

'My definition of a free society is a society where it is safe to be unpopular.'
  - Adlai Stevenson

'Politics, and the fate of mankind, are shaped by men without ideals and without greatness.'
  - Albert Camus

'The world is a dangerous place to live - not because of the people who are evil but because of the people who don't do anything about it.'
  - Albert Einstein

'There are two problems in my life. The political ones are insoluble and the economic ones are incomprehensible.'
  - Alexander Douglas-Home

'Party-spirit . . . which at best is but the madness of many for the gain of a few.'
  - Alexander Pope

'In politics a community of hatred is almost always the foundation of friendships.'
  - Alexis de Tocqueville

'All the ills of democracy can be cured by more democracy.'
  - Alfred E. Smith

'I have never regarded politics as the arena of morals. It is the arena of interests.'
  - Aneurin Bevan

'Politics is a blood sport.'
  - Aneurin Bevan

'It's nice to have four years between elections. It takes people that long to regain their faith.'
   - Anonymous

'When Cicero (Marcus Tullius Cicero 106-43 BC,) was in 64 BC running for consul of Rome he was reported to be advised by his "campaign manager" that the voters "had rather you lied to them than refused them."'
   - Anonymous

'A politician is an animal who can sit on a fence and yet keep both ears to the ground.'
   - Anonymous

'What obstructs the vision and is called smog in our big cities is called defining the issues in politics'
   - Anonymous

'Man is by nature a civic animal.'
   - Aristotle

'The worst form of inequality is to try to make unequal things equal.'
   - Aristotle

'Ultimately politics in a democracy reflects values much more than it shapes them.'
   - Arnold A. Rogow

'I'm proud to be paying taxes in the United States. The only thing is - I could be just as proud for half the money.'
   - Arthur Godfrey

'The statesman shears the sheep, the politician skins them.'
   - Austin O'Malley

'A majority is always better than the best repartee.'
   - Benjamin Disraeli

'Damn your principles! Stick to your party!'
   - Benjamin Disraeli

'Vote for the man who promises least; he'll be the least disappointing.'
   - Bernard Baruch

'The greatest blessing of our democracy is freedom. But in the last analysis, our only freedom is the freedom to discipline ourselves.'
   - Bernard Baruch

'What matters in Politics is what men actually do - sincerity is no excuse for acting unpolitically, and insincerity may be channelled by politics into good results.'
   - Bernard Crick

'I have the perfect simplified tax form for government. Why don't they just print our money with a return address on it?'
- Bob Hope

'Forgiving is all; forgetting is another thing.'
- Bob Rae

'Congress is so strange. A man gets up to speak and says nothing. Nobody listens, then everybody disagrees.'
- Boris Marshalov

'It would be folly to argue that the people cannot make political mistakes. They can and do make grave mistakes. They know it, they pay the penalty, but compared with the mistakes which have been made by every kind of autocracy they are unimportant.'
- Calvin Coolidge

'In order to become the master, the politician poses as the servant.'
- Charles de Gaulle

'It will not be any European statesman who will unite Europe: Europe will be united by the Chinese.'
- Charles de Gaulle

'In politics it is necessary either to betray one's country or the electorate. I prefer to betray the electorate.'
- Charles de Gaulle

'While democracy must have its organization and controls, its vital breath is individual liberty.'
- Charles Evans Hughes

'Like an armed warrior, like a plumed knight, James G. Blaine marched down the halls of American Congress and threw his shining lance full and fair against the brazen foreheads of the defamers of his country, and the maligners of his honor.'
- Charles J. Ingersoll

'When I was a boy, I was told that anybody could become president. I'm beginning to believe it.'
- Clarence Darrow

'Nothing is politically right which is morally wrong.'
- Daniel O'Connell

'We're eyeball to eyeball, and I think the other fellow just blinked.'
- Dean Rusk

'Instead of giving a politician the keys to the city, it might be better to change the locks.'
- Doug Larson

'Democracy is the recurrent suspicion that more than half of the people are right more than half of the time.'
- E. B. White

'Democracy is a festival of mediocrity.'
- E. M. Cioran

'Politics. The diplomatic name for the law of the jungle.'
- Ely Culbertson

'He's like a football coach who's smart enough to win the game, and dumb enough to think it's important.'
- Eugene McCarthy

'It is dangerous for a national candidate to say things that people might remember.'
- Eugene McCarthy

'The Senate is the last primitive society in the world. We still worship the elders of the tribe and honor the territorial imperative.'
- Eugene McCarthy

'Dirksen's Three Laws of Politics: 1. Get elected. 2. Get re-elected. 3. Don't get mad, get even.'
- Everett Dirksen

'I pledge you, I pledge myself, to a new deal for the American people. Let us all here assembled constitute ourselves prophets of a new order of competence and courage. This is a call to arms.'
- Franklin D. Roosevelt

'Democracy means government by the uneducated, while aristocracy means government by the badly educated.'
- G. K. Chesterton

'Unlike Churchill, I have no plans to shape history. . . . Socrates gave advice - and they poisoned him.'
- George Bush

'Politics is the diversion of trivial men who, when they succeed at it, become important in the eyes of more trivial men.'
- George Jean Nathan

'In our age there is no such thing as 'keeping out of politics'. All issues are political issues.'
- George Orwell

'It is a condition which confronts us - not a theory.'
- Grover Cleveland

'The job of a citizen is to keep his mouth open.'
- Gunter Grass

'What men value in the world is not rights, but privileges.'
- H. L. Mencken

'I have never found, in a long experience of politics, that criticism is ever inhibited by ignorance.'
- Harold Macmillan

'It was a storm in a tea cup, but in politics we sail in paper boats.'
  - Harold Macmillan

'In politics a week is a very long time.'
  - Harold Wilson

'Democracy is based upon the conviction that there are extraordinary possibilities in ordinary people.'
  - Harry Emerson

'Democracy is based on the conviction that man has the moral and intellectual capacity, as well as the inalienable right, to govern himself with reason and justice.'
  - Harry S. Truman

'Practical politics consists in ignoring facts.'
  - Henry Adams

'Politics, as a practice, whatever its professions, has always been the systematic organization of hatreds.'
  - Henry Adams

'This organization (United Nations) is created to prevent you from going to hell. It isn't created to take you to heaven.'
  - Henry Cabot Lodge

'Politics is the gizzard of society, full of gut and gravel.'
  - Henry David Thoreau

'There cannot be a crisis next week. My schedule is already full.'
  - Henry Kissinger

'Once upon a time my political opponents honored me as possessing the fabulous intellectual and economic power by which I created a worldwide depression all by myself.'
  - Herbert Hoover

'A politician is a person who can make waves and then make you think he's the only one who can save the ship.'
  - Ivern Ball

'Democracy is a small hard core of common agreement, surrounded by a rich variety of individual differences.'
  - James Bryant Conant

'A politician thinks of the next election; a statesman, of the next generation.'
  - James Freeman Clarke

'Democracy is good. I say this because other systems are worse.'
  - Jawaharlal Nehru

'Elections in L.A. are so different. Here you've got politicians with phony smiles making false promises to voters with fake boobs and bad toupees.'
   - Jay Leno

'As a politician he does everything to keep out of trouble, often by not asking questions. However, it does bother him that every time the doorbell rings his maid hides in the dryer.'
   - Jay Leno

'It is the greatest good to the greatest number which is the measure of right and wrong.'
   - Jeremy Bent ham

'Money is the mother's milk of politics.'
   - Jesse Unruh

'All political parties die at last of swallowing their own lies.'
   - John Arbuthnot

'Politics is not a good location or a vocation for anyone lazy, thin-skinned or lacking a sense of humor.'
   - John Bailey

'Damned Neuters, in their Middle way of Steering, Are neither Fish, nor Flesh, nor good Red Herring.'
   - John Dryden

'I just received the following wire from my generous Daddy "Dear Jack: Don't buy a single vote more than necessary. I'll be damned if I am going to pay for a landslide."'
   - John F. Kennedy

'If we cannot now end our differences, at least we can help make the world safe for diversity.'
   - John F. Kennedy

'Those who make peaceful revolution impossible will make violent revolution inevitable.'
   - John F. Kennedy

'A question which can be answered without prejudice to the government is not a fit question to ask.'
   - John G. Diefenbaker

'The purification of politics is an iridescent dream.'
   - John Ingalls

'Politics is a field where Taking Action is one long second best and where the choice constantly lies between two blunders.'
   - John Morley

'Vice president: A spare tire on the automobile of government.'
   - John Nance Garner

'In politics, a straight line is the shortest distance to disaster.'
   - John P. Roche

'Poetry was the maiden I loved, but politics was the harridan I married.'
- Joseph Howe

'All I know is I'm not a Marxist.'
- Karl Marx

'There is no worse heresy than that the office sanctifies the holder of it.'
- Lord Acton

'If people have to choose between freedom and sandwiches they will take sandwiches.'
- Lord Boyd-Orr

'As I learnt very early in my life in Whitehall, the acid test of any political question is: What is the alternative?'
- Lord Trent

'Politics is war without bloodshed, and war is politics with blood.'
- Mao Tse-Tung

'Liberals think you can reform an ax murderer. They don't want to kill anything. They want to change the Listerine labels to "Rehabilitate the germs that cause bad breath."'
- Marc Price

'Any woman who understands the problems of running a home will be nearer to understanding the problems of running a country.'
- Margaret Thatcher

'The lady's not for turning.'
- Margaret Thatcher

'The radical invents the views. When he has worn them out, the conservative adopts them.'
- Mark Twain

'Three people marooned on a desert island would soon reinvent politics.'
- Mason Cooley

'This proves what a purifying effect women would have on politics.'
- Nellie McClung

'Politics is not an exact science.'
- Otto von Bismarck

'The public is very fickle, as I was saying to my cabdriver, Gerald Ford.'
- Pat McCormick

'In academic life you seek to state absolute truths; in politics you seek to accommodate truth to the facts around you.'
- Pierre Elliott Trudeau

'The essential ingredient of politics is timing.'
- Pierre Elliott Trudeau

'The heaviest penalty for deciding to engage in politics is to be ruled by someone inferior to yourself.'
- Plato

'Deep down he is shallow.'
- Political saying

'There is a certain satisfTaking Action in coming down to the lowest ground of politics, for then we get rid of cant and hypocrisy.'
- Ralph Waldo Emerson

'I don't pick on politicians. They ain't done nothin'.'
- Red Skelton

'The sad duty of politics is to establish justice in a sinful world.'
- Reinhold Niebuhr

'You know very well that whether you are on page one or page thirty depends on whether they fear you. It is just as simple as that.'
- Richard Nixon

'Men in high levels of government seldom surf.'
- Rita Rudner

'One fifth of the people are against everything all the time.'
- Robert F. Kennedy

'Did you ever see that painting the Mona Lisa. It always reminds me of a reporter listening to a politician.'
- Robert Orben

'Politics is supposed to be the second oldest profession. I have come to realize that it bears a very close resemblance to the first.'
- Ronald Reagan

'A dictatorship is a country where they have taken the politics out of politics.'
- Sam Himmel

'Politics is the science of how who gets what, when and why.'
- Sidney Hillman

'If you want to understand democracy, spend less time in the library with Plato, and more time in the buses with people.'
- Simeon Strunsky

'Nobody is qualified to become a statesman who is entirely ignorant of the problems of wheat.'
- Socrates

'The great nations have always acted like gangsters, and the small nations like prostitutes.'
  - Stanley Kubrick

'A politician is a fellow who will lay down your life for his country.'
  - Texas Guinan

'Democracy means not "I am as good as you are," but "You are as good as I am."'
  - Theodore Parker

'My hat's in the ring. The fight is one and I'm stripped to the buff.'
  - Theodore Roosevelt

'There is no excitement anywhere in the world, short of war, to match the excitement of the American presidential campaign.'
  - Theodore White

'If a due participation of office is a matter of right, how are vacancies to be obtained? Those by death are few; by resignation, none.'
  - Thomas Jefferson

'The trouble with socialists is that they let their bleeding hearts go to their bloody heads.'
  - Tommy Douglas

'A conservative is a Democrat who's been mugged. I think we should just tip the government if it does a good job. Fifteen percent is the standard tip, isn't it?'
  - Vat Paulsen

'I always voted at my party's call, And I never thought of thinking for myself at all.'
  - W. S. Gilbert

'The prerequisites for being in the diplomatic corps are the ability to handle protocol, alcohol, and Geritol.'
  - Wallace Rowling

'People often say that, in a democracy, decisions are made by a majority of the people. Of course, that is not true. Decisions are made by a majority of those who make themselves heard and who vote - a very different thing.'
  - Walter H. Judd

'In a democracy, the opposition is not only tolerated as constitutional, but must be maintained because it is indispensable.'
  - Walter Lippmann

'Politics is but the common pulse beat.'
  - Wendell Phillips

'He is so aware of being politically correct he refers to a taco as Hispanic food.'
  - Wendy Morgan

'The Republicans have their splits right after election and Democrats have theirs just before an election.'
    - Will Rogers

'The more you read about politics, the more you got to admit that each party is worse than the other.'
    - Will Rogers

'Politics has got so expensive that it takes lots of money to even get beat with.'
    - Will Rogers

'If you ever injected truth into politics you would have no politics.'
    - Will Rogers

'A statesman is an easy man, He tells his lies by rote; A journalist makes up his lies And takes you by the throat; So stay at home and drink your beer And let the neighbours vote.'
    - William Butler Yeats

'To the victor belong the spoils of the enemy.'
    - William L. Marcy

'As long as I count the votes what are you going to do about it?'
    - William M. Tweed

'Something is rotten in the state of Denmark.'
    - William Shakespeare

'If nominated I will not accept; if elected I will not serve.'
    - William Tecumseh Sherman

'Who is the dark horse he has in his stable?'
    - William Thackeray

'The Labor Party is going about the country stirring up apathy.'
    - William White law

'Harold Wilson is going around the country stirring up apathy.'
    - William Whitelaw

'Politics is more dangerous than war, for in war you are only killed once.'
    - Winston Churchill

'It has been said that Democracy is the worst form of government except all those other forms that have been tried from time to time.'
    - Winston Churchill

'Nothing was ever done so systematically as nothing is being done now.'
    - Woodrow Wilson

'The world must be made safe for democracy.'
- Woodrow Wilson

'I believe in Democracy because it releases the energies of every human being.'
- Woodrow Wilson

POSITIVE

'The words "I am ..." are potent words; be careful what you hitch them to. The thing you're claiming has a way of reaching back and claiming you.'
- A. L. Kitselman

'Politeness is the art of choosing among one's real thoughts.'
- Abel Stevens

'If they do kill me, I shall never die another death.'
- Abraham Lincoln

'If you act like you're rich, you'll get rich.'
- Adnan Koashoggi

'Wit is the salt of conversation, not the food, and few things in the world are more wearying than a sarcastic attitude towards life.'
- Agnes Repplier

'All seems infected that the infected spy, as all looks yellow to the jaundiced eye.'
- Alexander Pope

'A person who doubts himself is like a man who would enlist in the ranks of his enemies and bear arms against himself. He makes his failure certain by himself being the first person to be convinced of it.'
- Alexandre Dumas

'We think in generalities, but we live in detail.'
- Alfred North Whitehead

'It is only in sorrow bad weather masters us; in joy we face the storm and defy it.'
- Amelia Barr

'The quality of our expectations determines the quality of our Taking Action.'
- Andre Godin

'Immense power is acquired by assuring yourself in your secret reveries that you were born to control affairs.'
- Andrew Carnegie

'Hate is like acid. It can damage the vessel in which it is stored as well as destroy the object on which it is poured.'
- Ann Landers

'God will help you if you try, and you can if you think you can.'
- Anna Delaney Peale

'Think of all the beauty that's still left in and around you and be happy!'
- Anne Frank

'I keep my ideals, because in spite of everything I still believe that people are really good at heart.'
- Anne Frank

'He was a "how" thinker, not an "if" thinker.'
- Anonymous

'Some folks think they are thinking when they are only rearranging their prejudices.'
- Anonymous

'Always imitate the behavior of the winner when you lose.'
- Anonymous

'People, by and large, will relate to the image you project.'
- Anonymous

'The only prison we need to escape from is the prison of our own minds.'
- Anonymous

'If you prepare for old age, old age comes sooner.'
- Anonymous

'Man is what he believes.'
- Anton Chekhov

'We become just by performing just Taking Actions, temperate by performing temperate Taking Actions, brave by performing brave Taking Actions.'
- Aristotle

'The way in which we think of ourselves has everything to do with how our world sees us.'
- Arlene Raven

'One of the most devastating experiences in human life is disillusionment.'
- Art Sisson

'I have found that if you love life, life will love you back.'
- Arthur Rubinstein

'Some folks never exaggerate-they just remember big.'
- Audrey Snead

'The evil of the world is made possible by nothing but the sanction you give it.'
- Ayn Rand

'Every man is free to rise as far as he's able or willing, but the degree to which he thinks determines the degree to which he'll rise.'
- Ayn Rand

'Attempt easy tasks as if they were difficult, and difficult as if they were easy; in the one case that confidence may not fall asleep, in the other that it may not be dismayed.'
- Baltasar Gracian

'Believe there is a great power silently working all things for good, behave yourself and never mind the rest.'
- Beatrix Potter

'We are what we believe we are.'
- Benjamin N. Cardozo

'What we love, we shall grow to resemble.'
- Bernard of Clairvaux

'Teenagers travel in droves, packs, swarms. ... To the librarian, they're a gaggle of geese. To the cook, they're a scourge of locusts. To department stores, they're a big beautiful exaltation of larks ... all lovely and loose and jingly.'
- Bernice Fitz-Gibbon

'The weak are the most treacherous of us all. They come to the strong and drain them. They are bottomless. They are insatiable. They are always parched and always bitter. They are everyone's concern and like vampires they suck our life's blood.'
- Bette Davis

'Whoso diggeth a pit shall fall therein.'
- Bible

'I never lost a game. I just ran out of time.'
- Bobby Layne

'All that we are is the result of what we have thought. The mind is everything. What we think, we become.'
- Buddha

'Fear breeds fear.'
- Byron Janis

'Always keep that happy attitude. Pretend that you are holding a beautiful fragrant bouquet.'
- Candice M. Pope

'Happiness is the ability to recognize it.'
- Carolyn Wells

'In rejecting secrecy I had also rejected the road to cynicism.'
- Catharine Marshall

'Power without [the people's] confidence is nothing.'
- Catherine the Great

'Life is raw material. We are artisans. We can sculpt our existence into something beautiful, or debase it into ugliness. It's in our hands.'
- Cathy Better

'If we are not responsible for the thoughts that pass our doors, we are at least responsible for those we admit and entertain.'
- Charles B. Newcomb

'It is good to act as if. It is even better to grow to the point where it is no longer an act.'
- Charles Caleb Colton

'The Wright brothers flew right through the smoke screen of impossibility.'
- Charles Franklin Kettering

'If a man plants melons he will reap melons; if he sows beans, he will reap beans.'
- Chinese proverb

'The person who says it cannot be done should not interrupt the person doing it.'
- Chinese proverb

'Journal writing is a voyage to the interior.'
- Christina Baldwin

'I don't believe in pessimism.'
- Clint Eastwood

'If you think it's going to rain, it will.'
- Clint Eastwood

'I invented my life by taking for granted that everything I did not like would have an opposite, which I would like.'
- Coco Chanel

'Work is either fun or drudgery. It depends on your attitude. I like fun.'
- Colleen C. Barrett

'Act as if you were already happy, and that will tend to make you happy.'
- Dale Carnegie

'Those who foresee the future and recognize it as tragic are often seized by a madness which forces them to commit the very acts which makes it certain that what they dread shall happen.'
- Dame Rebecca West

'I can't say I was ever lost, but I was bewildered once for three days.'
- Daniel Boone

'In the long run, the pessimist may be proved to be right, but the optimist has a better time on the trip.'
- Daniel L. Reardon

'Preparing for the worst is an activity I have taken up since I turned thirty-five, and the worst actually began to happen.'
- Delia Ephron

'We criticize and separate ourselves from the process. We've got to jump right in there with both feet.'
- Dolores Huerta

'Act as if it were impossible to fail.'
- Dorothea Brande

'There are seeds of self-destruction in all of us that will bear only unhappiness if allowed to grow.'
- Dorothea Brande

'You have to believe in happiness, or happiness never comes.'
- Douglas Malloch

'Our best friends and our worst enemies are our thoughts. A thought can do us more good than a doctor or a banker or a faithful friend. It can also do us more harm than a brick.'
- Dr. Frank Crane

'You can either give in to negative feelings or fight them, and I'm of the belief that you should fight them.'
- Dr. Ruth Westheimer

'No one can defeat us unless we first defeat ourselves.'
- Dwight D. Eisenhower

'Think positively and masterfully, with confidence and faith, and life becomes more secure, more fraught with Taking Action, richer in achievement and experience.'
- Eddie Rickenbacker

'I am dying, but otherwise I am quite well.'
- Edith Sitwell

'Dangers by being despised grow great.'
- Edmund Burke

'The biggest quality in successful people, I think, is an impatience with negative thinking ... my feeling was, even if it's as bad as I think it is, we'll make it work.'
- Edward McCabe

'The thing we fear we bring to pass.'
- Elbert Hubbard

'Where much is expected from an individual, he may rise to the level of events and make the dream come true.'
- Elbert Hubbard

'We awaken in others the same attitude of mind we hold toward them.'
- Elbert Hubbard

'If any has a stone to throw It is not I, ever or now.'
- Elinor Wylie

'Mankind's greatest gift... is that we have free choice.'
- Elisabeth Kubler-Ross

'If you look at life one way, there is always cause for alarm.'
- Elizabeth Bowen

'To know how to say what others only know how to think is what makes men poets or sages; and to dare to say what others only dare to think makes men martyrs or reformers-or both.'
- Elizabeth Charles

'We have learned that power is a positive force if it is used for positive purposes.'
- Elizabeth Dole

'It is easy enough to be pleasant, when life flows by like a song. But the man worthwhile is one who will smile, when everything goes dead wrong.'
- Ella Wheeler Wilcox

'A good heart will help you to a bonny face, my lad ... and a bad one will turn the bonniest into something worse than ugly.'
- Emily Bronte

'He that seeks trouble always finds it.'
- English proverb

'If you wish to live a life free from sorrow, think of what is going to happen as if it had already happened.'
- Epictetus

'However much we guard against it, we tend to shape ourselves in the image others have of us.'
- Eric Hoffer

'We are made kind by being kind.'
- Eric Hoffer

'Positive Thinking Is Practical There is in the worst of fortune the best of chances for a happy change.'
- Euripides

'You live with your thoughts-so be careful what they are.'
- Eva Arrington

'You end up as you deserve. In old age you must put up with the face, the friends, the health, and the children you have earned.'
- Fay Weldon

'Our minds can shape the way a thing will be because we act according to our expectations.'
- Federico Fellini

'Act so as to elicit the best in others and thereby in thyself.'
- Felix Adler

'Liberty cannot be caged into a charter and handed on ready-made to the next generation. Each generation must recreate liberty for its own times. Whether or not we establish freedom rests with ourselves.'
- Florence Ellinwood Allen

'I attribute my success to this: I never gave or took an excuse.'
- Florence Nightingale

'If one asks for success and prepares for failure, he will get the situation he has prepared for.'
- Florence Scovel Shinn

'Doubt indulged soon becomes doubt realized.'
- Frances Ridley Havergal

'It is healthier to see the good points of others than to analyze our own bad ones.'
- Franchise Sagan

'To expect defeat is nine-tenths of defeat itself.'
- Francis Marion Crawford

'There are more defects in temperament than in the mind.'
- Francois de La Rochefoucauld

'The confidence which we have in ourselves gives birth to much of that which we have in others.'
- Francois de La Rochefoucauld

'To establish oneself in the world, one has to do all one can to appear established.'
- Francois de La Rochefoucauld

'I will say this about being an optimist: even when things don't turn out well, you are certain they will get better.'
- Frank Hughes

'The thing always happens that you really believe in; and the belief in a thing makes it happen.'
- Frank Lloyd Wright

'Doubt breeds doubt.'
- Franz Grillparzer

'You just can't complain about being alive. It's self-indulgent to be unhappy.'
- Gena Rowland

'They've got us surrounded again, the poor bastards.'
- General Creighton W. Abrams

'Retreat? We're coming out of here as a Marine division. We're bring ... our dead. Retreat, hell! We're just advancing in another direction.'
- General Oliver Prince Smith

'It is never too late to be what you might have been.'
- George Eliot

'Play not with paradoxes. That caustic which you handle in order to scorch others may happen to sear your own fingers and make them dead to the quality of things.'
- George Eliot

'An ass may bray a good while before he shakes the stars down.'
- George Eliot

'No man can think clearly when his fists are clenched.'
- George Jean Nathan

'What you think means more than anything else in your life.'
- George Matthew Adams

'Cynicism is intellectual dandyism.'
- George Meredith

'Persistent prophecy is a familiar way of assuring the event.'
- George R. Gissing

'Knock the "t" off the "can't."'
- George Reeves

'It is by sitting down to write every morning that he becomes a writer. Those who do not do this remain amateurs.'
- Gerald Brenan

'Pessimism is a luxury that a Jew can never afford himself.'
- Golda Meir

'Rosiness is not a worse windowpane than gloomy gray when viewing the world.'
- Grace Paley

'Whatever the ups and downs of detail within our limited experience, the larger whole is primarily beautiful.'
- Gregory Bateson

'Make your judgement trustworthy by trusting it.'
- Grenville Kleiser

'Am I like the optimist who, while falling ten stories from a building, says at each story, "I'm all right so far"?'
- Gretel Ehrlich

'Beauty to me is being comfortable in your own skin.'
- Gwyneth Paltrow

'If you want your children to improve, let them overhear the nice things you say about them to others.'
- Haim Ginott

'Revolve your world around the customer and more customers will revolve around you.'
- Heather Williams

'After you're older, two things are possibly more important than any others: health and money.'
- Helen Gurley Brown

'I long to accomplish a great and noble task, but it is my chief duty to accomplish small tasks as if they were great and noble.'
- Helen Keller

'To keep our faces toward change, and behave like free spirits in the presence of fate, is strength undefeatable.'
- Helen Keller

'No pessimist ever discovered the secrets of the stars, or sailed to an uncharted land, or opened a new heaven to the human spirit.'
- Helen Keller

'Think like a man of Taking Action, act like a man of thought.'
- Henri Bergson

'The way a man's mind runs is the way he is sure to go.'
- Henry B. Wilson

'We are always paid for our suspicion by finding what we suspect.'
- Henry David Thoreau

'What a man thinks of himself, that is what determines, or rather indicates, his fate.'
- Henry David Thoreau

'The faultfinder will find faults even in paradise.'
- Henry David Thoreau

'Events, circumstances, etc., have their origin in ourselves. They spring from seeds which we have sown.'
- Henry David Thoreau

'I cannot discover that anyone knows enough to say definitely what is and what is not possible.'
- Henry Ford

'Think you can, think you can't; either way, you'll be right.'
- Henry Ford

'Keep your thoughts right, for as you think, so are you. Therefore, think only those things that will make the world better, and you unashamed.'
- Henry H. Buckley

'The only way to make a man trustworthy is to trust him.'
- Henry L. Stimson

'We create our fate every day ... most of the ills we suffer from are directly traceable to our own behavior.'
- Henry Miller

'The world is like a mirror; frown at it, and it frowns at you. Smile and it smiles, too.'
- Herbert Samuel

'If you would be powerful, pretend to be powerful.'
- Home Tooke

'When you look at the world in a narrow way, how narrow it seems! When you look at it in a mean way, how mean it is! When you look at it selfishly, how selfish it is! But when you look at it in a broad, generous, friendly spirit, what wonderful people you '
- Horace Rutledge

'Be careful of your thoughts; they may become words at any moment.'
- Ira Gassen

'If you keep saying things are going to be bad, you have a good chance of being a prophet.'
- Isaac Bashevis Singer

'Men have a trick of coming up to what is expected of them, good or bad.'
- Jacob A. Riis

'Never think any oldish thoughts. It's oldish thoughts that make a person old.'
- James A. Farley

'You can promote your healing by your thinking.'
- James E. Sweeney

'Like begets like; honesty begets honesty; trust, trust; and so on.'
- James F. Bell

'A man is literally what he thinks.'
- James Lane Allen

'Man's rise or fall, success or failure, happiness or unhappiness depends on his attitude ... a man's attitude will create the situation he imagines.'
- James Lane Allen

'As you think, you travel, and as you love, you attract. You are today where your thoughts have brought you; you will be tomorrow where your thoughts take you.'
- James Lane Allen

'We must dare to think unthinkable thoughts.'
- James W. Fulbright

'To make the world a friendly place, one must show it a friendly face.'
- James Whitcomb Riley

'What after all has maintained the human race on this old globe, despite all the calamities of nature and all the tragic failings of mankind, if not the faith in new possibilities and the courage to advocate them?'
- Jane Adams

'A person who can write a long letter with ease, cannot write ill.'
- Jane Austen

'Carry on, carry on, for the men and boys are gone, But the furrow shan't lie fallow while the women carry on.'
- Janet Begbie

'I made the decision. I'm accountable.'
- Janet Reno

'Fake feeling good. ... You're going to have to learn to fake cheerfulness. Believe it or not, eventually that effort will pay off: you'll actually start feeling happier.'
- Jean Bach

'We must laugh before we are happy, for fear of dying without having laughed at all.'
- Jean de la Bruyere

'There are certain people who so ardently and passionately desire a thing, that from dread of losing it they leave nothing undone to make them lose it.'
- Jean de la Bruyere

'The more wary you are of danger, the more likely you are to meet it.'
- Jean de la Fontaine

'Do not sit long with a sad friend. When you go to a garden do you look at the weeds? Spend more time with the roses and jasmines.'
- Jelaluddin Rumi

'My voice is still the same, and this makes me beside myself with Joy! Oh, mon Dieu, when I think what I might be able to do with it!'
- Jenny Lind

'The body manifests what the mind harbors.'
- Jerry Augustine

'You can't pay attention to your mistakes. I made a mistake today, I made a mistake yesterday. I think it's ... very important to ignore the negative.'
- Jerry Rubin

'The willingness to accept responsibility for one's own life is the source from which self-respect springs.'
- Joan Didion

'Exude happiness and you will feel it back a thousand times.'
- Joan Lunden

'Treat people as if they were what they should be, and you help them become what they are capable of becoming.'
- Johann von Goethe

'The basic success orientation is having an optimistic attitude.'
- John DePasquale

'You can't be pessimistic, because there are so many things that go wrong every day that if you were to be negative or pessimistic, you'd go out of business.'
- John DePasquale

'How much shall I be changed, before I am changed!'
- John Donnell

'What one believes to be true either is true or becomes true within limits to be found experientially and experimentally. These limits are beliefs to be transcended.'
- John Lilly

'What we see depends mainly on what we look for.'
- John Lubbock

'If fear is cultivated it will become stronger, if faith is cultivated it will achieve mastery.'
- John Paul Jones

'Any man will usually get from other men just what he is expecting of them. If he is looking for friendship he will likely receive it. If his attitude is that of indifference, it will beget indifference. And if a man is looking for a fight, he will in all '
- John Richelsen

'Dream lofty dreams, and as you dream, so shall you become. Your vision is the promise of what you shall at last unveil.'
- John Ruskin

'It is the nature of man to rise to greatness if greatness is expected of him.'
- John Steinbeck

'I couldn't hit a wall with a six-gun, but I can twirl one. It looks good.'
- John Wayne

'Opportunities multiply as they are seized; they die when neglected. Life is a long line of opportunities.'
- John Wicker

'Debt is a trap which man sets and baits himself, and then deliberately gets into.'
- Josh Billings

'When you're in love, you put up with things that, when you're out of love you cite.'
- Judith Martin

'Love is much nicer to be in than an automobile accident, a tight girdle, a higher tax bracket, or a holding pattern over Philadelphia.'
- Judith Viorst

'Look for the ridiculous in everything and you find it.'
- Jules Renard

'Being tall is an advantage, especially in business. People will always remember you. And if you're in a crowd, you'll always have some clean air to breathe.'
- Julia Child

'Who soweth good seed shall surely reap; The year grows rich as it groweth old, And life's latest sands are its sands of gold!'
- Julia Dorr

'We choose our joys and sorrows long before we experience them.'
- Kahlil Gibran

'The name we give to something shapes our attitude toward it.'
- Katherine Paterson

'Charm is the ability to make someone else think that both of you are pretty wonderful.'
- Kathleen Winsor

'We can destroy ourselves by cynicism and disillusion, just as affectively as by bombs.'
- Kenneth Clark

'Being an optimist after you've got everything you want doesn't count.'
- Kin Hubbard

'We are what we pretend to be, so we must be careful about what we pretend to be.'
- Kurt Vonnegut

'Isn't it splendid to think of all the things there are to find out about? It just makes me feel glad to be alive- it's such an interesting world.'
- L. M. Montgomery

'The pessimist sees the difficulty in every opportunity; the optimist sees the opportunity in every difficulty.'
- L. P. Jacks

'Any committee is only as good as the most knowledgeable, determined, and vigorous person on it. There must be somebody who provides the flame.'
- Lady Bird Johnson

'Children are likely to live up to what you believe of them.'
- Lady Bird Johnson

'He who has not faith in others shall find no faith in them.'
- Lao-Tzu

'Anyone can have an off decade.'
- Larry Cole

'If enough people think of a thing and work hard enough at it, I guess it's pretty nearly bound to happen, wind and weather permitting.'
- Laura Ingalls Wilder

'If you are going to think black, think positive about it. Don't think down on it, or think it is something in your way. And this way, when you really do want to stretch out and express how beautiful black is, everybody will hear you.'
- Leontyne Price

'The wisdom of all ages and cultures emphasizes the tremendous power our thoughts have over our character and circumstances.'
- Liane Cordes

'It is best to act with confidence, no matter how little right you have to it.'
- Lillian Hellman

'Here is where some entrepreneurs fail. They are filled with creative juices and total commitment to their business, but too often they don't understand that they must also be managers, administrators, even gofers-at least for a while.'
- Lillian Vernon

'This I conceive to be the chemical function of humor: to change the character of our thought.'
- Lin Yutang

'Choice is the essence of what I believe it is to be human.'
- Liv Ullmann

''Tis very certain the desire of life prolongs it.'
- Lord Byron

'There is no miraculous change that takes place in a boy that makes him a man. He becomes a man by being a man.'
- Louis L'Amour

'She was one of those happily created beings who please without effort, make friends everywhere, and take life so gracefully and easily that less fortunate souls are tempted to believe that such are born under a lucky star.'
- Louisa May Alcott

'True revolutions ... restore more than they destroy.'
- Louise Bogan

'Every thought we think is creating our future.'
- Louise L. Hay

'The mere apprehension of a coming evil has put many into a situation of the utmost danger.'
- Lucan

'One of the things I learned the hard way was that it doesn't pay to get discouraged. Keeping busy and making optimism a way of life can restore your faith in yourself.'
- Lucille Ball

'I expect some new phases of life this summer, and shall try to get the honey from each moment.'
- Lucy Stone

'Life has, indeed, many ills, but the mind that views every object in its most cheering aspect, and every doubtful dispensation as replete with latent good, bears within itself a powerful and perpetual antidote.'
- Lydia H. Sigourney

'1 Give to the world the best you have I and the best will come back to you.'
- Madeline Bridges

'Fear to let fall a drop and you spill a lot.'
- Malay proverb

'If you expect nothing, you're apt to be surprised. You'll get it.'
- Malcolm Forbes

'A man's life is what his thoughts make it.'
- Marcus Aurelius

'For years I wanted to be older, and now I am.'
- Margaret Atwood

'A voice is a human gift; it should be cherished and used, to utter as fully human speech as possible. Powerlessness and silence go together.'
- Margaret Atwood

'A word after a word after a word is power.'
- Margaret Atwood

'A sneer is like a flame; it may occasionally be curative because it cauterizes, but it leaves a bitter scar.'
- Margaret Deland

'I actually remember feeling delight, at two o'clock in the morning, when the baby woke for his feed, because I so longed to have another look at him.'
- Margaret Drabble

'We make our own criminals, and their crimes are congruent with the national culture we all share. It has been said that a people get the kind of political leadership they deserve. I think they also get the kinds of crime and criminals they themselves brin'
- Margaret Mead

'Live as if you like yourself, and it may happen.'
- Marge Piercy

'I am one of those people who are blessed ... with a nature which has to interfere. If I see a thing that needs doing I do it.'
- Margery Allingham

'The optimism of a healthy mind is indefatigable.'
- Margery Allingham

'We have seen too much defeatism, too much pessimism, too much of a negative approach.'
- Margo Jones

'If you don't like the way the world is, you change it. You have an obligation to change it. You just do it one step at a time.'
- Marian Wright Edelman

'If we choose to be no more than clods of clay, then we shall be used as clods of clay for braver feet to tread on.'
- Marie Corelli

'Give me good health and I'll take care of the rest.'
- Marilyn Home

'A man would prefer to come home to an unmade bed and a happy woman than to a neatly made bed and an angry woman.'
- Marlene Dietrich

'My center is giving way, my right is in retreat: situation excellent. I am attacking.'
- Marshal Ferdinand Foch

'They never raised a statue to a critic.'
- Martha Graham

'Lifting as they climb, onward and upward they go, struggling and striving and hoping that the buds and blossoms of their desires may burst into glorious fruition ere long.'
- Mary Church Terrell

'If you think you can, you can. And if you think you can't, you're right.'
- Mary Kay Ash

'Cease to be a drudge, seek to be an artist.'
- Mary McLeod Bethune

'The process of maturing is an art to be learned, an effort to be sustained. By the age of fifty, you have made yourself what you are, and if it is good, it is better than your youth.'
- Marya Mannes

'Nothing befalls us that is not of the nature of ourselves. There comes no adventure but wears to our soul the shape of our everyday thoughts.'
- Maurice Maeterlinck

'Self-image sets the boundaries of individual accomplishment.'
- Maxwell Maltz

'Our self-image, strongly held, essentially determines what we become.'
- Maxwell Maltz

'It was completely fruitless to quarrel with the world, whereas the quarrel with oneself was occasionally fruitful and always, she had to admit, interesting.'
- May Sarton

'When people asked, I used to tell them how sick I was. The more I talked about being sick, the worse I got. Finally, I started saying, "I'm getting better." It took a while, but then I started to feel better, too.'
- Michael Hirsch

'He who fears he shall suffer, already suffers what he fears.'
- Michel de Montaigne

'To believe in God is to yearn for His existence, and furthermore, it is to act as if He did exist.'
- Miguel de Unamuno

'I've never been poor, only broke. Being poor is a frame of mind. Being broke is a temporary situation.'
- Mike Todd

'Tragedy had its compensations. Once the worst misfortune occurred, one never worried about the minor ones.'
- Mildred Davis

'The best course was to buy a house across a road from a cemetery and look at it every morning. Reminding yourself where it all ended anyway, you'd never get upset about anything again.'
- Mildred Davis

'We are accountable only to ourselves for what happens to us in our lives.'
- Mildred Newman

'To find oneself jilted is a blow to one's pride. One must do one's best to forget it and if one doesn't succeed, at least one must pretend to.'
- Moliere

'While you don't need a formal written contract before you get married, I think it's important for both partners to spell out what they expect from each other.... There are always plenty of surprises-and lots of give and take-once you're married.'
- Muriel Fox

'I think there is a choice possible to us at any moment, as long as we live. But there is no sacrifice. There is a choice, and the rest falls away. Second choice does not exist. Beware of those who talk about sacrifice.'
- Muriel Rukeyser

'It is no use blaming the men-we made them what they are-and now it is up to us to try and make ourselves-the makers of men-a little more responsible.'
- Nancy Astor

'He who fears being conquered is sure of defeat.'
- Napoleon Bonaparte

'Circumstances-what are circumstances? I make circumstances.'
- Napoleon Bonaparte

'We planted flowers last year, and I didn't know if I'd be alive to see them come up.'
- Neal McHugh

'A vacant mind invites dangerous inmates, as a deserted mansion tempts wandering outcasts to enter and take up their abode in its desolate apartments.'
- Nicholas Hilliard

'Optimism is essential to achievement and is also the foundation of courage and of true progress.'
- Nicholas Murray Butler

'Success produces success, just as money produces money.'
- Nicolas de Chamfort

'Since the human body tends to move in the direction of its expectations-plus or minus-it is important to know that attitudes of confidence and determination are no less a part of the treatment program than medical science and technology.'
- Norman Cousins

'A human being fashions his consequences as surely as he fashions his goods or his dwelling. Nothing that he says, thinks or does is without consequences.'
- Norman Cousins

'Getting people to like you is merely the other side of liking them.'
- Norman Vincent Peale

'Change your thoughts and you change your world.'
- Norman Vincent Peale

'Our destiny changes with our thoughts; we shall become what we wish to become, do what we wish to do, when our habitual thoughts correspond with our desires.'
- Orison Swett Marden

'There is a very real relationship, both quantitatively and qualitatively, between what you contribute and what you get out of this world.'
- Oscar Hammerstein II

'How things look on the outside of us depends on how things are on the inside of us.'
- Park Cousins

'People are not going to love you unless you love them.'
- Pat Carroll

'Life is like a mirror. Smile at it and it smiles back at you.'
- Peace Pilgrim

'This is the way of peace-overcome evil with good, and falsehood with truth, and hatred with love.'
- Peace Pilgrim

'All things are possible until they are proved impossible-and even the impossible may only be so as of now.'
- Pearl S. Buck

'Your imagination has much to do with your life. ... It is for you to decide how you want your imagination to serve you.'
- Philip Conley

'I'm in a wonderful position: I'm unknown, I'm underrated, and there's nowhere to go but up.'
- Pierre S. DuPont IV

'The soul contains the event that shall befall it, for the event is only the actualization of its thoughts, and what we pray to ourselves for is always granted.'
- Ralph Waldo Emerson

'There are people who have an appetite for grief; pleasure is not strong enough and they crave pain. They have mithridatic stomachs which must be fed on poisoned bread, natures so doomed that no prosperity can sooth their ragged and disheveled desolation.'
- Ralph Waldo Emerson

'People only see what they are prepared to see.'
- Ralph Waldo Emerson

'A man is a method, a progressive arrangement; a selecting principle, gathering his like unto him wherever he goes. What you are comes to you.'
- Ralph Waldo Emerson

'Trust men and they will be true to you; treat them greatly and they will show themselves great.'
- Ralph Waldo Emerson

'A man is what he thinks about all day long.'
- Ralph Waldo Emerson

'Great men are they who see that the spiritual is stronger than any material force, that thoughts rule the world.'
- Ralph Waldo Emerson

'Skill to do comes of doing.'
- Ralph Waldo Emerson

'The principle of life is that life responds by corresponding; your life becomes the thing you have decided it shall be.'
- Raymond Charles Barker

'Illusory joy is often worth more than genuine sorrow.'
- Rene Descartes

'To heal ourselves we also have to heal society.'
- Riane Eisler

'Lead me not into temptation; I can find the way myself.'
- Rita Mae Brown

'It seems to me probably that any one who has a series of intolerable positions to put up with must have been responsible for them to some extent... they have contributed to it by impatience or intolerance, or brusqueness-or some provocation.'
- Robert Hugh Benson

'Positive thinking is the key to success in business, education, pro football, anything that you can mention. I go out there thinking that I am going to complete every pass.'
- Ron Jaworski

'I do think that being the second [female Supreme Court Justice] is wonderful, because it is a sign that being a woman in a place of importance is no longer extraordinary.'
- Ruth Bader Ginsberg

'Discussing how old you are is the temple of boredom.'
- Ruth Gordon

'People have a way of becoming what you encourage them to be-not what you nag them to be.'
- S. N. Parker

'If we live good lives, the times are also good. As we are, such are the times.'
- Saint Augustine

'Once you begin to believe there is help "out there," you will know it to be true.'
- Saint Bartholomew

'He who sows courtesy reaps friendship, and he who plants kindness gathers love.'
- Saint Basil

'Clear your mind of "can't."'
- Samuel Johnson

'If you make fun of bad persons you make yourself beneath them. ... Be kind to bad and good, for you don't know your own heart.'
- Sarah Winnemucca

'The saddest day hath gleams of light, The darkest wave hath bright foam beneath it, The twinkles o'er the cloudiest night, Some solitary star to cheer it.'
- Sarah Winnemucca

'If you constantly think of illness, you eventually become ill; if you believe yourself to be beautiful, you become so.'
- Shakti Gawain

'I'm not overweight, I'm just nine inches too short.'
- Shelley Winters

'Fortunately the family is a human institution: humans made it and humans can change it.'
- Shere Hite

'If I had a party to attend and didn't want to be there, I would play the part of someone who was having a lovely time.'
- Shirley MacLaine

'My gift is that I'm not beautiful. My career was never about looks. It's about health and being in good shape.'
- Shirley MacLaine

'If you haven't been happy very young, you can still be happy later on, but it's much harder. You need more luck.'
- Simone de Beauvoir

'One is not born a genius, one becomes a genius.'
- Simone de Beauvoir

'We are so outnumbered there's only one thing to do. We must attack.'
- Sir Andrew Cunningham

'I learned really to practice mustard seed faith, and positive thinking, and remarkable things happened.'
- Sir John Walton

'Kindness gives birth to kindness.'
- Sophocles

'I'll just hit the dry side of the ball.'
- Stan Musial

'Failure is impossible.'
- Susan B. Anthony

'My father instilled in me that if you don't see things happening the way you want them to, you get out there and make them happen.'
- Susan Powter

'They say, "You can't give a smile away; it always comes back." The same is true of a kind word or a conversation starter. What goes around, comes around.'
- Susan RoAne

'Although none of the rules for becoming alive is valid, it is healthy to keep on formulating them.'
- Susan Sontag

'Thoughts have power; thoughts are energy. And you can make your world or break it by your own thinking.'
- Susan Taylor

'Never say anything on the phone that you wouldn't want your mother to hear at your trial.'
- Sydney Biddle Barrows

'To think of losing is to lose already.'
- Sylvia Townsend Warner

'God prefers your health, and your obedience, to your penance.'
- Teresa of Avila

'The pessimist is half-licked before he starts.'
- Thomas A. Buckner

'Every noble work is at first impossible.'
- Thomas Carlyle

'The life each of us lives is the life within the limits of our own thinking. To have life more abundant, we must think in limitless terms of abundance.'
- Thomas Dreier

'The world is a great mirror. It reflects back to you what you are. If you are loving, if you are friendly, if you are helpful, the world will prove loving and friendly and helpful to you. The world is what you are.'
- Thomas Dreier

'Those see nothing but faults that seek for nothing else.'
- Thomas Fuller

'If you are possessed by an idea, you find it expressed everywhere, you even smell it.'
- Thomas Mann

'If you want to be a big company tomorrow, you have to start acting like one today.'
- Thomas Watson

'Most of the time we think we're sick it's all in the mind.'
- Thomas Wolfe

'My disease is one of the best things that has happened to me; it has pulled me out of a quietly desperate life toward one full of love and hope.'
- Tom O'Connor

'Our lives preserved. How it was; and how it will be. Passing it along in the relay. That is what I work to do: to produce stories that save our lives.'
- Toni Cade Bambara

'A critic is someone who never actually goes to the battle, yet who afterwards comes out shooting the wounded.'
- Tyne Daly

'Thoughts lead on to purposes; purposes go forth in Taking Action; Taking Actions form habits; habits decide character; and character fixes our destiny.'
- Tyron Edwards

'We are not interested in the possibilities of defeat.'
- Victoria, Queen of England

'Think of only three things: your God, your family and the Green Bay Packers-in that order.'
- Vince Lombardi

'Great things are not something accidental, but must certainly be willed.'
- Vincent van Gogh

'They can because they think they can.'
    - Virgil

'Once a human being has arrived on this earth, communication is the largest single factor determining what kinds of relationships he makes with others and what happens to him in the world about him.'
    - Virginia Satir

'We have a problem. "Congratulations." But it's a tough problem. "Then double congratulations."'
    - W Clement Stone

'If you've got it, flaunt it. If you do not, pretend.'
    - Wally Phillips

'I have learned to use the word impossible with the greatest caution.'
    - Wernher von Braun

'Focus is important. Focus on those parts of yourself that are working. Look at yourself as someone whose body is in the process of healing. Concentrate on the positive parts.'
    - Will Garcia

'Thousands upon thousands are yearly brought into a state of real poverty by their great anxiety not to be thought poor.'
    - William Cobbett

'All that a man does outwardly is but the expression and completion of his inward thought. To work effectively, he must think clearly; to act nobly, he must think nobly.'
    - William Ellery Channing

'The more we do, the more we can do; the more busy we are, the more leisure we have.'
    - William Hazlitt

'As is our confidence, so is our capacity.'
    - William Hazlitt

'Men will get no more out of life than they put into it.'
    - William J. H. Boetcker

'Our belief at the beginning of a doubtful undertaking is the one thing that ensures the successful outcome of our venture.'
    - William James

'The greatest discovery of my generation is that man can alter his life simply by altering his attitude of mind.'
    - William James

'If you want a quality, act as if you already had it.'
    - William James

'The world is a looking glass and gives back to every man the reflection of his own face. Frown at it and it will in turn look sourly upon you; laugh at it and with it, and it is a jolly, kind companion.'
- William Makepeace Thackeray

'Assume a virtue, if you have it not.'
- William Shakespeare

'Nothing can stop the man with the right mental attitude from achieving his goal; nothing on earth can help the man with the wrong mental attitude.'
- WW. Ziege

'Baseball is 90 percent mental. The other half is physical.'
- Yogi Berra

'Some patients I see are actually draining into their bodies the diseased thoughts of their minds.'
- Zachary T. Bercovitz

'Women forget all the things they don't want to remember, and remember everything they don't want to forget.'
- Zora Neale Hurston

PRAYER

'Help me to work and pray, Help me to live each day, That all I do may say, Thy kingdom come.'
- A. B. Simpson

'Prayer is the ascending vapor which supplies The showers of blessing, and the stream that flows Through earth's dry places, till on every side "The wilderness shall blossom as the rose."'
- A. B. Simpson

'Pray, always pray; beneath sins heaviest load, Prayer claims the blood from Jesus' side that flowed. Pray, always pray; though weary, faint, and lone, Prayer nestles by the Father's sheltering throne.'
- A. B. Simpson

'We cannot ask in behalf of Christ what Christ would not ask Himself if He were praying.'
- A. B. Simpson

'Pray, always pray; when sickness wastes thy frame, Prayer brings the healing power of Jesus' name.'
- A. B. Simpson

'You can do more than pray after you have prayed, but you cannot do more than pray until you have prayed.'
- A. J. Gordon

'Most Christians expect little from God, ask little, and therefore receive little and are content with little.'
- A. W. Pink

'Selfishness is never so exquisitely selfish as when it is on its knees. ... Self turns what would otherwise be a pure and powerful prayer into a weak and ineffective one.'
- A. W. Tozer

'Prayer at its best is the expression of the total life, for all things else being equal, our prayers are only as powerful as our lives'
- A. W. Tozer

'I have been driven many times to my knees by the overwhelming conviction that I had nowhere else to go. My own wisdom and that of all about me seemed insufficient for the day.'
- Abraham Lincoln

'Prayer requires more of the heart than of the tongue.'
- Adam Clarke

'God answers all true prayer, either in kind or in kindness.'
- Adoniram Judson

'Our prayers run along one road and God's answers by another, and by and by they meet.'
- Adoniram Judson

'To the man who himself strives earnestly, God also lends a helping hand.'
- Aeschylus

'It is vain to expect our prayers to be heard if we do not strive as well as pray.'
- Aesop

'Before we can pray, "Lord, Thy Kingdom come," we must be willing to pray, "My Kingdom go."'
- Alan Redpath

'If I am right, Thy grace impart, Still in the right to stay; If I am wrong, O teach my heart To find that better way!'
- Alexander Pope

'Prayer is a rising up and a drawing near to God in mind and in heart, and in spirit.'
- Alexander Whyte

'Incense is prayer That drives no bargain. Child, learn from incense How best to pray.'
- Alfred Barrett

'More things are wrought by prayer than this world dreams of.'
- Alfred, Lord Tennyson

'Seven days without prayer makes one weak.'
- Allen E. Bartlett

'Pray, v: to ask that the laws of the universe be annulled in behalf of a single petitioner confessedly unworthy.'
- Ambrose Bierce

'What I dislike least in my former self are the moments of prayer.'
- Andre Gide

'There is no hope but in prayer.'
- Andrew Bonar

'Nowhere can we get to know the holiness of God, and come under His influence and power, except in the inner chamber. It has been well said: "No man can expect to make progress in holiness who is not often and long alone with God."'
- Andrew Murray

'The great thing in prayer is to feel that we are putting our supplications into the bosom of omnipotent love.'
- Andrew Murray

'While others still slept, He went away to pray and to renew His strength in communion with His Father. He had need of this, otherwise He would not have been ready for the new day. The holy work of delivering souls demands constant renewal through fellowsh'
- Andrew Murray

'Let us thank God heartily as often as we pray that we have His Spirit in us to teach us to pray. Thanksgiving will draw our hearts out to God and keep us engaged with Him; it will take our attention from ourselves and give the Spirit room in our hearts.'
- Andrew Murray

'Do not strive in your own strength; cast yourself at the feet of the Lord Jesus, and wait upon Him in the sure confidence that He is with you, and works in you. Strive in prayer; let faith fill your heart-so will you be strong in the Lord, and in the powe'
- Andrew Murray

'When we pray for the Spirit's help ... we will simply fall down at the Lord's feet in our weakness. There we will find the victory and power that comes from His love.'
- Andrew Murray

'Let it be your business every day, in the secrecy of the inner chamber, to meet the holy God. You will be repaid for the trouble it may cost you. The reward will be sure and rich.'
- Andrew Murray

'Abiding fully means praying much.'
- Andrew Murray

'If a door slams shut it means that God is pointing to an open door further on down.'
- Anna Delaney Peale

'There are four ways God answers prayer: No, not yet; No, I love you too much; Yes, I thought you'd never ask; Yes, and here's more.'
- Anne Lewis

'Man is the only creature which rises by bowing, for he finds elevation in his subjection to his Maker.'
- Anonymous

'Productive prayer requires earnestness, not eloquence.'
- Anonymous

'It is impossible to lose your footing while on your knees.'
- Anonymous

'O God, if in the day of battle I forget Thee, do not Thou forget me.'
- Anonymous

'Always look for ways to act upon the faith you display in your prayers.'
- Anonymous

'Our thanks to God should always precede our requests.'
- Anonymous

'Asking for anything is allowed with the understanding that God's answers come from God's perspective. They are not always in harmony with our expectations, for only He knows the whole

story.'
- Anonymous

'Nothing is discussed more and practiced less than prayer.'
- Anonymous

'When you go to your knees, God will help you stand up to anything.'
- Anonymous

'Short prayers pierceth Heaven.'
- Anonymous

'Our prayers are often filled with selfish "wants"; God always answers with what we need.'
- Anonymous

'O Lord, forgive what I have been, sanctify what I am, and order what I shall be.'
- Anonymous

'Be not hot in prayer and cold in praise.'
- Anonymous

'Prayer changes things.'
- Anonymous

'Without the incense of heartfelt prayer, even the greatest of cathedrals is dead.'
- Anonymous

'Many words do not a good prayer make; what counts is the heartfelt desire to commune with God, and the faith to back it up.'
- Anonymous

''Mr. President, I am praying for you. 'Which way, Senator?''
- Anonymous

'God answers prayer with certainty. Wish fulfillment is something else.'
- Anonymous

'God eagerly awaits the chance to bless the person whose heart is turned toward Him.'
- Anonymous

'Fear of trouble, present and future, often blinds us to the numerous small blessings we enjoy, silencing our prayers of praise and thanksgiving.'
- Anonymous

'The greatest blessing of prayer is not receiving the answer, but being the kind of person God can trust with His answer.'
- Anonymous

'God's ear lies close to the believer's lip.'
- Anonymous

'Don't be timid when you pray; rather, batter the very gates of heaven with storms of prayer.'
- Anonymous

'The wings of prayer carry high and far.'
- Anonymous

'Prayer is the voice of faith.'
- Anonymous

'When at night you cannot sleep, talk to the Shepherd and stop counting sheep.'
- Anonymous

'True prayer brings a person's will into accordance with God's will, not the other way around.'
- Anonymous

'Amazing things start happening when we start praying!'
- Anonymous

'God receives little thanks, even for his greatest gifts.'
- Anonymous

'God deserves far more praise than any of us could ever give Him.'
- Anonymous

'When the knees are not often bent, the feet soon slide.'
- Anonymous

'Doubt not but God who sits on high, Thy secret prayers can hear; When a dead wall thus cunningly
Conveys soft whispers to the ear.'
- Anonymous

'God tells us to burden him with whatever burdens us.'
- Anonymous

'What men usually ask of God when they pray is that two and two not make four.'
- Anonymous

'The only way to pray is to pray, and the way to pray well is to pray much.'
- Anonymous

'Do not pray by heart, but with the heart.'
- Anonymous

'When my children do wrong, I ache to hear their stumbling requests for forgiveness. I'm sure our
heavenly Father aches even more deeply to hear from us.'
- Anonymous

'In the morning, prayer is the key that opens to us the treasures of God's mercies and blessings; in the evening, it is the key that shuts us up under His protection and safeguard.'
  - Anonymous

'How many of us will ever sit... bow our heads, and pray "Lord, show me where I'm wrong"?'
  - Anonymous

'Pray if thou canst with hope, but ever pray, though hope be weak or sick with long delay; pray in the darkness if there be no light; and if for any wish thou dare not pray, then pray to God to cast that wish away.'
  - Anonymous

'He who cannot pray when the sun is shining will not know how to pray when the clouds come.'
  - Anonymous

'We are going home to many who cannot read. So, Lord, make us to be Bibles so that those who cannot read the Book can read it in us.'
  - Anonymous Chinese woman

'The only prayer which a well-meaning man can pray is, O ye gods, give me whatever is fitting unto me!'
  - Appollonius of Tyana

'Prayer is the pillow of religion.'
  - Arab proverb

'Trust in Allah, but tie your camel first.'
  - Arab proverb

'Pray as if everything depended on God, and work as if everything depended upon man.'
  - Archbishop Francis J. Spellman

'When praying for healing, ask great things of God and expect great things from God. But let us seek for that healing that really matters, the healing of the heart, enabling us to trust God simply, face God honestly, and live triumphantly.'
  - Arlo F. Newell

'If we could all hear one another's prayers, God might be relieved of some of his burden.'
  - Ashleigh Brilliant

'Ordinarily when a man in difficulty turns to prayer, he has already tried every other means of escape.'
  - Austin O'Malley

'We are never more like Christ than in prayers of intercession.'
  - Austin Phelps

'Many people pray as if God were a big aspirin pill; they come only when they hurt.'
  - B. Graham Dienert

'Work as if you were to live one hundred years; pray as if you were to die tomorrow.'
- Benjamin Franklin

'They tell about a fifteen-year-old boy in an orphans' home who had an incurable stutter. One Sunday the minister was detained and the boy volunteered to say the prayer in his stead. He did it perfectly, too, without a single stutter. Later he explained, "'
- Bennett Cerf

'He who labors as he prays lifts his heart to God with his hands.'
- Bernard of Clairvaux

'Pray for one another.'
- Bible

'In the morning will I direct my prayer unto thee.'
- Bible

'Show me your ways, O Lord, teach me your paths; guide me in your truth and teach me, for you are God my Savior, and my hope is in you all day long.'
- Bible

'Cause me to hear thy loving kindness in the morning.'
- Bible

'Let us come before his presence with thanksgiving.'
- Bible

'And whatever ye shall ask in my name, that will I do.'
- Bible

'Confess your faults one to another, and pray one for another, that ye may be healed. The effectual, fervent prayer of a righteous man availeth much.'
- Bible

'When my soul fainted within me ... my prayer came in unto thee.'
- Bible

'Casting all your care upon Him; for he careth for you.'
- Bible

'Whatever things ye desire, when ye pray, believe that you receive them, and ye shall have them.'
- Bible

'If we ask anything according to his will, he heareth us.'
- Bible

'And in the morning, rising up a great while before day, he went out, and departed into a solitary place, and there prayed.'
- Bible

'When I am weak, then am I strong.'
    - Bible

'Being in an agony, he prayed more earnestly.'
    - Bible

'But thou, when thou prayest, enter into thy room, and when thou hast shut thy door, pray to thy Father who is in secret; and thy Father who seeth in secret, shall reward thee openly.'
    - Bible

'Let your requests be made known unto God.'
    - Bible

'O Lord, attend unto my cry.'
    - Bible

'Without faith it is impossible to please God, for he that cometh to God must believe that He is.'
    - Bible

'For we know not what we should pray for.'
    - Bible

'He will regard the prayer of the destitute.'
    - Bible

'May the Lord answer you when you are in distress; May the name of the God of Jacob protect you, May he send you help from the sanctuary and grant you support from Zion.'
    - Bible

'My strength is made perfect in weakness.'
    - Bible

'Pray without ceasing. In everything give thanks.'
    - Bible

'Create in me a clean heart, O God.'
    - Bible

'Ye ask, and receive not, because ye ask amiss.'
    - Bible

'The king shall joy in thy strength, O Lord; and in thy salvation how greatly shall he rejoice! Thou hast given him his heart's desire, and hast not withheld the request of his lips.'
    - Bible

'God is in heaven, and thou upon earth: therefore let thy words be few.'
    - Bible

'Evening, and morning, and at noon, will I pray.'
  - Bible

'Ye have not, because ye ask not.'
  - Bible

'Ask in faith.'
  - Bible

'Search me, O God, and know my heart: try me, and know my thoughts: and see if there be any wicked way in me.'
  - Bible

'Perhaps one of the greatest rewards of meditation and prayer is the sense of belonging that comes to us.'
  - Bill W.

'Our immediate temptation will be to ask for specific solutions to specific problems, and for the ability to help other people as we have already thought they should be helped. In that case, we are asking God to do it our way.'
  - Bill W.

'Lord, if any have to die this day, let it be me, for I am ready.'
  - Billy Bray

'O Lord, let me not live to be useless!'
  - Bishop John de Stratford

'Jesus Christ is a God whom we approach without pride, and before whom we humble ourselves without despair.'
  - Blaise Pascal

'Scream at God if that's the only thing that will get results.'
  - Brendan Francis

'A little lifting of the heart suffices; a little remembrance of God, one act of inward worship are prayers which, however short, are nevertheless acceptable to God.'
  - Brother Lawrence

'You need not cry very loud; he is nearer to us than we think.'
  - Brother Lawrence

'We ought to act with God in the greatest simplicity, speak to Him frankly and plainly, and implore His assistance in our affairs.'
  - Brother Lawrence

'True prayer always receives what it asks for-or something better.'
  - Bryon Edwards

'We must lay before him what is in us, not what ought to be in us.'
   - C. S. Lewis

'Prayer in the sense of petition, asking for things, is a small part of it; confession and penitence are its threshold, adoration its sanctuary, the presence and vision and enjoyment of God its bread and wine.'
   - C. S. Lewis

'It is quite useless knocking at the door of heaven for earthly comfort. It's not the sort of comfort they supply there.'
   - C. S. Lewis

'In Gethsemane the holiest of all petitioners prayed three times that a certain cup might pass from Him. It did not. After that the idea that prayer is recommended to us as a sort of infallible gimmick may be dismissed.'
   - C. S. Lewis

'Don't try to reach God with your understanding; that is impossible. Reach him in love; that is possible.'
   - Carlo Carretto

'No matter what may be the test, God will take care of you; Lean, weary one, upon His breast, God will take care of you.'
   - CD. Martin

'The man who says his prayers in the evening is a captain posting his sentries. After that, he can sleep.'
   - Charles Baudelaire

'Unless I had the spirit of prayer, I could do nothing.'
   - Charles G. Finney

'We ought not to tolerate for a minute the ghastly and grievous thought that God will not answer prayer.'
   - Charles Haddon Spurgeon

'Prayers are heard in heaven very much in proportion to your faith. Little faith will get very great mercies, but great faith still greater.'
   - Charles Haddon Spurgeon

'We cannot all argue, but we can all pray; we cannot all be leaders, but we can all be pleaders; we cannot all be mighty in rhetoric, but we can all be prevalent in prayer.'
   - Charles Haddon Spurgeon

'Sometimes we think we are too busy to pray. That is a great mistake, for praying is a saving of time.'
   - Charles Haddon Spurgeon

'Saints of the early church reaped great harvests in the field of prayer and found the mercy seat to be a mine of untold treasures.'
   - Charles Haddon Spurgeon

'The cry of a young raven is nothing but the natural cry of a creature, but your cry, if it be sincere, is the result of a work of grace in your heart.'
 - Charles Haddon Spurgeon

'The granting of prayer, when offered in the name of Jesus, reveals the Father's love to him, and the honor which he has put upon him.'
 - Charles Haddon Spurgeon

'One night alone in prayer might make us new men, changed from poverty of soul to spiritual wealth, from trembling to triumphing.'
 - Charles Haddon Spurgeon

'Whether we like it or not, asking is the rule of the Kingdom.'
 - Charles Haddon Spurgeon

'I sit beside my lonely fire and pray for wisdom yet: for calmness to remember or courage to forget.'
 - Charles Hamilton Aide

'The first purpose of prayer is to know God.'
 - Charles L. Allen

'Visualize, "prayerize," "Taking Actionize," and your wishes will come true.'
 - Charles L. Allen

'We, one and all of us, have an instinct to pray; and this fact constitutes an invitation from God to pray.'
 - Charles Sanders Peirce

'In Fellowship; alone To God, with Faith, draw near, Approach His Courts, besiege His Throne With all the power of Prayer.'
 - Charles Wesley

'To God your every Want In instant Prayer display, Pray always; Pray, and never faint; Pray, without ceasing, Pray.'
 - Charles Wesley

'Lord, till I reach that blissful shore, No privilege so dear shall be As thus my inmost soul to pour In prayer to thee.'
 - Charlotte Elliott

'Prayer opens our eyes that we may see ourselves and others as God sees us.'
 - Clara Palmer

'The purpose of prayer is not to inform God of our needs, but to invite Him to rule our lives.'
 - Clarence Bauman

'The right way to pray, then, is any way that allows us to communicate with God.'
 - Colleen Townsend Evans

'Any concern too small to be turned into a prayer is too small to be made into a burden.'
- Corrie ten Boom

'Pray till you pray.'
- D. M. McIntyre

'Ask God's blessing on your work, but don't ask him to do it for you.'
- Dame Flora Robson

'God listens to our weeping when the occasion itself is beyond our knowledge, but still within His love and power.'
- Daniel A. Poling

'What is the life of a Christian but a life of prayer!'
- David Brown

'Essentially prayer is based on a relationship. We don't converse freely with someone we don't know. We bare our souls and disclose our hidden secrets only to someone we trust.'
- Dean Register

'All who have walked with God have viewed prayer as the main business of their lives.'
- Delma Jackson

'Revival fires flame where hearts are praying.'
- Dick Eastman

'Prayer reaches out in love to a dying world and says, "I care."'
- Dick Eastman

'Prayer does not mean simply to pour out one's heart. It means rather to find the way to God and to speak with him, whether the heart is full or empty.'
- Dietrich Bonhoeffer

'The entire day receives order and discipline when it acquires unity. This unity must be sought and found in morning prayer. The morning prayer determines the day.'
- Dietrich Bonhoeffer

'When our will wholeheartedly enters into the prayer of Christ, then we pray correctly.'
- Dietrich Bonhoeffer

'Prayer has marked the trees across the wilderness of a skeptical world to direct the traveler in distress, and all paths lead to a single light.'
- Douglas Meador

'The influence of prayer on the human mind and body ... can be measured in terms of increased physical buoyancy, greater intellectual vigor, moral stamina, and a deeper understanding of the realities underlying human relationships.'
- Dr. Alexis Carrel

'Prayer is a cry of distress, a demand for help, a hymn of love.'
- Dr. Alexis Carrel

'When we pray we link ourselves with an inexhaustible motive power.'
- Dr. Alexis Carrel

'Prayer, like radium, is a luminous and self-generating form of energy.'
- Dr. Alexis Carrel

'All those football coaches who hold dressing-room prayers before a game should be forced to attend church once a week.'
- Duffy Daugherty

'This is what I found out about religion: It gives you courage to make decisions you must make in a crisis, and then the confidence to leave the result to a Higher Power. Only by trust in God can a man carrying responsibility find repose.'
- Dwight D. Eisenhower

'Prayer is a serious thing. We may be taken at our words.'
- Dwight L. Moody

'I firmly believe a great many prayers are not answered because we are not willing to forgive someone.'
- Dwight L. Moody

'Spread out your petition before God, and then say, "Thy will, not mine, be done." The sweetest lesson I have learned in God's school is to let the Lord choose for me.'
- Dwight L. Moody

'If we do not love one another, we certainly shall not have much power with God in prayer.'
- Dwight L. Moody

'God's chief gift to those who seek him is Himself.'
- E. B. Pusey

'Prayer puts God's work in His hands-and keeps it there.'
- E. M. Bounds

'If we would have God in the closet, God must have us out of the closet. There is no way of praying to God, but by living to God.'
- E. M. Bounds

'Prayer is our most formidable weapon, the thing which makes all else we do efficient.'
- E. M. Bounds

'Other duties become pressing and absorbing and crowd our prayer. "Choked to death" would be the coroner's verdict in many cases of dead praying if an inquest could be secured on this dire, spiritual calamity.'
- E. M. Bounds

'God's willingness to answer our prayers exceeds our willingness to give good and necessary things to our children, just as far as God's ability, goodness and perfection exceed our infirmities and evil.'
- E. M. Bounds

'Trouble and prayer are closely related. . . . Trouble often drives men to God in prayer, while prayer is but the voice of men in trouble.'
- E. M. Bounds

'By prayer, the ability is secured to feel the law of love, to speak according to the law of love, and to do everything in harmony with the law of love.'
- E. M. Bounds

'Non-praying is lawlessness, discord, anarchy.'
- E. M. Bounds

'The more praying there is in the world, the better the world will be; the mightier the forces against evil everywhere.'
- E. M. Bounds

'We can do nothing without prayer. All things can be done by importunate prayer. It surmounts or removes all obstacles, overcomes every resisting force and gains its ends in the face of invincible hindrances.'
- E. M. Bounds

'Prayer honors God, acknowledges His being, exalts His power, adores His providence, secures His aid.'
- E. M. Bounds

'Our praying, to be strong, must be buttressed by holy living. The life of faith perfects the prayer of faith.'
- E. M. Bounds

'It is only when the whole heart is gripped with the passion of prayer that the life-giving fire descends, for none but the earnest man gets access to the ear of God.'
- E. M. Bounds

'Prayer is the easiest and hardest of all things; the simplest and the sublimest; the weakest and the most powerful; its results lie outside the range of human possibilities-they are limited only by the omnipotence of God.'
- E. M. Bounds

'Men would pray better if they lived better. They would get more from God if they lived more obedient and well-pleasing to God.'
- E. M. Bounds

'I feel it is far better to begin with God, to see His face first, to get my soul near Him before it is near another. In general it is best to have at least one hour alone with God before engaging in anything else.'
- E. M. Bounds

'We cannot talk to God strongly when we have not lived for God strongly. The closet cannot be made holy to God when the life has not been holy to God.'
- E. M. Bounds

'Praying which does not result in pure conduct is a delusion. We have missed the whole office and virtue of praying if it does not rectify conduct. It is in the very nature of things that we must quit praying, or quit bad conduct.'
- E. M. Bounds

'God shapes the world by prayer. Prayers are deathless. They outlive the lives of those who uttered them.'
- E. M. Bounds

'Private place and plenty of time are the life of prayer.'
- E. M. Bounds

'The possibilities of prayer are found in its allying itself with the purposes of God, for God's purposes and man's praying are the combination of all potent and omnipotent forces.'
- E. M. Bounds

'Prayer is a trade to be learned. We must be apprentices and serve our time at it. Painstaking care, much thought, practice and labor are required to be a skillful tradesman in praying. Practice in this, as well as in all other trades, makes perfect.'
- E. M. Bounds

'Straight praying is never born of crooked conduct.'
- E. M. Bounds

'Prayer is of transcendent importance. Prayer is the mightiest agent to advance God's work. Praying hearts and hands only can do God's work. Prayer succeeds when all else fails.'
- E. M. Bounds

'It is hard to wait and press and pray, and hear no voice, but stay till God answers.'
- E. M. Bounds

'We can never know God as it is our privilege to know Him by brief repetitions that are requests for personal favors, and nothing more.'
- E. M. Bounds

'Prayer, like faith, obtains promises, enlarges their operation, and adds to the measure of their results.'
- E. M. Bounds

'Prayer means that we have come boldly into the throne room and we are standing in His presence.'
- E. W. Kenyon

'When you cannot pray as you would, pray as you can.'
- Edward M. Goulburn

'Prayer is exhaling the spirit of man and inhaling the spirit of God.'
- Edwin Keith

'I know not by what methods rare, But this I know: God answers prayer. I know not if the blessing sought Will come in just the guise I thought. I leave my prayer to Him alone Whose will is wiser than my own.'
- Eliza M. Hickok

'Though smooth be the heartless prayer, no ear in heaven will mind it; And the finest phrase falls dead, if there is no feeling behind it.'
- Ella Wheeler Wilcox

'It is vain to ask of the gods what man is capable of supplying for himself.'
- Epicurus

'There are no atheists on turbulent airplanes.'
- Erica Jong

'When life knocks you to your knees, and it will, why, get up! If it knocks you to your knees again, as it will, well, isn't that the best position from which to pray?'
- Ethel Barrymore

'The man who prays grows, and the muscles of the soul swell from this whipcord to iron bands.'
- F. B. Meyer

'Take my will, and make it Thine, It shall be no longer mine; Take my heart, it is Thine own; It shall be Thy royal throne.'
- Frances Ridley Havergal

'Heaven is never deaf but when man's heart is dumb.'
- Francis Quarles

'Time spent in prayer is never wasted.'
- Francois de Fenelon

'Even if no command to pray had existed, our very weakness would have suggested it.'
- Francois de Fenelon

'I would have no desire other than to accomplish thy will. Teach me to pray; pray thyself in me.'
- Francois de Fenelon

'We must pray for more prayer, for it is the world's mightiest healing force.'
- Frank C. Laubach

'A Chinese Christian prayed every day .... "Lord, reform Thy world, beginning with me."'
- Franklin Delano Roosevelt

'If you are swept off your feet, it's time to get on your knees.'
- Fred Beck

'The Lord's Prayer may be committed to memory quickly, but it is slowly learnt by heart.'
- Frederick Denison Maurice

'Every time you pray, if your prayer is sincere, there will be new feeling and new meaning in it which will give you fresh courage, and you will understand that prayer is an education.'
- Fyodor Dostoyevsky

'In the calm of sweet communion Let thy daily work be done; In the peace of soul-outpouring Care be banished, patience won; And if earth with its enchantments Seek thy spirit to enthrall, Ere thou listen, ere thou answer, Turn to Jesus, tell Him all.'
- G. M. Taylor

'There is a time for all things; a time to preach and a time to pray, but those times have passed away; there is a time to fight, and that time has come!'
- General Peter Muhlenberg

'Sincerity is the prime requisite in every approach to the God who ... hates all hypocrisy, falsehood, and deceit.'
- Geoffrey B. Wilson

'Most people do not pray; they only beg.'
- George Bernard Shaw

'Time spent on the knees in prayer will do more to remedy heart strain and nerve worry than anything else.'
- George David Stewart

'The deepest wishes of the heart find expression in secret prayer.'
- George E. Rees

'He that will learn to pray, let him go to Sea.'
- George Edward Herbert

'Thou who has given so much to me, give one thing more: a grateful heart.'
- George Herbert

'He that will learn to pray, let him to sea.'
- George Herbert

'My prayers, my God, flow from what I am not; I think Thy answers make me what I am.'
- George Macdonald

'She heard the snuffle of hypocrisy in her prayer. She had to cease to pray.'
- George Meredith

'Prayer for worldly goods is worse than fruitless, but prayer for strength of soul is that passion of the soul which catches the gift it seeks.'
- George Meredith

'Who rises from prayer a better man, his prayer is answered.'
- George Meredith

'The beginning of anxiety is the end of faith, and the beginning of true faith is the end of anxiety.'
- George Mueller

'Prayer, among sane people, has never superseded practical efforts to secure the desired end.'
- George Santayana

'Our rages, daughters of despair, creep and squirm like worms. Prayer is the only form of revolt which remains upright.'
- Georges Bernanos

'Prayer is an end to isolation. It is living our daily life with someone; with him who alone can deliver us from solitude.'
- Georges Lefevre

'Some people think that prayer just means asking for things, and if they fail to receive exactly what they asked for, they think the whole thing is a fraud.'
- Gerald Vann

'God gives the nuts, but he does not crack them.'
- German proverb

'It is in recognizing the actual presence of God that we find prayer no longer a chore, but a supreme delight.'
- Gordon Lindsay

'When the gods are angry with a man, they give him what he asks for.'
- Greek proverb

'No one is a firmer believer in the power of prayer than the devil; not that he practices it, but he suffers from it.'
- Guy H. King

'Prayer is not eloquence, but earnestness; not the definition of helplessness, but the feeling of it; not figures of speech, but earnestness of soul.'
- Hannah More

'Let me burn out for God ... prayer is the great thing. Oh, that I may be a man of prayer!'
- Henry Martyn

'Men of God are always men of prayer.'
- Henry T. Mahan

'It is not well for a man to pray cream and live skim milk.'
- Henry Ward Beecher

'I pray on the principle that wine knocks the cork out of a bottle. There is an inward fermentation, and there must be a vent.'
- Henry Ward Beecher

'Prayer, to the patriarchs and prophets, was more than the recital of well-known and well-worn phrases-it was the outpouring of the heart.'
- Herbert Lockyer

'How those holy men of old could storm the battlements above! When there was no way to look but up, they lifted up their eyes to God who made the hills, with unshakable confidence.'
- Herbert Lockyer

'He offered a prayer so deeply devout that he seemed kneeling and praying at the bottom of the sea.'
- Herman Melville

'Prayer indeed is good, but while calling on the gods, a man should himself lend a hand.'
- Hippocrates

'The prayers of the Christian are secret, but their effect cannot be hidden.'
- Howard Chandler Robbins

'Do I want to pray or only to think about my human problems? Do I want to pray or simply kneel there contemplating my sorrow? Do I want to direct my prayer toward God or let it direct itself towards me?'
- Hubert Van Zeller

'To avail yourself of His certain wisdom, ask of Him whatever questions you have. But do not entreat Him, for that will never be necessary.'
- Hugh Prather

'Call on God, but row away from the rocks.'
- Indian proverb

'A man's state before God may always be measured by his prayers.'
- J. C. Ryle

'No prayers can be heard which do not come from a forgiving heart.'
- J. C. Ryle

'No time is so well spent in every day as that which we spend upon our knees.'
- J. C. Ryle

'We must wrestle earnestly in prayer, like men contending with a deadly enemy for life.'
- J. C. Ryle

'Dealing in generalities is the death of prayer.'
- J. H. Evans

'Do not work so hard for Christ that you have no strength to pray, for prayer requires strength.'
- J. Hudson Taylor

'Just as an earthly father knows what is best for his children's welfare, so does God take into consideration the particular needs of His human family, and meets them out of His wonderful storehouse.'
- J. K. Maclean

'If our petitions are in accordance with His will, and if we seek His glory in the asking, the answers will come in ways that will astonish us and fill our hearts with songs of thanksgiving.'
- J. K. Maclean

'God is a rich and bountiful Father, and He does not forget His children, nor withhold from them anything which it would be to their advantage to receive.'
- J. K. Maclean

'When I have a problem I pray about it, and what comes to mind and stays there I assume to be my answer. And this has been right so often that I know it is God's answer.'
- J. L. Kraft

'Lord, you know how busy I must be this day. If I forget you, do not you forget me.'
- Jacob Astley

'They never sought in vain that sought the Lord aright!'
- James Drummond Burns

'Religion is no more possible without prayer than poetry without language or music without atmosphere.'
- James Martineau

'Not what we wish, but what we need, Oh! let your grace supply, The good unasked, in mercy grant; The ill, though asked, deny.'
- James Merrick

'O thou, by whom we come to God, The Life, the Truth, the Way, The path of prayer Thyself hast trod- Lord teach us how to pray.'
- James Montgomery

'Prayer is the soul's sincere desire.'
- James Montgomery

'I who still pray at morning and at eve Thrice in my life perhaps have truly prayed, Thrice stirred below conscious self Have felt that perfect disenthrallment which is God.'
- James Russell Lowell

'Grant us grace, Almighty Father, so to pray as to deserve to be heard.'
- Jane Austen

'With God there is no need for long speeches.'
- Jane Frances de Chantal

'In prayer, more is accomplished by listening than by talking.'
- Jane Frances de Chantal

'Follow your own way of speaking to our Lord sincerely, lovingly, confidently, and simply, as your heart dictates.'
- Jane Frances de Chantal

'The idea of thanking staff should mean giving them something that they would never buy for themselves.'
- Jayne Crook

'Help yourself and heaven will help you.'
- Jean de la Fontaine

'I have lived to thank God that all my prayers have not been answered.'
- Jean Ingelow

'Teach us to pray often, that we may pray oftener.'
- Jeremy Taylor

'In the war upon the powers of darkness, prayer is the primary and mightiest weapon, both in aggressive war upon them and their works; in the deliverance of men from their power; and against them as a hierarchy of powers opposed to Christ and His Church.'
- Jessie Penn-Lewis

'The minds of people are so cluttered up with every-day living these days that they don't, or won't, take time out for a little prayer-for mental cleansing, just as they take a bath for physical, outer cleansing. Both are necessary.'
- Jo Ann Carlson

'Prayer moves the hand that moves the world.'
- John Aikman Wallace

'No heart thrives without much secret converse with God and nothing will make amends for the want of it.'
- John Berridge

'No answer to prayer is an indication of our merit; every answer to prayer is an indication of God's mercy.'
- John Blanchard

'When you pray, rather let your heart be without words than your words without heart.'
- John Bunyan

'Prayer is a shield to the soul, a sacrifice to God, and a scourge for Satan.'
- John Bunyan

'In prayer it is better to have a heart without words than words without a heart.'
    - John Bunyan

'The best prayers have often more groans than words.'
    - John Bunyan

'A sensible thanksgiving for mercies received is a mighty prayer in the Spirit of God. It prevails with Him unspeakably.'
    - John Bunyan

'The answer of our prayers is secured by the fact that in rejecting them God would in a certain sense deny His own nature.'
    - John Calvin

'Keep us, Lord, so awake in the duties of our calling that we may sleep in thy peace and wake in thy glory.'
    - John Donne

'God be kind to all good Samaritans and also bad ones. For such is the kingdom of heaven.'
    - John Gardner

'The simple heart that freely asks in love, obtains.'
    - John Greenleaf Whittier

'Every chain that spirits wear crumbles in the breadth of prayer.'
    - John Greenleaf Whittier

'And help us, this and every day, to live more nearly as we pray.'
    - John Keble

'The main lesson about prayer is just this: Do it! Do it! Do it! You want to be taught to pray? My answer is: pray.'
    - John Laidlaw

'God warms his hands at man's heart when he prays.'
    - John Masefield

'Prayer is the great engine to overthrow and rout my spiritual enemies, the great means to procure the graces of which I stand in hourly need.'
    - John Newton

'You are coming to a King, Large petitions with you bring For his grace and power are such None can ever ask too much.'
    - John Newton

'Beyond our utmost wants His love and power can bless; To praying souls he always grants More than they can express.'
    - John Newton

'The spirit of prayer is the fruit and token of the Spirit of adoption.'
- John Newton

'He who prays as he ought, will endeavor to live as he prays.'
- John Owen

'Prayer is not artful monologue Of voice uplifted from the son; It is Love's tender dialogue Between the soul and God.'
- John Richard Moreland

'Prayer should be short, without giving God Almighty reasons why He should grant this or that; He knows best what is good for us.'
- John Selden

'God never denied that soul anything that went as far as heaven to ask it.'
- John Trapp

'Bear up the hands that hang down, by faith and prayer; support the tottering knees. Storm the throne of grace and persevere therein, and mercy will come down.'
- John Wesley

'Many pray with their lips for that for which their hearts have no desire.'
- Jonathan Edwards

'I always love to begin a journey on Sundays, because I shall have the prayers of the church to preserve all that travel by land, or by water.'
- Jonathan Swift

'God gives every bird its food, but he does not throw it into the nest.'
- Josiah G. Holland

'We should pray for a sane mind in a sound body.'
- Juvenal

'You pray in your distress and in your need; would that you might also pray in the fullness of your joy and in your days of abundance.'
- Kahlil Gibran

'Poverty, chastity, and obedience are extremely difficult. But there are always the graces if you will pray for them.'
- Katheryn Hulme

'The great tragedy of life is not unanswered prayer, but unoffered prayer.'
- KB. Meyer

'Praying is learned by praying.'
- L. A. T. van Dooren

'Oh, what a cause of thankfulness it is that we have a gracious God to go to on all occasions! Use and enjoy this privilege and you can never be miserable. Oh, what an unspeakable privilege is prayer!'
- Lady Maxwell

'I am used to praying when I am alone, thank God. But when I come together with other people, when I need more than ever to pray, I still cannot get used to it.'
- Leo Tolstoy

'I pray like a robber asking alms at the door of a farmhouse to which he is ready to set fire.'
- Leon Bloy

'Why is it when we talk to God we're said to be praying, but when God talks to us we're schizophrenic?'
- Lily Tomlin

'Women don't have halos built in.'
- Lorraine Hine

'I used to pray that God would do this or that; now I pray that God will make His will known to me.'
- Madame Chiang Kai-Shek

'To pray together, in whatever tongue or ritual, is the most tender brotherhood of hope and sympathy that man can contract in this life.'
- Madame de Stael

'Prayer is not asking. It is a longing of the soul.'
- Mahatma Gandhi

'Prayer is not an old woman's idle amusement. Properly understood and applied, it is the most potent instrument of Taking Action.'
- Mahatma Gandhi

'I find in the Psalms much the same range of mood and expression as I perceive within my own life of prayer.'
- Malcolm Boyd

'Our prayers must spring from the indigenous soil of our own personal confrontation with the Spirit of God in our lives.'
- Malcolm Boyd

'Our prayers must mean something to us if they are to mean anything to God.'
- Maltbie D. Babcock

'We must move from asking God to take care of the things that are breaking our hearts, to praying about the things that are breaking His heart.'
- Margaret Gibb

'Prayer begins where human capacity ends.'
- Marian Anderson

'Turn your doubts to question; turn your question to prayers; turn your prayers to God.'
- Mark R. Litteton

'In prayer we call ourselves 'worms of the dust', but it is only on a sort of tacit understanding that the remark shall not be taken at par.'
- Mark Twain

'Deep down in me I knowed it was a lie, and He knowed it. You can't pray a lie-I found that out.'
- Mark Twain

'In certain trying circumstances, urgent circumstances, desperate circumstances, profanity furnishes a relief denied even to prayer.'
- Mark Twain

'The less I pray, the harder it gets; the more I pray, the better it goes.'
- Martin Luther

'The fewer the words, the better the prayer.'
- Martin Luther

'I have to hurry all day to get time to pray.'
- Martin Luther

'Tomorrow I plan to work, work, from early until late. In fact I have so much to do that I shall spend the first three hours in prayer.'
- Martin Luther

'Prayer is not to be used as a confessional, to cancel sin. Such an error would impede true religion. Sin is forgiven only as it is destroyed by Christ - Truth and Light.'
- Mary Baker Eddy

'Ask, and it shall be given you; seek and ye shall find; knock, and it shall be opened unto you.'
- Matthew

'Every one that asketh receiveth; and he that seeketh findeth.'
- Matthew

'The essence of prayer, even of a mystical experience, is the way we are altered to see everything from its life-filled dimension.'
- Matthew Fox

'God's promises are to be our pleas in prayer.'
- Matthew Henry

'We read of preaching the Word out of season, but we do not read of praying out of season, for that is never out of season.'
- Matthew Henry

'Though we cannot by our prayers give God any information, yet we must by our prayers give him honor.'
- Matthew Henry

'It is good for us to keep some account of our prayers, that we may not unsay them in our practice.'
- Matthew Henry

'Prayer time must be kept up as duly as meal-time.'
- Matthew Henry

'God dwells where we let God in.'
- Menachem Mendel

'There are few men who dare to publish to the world the prayers they make to Almighty God.'
- Michel de Montaigne

'The Ancient Mariner said to Neptune during a great storm, "O God, you will save me if you wish, but I am going to go on holding my tiller straight."'
- Michel de Montaigne

'Prayer enlarges the heart until it is capable of containing God's gift of Himself.'
- Mother Teresa

'God bless all those that I love; God bless all those that love me; God bless all those that love those that I love and all those that love those that love me.'
- New England Sampler

'Today any successful and competent businessman will employ the latest and best-tested methods in production, distribution, and administration, and many are discovering that one of the greatest of all efficiency methods is prayer power.'
- Norman Vincent Peale

'The more helpless you are, the better you are fitted to pray, and the more answers to prayer you will experience.'
- O. Hallesby

'Prayer can assume very different forms, from quiet, blessed contemplation of God, in which eye meets eye in restful meditation, to deep sighs or sudden exclamations of wonder, joy, gratitude or adoration.'
- O. Hallesby

'We should say to God as we mingle with our dear ones each day, "God, give them each Thy blessing. They need it, because they live with me, and I am very selfish and unwilling to sacrifice very much for them, although I do love them."'
- O. Hallesby

'To pray is to open the door unto Jesus and admit Him into your distress. Your helplessness is the very thing which opens wide the door unto Him and gives Him access to all your needs.'
- O. Hallesby

'Prayer is a fine, delicate instrument. To use it right is a great art, a holy art. There is perhaps no greater art than the art of prayer. Yet the least gifted, the uneducated and the poor can cultivate the holy art of prayer.'
- O. Hallesby

'Our groanings, which cannot be uttered, rise to Him and tell Him better than words how dependent we are upon Him.'
- O. Hallesby

'Prayer is a condition of mind, an attitude of heart, which God recognizes as prayer whether it manifests itself in quiet thinking, in sighing or in audible words.'
- O. Hallesby

'As white snow flakes fall quietly and thickly on a winter day, answers to prayer will settle down upon you at every step you take, even to your dying day. The story of your life will be the story of prayer and answers to prayer.'
- O. Hallesby

'Do not forget that prayer is ordained for the purpose of glorifying the name of God. Therefore, whether you pray for big things or for little things, say to God, "If it will glorify Thy name, then grant my prayer and help me."'
- O. Hallesby

'A humble and contrite heart knows that it can merit nothing before God, and that all that is necessary is to be reconciled to one's helplessness and let our holy and almighty God care for us, just as an infant surrenders himself to his mother's care.'
- O. Hallesby

'Pray for whatsoever you will. In the name of Jesus you have permission, not only to stand in the presence of God, but also to pray for everything you need.'
- O. Hallesby

'If God does not give you something you ask for, wait on Him. He will speak with you tenderly and sympathetically about the matter until you yourself understand that He cannot grant your prayer.'
- O. Hallesby

'By prayer we couple the powers of heaven to our helplessness, the powers which can capture strongholds and make the impossible possible.'
- O. Hallesby

'Helplessness becomes prayer the moment that you go to Jesus and speak candidly and confidently with him about your needs. This is to believe.'
- O. Hallesby

'When we in prayer seek only the glorification of the name of God, then we are in complete harmony with the spirit of prayer. Then our hearts are at rest both while we pray and after we have prayed. Then we can wait for the Lord.'
- O. Hallesby

'Our prayer life will become restful when it really dawns upon us that we have done all we are supposed to do when we have spoken to Him about it. From the moment we have left it with Him, it is His responsibility.'
  - O. Hallesby

'When we go to our meeting with God, we should go like a patient to his doctor, first to be thoroughly examined and afterwards to be treated for our ailment. Then something will happen when you pray.'
  - O. Hallesby

'It is only when we pray for something according to the will of God that we have the promise of being heard and answered.'
  - O. Hallesby

'My praying friend, continue to make known your desires to God in all things. ... Let Him decide whether you are to receive what you ask for or not.'
  - O. Hallesby

'It is the will of our heavenly Father that we should come to Him freely and confidently and make known our desires to Him, just as we would have our children come freely and of their own accord and speak to us about the things they would like to have.'
  - O. Hallesby

'To pray is nothing more involved than to open the door, giving Jesus access to our needs and permitting Him to exercise His own power in dealing with them.'
  - O. Hallesby

'Prayer is something deeper than words. It is present in the soul before it has been formulated in words. And it abides in the soul after the last words of prayer have passed over our lips.'
  - O. Hallesby

'Be sure to remember that nothing in your daily life is so insignificant and so inconsequential that the Lord will not help you by answering your prayer.'
  - O. Hallesby

'We should not be afraid, when praying to God, to give expression to a definite desire, even though we are in doubt at the time we are praying whether it is really the right thing to pray for or not.'
  - O. Hallesby

'Helplessness is unquestionably the first and the surest indication of a praying heart. ... Prayer and helplessness are inseparable. Only he who is helpless can truly pray.'
  - O. Hallesby

'It is God's will not only to hear our prayer, but to give us the best and the richest answer which He, the almighty and omniscient God, can devise. He will send us the answer when it will benefit us and His cause the most.'
  - O. Hallesby

'We need to learn to know Him so well that we feel safe when we have left our difficulties with Him. To know Jesus in that way is a prerequisite of all true prayer.'
   - O. Hallesby

'At church, with meek and unaffected grace, His looks adorn'd the venerable place; Truth from his lips prevailed with double sway, And fools, who came to scoff, remain'd to pray.'
   - Oliver Goldsmith

'When the gods wish to punish us, they answer our prayers.'
   - Oscar Wilde

'It is by no haphazard chance that in every age men have risen early to pray. The first thing that marks decline in spiritual life is our relationship to the early morning.'
   - Oswald Chambers

'We impoverish God in our minds when we say there must be answers to our prayers on the material plane; the biggest answers to our prayers are in the realm of the unseen.'
   - Oswald Chambers

'We have to pray with our eyes on God, not on the difficulties.'
   - Oswald Chambers

'You say, "But He has not answered." He has, He is so near to you that His silence is the answer. His silence is big with terrific meaning that you cannot understand yet, but presently you will.'
   - Oswald Chambers

'Never say you will pray about a thing; pray about it.'
   - Oswald Chambers

'We look upon prayer as a means of getting things for ourselves; The Bible idea of prayer is that we may get to know God Himself.'
   - Oswald Chambers

'God's silences are His answers. If we only take as answers those that are visible to our senses, we are in a very elementary condition of grace.'
   - Oswald Chambers

'Do not have as your motive the desire to be known as a praying man. Get an inner chamber in which to pray where no one knows you are praying, shut the door, and talk to God in secret.'
   - Oswald Chambers

'The whole meaning of prayer is that we may know God.'
   - Oswald Chambers

'Prayer is often a temptation to bank on a miracle of God instead of on a moral issue, i.e., it is much easier to ask God to do my work than it is to do it myself. Until we are disciplined properly, we will always be inclined to bank on God's miracles and '
   - Oswald Chambers

'Prayer is not an exercise, it is the life.'
- Oswald Chambers

'The greatest answer to prayer is that I am brought into a perfect understanding with God, and that alters my view of actual things.'
- Oswald Chambers

'God does not exist to answer our prayers, but by our prayers we come to discern the mind of God.'
- Oswald Chambers

'The purpose of prayer is to reveal the presence of God equally present, all the time, in every condition.'
- Oswald Chambers

'When we pray "in the Name of Jesus" the answers are in accordance with His nature, and if we think our prayers are unanswered it is because we are not interpreting the answer along this line.'
- Oswald Chambers

'Prayer is the supreme activity of all that is noblest in our personality, and the essential nature of prayer is faith.'
- Oswald Chambers

'Every time we pray our horizon is altered, our attitude to things is altered, not sometimes but every time, and the amazing thing is that we don't pray more.'
- Oswald Chambers

'When a man is at his wits' end it is not a cowardly thing to pray, it is the only way he can get in touch with Reality.'
- Oswald Chambers

'Whenever the insistence is on the point that God answers prayer, we are off the track. The meaning of prayer is that we get hold of God, not of the answer.'
- Oswald Chambers

'Prayer is not only asking, it is an attitude of heart that produces an atmosphere in which asking is perfectly natural, and Jesus says, "every one that asketh receiveth."'
- Oswald Chambers

'Watch your motive before God; have no other motive in prayer than to know Him.'
- Oswald Chambers

'We pray pious blether, our will is not in it, and then we say God does not answer; we never asked Him for anything. Asking means that our wills are in what we ask.'
- Oswald Chambers

'God's "nothings" are His most positive answers. We have to stay on God and wait. Never try to help God to fulfill His word.'
- Oswald Chambers

'If you have ever prayed in the dawn you will ask yourself why you were so foolish as not to do it always: it is difficult to get into communion with God in the midst of the hurly-burly of the day.'
  - Oswald Chambers

'Prayer is the evidence that I am spiritually concentrated on God.'
  - Oswald Chambers

'One great effect of prayer is that it enables the soul to command the body. By obedience I make my body submissive to my soul, but prayer puts my soul in command of my body.'
  - Oswald Chambers

'If we rely on the Holy Spirit, we shall find that our prayers become more and more inarticulate; and when they are inarticulate, reverence grows deeper and deeper.'
  - Oswald Chambers

'It is impossible to conduct your life as a disciple without definite times of secret prayer.'
  - Oswald Chambers

'Our Lord never referred to unanswered prayer; he taught that prayers are always answered. He ever implied that prayers were answered rightly because of the Heavenly Father's wisdom.'
  - Oswald Chambers

'Prayer is God's answer to our poverty, not a power we exercise to obtain an answer.'
  - Oswald Chambers

'Pray because you have a Father, not because it quietens you, and give Him time to answer.'
  - Oswald Chambers

'Prayer is not logical, it is a mysterious moral working of the Holy Spirit.'
  - Oswald Chambers

'Our understanding of God is the answer to prayer; getting things from God is God's indulgence of us. When God stops giving us things, He brings us into the place where we can begin to understand Him.'
  - Oswald Chambers

'There is no need to get to a place of prayer; pray wherever you are.'
  - Oswald Chambers

'If God sees that my spiritual life will be furthered by giving the things for which I ask, then He will give them, but that is not the end of prayer. The end of prayer is that I come to know God Himself.'
  - Oswald Chambers

'A day without prayer is a boast against God.'
  - Owen Carr

'If we are willing to spend hours on end to learn to play the piano, operate a computer, or fly an airplane, it is sheer nonsense for us to imagine that we can learn the high art of getting guidance through communion with the Lord without being willing to '
  - Paul Rees

'Only man, among living things, says prayers. Or needs to.'
- Peter Bowman

'Prayers not felt by us are seldom heard by God.'
- Philip Henry

'Let prayer be the key of the morning and the bolt at night.'
- Philip Henry

'Prayer is the spirit speaking truth to Truth.'
- Philip James Bailey

'Trouble and perplexity drive me to prayer and prayer drives away perplexity and trouble.'
- Philipp Melanchthon

'Do not pray for easy lives, pray to be stronger men. Do not pray for tasks equal to your powers, pray for powers equal to your tasks.'
- Phillips Brooks

'Prayer, in its simplest definition, is merely a wish turned God-ward.'
- Phillips Brooks

'Cast thy burden upon the Lord, and he shall sustain thee.'
- Psalms ss:zx

'Though I am weak, yet God, when prayed, Cannot withhold his conquering aid.'
- Ralph Waldo Emerson

'Prayer is the contemplation of the facts of life from the highest point of view.'
- Ralph Waldo Emerson

'The wise man in the storm prays God not for safety from danger, but for deliverance from fear.'
- Ralph Waldo Emerson

'The Christian will find his parentheses for prayer even in the busiest hours of life.'
- Richard Cecil

'Two went to pray? Better to say one went to brag, the other to pray.'
- Richard Crashaw

'God punishes us mildly by ignoring our prayers, and severely by answering them.'
- Richard J. Needham

'They who have steeped their soul in prayer can every anguish calmly bear.'
- Richard M. Milnes

'God can pick sense out of a confused prayer.'
- Richard Sibbes

'Prayer serves as an edge and border to preserve the web of life from unraveling.'
- Robert Hall

'The prayer of faith is the only power in the universe to which the great Jehovah yields.'
- Robert Hall

'In prayer the lips ne'er act the winning part, without the sweet concurrence of the heart.'
- Robert Herrick

'We lie to God in prayer if we do not rely on him afterwards.'
- Robert Leighton

'Give us the strength to encounter that which is to come, that we may be brave in peril, constant in tribulation, temperate in wrath, and in all changes of fortune, and down to the gates of death, loyal and loving one to anther.'
- Robert Louis Stevenson

'A generous prayer is never presented in vain; the petition may be refused, but the petitioner is always, I believe, rewarded by some gracious visitation.'
- Robert Louis Stevenson

'Sometimes ... God answers our prayers in the way our parents do, who reply to the pleas of their children with "Not just now" or "I'll have to think about that for a little while."'
- Roy M. Pearson

'Nor it is an objection to say that we must understand a prayer if it is to have its true effect. That simply is not the case. Who understands the wisdom of a flower? Yet we can take pleasure in it.'
- Rudolph Steiner

'Pray to God, but keep rowing to shore.'
- Russian proverb

'Just pray for a tough hide and a tender heart.'
- Ruth Graham

'There are three answers to prayer: yes, no, and wait awhile. It must be recognized that no is an answer.'
- Ruth Stafford Peale

'To give pleasure to a single heart by a single kind act is better than a thousand head-bowings in prayer.'
- Sa'di

'He prays best who does not know that he is praying.'
- Saint Anthony of Padua

'Do what you can and pray for what you cannot yet do.'
- Saint Augustine

'There is no sinner in the world, however much at enmity with God, who cannot recover God's grace by recourse to Mary, and by asking her assistance.'
- Saint Bridget of Sweden

'Grant that we may not so much seek to be understood as to understand.'
- Saint Francis of Assisi

'Prayer is an all-efficient panoply, a treasure undiminished, a mine which is never exhausted, a sky unobscured by clouds, a heaven unruffled by the storm. It is the root, the fountain, the mother of a thousand blessings.'
- Saint John Chrysostom

'Prayer should be the means by which I, at all times, receive all that I need, and, for this reason, be my daily refuge, my daily consolation, my daily joy, my source of rich and inexhaustible joy in life.'
- Saint John Chrysostom

'The one concern of the devil is to keep Christians from praying. He fears nothing from prayerless studies, prayerless work, and prayer-less religion. He laughs at our toil, mocks at our wisdom, but trembles when we pray.'
- Samuel Chadwick

'Prayer is the acid test of devotion.'
- Samuel Chadwick

'Prayer may not change things for you, but it for sure changes you for things.'
- Samuel M. Shoemaker

'Don't pray to escape trouble. Don't pray to be comfortable in your emotions. Pray to do the will of God in every situation. Nothing else is worth praying for.'
- Samuel M. Shoemaker

'I did this night promise my wife never to go to bed without calling upon God, upon my knees, in prayer.'
- Samuel Pepys

'I seldom made an errand to God for another but I got something for myself.'
- Samuel Rutherford

'He prayeth well, who loveth well Both man and bird and beast. He prayeth best, who loveth best All things both great and small; For the dear God who loveth us, He made and loveth all.'
- Samuel Taylor Coleridge

'To have a curable illness and to leave it untreated except for prayer is like sticking your hand in a fire and asking God to remove the flame.'
- Sandra L. Douglas

'Don't pray when it rains if you don't pray when the sun shines.'
- Satchel Paige

'The first petition that we are to make to Almighty God is for a good conscience, the next for health of mind, and then of body.'
- Seneca

'"Oh, God, if I were sure I were to die tonight I would repent at once." It is the commonest prayer in all languages.'
- Sir James M. Barrie

'Pray devoutly, but hammer stoutly.'
- Sir William Gurney Benham

'He who ceases to pray ceases to prosper.'
- Sir William Gurney Benham

'Our prayers should be for blessings in general, for God knows best what is good for us.'
- Socrates

'Religion without humanity is a poor human stuff.'
- Sojourner Truth

'No one who has had a unique experience with prayer has a right to withhold it from others.'
- Soong Mei-ling

'Heaven ne'er helps the men who will not act.'
- Sophocles

'To stand on one leg and prove God's existence is a very different thing from going down on one's knees and thanking him.'
- Soren Kierkegaard

'Prayer does not change God, but it changes him who prays.'
- Soren Kierkegaard

'Teach me, O God, not to torture myself, not to make a martyr out of myself through stifling reflection, but rather teach me to breathe deeply in faith.'
- Soren Kierkegaard

'All the prayers in the Scripture you will find to be reasoning with God, not a multitude of words heaped together.'
- Stephen Charnock

'God has editing rights over our prayers. He will... edit them, correct them, bring them in line with His will and then hand them back to us to be resubmitted.'
- Stephen Crotts

'Answered prayers cover the field of providential history as flowers cover western prairies.'
- T. L. Cuyler

'The firmament of the Bible is ablaze with answers to prayer.'
- T. L. Cuyler

'He who prays for his neighbors will be heard for himself.'
- Talmud

'More tears are shed over answered prayers than unanswered ones.'
- Teresa of Avila

'From silly devotions and from sour-faced saints, good Lord, deliver us.'
- Teresa of Avila

'Let him never cease from prayer who has once begun it, be his life ever so wicked, for prayer is the way to amend it, and without prayer such amendment will be much more difficult.'
- Teresa of Avila

'Rejoice always, pray constantly, and in all circumstances give thanks.'
- The Desert Fathers

'Whatever you do in revenge against your brother will appear all at once in your heart at the time of payer.'
- The Desert Fathers

'Do not want things to turn out as they seem best to you, but as God pleases. Then you will be free from confusion, and thankful in prayer.'
- The Desert Fathers

'Constant prayer quickly straightens out our thoughts.'
- The Desert Fathers

'Pray not for lighter burdens, but for stronger backs.'
- Theodore Roosevelt

'O Lord, you know what is best for me. Let this or that be done, as you please. Give what you will, how much you will, and when you will.'
- Thomas a Kempis

'God hears no more than the heart speaks; and if the heart be dumb, God will certainly be dumb.'
- Thomas B. Brooks

'Cold prayers shall never have any warm answers.'
- Thomas B. Brooks

'Prayer crowns God with the honor and glory due to His name, and God crowns prayer with assurance and comfort. The most praying souls are the most assured souls.'
- Thomas B. Brooks

'Look, as a painted man is no man, and as painted fire is no fire, so a cold prayer is no prayer.'
- Thomas B. Brooks

'Prayer should be the key of the day and the lock of the night.'
    - Thomas Fuller

'None can pray well but he that lives well.'
    - Thomas Fuller

'I tremble for my country when I reflect that God is just.'
    - Thomas Jefferson

'I would rather stand against the cannons of the wicked than against the prayers of the righteous.'
    - Thomas Lye

'When we make self the end of prayer, it is not worship but self-seeking.'
    - Thomas Manton

'If we be empty and poor, it is not because God's hand is straitened, but ours is not opened.'
    - Thomas Manton

'Faith is the fountain of prayer, and prayer should be nothing else but faith exercised.'
    - Thomas Manton

'Prayer is the soul's breathing itself into the bosom of its heavenly Father.'
    - Thomas Watson

'The prayer that is faithless is fruitless.'
    - Thomas Watson

'A wicked man in prayer may lift up his hands, but he cannot lift up his face.'
    - Thomas Watson

'Prayer is the spiritual gymnasium in which we exercise and practice godliness.'
    - V. L. Crawford

'If you can't pray as you want to, pray as you can. God knows what you mean.'
    - Vance Havner

'A saint is to put forth his faith in prayer, and afterwards follow his prayer with faith.'
    - Vavasor Powell

'Those who always pray are necessary to those who never pray.'
    - Victor Hugo

'God prefers bad verses recited with a pure heart to the finest verses chanted by the wicked.'
    - Voltaire

'We offer up prayers to God only because we have made Him after our own image. We treat Him like a Pasha, or a Sultan, who is capable of being exasperated and appeased.'
    - Voltaire

'Our Father, let the spirit of gratitude so prevail in our hearts that we may manifest thy Spirit in our lives.'
- W. B. Slack

'Lord, take my lips and speak through them; take my mind and think through it; take my heart and set it on fire.'
- W. H. Aitken

'And since He bids me seek His face, Believe His word and trust His grace, I'll cast on Him my every care, And wait for thee, sweet hour of prayer.'
- W. W. Walford

'In seasons of distress and grief, My soul has often found relief, And oft escaped the tempter's snare, By thy return, sweet hour of prayer.'
- W. W. Walford

'Prayer is not merely an occasional impulse to which we respond when we are in trouble: prayer is a life attitude.'
- Walter A. Mueller

'Teach us to pray that we may cause The enemy to flee, That we his evil power may bind, His prisoners to free.'
- Watchman Nee

'To Mercy, Pity, Peace and Love All pray in their distress.'
- William Blake

'Work as if everything depended upon work and pray as if everything depended upon prayer.'
- William Booth

'Restraining prayer, we cease to fight; Prayer keeps the Christian's armor bright; And Satan trembles when he sees The weakest saint upon his knees.'
- William Cowper

'Be thankful that God's answers are wiser than your answers.'
- William Culbertson

'Never was a faithful prayer lost. Some prayers have a longer voyage than others, but then they return with their richer lading at last, so that the praying soul is a gainer by waiting for an answer.'
- William Gurnall

'The exercise of prayer, in those who habitually exert it, must be regarded by us doctors as the most adequate and normal of all the pacifiers of the mind and calmers of the nerves.'
- William James

'There must be fired affections before our prayers will go up.'
- William Jenkyn

'There is nothing that makes us love a man so much as praying for him.'
- William Law

'He who has learned to pray has learned the greatest secret of a holy and a happy life.'
- William Law

'The value of consistent prayer is not that He will hear us, but that we will hear Him.'
- William McGill

'O Lord, help me not to despise or oppose what I do not understand.'
- William Penn

'Just when I need Him, He is my all, Answering when upon Him I call; Tenderly watching lest I should fall.'
- William Poole

'We may as well not pray at all as offer our prayers in a lifeless manner.'
- William S. Plumer

'God may turn his ears from prattling prayers, or preaching prayers, but never from penitent, believing prayers.'
- William S. Plumer

'Real prayer seeks an audience and an answer.'
- William S. Plumer

'Those who trade with heaven by prayer grow rich by quick returns.'
- William S. Plumer

'My words fly up, my thoughts remain below; Words without thoughts never to heaven go.'
- William Shakespeare

'Now I am past all comforts here, but prayer.'
- William Shakespeare

'We do pray for mercy, and that same prayer doth teach us all to render the deeds of mercy.'
- William Shakespeare

'We, ignorant of ourselves, beg often our own harms, which the wise powers deny us for our good.'
- William Shakespeare

'If your prayer is selfish, the answer will be something that will rebuke your selfishness. You may not recognize it as having come at all, but it is sure to be there.'
- William Temple

'When I pray, coincidences happen, and when I don't, they don't.'
- William Temple

'Of all things, guard against neglecting God in the secret place of prayer.'
- William Wilberforce

'God help those who do not help themselves.'
- Wilson Mizner

'God give me work, till my life shall end And life, till my work is done.'
- Winifred Holtby

PROBLEMS

'The human mind prefers to be spoon fed with the thoughts of others, but deprived of such nourishment it will, reluctantly, begin to think for itself- and such thinking, remember, is original thinking and may have valuable results.'
  - Agatha Christie

'To overcome difficulties is to experience the full delight of existence.'
  - Arthur Schopenhauer

'It is a fact of history that those who seek to withdraw from its great experiments usually end up being overwhelmed by them.'
  - Barbara Ward

'Life is the acceptance of responsibilities or their evasion; it is a business of meeting obligations or avoiding them. To every man the choice is continually being offered, and by the manner of his choosing you may fairly measure him.'
  - Ben Ames Williams

'You can overcome anything if you don't bellyache.'
  - Bernard M. Baruch

'None of us can be free of conflict and woe. Even the greatest men have had to accept disappointments as their daily bread.'
  - Bernard M. Baruch

'There is no man in any rank who is always at liberty to act as he would incline. In some quarter or other he is limited by circumstances.'
  - Bonnie Blair

'Success is to be measured not so much by the position that one has reached in life as by the obstacles he has overcome trying to succeed.'
  - Booker T. Washington

'I used to believe that marriage would diminish me, reduce my options. That you had to be someone less to live with someone else when, of course, you have to be someone more.'
  - Candice Bergen

'Times of general calamity and confusion have ever been productive of the greatest minds. The purest ore is produced from the hottest furnace, and the brightest thunderbolt is elicited from the darkest storms.'
  - Charles Caleb Colton

'A problem well stated is a problem half solved.'
  - Charles F. Kettering

'When you approach a problem, strip yourself of preconceived opinions and prejudice, assemble and learn the facts of the situation, make the decision which seems to you to be the most honest, and then stick to it.'
  - Chester Bowles

'There is no other solution to a man's problems but the day's honest work, the day's honest decisions, the day's generous utterance, and the day's good deed.'
  - Clare Boothe Luce

'You often get a better hold upon a problem by going away from it for a time and dismissing it from your mind altogether.'
  - Dr. Frank Crane

'There is no movement without our own resistance.'
  - Dr. Laura Schlessinger

'When you can't solve the problem, manage it.'
  - Dr. Robert H. Schuller

'A good problem statement often includes: (a) what is known, (b) what is unknown, and (c) what is sought.'
  - Edward Hodnett

'Every path has its puddle.'
  - English proverb

'The greater the difficulty, the more glory in surmounting it.'
  - Epicurus

'It isn't that they can't see the solution, it's that they can't see the problem.'
  - G. K. Chesterton

'Can it be that man is essentially a being who loves to conquer difficulties, a creature whose function is to solve problems?'
  - Gorham Munson

'Conquering any difficulty always gives one a secret joy, for it means pushing back a boundary-line and adding to one's liberty.'
  - Henri Frederic Amiel

'Problems are only opportunities in work clothes.'
  - Henry J. Kaiser

'When I feel difficulty coming on, I switch to another book I'm writing. When I get back to the problem, my unconscious has solved it.'
  - Isaac Asimov

'What one decides to do in crisis depends on one's philosophy of life, and that philosophy cannot be changed by an incident. If one hasn't any philosophy in crises, others make the decision.'
  - Jeannette Rankin

'If we can really understand the problem, the answer will come out of it, because the answer is not separate from the problem.'
  - Jiddu Krishnamurti

'I wish I were with some of the wild people that run in the woods, and know nothing about accomplishments!'
  - Joanna Baillie

'Hiding leads nowhere except to more hiding.'
  - Margaret A. Robinson

'We must prepare and study truth under every aspect, endeavoring to ignore nothing, if we do not wish to fall into the abyss of the unknown when the hour shall strike.'
  - Marie von Ebner-Eschenbach

'Fear not those who argue but those who dodge.'
  - Marie von Ebner-Eschenbach

'I'll have to, as you say, take a stand, do something toward shaking up that system. ... Despair ... is too easy an out.'
  - Paule Marshall

'Difficulties exist to be surmounted.'
  - Ralph Waldo Emerson

'Life affords no higher pleasure than that of surmounting difficulties.'
  - Samuel Johnson

'What is difficulty? Only a word indicating the degree of strength requisite for accomplishing particular objects; a mere notice of the necessity for exertion ... a mere stimulus to men.'
  - Samuel Warren

'If the first woman God ever made was strong enough to turn the world upside down, these women together ought to be able to turn it right side up again.'
  - Sojourner Truth

'Every problem contains the seeds of its own solution.'
  - Stanley Arnold

'Real difficulties can be overcome, it is only the imaginary ones that are unconquerable.'
  - Theodore N. Vail

'All work of man is as the swimmer's: a vast ocean threatens to devour him; if he front it not bravely, it will keep its word.'
  - Thomas Carlyle

'The harder the conflict, the more glorious the triumph. What we obtain too cheap, we esteem too lightly; 'tis dearness only that gives everything it's value.'
  - Thomas Paine

'We must look for the opportunity in every difficulty, instead of being paralyzed at the thought of the difficulty in every opportunity.'
  - Walter E. Cole

'Half the unhappiness in life comes from people being afraid to go straight at things.'
  - William J. Lock

READING

'Reading after a certain (time) diverts the mind too much from its creative pursuits. Any man who reads too much and uses his own brain too little falls into lazy habits of thinking.'
  - Albert Einstein

'Everyone who knows how to read has it in their power to magnify themselves, to multiply the ways in which they exist, to make their life full, significant, and interesting.'
  - Aldous Huxley

'Books are the most mannerly of companions, accessible at all times, in all moods, frankly declaring the author's mind, without offense.'
  - Amos Bronson Alcott

'Never lend books - nobody ever returns them; the only books I have in my library are those which people have lent me.'
  - Anatole France

'I do not know any reading more easy, more fascinating, more delightful than a catalogue.'
  - Anatole France

'Book lovers never go to bed alone.'
  - Anonymous

'The possession of a book becomes a substitute for reading it.'
  - Anthony Burgess

'The habit of reading is the only enjoyment in which there is no alloy; it lasts when all other pleasures fade.'
  - Anthony Trollope

'He has only half learned the art of reading who has not added to it the even more refined accomplishments of skipping and skimming.'
  - Arthur Balfour

'Reading is sometimes an ingenious device for avoiding thought.'
  - Arthur Helps

'If you would understand your own age, read the works of fiction produced in it. People in disguise speak freely.'
  - Arthur Helps

'Any book which is at all important should be re-read immediately.'
  - Arthur Schopenhauer

'The delight of opening a new pursuit, or a new course of reading, imparts the vivacity and novelty of youth even to old age.'
- Benjamin Disraeli

'If you would not be forgotten as soon as you are dead, either write things worth reading or do things worth writing.'
- Benjamin Franklin

'One man is as good as another until he has written a book.'
- Benjamin Jowett

'Oh that my words were now written! Oh that they were printed in a book!'
- Bible

'The dust and silence of the upper shelf.'
- Bob Macaulay

'Books think for me.'
- Charles Lamb

'A book is like a garden carried in the pocket.'
- Chinese proverb

'When you read a classic you do not see in the book more than you did before. You see more in you than there was before.'
- Clifton Fadiman

'The first book of the nation is the dictionary of its language.'
- Contanitin, Comte de Volney

'A best-seller was a book which somehow sold well simply because it was selling well.'
- Daniel J. Boorstin

'My education was the liberty I had to read indiscriminately and all the time, with my eyes hanging out.'
- Dylan Thomas

'Reading is the work of the alert mind, is demanding, and under ideal conditions produces finally a sort of ecstasy. This gives the experience of reading a sublimity and power unequalled by any other form of communication.'
- E. B. White

'Laws die, books never.'
- Edward Bulwer-Lytton

'Master books, but do not let them master you. Read to live, not live to read.'
- Edward Bulwer-Lytton

'All good books are alike in that they are truer than if they really happened and after you are finished reading one you feel that it all happened to you and after which it all belongs to you.'
- Ernest Hemingway

'Literature is news that stays news.'
- Ezra Pound

'Properly we should read for power. Man reading should be man intensely alive. The book should be a ball of light in one's hand.'
- Ezra Pound

'Some books are to be tasted, others to be swallowed, and some few to be chewed and digested.'
- Francis Bacon

'To me the charm of an encyclopedia is that it knows - and I needn't.'
- Francis Yeats-Brown

'There are still a few of us booklovers around despite the awful warnings of Marshall McLuhan with his TV era and his pending farewell to Gutenberg.'
- Frank Davies

'A book is a mirror: if an ass peers into it, you can't expect an apostle to look out.'
- G. C. Lichtenberg

'The central theme of the novel is that they were glad to see each other.'
- Gertrude Stein

'Ordinary people know little of the time and effort it takes to learn to read. I have been eighty years at it, and have not reached my goal.'
- Goethe

"Sartor Resartus' is simply unreadable, and for me that always sort of spoils a book.'
- Harry S. Truman

'Where is human nature so weak as in the bookstore?'
- Henry Ward Beecher

'You should read it, though there is much that is skip-worthy.'
- Herbert Asquith

'First publication is a pure, carnal leap into that dark which one dreams is life.'
- Hortense Calisher

'The fact of knowing how to read is nothing, the whole point is knowing what to read.'
- Jacques Ellul

'What a sense of security in an old book which time has criticized for us!'
- James Russell Lowell

'The greatest masterpiece in literature is only a dictionary out of order.'
- Jean Cocteau

'I hate books; they teach us only to talk about what we do not know.'
- Jean-Jacques Rousseau

'Books give not wisdom where none was before. But where some is, there reading makes it more.'
- John Harington

'Having your book turned into a movie is like seeing your oxen turned into bouillon cubes.'
- John he Carri

'I am a part of all I have read.'
- John Kieran

'A good book is the precious life-blood of a master spirit, embalmed and treasured up on purpose to a life beyond life.'
- John Milton

'If a book is worth reading, it is worth buying.'
- John Ruskin

'Just the knowledge that a good book is awaiting one at the end of a long day makes that day happier.'
- Kathleen Norris

'Do give books - religious or otherwise - for Christmas. They're never fattening, seldom sinful, and permanently personal.'
- Lenore Hershey

'A publisher is somebody looking for someone who has something to say.'
- Lome Pierce

'Discretion is not the better part of biography.'
- Lytton Strachey

'There are perhaps no days of our childhood we lived so fully as those we believe we left without having lived them: those we spent with a favorite book.'
- Marcel Proust

'The man who does not read good books has no advantage over the man who can't read them.'
- Mark Twain

'A successful book cannot afford to be more than ten percent new.'
- Marshall McLuhan

'In the case of good books, the point is not to see how many of them you can get through, but rather how many can get through to you.'
- Mortimer J. Adler

'The telephone book is full of facts but it doesn't contain a single idea.'
  - Mortimer J. Adler

'The most technologically efficient machine that man has ever invented is the book.'
  - Northrop Frye

'It circulated for five years, through the halls of fifteen publishers, and finally ended up with Vanguard Press, which as you can see is rather deep into the alphabet.'
  - Patrick Dennis

'The responsibility of a dictionary is to record a language, not set its style.'
  - Phillip Babcock Gove

'A dictionary should be descriptive, not prescriptive.'
  - Phillip Babcock Gove

'A good book has no ending.'
  - R. D. Dimming

'Tis the good reader that makes the good book.'
  - Ralph Waldo Emerson

'Neither is a dictionary a bad book to read. There is no cant in it, no excess of explanation, and it is full of suggestions, the raw material of possible poems and histories.'
  - Ralph Waldo Emerson

'A good title is the title of a successful book.'
  - Raymond Chandler

'All the glory of the world would be buried in oblivion, unless God had provided mortals with the remedy of books.'
  - Richard De Bury

'To finish is both a relief and a release from an extraordinarily pleasant prison.'
  - Robert Burchfield

'The walls of books around him, dense with the past, formed a kind of insulation against the present world and its disasters.'
  - Ross MacDonald

'I read part of it all the way through.'
  - Sam Goldwyn

'The oldest books are still only just out to those who have not read them.'
  - Samuel Butler

'Books should be tried by a judge and jury as though they were crimes.'
  - Samuel Butler

'I keep my books at the British Museum and at Mudies.'
   - Samuel Butler

'Dictionaries are like watches. The worst is better than none at all and even the best cannot be expected to run quite true.'
   - Samuel Johnson

'A lexicographer, a writer of dictionaries, a harmless drudge.'
   - Samuel Johnson

'The true university of these days is a collection of books.'
   - Thomas Carlyle

'Some books are undeservedly forgotten; none are undeservedly remembered.'
   - W. H. Auden

'Camerado, this is no book. Who touches this, touches a man.'
   - Walt Whitman

'What is reading but silent conversation?'
   - Walter Savage Landor

'Nothing links man to man like the frequent passage from hand to hand of a good book.'
   - Walter Sickert

'Does it afflict you to find your books wearing out? I mean literally .. . the mortality of all inanimate things is terrible to me, but that of books most of all.'
   - William Dean Howells

'Reading, like prayer, remains one of our few private acts.'
   - William Jovanovich

RELATIONSHIPS

'We rarely confide in those who are better than we are.'
- Albert Camus

'I respect only those who resist me, but cannot tolerate them.'
- Charles de Gaulle

'With three or more people there is something bold in the air: direct things get said which would frighten two people alone and conscious of each inch of their nearness to one another. To be three is to be in public - you feel safe.'
- Elizabeth Bowen

'It is always safe to assume that people are more subtle and less sensitive than they seem.'
- Eric Hoffer

'The more you let yourself go, the less others let you go.'
- Friedrich Nietzsche

'Science may have found a cure for most evils: but it has found no remedy for the worst of them all - the apathy of human beings.'
- Helen Keller

'Though statisticians in our time have never kept the score man wants a great deal here below and Woman even more.'
- James Thurber

'It is a truth universally acknowledged, that a single man in possession of a good fortune, must be in want of a wife.'
- Jane Austen

'You know who must be very secure in their masculinity? Male ladybugs.'
- Jay Leno

'It is well to remember that the entire population of the universe, with one trifling exception, is composed of others.'
- John Andrew Holmes

'She has such a nice sense of rumor.'
- John Cutler

'There is no word equivalent to 'cuckold' for women.'
- Joseph Epstein

'What would we say if men changed the length of their trousers every year?'
- Lady Nancy Astor

'It women knew what we were thinking, they'd never stop slapping us.'
- Larry Miller

'Ginger Rogers did everything that Fred Astaire did. She just did it backwards and in high heels.'
- Linda Ellerbee

'I want to know why, if men rule the world, they don't stop wearing neckties.'
- Linda Ellerbee

'I present myself to you in a form suitable to the relationship I wish to achieve with you.'
- Luigi Pirandello

'When women go wrong, men go right after them.'
- Mae West

'The ultimate indignity is to be given a bedpan by a stranger who calls you by your first name.'
- Maggie Kuhn

'The opinions which we hold of one another, our relations with friends and kinsfolk are in no sense permanent, save in appearance, but are as eternally fluid as the sea itself.'
- Marcel Proust

'Man - a creature made at the end of the week's work when God was tired.'
- Mark Twain

'Manly men and womanly women are still here but feeling nervous.'
- Mason Cooley

'Flirtation - attention without intention.'
- Max O'Neil

'A woman is like a tea bag - only in hot water do you realize how strong she is.'
- Nancy Reagan

'I should like to see any kind of a man, distinguishable from a gorilla that some good and even pretty woman could not shape a husband out of.'
- Oliver Wendell Holmes

'Women are never disarmed by compliments. Men always are.'
- Oscar Wilde

'Tell me about yourself - your struggles, your dreams, your telephone number.'
- Peter Arno

'There are more men than women in mental hospitals - which just goes to show who's driving who crazy.'
- Peter Veale

'Make yourself necessary to somebody.'
- Ralph Waldo Emerson

'When the man is at home, his standing in society is well known and quietly taken; but when he is abroad, it is problematical, and is dependent on the success of his manners.'
- Ralph Waldo Emerson

'If you ever leave me, I'll go with you.'
- Rene Taylor

'If the world were a logical place, men would ride sidesaddle.'
- Rita Mae Brown

'Men who drink herbal teas are seldom serial killers.'
- Rita Rudner

'At bottom the world isn't a joke. We only joke about it to avoid an issue with someone, to let someone know that we know he's there with his questions; to disarm him by seeming to have heard and done justice to his side of the standing argument.'
- Robert Frost

'Women have one great advantage over men. It is commonly thought that if they marry they have done enough, and need career no further. If a man marries, on the other hand, public opinion is all against him if he takes this view.'
- Rose Macaulay

'Breathes there a man with hide so tough Who says two sexes aren't enough?'
- Samuel Hoffenstein

'As the faculty of writing has chiefly been a masculine endowment, the reproach of making the world miserable has always been thrown upon the women.'
- Samuel Johnson

'What is most beautiful in virile men is something feminine; what is most beautiful in feminine women is something masculine.'
- Susan Sontag

'Even the wisest men make fools of themselves about women, and even the most foolish women are wise about men.'
- Theodor Reik

'In our civilization, men are afraid that they will not be men enough and women are afraid that they might be considered only women.'
- Theodor Reik

'God has given you one face, and you make yourselves another.'
- William Shakespeare

'Macho does not prove mucho.'
   - Zsa Gabor

RISKS

'To get profit without risk, experience without danger and reward without work is as impossible as it is to live without being born.'
- A. P. Gouthey

'In danger there is great power.'
- Agnes Whistling Elk

'If one is forever cautious, can one remain a human being?'
- Aleksandr Solzhenitsyn

'Everything is sweetened by risk.'
- Alexander Smith

'It is the business of the future to be dangerous.'
- Alfred North Whitehead

'Adventure is worthwhile in itself.'
- Amelia Earhart

'I postpone death by living, by suffering, by error, by risking, by giving, by losing.'
- Anais Nin

'If man is not ready to risk his life, where is his dignity?'
- Andre Malraux

'Providence has hidden a charm in difficult undertakings, which is appreciated only by those who dare to grapple with them.'
- Anne-Sophie Swetchine

'Danger itself is the best remedy for danger.'
- Anonymous

'Take risks: if you win, you will be happy; if you lose, you will be wise.'
- Anonymous

'Without danger we cannot get beyond danger.'
- Anonymous

'He that is not in the war is not out of danger.'
- Anonymous

'If the risk-reward ratio is right, you can make big money buying trouble.'
- Anonymous

'No guts, no glory.'
- Anonymous

'The men who have done big things are those who were not afraid to attempt big things, who were not afraid to risk failure in order to gain success.'
- B. C. Forbes

'When you make a commitment to a relationship, you invest your attention and energy in it more profoundly because you now experience ownership of that relationship.'
- Barbara De Angelis

'Doing is a quantum leap from imagining.'
- Barbara Sher

'The defense force inside of us wants us to be cautious, to stay away from anything as intense as a new kind of Taking Action. Its job is to protect us, and it categorically avoids anything resembling danger. But it's often wrong.'
- Barbara Sher

'Be bold, and mighty forces will come to your aid.'
- Basil King

'To gain that which is worth having, it may be necessary to lose everything else.'
- Bernadette Devlin

'Attempt the impossible in order to improve your work.'
- Bette Davis

'Anything I've ever done that ultimately was worthwhile ... initially scared me to death.'
- Betty Bender

'What is necessary is never a risk.'
- Cardinal de Retz

'Speaking of Ted Turner The important thing is this: to be able at any moment to sacrifice what we are for what we could become.'
- Charles Du Bos

'The faster you go, the more chance there is of stubbing your toe, but the more chance you have of getting somewhere.'
- Charles F. Kettering

'No one would have crossed the ocean if he could have gotten off the ship in the storm.'
- Charles F. Kettering

'If you limit your Taking Actions in life to things that nobody can possibly find fault with, you will not do much.'
- Charles Lutwidge Dodgson

'What isn't tried won't work.'
- Claude McDonald

'I'll always push the envelope. To me, the ultimate sin in life is to be boring. I don't play it safe.'
- Cybil Shepherd

'All life is a chance. So take it! The person who goes furthest is the one who is willing to do and dare.'
- Dale Carnegie

'We fail far more often by timidity than by over-daring.'
- David Grayson

'Don't be afraid to take a big step if one is indicated. You can't cross a chasm in two small steps.'
- David Lloyd George

'If your life is ever going to get better, you'll have to take risks. There is simply no way you can grow without taking chances.'
- David Viscott

'You do not have to be superhuman to do what you believe in.'
- Debbi Fields

'It is better to die on your feet than to live on your knees!'
- Delores Ibarruri

'You risk just as much in being credulous as in being suspicious.'
- Denis Diderot

'In order to find the edge, you must risk going over the edge.'
- Dennis Dugan

'My favorite thing is to go where I have never gone.'
- Diane Arbus

'Life is a risk.'
- Diane von Furstenberg

'I compensate for big risks by always doing my homework and being well-prepared. I can take on larger risks by reducing the overall risk.'
- Donna E. Shalala

'There was never a place for her in the ranks of the terrible, slow army of the cautious. She ran ahead, where there were no paths.'
- Dorothy Parker

'An individual dies ... when, instead of taking risks and hurling himself toward being, he cowers within, and takes refuge there.'
- E. M. Cioran

'Life is either always a tightrope or a feather bed. Give me the tightrope.'
- Edith Wharton

'Into the darkness they go, the wise and the lovely.'
- Edna Saint Vincent Millay

'I feel very adventurous. There are so many doors to be opened, and I'm not afraid to look behind them.'
- Elizabeth Taylor

'The soul should always stand ajar, ready to welcome the ecstatic experience.'
- Emily Dickinson

'Better that we should die fighting than be outraged and dishonored. Better to die than to live in slavery.'
- Emmeline Pankhurst

'Danger and delight grow on one stalk.'
- English proverb

'And the trouble is, if you don't risk anything, you risk even more.'
- Erica Jong

'All serious daring starts from within.'
- Eudora Welty

'People who are born even-tempered, placid and untroubled-secure from violent passions or temptations to evil-those who have never needed to struggle all night with the angel to emerge lame but victorious at dawn, never become great saints.'
- Eva Le Gallienne

'You can't expect to hit the jackpot if you don't put a few nickels in the machine.'
- Flip Wilson

'Progress always involves risks. You can't steal second base and keep your foot on first.'
- Frederick B. Wilcox

'Defensive strategy never has produced ultimate victory.'
- General Douglas MacArthur

'Take calculated risks. That is quite different from being rash.'
- General George S. Patton

'The fixed determination to have acquired the warrior soul, to either conquer or perish with honor, is the secret of victory.'
- General George S. Patton

'Entrepreneurs, in accepting risk, achieve security for all. In embracing change, they ensure social and economic stability.'
- George Gilder

'We must dare, and dare again, and go on daring.'
- Georges Jacques Danton

'All reformations seem formidable before they are attempted.'
- Hannah Moore

'To be alive at all involves some risk.'
- Harold Macmillan

'Liberty is always dangerous, but it is the safest thing we have.'
- Harry Emerson Fosdick

'Of course people are afraid. But honestly facing that fear, seeing it for what it is, is the only way of putting it to rest.'
- Harvey Fierstein

'However well organized the foundations of life may be, life must always be full of risks.'
- Havelock Ellis

'Life is either a daring adventure or nothing.'
- Helen Keller

'Security is mostly superstition. It does not exist in nature.'
- Helen Keller

'Avoiding danger is no safer in the long run than outright exposure. The fearful are caught as often as the bold.'
- Helen Keller

'The follies which a man regrets most in his life are those which he didn't commit when he had the opportunity.'
- Helen Rowland

'Love, like a chicken salad or restaurant hash, must be taken with blind faith or it loses its flavor.'
- Helen Rowland

'Victories that are cheap are cheap. Those only are worth having which come as the result of hard fighting.'
- Henry Ward Beecher

'A leader must face danger. He must take the risk and the blame, and the brunt of the storm.'
- Herbert N. Casson

'Great deeds are usually wrought at great risks.'
- Herodotus

'Something must be left to chance; nothing is sure in a sea fight beyond all others.'
- Horatio Nelson

'What one has not experienced, one will never understand in print.'
- Isadora Duncan

'Our safety is not in blindness, but in facing our danger.'
- J. C. F. von Schiller

'To live without risk for me would be tantamount to death.'
- Jacqueline Cochran

'Nine times out of ten the best thing that can happen to a young man is to be tossed overboard and compelled to sink or swim.'
- James A. Garfield

'There is no memory with less satisfTaking Action than the memory of some temptation we resisted.'
- James Branch Cabell

'You might as well fall flat on your face as lean over too far backward.'
- James Thurber

'Unless you enter the tiger's den, you cannot take the cubs.'
- Japanese proverb

'Taking risks gives me energy.'
- Jay Chiat

'Every man has the right to risk his own life in order to preserve it. Has it ever been said that a man who throws himself out the window to escape a fire is guilty of suicide?'
- Jean-Jacques Rousseau

'You can no more win a war than you can win an earthquake.'
- Jeannette Rankin

'We owe something to extravagance, for thrift and adventure seldom go hand in hand.'
- Jennie Jerome Churchill

'It is so tempting to try the most difficult thing possible.'
- Jennie Jerome Churchill

'Be wary of the man who urges an Taking Action in which he himself incurs no risk.'
- Joaquin Setanti

'For of all sad words of tongues or pen the saddest are these: It might have been.'
- John Greenleaf Whittier

'If we are intended for great ends, we are called to great hazards.'
- John Henry Cardinal Newman

'To render ourselves insensible to pain we must forfeit also the possibilities of happiness.'
  - John Lubbock

'If you're never scared or embarrassed or hurt, it means you never take any chances.'
  - Julia Sorel

'A sharp knife cuts the quickest and hurts the least.'
  - Katharine Hepburn

'Any life truly lived is a risky business, and if one puts up too many fences against the risks one ends by shutting out life itself.'
  - Kenneth S. Davis

'Danger can never by overcome without taking risks.'
  - Latin proverb

'I don't think about risks much. I just do what I want to do. If you gotta go, you gotta go.'
  - Lillian Carter

'You have all eternity to be cautious in when you're dead.'
  - Lois Platford

'Between two evils, I always picked the one I never tried before.'
  - Mae West

'It is not manly to turn one's back on fortune.'
  - Marcus Annaeus Seneca

'Constant exposure to dangers will breed contempt for them.'
  - Marcus Annaeus Seneca

'It is not because things are difficult that we do not dare, it is because we do not dare that they are difficult.'
  - Marcus Annaeus Seneca

'We can only do what is possible for us to do. But still it is good to know what the impossible is.'
  - Maria Irene Fornes

'Competition can damage self-esteem, create anxiety, and lead to cheating and hurt feelings. But so can romantic love.'
  - Mariah Burton Nelson

'Risk always brings its own rewards: the exhilaration of breaking through, of getting to the other side; the relief of a conflict healed; the clarity when a paradox dissolves.'
  - Marilyn Ferguson

'Women must think strategically about creating ongoing pressure for change.'
  - Mary Baker Eddy

'Creativity is inventing, experimenting, growing, taking risks, breaking rules, making mistakes, and having fun.'
- Mary Lou Cook

'A dreamer-you know-it's a mind that looks over the edges of things.'
- Mary O'Hara

'The only things you regret are the things you don't do.'
- Michael Curtiz

'If you don't take chances, you can't do anything in life.'
- Michael Spinks

'The greater the obstacle, the more glory in overcoming it.'
- Moliere

'Do not follow where the path may lead. Go instead where there is no path and leave a trail.'
- Muriel Strode

'I love the challenge.'
- Nancy Lopez

'The torment of precautions often exceeds the dangers to be avoided. It is sometimes better to abandon one's self to destiny.'
- Napoleon Bonaparte

'There's no such thing as a sure thing. That's why they call it gambling.'
- Neil Simon

'One never finds anything perfectly pure and ... exempt from danger.'
- Niccolo Machiavelli

'We love because it is the only true adventure.'
- Nikki Giovanni

'The only things one never regrets are one's mistakes.'
- Oscar Wilde

'Every minute of life I take a risk; it's part of the enjoyment.'
- Otto Preminger

'To conquer without risk is to triumph without glory.'
- Pierre Corneille

'Every noble acquisition is attended with its risks; he who fears to encounter the one must not expect to obtain the other'
- Pietro Metastasio

'I am one of those people who can't help getting a kick out of life-even when it's a kick in the teeth.'
    - Polly Adler

'No one reaches a high position without daring.'
    - Publilius Syrus

'Dare to be naive.'
    - R. Buckminster Fuller

'Cadillacs are down at the end of the bat.'
    - Ralph Kiner

'As soon as there is life, there is danger.'
    - Ralph Waldo Emerson

'We may by our excessive prudence squeeze out of the life we are guarding so anxiously all the adventurous quality that makes it worth living.'
    - Randolph Bourne

'Living at risk is jumping off the cliff and building your wings on the way down.'
    - Ray Bradbury

'To play it safe is not to play.'
    - Robert Altman

'Only those who dare to fail greatly can ever achieve greatly.'
    - Robert F. Kennedy

'It is the risk element which ensures security. Risk brings out the ingenuity and resourcefulness which ensure success.'
    - Robert Rawls

'He gets a good hold on the paintbrush, then confidently has the ladder removed.'
    - Roger Vaughan

'Those lose least who have least to lose.'
    - Rose O'Neil

'Only those who dare, truly live.'
    - Ruth P. Freedman

'Prudence keeps life safe, but does not often make it happy.'
    - Samuel Johnson

'Life has no romance without risk.'
    - Sarah Doherty

'There is little place in the political scheme of things for an independent, creative personality, for a fighter. Anyone who takes that role must pay a price.'
- Shirley Chisholm

'Security is not the meaning of my life. Great opportunities are worth the risks.'
- Shirley Hufstedler

'Our whole way of life today is dedicated to the removal of risk. Cradle to grave we are supported, insulated, and isolated from the risks of life- and if we fall, our government stands ready with Band-Aids of every size.'
- Shirley Temple Black

'It's only when we have nothing else to hold onto that we're willing to try something very audacious and scary.'
- Sonia Johnson

'Sometimes I think we can tell how important it is to risk by how dangerous it is to do so.'
- Sonia Johnson

'Without risk, faith is an impossibility.'
- Soren Kierkegaard

'You can't catch trout with dry breeches.'
- Spanish proverb

'To achieve anything, you must be prepared to dabble on the boundary of disaster.'
- Stirling Moss

'The rewards go to the risk-takers, those who are willing to put their egos on the line and reach out to other people and to a richer, fuller life for themselves.'
- Susan RoAne

'I tore myself away from the safe comfort of certainties through my love for truth; and truth rewarded me.'
- Sylvia Ashton-Warner

'There could be no honor in a sure success, but much might be wrested from a sure defeat.'
- T. E. Lawrence

'Only those who will risk going too far can possibly find out how far one can go.'
- T. S. Eliot

'Make voyages. Attempt them. There's nothing else.'
- Tennessee Williams

'I prefer liberty with danger to peace with slavery.'
- The Palatine of Posnan

'It is impossible to win the great prizes of life without running risks.'
- Theodore Roosevelt

'The ambitious climb high and perilous stairs, and never care how to come down; the desire of rising hath swallowed up their fear of a fall.'
- Thomas Adams

'He that would have fruit must climb the tree.'
- Thomas Fuller

'He that will not sail till all dangers are over must never put to sea.'
- Thomas Fuller

'Better hazard once than always be in fear.'
- Thomas Fuller

'They are surely to be esteemed the bravest spirits who, having the clearest sense of both the pains and pleasures of life, do not on that account shrink from danger.'
- Thucydides

'Dancing on the edge is the only place to be.'
- Trisha Brown

'Those who cling to life die, and those who defy death live.'
- Uyesugi Kenshin

'There are those who have discovered that fear is death in life, and have willingly risked physical death and loss of all that is considered valuable in order to live in freedom.'
- Virginia Burden Tower

'It is only by risking ... that we live at all.'
- William James

'All great reforms require one to dare a lot to win a little.'
- William L. O'Neill

SADNESS

'Sadness is almost never anything but a form of fatigue.'
- Andre Gide

'Sadness is a state of sin.'
- Andre Gide

'Nothing is more sad than the death of an illusion.'
- Arthur Koestler

'Poverty makes you sad as well as wise.'
- Bertolt Brecht

'It is sad to grow old but nice to ripen.'
- Brigitte Bardot

'Proud people breed sad sorrows for themselves.'
- Emily Bronte

'A feeling of sadness and longing that is not akin to pain, and resembles sorrow only as the mist resembles the rain.'
- Henry Wadsworth Longfellow

'Sadness flies away on the wings of time.'
- Jean de la Fontaine

'Sadness flies on the wings of the morning, and out of the heart of darkness comes the light.'
- Jean Giraudoux

'No sadder proof can be given by a man of his own littleness, than disbelief in great men.'
- Thomas Carlyle

SELF-CONTROL

'I know too well the poison and the sting Of things too sweet.'
  - Adelaide Proctor

'There is only one corner of the universe you can be certain of improving, and that's your own self.'
  - Aldous Huxley

'Don't give advice unless you're asked.'
  - Amy Alcott

'Beware of allowing a tactless word, rebuttal, a rejection to obliterate the whole sky.'
  - Anais Nin

'Sweet words are like honey, a little may refresh, but too much gluts the stomach.'
  - Anne Bradstreet

'When one clings to the myth of superiority, one must constantly overlook the virtues and abilities of others.'
  - Anne Wilson Schaef

'Anger is only one letter short of danger.'
  - Anonymous

'What lies in our power to do, it lies in our power not to do.'
  - Aristotle

'I count him braver who overcomes his desires than him who conquers his enemies; the hardest victory is the victory over self.'
  - Aristotle

'I listen and give input only if somebody asks.'
  - Barbara Bush

'Don't confuse being stimulating with being blunt.'
  - Barbara Walters

'You've got to ensure that the holders of an opinion, however unpopular, are allowed to put across their points of view.'
  - Betty Boothroyd

'Gammy used to say, "Too much scrubbing takes the life right out of things."'
  - Betty MacDonald

'He that hath no rule over his own spirit is like a city that is broken down, and without walls.'
  - Bible

'I will write of him who fights and vanquishes his sins, who struggles on through weary years against himself ... and wins.'
- Caroline Begelow LeRow

'The silence of a man who loves to praise is a censure sufficiently severe.'
- Charlotte Lennox

'There is space within sisterhood for likeness and difference, for the subtle differences that challenge and delight; there is space for disappointment- and surprise.'
- Christine Downing

'Everybody's business is nobody's business, and nobody's business is my business.'
- Clara Barton

'If you can't write your message in a sentence, you can't say it in an hour.'
- Dianna Booher

'Talk uses up ideas. ... Once I have spoken them aloud, they are lost to me, dissipated into the noisy air like smoke. Only if I bury them, like bulbs, in the rich soil of silence do they grow.'
- Doris Grumbach

'No man is free who is not master of himself.'
- Epictetus

'It goes without saying that you should never have more children than you have car windows.'
- Erma Bombeck

'Next to entertaining or impressive talk, a thoroughgoing silence manages to intrigue most people.'
- Florence Hurst Harriman

'Love understands love; it needs no talk.'
- Frances Ridley Havergal

'All the feeling which my father could not put into words was in his hand- any dog, child, or horse would recognize the kindness of it.'
- Freya Stark

'Would that there were an award for people who come to understand the concept of enough. Good enough. Successful enough. Thin enough. Rich enough. Socially responsible enough. When you have self-respect you have enough.'
- Gail Sheehy

'Transformation also means looking for ways to stop pushing yourself so hard professionally or inviting so much stress.'
- Gail Sheehy

'Self-control is the quality that distinguishes the fittest to survive.'
- George Bernard Shaw

'Blessed is the man who, having nothing to say, abstains from giving wordy evidence of the fact.'
- George Eliot

'The desire to conquer is itself a sort of subjection.'
- George Eliot

'Leaders can be moral-and they should be moral-without imposing their morality on others.'
- Geraldine Ferraro

'To put a tempting face aside when duty demands every faculty is a lesson which takes most men longest to learn.'
- Gertrude Atherton

'Nothing could bother me more than the way a thing goes dead once it has been said.'
- Gertrude Stein

'What we do upon some great occasion will probably depend on what we already are; and what we are will be the result of previous years of self-discipline.'
- H. P. Liddon

'Silence is one of the great arts of conversation.'
- Hannah Moore

'Who is apt, on occasion, to assign a multitude of reasons when one will do? This is a sure sign of weakness in argument.'
- Harriet Martineau

'Never fail to know that if you are doing all the talking, you are boring somebody.'
- Helen Gurley Brown

'The highest result of education is tolerance.'
- Helen Keller

'A mind which really lays hold of a subject is not easily detached from it.'
- Ida Tarbell

'You must learn to be still in the midst of activity, and to be vibrantly alive in repose.'
- Indira Gandhi

'You were once wild here. Don't let them tame you!'
- Isadora Duncan

'Minimum information given with maximum politeness.'
- Jacqueline Kennedy Onassis

'The less said the better.'
- Jane Austen

'When we start deceiving ourselves into thinking not that we want something or need something, not that it is a pragmatic necessity for us to have it, but that it is a moral imperative that we have it. Then is when we join the fashionable madmen, and then '
- Joan Didion

'He who reigns within himself and rules his passions, desires, and fears is more than a king.'
- John Milton

'Many people have the ambition to succeed; they may even have a special aptitude for their job. And yet they do not move ahead. Why? Perhaps they think that since they can master the job, there is no need to master themselves.'
- John Stevenson

'You must have discipline to have fun.'
- Julia Child

'The strokes of the pen need deliberation as much as the sword needs swiftness.'
- Julia Ward Howe

'Without discipline, there's no life at all.'
- Katharine Hepburn

'The point of good writing is knowing when to stop.'
- L. M. Montgomery

'He who conquers others is strong; he who conquers himself is mighty.'
- Lao-Tzu

'We don't want to push our ideas on to customers, we simply want to make what they want.'
- Laura Ashley

'I like people who refuse to speak until they are ready to speak.'
- Lillian Hellman

'For fast-acting relief try slowing down.'
- Lily Tomlin

'A gossip is one who talks to you about others; a bore is one who talks to you about himself; and a brilliant conversationalist is one who talks to you about yourself.'
- Lisa Kirk

'There is little that can withstand a man who can conquer himself.'
- Louis XIV

'A little kingdom I possess, Where thoughts and feelings dwell; And very hard the task I find Of governing it well.'
- Louisa May Alcott

'It was enough just to sit there without words.'
    - Louise Erdrich

'Too often in ironing out trouble someone gets scorched.'
    - Marcelene Cox

'Most powerful is he who has himself in his own power.'
    - Marcus Annaeus Seneca

'There is no hierarchy of values by which one culture has the right to insist on all its own values and
deny those of another.'
    - Margaret Mead

'Temptations come, as a general rule, when they are sought.'
    - Margaret Oliphant

'To wear your heart on your sleeve isn't a very good plan; you should wear it inside, where it functions
best.'
    - Margaret Thatcher

'Waiting is one of the great arts.'
    - Margery Allingham

'The passion for setting people right is in itself an afflictive disease.'
    - Marianne Moore

'Superior people never make long visits.'
    - Marianne Moore

'Lack of discipline leads to frustration and self-loathing.'
    - Marie Chapian

'The fool shouts loudly, thinking to impress the world.'
    - Marie de France

'One sees intelligence far more than one hears it. People do not always say transcendental things, but
if they are capable of saying them, it is always visible.'
    - Marie Leneru

'A little of what you fancy does you good.'
    - Marie Lloyd

'As far as your self-control goes, as far goes your freedom.'
    - Marie von Ebner-Eschenbach

'In a society where the rights and potential of women are constrained, no man can be truly free. He
may have power, but he will not have freedom.'
    - Mary F. Robinson

'That is always our problem, not how to get control of people, but how all together we can get control of a situation.'
- Mary Parker Follett

'Talking too much, too soon, and with too much self-satisfTaking Action has always seemed to me a sure way to court disaster.'
- Meg Greenfield

'Not being able to govern events, I govern myself.'
- Michel de Montaigne

'The only people who would be in government are those who care more about people than they do about power.'
- Millicent Fenwick

'Violence of the tongue is very real- sharper than any knife.'
- Mother Teresa

'It is impossible to persuade a man who does not disagree, but smiles.'
- Muriel Spark

'When you borrow trouble you give your peace of mind as security.'
- Myrtle Reed

'Silence and reserve will give anyone a reputation for wisdom.'
- Myrtle Reed

'The strong man is the one who is able to intercept at will the communication between the senses and the mind.'
- Napoleon Bonaparte

'It isn't until you come to a spiritual understanding of who you are-not necessarily a religious feeling, but deep down, the spirit within-that you can begin to take control.'
- Oprah Winfrey

'A woman that's too soft and sweet is like tapioca pudding-fine for them as likes it.'
- Osa Johnson

'The longest absence is less perilous to love than the terrible trials of incessant proximity.'
- Ouida

'Handle them carefully, for words have more power than atom bombs.'
- Pearl Strachan Hurd

'Man who man would be, must rule the empire of himself.'
- Percy Bysshe Shelley

'He that would govern others should first be the master of himself.'
- Philip Massinger

'This is the gist of what I know: Give advice and buy a foe.'
  - Phyllis McGinley

'I am, indeed, a king, because I know how to rule myself.'
  - Pietro Aretino

'The man who masters his own soul will forever be called conqueror of conquerors.'
  - Plautus

'Self-command is the main elegance.'
  - Ralph Waldo Emerson

'When the fight begins within himself, a man's worth something.'
  - Robert Browning

'He that would be superior to external influences must first become superior to his own passions.'
  - Samuel Johnson

'The basic difference between being assertive and being aggressive is how our words and behavior affect the rights and well-being of others.'
  - Sharon Anthony Bower

'A story is told as much by silence as by speech.'
  - Susan Griffin

'Don't be curious of matters that don't concern you; never speak of them, and don't ask about them.'
  - Teresa of Avila

'Ambition, old as mankind, the immemorial weakness of the strong.'
  - Vita Sackville-West

SELF-REALIZATION

'One truth is clear, Whatever is is right.'
 - Alexander Pope

'We succeed in enterprises which demand the positive qualities we possess, but we excel in those which can also make use of our defects.'
 - Alexis de Tocqueville

'It is healthier, in any case, to write for the adults one's children will become than for the children one's "mature" critics often are.'
 - Alice Walker

'I don't tell the truth any more to those who can't make use of it. I tell it mostly to myself, because it always changes me.'
 - Anais Nin

'Nothing is good for everyone, but only relatively to some people.'
 - Andre Gide

'It is better to be hated for what you are than loved for what you are not.'
 - Andre Gide

'We live counterfeit lives in order to resemble the idea we first had of ourselves.'
 - Andre Gide

'Nobody is so miserable as he who longs to be somebody other than the person he is.'
 - Angelo Patri

'The most exhausting thing in life is being insincere.'
 - Anne Morrow Lindbergh

'Put your ear down close to your soul and listen hard.'
 - Anne Sexton

'It is possible to be different and still be all right.'
 - Anne Wilson Schaef

'Different people have different duties assigned to them by Nature; Nature has given one the power or the desire to do this, the other that. Each bird must sing with his own throat.'
 - Anonymous

'What one man does, another fails to do; what's fit for me may not be fit for you.'
 - Anonymous

"Tis a gift to be simple, 'tis a gift to be free. 'Tis a gift to come round to where we ought to be. And when we find a place that feels just right, We will be in the valley of love and delight.'
- Anonymous

'If I trim myself to suit others I will soon whittle myself away.'
- Anonymous

'Bloom where you are planted.'
- Anonymous

'Freedom and constraint are two aspects of the same necessity, the necessity of being the man you are, and not another. You are free to be that man, but not free to be another.'
- Antoine de Saint-Exupery

'Different men seek after happiness in different ways and by different means, and so make for themselves different modes of life.'
- Aristotle

'It is not a dreamlike state, but the somehow insulated state, that a great musician achieves in a great performance. He's aware of where he is and what he's doing, but his mind is on the playing of his instrument with an internal sense of Tightness-it is '
- Arnold Palmer

'The moment that any life, however good, stifles you, you may be sure it isn't your real life.'
- Arthur Christopher Benson

'The deepest personal defeat suffered by human beings is constituted by the difference between what one was capable of becoming, and what one has in fact become.'
- Ashley Montagu

'Are you doing the kind of work you were built for, so that you can expect to be able to do very large amounts of that kind and thrive under it? Or are you doing a kind of which you can do comparatively little?'
- B. C. Forbes

'There is a need to find and sing our own song, to stretch our limbs and shake them in a dance so wild that nothing can roost there, that stirs the yearning for solitary voyage.'
- Barbara Lazear Ascher

'I was the kind nobody thought could make it. I had a funny Boston accent. I couldn't pronounce my R's. I wasn't a beauty.'
- Barbara Walters

'Me, I'm just a hack. I'm just a schlep-per. I just do what I can do.'
- Bette Midler

'When she stopped conforming to the conventional picture of femininity she finally began to enjoy being a woman.'
- Betty Friedan

'To every man according to his ability.'
- Bible

'We don't see many fat men walking on stilts.'
- Bud Miller

'Any path is only a path, and there is no affront, to oneself or to others, in dropping it if that is what your heart tells you.'
- Carlos Castaneda

'True inward quietness ... is not vacancy, but stability-the steadfastness of a single purpose.'
- Caroline Stephen

'When a just cause reaches its flood-tide, as ours has done ..., whatever stands in the way must fall before its overwhelming power.'
- Carrie Chapman Catt

'The search for a new personality is futile; what is fruitful is the human interest the old personality can take in new activities.'
- Cesare Pavese

'We are sure to be losers when we quarrel with ourselves; it is civil war.'
- Charles Caleb Colton

'Happiness, that grand mistress of the ceremonies in the dance of life, impels us through all its mazes and meanderings, but leads none of us by the same route.'
- Charles Caleb Colton

'The white light streams down to be broken up by those human prisms into all the colors of the rainbow. Take your own color in the pattern and be just that.'
- Charles R. Brown

'The first duty of a human being is to assume the right relationship to society-more briefly, to find your real job, and do it.'
- Charlotte P. Gilman

'I searched through rebellion, drugs, diets, mysticism, religions, intellectualism and much more, only to begin to find ... that truth is basically simple-and feels good, clean and right.'
- Chick Corea

'If Heaven made him, earth can find some use for him.'
- Chinese proverb

'Live as you will wish to have lived when you are dying.'
- Christian Furchtegott Gellert

'There is only one success-to be able to spend your life in your own way.'
- Christopher Morley

'The door that nobody else will go in at, seems always to swing open widely for me.'
  - Clara Barton

'I was playing it like Willie Wilson, but I forgot that I'm in Clint Hurdle's body.'
  - Clint Hurdle

'We only do well the things we like doing.'
  - Colette

'Theories are like scaffolding: they are not the house, but you cannot build the house without them.'
  - Constance Fenimore Woolson

'Dedication to one's work in the world is the only possible sanctification. Religion in all its forms is dedication to Someone Else's work, not yours.'
  - Cynthia Ozick

'Be sure you are right, then go ahead.'
  - David Crockett

'All the discontented people I know are trying to be something they are not, to do something they cannot do.'
  - David Graydon

'Keep your promises to yourself.'
  - David Harold Fink

'Men are created different; they lose their social freedom and their individual autonomy in seeking to become like each other.'
  - David Riesman

'What I wanted was to be allowed to do the thing in the world that I did best-which I believed then and believe now is the greatest privilege there is. When I did that, success found me.'
  - Debbi Fields

'I don't go by the rule book-I lead from the heart, not the head.'
  - Diana, Princess of Wales

'Whatever you want in life, other people are going to want it too. Believe in yourself enough to accept the idea that you have an equal right to it.'
  - Diane Sawyer

'I'm not going to limit myself just because some people won't accept the fact that I can do something else.'
  - Dolly Parton

'I have the feeling when I write poetry that I'm doing what I'm supposed to do. You don't think about whether you're going to get money or fame, you just do it.'
  - Doris Lund

'No matter where I run, I meet myself there.'
- Dorothy Fields

'Success based on anything but internal fulfillment is bound to be empty.'
- Dr. Martha Friedman

'To be nobody-but-yourself-in a world which is doing its best, night and day, to make you everybody else-means to fight the hardest battle which any human being can fight; and never stop fighting.'
- e. e. cummings

'In efforts to soar above our nature, we invariably fall below it.'
- Edgar Allan Poe

'People are always neglecting something they can do in trying to do something they can't do.'
- Edgar Watson Howe

'Why not be oneself? That is the whole secret of a successful appearance. If one is a greyhound, why try to look like a Pekingese?'
- Edith Sitwell

'Criticism ... makes very little dent upon me, unless I think there is some real justification and something should be done.'
- Eleanor Roosevelt

'Remember always that you have not only the right to be an individual, you have an obligation to be one.'
- Eleanor Roosevelt

'Our concern must be to live while we're alive ... to release our inner selves from the spiritual death that comes with living behind a facade designed to conform to external definitions of who and what we are.'
- Elisabeth Kubler-Ross

'Dress to please yourself.... Forget you are what you wear.... Wear what you are.'
- Elizabeth Hawkes

'Like the winds of the sea are the ways of fate; As the voyage along thru life; 'Tis the will of the soul That decides its goal, And not the calm or the strife.'
- Ella Wheeler Wilcox

'I'll walk where my own nature would be leading; it vexes me to choose another guide.'
- Emily Bronte

'The world may take your reputation from you, but it cannot take your character.'
- Emma Dunham Kelley

'The history of human growth is at the same time the history of every new idea heralding the approach of a brighter dawn, and the brighter dawn has always been considered illegal, outside of the

law.'
- Emma Goldman

'Two wrongs can never make a right.'
- English proverb

'Do you know that disease and death must needs overtake us, no matter what we are doing? ... What do you wish to be doing when it overtakes you?... If you have anything better to be doing when you are so overtaken, get to work on that.'
- Epictetus

'I write lustily and humorously. It isn't calculated; it's the way I think. I've invented a writing style that expresses who I am.'
- Erica Jong

'Integrity simply means a willingness not to violate one's identity.'
- Erich Fromm

'Personality, too, is destiny.'
- Erik H. Erikson

'There is just one life for each of us: our own.'
- Euripides

'The same man cannot be skilled in everything; each has his special excellence.'
- Euripides

'Innovators are inevitably controversial.'
- Eva Le Gallienne

'There are as many ways to live and grow as there are people. Our own ways are the only ways that should matter to us.'
- Evelyn Mandel

'Let the world know you as you are, not as you think you should be, because sooner or later, if you are posing, you will forget the pose, and then where are you?'
- Fanny Brice

'I am a writer because writing is the thing I do best.'
- Flannery O'Connor

'Every man must get to heaven his own way.'
- Frederick the Great

'Every person is responsible for all the good within the scope of his abilities, and for no more.'
- Gail Hamilton

'The source of continuing aliveness was to find your passion and pursue it, with whole heart and single mind.'
- Gail Sheehy

'Until you know that life is interesting, and find it so, you haven't found your soul.'
- Geoffrey Fisher

'If you go to heaven without being naturally qualified for it, you will not enjoy it there.'
- George Bernard Shaw

'I'd rather be a failure at something I enjoy than a success at something I hate.'
- George Burns

'To feel that one has a place in life solves half the problem of contentment.'
- George E. Woodberry

'Each of us has some unique capability waiting for realization. Every person is valuable in his own existence, for himself alone ... each of us can bring to fruition these innate, God-given abilities.'
- George H. Bender

'We are betrayed by what is false within.'
- George Meredith

'The great enemy of clear language is insincerity. When there is a gap between one's real and one's declared aims, one turns, as it were, instinctively to long words and exhausted idioms, like a cuttlefish squirting out ink.'
- George Orwell

'Heaven itself has ordained the right.'
- George Washington

'When I was young, I said to God, "God, tell me the mystery of the universe." But God answered, "That knowledge is reserved for me alone." So I said, "God, tell me the mystery of the peanut." Then God said, "Well George, that's more nearly your size." And '
- George Washington Carver

'Follow what you love! Don't deign to ask what "they" are looking for out there. Ask what you have inside. Follow not your interests, which change, but what you are and what you love, which will and should not change.'
- Georgie Anne Geyer

'A rose is a rose is a rose.'
- Gertrude Stein

'Let me listen to me and not to them.'
- Gertrude Stein

'People are ridiculous only when they try or seem to be that which they are not.'
- Giacomo Leopardi

'A man like Verdi must write like Verdi.'
- Giuseppe Verdi

'Go ahead and do it. It's much easier to apologize after something's been done than to get permission ahead of time.'
- Grace Murray Hopper

'Starting out to make money is the greatest mistake in life. Do what you feel you have a flair for doing, and if you are good enough at it, the money will come.'
- Greer Garson

'The one thing that doesn't abide by majority rule is a person's conscience.'
- Harper Lee

'All I would tell people is to hold on to what was individual about themselves, not to allow their ambition for success to cause them to try to imitate the success of others. You've got to find in on your own terms.'
- Harrison Ford

'Philosophy is a purely personal matter. A genuine philosopher's credo is the outcome of a single complex personality; it cannot be transferred. No two persons, if sincere, can have the same philosophy.'
- Havelock Ellis

'Individuals learn faster than institutions and it is always the dinosaur's brain that is the last to get the new messages.'
- Hazel Henderson

'One can never consent to creep when one feels an impulse to soar.'
- Helen Keller

'Our whole life is an attempt to discover when our spontaneity is whimsical, sentimental irresponsibility and when it is a valid expression of our deepest desires and values.'
- Helen Merrell Lynd

'What's a man's first duty? The answer is brief: To be himself.'
- Henrik Ibsen

'Sir, I would rather be right than be President.'
- Henry Clay

'The question "Who ought to be boss" is like asking "Who ought to be tenor in the quartet?" Obviously, the man who can sing tenor.'
- Henry Ford

'The only success worth one's powder was success in the line of one's idiosyncrasy ... what was talent but the art of being completely whatever one happened to be?'
- Henry James

'Every man has his own destiny; the only imperative is to follow it, to accept it, no matter where it leads him.'
- Henry Miller

'What's important is finding out what works for you.'
- Henry Moore

'A door that seems to stand open must be of a man's size, or it is not the door that providence means for him.'
- Henry Ward Beecher

'Choose a subject equal to your abilities; think carefully what your shoulders may refuse, and what they are capable of bearing.'
- Horace

'Posterity weaves no garlands for imitators.'
- J. C. F. von Schiller

'Don't take anyone else's definition of success as your own. (This is easier said than done.)'
- Jacqueline Briskin

'No man can produce great things who is not thoroughly sincere in dealing with himself'
- James Russell Lowell

'Getting fit is a political act-you are taking charge of your life.'
- Jane Fonda

'To aim at the best and to remain essentially ourselves is one and the same thing.'
- Janet Erskine Stuart

'Don't compromise yourself. You are all you've got.'
- Janis Joplin

'The crow that mimics a cormorant gets drowned.'
- Japanese proverb

'I'm uncomfortable when I'm comfortable ... I can't help it, it's my personality.'
- Jay Chiat

'One should stick to the sort of thing for which one was made; I tried to be an herbalist, whereas I should keep to the butcher's trade.'
- Jean de la Fontaine

'Don't do anything that someone else can do for you because there are only so many things that only you can do.'
- Jinger Heath

'He who walks in another's tracks leaves no footprints.'
- Joan L. Brannon

'Man is not born to solve the problems of the universe, but to find out what he has to do ... within the limits of his comprehension.'
- Johann von Goethe

'Everybody undertakes what he sees another successful in, whether he has the aptitude for it or not.'
- Johann von Goethe

'That suit is best that best suits me.'
- John Clark

'The weakest among us has a gift, however seemingly trivial, which is peculiar to him and which worthily used will be a gift also to his race.'
- John Ruskin

'When men are rightfully occupied, then their amusement grows out of their work as the color petals out of a fruitful garden.'
- John Ruskin

'Brutes find out where their talents lie; a bear will not attempt to fly.'
- Jonathan Swift

'Abasement, degradation is simply the manner of life of the man who has refused to be what it is his duty to be.'
- Jose Ortega y Gasset

'All life is the struggle, the effort to be itself.'
- Jose Ortega y Gasset

'Be what you are. This is the first step toward becoming better than you are.'
- Julius Charles Hare

'If you have to support yourself, you had bloody well better find some way that is going to be interesting.'
- Katharine Hepburn

'To keep your character intact you cannot stoop to filthy acts. It makes it easier to stoop the next time.'
- Katharine Hepburn

'The best career advice given to the young ... is "Find out what you like doing best and get someone to pay you for doing it."'
- Katharine Whitehorn

'Keep integrity and your work ethics intact. So what if that means working a little harder; an honorable character is your best calling card, and that's something anyone can have!'
- Kathy Ireland

'Education should be the process of helping everyone to discover his uniqueness.'
- Leo Buscaglia

'For a long time the only time I felt beautiful-in the sense of being complete as a woman, as a human being, and even female-was when I was singing.'
- Leontyne Price

'The test of a vocation is the love of the drudgery it involves.'
- Logan Pearsall Smith

'A woman who is willing to be herself and pursue her own potential runs not so much the risk of loneliness as the challenge of exposure to more interesting men-and people in general.'
- Lorraine Hansbury

'The fun of being alive is realizing you have a talent and you can use it every day so it grows stronger.... And if you're in an atmosphere where this talent is appreciated instead of just tolerated, why, it's just as good as sex.'
- Lou Centlivre

'In the first grade, I already knew the pattern of my life. I didn't know the living of it, but I knew the line. ... From the first day in school until the day I graduated, everyone gave me one hundred plus in art. Well, where do you go in life? You go to '
- Louise Nevelson

'I think God rarely gives to one man, or one set of men, more than one great moral victory to win.'
- Lucy Stone

'As you go along your road in life, you will, if you aim high enough, also meet resistance ... but no matter how tough the opposition may seem, have courage still-and persevere.'
- Madeleine Albright

'Man has no nobler function than to defend the truth.'
- Mahalia Jackson

'The possibilities are unlimited as long as you are true to your life's purpose.'
- Marcia Wieder

'What does reason demand of a man? A very easy thing-to live in accord with his own nature.'
- Marcus Annaeus Seneca

'This is the chief thing: be not perturbed, for all things are according to the nature of the universal.'
- Marcus Aurelius

'Let them know a real man, who lives as he was meant to live.'
- Marcus Aurelius

'The great thing to learn about life is, first, not to do what you don't want to do, and, second, to do what you do want to do.'
- Margaret Anderson

'Any talent that we are born with eventually surfaces as a need.'
- Marsha Sinetar

'Do what you love, the money will follow.'
- Marsha Sinetar

'We don't know who we are until we see what we can do.'
- Martha Grimes

'While you cannot resolve what you are, at last you will be nothing.'
- Martial

'Here I stand. I can do no other. God help me. Amen.'
- Martin Luther

'Resolve to be thyself ... he who finds himself loses his misery!'
- Matthew Arnold

'The greatest thing in the world is to know how to be one's own self'
- Michel de Montaigne

'There's no right way of writing. There's only your way.'
- Milton Lomask

'Everyone has a right to his own course of Taking Action.'
- Moliere

'My mother said to me, "If you become a soldier, you'll be a general, if you become a monk you'll end up as the pope." Instead, I became a painter and wound up as Picasso.'
- Pablo Picasso

'The first and worst of all frauds is to cheat one's self. All sin is easy after that.'
- Pearl Bailey

'The first thing is to love your sport. Never do it to please someone else. It has to be yours.'
- Peggy Fleming

'Be not imitator; freshly act thy part; Through this world be thou an independent ranger; Better is the faith that springeth from thy heart Than a better faith belonging to a stranger.'
- Persian proverb

'Everything keeps its best nature only by being put to its best use.'
- Phillips Brooks

'Skills vary with the man. We must... strive by that which is born in us.'
- Pindar

'Learn what you are, and be such.'
- Pindar

'Each citizen should play his part in the community according to his individual gifts.'
- Plato

'With begging and scrambling we find very little, but with being true to ourselves we find a great deal more.'
- Rabindranath Tagore

'It is the soul's duty to be loyal to its own desires.'
- Rebecca West

'Ask yourself the secret of your success. Listen to your answer, and practice it.'
- Richard Bach

'Men can starve from a lack of self-realization as much as they can from a lack of bread.'
- Richard Wright

'To know what you prefer, instead of humbly saying "Amen" to what the world tells you you ought to prefer, is to keep your soul alive.'
- Robert Louis Stevenson

'Mountains should be climbed with as little effort as possible and without desire. The reality of your own nature should determine the speed. If you become restless, speed up. If you become winded, slow down. You climb the mountain in an equilibrium betwee'
- Robert M. Pirsig

'A man must be obedient to the promptings of his innermost heart.'
- Robertson Davies

'In my clinical experience, the greatest block to a person's development is his having to take on a way of life which is not rooted in his own powers.'
- Rollo May

'I had already learned from more than a decade of political life that I was going to be criticized no matter what I did, so I might as well be criticized for something I wanted to do.'
- Rosalynn Carter

'He will hew to the line of right, let the chips fly where they may.'
- Roscoe Conkling

'Do not wish to be anything but what you are.'
- Saint Francis de Sales

'God requires a faithful fulfillment of the merest trifle given us to do, rather than the most ardent aspiration to things to which we are not called.'
- Saint Francis de Sales

'You must be holy in the way God asks you to be holy. God does not ask you to be a Trappist monk or a hermit. He wills that you sanctify your everyday life.'
- Saint Vincent Pallotti

'I was raised to sense what someone wanted me to be and be that kind of person. It took me a long time not to judge myself through someone else's eyes.'
    - Sally Field

'No matter how ill we may be, nor how low we may have fallen, we should not change identity with any other person.'
    - Samuel Butler

'We will discover the nature of our particular genius when we stop trying to conform to our own or to other people's models, learn to be ourselves, and allow our natural channel to open.'
    - Shakti Gawain

'What really matters is what you do with what you have.'
    - Shirley Lord

'The pain of leaving those you grow to love is only the prelude to understanding yourself and others.'
    - Shirley MacLaine

'No amount of study or learning will make a man a leader unless he has the natural qualities of one.'
    - Sir Archibald Wavell

'Do what thy manhood bids thee do.'
    - Sir Richard Burton

'We must remember that one determined person can make a significant difference, and that a small group of determined people can change the course of history.'
    - Sonia Johnson

'All is disgust when one leaves his own nature and does things that misfit it.'
    - Sophocles

'I'm a salami writer. I try to write good salami, but salami is salami.'
    - Stephen King

'To have no set purpose in one's life is harlotry of the will.'
    - Stephen McKenna

'Whatever you are by nature, keep to it; never desert your own line of talent. Be what nature intended you for, and you will succeed; be anything else and you will be ten thousand times worse than nothing.'
    - Sydney Smith

'Men whose trade is rat-catching, love to catch rats; the bug destroyer seizes on his bug with delight; and the suppressor is gratified by finding his vice.'
    - Sydney Smith

'If you're gonna be a failure, at least be one at something you enjoy.'
    - Sylvester Stallone

'I believe there's an inner power that makes winners or losers. And the winners are the ones who really listen to the truth of their hearts.'
- Sylvester Stallone

'Truth has beauty, power, and necessity.'
- Sylvia Townsend Warner

'I wrote because I had to. I couldn't stop. There wasn't anything else I could do. If no one ever bought anything, anything I ever did, I'd still be writing. It's beyond a compulsion.'
- Tennessee Williams

'The great law of culture: Let each become all that he was created capable of being.'
- Thomas Carlyle

'The hole and the patch should be commensurate.'
- Thomas Jefferson

'The self is not something that one finds. It is something one creates.'
- Thomas Szasz

'If a man has a talent and cannot use it, he has failed. If he has a talent and uses only half of it, he has partly failed. If he has a talent and learns somehow to use the whole of it, he has gloriously succeeded, and won a satisfTaking Action and a triumph few '
- Thomas Wolfe

'I know that I haven't powers enough to divide myself into one who earns and one who creates.'
- Tillie Olsen

'I is who I is.'
- Tom Peterson

'We are traditionally rather proud of ourselves for having slipped creative work in there between the domestic chores and obligations. I'm not sure we deserve such big A-pluses for all that.'
- Toni Morrison

'There is always a certain peace in being what one is, in being that completely. The condemned man has that joy.'
- Ugo Betti

'The greatest achievement of the human spirit is to live up to one's opportunities and make the most of one's resources.'
- Vauvenargues

'I was and I always shall be hampered by what I think other people will say.'
- Violette Leduc

'We do not write as we want but as we can.'
- W. Somerset Maugham

'Right is the eternal sun; the world cannot delay its coming.'
  - Wendell Phillips

'We can't all be heroes, because someone has to sit on the curb and clap as they go by.'
  - Will Rogers

'I'd rather be a lamppost in Chicago than a millionaire in any other city.'
  - William A. Hulbert

'Every human being is intended to have a character of his own; to be what no others are, and to do what no other can do.'
  - William Ellery Channing

'Don't bother just to be better than your contemporaries or predecessors. Try to be better than yourself.'
  - William Faulkner

'Seek out that particular mental attitude which makes you feel most deeply and vitally alive, along with which comes the inner voice which says, "This is the real me," and when you have found that attitude, follow it.'
  - William James

'Whenever it is possible, a boy should choose some occupation which he should do even if he did not need the money.'
  - William Lyon Phelps

'This above all: to thine own self be true.'
  - William Shakespeare

'We would have to settle for the elegant goal of becoming ourselves.'
  - William Styron

'The things that one most wants to do are the things that are probably most worth doing.'
  - Winifred Holtby

'The driver knows how much the ox can carry, and keeps the ox from being overloaded. You know your way and your state of mind. Do not carry too much.'
  - Zen saying

'In the world to come they will not ask me, "Why were you not Moses?" They will ask me, "Why were you not Zusya?"'
  - Zusya of Hanipoli

SEX

'Accept every blind date you can get, even with a girl who wears jeans. Maybe you can talk her out of them.'
  - Abigail Van Buren

'Sex ought to be a wholly satisfying link between two affectionate people from which they emerge unanxious, rewarded, and ready for more.'
  - Alex Comfort

'Amoebas at the start were not complex -They tore themselves apart and started sex.'
  - Arthur Guiterman

'I'll wager that in ten years it will be fashionable again to be a virgin.'
  - Barbara Cartland

'The cable TV sex channels don't expand our horizons, don't make us better people, and don't come in clearly enough.'
  - Bill Maker

'Condoms aren't completely safe. A friend of mine was wearing one . . . and got hit by a bus.'
  - Bob Rubin

'I wasn't kissing her. I was whispering in her mouth.'
  - Chico Marx

'Sex - the poor man's polo.'
  - Clifford Odets

'When she raises her eyelids it's as if she were taking off all her clothes.'
  - Colette

'Sex is the great amateur art.'
  - David Cort

'The reason that husbands and wives do not understand each other is because they belong to different sexes.'
  - Dorothy Dix

'I am always looking for meaningful one-night stands.'
  - Dudley Moore

'I was with this girl the other night, and from the way she was responding to my skillful caresses, you would have sworn she was conscious from the top of her head to the tag on her toes.'
  - Emo Philips

'Sex, unlike justice, should not be seen to be done.'
- Evelyn Laye

'While a person does not give up on sex, sex does not give up on the person.'
- Gabriel Garcia Marquez

'Whatever else can be said about sex, it cannot be called a dignified performance.'
- Helen Lawrenson

'Sex is one of the nine reasons for reincarnation. The other eight are unimportant.'
- Henry Miller

'It's been so long since I made love I can't even remember who gets tied up.'
- Joan Rivers

'Sex is like money; only too much is enough.'
- John Updike

'Sara could commit adultery at one end and weep for her sins at the other, and enjoy both operations at once.'
- Joyce Carey

'Every animal is sad after intercourse.'
- Latin proverb

'My wife is a sex object - every time I ask for sex, she objects.'
- Les Dawson

'There will be sex after death; we just won't be able to feel it.'
- Lily Tomlin

'Sex is an emotion in motion.'
- Mae West

'It may be the cock that crows, but it is the hen that lays the eggs.'
- Margaret Thatcher

'Sex is a relatively recent addition to the dance of life. For more than 2,000,000,000 years, asexual reproduction was the rule. You know, if you were a creature, you just separated into two clones.'
- Mark Jerome Walters

'Two-parent sex appeared on the scene about 500,000,000 years ago.'
- Mark Jerome Walters

'Definition of a Jewish nymphomaniac: A woman who will make love the same day she has her hair done.'
- Maureen Lipman

'For birth control I rely on my personality.'
- Milt Abel

'Sex at eighty-four is terrific, especially the one in the winter.'
- Milton Berle

'There are a number of mechanical devices which increase sexual arousal, particularly in women. Chief among these is the Mercedes-Benz 380 SL convertible.'
- P. J. O'Rourke

'In opposition to sex education: Let the kids today learn it where we did - in the gutter.'
- Pat Paulsen

'Girls are much more psychic than guys. They're the first to know if you're going to get laid.'
- Paul Rodriguez

'When a man tells me he's run out of steam in the sex department, I'll tell him, 'Count your blessings; you've escaped from the clutches of a cruel tyrant. Enjoy!''
- Richard J. Needham

'Of all sexual aberrations, perhaps the most peculiar is chastity.'
- Rimy de Gourmont

'All men look at Dr. Ruth and wonder how she has gained all that sexual experience.'
- Rita Rudner

'I'm at the age when food has taken the place of sex in my life. In fact, I've just had a mirror put over my kitchen table.'
- Rodney Dangerfield

'If it weren't for pickpockets I'd have no sex life at all.'
- Rodney Dangerfield

'As a matter of biology, if something bites you it is probably female.'
- Scott M. Kruse

'Lord, make me chaste - but not yet.'
- St. Augustine

'I can't believe that out of a hundred thousand sperm, you were the quickest.'
- Steven Pearl

'A promiscuous person is someone who is getting more sex than you are.'
- Victor Lownes

'The natural man has only two primal passions - to get and beget.'
- William Osier

'Is sex dirty? Only if it's done right.'
- Woody Allen

'If there is reincarnation, I'd like to come back as Warren Beatty's fingertips.'
- Woody Allen

'I like American women. They do things sexually Russian girls would never dream of doing - like showering.'
- Yakov Smirnoff

'Personally, I know nothing about sex because I've always been married.'
- Zsa Gabor

SPORTS

'My best score is 103, but I've only been playing for fifteen years.'
- Alex Karras

'Golf and sex: Two things you can really enjoy without being that good at them.'
- Anonymous

'This guy is such an obvious cheater that once, when he had a hole in one, he wrote down zero on his scorecard.'
- Anonymous

'I'm not playing with my brother-in-law today. Would you play with a man who improves his lie and cheats on his score? Well, neither would he!'
- Anonymous

'He who has the fastest cart never has a bad lie.'
- Anonymous

'If people focused on life's really important matters, there'd be a shortage of golf clubs.'
- Anonymous

'It's not that I really cheat at golf. I play for my health, and a low score makes me feel better.'
- Anonymous

'I asked my instructor how I could cut ten strokes off my score. He told me to quit on hole 17!'
- Arlene Powers

'Golf is like a love affair: if you don't take it seriously, it's no fun; if you do take it seriously, it breaks your heart.'
- Arnold Daly

'If you watch a game, it's fun. If you play it, it's recreation. If you work at it, it's golf.'
- Bob Hope

'I want you all to line up in alphabetical order, according to your size.'
- Casey Stengel

'They X-rayed my head and found nothing.'
- Dizzy Dean

'Baseball, it is said, is only a game. True. And the Grand Canyon is only a hole in Arizona. Not all holes, or games, are created equal.'
- George Will

'All pro athletes are bilingual. They speak English and profanity.'
- Gordie Howe

'By the time a man can afford to lose a golf ball, he can't hit that far.'
- Jacob Braude

'When I see joggers go by, I shout, "Jim Fixx is dead. Fats Domino lives!"'
- Jason Chase

'I used to want to shoot my age. Now I would just like to shoot my temperature.'
- Jerry Feliciotto

'Gimme: An agreement between two losers who can't putt.'
- Jim Bishop

'Your brain commands your body to "Run forward! Bend! Scoop up the ball! Peg it to the infield!" Then your body says, "Who, me?"'
- Joe DiMaggio

'I play in the low eighties. If it's any hotter than that, I won't play.'
- Joe E. Lewis

'Nobody in football should be called a genius. Football players are not like Norman Einstein.'
- Joe Theisman

'player: Can I reach it with a five iron? caddie: Eventually.'
- John Adams

'Slumps in life are like soft beds. They're easy to get into and hard to get out of.'
- Johnny Bench

'You know you're getting old when you start watching golf on TV and enjoying it.'
- Larry Miller

'What a terrible round. I only hit two good balls all day and that was when I stepped on a rake in a bunker.'
- Lee Trevino

'Counting both times I cheated this week, I won at solitaire twice.'
- Mary Virginia Micka

'I don't say my golf game is bad, but if I grew tomatoes, they'd come up sliced.'
- Miller Barber

'The reason the pro tells you to keep your head down is so you can't see him laughing.'
- Phyllis Diller

'My golf has really improved even though my score hasn't. I'm missing the ball much closer now.'
- Richard Bull

'Men are very confident people. Even a sixty-year-old man with no arms thinks he could play in the Super Bowl if he had to.'
- Rita Rudner

'My father watched football with the sound off because he lived in fear of hearing the voice of Howard Cosell.'
- Rita Rudner

'Go jogging? And get hit by a meteor?'
- Robert Benchley

'Golf is not a matter of life or death. It is much more important than that.'
- Rod Powers

'You've got just one problem. You stand too close to the ball - after you've hit it.'
- Sam Snead

'Golf is a good preoccupation, but as the meaning of life ... it lacks a few things.'
- Scotty Brown

'Our team was surprisingly consistent this year. We closed with a seven-seven record. We lost seven at home, and seven on the road.'
- Steve Wheeler

'Everywhere is walking distance if you have the time.'
- Steven Wright

'He spends so much time in the sand trap you'd think he was in the cast of Baywatcb.'
- Tim Conway

'Stated to a running back after an overly exuberant display of celebration: Next time you make a touchdown, act like you've been there before.'
- Vince Lombardi

'I get confused with all the rules in golf. Let's say you're playing in L.A. and your ball lands on a dead body. Is your relief one or two club lengths?'
- Wendy Morgan

'As a woman I resent the fact that in golf if I have the highest score, I'm the loser.'
- Wendy Morgan

'My golf is getting better all the time. Today I parred all but sixteen holes.'
- Wendy Morga

SUCCESS

'The secret of every man who has ever been successful lies in the fact that he formed the bait of doing those things that failures don't like to do.'
  - A. Jackson King

'The only way to the top is by persistent, intelligent, hard work.'
  - A. T. Mercier

'God may allow His servant to succeed when He has disciplined him to a point where he does not need to succeed to be happy. The man who is elated by success and is cast down by failure is still a carnal man. At best his fruit will have a worm in it.'
  - A. W. Tozer

'With the catching ends the pleasures of the chase.'
  - Abraham Lincoln

'If your efforts are sometimes greeted with indifference, don't lose heart. The sun puts on a wonderful show at daybreak, yet most of the people in the audience go on sleeping.'
  - Ada Teixeira

'We would often be sorry if our wishes were gratified.'
  - Aesop

'Plodding wins the race.'
  - Aesop

'Sometimes "the fool who rushes in" gets the job done.'
  - Al Bernstein

'If, after all, men cannot always make history have a meaning, they can always act so that their own lives have one.'
  - Albert Camus

'A successful man is he who receives a great deal from his fellow men, usually incomparably more than corresponds to his service to them. The value of a man, however, should be seen in what he gives, and not in what he is able to receive.'
  - Albert Einstein

'Try not to become a man of success, but rather a man of value.'
  - Albert Einstein

'The way to succeed is never quit. That's it. But really be humble about it. ... You start out lowly and humble and you carefully try to learn an accretion of little things that help you get there.'
  - Alex Haley

'There are few successful adults who were not first successful children.'
- Alexander Chase

'Nothing succeeds like success.'
- Alexander Dumas

'Get place and wealth, if possible with grace; If not, by any means get wealth and place.'
- Alexander Pope

'Perseverance, n.: A lowly virtue whereby mediocrity achieves a glorious success.'
- Ambrose Bierce

'Achievement: The death of an endeavor, and the birth of disgust.'
- Ambrose Bierce

'There is no scientific answer for success. You can't define it. You've simply got to live it and do it.'
- Anita Roddick

'A winner never quits, and a quitter never wins.'
- Anonymous

'When asked how long I've worked here, I replied, "since the day they threatened to fire me."'
- Anonymous

'The two hardest things to handle in life are failure and success.'
- Anonymous

'Success comes before work only in the dictionary.'
- Anonymous

'Eagles may soar, but weasels don't get sucked into jet engines.'
- Anonymous

'The problem is not that you cannot have what you think you want. The problem is that when you get what you think you want, it won't satisfy.'
- Anonymous

'Success is not so much what you are, but rather what you appear to be.'
- Anonymous

'Success is getting what you want; happiness is wanting what you get.'
- Anonymous

'If at first you succeed, don't take any more stupid chances.'
- Anonymous

'My success is measured by my willingness to keep trying.'
- Anonymous

'If a man wants his dreams to come true, he must wake up.'
- Anonymous

'It takes time to be a success.'
- Anonymous

'It takes time to be a success, but time is all it takes.'
- Anonymous

'Make yourself indispensable and you'll be moved up. Act as if you're indispensable and you'll be moved out.'
- Anonymous

'Progress means taking risks, for you can't steal home and keep your foot on third base.'
- Anonymous

'Nothing except a battle lost can be half so melancholy as a battle won.'
- Arthur Wellesley

'Of course there is no formula for success except perhaps, an unconditional acceptance of life and what it brings.'
- Artur Rubinstein

'The man who has done his level best, and who is conscious that he has done his best, is a success, even though the world may write him down a failure.'
- B. C. Forbes

'Crime seems to change character when it crosses a bridge or a tunnel. In the city, crime is taken as emblematic of class and race. In the suburbs, though, it's intimate and psychological-resistant to generalization, a mystery of the individual soul.'
- Barbara Ehrenreich

'Success can make you go one of two ways. It can make you a prima donna, or it can smooth the edges, take away the insecurities, let the nice things come out.'
- Barbara Walters

'Success to me is having ten honeydew melons and eating only the top half of each one.'
- Barbra Streisand

'The way to rise is to obey and please.'
- Ben Johnson

'Success is a journey, not a destination.'
- Ben Sweetland

'You can imprison a man, but not an idea. You can exile a man, but not an idea. You can kill a man, but not an idea.'
- Benazir Bhutto

'The secret of success is constancy of purpose.'
  - Benjamin Disraeli

'The secret of success in life is for a man to be ready for his opportunity when it comes.'
  - Benjamin Disraeli

'What is the recipe for successful achievement? To my mind there are just four essential ingredients: Choose a career you love. ... Give it the best there is in you.... Seize your opportunities. ... And be a member of the team.'
  - Benjamin F. Fairless

'Thirteen virtues necessary for true success: temperance, silence, order, resolution, frugality, industry, sincerity, justice, moderation, cleanliness, tranquility, chastity, and humility.'
  - Benjamin Franklin

'Success has ruined many a man.'
  - Benjamin Franklin

'Unless a man has been taught what to do with success after getting it, the achievement of it must inevitably leave him a prey to boredom.'
  - Bertrand Russell

'He has achieved success, who has lived well, laughed often, and loved much; who has gained the respect of intelligent men and the love of little children.'
  - Bessie A. Stanley

'There are no shortcuts to any place worth going.'
  - Beverly Sills

'The struggle alone pleases us, not the victory.'
  - Blaise Pascal

'Behind every successful man there's a lot of unsuccessful years.'
  - Bob Brown

'The prospect of success in achieving our most cherished dream is not without its terrors. Who is more deprived and alone than the man who has achieved his dream?'
  - Brendan Francis

'The man who can own up to his error is greater than he who merely knows how to avoid making it.'
  - Cardinal de Retz

'The only thing that happens overnight is recognition. Not talent.'
  - Carol Haney

'An error gracefully acknowledged is a victory won.'
  - Caroline L. Gascoigne

'There is no point at which you can say, "Well, I'm successful now. I might as well take a nap."'
   - Carrie Fisher

'Most ball games are lost, not won.'
   - Casey Stengel

'So once I shut down my privilege of disliking anyone I choose and holding myself aloof if I could manage it, greater understanding, growing compassion came to me.'
   - Catharine Marshall

'To be ambitious for wealth, and yet always expecting to be poor; to be always doubting your ability to get what you long for, is like trying to reach east by traveling west. There is no philosophy which will help man to succeed when he is always doubting '
   - Charles Baudouin

'Success seems to be that which forms the distinction between confidence and conceit.'
   - Charles Caleb Colton

'Success generally depends upon knowing how long it takes to succeed.'
   - Charles de Montesquieu

'Success is that old ABC-Ability, Breaks and Courage.'
   - Charles Luckman

'Success is that old ABC- ability, breaks and courage.'
   - Charles Luckman

'I have always observed that to succeed in the world one should appear like a fool but be wise.'
   - Charles Montesquieu

'Sweat plus sacrifice equals success.'
   - Charles O. Finley

'Faith, mighty faith, the promise sees, And looks to that alone; Laughs at impossibilities, And cries it shall be done.'
   - Charles Wesley

'Successful minds work like a gimlet, - to a single point.'
   - Christian Nestell Bovee

'Big shots are only little shots who keep shooting.'
   - Christopher Morley

'Before you can win a game, you have to not lose it.'
   - Chuck Noll

'Success has made failures of many men.'
   - Cindy Adams

'Since everything is in our heads, we better not lose them.'
- Coco Chanel

'There are a lot of fellas with all the ability it takes to play in the major leagues, but they never make it, they always get stuck in the minor leagues because they haven't got the guts to make the climb.'
- Cookie Lavagetto

'Life is a succession of moments. To live each one is to succeed.'
- Corita Kent

'The haves and the have-nots can often be traced back to the dids and the did-nots.'
- D. O. Flynn

'Damon Runyon. A day-coach boy in a parlor car seat.'
- Damon Runyon

'There is always room at the top.'
- Daniel Webster

'Success has nothing to do with what you gain in life or accomplish for yourself. It's what you do for others.'
- Danny Thomas

'Striving for success without hard work is like trying to harvest where you haven't planted.'
- David Bly

'This guy put the suck in success.'
- David Letterman

'It's in the preparation-in those dreary pedestrian virtues they taught you in seventh grade and you didn't believe. It's making the extra call and caring a lot.'
- Diane Sawyer

'Noble deeds and hot baths are the best cures for depression.'
- Dodie Smith

'The successful people are the ones who think up things for the rest of the world to keep busy at.'
- Don Marquis

'Some aspects of success seem rather silly as death approaches.'
- Donald A. Miller

'The successful person is the individual who forms the habit of doing what the failing person doesn't like to do.'
- Donald Riggs

'Success is not a doorway, it's a staircase.'
- Dottie Walters

'Success is the progressive realization of a worthy ideal.'
- Earl Nightingale

'Success is simply a matter of luck. Ask any failure.'
- Earl Wilson

'It takes twenty years to make an overnight success.'
- Eddie Cantor

'No one can help you in holding a good job except Old Man You.'
- Edgar Watson Howe

'Some men succeed by what they know; some by what they do; and a few by what they are.'
- Elbert Hubbard

'Pray that success will not come any faster than you are able to endure it.'
- Elbert Hubbard

'Oh! Much may be done by defying The ghosts of Despair and Dismay And much may be gained by relying On "Where there's a Will There's a Way."'
- Eliza Cook

'Until they are of the age to use the brain.'
- Elizabeth Barrett Browning

'He must really be a big success - even his mother-in-law admits it.'
- Elmer Pasta

'Success is counted sweetest By those who ne'er succeed.'
- Emily Dickinson

'I place a high moral value on the way people behave. I find it repellent to have a lot, and to behave with anything other than courtesy in the old sense of the word-politeness of the heart, a gentleness of the spirit.'
- Emma Thompson

'The excursion is the same when you go looking for your sorrow as when you go looking for your joy.'
- Eudora Welty

'Along with success comes a reputation for wisdom.'
- Euripides

'We can never give up the belief that good guys always win. And that we are the good guys.'
- Faith Popcorn

'Vice Is nice But a little virtue Won't hurt you.'
- Felicia Lamport

'Football games aren't won, they're lost.'
- Fielding Yost

'Success didn't spoil me, I've always been insufferable.'
- Fran Lebowitz

'A wise man will make more opportunities than he finds.'
- Francis Bacon

'We should scarcely desire things ardently if we were perfectly acquainted with what we desire.'
- Francois de La Rochefoucauld

'A leading authority is anyone who has guessed right more than once.'
- Frank A. Clark

'Man is still responsible. ... His success lies not with the stars, but with himself. He must carry on the fight of self-correction and discipline.'
- Frank Curtis Williams

'I know the price of success: dedication, hard work and an unremitting devotion to the things you want to see happen.'
- Frank Lloyd Wright

'On earth we have nothing to do with success or results, but only with being true to God, and for God. Defeat in doing right is nevertheless victory.'
- Frederick W. Robertson

'I have found that it is much easier to make a success in life than to make a success of one's life.'
- G. W. Follin

'There are no secrets to success. It is the result of preparation, hard work, learning from failure.'
- General Colin L. Powell

'In war there is no second prize for the runner-up.'
- General Omar N. Bradley

'Success covers a multitude of blunders.'
- George Bernard Shaw

'There are two tragedies in life. One is to lose your heart's desire. The other is to gain it.'
- George Bernard Shaw

'The people who get on in this world are the people who get up and look for the circumstances they want, and, if they can't find them, make them.'
- George Bernard Shaw

'You can't have any successes unless you can accept failure.'
- George Cukor

'Nature gave men two ends-one to sit on, and one to think with. Ever since then man's success or failure has been dependent on the one he used most.'
- George R. Kirkpatrick

'Success is a great healer.'
- Gertrude Atherton

'The act of acting morally is behaving as if everything we do matters.'
- Gloria Steinem

'For me, writing is the only thing that passes the three tests of metal: (1) when I'm doing it, I don't feel that I should be doing something else instead; (2.) it produces a sense of accomplishment and, once in a while, pride; and (3) it's frightening.'
- Gloria Steinem

'Oddly enough, success over a period of time is more expensive than failure.'
- Grant Tinker

'Nothing worthwhile comes easily. Half effort does not produce half results. It produces no results. Work, continuous work and hard work, is the only way to accomplish results that last.'
- Hamilton Holt

'I realized early on that success was tied to not giving up. Most people in this business gave up and went on to other things. If you simply didn't give up, you would outlast the people who came in on the bus with you.'
- Harrison Ford

'Survival is triumph enough.'
- Harry Crews

'I studied the lives of great men and famous women; and I found that the men and women who got to the top were those who did the jobs they had in hand, with everything they had of energy and enthusiasm and hard work.'
- Harry S. Truman

'Always aim for achievement, and forget about success.'
- Helen Hayes

'If you rest, you rust.'
- Helen Hayes

'Success usually comes to those who are too busy to be looking for it.'
- Henry David Thoreau

'The man who will use his skill and constructive imagination to see how much he can give for a dollar, instead of how little he can give for a dollar, is bound to succeed.'
- Henry Ford

'Before everything else, getting ready is the secret of success.'
- Henry Ford

'The nice thing about being a celebrity is that when you bore people, they think it's their fault.'
- Henry Kissinger

'The conventional army loses if it does not win. The guerrilla wins if he does not lose.'
- Henry Kissinger

'Perseverance is a great element of success. If you only knock long enough and loud enough at the gate, you are sure to wake up somebody.'
- Henry Wadsworth Longfellow

'I cannot give you the formula for success, but I can give you the formula for failure, which is - try to please everybody.'
- Herbert Bayard Swope

'People are subject to moods, to temptations and fears, lethargy and aberration and ignorance, and the staunchest qualities shift under the stresses and strains of daily life.'
- Ilka Chase

'I've never sought success in order to get fame and money; it's the talent and the passion that count in success.'
- Ingrid Bergman

'The toughest thing about success is that you've got to keep on being a success. Talent is only a starting point in business. You've got to keep working that talent.'
- Irving Berlin

'Being frustrated is disagreeable, but the real disasters of life begin when you get what you want.'
- Irving Kristol

'My formula for success is rise early, work late, and strike oil.'
- J. Paul Getty

'Under normal periods, any man's success hinges about five percent on what others do for him and 95 percent on what he does.'
- James A. Worsham

'I have made mistakes, but I have never made the mistake of claiming that I never made one.'
- James Gordon Bennett

'In all human affairs there are efforts, and there are results, and the strength of the effort is the measure of the result.'
- James Lane Allen

'Granting our wish is one of Fate's saddest jokes.'
- James Russell Lowell

'Social advance depends as much upon the process through which it is secured as upon the result itself.'
- Jane Addams

'Now that I'm here, where am I?'
- Janis Joplin

'Certainly I believe in luck. How else do you explain the success of those you don't like?'
- Jean Cocteau

'There is no business in the world so troublesome as the pursuit of fame: life is over before you have hardly begun your work.'
- Jean de la Bruyere

'There are but two ways of rising in the world: either by one's own industry or profiting by the foolishness of others.'
- Jean de la Bruyere

'Sleep, riches, and health, to be truly enjoyed, must be interrupted.'
- Jean Paul Richter

'I feel that one must deliberate then act, must scan every life choice with rational thinking but then base the decision on whether one's heart will be in it.'
- Jean Shinoda Bolen

'I don't think success is harmful, as so many people say. Rather I believe it indispensable to talent: if for nothing else than to increase the talent.'
- Jeanne Moreau

'Success is like a liberation, or the first phase of a love affair.'
- Jeanne Moreau

'You have to block everything out and be extremely focused and be relaxed and mellow too.'
- Jennifer Capriati

'Problems arise in that one has to find a balance between what people need from you and what you need for yourself.'
- Jessye Norman

'The minute you think you've got it made, disaster is just around the corner.'
- Joe Paterno

'In the realm of ideas, everything depends on enthusiasm; in the real world, all rests on perseverance.'
- Johann von Goethe

'We are never further from our wishes than when we imagine that we possess what we have desired.'
- Johann von Goethe

'If you want to succeed, you must make your own opportunities as you go.'
- John B. Gough

'No matter how much a man can do, no matter how engaging his personality may be, he will not advance far in business if he cannot work through others.'
- John Craig

'Character is the real foundation of all worthwhile success.'
- John Hays Hammond

'There's such a thin line between winning and losing.'
- John R. Tunis

'Ideas are like rabbits. You get a couple and learn how to handle them, and pretty soon you have a dozen.'
- John Steinbeck

'We spend our time searching for security, and hate it when we get it.'
- John Steinbeck

'Success is peace of mind, which is a direct result of knowing you did your best to become the best that you are capable of becoming.'
- John Wooden

'If your ship doesn't come in, swim out to it.'
- Jonathan Winters

'If you wish success in life, make perseverance your bosom friend.'
- Joseph Addison

'Success and failure are both difficult to endure. Along with success come drugs, divorce, fornication, bullying, travel, meditation, medication, depression, neurosis and suicide. With failure comes failure.'
- Joseph Heller

'It takes time to succeed because success is merely the natural reward for taking time to do anything well.'
- Joseph Ross

'Success causes us to be more praised than known.'
- Joseph Roux

'When there is no feeling of accomplishment, children fail to develop properly and old people rapidly decline.'
- Joseph Whitney

'The measure of achievement is not winning awards. It's doing something that you appreciate, something you believe is worthwhile. I think of my strawberry souffle. I did that at least twenty-eight times before I finally conquered it.'
- Julia Child

'Out of the strain of the Doing, into the peace of the Done.'
- Julia Louise Woodruff

'Perseverance is failing nineteen times and succeeding the twentieth.'
- Julie Andrews

'I used to want the words "She tried" on my tombstone. Now I want "She did it."'
- Katherine Dunham

'Nothing fails like success because we don't learn from it. We learn only from failure.'
- Kenneth Boulding

'Once I decide to do something, I can't have people telling me I can't. If there's a roadblock, you jump over it, walk around it, crawl under it.'
- Kitty Kelley

'Vacillating people seldom succeed. They seldom win the solid respect of their fellows. Successful men and women are very careful in reaching decisions, and very persistent and determined in Taking Action thereafter.'
- L. G. Elliott

'Behind every successful man is a woman - with nothing to wear.'
- L. Grant Glickman

'Anyone who has gumption knows what it is, and anyone who hasn't can never know what it is.'
- L. M. Montgomery

'The penalty of success is to be bored by the people who used to snub you.'
- Lady Nancy Astor

'It is abundantly clear that success tends to negate humility.'
- Landrum P. Leavell

'If you lose, you're going to be fired, and if you win, you only put off the day you're going to be fired.'
- Leo Durocher

'If I do have some success, I'd like to enjoy it, for heaven's sake! What is the point of having it otherwise?'
- Leontyne Price

'The ultimate of being successful is the luxury of giving yourself the time to do what you want to do.'
- Leontyne Price

'If I had known what it would be like to have it all, I might have been willing to settle for less.'
- Lily Tomlin

'I wrote for twelve years and collected 250 rejection slips before getting any fiction published, so I guess outside reinforcement isn't all that important to me.'
- Lisa Alther

'Entrepreneurs average 3.8 failures before final success. What sets the successful ones apart is their amazing persistence. There are a lot of people out there with good and marketable ideas, but pure entrepreneurial types almost never accept defeat.'
- Lisa M. Amos

'The best thing that can come with success is the knowledge that it is nothing to long for.'
- Liv Ullmann

'If people knew what they had to do to be successful, most people wouldn't.'
- Lord Thomson of Fleet

'Pa, he always said a man had to look spry for himself, because nobody would do it for him; your opportunities didn't come knocking around, you had to hunt them down and hog-tie them.'
- Louis L'Amour

'Let me tell you the secret that has led me to my goal. My strength lies solely in my tenacity.'
- Louis Pasteur

'If at first you don't succeed, you're running about average.'
- M. H. Alderson

'Remember, the bread you meet each day is still rising. Don't scare the dough.'
- Macrina Wiederkehr

'The voice of conscience is so delicate that it is easy to stifle it; but it is also so clear that it is impossible to mistake it.'
- Madame de Stael

'She's the kind of woman who climbed the ladder of success, wrong by wrong.'
- Mae West

'Though a tree grow ever so high, the falling leaves return to the root.'
- Malay proverb

'How to succeed: try hard enough. How to fail: Try too hard.'
- Malcolm Forbes

'If you've had a good time playing the game, you're a winner even if you lose.'
- Malcolm Forbes

'Success follows doing what you want to do. There is no other way to be successful.'
- Malcolm Forbes

'The conditions of conquest are always easy. We have but to toil awhile, endure awhile, believe always, and never turn back.'
- Marcus Annaeus Seneca

'Success is not greedy, as people think, but insignificant. That's why it satisfies nobody.'
- Marcus Annaeus Seneca

'Tis the motive exalts the Taking Action, 'Tis the doing, and not the deed.'
- Margaret Junkin Preston

'I personally measure success in terms of the contributions an individual makes to his or her fellow human beings.'
- Margaret Mead

'Success is having a flair for the thing that you are doing, knowing that is not enough, that you have got to have hard work and a sense of purpose.'
- Margaret Thatcher

'Never face facts; if you do you'll never get up in the morning.'
- Mario Thomas

'Whoever said, "It's not whether you win or lose that counts," probably lost.'
- Martina Navratilova

'The man who goes fishing gets something more than the fish he catches.'
- Mary Astor

'That they can strengthen through the empowerment of others is essential wisdom often gathered by women.'
- Mary Field Belenky

'The insight to see possible new paths, the courage to try them, the judgment to measure results-these are the qualities of a leader.'
- Mary Parker Follett

'There must be more to life than having everything!'
- Maurice Sendak

'Despite the success cult, men are most deeply moved not by the reaching of the goal, but by the grandness of effort involved in getting there-or failing to get there.'
- Max Lerner

'To me success means effectiveness in the world, that I am able to carry my ideas and values into the world-that I am able to change it in positive ways.'
- Maxine Hong Kingston

'The only time you find success before work is in the dictionary.'
- May V. Smith

'Since when do grown men and women, who presume to hold high government office and exercise what they think of as "moral leadership," require ethics officers to tell them whether it is or isn't permissible to grab the secretary's behind or redirect public '
- Meg Greenfield

'Success has always been easy to measure. It is the distance between one's origins and one's final achievement.'
- Michael Korda

'You always pass failure on the way to success.'
- Mickey Rooney

'The brave man carves out his fortune, and every man is the sum of his own works.'
- Miguel de Cervantes

'Actually, I'm an overnight success. But it took twenty years.'
- Monty Hall

'I am not afraid of the pen, or the scaffold, or the sword. I will tell the truth whenever I please.'
- Mother Jones

'The journey is my home.'
- Muriel Rukeyser

'The closer one gets to the top, the more one finds there is no "top."'
- Nancy Barcus

'The penalty of success is to be bored by people who used to snub you.'
- Nancy, Lady Astor

'The lesser evil is also evil.'
- Naomi Mitchison

'Victory belongs to the most persevering.'
- Napoleon Bonaparte

'We're still not where we're going, but we're not where we were.'
- Natash Jasefowitz

'I know there will be spring, as surely as the birds know it when they see above the snow two tiny, quivering green leaves. Spring cannot fail us.'
- Olive Schreiner

'The reward of the general is not a bigger tent, but command.'
- Oliver Wendell Holmes

'Luck is a matter of preparation meeting opportunity.'
- Oprah Winfrey

'You wear yourself out in the pursuit of wealth or love or freedom, you do everything to gain some right, and once it's gained you take no pleasure in it.'
- Oriana Fallaci

'To have realized your dream makes you feel lost.'
- Oriana Fallaci

'The secret of all victory lies in the organization of the non-obvious.'
- Oswald Spengler

'Fame has only the span of the day, they say. But to live in the hearts of people-that is worth something.'
- Ouida

'The art of dealing with people is the foremost secret of successful men. A man's success in handling people is the very yardstick by which the outcome of his whole life's work is measured.'
- Paul C. Packe

'I don't eat junk food and I don't think junk thoughts.'
- Peace Pilgrim

'Creating success is tough. But keeping it is tougher. You have to keep producing, you can't ever stop.'
- Pete Rose

'Bad will be the day for every man when he becomes absolutely contented with the life he is living, when there is not forever beating at the doors of his soul some great desire to do something larger.'
- Phillips Brooks

'Nothing fails like success; nothing is so defeated as yesterday's triumphant cause.'
- Phyllis McGinley

'Success for the striver washes away the effort of striving.'
- Pindar

'One more such victory and we are undone.'
- Pyrrhus

'Success, which is something so simple in the end, is made up of thousands of things, we never fully know what.'
- Rainer Maria Rilke

'Whatever your grade or position, if you know how and when to speak, and when to remain silent, your chances of real success are proportionately increased.'
- Ralph C. Smedley

'Marconi invented radio, but Ted Husing knew what to do with it.'
- Ralph Edwards

'The reward of a thing well done is to have done it.'
- Ralph Waldo Emerson

'Self-trust is the first secret of success.'
- Ralph Waldo Emerson

'No one succeeds without effort.... Those who succeed owe their success to their perseverance.'
- Ramana Maharshi

'Will you be satisfied with the fruit of your life's work? Will the efforts you are making now bring you satisfTaking Action when the things of time are receding, and eternity looms ahead?'
- Raymond L. Cox

'Success is not the result of spontaneous combustion. You must set yourself on fire.'
- Reggie Leach

'There is some consolation in the fact that, even though your dreams don't come true, neither do your nightmares.'
- Richard Armour

'It's not that I'm not grateful for all this attention. It's just that fame and fortune ought to add up to more than fame and fortune.'
- Robert Fulghum

'All outward success, when it has value, is but the inevitable result of an inward success of full living, full play and enjoyment of one's faculties.'
- Robert Henri

'Is there anything in life so disenchanting as attainment?'
- Robert Louis Stevenson

'To travel hopefully is a better thing than to arrive, and the true success is to labor.'
- Robert Louis Stevenson

'To live only for some future goal is shallow. It's the sides of the mountain that sustain life, not the top.'
- Robert M. Pirsig

'It's the plugging away that will win you the day So don't be a piker, old pard! Just draw on your grit, it's so easy to quit- It's the keeping your chin up that's hard.'
- Robert W. Service

'Find a need and fill it.'
- Ruth Stafford Peale

'All you need in this life is ignorance and confidence, and then Success is sure.'
- S. L. Clemens

'Every man is the architect of his own fortune.'
- Sallust

'One of the first businesses of a sensible man is to know when he is beaten, and to leave off fighting at once.'
- Samuel Butler

'We grow weary of those things (and perhaps soonest) which we most desire.'
- Samuel Butler

'They who are the most persistent, and work in the true spirit, will invariably be the most successful.'
- Samuel Smiles

'The victory of success is half done when one gains the habit of work.'
- Sarah Knowles Bolton

'If you don't quit, and don't cheat, and don't run home when trouble arrives, you can only win.'
- Shelley Long

'I stopped believing in Santa Claus when I was six. Mother took me to see him in a department store and he asked for my autograph.'
- Shirley Temple

'If you live long enough, you'll see that every victory turns into a defeat.'
- Simone de Beauvoir

'Skill is fine, and genius is splendid, but the right contacts are more valuable than either.'
- Sir Archibald McIndoe

'The very first step towards success in any occupation is to become interested in it.'
- Sir William Osier

'Success ... depends on your ability to make and keep friends.'
- Sophie Tucker

'Success is dependent on effort.'
- Sophocles

'Our business in life is not to get ahead of others but to get ahead of ourselves-to break our own records, to outstrip our yesterdays by our today, to do our work with more force than ever before.'
- Steward B. Johnson

'It never pays to deal with the flyweights of the world. They take far too much pleasure in thwarting you at every turn.'
- Sue Grafton

'I think that wherever your journey takes you, there are new gods waiting there, with divine patience-and laughter.'
- Susan M. Watkins

'Respect for people is the cornerstone of communication and networking.'
- Susan RoAne

'Networking is an enrichment program, not an entitlement program.'
- Susan RoAne

'I am not the smartest or most talented person in the world, but I succeeded because I keep going, and going, and going.'
  - Sylvester Stallone

'Success is relative: It is what we can make of the mess we have made of things.'
  - T. S. Eliot

'Success is blocked by concentrating on it and planning for it.... Success is shy-it won't come out while you're watching.'
  - Tennessee Williams

'High station in life is earned by the gallantry with which appalling experiences are survived with grace.'
  - Tennessee Williams

'Success and failure are equally disastrous.'
  - Tennessee Williams

'Success has killed more men than bullets.'
  - Texas Guinan

'If a man be self-controlled, truthful, wise, and resolute, is there aught that can stay out of reach of such a man?'
  - The Panchatantra

'The most important single ingredient in the formula of success is knowing how to get along with people.'
  - Theodore Roosevelt

'Oh, how quickly the world's glory passes away.'
  - Thomas a Kempis

'The ambitious climbs high and perilous stairs and never cares how to come down; the desire of rising hath swallowed up his fear of a fall.'
  - Thomas Adams

'The most considerable difference I note among men is not in their readiness to fall into error, but in their readiness to acknowledge these inevitable lapses.'
  - Thomas Henry Huxley

'I'm a great believer in luck, and I find the harder I work the more I have of it.'
  - Thomas Jefferson

'You have reached the pinnacle of success as soon as you become uninterested in money, compliments, or publicity.'
  - Thomas Wolfe

'I've been polite and I've always shown up. Somebody asked me if I had any advice for young people entering the business. I said: "Yeah, show up."'
- Tom T. Hall

'There are three types of baseball players-those who make it happen, those who watch it happen, and those who wonder what happened.'
- Tommy Lasorda

'As soon as you find the key to success, somebody always changes the lock.'
- Tracey Ullman

'It is good to have an end to journey toward; but it is the journey that matters, in the end.'
- Ursula K. LeGuin

'Snowflakes are one of nature's most fragile things, but just look what they can do when they stick together.'
- Vesta M. Kelly

'A woman who is loved always has success.'
- Vicki Baum

'Fame always brings loneliness. Success is as ice cold and lonely as the North Pole.'
- Vicki Baum

'What it comes down to is that anybody can win with the best horse. What makes you good is if you can take the second or third best horse and win.'
- Vicky Aragon

'Everything bows to success, even grammar.'
- Victor Hugo

'If you can't accept losing, you can't win.'
- Vince Lombardi

'Never having been able to succeed in the world, he took his revenge by speaking ill of it.'
- Voltaire

'If at first you don't succeed, try, try, again. Then quit. There's no use being a damn fool about it.'
- W. C. Fields

'If at first you don't succeed, try, try, try again.'
- W. E. Hickson

'Excellence in any pursuit is the late, ripe fruit of toil.'
- W. M. L. Jay

'The common idea that success spoils people by making them vain, egotistic, and self-complacent is erroneous; on the contrary, it makes them, for the most part, humble, tolerant, and kind. Failure

makes people cruel and bitter.'
  - W. Somerset Maugham

'Out of every fruition of success, no matter what, comes forth something to make a new effort necessary.'
  - Walt Whitman

'Success makes men rigid and they tend to exalt stability over all the other virtues; tired of the effort of willing, they become fanatics about conservatism.'
  - Walter Lippman

'Nothing recedes like success.'
  - Walter Winchell

'If a man wakes up famous he hasn't been sleeping.'
  - Wes Izzard

'Four steps to achievement: plan purposefully, prepare prayerfully, proceed positively, pursue persistently.'
  - William A. Ward

'Success seems to be largely a matter of hanging on after others have let go.'
  - William Feather

'The exclusive worship of the bitch-goddess Success is our national disease.'
  - William James

'Need and struggle are what excite and inspire us; our hour of triumph is what brings the void.'
  - William James

'Three outstanding qualities make for success: judgement, industry, health. And the greatest of these is judgement.'
  - William Maxwell Aitken

'Great men have not been concerned with fame. The joy of achievement that comes from finding something new in the universe is by far their greatest joy.'
  - William P. King

'Men at some time are masters of their fates.'
  - William Shakespeare

'To climb steep hills Requires slow pace at first.'
  - William Shakespeare

'It isn't hard to be good from time to time in sports. What's tough is being good every day.'
  - Willie Mays

'It is no use saying "we are doing our best." You have got to succeed in doing what is necessary.'
  - Winston Churchill

'Continuous effort-not strength or intelligence-is the key to unlocking our potential.'
  - Winston Churchill

'Victory at all costs, victory in spite of all terror, victory however long and hard the hard may be; for without victory there is no survival.'
  - Winston Churchill

'The problems of victory are more agreeable than those of defeat, but they are no less difficult.'
  - Winston Churchill

TAKING ACTION

'Taking Action is the only reality, not only reality but morality, as well.'
- Abbie Hoffman

'I am not bound to win, but I am bound to be true. I am not bound to succeed, but I am bound to live up to what light I have.'
- Abraham Lincoln

'I claim not to have controlled events, but confess plainly that events have controlled me.'
- Abraham Lincoln

'One by one the sands are flowing, One by one the moments fall; Some are coming, some are going; Do not strive to grasp them all.'
- Adelaide Proctor

'It's astonishing in this world how things don't turn out at all the way you expect them to.'
- Agatha Christie

'I shall tell you a great secret, my friend. Do not wait for the last judgement, it takes place every day.'
- Albert Camus

'Life happens at the level of events, not words.'
- Alfred Adler

'Trust only movement. Life happens at the level of events, not of words. Trust movement.'
- Alfred Adler

'From the moment of birth we are immersed in Taking Action, and can only fitfully guide it by taking thought.'
- Alfred North Whitehead

'Life is made up of desires that seem big and vital one minute, and little and absurd the next. I guess we get what's best for us in the end.'
- Alice Caldwell Rice

'Events that are predestined require but little management. They manage themselves. They slip into place while we sleep, and suddenly we are aware that the thing we fear to attempt, is already accomplished.'
- Amelia Barr

'God's will is not an itinerary, but an attitude.'
- Andrew Dhuse

'Take time to deliberate; but when the time for Taking Action arrives, stop thinking and go in.'
- Andrew Jackson

'He nothing common did, or mean, Upon that memorable scene.'
- Andrew Marvell

'Keep doing what you're doing and you'll keep getting what you're getting.'
- Anonymous

'The man who has done nothing but wait for his ship to come in has already missed the boat.'
- Anonymous

'All glory comes from daring to begin.'
- Anonymous

'It is not yours to finish the task, but neither are you free to take no part in it.'
- Anonymous

'After all is said and done, more is said than done.'
- Anonymous

"Mean to' don't pick no cotton.'
- Anonymous

'Living upon a basis of unsatisfied demands, we were in a state of continual disturbance and frustration. Therefore, no peace was to be had unless we could find a means of reducing these demands.'
- Anonymous

'For peace of mind, resign as general manager of the universe.'
- Anonymous

'If faith without works is dead, willingness without Taking Action is fantasy.'
- Anonymous

'The door of opportunity won't open unless you do some pushing.'
- Anonymous

'Be God or let God.'
- Anonymous

'Go and wake up your cook.'
- Arabian proverb

'The only measure of what you believe is what you do. If you want to know what people believe, don't read what they write, don't ask them what they believe, just observe what they do.'
- Ashley Montagu

'It is a great piece of skill to know how to guide your luck, even while waiting for it.'
- Baltasar Gracian

'God helps them that helps themselves.'
- Benjamin Franklin

'If you want a thing done, go - if not, send.'
- Benjamin Franklin

'It is only in marriage with the world that our ideals can bear fruit; divorced from it, they remain barren.'
- Bertrand Russell

'The central problem of our age is how to act decisively in the absence of certainty.'
- Bertrand Russell

'Nothing fruitful ever comes when plants are forced to flower in the wrong season.'
- Bette Bao Lord

'You may be disappointed if you fail, but you are doomed if you don't try.'
- Beverly Sills

'But I trusted in thee, O Lord; I said, Thou art my God. My times are in thy hand.'
- Bible

'Here am I; send me.'
- Bible

'With us is the Lord our God, to help us and to fight our battles.'
- Bible

'It is better to trust in the Lord than to put confidence in man.'
- Bible

'Cast thy burden on the Lord, and he shall sustain thee.'
- Bible

'Go, and do thou likewise.'
- Bible

'Casting all your care upon Him, for He careth for you.'
- Bible

'Our nature consists in motion; complete rest is death.'
- Blaise Pascal

'You, yourself, must make the effort. The buddhas are only teachers.'
- Buddhist proverb

'There are two kinds of people: those who say to God, "Thy will be done," and those to whom God says, "All right, then, have it your way."'
- C. S. Lewis

'Let us act on what we have, since we have not what we wish.'
- Cardinal Newman

'We are the wire, God is the current. Our only power is to let the current pass through us.'
- Carlo Carretto

'If you can't help it, don't think about it.'
- Carmel Myers

'No day is so bad it can't be fixed with a nap.'
- Carrie Snow

'So much to do; so little done.'
- Cecil Rhodes

'Deliberation is the work of many men. Taking Action, of one alone.'
- Charles de Gaulle

'That man is blest who does his best and leaves the rest; do not worry.'
- Charles F. Deems

'If you can react the same way to winning and losing, that's a big accomplishment. That quality is important because it stays with you the rest of your life.'
- Chris Evert

'The superior man is modest in his speech, but excels in his Taking Actions.'
- Confucius

'Looking at small advantages prevents great affairs from being accomplished.'
- Confucius

'Having the world's best idea will do you no good unless you act on it. People who want milk shouldn't sit on a stool in the middle of a field in hopes that a cow will back up to them.'
- Curtis Grant

'You have striven so hard, and so long, to compel life. Can't you now slowly change, and let life slowly drift into you ... let the invisible life steal into you and slowly possess you.'
- D. H. Lawrence

'The fair request ought to be followed by the deed, in silence.'
- Dante Alighieri

'There is no genius in life like the genius of energy and activity.'
- Donald G. Mitchell

'It is the mark of great people to treat trifles as trifles and important matters as important.'
- Doris Lessing

'People who make some other person part of their job are dangerous.'
- Dorothy L. Sayers

'Coercion. The unpardonable crime.'
- Dorothy Miller Richardson

'He who is outside his door already has a hard part of his journey behind him.'
- Dutch proverb

'When you appeal to force, there's one thing you must never do - lose.'
- Dwight D. Eisenhower

'He started to sing as he tackled the thing That couldn't be done, and he did it.'
- Edgar A. Guest

'You always feel when you look it straight in the eye that you could have put more into it, could have let yourself go and dug harder.'
- Emily Carr

'The soul will take that love and put it where it can best be used.'
- Emmanuel

'As your faith is strengthened, you will find that there is no longer the need to have a sense of control, that things will flow as they will, and that you will flow with them, to your great delight and benefit.'
- Emmanuel

'An ounce of Taking Action is worth a ton of theory.'
- Friedrich Engels

'It is much easier to do and die than it is to reason why.'
- G. A. Studdert-Kennedy

'Do well and right, and let the world sink.'
- George Edward Herbert

''Tis God gives skill, but not without men's hands: he could not make Antonio Stradivarius violins without Antonio.'
- George Eliot

'To knock a thing down, especially if it is cocked at an arrogant angle, is a deep delight to the blood.'
- George Santayana

'Willfulness must give way to willingness and surrender. Mastery must yield to mystery.'
- Gerald G. May

'No way exists in the present to accurately determine the future effect of the least of our Taking Actions.'
- Gerald Jampolsky

'We will either find a way, or make one.'
  - Hannibal

'I come to the office each morning and stay for long hours doing what has to be done to the best of my ability. And when you've done the best you can, you can't do any better. So when I go to sleep I turn everything over to the Lord and forget it.'
  - Harry S. Truman

'For purposes of Taking Action nothing is more useful than narrowness of thought combined with energy of will.'
  - Henri Frederic Amiel

'Whate'er we leave to God, God does and blesses us.'
  - Henry David Thoreau

'Let each look to himself and see what God wants of him and attend to this, leaving all else alone.'
  - Henry Suso

'Let us then be up and doing, With a heart for any fate; Still achieving, still pursuing, Learn to labor and to wait.'
  - Henry Wadsworth Longfellow

'Trust no future, howe'er pleasant! Let the dead past bury its dead! Act, - act in the living Present! Heart within and God o'erhead.'
  - Henry Wadsworth Longfellow

''Tis man's to fight, but Heaven's to give success.'
  - Homer

'Life is God's novel. Let him write it.'
  - Isaac Bashevis Singer

'Between saying and doing many a pair of shoes is worn out.'
  - Italian proverb

'Let us do or die.'
  - James Drummond Burns

'Every man feels instinctively that all the beautiful sentiments in the world weigh less than a single lovely Taking Action.'
  - James Russell Lowell

'You take people as far as they will go, not as far as you would like them to go.'
  - Jeannette Rankin

'God doesn't make orange juice, God makes oranges.'
  - Jesse Jackson

'When you learn not to want things so badly, life comes to you.'
- Jessica Lange

'It is easy and dismally enervating to think of opposition as merely perverse or actually evil-far more invigorating to see it as essential for honing the mind, and as a positive good in itself. For the day that moral issues cease to be fought over is the '
- Jill Tweedie

'The best direction is the least possible direction.'
- Joan Manley

'I began to have an idea of my life, not as the slow shaping of achievement to fit my preconceived purposes, but as the gradual discovery and growth of a purpose which I did not know.'
- Joanna Field

'When written in Chinese, the word crisis is composed of two characters. One represents danger and the other represents opportunity.'
- John F. Kennedy

'A guru might say that spiritual deepening involves a journey toward the unselfconscious living of life as it unfolds, rather than toward a willful determination to make it happen.'
- John Fortunato

'Learn to do thy part and leave the rest to Heaven.'
- John Henry Cardinal Newman

'God alone can finish.'
- John Ruskin

'The worst thing you can do is to try to cling to something that's gone, or to recreate it.'
- Johnette Napolitano

'Taking Action is consolatory. It is the enemy of thought and the friend of flattering illusions.'
- Joseph Conrad

'O golden Silence, bid our souls be still, and on the foolish fretting of our care lay thy soft touch of healing unaware!'
- Julia Dorr

'Who can separate his faith from his Taking Actions, or his belief from his occupations?'
- Kahlil Gibran

'God tests His real friends more severely than the lukewarm ones.'
- Katheryn Hulme

'Much that I sought, I could not find; much that I found, I could not bind; much that I bound, I could not free; much that I freed, returned to me.'
- Lee Wilson Dodd

'Oh Lord, thou givest us everything, at the price of an effort.'
- Leonardo da Vinci

'The success of your presentation will be judged not by the knowledge you send but by what the listener receives.'
- Lily Walters

'Theirs not to make reply, Theirs not to reason why, Theirs but to do and die.'
- Lord Alfred Tennyson

'Blessed is he who carries within himself a god and an ideal and who obeys it - an ideal of art, of science, or gospel virtues. Therein lie the springs of great thoughts and great Taking Actions.'
- Louis Pasteur

'If it is your time, love will track you down like a cruise missile.'
- Lynda Barry

'Doing what is right isn't the problem; it's knowing what is right.'
- Lyndon B. Johnson

'I am not built for academic writings. Taking Action is my domain.'
- Mahatma Gandhi

'If thou workest at that which is before thee ... expecting nothing, fearing nothing, but satisfied with thy present activity according to Nature, and with heroic truth in every word and sound which thou utterest, thou wilt live happy. And there is no man who is able to prevent this.'
- Marcus Aurelius

'If you want something done right, get someone else to do it.'
- Marion Giacomini

'I see not a step before me as I tread on another year; But I've left the Past in God's keeping, the Future His mercy shall clear; And what looks dark in the distance may brighten as I draw near.'
- Mary Gardiner Brainard

'Trust in God and do something.'
- Mary Lyon

'The life of the spirit is centrally and essentially a life of Taking Action. Spirituality is something done, not merely something believed, or known or experienced.'
- Mary McDermott Shideler

'Coercive power is the curse of the universe; coactive power, the enrichment and advancement of every human soul.'
- Mary Parker Follett

'Letting people be okay without us is how we get to be okay without them.'
- Merrit Malloy

'Ideas are powerful things, requiring not a studious contemplation but an Taking Action, even if it is only an inner Taking Action.'
- Midge Dector

'So often we try to alter circumstances to suit ourselves, instead of letting them alter us.'
- Mother Maribel

'God hasn't called me to be successful. He's called me to be faithful.'
- Mother Teresa

'I am like a little pencil in God's hand. He does the writing. The pencil has nothing to do with it.'
- Mother Teresa

'There are only two forces that unite men - fear and interest.'
- Napoleon Bonaparte

'Stress is basically a disconnection from the earth, a forgetting of the breath. Stress is an ignorant state. It believes that everything is an emergency. Nothing is that important. Just lie down.'
- Natalie Goldberg

'On God for all events depend; You cannot want when God's your friend. Weigh well your part and do your best; Leave to your Maker all the rest.'
- Nathaniel Cotton

'It had been my repeated experience that when you said to life calmly and firmly (but very firmly!) "I trust you, do what you must," life had an uncanny way of responding to your need.'
- Olga Ilyin

'He who wants a rose must respect the thorn.'
- Persian proverb

'We cannot alter facts, but we can alter our ways of looking at them.'
- Phyllis Bottome

'Even now I am full of hope, but the end lies in God.'
- Pindar

'Play out the game, act well your part, and if the gods have blundered, we will not.'
- Ralph Waldo Emerson

'In Taking Action, be primitive; in foresight, a strategist.'
- Rene Char

'The only way to get positive feelings about yourself is to take positive Taking Actions. Man does not live as he thinks, he thinks as he lives.'
- Reverend Vaughan Quinn

'Somehow, when we no longer feel in control, we become available to deeper aliveness.'
- Richard Moss

'You have freedom when you're easy in your harness.'
- Robert Frost

'In vain our labours are, whatsoe'er they be, unless God gives the Benediction.'
- Robert Herrick

'A = r + p (or Adventure equals risk plus purpose.)'
- Robert McClure

'He will hew the line of right, let the chips fall where they may.'
- Roscoe Conkling

'Let us work as if success depended upon ourselves alone, but with heartfelt conviction that we are doing nothing, and God everything.'
- Saint Ignatius of Loyola

'Get good counsel before you begin: and when you have decided, act promptly.'
- Sallust

'If you have anything to tell me of importance, for God's sake begin at the end.'
- Sara Jeannette Duncan

'But search the land of living men, Where wilt thou find their like again.'
- Sir Walter Scott

'To create is to boggle the mind and alter the mood. Once the urge has surged, it maintains its own momentum. We may go along for the ride, but when we attempt to steer the course, the momentum dies.'
- Sue Atchley Ebaugh

'Through the picture, I see reality. Through the word, I understand it.'
- Sven Lidman

'The prayer of the chicken hawk does not get him the chicken.'
- Swahili proverb

'If people are suffering, then they must look within themselves. ... Happiness is not something ready-made [Buddha] can give you. It comes from your own Taking Actions.'
- The Dalai Lama

'I want to see you shoot the way you shout.'
- Theodore Roosevelt

'Everything comes to him who hustles while he waits.'
- Thomas A. Edison

'My life is ... a mystery which I do not attempt to really understand, as though 1 were led by the hand in a night where I see nothing, but can fully depend on the love and protection of Him who guides

me.'
  - Thomas Merton

'Wanna fly, you got to give up the shit that weighs you down.'
  - Toni Morrison

'Right Taking Action is the key to good living.'
  - Twelve Steps and

'Be like the bird that, passing on her flight awhile on boughs too slight, feels them give way beneath her, and yet sings, knowing that she hath wings.'
  - Victor Hugo

'Did nothing in particular And did it very well.'
  - W. S. Gilbert

'Nothing is often a good thing to do and always a good thing to say.'
  - Will Durant

'He who desires, but acts not, breeds pestilence.'
  - William Blake

'Men never cling to their dreams with such tenacity as at the moment when they are losing faith in them, and know it, but do not dare yet to confess it to themselves.'
  - William Graham Sumner

'Why, then the world's mine oyster Which I with sword will open.'
  - William Shakespeare

'What's done can't be undone.'
  - William Shakespeare

'To character and success, two things, contradictory as they may seem, must go together-humble dependence and manly independence: humble dependence on God, and manly reliance on self.'
  - William Wordsworth

'The men who act stand nearer to the mass of man than the men who write; and it is in their hands that new thought gets its translation into the crude language of deeds.'
  - Woodrow Wilson

TIME

'Enjoy the present hour, Be thankful for the past, And neither fear nor wish Th' approaches of the last.'
- Abraham Cowley

'Little by little does the trick.'
- Aesop

'This only is denied even to God: the power to undo the past.'
- Agathon

'When you sit with a nice girl for two hours, you think it's only a minute. But when you sit on a hot stove for a minute, you think it's two hours. That's relativity.'
- Albert Einstein

'I think and think for months, for years. Ninety-nine times the conclusion is false. The hundredth time I am right.'
- Albert Einstein

'Not to go back is somewhat to advance. And men must walk, at least, before they dance.'
- Alexander Pope

'Trifles make up the happiness or the misery of mortal life.'
- Alexander Smith

'You've got to think about "big things" while you're doing small things, so that all the small things go in the right direction.'
- Alvin Toffler

'There are very few human beings who receive the truth, complete and staggering, by instant illumination. Most of them acquire it fragment by fragment, on a small scale, by successive developments, cellularly, like a laborious mosaic.'
- Anais Nin

'One can get just as much exultation in losing oneself in a little thing as in a big thing. It is nice to think how one can be recklessly lost in a daisy.'
- Anne Morrow Lindbergh

'True worth is doing each day some little good, not dreaming of great things to do by and by.'
- Anonymous

'There was a young lady named Bright Who could travel much faster than light She started one day In the relative way And came back on the previous night.'
- Anonymous

'Yard by yard, it's very hard. But inch by inch, it's a cinch.'
- Anonymous

'One step and then another, and the longest walk is ended. One stitch and then another, and the longest rent is mended. One brick upon another, and the tallest wall is made. One flake and then another, and the deepest snow is laid.'
- Anonymous

'Every worthwhile accomplishment, big or little, has its stages of drudgery and triumph; a beginning, a struggle, and a victory.'
- Anonymous

'Sometimes the littlest things in life are the hardest to take. You can sit on a mountain more comfortably than on a tack.'
- Anonymous

'In time take time while time doth last, for time Is no time when time is past.'
- Anonymous

'It was only a sunny smile, But it scattered the night And little it cost in the giving; Like morning light, And made the day worth living.'
- Anonymous

'It is in trifles, and when he is off his guard, that a man best shows his character.'
- Arthur Schopenhauer

'Nothing really belongs to us but time, which even he has who has nothing else.'
- Baltasar Gracian

'Time and I against any two.'
- Baltasar Gracian

'You don't just luck into things. ... You build step by step, whether it's friendships or opportunities.'
- Barbara Bush

'A wonderful stream is the River Time, As it runs through the realms of Tears, With a faultless rhythm, and a musical rhyme, As it blends with the ocean of Years.'
- Benjamin F. Taylor

'A little neglect may breed great mischief. ... For want of a nail, the shoe was lost; for want of a shoe, the horse was lost; for want of a horse, the battle was lost; for want of the battle, the war was lost.'
- Benjamin Franklin

'Little strokes fell great oaks.'
- Benjamin Franklin

'Human felicity is produced not so much by great pieces of good fortune that seldom happen as by little advantages that occur every day.'
- Benjamin Franklin

'All movements go too far.'
- Bertrand Russell

'It's a long old road, but I know I'm gonna find the end.'
- Bessie Smith

'A thousand years in thy sight are but as yesterday when it is past, and as a watch in the night.'
- Bible

'My time has not yet come.'
- Bible

'He that is faithful in that which is least is faithful also in much; and he that is unjust in the least is unjust also in much.'
- Bible

'Though thy beginning was small, yet thy latter end should greatly increase.'
- Bible

'We spend our years as a tale that is told.'
- Bible

'The waters wear the stones.'
- Bible

'Inspiration does not come like a blot, nor is it kinetic energy striving, but it comes to us slowly and quietly all the time.'
- Brenda Euland

'Progress is the sum of small victories won by individual human beings.'
- Bruce Catton

'We cannot do everything at once, but we can do something at once.'
- Calvin Coolidge

'Nothing can be done except little by little.'
- Charles Baudelaire

'The only true time which a man can properly call his own, is that which he has all to himself; the rest, though in some sense he may be said to live it, is other people's time, not his.'
- Charles Lamb

'The smallest effort is not lost, Each wavelet on the ocean tost Aids in the ebb-tide or the flow; Each rain-drop makes some floweret blow; Each struggle lessens human woe.'
- Charles Mackay

'Life is made up of little things. It is very rarely that an occasion is offered for doing a great deal at once. True greatness consists in being great in little things.'
- Charles Simmons

'It is better to light a candle than to curse the darkness.'
- Chinese proverb

'O temporal O mores! O what times! what morals!'
- Cicero

'From a little spark may burst a mighty flame.'
- Dante Alighieri

'Large streams from little mountains flow, tall oaks from little acorns grow.'
- David Everett

'One third of the people of the world are asleep at any given moment. The other two thirds are awake and probably stirring up trouble somewhere.'
- Dean Rusk

'Instead of thinking about where you are, think about where you want to be. It takes twenty years of hard work to become an overnight success.'
- Diana Rankin

'Incident piled on incident no more makes life than brick piled on brick makes a house.'
- Edith Ronald Mirrielees

'Nobody makes a greater mistake than he who did nothing because he could only do a little.'
- Edmund Burke

'I cannot do everything, but still I can do something; and because I cannot do everything, I will not refuse to do something that I can do.'
- Edward Everett Hale

'Time is money.'
- Edward G. Bulwer-Lytton

'You have to accept whatever comes and the only important thing is that you meet it with the best you have to give.'
- Eleanor Roosevelt

'All that I have accomplished ... has been by that plodding, patient, persevering process of accretion which builds the ant heap particle by particle, thought by thought, fact by fact.'
- Elihu Burritt

'Backward, turn backward, O Time in your flight; Make me a child again just for tonight.'
- Elizabeth Akers Allen

'It is not the straining for great things that is most effective; it is the doing the little things, the common duties, a little better and better.'
- Elizabeth Stuart Phelps

'Time is a Test of Trouble - But not a Remedy - If such it proved, it proves too There was no Melody.'
- Emily Dickinson

'Time and tide wait for no man.'
- English proverb

'A stitch in time saves nine.'
- English proverb

'Practice yourself in little things, and thence proceed to greater.'
- Epictetus

'I am convinced that there are times in everybody's experience when there is so much to be done, that the only way to do it is to sit down and do nothing.'
- Fanny Fern

'Even a small star shines in the darkness.'
- Finnish proverb

'It is astonishing how short a time it takes for very wonderful things to happen.'
- Frances Hodgson Burnett

'Sow an act, reap a habit; sow a habit, reap a character; sow a character, reap a destiny.'
- G. D. Boardman

'In great matters men show themselves as they wish to be seen; in small matters, as they are.'
- Gamaliel Bradford

'Nothing is improbable until it moves into the past tense.'
- George Ade

'No matter how big and tough a problem may be, get rid of confusion by taking one little step toward solution. Do something.'
- George F. Nordenholt

'See Time has touched me gently in his race, And left no odious furrows in my face.'
- George Grabbe

'Time is the rider that breaks youth.'
- George Herbert

'I want to go ahead of Father Time with a scythe of my own.'
- H. G. Wells

'Time is a great legalizer, even in the fields of morals.'
- H. L. Mencken

'Time is a great legalizer, even in the field of morals.'
- H. L. Mencken

'A soul occupied with great ideas performs small duties.'
- Harriet Martineau

'If we take care of the inches, we will not have to worry about the miles.'
- Hartley Coleridge

'Time is a great teacher, but unfortunately it kills all its pupils.'
- Hector Berlioz

'The world is moved not only by the mighty shoves of the heroes, but also by the aggregate of the tiny pushes of each honest worker.'
- Helen Keller

'Almost everything comes from almost nothing.'
- Henri Frederic Amiel

'Time goes, you say? Ah no! Alas, Time stays, we go.'
- Henry Austin Dobson

'Nothing is particularly hard if you divide it into small jobs.'
- Henry Ford

'The greatest masterpieces were once only pigments on a palette.'
- Henry S. Haskins

'Most people would succeed in small things if they were not troubled with great ambitions.'
- Henry Wadsworth Longfellow

'Think not because no man sees, such things will remain unseen.'
- Henry Wadsworth Longfellow

'All things flow, nothing abides.'
- Heraclitus

'Those people work more wisely who seek to achieve good in their own small corner of the world ... than those who are forever thinking that life is in vain, unless one can ... do big things.'
- Herbert Butterfield

'If you only keep adding little by little, it will soon become a big heap.'
- Hesiod

'Enjoy the present day, trusting very little to the morrow.'
- Horace

'When you have a great and difficult task, something perhaps almost impossible, if you only work a little at a time, every day a little, suddenly the work will finish itself.'
- Isak Dinesen

'One thing at a time, all things in succession. That which grows slowly endures.'
- J. G. Hubbard

'Look at a stone cutter hammering away at his rock, perhaps a hundred times without as much as a crack showing in it. Yet at the hundred-and-first blow it will split in two, and I know it was not the last blow that did it, but all that had gone before.'
- Jacob A. Riis

'In life's small things be resolute and great To keep thy muscle trained; Know'st thou when Fate Thy measure takes, or when she'll say to thee, "I find thee worthy; do this deed for me?"'
- James Russell Lowell

'Time wounds all heels.'
- Jane Ace

'Home wasn't built in a day.'
- Jane Ace

'One sits down first; one thinks afterwards.'
- Jean Cocteau

'3 o'clock is always too late or too early for anything you want to do.'
- Jean-Paul Sartre

'I look at victory as milestones on a very long highway.'
- Joan Benoit Samuelson

'The growth of understanding follows an ascending spiral rather than a straight line.'
- Joanna Field

'It takes time to save time.'
- Joe Taylor

'Time was made for slaves.'
- John B. Buckstone

'Many strokes overthrow the tallest oaks.'
- John Lyly

'Respect the past in the full measure of its desserts, but do not make the mistake of confusing it with the present nor seek in it the ideals of the future.'
- Josi Incenieros

'To excel the past we must not allow ourselves to lose contact with it; on the contrary, we must feel it under our feet because we raised ourselves upon it.'
- Josi Ortega y Gasset

'Champions know there are no shortcuts to the top. They climb the mountain one step at a time. They have no use for helicopters!'
- Judi Adler

'No first step can be really great; it must of necessity possess more of prophecy than of achievement; nevertheless it is by the first step that a man marks the value, not only of his cause, but of himself.'
- Katherine Cecil Thurston

'A successful individual typically sets his next goal somewhat, but not too much, above his last achievement.'
- Kurt Lewin

'A terrace nine stories high begins with a pile of earth.'
- Lao-Tzu

'Better late than never.'
- Livy

'Events of great consequence often spring from trifling circumstances.'
- Livy

'The apparent serenity of the past is an oil spread by time.'
- Lloyd Frankenberg

'Know the true value of time; snatch, seize, and enjoy every moment of it. No idleness, no laziness, no procrastination: never put off till tomorrow what you can do today.'
- Lord Chesterfield

'I recommend you to take care of the minutes, for the hours will take care of themselves.'
- Lord Chesterfield

'Victory is won not in miles, but in inches. Win a little now, hold your ground, and later win a little more.'
- Louis L'Amour

'The distance doesn't matter; only the first step is difficult.'
- Madame Marquise du Deffand

'Time gives good advice.'
- Maltese proverb

'Time is a sort of river of passing events, and strong is its current; no sooner is a thing brought to sight than it is swept by and another takes its place, and this too will be swept away.'
- Marcus Aurelius

'The passing minute is every man's equal possession but what has once gone by is not ours.'
- Marcus Aurelius

'Connections are made slowly, sometimes they grow underground.'
- Marge Piercy

'If we take care of the moments, the years will take care of themselves.'
- Maria Edgeworth

'We must not... ignore the small daily differences we can make which, over time, add up to big differences that we often cannot foresee.'
- Marian Wright Edelman

'Happiness is a tide: it carries you only a little way at a time; but you have covered a vast space before you know that you are moving at all.'
- Mary Adams

'Let no one be deluded that a knowledge of the path can substitute for putting one foot in front of the other.'
- Mary Caroline Richards

'I never stop to plan. I take things step-by-step.'
- Mary McLeod Bethune

'The world doesn't come to the clever folks, it comes to the stubborn, obstinate, one-idea-at-a-time people.'
- Mary Roberts Rinehart

'The signs of the times.'
- Matthew

'We can do no great things-only small things with great love.'
- Mother Teresa

'Not all things are blest, but the seeds of all things are blest.'
- Muriel Rukeyser

'Life is denied by lack of attention, whether it be to cleaning windows or trying to write a masterpiece.'
- Nadia Boulanger

'Great issues develop from small beginnings.'
- Norman Vincent Peale

'Life is a great bundle of little things.'
- Oliver Wendell Holmes

'Take your needle, my child, and work at your pattern; it will come out a rose by and by. Life is like that; one stitch at a time taken patiently, and the pattern will come out all right, like embroidery.'
- Oliver Wendell Holmes

'The bird of time has but a little way To flutter - and the bird is on the wing.'
 - Omar Khayyam

'Punctuality is the thief of time.'
 - Oscar Wilde

'Human successes, like human failures, are composed of one Taking Action at a time and achieved by one person at a time.'
 - Patty H. Sampson

'Every minute starts an hour.'
 - Paul Gondola

'Time is the wisest counselor.'
 - Pericles

'Seize time by the forelock.'
 - Pittacus of Mitylene

'Many things which cannot be overcome when they are together, yield themselves up when taken little by little.'
 - Plutarch

'If you wish to reach the highest, begin at the lowest.'
 - Publilius Syrus

'Most of the critical things in life, which become the starting points of human destiny, are little things.'
 - R. Smith

'The butterfly counts not months but moments, And has time enough.'
 - Rabindranath Tagore

'Gather ye rose-buds while ye may, Old Time is still aflying, And this same flower that smiles today, Tomorrow will be dying.'
 - Robert Herrick

'Start by doing what's necessary, then what's possible, and suddenly you are doing the impossible.'
 - Saint Francis of Assisi

'A harbor, even if it is a little harbor, is a good thing.... It takes something from the world, and has something to give in return.'
 - Sarah Orne Jewett

'What may be done at any time will be done at no time.'
 - Scottish proverb

'An age builds up cities: an hour destroys them.'
 - Seneca

'Time discovered truth.'
- Seneca

'Longevity conquers scandal every time.'
- Shelby Foote

'Time is a kindly god.'
- Sophocles

'Put your heart, mind, intellect, and soul even to your smallest acts. This is the secret of success.'
- Swami Sivananda

'I don't ask for your pity, but just your understanding - no, not even that -no. Just for your recognition of me in you, and the enemy, time, in us all.'
- Tennessee Williams

'Once in Persia reigned a king Who upon his signet ring Graved a maxim true and wise, Which if held before the eyes Gave him counsel at a glance Fit for every change and chance. Solemn words, and these are they: "Even this shall pass away."'
- Theodore Tilton

'What a day may bring, a day may take away.'
- Thomas Fuller

'Time cools, time clarifies; no mood can be maintained quite unaltered through the course of hours.'
- Thomas Mann

'These are the times that try men's souls.'
- Thomas Paine

'Let time that makes you homely, make you sage.'
- Thomas Parnell

'Inches make a champion.'
- Vince Lombardi

'Great things are not done by impulse, but by a series of small things brought together.'
- Vincent van Gogh

'The mind of man works with strangeness upon the body of time. An hour, once it lodges in the queer element of the human spirit, may be stretched to fifty or a hundred times its clock length; on the other hand, an hour may be accurately represented by the '
- Virginia Woolf

'It is by attempting to reach the top at a single leap that so much misery is caused in the world.'
- William Cobbett

'The big things that come our way are ... the fruit of seeds planted in the daily routine of our work.'
- William Feather

'The way a chihuahua goes about eating a dead elephant is to take a bite and be very present with that bite. In spiritual growth, the definitive act is to take one step and let tomorrow's step take care of itself!'
- William H. Houff

'Make use of time, let not advantage slip.'
- William Shakespeare

'There's a time for all things.'
- William Shakespeare

'Many strokes, though with a little axe, hew down and fell the hardest-timber'd oak.'
- William Shakespeare

'The time is out of joint.'
- William Shakespeare

'O, call back yesterday, bid time return.'
- William Shakespeare

'Much rain wears the marble.'
- William Shakespeare

'How far that little candle throws his beams! So shines a good deed in a naughty world.'
- William Shakespeare

'Well-being is attained little by little, and is no little thing itself.'
- Zeno

TRUST

'Time is precious, but truth is more precious than time.'
- Benjamin Disraeli

'When praying does no good, insurance does help.'
- Bertolt Brecht

'There is no truth in him.'
- Bible

'And ye shall know the truth, and the truth shall make you free.'
- Bible

'In God have I put my trust: I will not be afraid what man can do unto me.'
- Bible

'Thou trustest in the staff of this broken reed.'
- Bible

'Never trust the teller. Trust the tale.'
- D. H. Lawrence

'Public office is a public trust.'
- Dan S. Lamont

'There is nothing more likely to start disagreement among people or countries than an agreement.'
- E. B. White

'My way of joking is to tell the truth. It's the funniest joke in the world.'
- George Bernard Shaw

'All great truths began as blasphemies.'
- George Bernard Shaw

'To be trusted is a greater compliment than to be loved.'
- George Macdonald

'Government is a trust, and the officers of the government are trustees; and both the trust and the trustees are created for the benefit of the people.'
- Henry Clay

'It takes two to speak the truth - one to speak, and another to hear.'
- Henry David Thoreau

'I think that we may safely trust a good deal more than we do.'
- Henry David Thoreau

'Trust me, but look to thyself.'
- Irish proverb

'Truth forever on the scaffold. Wrong forever on the throne.'
- James Russell Lowell

'For truth has such a face and such a mien, As to be lov'd needs only to be seen.'
- John Dryden

''Tis strange - but true; for truth is always strange, Stranger than fiction.'
- Lord Byron

'The greater the truth the greater the libel.'
- Lord Ellenborough

'Truth is immortal; error is mortal.'
- Mary Baker Eddy

'Trust in God, and keep your powder dry.'
- Oliver Cromwell

'A promise made is a debt unpaid.'
- Robert W. Service

'To put one's trust in God is only a longer way of saying that one will chance it.'
- Samuel Butler

'Loyalty is still the same, Whether it win or lose the game; True as a dial to the sun, Although it be not shined upon.'
- Samuel Butler

'It is better to suffer wrong than to do it, and happier to be sometimes cheated than not to trust.'
- Samuel Johnson

'Truth ever lovely - since the world began, The foe of tyrants, and the friend of man.'
- Thomas Campbell

'Trust thyself only, and another shall not betray thee.'
- Thomas Fuller

'When a man assumes a public trust, he should consider himself as public property.'
- Thomas Jefferson

'Trust one who has tried.'
- Virgil

'Truth crushed to earth shall rise again.'
- William Cullen Bryant

'My man's as true as steel.'
   - William Shakespeare

''Tis true, 'tis pity; And pity 'tis 'tis true.'
   - William Shakespeare

TRUTH

'We call first truths those we discover after all the others.'
- Albert Camus

'If you are out to describe the truth, leave elegance to the tailor.'
- Albert Einstein

'Facts do not cease to exist because they are ignored.'
- Aldous Huxley

'No one can bar the road to truth, and to advance its cause I'm ready to accept even death.'
- Aleksandr Solzhenitsyn

'There are no whole truths. All truths are half-truths. It is trying to treat them as whole truths that plays the devil.'
- Alfred North Whitehead

'Pretty much all the honest truth telling there is in the world is done by children.'
- Anonymous

'Some people handle the truth carelessly; Others never touch it at all.'
- Anonymous

'Every truth passes through three stages before it is recognized. In the first it is ridiculed, in the second it is opposed, in the third it is regarded as self-evident.'
- Arthur Schopenhauer

'Truth always lags last, limping along on the arm of Time.'
- Baltasar Gracian

'We shall return to proven ways - not because they are old, but because they are true.'
- Barry Goldwater

'In every generation there has to be some fool who will speak the truth as he sees it.'
- Boris Pasternak

'Pure truth, like pure gold, has been found unfit for circulation because men have discovered that it is far more convenient to adulterate the truth than to refine themselves.'
- Charles Caleb Colton

'"It was as true", said Mr. Barkus, "as taxes is. And nothing is truer than them."'
- Charles Dickens

'Truth is a child of Time'
- Don Ford

'Many people would be more truthful were it not for their uncontrollable desire to talk.'
- Edgar Watson Howe

'Time trieth truth.'
- English proverb

'Truth emerges more readily from error than from confusion.'
- Francis Bacon

'Too much truth Is uncouth.'
- Franklin P. Adams

'One can live in this world on soothsaying but not on truth saying.'
- G. C. Lichtenberg

'The truth is cruel, but it can be loved and it makes free those who have loved it.'
- George Santayana

'Truth exists. Only lies are invented.'
- Georges Braque

'Truth has a handsome countenance but torn garments.'
- German proverb

'I don't give them hell. I just tell the truth and they think it is hell.'
- Harry S. Truman

'No one means all he says and yet very few say all they mean.'
- Henry Adams

'Between whom there is hearty truth, there is love.'
- Henry David Thoreau

'Truth for him was a moving target; he never aimed for the bull and rarely pierced the outer ring.'
- Hugh Cudlipp

'Seeing's believing - but feeling is God's own truth.'
- Irish proverb

'Every emancipation has in it the seeds of a new slavery, and every truth easily becomes a lie.'
- J. F. Stone

'Truth is something you stumble into when you think you're going some place else.'
- Jerry Garcid

'He who, when called upon to speak a disagreeable truth, tells it boldly and has done, is both bolder and milder than he who nibbles in a low voice and never ceases nibbling.'
- Johann Kaspar Lavater

'It makes all the difference in the world whether we put truth in the first place, or in the second place.'
- John Morley

'As scarce as truth is, the supply has always been in excess of the demand.'
- Josh Billings

'An exaggeration is a truth that has lost its temper.'
- Kahlil Gibran

'What I tell you three times is true.'
- Lewis Carroll

'As a rule, I am very careful to be shallow and conventional where depth and originality are wasted.'
- Lucy Maud Montgomery

'If you tell the truth you don't have to remember anything.'
- Mark Twain

'Peace if possible, but truth at any rate.'
- Martin Luther

'I speak the truth, not so much as I would, but as much as I dare; and I dare a little more, as I grow older.'
- Michel de Montaigne

'Don't be consistent, but be simply true.'
- Oliver Wendell Holmes

'Rough work, iconoclasm, but the only way to get at the truth.'
- Oliver Wendell Holmes

'The truth is rarely pure, and never simple.'
- Oscar Wilde

'A thing is not necessarily true because a man dies for it.'
- Oscar Wilde

'For my part, whatever anguish of spirit it may cost, I am willing to know the whole truth - to know the worst and provide for it.'
- Patrick Henry

'The passion for truth is silenced by answers which have the weight of undisputed authority.'
- Paul Tillich

'The man who speaks the truth is always at ease.'
- Persian proverb

'It is a difficult task, Oh citizens, to make speeches to the belly, which has no ears.'
- Plutarch

'When one has no design but to speak plain truth, he may say a great deal in a very narrow compass.'
- Richard Steele

'Every man has a right to utter what he thinks is truth, and every other man has a right to knock him down for it.'
- Samuel Johnson

'A misleading impression, not a lie. It was being economical with the truth.'
- Sir Robert Armstrong

'The man who fears no truths has nothing to fear from lies.'
- Thomas Jefferson

'Everything has to be taken on trust; truth is only that which is taken to be true. It's the currency of living. There may be nothing behind it, but it doesn't make any difference so long as it is honored.'
- Tom Stoppard

'If you speak the truth have a foot in the stirrup.'
- Turkish proverb

'There's such a thing as moderation, even in telling the truth.'
- Vera Johnson

'There are truths that are not for all men, nor for all times.'
- Voltaire

'What a myth never contains is the critical power to separate its truth from its errors.'
- Walter Lippman

'A truth that's told with bad intent Beats all the lies you can invent.'
- William Blake

'One truth discovered, one pang of regret at not being able to express it, is better than all the fluency and flippancy in the world.'
- William Hazlitt

'Truth never dies but lives a wretched life.'
- Yiddish proverb

VISUALIZATION

'Who would ever give up the reality of dreams for relative knowledge?'
   - Alice James

'The artist doesn't see things as they are, but as he is.'
   - Anonymous

'A couple of times a day I sit quietly and visualize my body fighting the AIDS virus. It's the same as me sitting and seeing myself hit the perfect serve. I did that often when I was an athlete.'
   - Arthur Ashe

'Our visions begin with our desires.'
   - Audre Lorde

'The very least you can do in your life is to figure out what you hope for. And the most you can do is live inside that hope. Not admire it from a distance but live right in it, under its roof.'
   - Barbara Kingsolver

'Nothing happens unless first a dream.'
   - Carl Sandburg

'Envisioning the end is enough to put the means in motion.'
   - Dorothea Brande

'Leaders are visionaries with a poorly developed sense of fear and no concept of the odds against them. They make the impossible happen.'
   - Dr. Robert Jarvik

'I think, at a child's birth, if a mother could ask a fairy godmother to endow it with the most useful gift, that gift should be curiosity.'
   - Eleanor Roosevelt

'I've dreamt in my life dreams that have stayed with me ever after, and changed my ideas: they've gone through and through me, like wine through water, and altered the color of my mind.'
   - Emily Bronte

'When we can't dream any longer, we die.'
   - Emma Goldman

'The best antidote I have found is to yearn for something. As long as you yearn, you can't congeal: there is a forward motion to yearning.'
   - Gail Godwin

'No vision and you perish; No ideal, and you're lost; Your heart must ever cherish Some faith at any cost. Some hope, some dream to cling to, Some rainbow in the sky, Some melody to sing to, Some

service that is high.'
- Harriet Du Autermont

'Imagination has always had powers of resurrection that no science can match.'
- Ingrid Bengis

'You know, my children, that humanity advances only by forming itself an ideal and endeavoring to realize it. Every passion has its ideal, which is modified by that of the whole.'
- Jenny R d'Hericourt

'Hold fast to dreams, for if dreams die, life is a broken-winged bird that cannot fly.'
- Langston Hughes

'Imagination is the highest kite that can fly.'
- Lauren Bacall

'When your dreams tire, they go underground and out of kindness that's where they stay.'
- Libby Houston

'Within your heart, keep one still, secret spot where dreams may go.'
- Louise Driscoll

'The history of all times, and of today especially, teaches that... women will be forgotten if they forget to think about themselves.'
- Louise Otto

'One of your most powerful inner resources is your own creativity. Be willing to try on something new and play the game full-out.'
- Marcia Wieder

'One must desire something to be alive: perhaps absolute satisfTaking Action is only another name for Death.'
- Margaret Deland

'It's our dreams that keep us going, that separate us from the beasts. I wouldn't even want to live if I thought it was all just eating and sleeping and taking off my clothes.'
- Mary Chase

'To the lack of incentive to effort, which is the awful shadow under which we live, may be traced the wreck and ruin of scores of colored youth.'
- Mary Church Terrell

'We are governed not by armies, but by ideas.'
- Mona Caird

'Dreams are the sources of Taking Action, the meeting and the end, a resting place among the flight of things.'
- Muriel Rukeyser

'The truth isn't always beauty, but the hunger for it is.'
- Nadine Gordimer

'What man can imagine he may one day achieve.'
- Nancy Hale

'With our progress we have destroyed our only weapon against tedium: that rare weakness we call imagination.'
- Oriana Fallaci

'Every woman dreams of her own political career and her own place in life.'
- Raisa M. Gorbachev

'When there is no vision, people perish.'
- Ralph Waldo Emerson

'If we have not achieved our early dreams, we must either find new ones or see what we can salvage from the old. If we have accomplished what we set out to do in our youth, we need not weep like Alexander the Great that we have no more worlds to conquer.'
- Rosalynn Carter

'All prosperity begins in the mind and is dependent only upon the full use of our creative imagination.'
- Ruth Ross

'It may be that those who do most, dream most.'
- Stephen Leacock

'The moment of enlightenment is when a person's dreams of possibilities become images of probabilities.'
- Vic Braden

'It is in our idleness, in our dreams, that the submerged truth sometimes comes to the top.'
- Virginia Woolf

WAR

'The ballot is stronger than the bullet.'
- Abraham Lincoln

'I have never understood disliking for war. It panders to instincts already catered for within the scope of any respectable domestic establishment.'
- Alan Bennett

'God how the dead men Grin by the wall, Watching the fun Of the Victory Ball.'
- Alfred Noyes

'A war regarded as inevitable or even probable, and therefore much prepared for, has a very good chance of eventually being fought.'
- Anais Nin

'Today the real test of power is not capacity to make war but capacity to prevent it.'
- Anne O'Hare McCormick

'War does not determine who is right - only who is left.'
- Anonymous

'The inevitableness, the idealism, and the blessing of war, as an indispensable and stimulating law of development, must be repeatedly emphasized.'
- Anonymous

'Wars are not fought for territory, but for words. Man's deadliest weapon is language. He is as susceptible to being hypnotized by slogans as he is to infectious diseases. And where there is an epidemic, the group-mind takes over.'
- Arthur Koestler

'All wars are popular for the first 30 days.'
- Arthur Schlesinger

'Good things, when short, are twice as good.'
- Baltasar Gracian

'War is the unfolding of miscalculations.'
- Barbara Tuchman

'There never was a good war or a bad peace.'
- Benjamin Franklin

'Let us not be deceived - we are today in the midst of a cold war.'
- Bernard Baruch

'War is like love, it always finds a way.'
- Bertolt Brecht

'If a house be divided against itself, that house cannot stand.'
- Bible

'In time of war the first casualty is truth.'
- Boake Carter

'There is no such thing as inevitable war. If war comes it will be from failure of human wisdom.'
- Bonar Law

'What the hell difference does it make, left or right? There were good men lost on both sides.'
- Brendan Behan

'Either war is obsolete, or men are.'
- Buckminster Fuller

'War hath no fury like a noncombatant.'
- C. E. Montague

'Sometime they'll give a war and nobody will come.'
- Carl Sandburg

'It would indeed be a tragedy if the history of the human race proved to be nothing more than the story of an ape playing with a box of matches on a petrol dump.'
- David Ormsby Gore

'I don't know what effect these men will have on the enemy, but by God, they frighten me.'
- Duke of Wellington

'The whole art of war consists of guessing at what is on the other side of the hill.'
- Duke of Wellington

'War hath no fury like a non-combatant.'
- E. C. Montague

'War never leaves, where it found a nation.'
- Edmund Burke

'It simply is not true that war never settles anything.'
- Felix Frankfurter

'When after many battles past, Both tir'd with blows, make peace at last, What is it, after all, the people get? Why! taxes, widows, wooden legs, and debt.'
- Francis Moore

'Modern warfare is an intricate business about which no one knows everything and few know very much.'
- Frank Knox

'We don't want to fight, but by jingo if we do, We've got the ships, we've got the men, we've got the money too. We've fought the Bear before and while we're Britons true, The Russians shall not have Constantinople.'
- G. W. Hunt

'We give up the fort when there's not a man left to defend it.'
- General Croghan

'The quickest way of ending a war is to lose it.'
- George Orwell

'World War II was the last government program that really worked.'
- George Will

'War is much too important a matter to be left to the generals.'
- Georges Clemenceau

'War is a series of catastrophes which result in victory.'
- Georges Clemenceau

'In time of war the devil makes more room in hell.'
- German proverb

'I have prayed in her fields of poppies, I have laughed with the men who died - But in all my ways and through all my days Like a friend He walked beside. I have seen a sight under Heaven That only God understands, In the battle's glare I have seen Christ '
- Gordon Johnstone

'Hang yourself, brave Crillon. We fought at Arques, and you were not there.'
- Henry IV

'In peace, sons bury their fathers; in war, fathers bury their sons.'
- Herodotus

'Men grow tired of sleep, love, singing and dancing sooner than of war.'
- Homer

'It is not right to exult over slain men.'
- Homer

'But, in case signals can neither be seen or perfectly understood, no captain can do very wrong if he places his ship alongside the enemy.'
- Horatio Nelson

'The weak against the strong, Is always in the wrong.'
  - Ivan Krylov

'When the rich wage war, it's the poor who die.'
  - Jean-Paul Sartre

'Boys are the cash of war. Whoever said: we're not free spenders- doesn't know our like.'
  - John Ciardi

'War is the trade of kings.'
  - John Dryden

'War, he sung, is toil and trouble; Honor but an empty bubble.'
  - John Dryden

'War will exist until that distant day when the conscientious objector enjoys the same reputation and prestige that the warrior does today.'
  - John F. Kennedy

'The world will never have lasting peace so long as men reserve for war the finest human qualities.'
  - John Foster Dulles

'Men love war because it allows them to look serious; because it is the only thing that stops women laughing at them.'
  - John Fowles

'Take up our quarrel with the foe! To you from failing hands we throw The torch; be yours to hold it high. If ye break faith with us who die We shall not sleep, though poppies grow In Flanders' fields.'
  - John McCrae

'The brazen throat of war.'
  - John Milton

'War is the science of destruction.'
  - John S. C. Abbott

'Most sorts of diversion in men, children and other animals, are in imitation of fighting.'
  - Jonathan Swift

'And this I hate - not men, nor flag nor race, But only War with its wild, grinning face.'
  - Joseph Dana Miler

'Frankly I'd like to see the government get out of war altogether and leave the whole field to private industry.'
  - Joseph Heller

'Mine eyes have seen the glory of the coming of the Lord: He is trampling out the vintage where the grapes of wrath are stored: He hath loosed the fateful lightning of his terrible swift sword: His truth is

marching on.'
- Julia Ward Howe

'Veni, vidi, vici. (I came, I saw, I conquered.)'
- Julius Caesar

'In war the will is directed at an animate object that reacts.'
- Karl von Clausewitz

'Sweet is war to those who have never experienced it.'
- Latin proverb

'Tweedle Dum and Tweedle Dee Agreed to have a battle; For Tweedle Dum said Tweedle Dee Had spoiled his nice new rattle.'
- Lewis Carroll

'It's one of the most serious things that can possibly happen to one in a battle - to get one's head cut off.'
- Lewis Carroll

'Morality is contraband in war.'
- Mahatma Gandhi

'The guerilla must live amongst the people as the fish lives in the water.'
- Mao Tse-Tung

'Television brought the brutality of war into the comfort of the living room. Vietnam was lost in the living rooms of U.S.A. - not on the battlefields of Vietnam.'
- Marshall McLuhan

'War is the greatest plague that can afflict humanity; it destroys religion, it destroys states, it destroys families. Any scourge is preferable to it.'
- Martin Luther

'Wars and rumors of wars.'
- Matthew

'They will conquer, but they will not convince.'
- Miguel de Unamuno

'War is the national industry of Prussia.'
- Mirabeau

'Above all, Vietnam was a war that asked everything of a few and nothing of most in America.'
- Myra McPherson

'If they want peace, nations should avoid the pinpricks that precede cannon shots.'
- Napoleon Bonaparte

'A man who experiences no genuine satisfTaking Action in life does not want peace. People court war to escape meaninglessness and boredom, to be relieved of fear and frustration.'
- Nels F. S. Ferre

'The possibility of war increases in direct proportion to the effectiveness of the instruments of war.'
- Norman Cousins

'War appeals to young men because it is fundamentally auto-eroticism.'
- Northrop Frye

'As long as war is regarded as wicked, it will always have its fascination. When it is looked upon as vulgar, it will cease to be popular.'
- Oscar Wilde

'(The great questions of the day) are not decided by speeches and majority votes, but by blood and iron.'
- Otto von Bismarck

'Better pointed bullets than pointed speeches.'
- Otto von Bismarck

'0 God assist our side: at least, avoid assisting the enemy and leave the rest to me.'
- Prince Leopold

'We only win at war because we fight another government. If we fought private industry we would not last until noontime.'
- R. I. Fitzhenry

'By the rude bridge that arched the flood, Their flag to April's breeze unfurl'd; Here once the embattl'd farmers stood, And fired the shot heard round the world.'
- Ralph Waldo Emerson

'Human war has been the most successful of all our cultural traditions.'
- Robert Ardrey

'It is well that war is so terrible - we would grow too fond of it.'
- Robert E. Lee

'To arms! to arms! ye brave! The avenging sword unsheathe, March on! march on! all hearts resolved On victory or death!'
- Rouget de Lisle

'War would end if the dead could return.'
- Stanley Baldwin

'If you know the enemy and know yourself you need not fear the results of a hundred battles.'
- Sun Tzu

'The supreme excellence is not to win a hundred victories in a hundred battles. The supreme excellence is to subdue the armies of your enemies without even having to fight them.'
- Sun Tzu

'A bad peace is even worse than war.'
- Tacitus

'Great Britain was going to make war on a kindred nation who desired nothing better than to be friends with her.'
- Theobald von Bethmann-Hollweg

'What millions died - that Caesar might be great!'
- Thomas Campbell

'War is as much a punishment to the punisher as to the sufferer.'
- Thomas Jefferson

'General Taylor never surrenders.'
- Thomas L. Crittenden

'Vice stirs up war; virtue fights.'
- Vauvenargues

'There will be no veterans of World War III.'
- Walter Mondale

'What distinguishes war is, not that man is slain, but that he is slain, spoiled, crushed by the cruelty, the injustice, the treachery, the murderous hand of man.'
- William Ellery Channing

'So far war has been the only force that can discipline a whole community, and until an equivalent discipline is organized, I believe that war must have its way.'
- William James

'So long as the anti-militarists propose no substitute for war's disciplinary function, no moral equivalent of war, analogous, as one might say, to the mechanical equivalent of hate, so long they fail to realize the full equities of the situation.'
- William James

'We few, we happy few, we band of brothers; For he today that sheds his blood with me; Shall be my brother.'
- William Shakespeare

'O war! thou son of Hell!'
- William Shakespeare

'There is many a boy here today who looks on war as all glory, but boys, it is all hell.'
- William T. Sherman

'There are no atheists in the foxholes.'
- William Thomas Cummings

'No one can guarantee success in war, but only deserve it.'
- Winston Churchill

'Let us therefore brace ourselves to our duties, and so bear ourselves that, if the British Empire and its Commonwealth last for a thousand years, men will still say: "This was their finest hour."'
- Winston Churchill

'War is mainly a catalogue of blunders.'
- Winston Churchill

'Do not let us speak of darker days; let us speak rather of sterner days. These are not dark days: these are great days - the greatest days our country has ever lived.'
- Winston Churchill

WEALTH

'Surplus wealth is a sacred trust which its possessor is bound to administer in his life-time for the good of the community.'
- Andrew Carnegie

'I glory more in the coming purchase of my wealth than in the glad possession.'
- Ben Jonson

'If you would be wealthy, think of saving as well as of getting.'
- Benjamin Franklin

'Wealth is not his that has it, but his who enjoys it.'
- Benjamin Franklin

'Who is rich? He that rejoices in his portion.'
- Benjamin Franklin

'He heapeth up riches, and knoweth not who shall gather them.'
- Bible

'Wealth ... is a relative thing since he that has little and wants less is richer than he that has much but wants more.'
- Charles Caleb Colton

'Sometimes when you have everything, you can't really tell what matters.'
- Christina Onassis

''Let us not get so busy or live so fast that we can't listen to the music of the meadow or the symphony that glorifies the forest. Some things in the world are far more important than wealth; one of them is the ability to enjoy simple things.'
- Dale Carnegie

'Australia is so kind that, just tickle her with a hoe, and she laughs with a harvest.'
- Douglas Jerrold

'I am rich beyond the dreams of avarice.'
- Edward Moore

'In big houses in which things are done properly, there is always the religious element. The diurnal cycle is observed with more feeling when there are servants to do the work.'
- Elizabeth Bowen

'It is good to have things that money can buy, but it is also good to check up once in awhile and be sure we have the things money can't buy.'
- George Horace Lorimer

'The ideal social state is not that in which each gets an equal amount of wealth, but in which each gets in proportion to his contribution to the general stock.'
- Henry George

'Prosperity is just around the corner.'
- Herbert Hoover

'Riches either serve or govern the possessor.'
- Horace

'Sleep, riches and health to be truly enjoyed must be interrupted.'
- Jean Paul Richter

'I was born into it and there was nothing I could do about it. It was there, like air or food, or any other element. The only question with wealth is what you do with it.'
- John D. Rockefeller

'All wealth is the product of labor'
- John Locke

'The smell of profit is clean and sweet, whatever the source.'
- Juvenal

'Having given all he had, He then is very rich indeed.'
- Lao-Tzu

'It is wealth to be content.'
- Lao-Tzu

'It is the wretchedness of being rich that you have to live with rich people.'
- Logan Pearsall Smith

'We can have democracy in this country or we can have great wealth concentrated in the hands of a few, but we can't have both.'
- Louis D. Brandeis

'I wish to become rich, so that I can instruct the people and glorify honest poverty a little, like those kind-hearted, fat, benevolent people do.'
- Mark Twain

'I am opposed to millionaires, but it would be dangerous to offer me the position.'
- Mark Twain

'Our Lord commonly giveth Riches to such gross asses, to whom he affordeth nothing else that is good.'
- Martin Luther

'True abundance is not about gathering more things, it's about touching the place in us that is connected to the divine source of abundance, so that we know what we need in the moment will be

provided.'
- Mary Manin Morrissey

'It is easier for a camel to go through the eye of a needle, than for a rich man to enter into the kingdom of God.'
- Matthew

'I have enough money to get by. I'm not independently wealthy, just independently lazy, I suppose.'
- Montgomery Clift

'Riches do not consist in the possession of treasures, but in the use made of them.'
- Napoleon Bonaparte

'Riches serve a wise man but command a fool.'
- Old saying

'Poor men seek meat for their stomach, rich men stomach for their meat.'
- Old saying

'I'll fares the land, to hastening ills of prey Where wealth accumulates, and men decay.'
- Oliver Goldsmith

'Ordinary riches can be stolen, real riches cannot. In your soul are infinitely precious things that cannot be taken from you.'
- Oscar Wilde

'I have no complex about wealth. I have worked hard for my money, producing things people need. I believe that the able industrial leader who creates wealth and employment is more worthy of historical notice than politicians or soldiers.'
- Paul Getty

'Riches certainly make themselves wings.'
- Proverbs

'The wealth of nations is men, not silk and cotton and gold.'
- Richard Hovey

'If you see yourself as prosperous, you will be. If you see yourself as continually hard up, that is exactly what you will be.'
- Robert Collier

'The rich man is not one who is in possession of much, but one who gives much.'
- Saint John Chrysostom

'It is better to live rich than to die rich.'
- Samuel Johnson

'Life is short. The sooner that a man begins to enjoy his wealth the better.'
- Samuel Johnson

'It's time we put thoughts of lack behind us. It's time for us to discover the secrets of the stars, to sail to an uncharted land, to open up a new heaven where our spirits can soar.'
- Sarah Ban Breathnach

'If you're happy, you're wealthy! Happiness doesn't need a bank account.'
- Sr. Mary Christelle Macaluso

'No good man ever became suddenly rich.'
- Syrus

'Riches enlarge, rather than satisfy appetites.'
- Thomas Fuller

'I have mental joys and mental health, Mental friends and mental wealth, I've a wife that I love and that loves me; I've all but riches bodily.'
- William Blake

WISDOM

'Let weakness learn meekness.'
- A. C. Swinburne

'What a man knows at fifty that he did not know at twenty is for the most part incommunicable.'
- Adlai Stevenson

'Wisdom comes alone through suffering.'
- Aeschylus

'Experience is not what happens to a man. It is what a man does with what happens to him.'
- Aldous Huxley

'Experience teaches only the teachable.'
- Aldous Huxley

'All human wisdom is summed up in two words - wait and hope.'
- Alexandre Dumas

'Experience is the name men give to their follies or their sorrows.'
- Alfred de Musset

'Knowledge comes, but wisdom lingers.'
- Alfred, Lord Tennyson

'Good judgement comes from experience, and experience - well, that comes from poor judgement.'
- Anonymous

'Never since the time of Copernicus have so many experts been so wrong so often with so little humility.'
- Anonymous

'A word to the wise is infuriating.'
- Anonymous

'Experience is the extract of suffering.'
- Arthur Helps

'A sage has one advantage; he is immortal. If this is not his century, many others will be.'
- Baltasar Gracian

'A wise man gets more use from his enemies than a fool from his friends.'
- Baltasar Gracian

'The wise have a solid sense of silence and the ability to keep a storehouse of secrets. Their capacity and character are respected.'
- Baltasar Gracian

'Who is wise? He that learns from everyone. Who is powerful? He that governs his passions. Who is rich? He that is content. Who is that? Nobody.'
- Benjamin Franklin

'Age is only a number, a cipher for the records. A man can't retire his experience. He must use it. Experience achieves more with less energy and time.'
- Bernard Baruch

'Through wisdom a house is built and through understanding it is established.'
- Bible

'In much wisdom is much grief: and he that increaseth knowledge increaseth sorrow.'
- Bible

'I gave my beauty and my youth to men. I am going to give my wisdom and experience to animals.'
- Brigitte Bardot

'Any man worth his salt has by the time he is forty-five accumulated a crown of thorns, and the problem is to learn to wear it over one ear.'
- Christopher Morley

'The more specific you are, the more general it'll be.'
- Diane Arbus

'Strange how few After all's said and done, the things that are Of moment.'
- Edna St. Vincent Millay

'A man's ruin lies in his tongue.'
- Egyptian saying

'Every man is a damn fool for at least five minutes every day; wisdom consists in not exceeding the limit.'
- Elbert Hubbard

'Not to transmit an experience is to betray it.'
- Elie Wiesel

'A burnt child dreads the fire.'
- English proverb

'Many of the insights of the saint stem from his experience as a sinner.'
- Eric Hoffer

'Experience has two things to teach: The first is that we must correct a great deal; the second that we must not correct too much.'
- Eugene Delacroix

'Let my heart be wise. It is the gods' best gift.'
- Euripides

'Experience enables you to recognize a mistake when you make it again.'
- Franklin P. Jones

'Men are wise in proportion, not to their experience, but to their capacity for experience.'
- George Bernard Shaw

'Everything happens to everybody sooner or later if there is time enough.'
- George Bernard Shaw

'Night is the mother of counsels.'
- George Herbert

'Almost every wise saying has an opposite one, no less wise, to balance it.'
- George Santayana

'All that I know I learned after I was thirty.'
- Georges Clemenceau

'It is characteristic of wisdom not to do desperate things.'
- Henry David Thoreau

'Experience is in the fingers and the head. The heart is inexperienced.'
- Henry David Thoreau

'Motives and purposes are in the brain and heart of man. Consequences are in the world of fact.'
- Henry Geaye

'Deep experience is never peaceful.'
- Henry James

'Knowledge can be communicated but not wisdom.'
- Hermann Hesse

'It wasn't raining when Noah built the ark.'
- Howard Ruff

'Not to know certain things is a great part of wisdom.'
- Hugo Grotius

'Experience, which destroys innocence, also leads one back to it.'
- James Baldwin

'One thorn of experience is worth a whole wilderness of warning.'
- James Russell Lowell

'Ah, men do not know how much strength is in poise, That he goes the farthest who goes far enough.'
- James Russell Lowell

'The question of commonsense is always "what is it good for?" - a question which would abolish the rose and be answered triumphantly by the cabbage.'
- James Russell Lowell

'A wise man hears one word and understands two.'
- Jewish proverb

'A proverb is one man's wit and all men's wisdom.'
- John Russell

'There was only one catch and that was Catch-22, which specified the concern for one's own safety in the face of dangers that were real and immediate was the process of a rational mind.'
- Joseph Heller

'Deliberate often - decide once.'
- Latin proverb

'When choosing between two evils, I always like to take the one I've never tried before.'
- Mae West

'A wise man sees as much as he ought, not as much as he can.'
- Michel de Montaigne

'The life of the law has not been logic, it has been experience.'
- Oliver Wendell Holmes

'The number of people who will not go to a show they do not want to see is unlimited.'
- Oscar Hammerstein

'Experience is the name so many people give to their mistakes.'
- Oscar Wilde

'A wise man, to accomplish his end, may even carry his foe on his shoulder.'
- Panchatantra

'I have but one lamp by which my feet are guided, and that is the lamp of experience.'
- Patrick Henry

'Wisdom is always an overmatch for strength.'
- Phaedrus

'It is not wise to be wiser than is necessary.'
- Philippe Quinault

'Le raison avant la passion - Reason over passion.'
- Pierre Elliott Trudeau

'The road to wisdom? Well, it's plain And simple to express: Err And err And err again But less And less And less.'
- Piet Hein

'Do not be too timid and squeamish about your Taking Actions. All life is an experience.'
- Ralph Waldo Emerson

'A wise man always throws himself on the side of his assailants. It is more his interests than it is theirs to find his weak point.'
- Ralph Waldo Emerson

'It's taken me all my life to understand that it is not necessary to understand everything.'
- Rent Coty

'My father used to say: Son, if you are not bright, you've got to be methodical, (defusing argument when challenged and proved right)'
- Robert Sachs

'Life is like playing a violin solo in public, and learning the instrument as one goes on.'
- Samuel Butler

'To most men, experience is like the stern lights of a ship, which illumine only the track it has passed.'
- Samuel Taylor Coleridge

'The wise only possess ideas; the greater part of mankind are possessed by them.'
- Samuel Taylor Coleridge

'From error to error one discovers the entire truth.'
- Sigmund Freud

'Everyone whose deeds are more than his wisdom, his wisdom endures. And everyone whose wisdom is more than his deeds, his wisdom does not endure.'
- The Talmud

'Nine-tenths of wisdom consists in being wise in time.'
- Theodore Roosevelt

'Experience is the best of schoolmasters, only the school-fees are heavy.'
- Thomas Carlyle

'Today is yesterday's pupil.'
- Thomas Fuller

'Some folks are wise and some are otherwise.'
- Tobias Smollett

'Experience is the worst teacher; it gives the test before presenting the lesson.'
  - Vernon Law

'Is there anyone so wise as to learn by the experience of others?'
  - Voltaire

'To a great experience one thing is essential - an experiencing nature.'
  - Walter Bagehot

'The tigers of wrath are wiser than the horses of instruction.'
  - William Blake

'The art of being wise is the art of knowing what to overlook.'
  - William James

'I embrace emerging experience. I participate in discovery. I am a butterfly. I am not a butterfly collector. I want the experience of the butterfly.'
  - William Stafford

'Learning passes for wisdom among those who want both.'
  - William Temple

WITTY

'When wealth is lost, nothing is lost; When health is lost, something is lost; When character is lost, all is lost!'
- Anonymous

'The rich can be "eccentric," the poor have to be considered "nuts."'
- Anonymous

'The best way to save face is keep the bottom half shut.'
- Anonymous

'What do you call a woman who knows where her husband is at all times? A widow.'
- Anonymous

'No woman ever shot her husband while he was doing the dishes.'
- Anonymous

'In the game of life nothing is less important than the score at half time.'
- Anonymous

'Retirement must be wonderful. I mean, you can suck in your stomach for only so long.'
- Burt Reynolds

'Do not free a camel of the burden of his hump; you may be freeing him from being a camel.'
- G. K. Chesterton

'When I was born I was so surprised I didn't talk for a year and a half.'
- Grade Allen

'When a man brings his wife flowers for no reason - there's a reason.'
- Molly McGee

'The only thing I regret about my past is the length of it. If I had to live my life again, I'd make the same mistakes, only sooner.'
- Tallulah Bankhead

WOMEN

'But what is woman? Only one of nature's agreeable blunders.'
- Abraham Cowley

'A woman is the only thing I am afraid of that I know will not hurt me.'
- Abraham Lincoln

'You don't know a woman until you have had a letter from her.'
- Ada Levenson

'Why should human females become sterile in their forties, while female crocodiles continue to lay eggs into their third century?'
- Aldous Huxley

'Woman's at best a contradiction still.'
- Alexander Pope

'Offend her, and she knows not to forgive; Oblige her, and she'll hate you while you live.'
- Alexander Pope

'We don't love a woman for what she says, but we like what she says because we love her.'
- Andri Maurois

'I dress for women - and I undress for men.'
- Angle Dickinson

'Woman's normal occupations in general run counter to creative life, or contemplative life, or saintly life.'
- Anne Morrow Lindbergh

'Why did God make man before he made woman? Because he didn't want any advice on how to do it.'
- Anonymous

'Outside every thin girl is a fat man, trying to get in.'
- Anonymous

'The cleverest woman finds a need for foolish admirers.'
- Anonymous

'Some women blush when they are kissed; some call for the police; some swear; some bite. But the worst are those who laugh.'
- Anonymous

'Oh, the shrewdness of their shrewdness when they're shrewd. And the rudeness of their rudeness when they're rude; But the shrewdness of their shrewdness and the rudeness of their rudeness, Are

nothing to their goodness when they're good.'
  - Anonymous

'When Eleanor Roosevelt was asked if she had any regrets about her life she replied "Just one. I wish I had been prettier."'
  - Anonymous

'She was not a woman likely to settle for equality when sex gave her an advantage.'
  - Anthony Delano

'A beautiful woman should break her mirror early.'
  - Baltasar Gracian

'Next to the wound, what women make best is the bandage.'
  - Barbey d'Aurevilly

'A woman, the more careful she is about her face, is commonly the more careless about her house.'
  - Ben Jonson

'Simpson succeeded in proving that there was no harm in giving anesthetics to men, because God put Adam into a deep sleep when He extracted his rib. But male ecclesiastics remained unconvinced as regards the sufferings of women, at any rate in childbirth.'
  - Bertrand Russell

'A woman past forty should make up her mind to be young - not her face.'
  - Billie Burke

'O wild, dark flower of woman, Deep rose of my desire, An Eastern wizard made you Of earth and stars and fire.'
  - C. G. D. Roberts

'No woman marries for money; they are all clever enough, before marrying a millionaire, to fall in love with him first.'
  - Cesare Pavese

'Where young boys plan for what they will achieve and attain, young girls plan for whom they will achieve and attain.'
  - Charlotte Perkins

'Whatever women do they must do twice as well as men to be thought half as good. Luckily, this is not difficult.'
  - Charlotte Whitton

'The woman who thinks she is intelligent demands equal rights with men. A woman who is intelligent does not.'
  - Colette

'Women do not find it difficult nowadays to behave like men, but they often find it extremely difficult to behave like gentlemen.'
- Compton Mackenzie

'Women keep a special corner of their hearts for sins they have never committed.'
- Cornelia Otis Skinner

'The great fault in women is to desire to be like men.'
- De Maistre

'Men say of women what pleases them! women do with men what pleases them.'
- De Segur

'Women are the cowards they are because they have been semi-slaves for so long. The number of women prepared to stand up for what they really think, feel, experience, with a man they are in love with is still very small.'
- Doris Lessing

'Time and trouble will tame an advanced young woman. But an advanced old woman is uncontrollable by any force.'
- Dorothy L. Sayers

'A woman is as old as she looks before breakfast.'
- Edgar Watson Howe

'For a single woman, preparing for company means wiping the lipstick off the milk carton.'
- Elayne Boosler

'Social science affirms that a woman's place in society marks the level of civilization.'
- Elizabeth Cady Stanton

'There is but an hour a day between a good housewife and a bad one.'
- English proverb

'There is no worse evil than a bad woman; and nothing has ever been produced better than a good one.'
- Euripides

'Housework is what woman does that nobody notices unless she hasn't done it.'
- Evan Esar

'No man is as anti-feminist as a really feminine woman.'
- Frank O'Connor

'The great and almost only comfort about being a woman is that one can always pretend to be more stupid than one is and no one is surprised.'
- Freya Stark

'A woman may very well form a friendship with a man, but for this to endure, it must be assisted by a little physical antipathy.'
- Friedrich Nietzsche

'Has a woman who knew that she was well dressed ever caught a cold?'
- Friedrich Nietzsche

'When thou goest to woman, take thy whip.'
- Friedrich Nietzsche

'Honor women! they entwine and weave heavenly roses in our earthly life.'
- Friedrich von Schiller

'Woman's dearest delight is to wound Man's self-conceit, though Man's dearest delight is to gratify hers.'
- George Bernard Shaw

'A woman never sees what we do for her, she only sees what we don't do.'
- Georges Courteline

'Most women still need a room of their own and the only way to find it may be outside their own home.'
- Germaine Greer

'A woman without a man is like a fish without a bicycle.'
- Gloria Steinem

'The society of women is the foundation of good manners.'
- Goethe

'Whether women are better than men I cannot say - but I can say they are certainly no worse.'
- Golda Meir

'Can we today measure devotion to husband and children by our indifference to everything else?'
- Golda Meir

'Women have simple tastes. They get pleasure out of the conversation of children in arms and men in love.'
- H. L. Mencken

'Woman is at once apple and serpent.'
- Heinrich Heine

'You have to go back to the Children's Crusade in 1212 AD to find as unfortunate and fatuous an attempt at manipulated hysteria as the Women's Liberation Movement.'
- Helen Lawrenson

'Failing to be there when a man wants her is a woman's greatest sin, except to be there when he doesn't want her.'
- Helen Rowland

'There are no ugly women, only lazy ones.'
- Helena Rubinstein

'Too fair to worship, too divine to love.'
- Henry Hart Milman

'The crown of creation.'
- Herdeb

'If a woman likes another woman, she's cordial. If she doesn't like her, she's very cordial.'
- Irvin S. Cobb

'The more underdeveloped the country, the more overdeveloped the women.'
- J. K. Galbraith

'Earth's noblest thing, a Woman perfected.'
- James Russell Lowell

'Woman's place is in the wrong.'
- James Thurber

'There are no ugly women; there are only women who do not know how to look pretty.'
- Jean de la Bruyere

'I have met with women who I really think would like to be married to a poem, and to be given away by a novel.'
- John Keats

'Grace was in all her steps, heaven in her eye, In every gesture dignity and love.'
- John Milton

'When a woman dressed up for an occasion, the man should become the black velvet pillow for the jewel.'
- John Weitz

'There is nothing enduring in life for a woman except what she builds in a man's heart.'
- Judith Anderson

'Women are perfectly well aware that the more they seem to obey the more they rule.'
- Jules Michelet

'I don't know of anything better than a woman if you want to spend money where it will show.'
- Kin Hubbard

'Educating a beautiful woman is like pouring honey into a fine Swiss watch: everything stops.'
  - Kurt Vonnegut

'One can find women who have never had a love affair, but it is rare indeed to find any who have had only one.'
  - La Rochefoucauld

'The worst thing about work in the house or home is that whatever you do is destroyed, laid waste or eaten within twenty-four hours.'
  - Lady Kasluck

'The cave-dweller's wife complained that he hadn't dragged her anywhere in months.'
  - Laurence J. Peter

'Regard the society of women as a necessary unpleasantness of social life, and avoid it as much as possible.'
  - Leo Tolstoy

'Nobody objects to a woman being a good writer or sculptor or geneticist if at the same time she manages to be a good wife, good mother, good looking, good tempered, well groomed and unaggressive.'
  - Leslie M. McIntyre

'Boys don't make passes at female smart-asses.'
  - Letty Cottin Pogrebin

'All women's dresses are merely variations on the eternal struggle between the admitted desire to dress and the unadmitted desire to undress.'
  - Lin Yutang

'In her first passion woman loves her lover; In all the others, all she loves is love.'
  - Lord Byron

'Women always have some mental reservation.'
  - Louis Ferdinand Destouches

'Women are most adorable when they are afraid; that's why they frighten so easily.'
  - Ludwig Borne

'Each suburban housewife spends her time presiding over a power plant sufficient to have staffed the palace of a Roman emperor with a hundred slaves.'
  - Margaret Mead

'No woman can call herself free who does not own and control her body. No woman can call herself free until she can choose consciously whether she will or will not be a mother.'
  - Margaret Sanger

'The battle for women's rights has been largely won.'
  - Margaret Thatcher

'I've got a woman's ability to stick to a job and get on with it when everyone else walks off and leaves it.'
- Margaret Thatcher

'As a woman, to be competitive is to be passive.'
- Marianne Partridge

'Can you imagine a world without men? No crime and lots of happy fat women.'
- Marion Smith

'A kiss can be a comma, a question mark or an exclamation point. That's a basic spelling that every woman should know.'
- Mistinguette

'The mirror is the conscience of women; they never do a thing without first consulting it.'
- Morltz G. Saphlr

'My vigor, vitality and cheek repel me. I am the kind of woman I would run from.'
- Nancy Lady Astor

'The economic dependence of women is perhaps the greatest injustice that has been done to us, and has worked the greatest injury to the race.'
- Nellie McClung

'By nice women . . . you probably mean selfish women who have no more thought for the underprivileged, overworked women than a pussycat in a sunny window for the starving kitten in the street. Now in that sense I am not a nice woman, for I do care.'
- Nellie McClung

'Women who set a low value on themselves make life hard for all women.'
- Nellie McClung

'If you can make a woman laugh you can do anything with her.'
- Nicol Williamson

'A modest woman, dressed out in all her finery, is the most tremendous object of the whole creation.'
- Oliver Goldsmith

'Man has his will, - but woman has her way.'
- Oliver Wendell Holmes

'Nature is in earnest when she makes a woman.'
- Oliver Wendell Holmes

'There is no such thing as romance in our day, women have become too brilliant; nothing spoils a romance so much as a sense of humor in the woman.'
- Oscar Wilde

'A woman is always buying something.'
- Ovid

'Whether they give or refuse, women are glad to have been asked.'
- Ovid

'What one beholds of a woman is the least part of her.'
- Ovid

'The toughest thing about being a housewife is you have no place to stay home from.'
- Patricia C. Beudoin

'It takes all the fun out of a bracelet if you have to buy it yourself.'
- Peggy Joyce

'Nature says to a woman: 'Be beautiful if you can, wise if you want to, but be respected, that is essential.''
- Pierre Beaumarchais

'Feminism is the most revolutionary idea there has ever been. Equality for women demands a change in the human psyche, more profound than anything Marx dreamed of. It means valuing parenthood as much as we value banking.'
- Polly Toynbee

'A woman's strength is the irresistible might of weakness.'
- Ralph Waldo Emerson

'People call me a feminist whenever I express sentiments that differentiate me from a doormat or a prostitute.'
- Rebecca West

'Most men who run down women are running down one woman only.'
- Remy de Gourmont

'Such, Polly, are your sex - part truth, part fiction; Some thought, much whim, and all contradiction.'
- Richard Savage

'What will not woman, gentle woman dare When strong affection stirs her spirit up?'
- Robert Southey

'It is easier for a woman to defend her virtue against men than her reputation against women.'
- Rochebrune

'For the female of the species is more deadly than the male.'
- Rudyard Kipling

'A woman's guess is much more accurate than a man's certainty.'
- Rudyard Kipling

'The colonel's lady and Judy O'Grady Are sisters under their skins.'
    - Rudyard Kipling

'An' I learned about women from 'er.'
    - Rudyard Kipling

'A rag and a bone and a hank of hair.'
    - Rudyard Kipling

'Women can do everything; men can do the rest.'
    - Russian proverb

'Even the most respectable woman has a complete set of clothes in her wardrobe ready for a possible abduction.'
    - Sacha Guitry

'My sister says she never seems to get it together . . . either her rear looks good or her face does.'
    - Sally Bucko

'Women are the true maintenance class. Society is built upon their acquiescence and upon their small and necessary labours.'
    - Sally Kempton

'It is hard to fight an enemy who has outposts in your head.'
    - Sally Kempton

'Men know that women are an overmatch for them, and therefore they choose the weakest or the most ignorant. If they did not think so, they never could be afraid of women knowing as much as themselves.'
    - Samuel Johnson

'Music and women I cannot but give way to, whatever my business is.'
    - Samuel Pepys

'The weakness of their reasoning faculty also explains why women show more sympathy for the unfortunate than men;... and why, on the contrary, they are inferior to men as regards justice, and less honorable and conscientious.'
    - Schopenhauer

'A woman is like your shadow; follow her, she flies; fly from her, she follows.'
    - Sebastien Chamfort

'Of my two 'handicaps', being female put many more obstacles in my path than being black.'
    - Shirley Chisholm

'The great question which I have not been able to answer, despite my 30 years of research into the feminine soul, is "what does a woman want"?'
    - Sigmund Freud

'One is not born a woman - one becomes one.'
- Simone de Beauvoir

'You see, dear, it is not true that woman was made from man's rib; she was really made from his funny bone.'
- Sir James Matthew Barrie

'From birth to 18 a girl needs good parents. From 18 to 35, she needs good looks. From 35 to 55, good personality. From 55 on, she needs good cash. I'm saving my money.'
- Sophie Tucker

'The only question left to be settled now is, are women persons?'
- Susan B. Anthony

'A woman either loves or hates: she knows no medium.'
- Syrus

'I know the nature of women; When you want to, they don't want to; And when you don't want to, they desire exceedingly.'
- Terence

'Women forgive injuries, but never forget slights.'
- Thomas Haliburton

'It is God who makes woman beautiful, it is the devil who makes her pretty.'
- Victor Hugo

'Have you any notion how many books are written about women in the course of one year? Have you any notion how many are written by men? Are you aware that you are, perhaps, the most discussed animal in the universe?'
- Virginia Woolf

'If woman had no existence save in the fiction written by men, one would imagine her a person of the utmost importance; very various; heroic and mean; splendid and sordid; infinitely beautiful and hideous in the extreme; as great as a man, some think even '
- Virginia Woolf

'Women are like elephants. They are interesting to look at, but I wouldn't like to own one.'
- W. C. Fields

'It was a woman who drove me to drink - and, you know, I never even thanked her.'
- W. C. Fields

'American women expect to find in their husbands a perfection that English women only hope to find in their butlers.'
- W. Somerset Maugham

'O Woman! in our hours of ease, Uncertain coy, and hard to please, And variable as the shade By the light quivering aspen made; When pain and anguish wring the brow, A ministering angel thou!'
- Walter Scott

'There is in every true woman's heart a spark of heavenly fire, which lies dormant in the broad daylight of prosperity, but which kindles up and beams and blazes in the dark hour of adversity.'
- Washington Irving

'A man is a person who will pay two dollars for a one-dollar item he wants. A woman will pay one dollar for a two-dollar item she doesn't want.'
- William Binger

'Age cannot wither her, nor custom stale her infinite variety; other women cloy the appetites they feed, but she makes hungry where most she satisfies.'
- William Shakespeare

'Frailty, thy name is woman!'
- William Shakespeare

'She was a Phantom of delight When first she gleamed upon my sight; A lovely Apparition, sent To be a moment's ornament.'
- William Wordsworth

'A beautiful woman who is pleasing to men is good only for frightening fish when she falls into the water.'
- Zen proverb

WORK

'There is no more dreadful punishment than futile and hopeless labor.'
- Albert Camus

'There is dignity in work only when it is work freely accepted.'
- Albert Camus

'How do I work? I grope.'
- Albert Einstein

'They intoxicate themselves with work so they won't see how they really are.'
- Aldous Huxley

'Routine is the god of every social system; it is the seventh heaven of business, the essential component in the success of every factory, the ideal of every statesman.'
- Alfred North Whitehead

'Work is a world apart from jobs. Work is the way you occupy your mind and hand and eye and whole body when they're informed by your imagination.'
- Alice Koller

'I always feel the movement is a sort of mosaic. Each of us puts in one little stone, and then you get a great mosaic at the end.'
- Alice Paul

'A professional is someone who can do his best work when he doesn't feel like it.'
- Alistair Cooke

'The effectiveness of work increases according to geometric progression if there are no interruptions.'
- Andri Maurois

'Whether we call it a job or a career, work is more than just something we do. It is a part of who we are.'
- Anita Hill

'Nobody ever drowned in his own sweat.'
- Ann Landers

'Work ... has always been my favorite form of recreation.'
- Anna Howard Shaw

'Work in some form or other is the appointed lot of all.'
- Anna Jameson

'Success depends in a very large measure upon individual initiative and exertion, and cannot be achieved except by a dint of hard work.'
 - Anna Pavlova

'Most leaders are indispensable, but to produce a major social change, many ordinary people must also be involved.'
 - Anne Firor Scott

'Good communication is as stimulating as black coffee, and just as hard to sleep after.'
 - Anne Morrow Lindbergh

'There must be bands of enthusiasts for everything on earth-fanatics who shared a vocabulary, a batch of technical skills and equipment, and, perhaps, a vision of some single slice of the beauty and mystery of things, of their complexity, fascination, and '
 - Annie Dillard

'Before I started working here, I drank, smoked, and used bad language. Thanks to this job, I now have good reason.'
 - Anonymous

'A secretary must think like a man, act like a lady, look like a girl and work like a dog.'
 - Anonymous

'One machine can do the work of 50 ordinary men. No machine can do the work of one extraordinary man.'
 - Anonymous

'A hobby is hard work you wouldn't do for a living.'
 - Anonymous

'Work! Thank God for the swing of it, for the clamoring, hammering ring of it.'
 - Anonymous

'A man's work is from sun to sun, but a mother's work is never done.'
 - Anonymous

'Work, alternated with needful rest, is the salvation of man or woman.'
 - Antoinette Brown Blackwell

'Congenial labor is essence of happiness.'
 - Arthur Christopher Benson

'There are certain natures to whom work is nothing, the act of work everything.'
 - Arthur Symons

'Duty is an icy shadow. It will freeze you. It cannot fill the heart's sanctuary.'
 - Augusta Evans

'Productive work is the central purpose of a rational man's life, the central value that integrates and determines the hierarchy of all his other values. Reason is the source, the precondition of his productive work - pride is the result.'
   - Ayn Rand

'We learn best to listen to our own voices if we are listening at the same time to other women-whose stories, for all our differences, turn out, if we listen well, to be our stories also.'
   - Barbara Deming

'A job is not a career. I think I started out with a job. It turned into a career and changed my life.'
   - Barbara Walters

'Diligence is the mother of good luck, and God gives all things to industry.'
   - Benjamin Franklin

'A ploughman on his legs is higher than a gentleman on his knees.'
   - Benjamin Franklin

'Handle your tools without mittens.'
   - Benjamin Franklin

'Today whenever women gather together it is not necessarily nurturing. It is coalition building. And if you feel the strain, you may be doing some good work.'
   - Bernice Johnson Reagon

'Work is of two kinds: first, altering a position of matter at or near the earth's surface relatively to other such matter; second, telling other people to do so. The first kind is unpleasant and ill-paid; the second is pleasant and highly paid.'
   - Bertrand Russell

'When people go to work, they shouldn't have to leave their hearts at home.'
   - Betty Bender

'Neither woman nor man lives by work, or love, alone.... The human self defines itself and grows through love and work: All psychology before and after Freud boils down to that.'
   - Betty Friedan

'In the sweat of thy face shalt thou eat bread.'
   - Bible

'If a man will not work, he shall not eat.'
   - Bible

'The laborer is worthy of his hire.'
   - Bible

'There's no labor a man can do that's undignified, if he does it right.'
   - Bill Cosby

'Better to wear out than to rust out.'
- Bishop Cumberland

'The sport I love has taken me around the world and shown me many things.'
- Bonnie Blair

'Work expands so as to fill the time available for its completion.'
- C. Northcote Parkinson

'When white-collar people get jobs, they sell not only their time and energy, but their personalities as well. They sell by week, or month, their smiles and their kindly gestures, and they must practise prompt repression of resentment and aggression.'
- C. Wright Mills

'When more and more people are thrown out of work, unemployment results.'
- Calvin Coolidge

'Miracles sometimes occur, but one has to work terribly hard for them.'
- Chaim Weizmann

'As a remedy against all ills - poverty, sickness, and melancholy - only one thing is absolutely necessary: a liking for work.'
- Charles Baudelaire

'Everything considered, work is less boring than amusing oneself.'
- Charles Baudelaire

'How many years of fatigue and punishment it takes to learn the simple truth that work, that disagreeable thing, is the only way of not suffering in life, or at all events, of suffering less.'
- Charles Baudelaire

'Chance favors only those who know how to court her.'
- Charles Nicolle

'I realized that with hard work, the world was your oyster. You could do anything you wanted to do. I learned that at a young age.'
- Chris Evert

'Remember the dignity of your womanhood. Do not appeal, do not beg, do not grovel. Take courage, join hands, stand beside us, fight with us.'
- Christabel Pankhurst

'For it is commonly said: accomplished labours are pleasant.'
- Cicero

'What a man sows, that shall he and his relations reap.'
- Clarissa Graves

'Now men and women are separate and unequal. We should be hand in hand; in fact, we should have our arms around one another.'
- Cloris Leachman

'When I can no longer create anything, I'll be done for.'
- Coco Chanel

'A task becomes a duty from the moment you suspect it to be an essential part of that integrity which alone entitles a man to assume responsibility.'
- Dag Hammarskjold

'Work is man's most natural form of relaxation.'
- Dagobert Runes

'Every woman is a human being-one cannot repeat that too often-and a human being must have occupation if he or she is not to become a nuisance to the world.'
- Dorothy L. Sayers

'Work is the province of cattle.'
- Dorothy Parker

'Workaholics commit slow suicide by refusing to allow the child inside them to play.'
- Dr. Laurence Susser

'It is not hard work that is dreary; it is superficial work'
- Edith Hamilton

'We work to become, not to acquire.'
- Elbert Hubbard

'If you want a work well done, select a busy man: the other kind has no time.'
- Elbert Hubbard

'Work means so many things! So many! Among other things, work also means freedom. ... Without it even the miracle of love is only a cruel deception.'
- Eleonora Duse

'For what is done or learned by one class of women becomes, by virtue of their common womanhood, the property of all women.'
- Elizabeth Blackwell

'It's not the having, it's the getting.'
- Elizabeth Taylor

'Work is the thing that stays. Work is the thing that sees us through.'
- Ellen Gilchrist

'I slept, and dreamed that life was Beauty; I woke, and found that life was Duty.'
- Ellen Sturgis Hooper

'If I could I would always work in silence and obscurity, and let my efforts be known by their results.'
- Emily Bronte

'Elbow grease is the best polish.'
- English proverb

'It's all in the day's work.'
- English Saying

'He who shuns the millstone, shuns the meal.'
- Erasmus

'Busy people are never busybodies.'
- Ethel Watts Mumford

'The workers are the saviors of society, the redeemers of the race.'
- Eugene V. Debs

'Chop your own wood and it will warm you twice.'
- Fairlane

'Most people like hard work, particularly when they're paying for it.'
- Franklin P. Jones

'Originality and the feeling of one's own dignity are achieved only through work and struggle.'
- Fyodor Dostoyevsky

'A man must love a thing very much if he not only practices it without any hope of fame and money, but even practices it without any hope of doing it well.'
- G. K. Chesterton

'Employment is nature's physician, and is essential to human happiness.'
- Galen

'Amateurs hope. Professionals work.'
- Garson Kanin

'In a professional once engaged, the performance of the job comes first.'
- Garson Kanin

'A people so primitive that they did not know how to get money except by working for it.'
- George Ade

'I work as my father drank.'
- George Bernard Shaw

'When I was a young man I observed that nine out of ten things I did were failures. I didn't want to be a failure, so I did ten times more work.'
- George Bernard Shaw

'Work is not man's punishment. It is his reward and his strength, his glory and his pleasure.'
- George Sand

'Every time a man unburdens his heart to a stranger he reaffirms the love that unites humanity.'
- Germaine Greer

'Energy is the power that drives every human being. It is not lost by exertion but maintained by it, for it is a faculty of the psyche.'
- Germaine Greer

'The only way to enjoy anything in this life is to earn it first.'
- Ginger Rogers

'When I die, my epitaph should read: She Paid the Bills.'
- Gloria Swanson

'I've always believed that one woman's success can only help another woman's success.'
- Gloria Vanderbilt

'We can redeem anyone who strives unceasingly.'
- Goethe

'Most people work the greater part of their time for a mere living; and the little freedom which remains to them so troubles them that they use every means of getting rid of it.'
- Goethe

'Unionism, seldom if ever, uses such powers as it has to ensure better work; almost always it devotes a large part of that power to safeguarding bad work.'
- H. L. Mencken

'The monarchy is a labor-intensive industry.'
- Harold Wilson

'Cooking is like love. It should be entered into with abandon or not at all.'
- Harriet Van Home

'The only thing that separates successful people from the ones who aren't is the willingness to work very, very hard.'
- Helen Gurley Brown

'Alone we can do so little; together we can do so much.'
- Helen Keller

'I believe in hard work. It keeps the wrinkles out of the mind and spirit.'
- Helena Rubinstein

'Beware all enterprises that require new clothes.'
- Henry David Thoreau

'Only he is successful in his business who makes that pursuit which affords him the highest pleasure sustain him.'
  - Henry David Thoreau

'When your work speaks for itself, don't interrupt.'
  - Henry J. Kaiser

'Heaven is blessed with perfect rest but the blessing of earth is toil.'
  - Henry Van Dyke

'The heights by great men reached and kept Were not attained by sudden flight, But they, while their companions slept, Were toiling upward in the night.'
  - Henry Wadsworth Longfellow

'Neither snow, nor rain, nor heat, nor gloom of night stay these couriers from the swift completion of their appointed rounds.'
  - Herodotus

'The Gods rank work above virtues.'
  - Hesiod

'The work praises the man.'
  - Irish proverb

'We seldom stop to think how many people's lives are entwined with our own. It is a form of selfishness to imagine that every individual can operate on his own or can pull out of the general stream and not be missed.'
  - Ivy Baker Priest

'There is a kind of victory in good work, no matter how humble.'
  - Jack Kemp

'Ideally, couples need three lives; one for him, one for her, and one for them together.'
  - Jacqueline Bisset

'All work and no play makes Jack a dull boy.'
  - James Howell

'No man is born into the world whose work Is not born with him; there is always work, And tools to work withal, for those who will; And blessed are the horny hands of toil!'
  - James Russell Lowell

'By the work one knows the workman.'
  - Jean de la Fontaine

'Men and women are like right and left hands: it doesn't make sense not to use both.'
  - Jeannette Rankin

'Work is creativity accompanied by the comforting realization that one is bringing forth something really good and necessary, with a conviction that a sudden, arbitrary cessation would cause a sensitive void, produce a loss.'
- Jenny Heynrichs

'I like work; it fascinates me. I can sit and look at it for hours. I love to keep it by me: the idea of getting rid of it nearly breaks my heart.'
- Jerome K. Jerome

'I want a house that has gotten over all its troubles; I don't want to spend the rest of my life bringing up a young and inexperienced house.'
- Jerome K. Jerome

'It is impossible to enjoy idling thoroughly unless one has plenty of work to do.'
- Jerome K. Jerome

'Ambition is destruction, only competence matters.'
- Jill Robinson

'Anyone who is honestly seeking a job and can't find it, deserves the attention of the United States government, and the people.'
- John F. Kennedy

'When love and skill work together, expect a masterpiece.'
- John Ruskin

'The highest reward for man's toil is not what he gets for it, but what he becomes by it.'
- John Ruskin

'If one defines the term 'dropout' to mean a person who has given up serious effort to meet his responsibilities, then every business office, government agency, golf club and university faculty would yield its quota.'
- John W. Gardner

'If your dream is a big dream, and if you want your life to work on the high level that you say you do, there's no way around doing the work it takes to get you there.'
- Joyce Chapman

'The simple idea that everyone needs a reasonable amount of challenging work in his or her life, and also a personal life, complete with noncompetitive leisure, has never really taken hold.'
- Judith Martin

'If you're in a good profession, it's hard to get bored, because you're never finished-there will always be work you haven't done.'
- Julia Child

'Find something you're passionate about and keep tremendously interested in it.'
- Julia Child

'Never turn down a job because you think it's too small; you never know where it may lead.'
- Julia Morgan

'Some people regard discipline as a chore. For me, it is a kind of order that sets me free to fly.'
- Julie Andrews

'Work is love made visible. And if you cannot work with love but only with distaste, it is better that you should leave your work and sit at the gate of the temple and take alms of those who work with joy.'
- Kahlil Gibran

'I don't think that work ever really destroyed anybody. I think that lack of work destroys them a hell of a lot more.'
- Katharine Hepburn

'As for me, prizes mean nothing. My prize is my work.'
- Katharine Hepburn

'For the last third of life there remains only work. It alone is always stimulating, rejuvenating, exciting and satisfying.'
- Kathe Kollwitz

'To love what you do and feel that it matters-how could anything be more fun?'
- Katherine Graham

'The only genius that's worth anything is the genius for hard work.'
- Kathleen Winsor

'Maintain a good balance. A personal life adds dimensions to your professional life and vice versa. It helps nurture creativity through a deeper understanding of yourself.'
- Kathy Ireland

'To industry, nothing is impossible.'
- Latin proverb

'Skilled labor teaches something not to be found in books or in colleges.'
- Laura Towne

'People should tell their children what life is all about-it's about work.'
- Lauren Bacall

'Work is accomplished by those employees who have not yet reached their level of incompetence.'
- Laurence J. Peter

'Work is the inevitable condition of human life, the true source of human welfare.'
- Leo Tolstoy

'God sells us all things at the price of labor.'
- Leonardo da Vinci

'No thoroughly occupied man was ever yet very miserable.'
- Letitia Landon

'Marriage ain't easy but nothing that's worth much ever is.'
- Lillian Carter

'The sentimentalist ages far more quickly than the person who loves his work and enjoys new challenges.'
- Lillie Langtry

'I have worked all my life, wanted to work all my life, needed to work all my life.'
- Liz Carpenter

'To deny we need and want power is to deny that we hope to be effective.'
- Liz Smith

'It is better to have no emotion when it is work. Do what needs to be done, and do it coolly.'
- Louis L'Amour

'Here I am, where I ought to be.'
- Louise Erdrich

'I believe in my work and in the joy of it. You have to be with the work and the work has to be with you. It absorbs you totally and you absorb it totally.'
- Louise Nevelson

'If you want something done, ask a busy person to do it. The more things you do, the more you can do.'
- Lucille Ball

'You have to do what you love to do, not get stuck in that comfort zone of a regular job. Life is not a dress rehearsal. This is it.'
- Lucinda Basset

'Whatever the job you are asked to do at whatever level, do a good job because your reputation is your resume.'
- Madeleine Albright

'Be strong! We are not here to play, to dream, to drift; We have hard work to do and loads to lift; Shun not the struggle-face it; 'tis God's gift.'
- Maltbie D. Babcock

'I was brought up to believe that the only thing worth doing was to add to the sum of accurate information in the world.'
- Margaret Mead

'Work is its own cure. You have to like it better than being loved.'
- Marge Piercy

'The one important thing I have learned over the years is the difference between taking one's work seriously, and taking one's self seriously. The first is imperative, and the second is disastrous.'
- Margot Fonteyn

'Winning the [Nobel] prize wasn't half as exciting as doing the work itself.'
- Maria Goeppert Mayer

'There can be no substitute for work, neither affection nor physical well-being can replace it.'
- Maria Montessori

'Don't be afraid of hard work.'
- Marian Wright Edelman

'Do your duty until it becomes your joy.'
- Marie von Ebner-Eschenbach

'Workaholics are energized rather than enervated by their work-their energy paradoxically expands as it is expended.'
- Marilyn Machlowitz

'Because it is less structured than work, leisure time leaves workaholics at a loss for what to do. Workaholics practically climb the wall when they can't work.'
- Marilyn Machlowitz

'Work and play are words used to describe the same thing under differing conditions.'
- Mark Twain

'Work consists of whatever a body is obliged to do, and play consists of whatever a body is not obliged to do.'
- Mark Twain

'You can have unbelievable intelligence, you can have connections, you can have opportunities fall out of the sky. But in the end, hard work is the true, enduring characteristic of successful people.'
- Marsha Evans

'To find in ourselves what makes life worth living is risky business, for it means that once we know we must seek it. It also means that without it life will be valueless.'
- Marsha Sinetar

'If a man is called to be a street sweeper, he should sweep streets even as Michelangelo painted, or Beethoven composed music or Shakespeare wrote poetry. He should sweep streets so well that all the hosts of heaven and earth will pause to say, here lived '
- Martin Luther King, Jr.

'Work is a substitute "religious" experience for many workaholics.'
- Mary Daly

'Manual labor to my father was not only good and decent for its own sake, but as he was given to saying, it straightened out one's thoughts.'
- Mary Ellen Chase

'Some people are born to lift heavy weights, some are born to juggle golden balls.'
- Max Beerbohm

'No fine work can be done without concentration and self-sacrifice and toil and doubt.'
- Max Beerbohm

'He who labors diligently need never despair, for all things are accomplished by diligence and labor.'
- Menander

'Pears cannot ripen alone. So we ripened together.'
- Meridel Le Sueur

'We must stand together; if we don't, there will be no victory for any one of us.'
- Mother Jones

'Give the laborer his wage before his perspiration be dry.'
- Muhammad

'Women and men have to fight together to change society-and both will benefit.'
- Muriel Fox

'Exchange is creation.'
- Muriel Rukeyser

'Hard work has made it easy. That is my secret. That is why I win.'
- Nadia Comaneci

'Men take only their needs into consideration, never their abilities.'
- Napoleon Bonaparte

'Hasten slowly, and without losing heart, put your work twenty times upon the anvil.'
- Nicolas Boileau

'Work is more fun than fun.'
- Noel Coward

'People who work sitting down get paid more than people who work standing up.'
- Ogden Nash

'Fortune is ever seen accompanying industry.'
- Oliver Goldsmith

'Work is the curse of the drinking classes.'
- Oscar Wilde

'With the power of conviction, there is no sacrifice.'
- Pat Benatar

'The joy about our work is spoiled when we perform it not because of what we produce but because of the pleasure with which it can provide us, or the pain against which it can protect us.'
- Paul Tillich

'There are two kinds of talents, man-made talent and God-given talent. With man-made talent you have to work very hard. With God-given talent, you just touch it up once in a while.'
- Pearl Bailey

'We all act as hinges-fortuitous links between other people.'
- Penelope Lively

'Unless I am a part of everything I am nothing.'
- Penelope Lively

'Rest is the sweet sauce of labor.'
- Plutarch

'My whole life, whether it be long or short, shall be devoted to your service and the service of our great imperial family to which we all belong. But I shall not have the strength to carry out this resolution alone unless you join in it with me.'
- Queen Elizabeth II

'It is the privilege of any human work which is well done to invest the doer with a certain haughtiness. He can well afford not to conciliate, whose faithful work will answer for him.'
- Ralph Waldo Emerson

'Man's usual routine is to work and to dream and work and dream.'
- Raymond Queneau

'The more I want to get something done, the less I call it work.'
- Richard Bach

'I believe you are your work. Don't trade the stuff of your life, time, for nothing more than dollars. That's a rotten bargain'
- Rita Mae Brown

'Anyone can do any amount of work provided it isn't the work he is supposed to be doing at that moment.'
- Robert Benchley

'By working faithfully eight hours a day you may eventually get to be a boss and work 12 hours a day.'
- Robert Frost

'Laziness is a secret ingredient that goes into failure. But it's only kept a secret from the person who fails.'
- Robert Half

'If a little labor, little are our gains. Man's fortunes are according to his pains.'
- Robert Herrick

'If a man loves the labor of his trade, apart from any question of success or fame, the gods have called him.'
- Robert Louis Stevenson

'They say hard work never hurt anybody, but I figure why take the chance.'
- Ronald Reagan

'Whatever my individual desires were to be free, I was not alone. There were others who felt the same way.'
- Rosa Parks

'And only the Master shall praise us, and only the Master shall blame; And no one shall work for money, and no one shall work for fame; But each for the joy of the working, and each, in his separate star, Shall draw the Thing as he sees It, for the God of '
- Rudyard Kipling

'The worst crime against working people is a company which fails to operate at a profit.'
- Samuel Gompers

'Love of bustle is not industry.'
- Seneca

'When you're following your energy and doing what you want all the time, the distinction between work and play dissolves.'
- Shakti Gawain

'While I am busy with little things, I am not required to do greater things.'
- St. Francis de Sales

'When I stop [working], the rest of the day is posthumous. I'm only really alive when I'm working.'
- Tennessee Williams

'It is not upon thee to finish the work; neither art thou free to abstain from it.'
- The Talmud

'I am only an average man, but, by George, I work harder at it than the average man.'
- Theodore Roosevelt

'One's lifework, I have learned, grows with the working and the living. Do it as if your life depended on it, and first thing you know, you'll have made a life out of it. A good life, too.'
- Theresa Helburn

'Opportunity is missed by most people because it is dressed in overalls, and looks like work.'
- Thomas A. Edison

'I never did anything worth doing by accident, nor did any of my inventions come by accident; they came by work.'
- Thomas Alva Edison

'He that can work is a born king of something.'
- Thomas Carlyle

'All work is seed sown. It grows and spreads, and sows itself anew.'
- Thomas Carlyle

'Work is the grand cure of all the maladies and miseries that ever beset mankind.'
- Thomas Carlyle

'Honest labor bears a lovely face.'
- Thomas Dekker

'A good horse should be seldom spurred.'
- Thomas Fuller

'After fifty years of living, it occurs to me that the most significant thing that people do is go to work, whether it is to go to work on their novel or at the assembly plant or fixing somebody's teeth.'
- Thomas McGuane

'Passion is never enough; neither is skill.'
- Toni Morrison

'I know a lot of people think it's monotonous, down the black lines over and over, but it's not if you're enjoying what you're doing. I love to swim and I love to train.'
- Tracy Caulkins

'Labor disgraces no man; unfortunately, you occasionally find men who disgrace labor.'
- Ulysses S. Grant

'A person who believes ... that there is a whole of which one is a part, and that in being a part one is whole: such a person has no desire whatever, at any time, to play God. Only those who have denied their being yearn to play at it.'
- Ursula K. LeGuin

'The only place where success comes before work is a dictionary.'
- Vidal Sassoon

'Cooperation is an intelligent functioning of the concept of laissez faire-a thorough conviction that nobody can get there unless everybody gets there.'
- Virginia Burden Tower

'Work banishes those three great evils, boredom, vice, and poverty.'
- Voltaire

'I love Mickey Mouse more than any woman I've ever known.'
   - Walt Disney

'Industry is a better horse to ride than genius.'
   - Walter Lippman

'God gave man work, not to burden him, but to bless him, and useful work, willingly, cheerfully, effectively done, has always been the finest expression of the human spirit.'
   - Walter R. Courtenay

'If a man wakes up famous, he hasn't been sleeping.'
   - Wes Izzard

'Tools were made and born were hands, Every farmer understands.'
   - William Blake

'I get satisfTaking Action of three kinds. One is creating something, one is being paid for it and one is the feeling that I haven't just been sitting on my ass all afternoon.'
   - William F. Buckley

'One of the saddest things is, the only thing a man can do for 8 hours a day, day after day, is work. You can't eat 8 hours a day nor drink for 8 hours a day, nor make love for 8 hours.'
   - William Faulkner

'Work is the best method devised for killing time.'
   - William Feather

'Many hands make light work.'
   - William Patten

'If all the year were playing holidays To sport would be as tedious as to work.'
   - William Shakespeare

'I am fierce for work. Without work I am nothing.'
   - Winifred Holtby

'No task, rightly done is truly private. It is part of the world's work.'
   - Woodrow Wilson

WORRY

'Worry never robs tomorrow of its sorrow, but only saps today of its strength.'
  - A. J. Cronin

'It ain't no use putting up your umbrella till it rains!'
  - Alice Caldwell Rice

'Of course I realized there was a measure of danger. Obviously I faced the possibility of not returning when I first considered going. Once faced and settled there really wasn't any good reason to refer to it again.'
  - Amelia Earhart

'Worry is a complete cycle of inefficient thought revolving about a pivotal fear.'
  - Anonymous

'If you worry about what might be, and wonder what might have been, you will ignore what is.'
  - Anonymous

'A problem not worth praying about is not worth worrying about.'
  - Anonymous

'Worry doesn't help tomorrow's troubles, but it does ruin today's happiness.'
  - Anonymous

'Worry is the sin we're not afraid to commit.'
  - Anonymous

'Worry never climbed a hill, worry never paid a bill, Worry never dried a tear, worry never calmed a fear, Worry never darned a heel, worry never cooked a meal, It never led a horse to water, nor ever did a thing it "oughter."'
  - Anonymous

'Worry is a futile thing, it's somewhat like a rocking chair, Although is keeps you occupied, it doesn't get you anywhere.'
  - Anonymous

'Worry is evidence of an ill-controlled brain; it is merely a stupid waste of time in unpleasantness.'
  - Arnold Bennett

'You'll break the worry habit the day you decide you can meet and master the worse that can happen to you.'
  - Arnold Glasow

'Worry is a thin stream of fear trickling through the mind. If encouraged, it cuts a channel into which all other thoughts are drained.'
  - Arthur Somers Roche

'Turn resolutely to work, to recreation, or in any case to physical exercise till you are so tired you can't help going to sleep, and when you wake up you won't want to worry.'
- B. C. Forbes

'Stop worrying about the potholes in the road and celebrate the journey!'
- Barbara Hoffman

'We can always get along better by reason and love of truth than by worry of conscience and remorse. Harmful are these, and evil.'
- Baruch Spinoza

'Worry is a god, invisible but omnipotent. It steals the bloom from the cheek and lightness from the pulse; it takes away the appetite, and turns the hair gray.'
- Benjamin Disraeli

'Worry is a form of fear.'
- Bertrand A. Russell

'A great many worries can be diminished by realizing the unimportance of the matter which is causing anxiety.'
- Bertrand Russell

'Be, therefore, not anxious about tomorrow; for tomorrow will be anxious for the things of itself.'
- Bible

'Which of you by being anxious can add one cubit unto his stature?'
- Bible

'If you see ten troubles coming down the road, you can be sure that nine will run into the ditch before they reach you.'
- Calvin Coolidge

'That man is blest Who does his best And leaves the rest, Then-do not worry.'
- Charles F. Deems

'Worry affects the circulation, the heart, the glands, the whole nervous system, and profoundly affects the health. You have never known a man who died from overwork, but many who died from doubt.'
- Charles W. Mayo

'Worry is like a rocking chair-it keeps you moving but doesn't get you anywhere.'
- Corrie ten Boom

'Worry is like racing the engine of an automobile without letting in the clutch.'
- Corrie ten Boom

'Worry compounds the futility of being trapped on a dead-end street. Thinking opens new avenues.'
- Cullen Hightower

'Most people go through life dreading they'll have a traumatic experience.'
- Diane Arbus

'The really frightening thing about middle age is that you know you'll grow out of it!'
- Doris Day

'A man ninety years old was asked to what he attributed his longevity. "I reckon," he said, with a twinkle in his eye, "it's because most nights I went to bed and slept when I should have sat up and worried."'
- Dorothea Kent

'"Worry" is a word that I don't allow myself to use.'
- Dwight D. Eisenhower

'I am reminded of the advice of my neighbor. "Never worry about your heart 'til it stops beating."'
- E. B. White

'Some men storm imaginary Alps all their lives, and die in the foothills cursing difficulties which do not exist.'
- Edgar Watson Howe

'Needless fear and panic over disease or misfortune that seldom materialize are simply bad habits. By proper ventilation and illumination of the mind it is possible to cultivate tolerance, poise and real courage.'
- Elie Metchnikoff

'To be rich is not the end, but only a change, of worries.'
- Epicurus

'We have to fight them daily, like fleas, those many small worries about the morrow, for they sap our energies.'
- Etty Hillesum

'Worry less about what other people think about you, and more about what you think about them.'
- Fay Weldon

'Worry is the cross which we make for ourselves by overanxiety.'
- Francois de Fenelon

'A hundred load of worry will not pay an ounce of debt.'
- George Herbert

'If things happen all the time you are never nervous. It is when they are not happening that you are nervous.'
- Gertrude Stein

'Everybody knows if you are too careful you are so occupied in being careful that you are sure to stumble over something.'
- Gertrude Stein

'Anxiety never yet successfully bridged any chasm.'
  - Giovanni Ruffini

'What worries you, masters you.'
  - Haddon W. Robinson

'A worried man could borrow a lot of trouble with practically no collateral.'
  - Helen Nielsen

'Worry is the only insupportable misfortune of life.'
  - Henry Saint John

'It is not work that kills men, it is worry. Work is healthy; you can hardly put more upon a man that he can bear. Worry is rust upon the blade.'
  - Henry Ward Hughes

'Our worst misfortunes never happen, and most miseries lie in anticipation.'
  - Honore de Balzac

'Worry is most apt to ride you ragged not when you are in Taking Action, but when the day's work is done. Your imagination can run riot then ... your mind is like a motor operating without its load.'
  - James L. Muresell

'This was a great year for preventive worrying. Seldom in recent history have so many people worried about so many things that didn't happen in the end.'
  - James Reston

'The misfortunes hardest to bear are those which never happen.'
  - James Russell Lowell

'We poison our lives with fear of burglary and shipwreck, and the house is never burgled, and the ship never goes down.'
  - Jean Anouilh

'If your eyes are blinded with your worries, you cannot see the beauty of the sunset.'
  - Jiddu Krishnamurti

'A day of worry is more exhausting than a day of work.'
  - John Lubbock

'What is there to be afraid of? The worst thing that can happen is you fail. So what? I failed at a lot of things. My first record was horrible.'
  - John Mellencamp

'It is the little things that fret and worry us; you can dodge an elephant, but not a fly.'
  - Josh Billings

'There are people who are always anticipating trouble, and in this way they manage to enjoy many sorrows that never really happen.'
- Josh Billings

'It only seems as if you are doing something when you're worrying.'
- L. M. Montgomery

'You can't start worrying about what's going to happen. You get spastic enough worrying about what's happening now.'
- Lauren Bacall

'Bacteria and other microorganisms find it easier to infect people who worry and fret.'
- Leo Rangell

'A wise man fights to win, but he is twice a fool who has no plan for possible defeat.'
- Louis L'Amour

'There is nothing so wretched or foolish as to anticipate misfortunes. What madness is it in expecting evil before it arrives?'
- Marcus Annaeus Seneca

'The expectation of an unpleasantness is more terrible than the thing itself.'
- Marie Bashkirtseff

'Every faculty and virtue I possess can be used as an instrument with which to worry myself.'
- Mark Rutherford

'I am an old man and have known a great many troubles, but most of them never happened.'
- Mark Twain

'Worry a little bit every day and in a lifetime you will lose a couple of years. If something is wrong, fix it if you can. But train yourself not to worry. Worry never fixes anything.'
- Mary Hemingway

'Do we not all spend the greater part of our lives under the shadow of an event that has not yet come to pass?'
- Maurice Maeterlinck

'Worry is a funky luxury when a lot has to be done.'
- Melvin Peebles

'My life has been full of terrible misfortunes, most of which never happened.'
- Michel de Montaigne

'A request not to worry ... is perhaps the least soothing message capable of human utterance.'
- Mignon G. Eberhart

'The crisis you have to worry about most is the one you don't see coming.'
- Mike Mansfield

'Worry is as useless as a handle on a snowball.'
  - Mitzi Chandler

'Worry is a state of mind based on fear.'
  - Napoleon Hill

'Though life is made up of mere bubbles 'Tis better than many have, For while we've a whole lot of troubles The most of them never occur.'
  - Nixon Waterman

'No good work is ever done while the heart is hot and anxious and fretted.'
  - Olive Schreiner

'Happy the man who has broken the chains which hurt the mind, and has given up worrying, once and for all.'
  - Ovid

'Anxiety is the poison of human life, the parent of many sins and of more miseries.... Can it alter the cause, or unravel the mystery of human events?'
  - Paxton Blair

'Some of your hurts you have cured, And the sharpest you still have survived, But what torments of grief you endured From the evil which never arrived.'
  - Ralph Waldo Emerson

'What torments of grief you endured, from evils that never arrived.'
  - Ralph Waldo Emerson

'Rule No. i is, don't sweat the small stuff. Rule No. 2 is, it's all small stuff.'
  - Robert Eliot

'The reason why worry kills more people than work is that more people worry than work.'
  - Robert Frost

'If you are doing your best, you will not have time to worry about failure.'
  - Robert Hillyer

'There are two days in the week about which and upon which I never worry. ... One of these days is Yesterday ... And the other day I do not worry about is Tomorrow.'
  - Robert Jones Burdette

'Worry is a morbid anticipation of events which never happen.'
  - Russell Green

'When speculation has done its worst, two and two still make four.'
  - Samuel Johnson

'T'ain't worthwhile to wear a day all out before it comes.'
  - Sarah Orne Jewett

'Other Definitions of Worry Anxiety is the great modern plague. But faith can cure it.'
- Smiley Blanton

'Worry often gives a small thing a big shadow.'
- Swedish proverb

'When you first learn to love hell, you will be in heaven.'
- Thaddeus Golas

'As a cure for worrying, work is better than whiskey.'
- Thomas A. Edison

'Cast away care; he that loves sorrow lengthens not a day, nor can he buy tomorrow.'
- Thomas Dekker

'How much pain they have cost us, the evils which have never happened.'
- Thomas Jefferson

'Worries are the most stubborn habits in the world. Even after a poor man has won a huge lottery prize, he will still for months wake up in the night with a start, worrying about food and rent.'
- Vicki Baum

'Don't hurry, don't worry. You're only here for a short visit. So be sure to stop and smell the flowers.'
- Walter Hagen

'Worry is interest paid on trouble before it comes due.'
- William Ralph Inge

'The worst is not so long as we can say, "This is the worst."'
- William Shakespeare

'I remember the story of the old man who said on his deathbed that he had had a lot of trouble in his life, most of which never happened.'
- Winston Churchill

WRITING

'Nature, not content with denying him the ability to think, has endowed him with the ability to write.'
  - A. E. Housman

'I can write better than anyone who can write faster, and I can write faster than anyone who can write better.'
  - A. J. Liebling

'To write is to become disinterested. There is a certain renunciation in art.'
  - Albert Camus

'Writers write to influence their readers, their preachers, their auditors, but always, at bottom, to be more themselves.'
  - Aldous Huxley

'Please, never despise the translator. He's the mailman of human civilization.'
  - Alexander Pushkin

'A man really writes for an audience of about ten persons. Of course if others like it, that is clear gain. But if those ten are satisfied, he is content.'
  - Alfred North Whitehead

'It is the function of art to renew our perception. What we are familiar with we cease to see. The writer shakes up the familiar scene, and, as if by magic, we see a new meaning in it.'
  - Anais Nin

'Style is the hallmark of a temperament stamped upon the material at hand.'
  - Andre Maurois

'John the Baptist pretending to be Karl Marx.'
  - Anonymous

'The beginning is easy; what happens next is much harder.'
  - Anonymous

'Write something, even if it's just a suicide note.'
  - Anonymous

'In Ireland, a writer is looked upon as a failed conversationalist.'
  - Anonymous

'I am what libraries and librarians have made me, with a little assistance from a professor of Greek and a few poets.'
  - B. K. Sandwell

'Begin with another's to end with your own.'
- Baltasar Gracian

'Autobiography is a preemptive strike against biographers.'
- Barbara G. Harris

'Words and sentences are subjects of revision; paragraphs and whole compositions are subjects of prevision.'
- Barrett Wendell

'There is an accuracy that defeats itself by the overemphasis of details. I often say that one must permit oneself, and quite advisedly and deliberately, a certain margin of misstatement.'
- Benjamin N. Cardozo

'I have only made this letter rather long because I have not had time to make it shorter.'
- Blaise Pascal

'There are three difficulties in authorship: to write anything worth the publishing, to find honest men to publish it, and to get sensible men to read it.'
- C. C. Colton

'I have cultivated my hysteria with joy and terror.'
- Charles Baudelaire

'I have tried lately to read Shakespeare, and found it so intolerably dull that it nauseated me.'
- Charles Darwin

'Make'em laugh; make 'em cry; make 'em wait.'
- Charles Reade

'There are two kinds of writers - the great ones who can give you truths, and the lesser ones, who can only give you themselves.'
- Clifton Fadiman

'Better to write for yourself and have no public, than to write for the public and have no self.'
- Cyril Connolly

'Tennessee Williams said if he got rid of his demons, he would lose his angels.'
- Dakin Williams

'Writers should be read - but neither seen nor heard.'
- Daphne du Maurier

'A memorandum is written to protect the writer - not to inform his reader.'
- Dean Acheson

'When my journal appears, many statues must come down.'
- Duke of Wellington

'Advice to young writers who want to get ahead without any annoying delays: don't write about Man, write about a man.'
- E. B. White

'How can I know what I think till I see what I say?'
- E. M. Forster

'A great many people now reading and writing would be better employed in keeping rabbits.'
- Edith Sitwell

'In any really good subject, one has only to probe deep enough to come to tears.'
- Edith Wharton

'Every writer, without exception, is a masochist, a sadist, a peeping Tom, an exhibitionist, a narcissist, an injustice collector and a depressed person constantly haunted by fears of unproductivity.'
- Edmund Bergler

'I think with my right hand.'
- Edmund Wilson

'Life cannot defeat a writer who is in love with writing - for life itself is a writer's love until death.'
- Edna Ferber

'A person who publishes a book appears willfully in public with his pants down.'
- Edna St. Vincent Millay

'The pen is mightier than the sword.'
- Edward Bulwer-Lytton

'Many a fervid man writes books as cold and flat as graveyard stones.'
- Elizabeth Barrett Browning

'If you would be a reader, read; if a writer, write.'
- Epictetus

'The writer must write what he has to say, not speak it.'
- Ernest Hemingway

'The most essential gift for a good writer is a built-in, shockproof shit detector. This is the writer's radar and all great writers have had it.'
- Ernest Hemingway

'His (the writer's) standard of fidelity to the truth should be so high that his invention, out of his experience, should produce a truer account than anything factual can be.'
- Ernest Hemingway

'The business of writing is one of the four or five most private things in the world.'
- Ethel Wilson

'No man understands a deep book until he has seen and lived at least part of its contents.'
- Ezra Pound

'Writers aren't exactly people, they're a whole lot of people trying to be one person.'
- F. Scott Fitzgerald

'An original writer is not one who imitates nobody, but one whom nobody can imitate.'
- Francois Rene De Chateaubriand

'The life of a writer is tragic: the more we advance, the farther there is to go and the more there is to say, the less time there is to say it.'
- Gabrielle Roy

'Writing is easy: all you do is sit staring at the blank sheet of paper until the drops of blood form on your forehead.'
- Gene Fowler

'My method is to take the utmost trouble to find the right thing to say, and then to say it with the utmost levity.'
- George Bernard Shaw

'Never believe anything a writer tells you about himself. A man comes to believe in the end the lies he tells himself about himself.'
- George Bernard Shaw

'Memoirs: the backstairs of history.'
- George Meredith

'Writing is not a profession but a vocation of unhappiness.'
- Georges Simenon

'I write for myself and strangers. The strangers, dear Readers, are an afterthought.'
- Gertrude Stein

'We like that a sentence should read as if its author, had he held a plough instead of a pen, could have drawn a furrow deep and straight to the end.'
- Henry David Thoreau

'How vain it is to sit down to write when you have not stood up to live.'
- Henry David Thoreau

'As for style of writing, if one has anything to say, it drops from him simply and directly, as a stone falls to the ground.'
- Henry David Thoreau

'Dr. Johnson's sayings would not appear so extraordinary were it not for his bow-wow way.'
- Henry Herbert

'I am being frank about myself in this book. I tell of my first mistake on page 850.'
- Henry Kissinger

'I struggled in the beginning. I said I was going to write the truth, so help me God. And I thought I was. I found I couldn't. Nobody can write the absolute truth.'
- Henry Miller

'Caesar had perished from the world of men Had not his sword been rescued by his pen.'
- Henry Vaughan

'When I am dead, I hope it may be said: 'His sins were scarlet, but his books were read.''
- Hilaire Belloc

'Just as there is nothing between the admirable omelets and the intolerable, so with autobiography.'
- Hilaire Belloc

'A novel must be exceptionally good to live as long as the average cat.'
- Hugh MacLennan

'He claimed his modest share of the general foolishness of the human race.'
- Irving Howe

'Writing has power, but its power has no vector. Writers can stir the mind, but they can't direct it. Time changes things, God changes things, the dictators change things, but writers can't change anything.'
- Isaac Bashevis Singer

'The waste basket is a writer's best friend.'
- Isaac Bashevis Singer

'A good writer is basically a story-teller, not a scholar or a redeemer of mankind.'
- Isaac Bashevis Singer

'The most lasting reputation I have is for an almost ferocious aggressiveness, when in fact I am amiable, indulgent, affectionate, shy and rather timid at heart.'
- J. B. Priestley

'It is a sobering thought that each of us gives his hearers and his readers a chance to look into the inner working of his mind when he speaks or writes.'
- J. M. Barker

'There is nothing more dangerous to the formation of a prose style than the endeavour to make it poetic.'
- J. Middleton Murry

'Writing is turning one's worst moments into money.'
- J. P. Donleavy

'The writer is committed when he plunges to the very depths of himself with the intent to disclose, not his individuality, but his person in the complex society that conditions and supports him.'
- Jean-Paul Sartre

'There is one last thing to remember: writers are always selling somebody out.'
- Joan Didion

'Journalism allows it's readers to witness history. Fiction gives its readers an opportunity to live it.'
- John Hersey

'A writer and nothing else: a man alone in a room with the English language, trying to get human feelings right.'
- John K. Hutchens

'It is in the hard rockpile labor of seeking to win, hold, or deserve a reader's interest that the pleasant agony of writing comes in.'
- John Mason Brown

'Proper words in proper places, make the true definition of a style.'
- Jonathan Swift

'Writers are the engineers of human souls.'
- Joseph Stalin

'My novels point out that the world consists entirely of exceptions.'
- Joyce Carey

'Thought flies and words go on foot.'
- Julien Green

'A writer is someone who can make a riddle out of an answer.'
- Karl Kraus

'Writing is a solitary occupation. Family, friends and society are the natural enemies of a writer. He must be alone, uninterrupted and slightly savage if he is to sustain and complete an undertaking.'
- Laurence Clark Powell

'Writing, when properly managed (as you may be sure I think mine is) is but a different name for conversation.'
- Laurence Sterne

'Take care of the sense and the sounds will take of care themselves.'
- Lewis Carroll

'They're fancy talkers about themselves, writers. If I had to give young writers advice, I would say don't listen to writers talking about writing or themselves.'
- Lillian Hellman

'What I like in a good author is not what he says, but what he whispers.'
- Logan Pearsall Smith

'Every author, however modest, keeps a most outrageous vanity chained like a madman in the padded cell of his breast.'
- Logan Pearsall Smith

'I like prefaces. I read them. Sometimes I do not read any further.'
- Malcolm Lowry

'I conceive that the right way to write a story for boys is to write so that it will not only interest boys but strongly interest any man who has ever been a boy. That immensely enlarges the audience.'
- Mark Twain

'Publication is a self-invasion of privacy.'
- Marshall McLuhan

'(Writing) - the art of applying the seat of the pants to the seat of the chair.'
- Mary Heaton Worse

'Every word she writes is a lie, including 'and' and 'the'.'
- Mary McCarthy

'I believe the writer... should always be the final judge. I have always held to that position and have sometimes seen books hurt thereby, but at least as often helped. The book belongs to the author.'
- Maxwell Perkins

'Just get it down on paper, and then we'll see what to do with it.'
- Maxwell Perkins

'You have to throw yourself away when you write.'
- Maxwell Perkins

'Every human being has hundreds of separate people living under his skin. The talent of a writer is his ability to give them their separate names, identities, personalities and have them relate to other characters living with him.'
- Mel Brooks

'I quote others in order to better express my own self.'
- Michel de Montaigne

'I work every day - or at least I force myself into office or room. I may get nothing done, but you don't earn bonuses without putting in time. Nothing may come for three months, but you don't earn the fourth without it.'
- Mordecai Richler

'Fundamentally, all writing is about the same thing: it's about dying, about the brief flicker of time we have here, and the frustrations that it creates.'
- Mordecai Richler

'Agatha Christie has given more pleasure in bed than any other woman.'
- Nancy Banks-Smith

'It is only through fiction and the dimension of the imaginary that we can learn something real about individual experience. Any other approach is bound to be general and abstract.'
- Nicola Chiaromonte

'I think it's bad to talk about one's present work, for it spoils something at the root of the creative act. It discharges the tension.'
- Norman Mailer

'Beauty and truth may be attributes of good writing, but if the writer deliberately aims at truth, he is likely to find that what he has hit is the didactic.'
- Northrop Frye

'Writing: I certainly do rewrite my central myth in every book, and would never read or trust any writer who did not also do so.'
- Northrop Frye

'When the style is fully formed, if it has a sweet under song, we call it beautiful, and the writer may do what he likes in words or syntax.'
- Oliver Wendell Holmes

'This morning I took out a comma and this afternoon I put it back again.'
- Oscar Wilde

'I've put my genius into my life; I've only put my talent into my works.'
- Oscar Wilde

'On the trail of another man, the biographer must put up with finding himself at every turn: any biography uneasily shelters an autobiography within it.'
- Paul Murray Kendall

'The work of Henry James has always seemed divisible by a simple dynastic arrangement into three reigns: James 1st, James 2nd, and the Old Pretender.'
- Philip Guedalla

'The obscurity of a writer is generally in proportion to his incapacity.'
- Quintilian

'Writing is one of the easiest things: erasing is one of the hardest.'
- Rabbi Israel Salanter

'We are as much informed of a writer's genius by what he selects as by what he originates.'
- Ralph Waldo Emerson

'It makes a great difference in the force of a sentence whether a man be behind it or no.'
- Ralph Waldo Emerson

'At least half the mystery novels published violate the law that the solution, once revealed, must seem to be inevitable.'
- Raymond Chandler

'How can you write if you can't cry?'
- Ring Lardner

'Less is more.'
- Robert Browning

'No tears and the writer, no tears and the reader.'
- Robert Frost

'There is but one art, to omit.'
- Robert Louis Stevenson

'The most original thing a writer can do is write like himself. It is also his most difficult task.'
- Robertson Davies

'Flaubert had infinite correction to perform.'
- Roland Barthes

'You praise the firm restraint with which they write - I'm with you, there, of course: They use the snaffle and the curb all right, But where's the bloody horse?'
- Roy Campbell

'I keep six honest serving men. (They taught me all I know); Their names are What and Why and When and How and Where and Who.'
- Rudyard Kipling

'You cannot write in the chimney with charcoal.'
- Russian proverb

'The editorial job has become, unlike the ancient age when one judged what one read, a job of making judgements on outlines, ideas, reputations, previous books, scenarios, treatments, talk and promises.'
- Sam Vaughan

'The best part of every author is in general to be found in his book, I assure you.'
- Samuel Johnson

'Read over your compositions, and when you meet a passage which you think is particularly fine, strike it out.'
- Samuel Johnson

'When an author is yet living, we estimate his powers by his worst performance; and when he is dead, we rate them by his best.'
- Samuel Johnson

'What is written without effort is in general read without pleasure.'
- Samuel Johnson

'Your manuscript is both good and original; but the parts that are good are not original, and the parts that are original are not good.'
- Samuel Johnson

'Every other author may aspire to praise; the lexicographer can only hope to escape reproach.'
- Samuel Johnson

'The man who is asked by an author what he thinks of his work is put to the torture and is not obliged to speak the truth.'
- Samuel Johnson

'Our society, like decadent Rome, has turned into an amusement society, with writers chief among the court jesters - not so much above the clatter as part of it.'
- Saul Bellow

'All a writer has to do to get a woman is to say he's a writer. It's an aphrodisiac.'
- Saul Bellow

'The truth is, we've not really developed a fiction that can accommodate the full tumult, the zaniness and crazed quality of modern experience.'
- Saul Bellow

'It has been said that writing comes more easily if you have something to say.'
- Sholem Asch

'Writing is no trouble: you just jot down ideas as they occur to you. The jotting is simplicity itself- it is the occurring which is difficult.'
- Stephen Leacock

'An editor should tell the author his writing is better than it is. Not a lot better, a little better.'
- T. S. Eliot

'I suppose some editors are failed writers - but so are most writers.'
- T. S. Eliot

'The reason a writer writes a book is to forget a book and the reason a reader reads one is to remember it.'
- Thomas Wolfe

'That's not writing, that's typing.'
- Truman Capote

'Self-expression is for babies and seals, where it can be charming. A writer's business is to affect the reader.'
- Vincent McHugh

'A woman must have money and a room of her own if she is to write fiction.'
- Virginia Woolf

'As for my next book, I am going to hold myself from writing it till I have it impending in me: grown heavy in my mind like a ripe pear, pendant, gravid, asking to be cut or it will fall.'
- Virginia Woolf

'He is limp and damp and milder than the breath of a cow.'
- Virginia Woolf

'It is a sad fact about our culture that a poet can earn much more money writing or talking about his art than he can by practicing it.'
- W. H. Auden

'I am always at a loss to know how much to believe of my own stories.'
- Washington Irving

'When you put down the good things you ought to have done, and leave out the bad things you did do - well, that's memoirs.'
- Will Rogers

'Footnotes, the little dogs yapping at the heels of the text.'
- William James

'I am not learning definitions as established in even the latest dictionaries. I am not a dictionary-maker. I am a person a dictionary-maker has to contend with. I am a living evidence in the development of language.'
- William Stafford

'Every great and original writer, in proportion as he is great and original, must himself create the taste by which he is to be relished.'
- William Wordsworth

'Now as through this world I ramble, I see lots of funny men, Some rob you with a six gun Some with a fountain pen.'
- Woody Guthrie

YOUTH

'We think our fathers fools, so wise we grow; Our wiser sons, no doubt, will think us so.'
- Alexander Pope

'The deepest definition of youth is life as yet untouched by tragedy.'
- Alfred North Whitehead

'If one could recover the uncompromising spirit of one's youth, one's greatest indignation would be for what one has become.'
- Andre Gide

'This is a youth-oriented society, and the joke is on them because youth is a disease from which we all recover.'
- Anonymous

'Young men think old men fools and old men know young men to be so.'
- Anonymous

'In early youth, as we contemplate our coming life, we are like children in a theatre before the curtain is raised, sitting there in high spirits and eagerly waiting for the play to begin.'
- Arthur Schopenhauer

'I do beseech you to direct your efforts more to preparing youth for the path and less to preparing the path for the youth.'
- Ben Lindsey

'Reckless youth makes rueful age.'
- Benjamin Franklin

'I am constantly amazed when I talk to young people to learn how much they know about sex and how little about soap.'
- Billie Burke

'Trouble is, kids feel they have to shock their elders and each generation grows up into something harder to shock.'
- Cal Craig

'One boy's a boy, two boys are half a boy; three boys are no boy at all.'
- Charles A. Lindbergh

'As I approve of a youth that has something of the old man in him, so I am no less pleased with an old man that has something of the youth. He that follows this rule may be old in body, but can never be so in mind.'
- Cicero

'The 'teenager' seems to have replaced the Communist as the appropriate target for public controversy and foreboding.'
- Edgar Z. Friedenberg

'The interests of childhood and youth are the interests of mankind.'
- Edmund Storer James

'In the lexicon of youth, which fate reserves For a bright manhood, there is no such word As fail.'
- Edward G. Bulwer-Lytton

'Whom the gods love, die young, no matter how long they live.'
- Elbert Hubbard

'Youth will be served.'
- English proverb

'Keep true to the dreams of thy youth.'
- Friedrich von Schiller

'It's all that the young can do for the old, to shock them and keep them up to date.'
- George Bernard Shaw

'Everyone believes in his youth that the world really began with him, and that all merely exists for his sake.'
- Goethe

'It is not possible for civilization to flow backward while there is youth in the world. Youth may be headstrong, but it will advance its allotted length.'
- Helen Keller

'Yes, you may depend upon it he has the ability! He is the younger generation that stands ready to knock at my door - to make an end of Halvard Solness.'
- Henrik Ibsen

'The youth gets together this material to build a bridge to the moon, or perchance, a palace or temple on earth, and at length, the middle-aged man concludes to build a woodshed with them.'
- Henry David Thoreau

'How beautiful is youth! how bright it gleams With its illusions, aspirations, dreams! Book of Beginnings, Story without End, Each maid a heroine, and each man a friend!'
- Henry Wadsworth Longfellow

'Youth comes but once in a lifetime.'
- Henry Wadsworth Longfellow

'Blessed are the young, for they shall inherit the national debt.'
- Herbert Hoover

'The joy of the young is to disobey - but the trouble is that there are no longer any orders.'
- Jean Cocteau

'Youth! youth! how buoyant are thy hopes; they turn, Like marigolds, toward the sunny side.'
- Jean Ingelow

'Every generation is a secret society and has incommunicable enthusiasms, tastes, and interests which are a mystery both to its predecessors and to posterity.'
- John Jay Chapman

'I remember my youth and the feeling that will never come back any more - the feeling that I could last forever, outlast the sea, the earth, and all men.'
- Joseph Conrad

'When a man of 40 falls in love with a girl of 20, it isn't her youth he is seeking but his own.'
- Lenore Coffee

'Don't laugh at a youth for his affectations; he's only trying on one face after another till he finds his own.'
- Logan Pearsall Smith

'Ah! happy years! once more who would not be a boy!'
- Lord Byron

'In youth we learn; in age we understand.'
- Marie von Ebner-Eschenbach

'When I was younger, I could remember anything, whether it had happened or not.'
- Mark Twain

'You never see the old austerity That was the essence of civility; Young people hereabouts, unbridled, now Just want.'
- Moliere

'It is essential that we enable young people to see themselves as participants in one of the most exciting eras in history, and to have a sense of purpose in relation to it.'
- Nelson Rockefeller

'Young folk, silly folk; old folk, cold folk.'
- Old saying

'Only the young die good.'
- Oliver Herford

'It takes a long time to become young.'
- Pablo Picasso

'If youth but knew, and age were able, Then poverty would be a fable.'
- Proverbs

'Oh, to be only half as wonderful as my child thought I was when he was small, and only half as stupid as my teenager now thinks I am.'
- Rebecca Richards

'It is always self-defeating to pretend to the style of a generation younger than your own; it simply erases your own experience in history.'
- Renata Adler

'Ah sorts of allowances are made for the illusions of youth; and none, or almost none, for the disenchantments of age.'
- Robert Louis Stevenson

'For God's sake give me the young man who has brains enough to make a fool of himself.'
- Robert Louis Stevenson

'Live as long as you may, the first twenty years are the longest half of your life.'
- Robert Southey

'Youth has become a class.'
- Roger Vadim

'Much may be made of a Scotchman if he be caught young.'
- Samuel Johnson

'What though youth gave love and roses Age still leaves us friends and wine.'
- Thomas More

'All the world's a mass of folly, Youth is gay, age melancholy: Youth is spending, age is thrifty, Mad at twenty, cold at fifty; Man is naught but folly's slave, From the cradle to the grave.'
- W. H. Ireland

'She bid me take love easy, as the leaves grow on the tree; But I, being young and foolish, with her would not agree.'
- William Butler Yeats

'The belief that youth is the happiest time of life is founded upon a fallacy. The happiest person is the person who thinks the most interesting thoughts, and we grow happier as we grow older.'
- William Lyon Phelps

ABOUT THE AUTHOR

Joanne Kelly is married and lives in the city of London in the United Kingdom with her husband, Ben, their three children, Michael, Douglas and Jessica - and their wonderful labrador, Barney.